Developing the Curriculum

Third Edition

Peter F. Oliva
Author, *Supervision for Today's Schools*

HarperCollins*Publishers*

Grandson Cory, age 11, I'm sure you won't mind sharing this dedication with grandson Anthony, age 3, and newly arrived granddaughter Amanda, who will share with you many of the same curricular needs.

Cover Design and Illustration: Darrin Drda, Publication Services, Inc.
Executive Editor: Christopher Jennison
Full-Service Manager: Michael Weinstein
Production Coordinator: Cindy Funkhouser
Production Manager: Priscilla Taguer
Compositor: Publication Services, Inc.
Printer and Binder: R. R. Donnelley & Sons Company
Cover Printer: The Lehigh Press, Inc.

Developing the Curriculum, Third Edition

Library of Congress Cataloging-in-Publication Data
Oliva, Peter F.
    Developing the curriculum / by Peter F. Oliva. – 3rd ed.
      p. cm.
    Includes bibliographical references (p.) and index.
    ISBN 0-673-52195-8
    1. Curriculum planning–United States. 2. School supervision—
United States. I. Title.
LB2806.15.O45 1991
375'.001'0973–dc20

                                 91-28681
                                    CIP

95 94 93 92 9 8 7 6 5 4 3 2 1

CREDITS

(*continued on p. 609*)

Brief Contents

Contents

PREFACE

In its third edition, this textbook remains a comprehensive analysis of the process of curriculum development. The substance of the text that delineates the process has not changed. The passing of time has not altered the process described in the first and second editions. The book has, however, been thoroughly updated with the inclusion of selected movements, practices, and issues of the 1990s and the deletion of certain past movements, practices, and issues.

Like its preceding editions this book is intended for students in courses such as Curriculum Development, Curriculum Planning, and Curriculum Improvement. It is meant to be especially helpful to preservice and in-service curriculum coordinators, principals, assistant principals for curriculum, department chairpersons, instructional team leaders, and grade coordinators, who will find the book to be a practical guide to curriculum development.

This text has proved useful at the master's degree level through the doctoral level. It fits especially well those courses in curriculum development that are required of persons preparing to be instructional leaders, administrators, and supervisors. In addition, the book contains a great deal of information and suggestions suitable to in-service professionals.

The text begins with an examination of the theoretical dimensions of curriculum development. After curriculum has been defined and its relationship to instruction discussed, the text looks at the roles of various personnel who have primary responsibility for developing the curriculum. Models of curriculum development are then described and the use of one integrated model is suggested. A step-by-step process for using this model is delineated. This process is examined all the way from stating philosophical beliefs and broad aims of education to specifying curriculum and instructional goals and objectives, implementing the curriculum and instruction, and evaluating instruction and the curriculum.

Because the primary focus of this book is on curriculum development, less emphasis is given to instruction, a whole area of study in itself (Chapters 10 through 12). The theme of this book is the process of curriculum development, not curriculum content; for example, analysis of the various disciplines is not included. Nor is there heavy treatment of the foundations of curriculum. Foundation areas are discussed and interwoven into the text. Process is the main feature that distinguishes this text from many other curriculum texts.

Each chapter begins with a number of cognitive objectives (competencies) to be achieved by the student on the completion of study of the chapter. Several questions for discussion are found at the end of each chapter. The supplementary exercises that follow the questions for discussion are designed to serve two purposes: (1) to reinforce the goals and content of each chapter and (2) to extend the treatment of topics beyond the material presented in this book. These exercises range in difficulty from simple to complex. Some provide for individual student work, others for group work. Some require only thought and opinion; others call for extensive research. Instructors are encouraged to select those exercises most appropriate for their own students. Instructors who wish to do so can easily turn many of the supplementary exercises into questions for class discussion. To further enhance the usefulness of the text, each chapter concludes with a bibliography of pertinent books, journal articles, and other media.

Both old and new references have been deliberately woven into the text to clarify and support points under discussion. The old references are included in order to (1) acquaint the student with persons who have contributed to the field, (2) trace the development of curricular thought, and (3) show that earlier thinking was often ahead of its time. The new references are included, of course, to present current views of the curriculum.

In the media sections of the bibligraphies at the end of chapters you will find some references to dated materials. I debated whether to remove these. However, I decided to leave those that I feel are still useful in the hope that college, university, and practitioners' libraries may have the items in their collections.

At the end of the text book are six appendices. Appendix A is a list of exit competencies, a summary of behaviors student should be able to demonstrate at the end of the course. Appendix B lists Educational Resources Information Center (ERIC) clearinghouses; Appendix C, facilitators of the National Diffusion Network; Appendix D, regional educational laboratories; Appendix E, national research and development centers; and Appendix F, curriculum journals. Readers are cautioned that these lists are current as of the publication of this edition. However, I felt it useful to include the most current sources even though persons in charge do change over time.

I would like to emphasize that this textbook, with its questions for discussion, exercises, and extensive bibliographies, is meant to be used, not just read. It is, therefore, designed as a teaching aid for the instructor and a sourcebook for the student.

Many people have contributed to the writing and publishing of this edition. Through their insights into curriculum and instruction, teachers, administrators, and students with whom I have worked have helped to shape my thinking. I again want to thank all those persons mentioned in the prefaces to the first two editions, especially Mylan Jaixen, then my editor at Little, Brown and Company, and Christopher Jennison, my present editor at HarperCollins. Those readers who keep up with mergers in the publishing business will recognize that Little, Brown, publisher of the first edition of this book, was bought out by Scott, Foresman, publisher of the second edition, which was, in turn, bought out by HarperCollins, publisher of the third edition. I appreciate as well the reviews and suggestions made by Cynthia Kruger of Southeastern Massachusetts University and James Johnson of the University of Toledo. In addition, I want to thank John Walters, Documents Librarian, and the staff of the university library at the University of Central Florida, especially the interlibrary loan, serials/AV, and reference departments, for all the help they gave me.

As always, I welcome comments from readers and users of the book.

Peter F. Oliva
Casselberry, Florida

PART I

The Curriculum: Theoretical Dimensions

CHAPTER ONE

Curriculum and Instruction Defined

After studying this chapter you should be able to:

1. Define curriculum.
2. Define instruction.
3. Explain in what ways curriculum can be considered a discipline.
4. Create or select a model of the relationship between curriculum and instruction and describe your creation or selection.

CONCEPTIONS OF CURRICULUM

Gaius Julius Caesar and his cohorts of the first century before Christ had no idea that the oval track upon which the Roman chariots raced would bequeath a word used almost daily by educators 21 centuries later. That track—*the curriculum*—has become one of the key concerns of today's schools, and its meaning has expanded from a race course to an abstract concept.

In the world of professional education, the word "curriculum" has taken on an elusive, almost esoteric connotation. This poetic, neuter word does possess an aura of mystery. By contrast, other dimensions of the world of professional education like administra*tion*, instruc*tion*, and supervi*sion* are strong, action-oriented words. Administration is the *act* of administering: instruction is the *act* of instructing; and supervision is the *act* of supervising. But in what way is "curriculum" an act? While administrators administer, instructors instruct, and supervisors supervise, no school person "curricules," and it is only a rare individual who "curricularizes."

The quest for a definition of curriculum has taxed many an educator. Dwayne Huebner ascribed ambiguity and a lack of precision to the term "curriculum,"[1] Elizabeth Vallance observed, "The curriculum field is by no means clear; as a discipline of study and as a field of practice, 'curriculum' lacks clean boundaries. . . . "[2] Indeed, curriculum seems at times analogous to the blind men's elephant. It is the pachyderm's trunk to some; its thick legs to others; its pterodactyl-like flopping ears to some people; its massive, rough sides to other persons; and its ropelike tail to still others.

Though it may be vehemently denied, no one has ever seen a curriculum, not a real, total, tangible, visible entity called a curriculum. The interested observer may have seen a written plan that may have been called a curriculum. Somehow the observer knows, probably by word of mouth, that in every school in which teachers are instructing students a curriculum exists. A written plan provides the observer with an additional clue to the existence of a certain something called a curriculum. But if by some bit of magic the observer could lift the roof of a school in session and examine the cross section thereof, the curriculum would not be apparent. What the observer would immediately perceive would be many instances of teacher-pupil interaction which we call *instruction*.

The search for evidence of the mysterious creation called curriculum is not unlike efforts to track down Bigfoot, the Yeti, Sasquatch, South Bay Bessie, or the Loch Ness Monster. Bigfoot, Sasquatch, and the Yeti have left their tracks in the mud and the snow; Bessie and Nessie have rippled the waters of their lakes; but no one has yet succeeded in producing incontrovertible

---

[1]Dwayne Huebner, "The Moribund Curriculum Field: Its Wake and Our Work," *Curriculum Inquiry* 6, no. 2 (1976): 156.

[2]Elizabeth Vallance, "Curriculum As a Field of Practice," in Fenwick W. English, ed., *Fundamental Curriculum Decisions,* 1983 Yearbook (Alexandria, Va.: Association for Supervision and Curriculum Development, 1983), p. 159.

photographs of these reputed creatures. Nor has anyone ever photographed a curriculum. Shutterbugs have instead photographed pupils, teachers, and other school personnel. Perhaps if someone photographed every instance of behavior in every classroom, corridor, office, and auxiliary room of a school every day and then investigated this record as thoroughly as military leaders analyze air reconnaissance photos, a curriculum could be deduced.

Certification and Curriculum

State certification laws compound the problem of defining curriculum, because few if any professionals can become certified in "curriculum." Whereas all professionals in training must take courses of one type or another called "curriculum," there is not a certifiable field labeled "curriculum." Professionals are certified in administration, guidance, supervision, school psychology, elementary education, and many fields of teaching. But in "curriculum" per se? Not as a rule, although courses in the field of curriculum are mandated for certification in certain fields of specialization, such as administration and supervision.

Nevertheless, numbers of curriculum workers, consultants, coordinators, and even professors of curriculum can be identified. These specialists, even though they may be certified in one or more fields, cannot customarily hang on the wall a certificate which shows that state approval has been granted in a field called "curriculum."

While a certifiable field of specialization called curriculum may be lacking, the word itself is treated as if it had tangible substance, for it can undergo a substantial variety of processes. Curriculum—or its plural, curricula or curriculums (depending on the user's penchant or abhorrence for the Latin)—is built, planned, designed, and constructed. It is improved, evaluated, and revised. Like photographic film and muscles, the curriculum is developed. It is also organized and, like a wayward child, reformed—or, using today's language, restructured. With considerable ingenuity the curriculum planner—another specialist—can mold, shape, and tailor the curriculum.

Interpretations of Curriculum

The amorphous nature of the word curriculum has given rise over the years to many interpretations. Depending on their philosophical beliefs, persons have conveyed these interpretations, among others:

☐ Curriculum is that which is taught in school.
☐ Curriculum is a set of subjects.
☐ Curriculum is content.
☐ Curriculum is a program of studies.
☐ Curriculum is a set of materials.
☐ Curriculum is a sequence of courses.
☐ Curriculum is a set of performance objectives.
☐ Curriculum is a course of study.

□ Curriculum is everything that goes on within the school, including extra-class activities, guidance, and interpersonal relationships.
□ Curriculum is that which is taught both inside and outside of school directed by the school.
□ Curriculum is everything that is planned by school personnel.
□ Curriculum is a series of experiences undergone by learners in school.
□ Curriculum is that which an individual learner experiences as a result of schooling.

In the foregoing definitions you can see that curriculum can be conceived in a narrow way (as subjects taught) or in a broad way (as all the experiences of learners, both in school and out, directed by the school). The implications for the school to be drawn from the differing conceptions of curriculum can vary considerably. The school that accepts the definition of curriculum as a set of subjects faces a much simpler task than the school that takes upon itself responsibilities for experiences of the learner both inside and outside of school.

A variety of nuances *is* perceived when the professional educators define curriculum. The first definition, for example, given in Carter V. Good's *Dictionary of Education* describes curriculum as "a systematic group of courses or sequences of subjects required for graduation or certification in a major field of study, for example, social studies curriculum, physical education curriculum. . . ."[3]

Hollis L. Caswell and Doak S. Campbell viewed curriculum not as a group of courses but as "all the experiences children have under the guidance of teachers."[4] J. Galen Saylor, William M. Alexander, and Arthur J. Lewis offered this definition: "We define curriculum as a plan for providing sets of learning opportunities for persons to be educated."[5]

The Saylor, Alexander, and Lewis definition parallels the one given by Hilda Taba in a discussion of criteria for curriculum development: "A curriculum is a plan for learning."[6] She defined curriculum by listing its elements:

> All curricula, no matter what their particular design, are composed of certain elements. A curriculum usually contains a statement of aims and of specific objectives; it indicates some selection and organization of content; it either implies or manifests certain patterns of learning and teaching, whether because the objectives demand them or because the content organization requires them. Finally, it includes a program of evaluation of the outcomes.[7]

---

[3]From *Dictionary of Education*, 3rd ed., p. 157, by Carter V. Good, ed. Copyright ©1973 by McGraw-Hill. Used with the permission of McGraw-Hill book Company.
[4]Hollis L. Caswell and Doak S. Campbell, *Curriculum Development* (New York: American Book Company, 1935), p. 66.
[5]Excerpts from *Curriculum Planning for Better Teaching and Learning,* p. 8., and by J. G. Saylor and W. M. Alexander, copyright ©1954 by Holt, Rinehart and Winston, Inc. and renewed 1982 by J. G. Saylor and W. M. Alexander, reprinted by permission of the publisher.
[6]Excerpts from *Curriculum Development: Theory and Practice,* p. 11, by Hilda Taba, copyright ©1962 by Harcourt Brace Jovanovich, Inc. and renewed 1990 by Margaret J. Spalding, reprinted by permission of the publisher.
[7]Ibid., p. 10.

Ronald C. Doll defined the curriculum of a school as:

> the formal and informal content and process by which learners gain knowledge and understanding, develop skills, and alter attitudes, appreciations, and values under the auspices of that school. [8]

Daniel Tanner and Laurel N. Tanner proposed the following definition:

> The authors regard curriculum as *that reconstruction of knowledge and experience systematically developed under the auspices of the school (or university), to enable the learner to increase his or her control of knowledge and experience.* [9]

Albert I. Oliver equated curriculum with the educational program and divided it into four basic elements: "(1) the program of studies, (2) the program of experiences, (3) the program of services, and (4) the hidden curriculum."[10]

The programs of studies, experiences, and services are readily apparent. To these elements Oliver has added the concept of a hidden curriculum, which encompasses values promoted by the school, differing emphases given by different teachers within the same subject areas, the degree of enthusiasm of teachers, and the physical and social climate of the school.

A different approach to defining curriculum was taken by Robert M. Gagné, who wove together subject matter (content), the statement of ends (terminal objectives), sequencing of content, and preassessment of entry skills required of students when they begin the study of the content.[11] Mauritz Johnson, Jr., agreed basically with Gagné when he defined curriculum as a "structured series of intended learning outcomes."[12] Johnson perceived curriculum as "the output of a 'curriculum development system' and as an input into an 'instructional system'."[13]

Geneva Gay, writing on desegregating the curriculum, offered a broad interpretation of curriculum:

> If we are to achieve equality, we must broaden our conceptions of curriculum to include the entire culture of the school—not just subject matter content.[14]

---

[8]From Ronald C. Doll, *Curriculum Improvement: Decision Making and Process,* seventh ed., p. 8. Copyright ©1989 by Allyn & Bacon. Reprinted with permission.

[9]Reprinted by permission of Macmillan Publishing Company from *Curriculum Development: Theory into Practice,* 2nd ed., p. 43, by Daniel Tanner and Laurel N. Tanner. Copyright ©1980 by Macmillan Publishing Company.

[10]Excerpts from *Curriculum Improvement: A Guide to Problems, Principles, and Process,* 2nd ed., p. 8, by Albert I. Oliver. Copyright ©1965 by Harper & Row Publishers, Inc. Reprinted by permission of HarperCollins Publishers.

[11]See Robert M. Gagné, "Curriculum Research and the Promotion of Learning," *AERA Monograph Series on Evaluation: Perspectives of Curriculum Evaluation,* no. 1 (Chicago: Rand McNally, 1967), p. 21.

[12]Mauritz Johnson, Jr., "Definitions and Models in Curriculum Theory," *Educational Theory* 17, no. 2 (April 1967): 130.

[13]Ibid., p. 133.

[14]Geneva Gay, "Achieving Educational Equality Through Curriculum Desegregation," *Phi Delta Kappan* 72, no. 1 (September 1990): 61–62.

Definitions by Purposes, Contexts, and Strategies

Differences in substance of definitions of curriculum, while they exist, are not as great or as common as differences in what the curriculum theorists include in their conceptions of the term. Some theorists elaborate more than others. Some combine elements of both curriculum and instruction, a conceptual problem that will be examined later in this chapter. Others find a definition of curriculum in (1) purposes or goals of the curriculum, (2) contexts within which the curriculum is found, or (3) strategies used throughout the curriculum.

Purposes.   The search for a definition of curriculum is clouded when the theoretician responds to the term not in the context of what curriculum *is* but what it *does* or *should do*—that is, its purpose. On the purposes of the curriculum we can find many varying statements.

When curriculum is conceptualized as "the development of reflective thinking on the part of the learner" or as "the transmission of the cultural heritage," purpose is confused with entity. This concept could be stated more correctly: "The purpose of the curriculum is transmission of the cultural heritage," or "The purpose of the curriculum is the development of reflective thinking on the part of the learner." A statement of what the curriculum is meant to achieve does little to help us sharpen a definition of what the curriculum is.

Contexts.   Definitions of curriculum sometimes state the settings within which it takes shape. When the theoreticians speak of an essentialist curriculum, a child-centered curriculum, or a reconstructionist curriculum, they are invoking two characteristics of the curriculum at the same time—purpose and context. For example, an essentialistic curriculum is designed to transmit the cultural heritage, to school young people in the organized disciplines, and to prepare boys and girls for the future. This curriculum arises from a special philosophical context, that of the essentialistic school of philosophy.

A child-centered curriculum clearly reveals its orientation—the learner, who is the primary focus of the progressive school of philosophy. The development of the individual learner in all aspects of growth may be inferred but the plans for that development may vary considerably from school to school. The curriculum of a school following reconstructionist philosophical beliefs aims to educate youth in such a way that they will be capable of solving some of society's pressing problems and therefore change society for the better. Again we see a particular orientation or context within which the curriculum is lodged.

Strategies.   While purpose and context are sometimes offered as definitions of curriculum, an additional complexity arises when the theoretician equates curriculum with instructional strategy. Some theoreticians isolate certain instructional variables such as processes, strategies, and techniques and then proceed to equate them with curriculum. The curriculum as a problem-solving process illustrates an attempt to define curriculum in terms of an instructional process— problem-solving techniques, the scientific method, or reflective thinking. The curriculum as group living, for example, is an effort at definition built around certain instructional techniques that must be used to provide opportunities for group living. The curriculum as individualized learning and the curriculum as programmed instruction are, in reality, specifications of systems by which the learners encounter curricular content through the process of instruction. Neither purpose, context, nor strategy provides a clear basis for defining curriculum.

In a class by itself is the definition of curriculum as ends or terminal objectives. W. James Popham and Eva L. Baker classified curriculum as ends and instruction as means when they said: "Curriculum is all the planned learning outcomes for which the school is responsible."[15] In designing the curriculum, planners would cast these outcomes or objectives in operational or behavioral terms.

The operational or behavioral objectives are, in effect, instructional objectives. According to the proponents of behavioral objectives, a compilation of all the behavioral objectives of all the programs and activities of the school would constitute the curriculum. The curriculum then would be the sum total of all instructional objectives. You will encounter in this text an approach that distinguishes curricular goals and objectives from instructional goals and objectives.

Both curriculum goals and objectives and instructional goals and objectives can be specified in behavioral terms. Some advocates of behavioral objectives seem comfortable with the notion that once the terminal objectives (the ends) are clearly specified, the curriculum has been defined. From that point on instruction takes over. This view of curriculum as specification of objectives is quite different, for example, from the concept of the curriculum as a plan, a program, or a sequence of courses.[16]

In this text curriculum is perceived as a plan or program for all the experiences which the learner encounters under the direction of the school. In practice, the curriculum consists of a number of plans, in written form and of varying scope, that delineate the desired learning experiences. The curriculum, therefore, may be a unit, a course, a sequence of courses, the school's entire program of studies—and may take place outside of class or school when directed by the personnel of the school.

RELATIONSHIPS BETWEEN CURRICULUM AND INSTRUCTION

The search to clarify the meaning of curriculum reveals uncertainty about the distinctions between curriculum and instruction and their relationships to each other. We may simplistically view curriculum as that which is taught and instruction as the means used to teach that which is taught. Even more simply,

---

[15]W. James Popham and Eva L. Baker, *Systematic Instruction* (Englewood Cliffs, N.J.: Prentice-Hall, 1970), p. 48.

[16]See, for example, Gagné, "Curriculum Research."

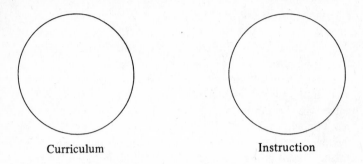

Curriculum   Instruction

FIGURE 1–1   The dualistic model

curriculum can be conceived as the "what" and instruction as the "how." We
may think of the curriculum as a program, a plan, content, and learning experiences, whereas we may characterize instruction as methods, the teaching act,
implementation, and presentation.

Distinguishing instruction from curriculum, Johnson defined instruction as
"the interaction between a teaching agent and one or more individuals intending
to learn."[17] James B. Macdonald viewed curricular activity as the production of
plans for further action and instruction as the putting of plans into operation.
Thus, according to Macdonald, curriculum planning precedes instruction, a
premise with which I am in agreement.[18]

In the course of planning for either the curriculum or instruction, decisions are made. Decisions about the curriculum relate to plans or programs
and thus are *programmatic,* while those about instruction (and thereby implementation) are *methodological.* Both curriculum and instruction are subsystems of a larger system called schooling or education.

Models of the Curriculum-Instruction Relationship

Definitions of the two terms are valuable but can obscure the interdependence of
these two subsystems. They may be recognized as two entities, but like Siamese
twins who are joined together, one may not function without the other. That the
relationship between the "what" and the "how" of education is not easily determined can be seen in several different models of this relationship. For lack of
better terminology, the following labels are coined for these models: (1) dualistic model, (2) interlocking model, (3) concentric models, (4) cyclical model.

Dualistic Model.   Figure 1–1 depicts the dualistic model. Curriculum sits on
one side and instruction on the other, and never the twain shall meet. Between

[17]Johnson, "Definitions," p. 138. See also Saylor, Alexander, and Lewis, *Curriculum Planning,* pp. 9–10, for a definition of instruction.
[18]James B. Macdonald and Robert R. Leeper, eds., *Theories of Instruction* (Alexandria, Va.:
Association for Supervision and Curriculum Development, 1965), pp. 5–6.

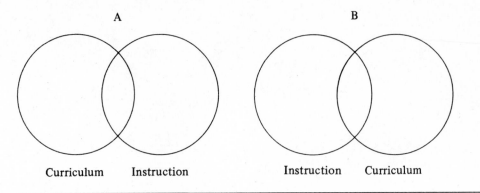

A   B

Curriculum   Instruction   Instruction   Curriculum

FIGURE 1–2   The interlocking model

the two entities lies a great gulf. What takes place in the classroom under the direction of the teacher seems to have little relationship to what the master plan says should go on in the classroom. The planners ignore the instructors and in turn are ignored by them. Discussions of curriculum are divorced from their practical application to the classroom. Under this model the curriculum and the instructional process may change without significantly affecting one another.

Interlocking Model.   When curriculum and instruction are shown as systems entwined, an interlocking relationship exists. No particular significance is given to the position of instruction or curriculum in either of the versions of this model presented in Figure 1–2. The same relationship is implied no matter which element appears on the left or the right. These models clearly demonstrate an integrated relationship between these two entities. The separation of one from the other would do serious harm to both.

Curriculum planners would find it difficult to regard instruction as paramount to curriculum and to determine teaching methods before program objectives. Nevertheless, some faculties proceed as if instruction were primary by dispensing with advance planning of the curriculum and by letting it more or less develop as it unfolds in the classroom.

Concentric Models.   The preceding models of the relationship between curriculum and instruction reveal varying degrees of independence from complete detachment to interlocking relationships. Mutual dependence is the key feature of concentric models. Two conceptions of the curriculum-instruction relationship that show one as the subsystem of the other can be sketched (see Figure 1–3). Variations A and B both convey the idea that one of the entities occupies a superordinate position while the other is subordinate.

Concentric model A makes instruction a subsystem of curriculum, which is itself a subsystem of the whole system of education. Concentric model B subsumes curriculum within the subsystem instruction. A clear hierarchical relationship comes through in both these models. Curriculum ranks above in-

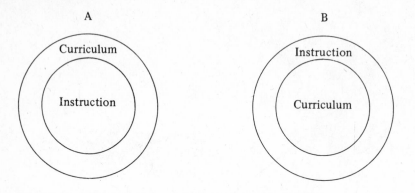

FIGURE 1–3   Concentric models

struction in model A, and instruction is predominant in model B. In model A instruction is a very dependent portion of the entity curriculum. Model B makes curriculum subservient to and derivative from the more global instruction.

Cyclical Model.   The cyclical conception of the curriculum-instruction relationship is a simplified systems model that stresses the essential element of feedback. Curriculum and instruction are separate entities with a continuing circular relationship. Curriculum makes a continuous impact on instruction, and, vice versa, instruction impacts on curriculum. This relationship can be schematically represented as in Figure 1–4. This cyclical model implies that instructional decisions are made after curricular decisions, which in turn are modified after instructional decisions are implemented and evaluated. This process is continuous, repetitious, and never-ending. The evaluation of instructional procedures affects the next round of curricular decision making, which again affects instructional implementation. While curriculum and instruction are diagrammed as separate entities, with this model they are not to be conceived

FIGURE 1–4   The cyclical model

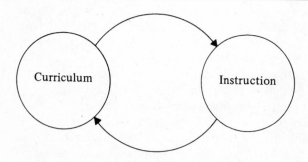

as separate entities but as part of a sphere—a circle that revolves, causing continuous adaptations and improvements of both entities.

Each curriculum-instruction model has its champions who espouse it in part or in whole, in theory or in practice. Yet how can we account for these numerous conceptions, and how do we know which is the "right" one to hold?

Common Beliefs. As newer developments occur in education, as research adds new insights on teaching and learning, as new ideas are developed, and as times change, beliefs about curriculum and instruction also undergo transformation. The "rightness" or "wrongness" of concepts like curriculum and instruction cannot be established by an individual educator or even by a group of educators. One index of "correctness" might be the prevailing opinion of most educators at a particular stage in history—a rather pragmatic but nevertheless viable and defensible position. Though no one to my knowledge has made a count of prevailing postulates regarding curriculum and instruction, most theoreticians today appear to agree with the following statements:

- □ Curriculum and instruction are related but different.
- □ Curriculum and instruction are interlocking and interdependent.
- □ Curriculum and instruction may be studied and analyzed as separate entities but cannot function in mutual isolation.

In my judgement, serious problems are posed by the dualistic conceptual model of the relationship between curriculum and instruction with its separation of the two entities and by concentric models that make one a subsystem of the other.

Some curriculum workers feel comfortable with an interlocking model because it shows a close relationship between the two entities. Of all the curriculum-instruction models that have crossed my path, however, the cyclical has much to recommend it for its simplicity and for its stress on the need for the continuous influence of each entity on the other.

CURRICULUM AS A DISCIPLINE

In spite of its elusive character, curriculum is viewed by many, including me, as a discipline—a subject of study—and even, on the graduate level of higher education, as a major field of study. Curriculum is then both a field within which people work and a subject to be taught. Graduate and, to some extent, undergraduate students take courses in curriculum development, curriculum theory, curriculum evaluation, secondary school curriculum, elementary school curriculum, middle school curriculum, community college curriculum, and, on rare occasions, university curriculum.

Can there be a discipline called curriculum? Are the many college courses in curriculum mere frosting, as some of the critics of teacher education maintain, or is there cake beneath the surface? Is there a curriculum field or occupation to which persons can devote their lives?

The Characteristics of a Discipline

To arrive at a decision as to whether an area of study is a discipline, the question might be raised, "What are the characteristics of a discipline?" If the characteristics of a discipline could be spelled out, we could determine whether curriculum, for example, is a discipline or not.

Principles.   *Any discipline worthy of study has an organized set of theoretical constructs or principles that govern it.* Certainly the field of curriculum has developed a significant number of principles, tried and untried, proved and unproved, many of which are appropriately the subjects of discussion in this text. Balance in the curriculum, discussed in Chapter 14, is a construct or concept. Curriculum itself is a construct or concept, a verbalization of an extremely complex idea or set of ideas. Using the constructs of balance and curriculum, we can derive a principle or rule which, stated in simple terms, says, "A curriculum that provides maximum opportunities for learners incorporates the concept of balance." Sequencing of courses, career education, open-space education, behavioral objectives, and a systems approach to teaching reading are examples of constructs incorporated into one or more curriculum principles.

A major characteristic of any theoretical principle is its capacity for being generalized and applied in more than one situation. Were curriculum theories but one-shot solutions to specific problems, it would be difficult to defend the concept of curriculum as a discipline. But the principles of curriculum theory are often successful efforts to establish rules that can be repeated in similar situations and under similar conditions. Many people will agree, for example, that the concept of balance should be incorporated into every curriculum. We encounter more controversy, however, over a principle that might be stated as "The first step in curriculum planning is the specification of behavioral objectives." Though some maintain that this principle has become universal practice and therefore might be labeled "truth," it has been tried and accepted by many schools, rejected by some, and tried and abandoned by others.

Knowledge and Skills.   *Any discipline encompasses a body of knowledge and skills pertinent to that discipline.* The field of curriculum has adapted and borrowed subject matter from a number of pure and derived disciplines. Figure 1–5 schematically shows areas from which the field of curriculum has borrowed constructs, principles, knowledge, and skills. Selection of content for study by students, for example, cannot be done without referring to the disciplines of sociology, psychology, and subject areas. Organization of the curriculum depends upon knowledge from organizational theory and management, which are aspects of administration. The fields of supervision, systems theory, technology, and communications theory are called on in the process of curriculum development. Knowledge from many fields is selected and adapted by the curriculum field.

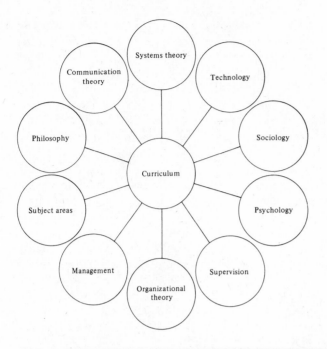

FIGURE 1–5   Sources of the curriculum field

The "child-centered curriculum" as a concept draws heavily on what is known about learning, growth, and development (psychology and biology), on philosophy (particularly from one school of philosophy, progressivism), and on sociology. The "essentialist curriculum" borrows from the subject areas of philosophy, psychology, and sociology.

You might ask whether the field of curriculum contributes any knowledge of its own to that borrowed from other disciplines. Certainly, a good deal of thinking and research is going on in the name of curriculum. New curricular ideas are being generated continuously. These ideas, whether they be cooperative learning, interactive video, or environmental education (to mention but three fairly recent concepts), borrow heavily from other disciplines.

The skills used by curriculum specialists are also borrowed from other fields. Let's take an example from the field of social psychology. Generally accepted is the notion that a curriculum changes only when the people affected have changed. This principle, drawn from the field of social psychology and applied in the field of curriculum development, was perhaps most dramatically demonstrated by the Western Electric researches conducted by industry in the 1930s.[19] Here researchers discovered that factory workers assembling telephone

---

[19] See F. J. Roethlisberger and William J. Dickson, *Management and the Worker* (Cambridge, Mass.: Harvard University Press, 1939) for discussion of the Western Electric researches.

relays were more productive when they were consulted and made to feel of value to the organization. Making the workers feel important resulted in greater productivity than manipulating the physical environment, for example, lighting in the factory. The feeling of being a part of the research studies also created its own aura, the so-called Hawthorne Effect, named for Western Electric's Hawthorne plant in Chicago. Since the feeling of involvement can in itself contribute to high productivity, this effect is one that researchers learn to discount, for it can obscure the hypothesized or real causes for change. However, the educational practitioner who is aware of the Hawthorne Effect may take advantage of it to promote learning.

Criticisms have been made of the Western Electric researches.[20] In spite of the criticisms, however, the findings still appear generally sound. An instructional leader—let's call him or her a supervisor—is the person who acts as a catalyst or agent for bringing about change in people. How does the supervisor do this? He or she makes use of knowledge and skills from a number of fields: communications theory, psychology of groups, and other areas. How does the supervisor help teachers to carry out the change once they have subscribed to it? He or she applies principles and skills from management, from knowledge of the structure of disciplines, and from other areas.

Consequently, we can conclude that the field of curriculum requires the use of an amalgamation of knowledge and skills from many disciplines. That curriculum theory and practice are derived from other disciplines does not in any way diminish the importance of the field. The observation of its derived nature simply characterizes its essence. Curriculum's synthesis of elements from many fields in some ways makes it both a demanding and an exciting area in which to work.

In a cyclical fashion the derived discipline of "curriculum" in turn makes its own potent impact upon the disciplines from which it is derived. Through curricular research, experimentation, and application, subject areas are modified; learning theories are corroborated, revised, or rejected; administrative and supervisory techniques are implemented or changed; and philosophical positions are subjected to examination.

Theoreticians and Practitioners.   *A discipline has its theoreticians and its practitioners.* Certainly, the field of curriculum has an array of workers laboring in its name. Mention has already been made of some of the titles they go by: planners, consultants, coordinators, directors, and professors of curriculum, to recall but a few. We can include them all under the generic title of curriculum worker or curriculum specialist.

Curriculum specialists make a number of distinctive contributions to their field. Specialists know what types of curricula have worked in the past, under

---

[20]Berkeley Rice, "The Hawthorne Defect: Persistence of a Flawed Theory," *Psychology Today* 16, no. 2 (February 1982): 70–74.

what conditions, and with what success. Since the name of the game is improvement, specialists must be well-grounded in the historical development of the curriculum and must possess the capacity to use that knowledge to help the schools avoid historic pitfalls.

Curriculum specialists generate or help to generate new curriculum concepts. In this capacity specialists draw on the past and conceive new arrangements, adaptations of existing approaches, or completely new approaches. Alternative forms of schooling, for example, are newer arrangements and approaches for the same general goal—education of the young.

While curriculum specialists are indulging in the "big think," hoping to bring to light new theories—a worthy goal not to be dismissed lightly—other, and perhaps more, curriculum specialists are experts in application. They know techniques of curriculum planning that are most likely to result in higher achievement on the part of learners. They are familiar with variations in organizational patterns. They must be not only knowledgeable but also creative and able to spark innovations that give promise of bringing about higher achievement in learners.

In its day the concept of a "core" curriculum, for example, that integrated two or more subjects, was a promising, creative innovation. In one of its shapes the core curriculum, which we will discuss in Chapter 9, fused English and social studies into a block of time—ordinarily two to three periods—at the junior high school level, using content based on adolescent needs and interests. But was this innovative concept truly original, unique to the field of curriculum, or was it adapted and drawn from a variety of disciplines? Examination of the subconcepts of the core curriculum shows that it owed a great deal to other disciplines. The adolescent needs base followed in some core programs came from student-centered, progressive learning theories, as did the problem-solving approach used in instruction. One reason for the inauguration of this type of core curriculum in schools in the 1930s and 1940s could be attributed to dissatisfaction with the subject matter curriculum as evidenced by, among other factors, the low holding power of schools of the times.

CURRICULUM PRACTITIONERS

Curriculum Specialists

Curriculum specialists often make a unique contribution by creatively transforming theory and knowledge into practice. Through their efforts a new, at first experimental, approach gradually becomes a widespread practice. As students of the discipline of curriculum, they also examine and reexamine theory and knowledge from their field and related fields. Their awareness of past successes and failures elsewhere helps them to chart directions for their own curricula.

Curriculum specialists are in the best position to stimulate research on curricular problems. Specialists carry out and encourage study of curricular problems, comparisons of plans and programs, results of new patterns of curriculum organization, and history of curriculum experiments, to indicate but a few areas of research. Specialists encourage the use of results of research to continue efforts to improve the curriculum.

While classroom teachers daily concern themselves with problems of curriculum and instruction, the curriculum specialist is charged with the task of providing leadership to the teachers. Since there are so many different types of specialists in so many different locations, you will find it difficult to generalize their roles. Some curriculum workers are generalists whose roles may be limited to leadership in curricular or programmatic planning or whose roles may also encompass instructional planning and decision making.

Some curriculum workers confine their spheres of action to certain levels or subjects, such as secondary school curriculum, elementary school curriculum, community college curriculum, special education, science education, early childhood education, and others. What can be observed is that the roles the curriculum leader plays are shaped by the job, by the supervising administrator, and by the specialist himself or herself. At varying times the curriculum specialist must be

- a philosopher
- a psychologist
- a sociologist
- a supervisor
- a human relations expert
- a theoretician
- a historian
- a scholar in one or more disciplines
- an evaluator
- a researcher
- an instructor
- a system analyst

Teachers

Up to this point the discussion has centered on the curriculum specialists and their place in the scheme of the field called curriculum. We must not deemphasize an even larger group of professionals—the teachers. Just as the curriculum leader works primarily in the curriculum realm of the continuum that we call curriculum-instruction and secondarily in the instructional realm, so too the teacher works primarily in one realm (instructional) and secondarily in the other (curriculum).

The teacher, too, is a curriculum worker who engages in curriculum planning in varying degrees, in varying settings, on different occasions, generally under the leadership of a specialist, be that person a coordinator, consultant, supervisor, team leader, department head, or assistant principal. How the teacher-instructor and the curriculum specialist work together in the two fields of curriculum and instruction is a recurrent theme of this book.

Supervisors

An additional clarification should be made at this point—that is, the relationship between the roles of persons designated as curriculum specialists and those persons who are called supervisors. Some consider the titles synonomous.

In this text a *supervisor* is perceived as a specialist who works in three domains: instructional development, curriculum development, and teacher development.[21] When the supervisor works in the first two domains, he or she is an instructional/curriculum specialist or, in common but somewhat inaccurate parlance, a curriculum specialist. Thus the curriculum worker or specialist is a particular type of supervisor, one with more limited responsibilities than a "complete" supervisor. Both the curriculum specialist and the supervisor fulfill similar roles when they work with teachers in curriculum development and instructional development, but the curriculum specialist is not primarily concerned with such activities as organizing in-service programs and evaluating teachers, which are more properly responsibilities of the supervisor or administrator.

Role Variations

As with so many jobs in the field of education, difficulty arises in attempting to draw firm lines that apply under all conditions and in all situations. To understand more fully the roles and functions of educational personnel, we must examine local practice. Teachers, curriculum specialists, and supervisors all engage in activities to improve both the curriculum and instruction. At times their roles are different and at other times their roles are similar. These personnel, all specialists in their own right, frequently trade places to accomplish the task of improvement. Sometimes they are one and the same person—the teacher who is his or her own curriculum specialist and supervisor. Other times they are two persons—the teacher and curriculum specialist/supervisor. At still other times they are a team of three—the teacher, the curriculum specialist, and the supervisor. Whatever the structure of leadership for the improvement of curriculum and instruction, all teachers and all specialists must ultimately participate in this challenging task. Since curriculum and instruction are the mind and heart of schooling, all personnel, all students, and the community as

---

[21] See Peter F. Oliva, *Supervision for Today's Schools,* 3rd ed. (White Plains, N.Y.: Longman, 1989).[4th ed. in process.]

well participate in the improvement of what is offered in the school and how it is implemented.

Chapters 3 and 4 will describe roles of personnel involved in curriculum development, including teachers, students, department heads, team leaders, grade coordinators, administrators, curriculum specialists, supervisors, and lay persons.

SUMMARY

Curriculum and instruction are viewed as separate but dependent concepts. Curriculum is defined in a variety of ways by theoreticians. This text follows the concept of curriculum as a plan or program for the learning experiences that the learner encounters under the direction of the school.

Instruction is perceived in these pages as the means for making the curriculum operational: the techniques that teachers use to make the curriculum available to the learners. In short, curriculum is program and instruction is method.

A number of models showing the relationship between curriculum and instruction have been discussed. While all models have their strengths and weaknesses, the cyclical model seems to have particular merit for its emphasis on the reciprocity between curriculum and instruction.

Planning should begin with the programmatic—that is, with curricular decisions, rather than with instructional decisions. Appropriate planning begins with the broad aims of education and proceeds through a continuum that leads to the most detailed objectives of instruction.

Curriculum is perceived as a discipline, albeit a derived one that borrows concepts and principles from many disciplines.

Many practitioners work in the field of curriculum, including specialists who make a career of curriculum planning and development. Teachers, curriculum specialists, and supervisors share leadership responsibilities in efforts to develop the curriculum.

As a discipline, curriculum possesses (1) an organized set of principles, (2) a body of knowledge and skills for which training is needed, and (3) its theoreticians and practitioners.

QUESTIONS FOR DISCUSSION

1. Does it make any difference which definition of curriculum you adopt? Why? Give examples of the effect of following different definitions of curriculum.
2. Should curriculum be an area certified by the state? Why?

3. What is the purpose of distinguishing curriculum from instruction?
4. What would you include in a preparation program for curriculum special-ists?
5. Does planning start with the curriculum or with instruction? Why?

SUPPLEMENTARY EXERCISES

1. Locate and report three definitions of curriculum that differ from those quoted in this chapter.
2. Describe the characteristics of a discipline.
3. Describe whether curriculum is a discipline, a pseudodiscipline, a de-rived discipline, or not a discipline, and state your reasons for your deci-sion.
4. Make a brief presentation on the distinctions between a curriculum spe-cialist and a supervisor, using selected quotations from the professional literature or from persons in positions with those titles.
5. Define: curriculum worker, curriculum specialist, curriculum planner, curriculum coordinator, curriculum consultant, and instructional super-visor.
6. Locate in the literature and describe one or more models of the relationship between curriculum and instruction that are different from those that appear in this chapter.
7. Create and describe your own model of the relationship between curriculum and instruction.
8. Evaluate the model of the relationship between curriculum and instruc-tion below suggested by Deborah Westcot, graduate student in the Geor-gia Southern College–University of Georgia Cooperative Doctoral Program winter 1986:

In the field of mathematics known as topology, the Möbius strip [see the illustration] presents only one continuous surface. When applied to the rela-tionship between curriculum and instruction, curriculum flows into instruction and instruction flows into curriculum.

The Möbius strip

9. Take each of the disciplines from which the field of curriculum borrows and explain at least one contribution (principle, construct, or skill) borrowed from that discipline.
10. Decide whether there are any sources of the curriculum field not shown in Figure 1–5.
11. State what you believe is meant by the following terms: curriculum planning, curriculum development, curriculum revision, curriculum improvement, curriculum reform, and curriculum evaluation.
12. Report on the Western Electric researchers mentioned in this chapter and explain their significance for curriculum development. Include in your answer your description of the Hawthorne Effect. Evaluate some of the criticisms of the Western Electric researches.
13. Consult one or more of the following references (see bibliography) on the meaning of "hidden curriculum:" James A. Bean et al.; Henry Giroux and David Purpel; John D. McNeil; Albert I. Oliver.
14. Define types of curricula described by Allan A. Glatthorn (see bibliography) and by John I. Goodlad and associates (see bibliography).

BIBLIOGRAPHY

Armstrong, David G. *Developing and Documenting the Curriculum*. Boston: Allyn and Bacon, 1989.

Bean, James A., Toepfer, Conrad F., Jr., and Alessi, Samuel J., Jr. *Curriculum Planning and Development*. Boston: Allyn and Bacon, 1986.

Beauchamp, George A. *Curricular Theory,* 4th ed. Itasca, Ill.: F. E. Peacock, 1981.

Caswell, Hollis L. and Campbell, Doak S. *Curriculum Development*. New York: American Book Company, 1935.

Doll, Ronald C. *Curriculum Improvement: Decision Making and Process*. 7th ed. Boston: Allyn and Bacon, 1989.

Eisner, Elliot W., ed. *Confronting Curriculum Reform*. Boston: Little, Brown 1971.

———. *The Educational Imagination: On the Design and Evaluation of School Programs,* 2nd ed. New York: Macmillan, 1985.

Eisner, Elliot W. and Vallance, Elizabeth, eds. *Conflicting Conceptions of Curriculum*. Berkeley, Calif.: McCutchan, 1974.

Foshay, Arthur W. *Curriculum for the 70's: An Agenda for Invention*. Washington, D.C.: National Education Association, 1970.

Frymier, Jack R. and Hawn, Horace C. *Curriculum Improvement for Better Schools*. Worthington, Ohio: Charles A. Jones, 1970.

Giroux, Henry A., Penna, Anthony N., and Pinar, William F., eds. *Curriculum and Instruction: Alternatives in Education*. Berkeley, Calif.: McCutchan, 1981.

Giroux, Henry and Purpel, David, eds. *The Hidden Curriculum and Moral Education*. Berkeley, Calif.: McCutchan, 1983.

Glatthorn, Allan A. *Curriculum Leadership*. Glenview, Ill.: Scott, Foresman, 1987.

Goodlad, John I. and associates. *Curriculum Inquiry: The Study of Curriculum Practice*. New York: McGraw-Hill, 1979.

Gress, James R. and Purpel, David E. *Curriculum: An Introduction to the Field,* 2nd ed. Berkeley, Calif.: McCutchan, 1988.

Johnson, Harold T. *Foundations of Curriculum.* Columbus, Ohio: Charles E. Merrill, 1968.

Johnson, Mauritz, Jr. "Definitions and Models in Curriculum Theory." *Educational Theory* 17, no. 2 (April 1967): 127–140.

Kelly, A. V. *The Curriculum: Theory and Practice.* New York: Harper & Row, 1977.

Macdonald, James B. and Leeper, Robert R., eds. *Theories of Instruction.* Alexandria, Va.: Association for Supervision and Curriculum Development, 1965.

McNeil, John D. *Curriculum: A Comprehensive Introduction,* 4th ed. Glenview, Ill.: Scott, Foresman/Little, Brown, 1990.

Molnar, Alex, ed. *Current Thought on Curriculum,* 1985 Yearbook. Alexandria, Va.: Association for Supervision and Curriculum Development, 1985.

Oliver, Albert I. *Curriculum Improvement: A Guide to Problems, Principles, and Process,* 2nd ed. New York: Harper & Row, 1977.

Pratt, David. *Curriculum: Design and Development.* New York: Harcourt Brace Jovanovich, 1980.

Roethlisberger, F. J. and Dickson, William J. *Management and the Worker.* Cambridge, Mass.: Harvard University Press, 1939.

Saylor, J. Galen, Alexander, William M., and Lewis, Arthur J. *Curriculum Planning for Better Teaching and Learning,* 4th ed. New York: Holt, Rinehart and Winston, 1981.

Schiro, Michael. *Curriculum for Better Schools.* Englewood Cliffs, N.J.: Educational Technology Publications, 1978.

Schubert, William H. *Curriculum: Perspective, Paradigm, and Possibility.* New York: Macmillan, 1986.

Schwab, Joseph J. *The Practical: A Language for Curriculum.* Washington, D.C.: National Education Association, Center for the Study of Instruction, 1970.

Taba, Hilda. *Curriculum Development: Theory and Practice.* New York: Harcourt Brace Jovanovich, 1962.

Tanner, Daniel and Tanner, Laurel N. *Curriculum Development: Theory into Practice.* New York: Macmillan, 1975; 2nd ed., 1980.

Taylor, Philip H. and Richards, Colin M. *An Introduction to Curriculum Studies.* Windsor, England: NFER Publishing Company, 1979.

Tyler, Ralph W. *Basic Principles of Curriculum and Instruction.* Chicago: University of Chicago Press, 1949.

Unruh, Glenys G. and Unruh, Adolph. *Curriculum Development: Problems, Processes, and Progress.* Berkeley, Calif.: McCutchan, 1984.

Vallance, Elizabeth. "Curriculum As a Field of Practice." In Fenwick W. English, ed. *Fundamental Curriculum Decisions,* 1983 Yearbook, 154–164. Alexandria, Va.: Association for Supervision and Curriculum Development, 1983.

Wiles, Jon and Bondi, Joseph C. *Curriculum Development: A Guide to Practice,* 2nd ed. Columbus, Ohio: Charles E. Merrill, 1984.

Zais, Robert S. *Curriculum: Principles and Foundations.* New York: Harper & Row, 1976.

CHAPTER TWO

Principles of Curriculum Development

After studying this chapter you should be able to:

1. Describe the ten axioms for curriculum development discussed in this chapter.

2. Illustrate in what way the curriculum is influenced by changes in society.

3. Describe limitations affecting curriculum changes in a school system and within which curriculum workers must function.

CLARIFICATION OF TERMS

Education is one of the institutions the human race has created to serve certain needs, and, like all human institutions, it responds or should respond to changes in the environment. The institution of education is activated by a curriculum that itself changes in response to forces affecting it. The curriculum of the cave dweller, albeit informal and unstructured, was quite different from increasingly formal types of schooling that the human race invented over subsequent periods of history. Techniques for coping with the woolly mammoth may well have been of paramount concern to prehistoric man.[1] But the woolly mammoth has disappeared, and men and women today must learn to cope with other sources of anxiety like decreasing natural resources; increasing population; lack of housing; drug addiction; pollution of air, land, and sea; unemployment; crime; health problems; malnutrition; and the military and industrial hazards of nuclear power. At the same time humankind must learn to apply the technological tools at its disposal to solve these and other problems.

Although no educator—teacher, curriculum coordinator, administrator, or professor—would dream of arguing that techniques of coping with the woolly mammoth should be a part of the curriculum of schools at the dawn of the twenty-first century A.D., in the third century of the American republic, the woolly mammoth syndrome still persists. Schools "woolly mammoth" children when they offer a curriculum that does the following things:

- ☐ Allows learners to leave school without an adequate mastery of the basic skills.
- ☐ Omits exposure to the fine arts, including the development of aesthetic appreciation.
- ☐ Portrays the average American child as being of Caucasian extraction; living with a father, mother, and one sibling of the opposite sex; residing in a $150,000 single-family home equipped with all the modern conveniences and two cars in the garage.
- ☐ Uses materials that show all children as members of healthy, happy, white, Anglo-Saxon Protestant families joyously living in suburbs.
- ☐ Ill equips its learners to find employment when they leave school.
- ☐ Fails to promote attitudes of concern for others, cooperation with others, responsibility for one's actions, tolerance of others, and conservation of resources.
- ☐ Leaves out the practical knowledge and skills necessary for survival and success in a complex society, such as knowledge about insurance and income taxes, writing a letter of application for a job, interviewing for a job, typing, and discussion and listening skills.

---

[1]For delightful reading, the little classic by Harold Benjamin (J. Abner Peddiwell) entitled *The Saber-Tooth Curriculum* (New York: McGraw-Hill, 1939) is recommended.

   □ Appeals to short-term interests of students and ignores long-range needs; or, vice versa, it may appeal to long-range needs and ignore short-term interests.

   □ Distorts truths of the past ("Honest Abe had no faults"), the present ("Every person who is willing to work can find a job"), and the future ("There is no need for residents of growing sections of the United States to worry about running out of potable water.").

   □ Ignores the use of computers.

If the curriculum is perceived as a plan for the learning experiences that young persons encounter under the direction of the school, its purpose is to provide a vehicle for ordering and directing these experiences. This process of providing the vehicle and keeping it running smoothly is known as curriculum development.

It may be helpful at this point to review the slight distinctions among the following terms: curriculum development, curriculum planning, curriculum implementation, curriculum improvement, and curriculum evaluation. *Curriculum development* is the more comprehensive term, which includes planning, implementation, and evaluation. Since curriculum development implies change and betterment, *curriculum improvement* is often used synonymously with curriculum development, though in some cases improvement is viewed as the result of development.

Curriculum planning is the preliminary phase of curriculum development when the curriculum workers make decisions and take actions to establish the plan that teachers and students will carry out. Planning is the thinking or design phase.

Curriculum implementation is translating plans into action. During the stage of curriculum planning, certain patterns of curriculum organization or reorganization are chosen. These patterns are put into operation at the implementation stage. Ways of delivering the learning experiences, for example, using teaching teams, are taken out of the planning context and made operational. Since curriculum implementation translates plans into action in the classroom, thereby transforming the realm of curriculum into the realm of instruction, the role of the teacher changes from curriculum worker to instructor.

Curriculum evaluation is the final phase of development in which results are assessed and successes of both the learners and the programs are determined. On occasion, *curriculum revision* is used to refer to the process for making changes in the curriculum or to the changes themselves and is substituted for *curriculum development* or *improvement*. We shall return to the distinctions among curriculum planning, implementation, and evaluation when models of curriculum development are diagrammed and discussed in Chapter 5.

Through the process of curriculum development, we can discover new ways for providing more effective pupil learning experiences. The curriculum developer continuously strives to find newer, better, and more efficient means to accomplish the task of educating the young.

TYPES OF CURRICULUM DEVELOPERS

Some curriculum developers excel in the conceptualizing phase (planning), others in carrying out the curricular plan (implementation), and still others in assessing curriculum results (evaluation). Over the centuries the human race has had no shortage of curriculum developers. In a positive vein Moses, Jesus, Buddha, Confucius, and Muhammad could all be called curriculum consultants. They had their respective conceptions of the goals of the human race and recommended behavior that must be learned and practiced to achieve these goals. On the negative side, at a later period in history Hitler, Stalin, Mussolini, and Mao Zedong had definite notions and programs to train the young in what to believe and how to behave in a totalitarian society.

The ranks of the politicians in a democracy have produced curriculum consultants, some more astute than others. To the weary professional curriculum worker, it sometimes seems that every federal, state, and local legislator is a self-appointed, self-trained curriculum consultant who has his or her own pet program to promulgate. The statutes of the state legislatures, as we shall see in Chapter 3, provide numerous examples of legislative curriculum making.

Singling out all the politicians who have turned themselves into curriculum consultants through the years would be difficult. But the kite flier who experimented with electricity, invented a stove, created a new educational institution called the Academy, and in between found time to participate in a revolution—Benjamin Franklin—made some farsighted curriculum proposals for his academy. Franklin's statement of recommendations almost seems to have been drawn out of a report on a high school's program of studies by a present-day visiting committee of a regional accreditation association. Franklin proposed for his academy (later to become the University of Pennsylvania) a curriculum much more suited to its time than its predecessor, the Latin Grammar School.[2]

Curriculum advisers have been found not only among politicians but also among academicians, journalists, the clergy, and the public at large. Professional educators have received a great deal of both wanted and unwanted help in shaping the school's curricula. An unending procession of advisers from both within and outside the profession of education over the years has not been at a loss to advocate curriculum proposals. No matter how significant or minor these proposals, no matter how mundane or bizarre, all proposals have shared one common element: advocacy of change.

What has led so many people to be dissatisfied with so much of what education is all about? Why is the status quo rarely a satisfactory place to be? And why does it turn out, as will be illustrated, that yesterday's status

---

[2]For discussion of the Academy, see Nelson L. Bossing, *Principles of Secondary Education* (Englewood Cliffs, N.J.: Prentice-Hall, 1955), pp. 97–107.

quo is sometimes tomorrow's innovation? For answers to these questions some general principles of curriculum development must be considered by teachers and specialists who participate in efforts to improve the curriculum.

SOURCES OF CURRICULUM PRINCIPLES

Principles serve as guidelines to direct the activity of persons working in a particular area. Curriculum principles are derived from many sources: (1) empirical data, (2) experimental data, (3) the folklore of curriculum, composed of unsubstantiated beliefs and attitudes, and (4) common sense. In an age of science and technology, the attitude often prevails that all principles must be scientifically derived from the results of research. Yet even folklore and common sense can have their usage. The scientist has discovered, for example, that some truths underlie ancient folk remedies for human maladies and that old wives' tales are not always the ravings of demented witches. While a garland of garlic hung around the neck may or may not fend off werewolves and asafetida on the end of a fishline may or may not lure fish onto the hook, the aloe plant does, after all, yield a soothing ointment for burns, and the peppermint herb has relieved many a stomachache.

Common sense, which is often distrusted, combines folklore, generalizations based on observation, and learnings discovered through experimentation with intuition and reasoned guesses. It can function not only as a source of curriculum principles but as a methodology as well. For example, Joseph J. Schwab proposed a common-sense process he called "deliberation" to deal with curriculum problems. Minimizing the search for theoretical constructs and principles, his method depends more on practical solutions to specific problems.[3] Schwab pointed out the pitfalls of relying on theory alone. He rejected "the pursuit of global principles and comprehensive patterns, the search for stable sequences and invariant elements, the construction of taxonomies of supposedly fixed or recurrent kinds" and recommended "three other modes of operation . . . the practical, the quasi-practical, and the eclectic."[4]

Of particular interest is Schwab's contrast of the theoretical and practical modes. Schwab explained:

> The end or outcome of the theoretical is knowledge, general or universal statements which are supposed to be true, warranted, confidence-inspiring. Their truth, warrant, or untrustworthiness is held, moreover, to be durable and extensive. . . . The end or outcome of the practical, on the other hand, is a *decision,* a selection and a guide to possible action. Decisions are never true or trustworthy. Instead a decision (before it is put into effect) can be

---

[3] Joseph J. Schwab, *The Practical: A Language for Curriculum* (Washington, D.C.: National Education Association, Center for the Study of Instruction, 1970).
[4] Ibid., p. 2. Reprinted with permission.

judged only comparatively, as probably better or worse than alternatives. . . . A decision, moreover, has no great durability or extensive application. It applies unequivocally only to the case for which it is sought.[5]

When curriculum planning is based on deliberation, judgment and common sense are applied to decision making. Some professional educators have faulted the application of common sense or judgment as a methodology, so imbued are they with a scientific approach to problem solving. In 1918 Franklin Bobbitt took note of scientific methodology in curriculum making, citing the application of measurement and evaluation techniques, diagnosis of problems, and prescription of remedies.[6] At a later date Arthur W. Combs was moved to warn against too great a reliance on science for the solution of all educational problems.[7] Whereas science may help us find solutions to some problems, not all answers to educational problems of the day can be found this way. Certainly, hard data are preferred over beliefs and judgments. But there are times in the absence of hard data when curriculum workers must rely on their intuition and make judgments on the best available evidence.

Unless a principle is established that is irrefutable by reason of objective data, some degree of judgment must be brought into play. Whenever judgment comes into the picture, the potential for controversy also arises. Consequently, some of the principles for curriculum development provoke controversy while others are generally accepted as reasonable guidelines. Controversy occurs as often as a result of differing values and philosophical orientations of curriculum workers as it does from lack of hard data for making decisions.

TYPES OF PRINCIPLES

Curriculum principles may be viewed as whole truths, partial truths, or hypotheses. While all function as operating principles, they are distinguished by their known effectiveness or by degree of risk. An understanding of these differences is important before examination of the major guiding principles for curriculum development.

Whole Truths

Whole truths are either obvious facts or concepts proved through experimentation, and they are usually accepted without challenge. For example, few will dispute that students will be able, as a rule, to master an advanced body of content only after they have developed the prerequisite skills. From this principle come the practices of preassessment of entry skills and sequencing of content.

---

[5]Ibid., pp. 2–3.
[6]See Franklin Bobbitt, *The Curriculum* (Boston: Houghton Mifflin, 1918), pp. 41–42.
[7]See Arthur W. Combs, *The Professional Education of Teachers* (Boston: Allyn and Bacon, 1965), p. 74.

Partial Truths

Partial truths are based on limited data and can apply to some, many, or most situations, but they are not always universal. Some educators assert, for example, that student achievement is higher when students are grouped homogeneously for instruction. Some learners may achieve better results when placed in groups of like ability, but others may not. The practice of homogeneous or ability grouping may be successful with some groups but not with others. It may permit schools to achieve certain goals of education, such as mastery of content, but prevent them from achieving other goals, such as learning to live and work with persons of differing levels of ability. Partial truths are not "half-truths," containing falsehoods, but they do not tell the whole story.

Hypotheses

Finally, some principles are neither whole nor partial truths but are *hypotheses* or tentative working assumptions. Curriculum workers base these ideas on their best judgments, folklore, and common sense. As one example, teachers and administrators have talked for many years about optimum size for classes and for schools. The magic ratio of 1 teacher to 25 pupils has been repeatedly advocated as a standard for class size. Educators have been less certain as to how many pupils should be housed in a single school. Figures used as recommendations for class and school size are but estimates based on best judgments. School planners have reasoned that for purposes of economy and efficiency, class and school sizes can be too small. They also know from intuition or experience that class and school sizes can grow so large as to create situations that reduce educational productivity. However, the research recalls no magic number that will guarantee success in every course, classroom, and school.

While practice based on whole truth is a desideratum, the use of partial truths and the application of hypotheses contribute to the development of the field. Growth would be stymied if the field waited until all truths were discovered before any changes were made. Judgments, folklore, and common sense make the curriculum arena a far more stimulating place to work than if everything were already predetermined. If all theories, beliefs, and hypotheses could be either proved or disproved—a most improbable event—we would have reached that condition of perfection that would make life among the curriculum developers exceedingly dull.

TEN AXIOMS

Instead of talking in terms of whole truths and partial truths, since so many of the principles practitioners subscribe to have not been fully tested, we might be more accurate if we speak of "axioms." *Webster's Ninth New Collegiate Dic-*

tionary defines an axiom as "**1:** a maxim widely accepted on its intrinsic merit **2:** a statement accepted as true as the basis for argument or inference: POSTULATE **3:** an established rule or principle or a self-evident truth." [8] Or perhaps "axiom" should be replaced with "theorem." The first two definitions of "theorem" in this dictionary are "**1:** a formula, proposition, or statement in mathematics or logic deduced or to be deduced from other formulas or propositions   **2:** an idea accepted or proposed as a demonstrable truth often as a part of a general theory: PROPOSITION." [9] As students of mathematics know well, even though an axiom may be a postulate and a theorem may be a proposition, both axioms and theorems serve the field well. They offer guidelines that establish a frame of reference for workers seeking ways of operating and resolving problems. Several generally accepted axioms that apply to the curriculum field may serve to guide efforts that curriculum workers make for the purpose of improving the curriculum.

Inevitability of Change

Axiom 1: *Change is both inevitable and necessary, for it is through change that life forms grow and develop.* Human institutions, like human beings themselves, grow and develop in proportion to their ability to respond to change and to adapt to changing conditions. Society and its institutions continuously encounter problems to which they must respond or perish. Glen Hass called attention to the following major contemporary problems facing society:

- □ environment
- □ changing values and morality
- □ the family
- □ the Microelectronics Revolution
- □ the changing world of work
- □ equal rights
- □ urban and suburban crises
- □ crime and violence
- □ alienation and anxiety
- □ international tensions[10]

The public school, one of our society's fundamental institutions, faces a plethora of contemporary problems, some of which threaten its very existence. We need cite only the intense competition from both secular and sectarian private schools, proposals for tax credits and vouchers, and the existence of home schools to illustrate the scope of problems currently confronting the public

---

[8]By permission. From *Webster's Ninth New Collegiate Dictionary* ©1989 by Merriam-Webster Inc., publisher of the Merriam-Webster®Dictionaries.

[9]By permission. From *Webster's Ninth New Collegiate Dictionary* ©1989 by Merriam-Webster Inc., publisher of the Merriam-Webster®Dictionaries.

[10]Glen Hass, *Curriculum Planning: A New Approach,* 5th ed. (Boston: Allyn and Bacon, 1987), pp. 45–48.

school. Change in the form of responses to contemporary problems must be foremost in the minds of curriculum developers.

Curriculum as a Product of Its Time

Axiom 2: The second axiom is a corollary of the first axiom. Quite simply, *a school curriculum not only reflects but is a product of its time.* Though it may seem to some that the curriculum is a tortoise moving infernally s-l-o-w-l-y, it has really undergone more transformations than the number of disguises assumed by a skilled master change artist.

David Turney, for example, commented on the slowness of change when he said:

> Real social change is painfully slow. It proceeds like a glacier whose movement is measured in feet per year. Educational and especially curriculum change is a part and parcel of social change and proceeds at about the same rate.[11]

Turney felt that at least a decade must be allowed as a minimum period of time for a basic change in education to be made. The reader has no doubt heard the comment (itself now an axiom) that it takes 50 years to effect an innovation in the school's curriculum. Many also believe it takes an additional 50 years before the innovation is universally adopted by the schools. The 50-year axiom illustrates well that axioms, which are created by human beings, are themselves subject to change as conditions change. Prior to the advent of television, the computer, and sophisticated media, this axiom may have had an element of truth; but today news and ideas flash across the country instantaneously. 50 years were certainly not required for thousands of schools across the country to put into practice team teaching, open-space education, values clarification, behavioral objectives, computer literacy, cooperative learning, and whole language, to mention only a few relatively recent innovations. But as a word of caution, although an innovation may not require 50 to 100 years, it may require three, five, or ten years or more—to some a long period of time—before it becomes a relatively common practice.

Clearly, the curriculum responds to and is changed by social forces, philosophical positions, psychological principles, accumulating knowledge, and educational leadership at its moment in history. The impact of the rapid accumulation of knowledge may be one of the more dramatic illustrations of forces affecting the curriculum. Certainly some adaptations in the school's program ought to be made as a result of discoveries of lifesaving vaccines; inventions such as the computer, the laser, and interactive video; and scientific accomplishments like the moon landings, the Mars flights, the Jupiter, Saturn, Uranus, and Venus probes, and other space explorations.

---

[11]David Turney, "Sisyphus Revisited," *Perspectives on Curriculum Development 1776–1976.* 1976 ASCD Yearbook (Alexandria, Va.: Association for Supervision and Curriculum Development, 1976), p. 232.

The presence of persuasive educational groups and individuals has been responsible for the adoption of curricular innovations at given moments in history and in numerous cases has caused permanent and continuing curriculum change. The effects of the famous Seven Cardinal Principles of Secondary Education by the Commission on the Reorganization of Secondary Education,[12] the Ten Imperative Needs of Youth by the Educational Policies Commission,[13] and *A Nation at Risk* by the National Commission on Excellence in Education[14] are illustrations of the impact persuasive groups have on the curriculum.

We may even point to individuals over the course of history, speaking either for themselves or for groups that they represented, who can be credited (or blamed, depending on one's perspective) for changes that have come about in the curriculum. Who can calculate the impact on education, for example, of Benjamin Franklin in the eighteenth century or Horace Mann in the nineteenth? What would the progressive education movement of the early twentieth century have been without John Dewey, William H. Kilpatrick, and Boyd Bode? How many secondary schools in the late 1950s and early 1960s "Conantized" their programs on the recommendations of James B. Conant, the former president of Harvard University? What impact has Maria Montessori had on elementary school programs? What responses of the curriculum in the latter half of the twentieth century can be traced to the teachings of Jean Piaget and of B. F. Skinner? What changes will come about as a result of recommendations made by Mortimer J. Adler,[15] Ernest L. Boyer,[16] John I. Goodlad,[17] and Theodore R. Sizer?[18] (In Chapter 9 we will examine many of these recommendations.)

We could fashion for ourselves a little chart—see Table 2–1—to illustrate the effects of several forces during periods of history on both the curriculum and instruction. In barest skeletal form we might break American educational history into three historical periods: 1650–1750, 1750–1850, and 1850 to the present. We might then chart some of the curricular and instructional responses to philosophical, psychological, and sociological forces of their time as the

---

[12]Commission on the Reorganization of Secondary Education, *Cardinal Principles of Secondary Education* (Washington, D.C.: U.S. Office of Education, Bulletin 35, 1918). See Chapter 3 of this text.

[13]Educational Policies Commission, *Education for All American Youth* (Washington, D.C.: National Education Association, 1944). See Chapter 3 of this text.

[14]The National Commission on Excellence in Education, David P. Gardner, chairman, *A Nation at Risk: The Imperative for Educational Reform* (Washington, D.C.: U.S. Government Printing Office, 1983). See Chapter 9 of this text.

[15]Mortimer J. Adler, *The Paideia Proposal: An Educational Manifesto* (New York: Macmillan, 1982).

[16]Ernest L. Boyer, *High School: A Report on Secondary Education in America* (New York: Harper & Row, 1983).

[17]John I. Goodlad, *A Place Called School: Prospects for the Future* (New York: McGraw-Hill, 1984).

[18]Theodore R. Sizer, *Horace's Compromise: The Dilemma of the American High School* (Boston: Houghton Mifflin, 1984).

TABLE 2–1   Forces affecting curriculum and instruction

PERIOD	FORCES	CURRICULAR RESPONSES	INSTRUCTIONAL RESPONSES
1650–1750	*Philosophy* Essentialism *Psychology* Faculty psychology— mind as a muscle *Sociology* Theocracy-Calvinist Male chauvinism Agrarian society Rich-poor dichotomy	Latin Grammar School: School for boys *The Bible* The three R's Classical curriculum	Strict discipline Rote learning Use of sectarian materials Mental discipline
1750–1850	*Philosophy* Essentialism Utilitarianism *Psychology* Faculty psychology *Sociology* Industrial Revolution Westward movement Rise of middle class Increased urbanization	Academy: Education for girls Instruction in: English Natural history Modern languages plus three R's and classical curriculum Tax-supported schools Kindergartens	Mental discipline Recitation Strict discipline Some practical applications
1850 to present:	*Philosophy* Essentialism Progressivism *Psychology* Behavioristic Experimental Gestalt Perceptual	**1850–1925:** High schools **1925–1950:** Child-centered curriculum Experimentalism Centralization and consolidation of schools Life adjustment	Practical applications Electives Problem-solving methods Attention to whole child

TABLE 2–1   continued

Period	FORCES	CURRICULAR RESPONSES	INSTRUCTIONAL RESPONSES
	Sociology	**1950 to present:**	Individualization and groupings for instruction
	Settling the West	Career education	Instructional technology
	Mechanized society	Open-space education	Opportunities for self-discipline
	Internationalism	Alternative schools	Achievement testing
	Urbanization	Magnet schools	Effective teaching models
	Immigration	Basic skills	Cooperative learning
	Armed conflicts	Global education	Whole language
	Civil rights	Middle schools	
	Big business	Computer education	
	Big labor	Values education	
	Equal rights	Special education	
	Changes in family	Environmental education	
	Environmental problems	Multi-cultural education	
	Diminishing resources	Health education/clinics	
	Rapid growth of technology	Sex education	
	Space exploration	Adult education	
	Public demand for schools' accountability	Literacy education	
	Unemployment	Bilingual education	
	Drug and alcohol abuse	Consumer education	
	Increase in crime		
	Homeless persons		
	Racial tensions/Ethnic conflicts		
	Movements for human rights		
	Handicapped persons		
	Aging population		
	Sexual behavior		
	Religious differences		
	Growth of democratic movements worldwide		
	Economic crises		

table shows. These forces and responses often overlap from one period to the next.

We could embellish the chart by refining the period of history and by adding other elements, but this skeletal description serves to illustrate that a curriculum is the product of its own time. James B. Macdonald made this point in this way:

> It should be clear to most knowledgeable and thoughtful observers of the American scene during the past twenty-five years, that any reforms in institutional setting, whether in education, occupations, churches, families, recreation, or whatever, are intricately related to multiple social pressures and set in the context of a general cultural ethos.[19]

Consequently, the curriculum planner of today must identify and be concerned with forces that impinge on the schools and must carefully decide how the curriculum should change in response to these often conflicting forces.

Concurrent Changes

Axiom 3: *Curriculum changes made at an earlier period of time can exist concurrently with newer curriculum changes at a later period of time.* The classical curriculum of the Latin Grammar School was continued, in spite of the reluctance of Benjamin Franklin, in the Academy. Indeed, even the first high school, established in Boston in 1821, was known as the English Classical School. It was not until three years later that the English Classical School became the English High School.

Curriculum revision rarely starts and ends abruptly. Changes coexist and overlap for long periods of time. Ordinarily, curricular developments are phased in gradually and phased out the same way. Because competing forces and responses occur at different periods of time and continue to exist, curriculum development becomes a frustrating yet challenging task.

Philosophical positions that differ on the nature of humankind, the destiny of the human race, good and evil, and the purposes of education have existed at every period of history. The powerful schools of essentialism and progressive thought continually strive to capture the allegiance of the profession and the public. The college preparatory curriculum, for example, vies with the vocational curriculum for primacy. Instructional strategies that are targeted at the development of the intellect compete with strategies for treating the child in body, mind, and spirit.

The competing responses to changing conditions have almost mandated an eclecticism, especially in the public schools. Curriculum developers select the

---

[19]James B. Macdonald, "Curriculum Development in Relation to Social and Intellectual Systems," in Robert M. McClure, ed., *The Curriculum: Retrospect and Prospect*, 70th Yearbook, Part I, National Society for the Study of Education. (Chicago: University of Chicago Press, 1971), pp. 98–99. Reprinted with permission.

best responses from previous times or modify them for future times. Except at the most trivial level, either/or choices are almost impossible to make in complex social areas like education. Yet some people continue to look for and argue for either/or solutions. To some, education will perish if all teachers do not write behavioral objectives. To others, the growth of preadolescents will surely be stunted unless they are educated in a middle school. Some elementary school administrators seek to provide a quality education with teaching teams. Others hold firmly to the traditional self-contained classroom.

Some themes are repeated through history. Critics have, for example, lambasted the schools periodically for what they conceive as failure to stress fundamental subject matter.[20] The history of curriculum development is filled with illustrations not only of recurrent philosophical themes, like the subject matter cacophony, but also with recurrent and cyclical curricular responses. Many of our schools have changed from an essentialistic to a progressive curriculum and back again.

Schools have moved from self-contained to open-space to self-contained; they have taught "old math," then "new math," and then reverted to the former; they have followed the phonics method of teaching reading, shifted to "look/say" methods, then reverted to phonics; they have stressed modern languages, then abandoned them, then reincorporated them in the curriculum. On the other hand, some schools, particularly the essentialistic, have remained unchanged while social change has swirled around them.

The schools of the early days in America stressed basic skills taught in a strict disciplinary climate. The early twentieth century schools went beyond basic skills—some would say away from basic skills—to concern for pupils' diverse needs and interests appealed to in a more permissive environment. Schools are now stressing the basic skills, subject matter, homework, academic achievement, pupil assessment, and codes of conduct.

As curricular themes are often recapitulated, some teachers and curriculum developers are disposed to maintain the status quo, concluding that their current mode of operation, while it may be out of favor at the present moment, will be in style again sometime in the future. "Why change and then have to change back?" they ask.

When the status quo no longer serves the needs of the learners nor of society, the maintenance of the status quo is inexcusable, for it prohibits responses appropriate to the times. Even if prior responses return at a later date, they should result from a reexamination of the forces of that particular time. Thus the reemergence of prior responses will be *new* responses, not *old* in the sense of being unchanging and unchangeable.

---

[20]See, for example, Arthur Bestor, *Educational Wastelands: The Retreat from Learning in Our Public Schools* (Urbana, Ill.: University of Illinois Press, 1953); Hyman Rickover, *Swiss Schools and Ours: Why Theirs Are Better* (Boston: Little, Brown, 1962); and Richard Mitchell, *The Graves of Academe* (Boston: Little, Brown, 1981).

Change in People

Axiom 4: *Curriculum change results from changes in people*. Thus curriculum developers should begin with an attempt to change the people who must ultimately effect curriculum change. This effort implies involving people in the process of curriculum development to gain their commitment to the change. Sad experience over a long period of time has demonstrated that changes handed down from on high to subordinates do not work well as a rule. Not until the subordinates have internalized the changes and accepted them as their own can the changes be effective and long lasting. Many school personnel lack commitment because they are denied this involvement in change and their contributions to change have been deprecated.

The importance of effecting change in people has been stressed by the curriculum experts for many years. Alice Miel, for example, wrote:

> To change the curriculum of the school is to change the factors interacting to shape that curriculum. In each instance this means bringing about changes in people — in their desires, beliefs, and attitudes, in their knowledge and skill. Even changes in the physical environment, to the extent that they can be made at all, are dependent upon changes in the persons who have some control over that environment. In short, the nature of curriculum change should be seen for what it really is — a type of social change, change in people, not mere change on paper.[21]

Vernon Anderson advised curriculum developers that no curriculum change could be lasting without a change in the way people think. He gave this principle paramount importance.[22]

Jack Frymier and Horace Hawn spoke to the same theme:

> Tinkering with minutiae in curriculum may cause some minor changes to occur in the educational process, but for anyone seriously interested in effecting significant change, the people who are involved must be themselves changed.[23]

An interested observer does not have to look far in most school systems to find evidence of curricular decisions being made without the participation of those affected by the decisions. For example, how many school buildings that impact heavily on curriculum are planned in cooperation with the teachers and curriculum workers?

When curricular prescriptions are handed down and mandated, programs may exist and even grow but, as a rule, those who must translate the mandated programs into action — the teachers — do so with less enthusiasm and fidelity.

---

[21] Alice Miel, *Changing the Curriculum: A Social Process* (New York: D. Appleton-Century, 1946), p. 10.

[22] See Vernon E. Anderson, *Curriculum Guidelines in an Era of Change* (New York: Ronald Press, 1969), p. 19.

[23] Jack R. Frymier and Horace C. Hawn, *Curriculum Improvement for Better Schools* (Worthington, Ohio: Charles A. Jones, 1970), p. 24. Reprinted with permission.

This lack of enthusiastic support spills over to the students, who often adopt negative attitudes as a result.

Some curriculum planners interpret this axiom to mean that 100 percent commitment of all affected parties must be achieved before a curriculum change can be implemented. Would that it were possible to obtain 100 percent consensus on any issue in education! Somewhere between a simple majority and universal agreement would appear to be a reasonable expectation. Involvement of persons affected in the process itself will succeed in garnering some support even from those who may disagree with the final curricular product.

The curriculum planner should ensure that all persons have an opportunity to contribute to a proposed change before it is too far along and irreversible. No persons should be involved in the charade practiced in some school systems whereby teachers and others are brought into the planning process for window dressing when it is a foregone conclusion that the curriculum change will be implemented whether the participants accept it or not. The "curriculum planner knows best" attitude has no place in curriculum design and implementation. In recent years we have been witnessing a pronounced movement toward empowering teachers, that is, enabling them to exercise a degree of control over what happens in their schools. For further discussion of empowerment of teachers, see Chapter 4, which expands on the process for instituting and effecting curriculum change.

Cooperative Endeavor

Axiom 5: *Curriculum change is effected as a result of cooperative endeavor on the part of groups.* Albert I. Oliver underscored the group nature of curriculum development when he said:

> It cannot be stressed too strongly that curriculum improvement is a cooperative endeavor. In the past, action on the curriculum was often limited to small-group work or to administrative decree; today, on the other hand, many groups and individuals are being encouraged to participate in a spirit of genuine cooperation.[24]

Oliver saw the cooperative nature of curriculum development as "more a matter of growth of individuals" than as "the installation or construction of certain materials."[25] Therefore, according to Oliver, "the more individuals can identify themselves with a curriculum activity, the more readily will they accept new phases. Genuine participation tends to generate 'psychological ownership' of the resulting program."[26]

---

[24]Excerpts from *Curriculum Improvement: A Guide to Problems, Principles, and Process,* 2nd ed., p. 37, by Albert I. Oliver. Copyright ©1965 by Harper & Row, Inc. Reprinted by permission of HarperCollins Publishers.
[25]Ibid.
[26]Ibid.

Although an individual teacher working in isolation might conceivably effect changes in the curriculum by himself or herself, large and fundamental changes are brought about as a result of group decision.

Several groups or constituencies are involved in curriculum development in differing roles and with differing intensities. Students and lay persons often, though perhaps not as frequently as might be desired, join forces with educational personnel in the complex job of planning a curriculum.

Teachers and curriculum specialists constitute the professional core of planners. These professionally trained persons carry the weight of curriculum development. They work together under the direction of the school administrator whose task it is to oversee their activities and to facilitate their efforts at all stages of development. The administrator may take the bows for the school's successful activities but by the same token will also encounter criticism for efforts gone awry.

Students enter the process of curriculum development as direct recipients of both benefits and harm which result from curriculum change, and parents are brought in as the persons most vitally concerned with the welfare of their young. Most often and more willingly than in days gone by, administrators invite students and parents to participate in the process of curriculum planning. Some school systems go beyond parents of children in their schools and seek representation from the total community, parents and nonparents alike. People from the community are asked more frequently now what they feel the schools should offer and what they believe the schools are omitting from their programs.

Generally, any significant change in the curriculum should involve all the aforementioned constituencies, as well as the school's noncertificated personnel. The more people affected by the change, the greater its complexity and the greater its costs, the greater the number of persons and groups that should be involved. The roles of various individuals and groups in curriculum development are examined in Chapter 4.

Although some limited gains certainly take place through independent curriculum development within the walls of a classroom, significant curriculum improvement comes about through group activity. Results of group deliberation are not only more extensive than individual efforts, but the process by which the group works together allows group members to share their ideas and to reach group consensus. In this respect group members help each other to change and to achieve commitment to change.

Decision-making Process

Axiom 6: *Curriculum development is basically a decision-making process.* The curriculum planner in cooperation with those involved must make a variety of choices, including the following:

1. Choices among disciplines. The absence of philosophy, anthropology, Chinese, and sometimes even art and music from the curriculum of schools indicates that choices have been made about the subjects to which students will be exposed.
2. Choices among competing viewpoints. Planners must decide, for example, whether they agree that bilingual education best serves the needs of segments of society. They must make decisions about programs such as interscholastic athletics for girls, whether pupils with learning disabilities should be assigned to special classes, whether to group pupils by ability, and whether programs of sex education should be offered.
3. Choices of emphases. Shall a school system, for example, give extra help to poor readers? Shall school systems provide programs for the gifted? Shall extra efforts be made for disadvantaged youngsters? Should school funds be diverted from one group of students to aid another group?
4. Choices of methods. What is the best way, for example, of teaching reading? phonics? look/say? "systems" reading? whole language? What are the more effective materials to use? How is cultural bias eliminated from the program?
5. Choices in organization. Is a nongraded school, for example, the better approach to an organizational arrangement that will provide maximum opportunities for learners? Should alternative forms of schooling within and outside the system be provided? Shall elementary programs be delivered in an open-space or pod setting, with totally self-contained classrooms, or with the use of resource persons to assist a teacher in a self-contained classroom?

Two necessary characteristics of a curriculum planner are the ability to effect decisions after sufficient study of a problem and the willingness to make decisions.[27] The indecisive person had best not gravitate to a career as a curriculum planner. Those persons for whom every *i* must be dotted and every *t* crossed before a move can be made are far too cautious for curriculum planning. Every decision involves calculated risk, for no one—in spite of what some experts may claim—has all the answers to all the problems or a single panacea for every problem. Some decisions will end in dismal failure. But unless the test is made, it can never be known what will succeed and what will not. The most that can be expected of a fallible human being is that decisions will be made on available evidence that suggests success for the learners and that promises no serious harm for them as a result of a decision taken. In the history of curriculum development we can find evidence of many roads that were not taken. Those roads might have turned out to be expressways to

---

[27]For description of a decision-making process, see Chapter 13 of this text regarding material from Phil Delta Kappa National Study Committee on Evaluation, Daniel L. Stufflebeam, committee chairman, *Educational Evaluation and Decision Making* (Itasca, Ill.: F. E. Peacock, 1971).

learning, though, of course, the pessimistic champion of the status quo would assure us that the roads not taken would have been overgrown ruts that ended at the brink of a precipice or circular paths that would lead us right back to where we were.

Although the task of making curricular choices may be difficult in complex, advanced societies, the opportunity to make choices from among many alternatives is a luxury not found in every country.

Continuous Process

Axiom 7: *Curriculum development is a never-ending process*. Curriculum planners constantly strive for the ideal, yet the ideal eludes them. John R. Verduin, Jr., made this point succinctly: "Continuous examination, evaluation, and improvement of the curriculum is, therefore, of vital importance."[28] Perfection in the curriculum will never be obtained. The curriculum can always be improved, and better solutions can always be found to accomplish specific objectives. As the needs of learners change, as society changes, and as new knowledge appears, the curriculum must change. Curriculum evaluation should affect subsequent planning and implementation. Curriculum goals and objectives and plans for curricular organization should be modified as feedback reveals the need for modification.

Curriculum development is not finished when a single curricular problem has been temporarily resolved nor when a new or revised program has been instituted. Continual monitoring is necessary to assure that the program is on track and the problem does not recur. Further, adequate records should be kept by curriculum committees so that curriculum workers in future years will know what has been attempted and with what results.

Comprehensive Process

Axiom 8: *Curriculum development is a comprehensive process*. Historically, much of curriculum development has been a hit-or-miss procedure: patching, cutting, adding, plugging in, shortening, lengthening, and troubleshooting. In agreeing with the necessity for comprehensive planning, Hilda Taba explained:

> Some commentators have pointed out that the whole history of our curriculum revision has been piecemeal—a mere shifting of pieces from one place to another, taking out one piece and replacing it with another without a reappraisal of the whole patterns. The curriculum has become "the amorphous product of generations of tinkering"—a patchwork. This piecemeal approach is continuing today, when additions and revisions in

---

[28]John R. Verduin, Jr., *Cooperative Curriculum Improvement* (Englewood Cliffs, N.J.: Prentice-Hall, 1967), p. 33.

certain areas are made without reconsidering the entire pattern, and when acceleration in one part of the school system is recommended without corresponding changes in the next.[29]

Curriculum planning has often been too fragmentary rather than comprehensive or holistic. Too many curriculum planners have focused on the trees and not seen the forest.

Curriculum development spills not only into the forest but beyond. A comprehensive view encompasses an awareness of the impact of curriculum development not only on the students, teachers, and parents directly concerned with a programmatic change but also on the innocent bystanders, those not directly involved in the curriculum planning but affected in some way by the results of planning.[30] Sex education, for example, may affect not only teachers, students, and parents of students for whom the program is intended but also students, teachers, and parents of those who are not scheduled for the instruction. Some from the groups involved may not wish to be included. Some from the groups not in the program may wish to receive the instruction. Some from both groups may reject the subject as inappropriate for the school.

The comprehensive approach to curriculum planning requires a generous investment of physical and human resources. Curriculum workers must engage in, without meaning to be redundant, planning for curriculum planning or what some people might refer to as "preplanning." Some predetermination must be made prior to initiating curriculum development as to whether the tangible resources, the personnel, and sufficient time will be available to allow a reasonable expectation of success. Not only must personnel be identified, but their sense of motivation, energy level, and other commitments must also be taken into consideration by the curriculum leaders. Perhaps one of the reasons why curriculum development has historically been fragmentized and piecemeal is the demand the comprehensive approach places on the school's resources.

Systematic Development

Axiom 9: *Systematic curriculum development is more effective than trial and error.* Curriculum development should ideally be made comprehensive by looking at the whole canvas and should be made systematic by following an established set of procedures. That set of procedures should be agreed upon and known by all those who participate in the development of the curriculum. Curriculum planners are more likely to be productive and successful if they follow

---

[29]Excerpts from *Curriculum Development: Theory and Practice,* p. 8, by Hilda Taba, copyright ©1962 by Harcourt Brace Jovanovich, Inc. and renewed 1990 by Margaret J. Spalding, reprinted by permission of the publisher.

[30]See Michael Scriven, "The Methodology of Evaluation," *Perspectives of Curriculum Evaluation,* AERA Monograph Series on Curriculum Evaluation no. 1 (Chicago: Rand McNally, 1967), p. 77.

an agreed-upon model for curriculum development that outlines or charts the sequence of steps to be followed. In Chapter 5 we will examine several models for curriculum development.

If the curriculum worker subscribes to the foregoing axioms and consents to modeling his or her behavior on the basis of these axioms, will success be inevitable? The answer is an obvious no, for there are many limitations on curriculum workers, some of which are beyond their control. Among the restrictions on the curriculum planner are the style and personal philosophy of the administrator, the resources of the school system, the degree of complacency in the school system and community, the presence or absence of competent supervisory leadership, the fund of knowledge and skills possessed by the participants in curriculum development, and the availability of professional materials and resource persons.

One of the great limitations—sometimes overlooked because it is so obvious and encompassing—is the existing curriculum. Many treatises have been written by the curriculum experts on the characteristics of different types of curriculum. The earmarks of an activity curriculum, a subject matter curriculum, a broad-fields curriculum, and variations of core curricula are described in the literature in detail.[31] From a purely cognitive base such discussions are useful. But the inference is sometimes drawn that the choice of a type of curriculum is an open one—that if the planners know and believe in the characteristics of an activity curriculum, for example, they will have the option of organizing and implementing that type of curriculum. It is as if a curriculum planner could start from scratch and design a totally new curriculum, which is rarely the case, and which leads us to the tenth axiom.

Starting from the Existing Curriculum

Axiom 10: *The curriculum planner starts from where the curriculum is just as the teacher starts from where the students are.* Curriculum change does not take place overnight. Few overnight quantum leaps can be found in the field of curriculum, and this condition may be a positive value rather than a negative one, for slow but steady progress toward change allows time for testing and reflection.

Since most curriculum planners begin with already existing curricula, we would be more accurate if, instead of talking about curriculum organization, we talked about curriculum reorganization. The investment of thought, time, money, and work by previous planners cannot be thrown out even if such a drastic remedy appeared valid to a new set of planners. The curriculum worker

---

[31] See B. O. Smith, William O. Stanley, and J. Harlan Shores, *Fundamentals of Curriculum Development,* rev. ed. (New York: Harcourt Brace Jovanovich, 1957). See also Chapter 9 of this text.

might well follow the advice in the *Book of Common Prayer* where the believer is told to "hold fast to that which is good."

SUMMARY

The system that we call education responds to change as conditions in its suprasystem (society) change. Curriculum change is a normal, expected consequence of changes in the environment.

The curriculum worker's responsibility is to seek ways of making continuous improvement in the curriculum. The task of the curriculum worker is facilitated if the worker follows some generally accepted principles for curriculum development. Ten general principles or axioms are presented. The principles stem not only from disciplines outside of professional education but also from the folklore of curriculum, observation, experimental data, and common sense.

Axioms suggested as guides to curriculum developers are:

- ☐ Curriculum change is inevitable and desirable.
- ☐ The curriculum is a product of its time.
- ☐ Curriculum changes of earlier periods often coexist with and overlap curriculum changes of later periods.
- ☐ Curriculum change results only as people are changed.
- ☐ Curriculum development is a cooperative group activity.
- ☐ Curriculum development is basically a process of making choices from among alternatives.
- ☐ Curriculum development never ends.
- ☐ Curriculum development is more effective if it is a comprehensive, not a piecemeal, process.
- ☐ Curriculum development is more effective when it follows a systematic process.
- ☐ Curriculum development starts from where the curriculum is.

Both teachers and curriculum specialists fill roles as curriculum workers in cooperation with other school personnel. Teachers, curriculum specialists, supervisors, administrators, students, parents, and other community representatives can all play significant roles in effecting curricular change.

Curriculum developers start from the given and work within specific parameters. Ordinarily, change is relatively slow, limited, and gradual.

QUESTIONS FOR DISCUSSION

1. In what ways is today's public school curriculum suitable for the times?
2. In what ways is today's public school curriculum not suitable for the times?
3. What are some curriculum principles derived from common sense?

4. Are there any curriculum developments that have been based on whole truth? If so, give examples.
5. Are there any curriculum developments that have been based on false premises? If so, give examples.

SUPPLEMENTARY EXERCISES

1. Develop your own chart of the effects of forces on curriculum and instruction by periods of history of the United States. Your chart should expand on the periods of history and present additional details.
2. Formulate and support one or two additional axioms pertaining to curriculum development. These may be original ones that you will be able to defend, or they may be axioms drawn from the professional literature.
3. Write a paper on the contributions of one of the following persons to the development of curriculum thought or practice: Horace Mann, William James, John Dewey, William H. Kilpatrick, Boyd Bode, B. F. Skinner, Jean Piaget, Ralph Tyler, and Robert Hutchins.
4. Write a paper on one of the following groups and describe its impact on curriculum development in the United States: the Commission on the Reorganization of Secondary Education, the Committee of Ten, the Educational Policies Commission, and the National Science Foundation.
5. Choose three social developments, events, pressures, or forces in the United States within the last 15 years that have caused changes in the school's curriculum, and briefly describe those changes.
6. Look up one or more books or articles by an author who has been critical of public education (such as Arthur Bestor, Rudolph Flesch, Paul Goodman, John Holt, John Keats, James D. Koerner, Jonathan Kozol, Max Rafferty, Hyman Rickover, and Mortimer Smith in the 1950s and 1960s; Paul Copperman, Ivan Illich, and Charles E. Silberman in the 1970s; Richard Mitchell, E. D. Hirsch, Jr., Diane Ravitch, and Chester E. Finn, Jr. in the 1980s; and Lynne V. Cheney of the National Endowment for the Humanities in 1990) and summarize the criticisms in a written or oral report. Tell where you believe the critics were right and where you believe they were wrong. (You will be given an opportunity in the exercises at the end of Chapter 9 to report on some of the recent studies on the reform of education.)
7. Read *The Practical: A Language for Curriculum* by Joseph J. Schwab and explain to the class what Schwab means by three modes of operation for curriculum development: the practical, the quasi-practical, and the eclectic. Tell what Schwab means when he says, "The field of curriculum is moribund." State whether you agree with Schwab. (See reference to Schwab's book in the bibliography.)
8. Consult some books on the history of American education and prepare comparative descriptions of the curriculum of (1) the Latin Grammar School, (2) the Academy, and (3) the English High School.

BIBLIOGRAPHY

Anderson, Vernon E. *Curriculum Guidelines in an Era of Change.* New York: Ronald Press, 1969.

———. *Principles and Procedures of Curriculum Improvement,* 2nd ed. New York: Ronald Press, 1965.

Beane, James A., Toepfer, Conrad F., Jr., and Alessi, Samuel J., Jr. *Curriculum Planning and Development.* Boston: Allyn and Bacon, 1986.

Benjamin, Harold R. W. [Peddiwell, J. Abner]. *The Saber-Tooth Curriculum.* New York: McGraw-Hill, 1939.

Berman, Louise M. and Roderick, Jessie A. *Curriculum: Teaching the What, How, and Why of Living.* Columbus, Ohio: Charles E. Merrill, 1977.

Bobbitt, Franklin. *The Curriculum.* Boston: Houghton Mifflin, 1918. Also, New York: Arno Press and *The New York Times,* 1975.

Charters, W. W. *Curriculum Construction.* New York: Macmillan, 1923. Also, New York: Arno Press and *The New York Times,* 1971.

Combs, Arthur W. *The Professional Education of Teachers: A Perceptual View of Teacher Preparation.* Boston: Allyn and Bacon, 1965.

Davis, O. L., Jr., ed. *Perspectives on Curriculum Development 1776–1976,* 1976 Yearbook. Alexandria, Va.: Association for Supervision and Curriculum Development, 1976.

Doll, Ronald C. *Curriculum Improvement: Decision Making and Process,* 7th ed. Boston: Allyn and Bacon, 1989.

Draper, Edgar Marion. *Principles and Techniques of Curriculum Making.* New York: D. Appleton-Century, 1936.

Firth, Gerald R. and Kimpston, Richard D. *The Curricular Continuum in Perspective.* Itasca, Ill.: F. E. Peacock, 1973.

Frymier, Jack R. and Hawn, Horace C. *Curriculum Improvement for Better Schools.* Worthington, Ohio: Charles A. Jones, 1970.

Gagné, Robert M. *The Conditions of Learning,* 2nd ed. New York: Holt, Rinehart and Winston, 1970; 3rd ed., 1977.

Gwynn, J. Minor and Chase, John B., Jr. *Curriculum Principles and Social Trends,* 4th ed. New York: Macmillan, 1969.

Hass, Glen. *Curriculum Planning: A New Approach,* 5th ed. Boston: Allyn and Bacon, 1987.

Herrick, Virgil E. and Tyler, Ralph W. *Toward Improved Curriculum Theory.* Supplementary Educational Monograph, no. 71, March, 1950. Chicago: University of Chicago Press, 1950.

Knezevich, Stephen J. *Administration of Public Education,* 4th ed. New York: Harper & Row, 1984.

McClure, Robert M., ed. *The Curriculum: Retrospect and Prospect,* 70th Yearbook. Chicago: National Society for the Study of Education, University of Chicago Press, 1971.

Macdonald, James B., Anderson, Dan W., and May, Frank B. *Strategies of Curriculum Development: Selected Writings of the Late Virgil E. Herrick.* Columbus, Ohio: Charles E. Merrill, 1965.

Oliver, Albert I. *Curriculum Improvement: A Guide to Problems, Principles, and Process,* 2nd ed. New York: Harper & Row, 1977.

Orlofsky, Donald E. and Smith, B. Othanel. *Curriculum Development: Issues and Insights.* Chicago: Rand McNally, 1978.

Rubin, Louis, ed. *Curriculum Handbook: The Disciplines, Current Movements, and Instructional Methodology.* Boston: Allyn and Bacon, 1977.

———. *Curriculum Handbook: Administration and Theory.* Boston: Allyn and Bacon, 1977.

———. *Curriculum Handbook: The Disciplines, Current Movements, Instructional Methodology, Administration and Theory,* abridged ed. Boston: Allyn and Bacon, 1977.

Saylor, J. Galen, Alexander, William M., and Lewis, Arthur J. *Curriculum Planning for Better Teaching and Learning,* 4th ed. New York: Holt, Rinehart and Winston, 1981.

Schwab, Joseph J. *The Practical: A Language for Curriculum.* Washington, D.C.: National Education Association, Center for the Study of Instruction, 1970.

Short, Edmund C. and Marconnit, George D., eds. *Contemporary Thought on Public School Curriculum.* Dubuque, Iowa: William C. Brown, 1968.

Taba, Hilda. *Curriculum Development: Theory and Practice.* New York: Harcourt Brace Jovanovich, 1962.

Tanner, Daniel and Tanner, Laurel N. *Curriculum Development: Theory Into Practice,* 2nd ed. New York: Macmillan, 1980.

Unruh, Glenys H. *Responsive Curriculum Development: Theory and Action.* Berkeley, Calif.: McCutchan, 1975.

Verduin, John R., Jr. *Cooperative Curriculum Improvement.* Englewood Cliffs, N.J.: Prentice-Hall, 1967.

Walker, Decker. *Fundamentals of Curriculum.* Orlando, Fla.: Harcourt, Brace Jovanovich, 1990.

Wiles, Jon and Bondi, Joseph C. *Curriculum Development: A Guide to Practice,* 2nd ed. Columbus Ohio: Charles E. Merrill, 1984.

Zais, Robert S. *Curriculum: Principles and Foundations.* New York: Harper & Row, 1976.

PART II

Curriculum Development: Roles of School Personnel

CHAPTER THREE

Curriculum Planning: A Multilevel, Multisector Process

After studying this chapter you should be able to:

1. Describe types of curriculum planning that are conducted at five levels and in three sectors.

2. Design an organizational pattern for curriculum development at the individual school level.

3. Design an organizational pattern for curriculum development at the school district level.

ILLUSTRATIONS OF CURRICULUM DECISIONS

Daily, curriculum decisions like the following are being made in some school district somewhere in the United States:

- ☐ An elementary school uses computer-assisted instruction in teaching the basic skills. Computer laboratories have been established in both the junior and senior high schools of this same school district.
- ☐ An entire school district has decided to put a program of sex education into the curriculum at all levels.
- ☐ A junior high school has decided to incorporate more material on the achievements of various ethnic groups into its social studies program.
- ☐ A senior high school faculty is concentrating on the development of students' thinking skills.
- ☐ A school system has adopted a plan for bilingual education.
- ☐ An elementary school has decided to replace its reading series with that of another publisher.
- ☐ A school district has put into operation a program of writing across the curriculum.
- ☐ A school system has approved a plan for meeting the needs of the academically talented and gifted.
- ☐ The secondary schools of a district have put into operation a plan for increasing opportunities for girls to participate in team sports and for placing these sports on a par with boys' athletic activities.
- ☐ An urban school district is establishing a magnet secondary school that will emphasize science, mathematics, and technology.

Variations Among Schools

Countless curricular decisions like those in the preceding examples are made constantly. Some decisions are relatively simple—adding a course here, deleting a course there, or making some minor change of content. Other decisions are sweeping and far-reaching—for example, the institution or abandonment of open-education plans or the conversion of a 6–3–3 plan for school organization (six years of elementary school, three of junior high, and three of senior high) to a 4–4–4 plan (four years each of elementary school, middle school, and high school). These changes are both administrative and curricular decisions.

Some of the more dynamic school systems maintain a lively pace of curriculum decision making and are continuously effecting changes in the curriculum as a result of these decisions. Often more than one type of change occurs simultaneously in some districts and schools.

Some systems follow a reasoned, measured process for arriving at planning decisions and carrying out those decisions; others enter into an almost frenzied, superheated process in which dozens of curricular ideas are dancing around without decision or resolution; other school districts demonstrate lethargy and apathy toward curricular decision making and are, for all intents and purposes, stagnant.

The foregoing illustrations of curriculum decisions are typical examples occurring within individual school districts. These illustrations might have been stated to show that the same kinds of decisions were being made at the same time in more than one school district. These illustrations of curriculum decisions could apply to multiple school districts scattered throughout the United States and might be reported as follows:

☐ A number of elementary schools have decided to replace their reading series with that of another publisher. We might extend this illustration by pointing out that they have all chosen the same publisher!

☐ Several school districts have decided to put a program of sex education into the curriculum at all levels.

☐ Several middle schools have decided to incorporate more material on the achievements of various ethnic groups in their social studies programs.

How can we account for the simultaneous development of curriculum plans in different parts of the country? Shall we attribute it to legal pressures from federal or state sources? Among the foregoing illustrations only two—bilingual education programs and increased opportunities for girls to participate in team sports—may be said to have evolved as a result of legal processes. In 1974 the United States Supreme Court opened the doors to bilingual education programs with its decision in the *Lau* v. *Nichols* case.[1] As a consequence of this decision the San Francisco school system was required to provide special instruction to children of Chinese ancestry who were having difficulty with the English language. Furthermore, federal funds have been appropriated to assist school systems to develop and implement bilingual education programs. The participation of girls in team sports has been advanced through enactment by the U.S. Congress of Title IX of the Educational Amendments of 1972, which bars discrimination on the basis of sex. Certainly, federal and state legislation and court decisions have brought about curricular change, as we will explore more fully later. But we must also look elsewhere for other causes or partial causes of simultaneous development of curricular plans.

Simultaneous Developments

Though it is unlikely, similar curriculum developments in different school systems may unfold at the same time by pure chance. This situation resembles that of two astronomers, unknown to each other and separated by oceans and continents, who suddenly discover the same star, or two scientific researchers who find within days or weeks of each other a cure for a disease plaguing humankind.

---

[1] *Lau* v. *Nichols,* 414 U.S. 563 (1974).

It is more likely that our country's efficient systems of transportation and communication can be pointed to as principal reasons for concurrent curriculum development. These pervasive technological systems make possible the rapid transmission of the beneficial pollen (or not so beneficial virus, depending on one's point of view) of curricular ideas.

These gigantic systems have an impact on all the constituencies of a school district—the administrators, teachers, students, parents, and other members of the community. Transportation makes it possible for people from all parts of the country to get together in formal and informal settings and discuss contemporary problems of the schools. It would be interesting, for example, to measure the effects of national professional education conferences on the spread of curricular innovation. Although the pessimist would assert that a great deal of drivel flows at many professional conferences, enough kernels of wisdom are shared that are taken back home where they are planted and brought to fruition. Could not several of the preceding illustrations have come about through the exchange of ideas on a person-to-person basis at a state, regional, or national meeting?

With possibly an even greater impact, communication systems permit the dissemination of reports of educational and social problems in various parts of the country and descriptions of how communities have sought to cope with these problems. The commercial press and television consistently make the public aware of social problems that call for some curricular responses, such as drug abuse, unemployment, racial problems, environmental problems, and the lack of basic skills on the part of young people. The media have been instrumental in revealing widespread citizen dissatisfaction with the public schools to the point where lay constituencies are demanding that curricular changes be made.

While the commercial media are pointing out social problems and, on occasion, educational responses to these problems, the professional media are engaged in healthy dialogue. The United States is blanketed with professional journals filled with educators' philosophical positions, proposals for change, and reports of projects, research, and experimentation. National and state professional organizations, the United States Department of Education, and state departments of education frequently release monographs, guides, and research reports of promising curricular projects. Both popular and professional books on education make their contributions to the quest for curricular solutions to many social and educational problems. Who is to assess, for example, the impact made on the schools by writers and educators such as Earl Kelley, who stressed the importance of an individual's self-concept;[2] Ralph Tyler, who suggested a systematic way of arriving at instructional objectives;[3] Benjamin Bloom and his associates, who offered a way of classifying educational objectives and ad-

---

[2]Earl C. Kelley, *Education for What Is Real* (New York: Harper & Row, 1947).
[3]Ralph W. Tyler, *Basic Principles of Curriculum and Instruction* (Chicago: University of Chicago Press, 1949).

vocated mastery learning;[4] James B. Conant, who made recommendations that were widely adopted by secondary schools;[5] Jerome S. Bruner, who wrote on the structure of disciplines;[6] Charles E. Silberman, who painted a grim picture of schools;[7] and John I. Goodlad, who directed an extensive study of schools and made recommendations for improvement?[8]

Through modern means of communication and transportation, curriculum innovations—good, bad, and indifferent—are transmitted rapidly to a world thirsty for new and better ways of meeting its educational obligations to children and youth. It is extremely difficult in an enterprise as large as education to pinpoint the source of a particular curriculum change, and it is not usually necessary to do so. What is important to the student and practitioner in curriculum planning is to understand that processes for effecting change are in operation. These processes extend beyond the classroom, the school, even the school district.

LEVELS OF PLANNING

Curriculum planning occurs on many levels, and curriculum workers— teachers, supervisors, administrators, or others—may be engaged in curriculum efforts on several levels at the same time. The levels of planning on which teachers function can be conceptualized as shown in Figure 3–1.[9] All teachers are involved in curriculum planning at the classroom level, most teachers participate in curriculum planning at the school level, some take part at the district level, and fewer and fewer engage in the planning process at state, regional, national, and international levels. A few teachers, however, do participate in curriculum planning at all levels.

Importance of Classroom Level

The model in Figure 3–1, with its ascending stairs and even with its use of the term "levels," may lead to some erroneous conclusions. You might conclude, since the steps clearly sketch a hierarchy, that planning at the

---

[4]Benjamin S. Bloom, ed., *Taxonomy of Educational Objectives: The Classification of Educational Goals: Handbook I: Cognitive Domain* (New York: Longman, 1956).

Benjamin S. Bloom, J. Thomas Hastings, and George F. Madans, *Handbook on Formative and Summative Evaluation of Student Learning* (New York: McGraw-Hill, 1971).

[5]James B. Conant, *The American High School Today* (New York: McGraw-Hill, 1959).

[6]Jerome S. Bruner, *The Process of Education* (Cambridge, Mass.: Harvard University Press, 1960).

[7]Charles E. Silberman, *Crisis in the Classroom: The Remaking of American Education* (New York: Random House, 1970).

[8]John I. Goodlad, *A Placed Called School: Prospects for the Future* (New York: McGraw-Hill, 1984).

[9]Adapted from Peter F. Oliva, *The Secondary School Today*, 2nd ed. (New York: Harper & Row, 1972), p. 280.

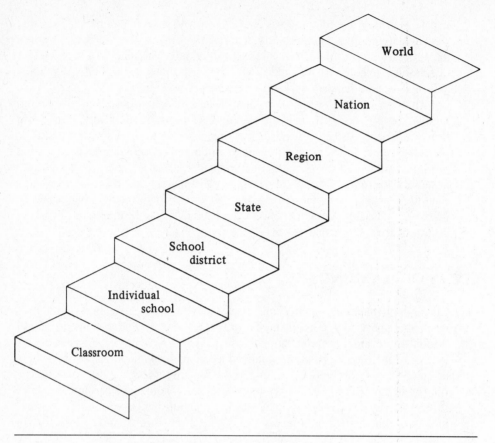

FIGURE 3–1   Levels of planning

classroom level is least important and planning at each successive level is increasingly more important. Nothing could be further from the truth. If we are concerned about levels of importance, and indeed we are, we should concede that classroom planning is far more important than any of the successive steps. At the classroom level, the results of curriculum planning make their impact on the learners.

In some ways it would appear more pertinent if we turned the model around and placed classroom planning at the top and international planning at the bottom. Unfortunately, reversing the step model would introduce another possible misinterpretation. Since the classroom is the focal point for curriculum planning and the main locale for curriculum development efforts, this stage is shown as the first step. Designating the international level as the initial step would be extremely inaccurate since very few teachers or curriculum specialists work at that level and then usually only after they have demonstrated competence at the other levels.

The step model may convey to some readers that curriculum workers move through each stage or level in a fixed sequence. Although most teachers are involved in curriculum planning at both the classroom and school levels, some will proceed no further than these two levels. Some teachers and curriculum specialists work in sequence from one level to the next or simultaneously at all levels, whereas others may skip whole levels. Although curriculum planning usually begins in the classroom, it may start at whatever level curriculum workers feel a need to initiate change.

Since the steps in the preceding model are of equal width and rise, the model can give the impression that curriculum planners have an equal opportunity to participate at all levels and spend equal amounts of time in planning at each level. Opportunities for curriculum planning become fewer at each successive step up the staircase. Consequently, if the step model is retained to show the levels of planning, it would be better to visualize the rise between steps as progressively higher and the width of each step as progressively narrower.

The persons with whom we are most concerned in this textbook—the curriculum workers at the school and district levels—will be able to devote only limited time to curriculum planning at levels beyond the district.

As long as we conceptualize levels of planning as loci of work rather than of importance and understand that curriculum specialists do not necessarily work at all levels or in a fixed sequence of levels, the concept of levels of planning is valid and useful.

SECTORS OF PLANNING

Some curriculum theorists might feel somewhat more comfortable if, instead of speaking of levels of planning, we talked of sectors of planning. The concept of sectors eliminates the hierarchical and sequence problems of the step model and says simply that curriculum planning goes on in eight sectors: the classroom, the team/grade/department, the individual school, the school district, the state, the region, the nation, and the world. The sector model, illustrated in Figure 3–2, shows teachers and curriculum workers spending the largest part of their planning time in the individual school and school district and decreasing amounts of their time in sectors beyond the district boundaries. The broken lines signify that an individual teacher or curriculum planner may work at separate times or simultaneously in more than one sector. On the other hand, the teacher or curriculum planner may confine himself or herself to the classroom sector.

Models of levels or of sectors of planning address the question of where decisions are made and what organizational processes are used for developing

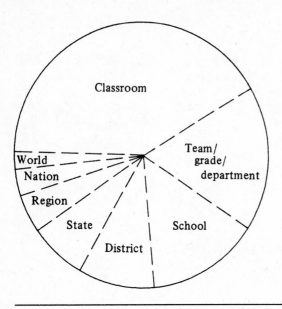

FIGURE 3–2   Sectors of planning

,plans. These models do not, of course, answer the question of why decisions are made, a topic explored in later chapters.

In discussing levels or sectors of planning, we should distinguish between levels or sectors in which individual planners work and those where decisions are actually made. These are not necessarily the same. Let's take, for example, the case of a fifth-grade teacher. This teacher may possess sufficient leadership skills, motivation, and knowledge to become involved in curriculum planning either at successive times or simultaneously in the classroom, team/grade/department, school, and district levels. This individual may be involved at each level in making curriculum decisions that affect him or her as well as others in the school system.

On the other hand, this fifth-grade teacher may be engaged in curriculum planning at only the classroom level and may not be actively involved in the process above that level. Nevertheless, decisions about classroom curriculum that the individual teacher wishes to make must often be referred to a higher level of decision making, especially if these decisions will affect other teachers. For example, the individual teacher cannot unilaterally replace an adopted textbook that is part of an articulated series used at several grade levels. Decision making, then, will and must take place at higher levels whether or not the individual teacher actively participates in them.

A Hierarchical Structure

Since many curriculum decisions must be, in effect, ratified at successive levels, we do have a hierarchical structure in operation throughout the United States. Each successive level of the hierarchy, up to and including the state level, possesses the power to approve or reject curriculum proposals of the level below it.

In practice, responsibility for curriculum planning is spread across the levels of classroom, school, district, and state. Whereas teachers and curriculum specialists may participate in curriculum projects at the state level, their curriculum efforts at that level are purely advisory. Only the state board of education, the state department of education, or the state legislature can mandate incorporating the projects' results in the schools' program. School systems must follow specific state regulations and statutes, after which, allowing for state curricular mandates, they may demonstrate initiative in curriculum planning.

Limitations of Hierarchical Structure

Beyond the state level, hierarchical power structure does not hold true. In our decentralized system of education, authority for education is reserved to the states. The regional, national (with appropriate qualifications), and international sectors may seek to bring about curriculum change only through persuasion by working through state and local levels.

The national level represents a unique blend of control through both authority and persuasion. Some maintain that in spite of our decentralized system the federal government exercises too much control over the schools, including the curriculum of those schools.

The history of federal legislation in support of vocational education and education of the handicapped, for example, reveals that the national level exerts a potent influence on the curriculum of schools throughout the country. The dollar, distributed by the federal government, is, of course, in itself a powerfully persuasive instrument. However, officials at the national level can intervene in state and local school matters only subsequent to federal legislation that they are empowered and required to enforce.

It is a moot question, however, whether the enactment of federal legislation and the enforcement of federal decisions can be called curriculum planning in its true sense. Whereas school districts must comply with federal legislation, for example, that bans all forms of discrimination in the schools' programs, they are under no obligation to submit grant proposals for optional types of aid. Consequently, we might design a model that shows the levels of curriculum planning through the state level and the sectors beyond the state level. Such a model is shown in Figure 3–3.

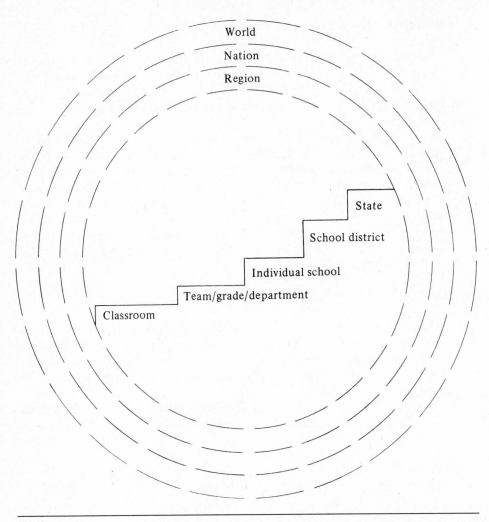

FIGURE 3–3   Levels and sectors of planning. For purposes of simplicity this figure does not show two levels—the area level that is a subdivision of the district and the intermediate unit that is a level between the district and the state. The area level is found in large urban school systems and the intermediate level, primarily a service unit, in some states.

CURRICULUM EFFORTS AT THE VARIOUS LEVELS

When the graduates of teacher education programs, with degrees and state certificates fresh in hand, sign contracts for their first teaching positions, they generally have only the vaguest of notions of the extent to which they will be involved in curriculum planning and development. Teacher education institutions do not ordinarily require courses in curriculum development at the undergraduate level. A typical preservice training program, ignoring the problem of differing delivery systems, consists of general education (liberal studies), foundations of education (social, psychological, philosophical, and historical) or introduction to education, methods of teaching (both general and specific), and student teaching in addition to a major in a teaching field. Some teacher candidates are exposed to an undergraduate course in curriculum, which provides them with an overview of the sources of the curriculum, presents a survey of programs in elementary and secondary education, and raises some curriculum issues. Despite their limited undergraduate training in curriculum development, teachers engage in instructional and curricular decision making from day one. Novice teachers are, as a rule, reasonably well trained to make the instructional or methodological decisions but are less well equipped to make the curricular or programmatic decisions, even though they may be well grounded in subject matter.

Teachers and curriculum specialists work within and across many levels and sectors. Each level performs distinct curricular efforts and has its own organizational processes for making curriculum decisions. Let's examine these levels more fully and point to the internal structures professionals have created to improve the curriculum. By contrast, in Chapters 4 and 7 you will see how external structures—those outside the teaching profession itself—impinge on internal structures.

For curriculum decision making to take place, appropriate organizational structures are essential. In the following pages of this chapter we will examine such structures in some detail. In Chapter 4 you will find a fuller treatment of the roles of various individuals and groups in the curriculum development process.

The Classroom Level

At first blush it seems that all programmatic decisions have been made for the teacher at the time he or she is employed. A full-blown program is already in operation at the school where the teacher is to be assigned. The principal contracts with the applicant to fill an advertised position, be it early childhood education, sixth grade, middle school English, or senior high school chemistry; designates the grade or subject(s) to be taught; and informs the teacher about school policies and regulations. If the school is large enough to require the services of supervisory personnel other than the principal, the teacher may be referred to one of the supervisors for further orientation. The supervisor designated by the principal (for example, the assistant principal, a grade coordinator, or a department head) acquaints the teacher with the adopted textbooks and whatever other curriculum materials are used, such as statements of objectives, syllabi, and curriculum guides.

The new teacher begins to feel as if all the important decisions about the curriculum have been made. Perhaps the life of the teacher would be easier and certainly less complicated were that the case. On the other hand, it is safe to say that the teacher's life would be immensely duller were there no curriculum decisions to be made. If the teacher subscribes to the axioms that change is inevitable and never-ending, he or she will come to view his or her role first and foremost as a decision maker. The teacher then not only makes decisions or participates in shared decision making but also gathers data on which to base decisions, implements decisions, and evaluates programs. In what specific curriculum endeavors, we may ask, is the individual classroom teacher likely to participate? Let's respond to that question in two ways.

Two Cases.   First, let us take the hypothetical cases of two high-powered, experienced, highly motivated teachers—a fourth-grade teacher and a ninth-grade teacher of social studies. We will further posit that (1) the fourth-grade teacher is a male and the ninth-grade teacher a female, (2) both are employed in the same school district, and (3) both participate in curriculum planning at all levels and in all sectors. Our fourth-grade teacher, whom we will refer to as Teacher F, is the leader of a team of three teachers who have responsibility for a group of 90 students in an open-area setting. Our ninth-grade teacher, Teacher N, is a member of a social studies department numbering eight faculty members. We will examine their curriculum development activities at one point in time—the cool and windy month of March.

During this period Teacher F was reviewing with the other teachers the next day's mathematics lesson for the slower students in the class and examining a new fourth-grade reading program (team/grade level). He was also participating in making recommendations for implementing a new human growth and development program in the school (school level), serving on a committee studying ways to implement federal legislation regarding the handicapped (district level), serving on a statewide committee to define minimal competencies in reading (state level), taking part in a panel discussion at a regional conference on effective schools (regional sector), finishing a proposal for federal funding of a project for the socially disadvantaged (national sector and local level), and planning activities for a program on contributions of immigrants to American culture (international sector and local level).

While Teacher F has been making his contribution toward keeping the curriculum of his school system lively, Teacher N has been no less occupied. She has just finished resequencing the content of a course in geography that she regularly teaches (classroom level), is planning together with all the other ninth-grade teachers a new course in consumer economics (grade level), will attend later in the week as her grade representative a meeting of the school's curriculum committee to discuss ways of using community resources more effectively (school level), has been serving on the same district committee as

Teacher F, which is charged with the task of making recommendations for implementing curricula for the handicapped (district level), has been invited to participate in a committee to consider changes in the state's minimal requirements for high school graduation (state level), served a week ago on the visiting committee for a distant high school that is seeking regional accreditation (regional sector), has been notified by the National Endowment for the Humanities that a proposal she submitted will be funded (national sector and local level), and has been invited by the World Council for Gifted and Talented Children to present a paper at a conference in Europe (international sector). While relatively few teachers have the opportunity, ability, or perhaps the inclination to participate in curriculum efforts at all the levels and sectors suggested in these two hypothetical cases, none of these curricular activities is beyond the realm of possibility. Teachers have engaged in all these activities at some time or other.

A second way to respond to the question "In what specific endeavors is the individual classroom teacher likely to participate?" is to survey typical curriculum efforts that take place at each level and in each sector. An examination of some of the curriculum responsibilities of the classroom level reveals that the individual teacher has a rather large task cut out for him or her. A number of tasks in curriculum development may be identified at the classroom level. They can be classified into three categories: curriculum planning or design, curriculum implementation, and curriculum and instructional evaluation.

Tasks of Teachers.   Teachers carry out activities in curriculum design when they write curricular goals and objectives, select subject matter (content), choose materials, identify resources in the school and community, sequence or resequence the subject matter, decide on the scope of the topics or course, revise the content, decide on types of instructional plans to use, construct the plans, try out new programs, create developmental and remedial programs in reading or other subject matter, seek ways to provide for all kinds of individual differences in the classroom, incorporate content mandated by levels above the classroom, and develop their own curricular materials.

Curriculum implementation is equated by some curriculum experts with instruction. Some hold the view that curriculum implementation does not start until the teacher interacts with the students. I would include in this concept the final stages of curriculum planning or design when the nitty-gritty decisions are made about how programs will be put into operation and how instruction will be designed and presented. Within this context teachers are occupied at the classroom level when they select appropriate emphases within the subjects, decide which students will pursue what subject matter, allot times for the various topics and units to be taught, determine if the facilities are appropriate and how they may be modified (if necessary), decide how materials and resources may best be made available to the learners, assign duties to volunteer aides, write instructional goals and objectives, and select and carry out strategies for classroom presentation and interaction.

Teachers have the responsibility of evaluating both the curriculum and instruction. In some ways it is difficult to separate the two dimensions of evaluation and to tell where instructional evaluation ceases and curriculum evaluation begins. In a very real sense evaluating instruction is evaluating curriculum implementation. We may clarify the distinctions between the two dimensions of evaluation in the following way: *Curriculum evaluation* is the assessment of programs, processes, and curricular products (material, not human). *Instructional evaluation* is (1) the assessment of student achievement before, during, and at the end of instruction and (2) the assessment of the effectiveness of the instructor. Thus, teachers work at the task of curriculum evaluation when they seek to find out if the programs are meeting the curriculum objectives; try to learn if the programs are valid, relevant, feasible, of interest to the learners, and in keeping with the learners' needs; review the choices of delivery systems, materials, and resources; and examine the finished curriculum products, such as guides, unit plans, and lesson plans, that they have created. Teachers conduct instructional evaluation when they assess the learners' entry skills before the start of instruction; give progress tests; write, administer, score, and interpret final achievement tests; and permit students to evaluate their performance as instructors.

These examples of activities transpiring at the classroom level demonstrate that curriculum planning and development are complex and demanding responsibilities for the teacher. As we discuss curriculum planning at the various levels in the following pages of this chapter, it may seem that individual teachers have little autonomy. Surely, many hold that view, and to some extent there is truth in that belief. The impingement of federal, state, and local school system mandates affecting the teacher's prerogatives in the areas of curriculum and instruction is a serious concern. In spite of the infringement on the teacher's professional responsibilities, many curricular and instructional decisions remain to be made, especially in selecting delivery systems, adapting techniques to students' learning styles, diagnosing student problems, and prescribing remediation.

Teachers may take comfort from the fact that they have at least as a group, if not individually, considerable opportunity to shape curricular decisions at the local school and district levels and some opportunity at the state level.

The Team, Grade, and Department Level

One of the axioms in Chapter 2 stated that curriculum development is essentially a group undertaking. Once the teacher leaves the sanctuary of the self-contained elementary or secondary school classroom and joins other teachers, curriculum development takes a new turn. It calls for a cooperative effort on the part of each teacher, places a limit on solitary curriculum planning, and calls for a more formal organizational structure. It is at the team, grade, or department level that curriculum leadership begins to emerge and leaders come to be distinguished from followers.

For decades the graded school system with its orderly hierarchical structure and self-contained classrooms has been and continues to be the prevailing model of school organization. In the late 1970s, however, the self-contained classroom was jostled by the appearance of open-space or open-area schools. Scores of elementary, middle, and junior high schools were built as or converted into open-space facilities. In these schools, in the place of walled, self-contained classrooms came large open spaces in which the learning activities of a large group of youngsters were directed by a team of teachers assisted in some cases by paraprofessionals. A semblance of territoriality was created by assigning each of the team members to a particular group of youngsters whose home base was a sector of the large open area. In theory and in practice, groups and subgroups were formed and reformed continuously depending on their learning needs, goals, and interests. Although open-space schools can still be found, the movement has abated, and in many cases open classrooms have been converted or reconverted into self-contained classrooms. Sentiment among teachers, parents, and students has continued to favor the self-contained classroom.

Specific curriculum innovations are discussed in this text primarily to delineate the process of curriculum development and to help the curriculum worker to effect and evaluate curriculum change.[10] Two organizational patterns—the self-contained classroom and open space—are mentioned in this chapter to point out that teachers in an open-space school, unlike their counterparts in the self-contained classroom, participate in curriculum planning at the team level. In cases where there is more than one team at the same grade level, teachers in open-space schools engage in planning on two levels: team and grade. When only one team exists at a particular grade level—for example, one fourth-grade team consisting of three teachers for 90 students—teachers serve as planners at both the team and grade level simultaneously. Teachers in both open-space schools and in the self-contained classroom participate in curriculum planning at the grade level.

Elementary school teachers in open-space schools, therefore, participate in curriculum planning at both the team and grade levels, whereas secondary school teachers usually join with their colleagues in curriculum planning at both the grade and department levels. With the children for whom they are specifically responsible in mind, the teachers in a team, a given grade, or a particular department are called on to make curriculum decisions like the following:

---

[10] See Chapter 9 of this text for a discussion of the graded school, open-space schools, and other organizational arrangements.

- determining content to be presented
- sequencing of subject matter
- adapting instruction for exceptionalities
- establishing team, grade, or departmental objectives
- selecting materials and resources suitable to the children under their supervision
- creating groupings of learners
- establishing a means of coordinating progress of students in the various sections and classrooms
- writing tests to be taken by all students of the team, grade, or department
- writing curriculum materials for use by all teachers
- agreeing on team-wide, grade-wide, and department-wide programs that all students and teachers will attend
- agreeing on ways students can learn to demonstrate socially responsible behavior and self-discipline
- agreeing on minimal standards that pupils must demonstrate in the basic skills
- cooperating in the establishment and use of laboratories and learning centers
- agreeing on marking practices
- agreeing on the institution of new programs and abandonment of old programs within their area of jurisdiction
- evaluating their own programs, students, and instructors

These are but a sampling of the many kinds of cooperative decisions that members who constitute the team, grade, or department must make. Individual classroom teachers are generally free to make many, though not all, decisions that affect only their classes. When a decision is likely to have an impact on teachers other than the individual classroom teacher, it becomes a matter for joint deliberation by the parties to be affected or, at higher levels, by their representatives.

To make the decision-making process more efficient, curriculum leaders either emerge or need to be designated. Team leaders or lead teachers, grade coordinators or chairpersons, and the department heads or chairpersons are appointed by the principal or elected by the teachers themselves. Those administrators who are inclined to a bureaucratic approach to administration prefer the former system, and those who are disposed to a collegial approach permit the latter system. In either case, if the most experienced and skilled teachers are chosen for these leadership positions, they may establish themselves as curriculum specialists, key members of a cooperating group of curriculum workers.

Although many schools have their own unique organizational arrangements, we might diagram common organizational patterns for curriculum planning through the team, grade, and departmental levels. Later in this chapter we will look at parallel patterns of organization for curriculum development on a school-wide and district-wide basis.

Patterns 1 through 4 reveal ways in which individual classroom teachers, teams, grades, and departments are organized for carrying out their assigned tasks, a major one of which is curriculum development. Each pattern should be viewed in the mind's eye as expanded to include all teachers, teams, grades, and departments in the school. The channels shown in the charts can be followed for both administrative and curricular decision making, limited, of course, in these illustrations to decisions affecting only one teacher, team, grade, or department. In a moment we will look at the means of organizing on a school-wide basis and for making decisions that affect more than one teacher, team, grade, or department.

The arrowheads at both ends of the lines in the diagrams convey a philosophy and practice of collegiality. This element of collegiality extends even to the various leaders' relationships with the administrator. Many charts, especially those showing administrative decision making in a bureaucratic model, include lines with no arrows or arrows in only one direction—from the top down. Interchange among all participants is absolutely essential to intelligent and effective curriculum planning.

In the less common small school with one class of each grade with one teacher in a self-contained unit, the individual teacher is the curriculum leader (and follower, for that matter) and has sole responsibility for making curriculum decisions (with the administrator's cooperation and approval) for the classroom and grade levels, in this case identical. The teacher and principal relate to each other directly. Whereas the absence of multiple sections of grades prevents cooperative curriculum planning within grade levels, cooperation is possible, if the principal permits, at the school level and across grade levels.

In some schools housing multiple sections of each grade the principal follows the model of the less common small school, trying to relate to each teacher on an individual basis and not encouraging cooperative planning by the faculty within grade levels and across grade levels.

Patterns 1 through 4 introduce a dimension of cooperative planning. Pattern 1 shows an open-space team arrangement in a small school in which this one team also constitutes the grade faculty. Since there is but one team-taught section of the grade in this school, the team leader is, in effect, the grade coordinator. All members of the team interact with one another, while the team leader serves as the team's liaison to the principal's office. If we wished to visualize the extension of this pattern school-wide, we might in a simplistic fashion, hypothesize one section at each grade level—K through 6—figuratively adding five more identical teams.

The organizational arrangements for curriculum planning become more complex and at the same time more common with the presence of multiple sections at the various grade levels. Pattern 2 depicts the structure in an open-space school that has two sections of a particular grade, each made up of a team of three teachers. In this model we see two team leaders, one of whom happens to be serving also as grade coordinator. Members of each team interact with one another and with the grade coordinator.

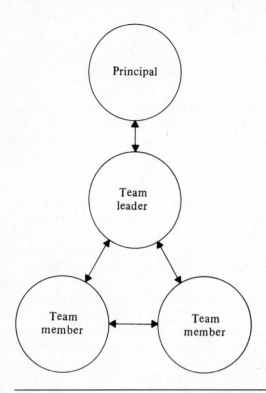

PATTERN 1   Team in an open-space school. There is only one section of this grade level in the school.

PATTERN 2   Two teams of one grade level in an open-space elementary school.

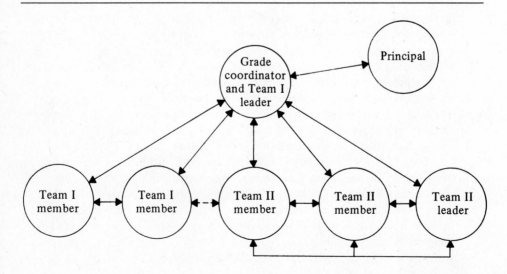

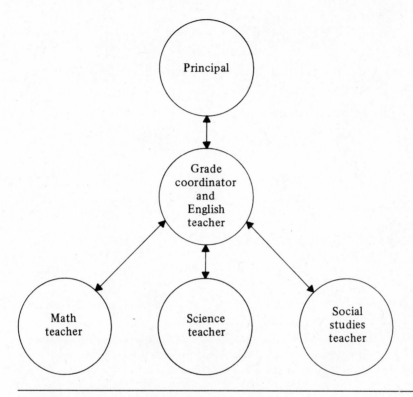

PATTERN 3   Grade-level organization of those teachers who are assigned primarily to teach students at a particular level of a secondary school.

The broken line between Teams I and II is significant. Although there may be no walls between groups of children of one team, there are walls between teams. Furthermore, the interaction among teachers is more limited across than within teams.

Alternatively, we might have charted a situation that is less complicated and even more common: the grade level organization in an elementary school with self-contained classrooms. For example, the pattern for one grade consisting of three sections, each in a self-contained unit under a single teacher, would be identical to the diagram for Team I, Pattern 2, with only the labels changed. We would have one teacher who is grade coordinator and two grade teachers. The three teachers would interact with one another, and the grade coordinator would serve as the link to the principal.

Two ways of organizing grade and departmental faculty of a secondary school for administrative purposes and for curriculum planning are represented by Patterns 3 and 4. Of these two models Pattern 4 is the typical, traditional, standard vehicle by which much of the work of the secondary school is conducted. Pattern 3 is followed only when the grade structure becomes particularly

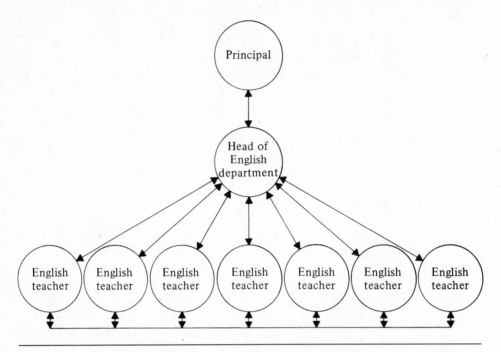

PATTERN 4   Organizational pattern of all members of a secondary school department. One faculty member happens to also serve as a grade coordinator.

significant, as in the case of schools implementing team concepts such as the core curriculum, interdisciplinary team teaching, differentiated staffing,[11] and the school-within-the-school.[12]

These last two patterns can exist concurrently in the same school. Departmental organization, however, is the prevailing pattern in the secondary school, and most high school administrators would feel at a loss without it. Grade-level organization in the secondary school, unless provided for specific and innovative undertakings such as those just mentioned, tends to be weak, loose, and relatively nonexistent as far as curriculum planning is concerned. As an added hurdle to grade-level planning as opposed to departmental planning in the secondary school, many teachers teach at more than one grade level. There will be times when the principal of a secondary school will wish to meet with the faculty of one grade level—ninth-grade teachers, for example—to discuss matters pertinent to just that level. Unless plans are consciously drawn to provide for curriculum planning, grade level faculty meetings, like meetings

---

[11]For discussion of the core curriculum, team teaching, and differentiated staffing, see Chapter 9 of this text.

[12]See David W. Beggs III, ed., *Team Teaching: Bold New Venture* (Indianapolis: Unified College Press, 1964), p. 20; *Education by Choice,* 16-mm film that shows seven schools within Quincy (Illinois) High School (Media Five, 1011 North Cole Avenue, Hollywood, Calif., 1976); and Oliva, *Secondary School,* p. 193.

of the entire faculty of a school, generally offer only limited opportunity for curriculum decision making.

Patterns 2 through 4 show structures for curriculum development at the team, grade, and department level. Curriculum matters that can be settled and contained within a team, grade, or department are handled at that level. However, curriculum planning sends out waves that affect, sometimes even engulf, persons beyond the planners and the client group for whom the plans were made. Hence, we must look to the next level—the school level—for curriculum decision making that transcends the team, grade, or department level.

The School Level

Although many curriculum decisions may be made at the classroom or team/grade/department level, other decisions can be reached only at a school-wide level. The institution must provide some mechanism by which the curriculum is articulated and integrated. The administrator must ensure a process whereby the implications of curriculum decisions made anywhere within the institution will be understood and, hopefully, agreed to by the faculty as a whole.

Of all the levels and sectors of curriculum planning, the individual school has emerged as the most critical. Current administrative philosophy promotes an approach to school administration known generally as "school-based management" in which authority is decentralized and the school principal is granted considerable autonomy over not only curriculum planning but also the budget, hiring and firing of school personnel, in-service education of staff, supervision of personnel, and evaluation of staff.[13] Several writers have identified the individual school as the primary locus for curriculum change. Alice Miel long ago observed, "If really widespread participation is desirable, there appears to be no better way than to make the individual school the unit of participation, the primary action agency in curriculum development."[14] Almost 40 years later Goodlad endorsed the concept of the school as the unit for improvement.[15]

The decade of the 1980s, with its quest for reform of the schools, saw many states shift more and more decision making to the state level as they grappled for ways to improve their schools. Local schools felt the pressure of state curricular mandates that in some cases went beyond the specification of subjects and units to the specification of instructional objectives to be accomplished at every level in every course.

---

[13] See Barbara Parker, "School Based Management: Improve Education by Giving Parents, Principals More Control of Your Schools," *American School Board Journal* 166, no. 7 (July 1979): 20–21. See also Jane L. David, "Synthesis of Research on School-Based Management," *Educational Leadership* 46, no. 8 (May 1989): 45–53.

[14] Alice Miel, *Changing the Curriculum: A Social Process* (New York: D. Appleton-Century, 1946), p. 69.

[15] Goodlad, *A Place Called School,* pp. 31 and 318–319.

Emphasis is now shifting away from heavy centralized state and district administration and toward more responsibility for operation of the schools on the local school level. For example, in 1990, the governor-elect of Florida voiced the desire to return more control over the schools to the local school systems. In the spring of 1991 the Florida House Appropriations Committee approved a plan to reduce state control over aid for specific educational categories and to extend more authority to local school boards, teachers, and parents. Tight state budgets as well as educational reasons may accelerate the move toward decentralization from state to local level.

Two widely recognized models for school-based management within urban school systems are those of the Dade County (Florida) schools and the Chicago Public Schools. In 1988 the Dade County schools initiated a four-year, voluntary program of School-Based Management and Shared Decision Making in 33 of its over 300 schools. In 1991, the program had been expanded to include 157 schools. Many of the decisions that were formerly made at the central office are now made at the individual school level through the school's decision-making group of 5 to 12 persons, which includes teachers, administrators, staff, parents, other citizens of the community, and, in the case of secondary schools, students.

In 1988 the Chicago public school system was empowered by law to decentralize its administrative structure, placing decision making in the hands of 11-member councils at each of its over 600 schools. These councils were composed of six parents with children in the school, two members of the community who did not have children in the school, two teachers of that school, and the principal. Tensions ensued when, among other actions, the councils hired and fired principals. In 1989 Chicago school administrators filed suit, challenging the method of constituting the councils. In November 1990 the Illinois Supreme Court ruled the process of forming the councils unconstitutional. Reports indicate that the Chicago schools will restructure the councils and continue with school-based management.

The preceding chapter demonstrated that curriculum specialists conceive of curriculum development as a cooperative group undertaking. Given the many dimensions of the school administrator's job, intensified by the concept of school-based management, a participatory approach to administration is sound not only philosophically but also practically. Shared decision making, whether in respect to curriculum planning or other aspects of the administrator's job, makes for a more efficient and effective school.

Foreign observers are often disturbed, if not shocked, by the uniqueness of each American school. Two elementary schools in the same community, for example, may be completely different in ambience, student body, staffing, and neighborhood setting. Achievement levels, motivation of the students, enthusiasm of the faculty, leadership skills of the principal, and curricular emphases differ school by school. Consequently, we may anticipate that organizational arrangements for curriculum development will differ school by school.

Constituencies of the School.   To varying degrees, the democratic process is accepted more and more in school systems across the country. Nowhere is its presence more clearly felt than in the participatory procedures that seek to involve the major constituencies of the school in curriculum development. Usually identified as the principal constituencies are the administrators and their staffs, teachers, students, and citizens of the community. On occasion, nonprofessional employees of the school system are acknowledged in this way and become involved in the planning process—but rarely as major participants.

Jack R. Frymier and Horace C. Hawn stated a principle that summarizes their belief in the necessity for involving persons in curriculum planning on a broad scale:

> *People Who Are Affected Must Be Involved*. Involvement is a principle fundamental to democracy and to learning theory. The very essence of democracy is predicated upon the assumption that those who are affected by any change should have some say in determining just what that change shall be. This is guaranteed in our political-social system through citizen participation and through our efforts to persuade elected representatives once they have been chosen. Devising ways of involving people in decision-making is a difficult and time-consuming chore, but *unless decisions are made democratically they will be less than the best.* . . . Significant and lasting change can only come about by such involvement. All who are affected by curriculum development and change must have a genuine opportunity to participate in the process.[16]

Robert S. Zais raised a question about the validity of the participatory model of curriculum decision making. Speaking of the democratic "grass-roots model,"[17] Zais said:

> The grass-roots model of curriculum engineering[18] . . . is initiated by teachers in individual schools, employs democratic group methods of decision making, proceeds on a "broken front," and is geared to the specific curriculum problems of particular schools or even classrooms.
>
> The intensely democratic orientation of the grass-roots model is responsible for generating what have probably become the curriculum establishment's two least-questioned axioms: First, that a curriculum can be successfully implemented only if the teachers have been intimately involved in the construction and development processes, and second, that not only professional

---

[16]Jack R. Frymier and Horace C. Hawn, *Curriculum Improvement for Better Schools* (Worthington, Ohio: Charles A. Jones, 1970), pp. 28–29. Reprinted with permission.

[17]Zais attributes the classification "grass-roots model" to B. Othanel Smith, William O. Stanley, and J. Harlan Shores, *Fundamentals of Curriculum Development* (New York: Harcourt Brace Jovanovich, 1957). See Robert S. Zais, *Curriculum: Principles and Foundations* (New York: Harper & Row, 1976), p. 448.

[18]Zais refers to the definition of "curriculum engineering" by George A. Beauchamp, *Curriculum Theory,* 2nd ed. (Wilmette, Ill.: Kagg Press, 1968), and uses the term to encompass "curriculum construction," "curriculum development," and "curriculum implementation," Zais, *Curriculum,* p. 18. See also the third edition of Beauchamp's *Curriculum Theory* (1975), Chapter 7.

personnel, but students, parents, and other lay members of the community must be included in the curriculum planning process. To deny the validity of either of these claims (neither of which has been satisfactorily demonstrated) is not necessarily to deny *any* role to teachers or lay participants; rather it is to suggest the need to define more precisely the *appropriate* role that administrators, teachers, curriculum specialists, and non-professionals should play in curriculum engineering.[19]

Decisions and Organizational Patterns. Curriculum committees or councils exist in many schools. The school's curriculum committee meets and makes recommendations on such matters as the following:

- □ adding new programs for the school, including interdisciplinary programs
- □ deleting existing programs
- □ revising existing programs
- □ conducting school-wide surveys of teacher, student, and parental opinion
- □ evaluating the school's curriculum
- □ planning ways to overcome curricular deficiencies
- □ planning for school accreditation
- □ choosing articulated series of textbooks
- □ using library and learning centers
- □ planning for exceptional children
- □ verifying the school's compliance with state mandates and federal legislation
- □ sanctioning school-wide events like career days and science fairs
- □ supervising assessment of student achievement
- □ reviewing recommendations of accrediting committees and planning for removal of deficiencies
- □ reducing absenteeism
- □ increasing the holding power of the school

Although curriculum specialists may not agree to what degree they should encourage or permit the involvement of various constituencies, how each group will be constituted, and which group has the primary role, the literature on curriculum development almost unanimously endorses the concept of the democratic, participatory approach. Although it is possible that the collective judgment of specialists in the field could be in error, their judgments—based on experience, training, observation, and research—provide a foundation for accepting the validity of the democratic approach to curriculum development.

There are several organizational arrangements on the school level for considering curriculum matters. The diagrams that follow depict some of these patterns of organization. In Patterns A1 and A2 the administrator(s) shares decision making with the group that most curriculum experts agree is of pri-

---

[19]Excerpts from *Curriculum: Principles and Foundations*, pp. 448–449, by Robert F. Zais. Copyright©1976 by Harper & Row, Publishers, Inc. Reprinted by permission of Harper Collins Publishers.

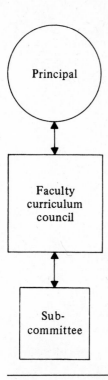

PATTERN A1   Principal works with a faculty curriculum council. Subcommittees of the faculty curriculum council are appointed as needed.

mary importance in curriculum development—the teachers. Patterns A3 and A4 expand cooperation into collaborative models that include other groups in addition to teachers.

We should not forget that in any organizational model in which decision making is shared, groups other than the duly appointed administrators serve only in advisory capacities. Both professionally and legally the administrator does not and cannot surrender "line" authority for making ultimate decisions and supervising the staff.

The following patterns of organizing for curriculum development at the local school level maintain the customary line-and-staff relationship that we have already seen at the team/grade/department level and will see again at the school district level. They also serve as illustrations of ways schools may be organized for carrying out curriculum development and convey a sense of the variations possible for accomplishing this task.

The principals in Patterns A1 and A2 use a faculty curriculum council or faculty curriculum committee. In practice, faculty committees that serve to advise school administrators on curriculum matters are constituted either by election of teachers by their colleagues or by appointment of teachers by school administrators. In some cases, team leaders, grade coordinators, or

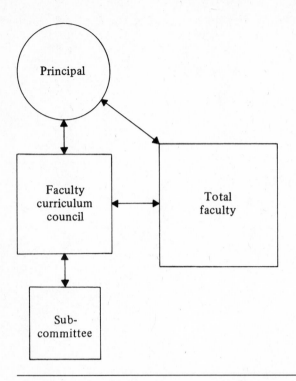

PATTERN A2   Principal works with a faculty curriculum council and involves total faculty.

department heads—elected in some schools, appointed in others—may make up the faculty curriculum committee. I would advocate the democratic election of representatives to curriculum committees and councils at all levels of the school system.

The principal in Pattern A2 has provided a systematic way by which the total faculty acting as a body approves or disapproves decisions of the faculty curriculum council. Although only one subcommittee is pictured in each of these figures, it is understood that the faculty curriculum council would appoint as many subcommittees of the faculty as needed.

Citizens of the community and students join forces with the faculty and administrators to produce collaborative Patterns A3 and A4. The principal of Pattern A3 keeps the three constituencies separate. The model shows, however, the possibility of interaction among the several working groups. Pattern A4 integrates all three constituencies into one expanded curriculum committee. Patterns A2, A3, and A4 all incorporate the total faculty within the model.

Pattern A4, an integrated, collaborative model, appears the most democratic, but it would be wrong to conclude that it is therefore the most efficient. As anyone who has grappled with the concept of "parity" as dictated by some federal programs—public school teachers, university specialists, and lay people

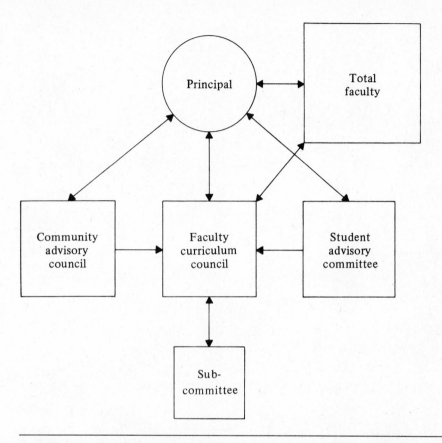

PATTERN A3   Principal involves lay citizens and students as well as faculty.

working together as equal partners from proposal stage to final evaluation—has discovered, "parity" is not necessarily the most efficient way to do business. In reference to the expanded curriculum committee the professionals—the teachers and administrators—must often talk a language filled with concepts that must be explained to lay citizens and students and must make distinctions between desired outcomes and processes. Technical decisions that must be made are often beyond the competence of lay citizens and students. Only if an expanded curriculum committee is composed of persons who are well informed about the processes of education and are highly motivated can this pattern meet with any degree of success.

Students and lay persons often participate with teachers and administrators on school-level curriculum committees. In the next chapter, we will examine the roles of these constituent groups in curriculum development. We might ask at this point: What are typical curriculum tasks of the school-wide curriculum committee? The school curriculum committee or council must ar-

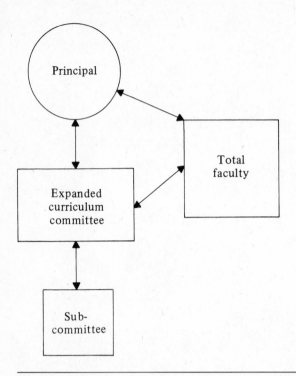

PATTERN A4   Principal involves lay citizens, students, and faculty in a combined curriculum committee.

ticulate its work with curriculum development efforts at the classroom and team/grade/department levels and, in effect, coordinate the work of the lower levels. It receives proposals for curricular change from the lower levels, especially proposals that affect more than one team, grade, or department or that are interdisciplinary in nature.

The school curriculum council considers proposals that require human and material resources, budgetary expenditures, and changes in staffing. The council conducts or supervises assessment of the educational needs of pupils. It coordinates the development of a statement of school philosophy. It specifies and regularly reviews curriculum goals and objectives for the school.

The curriculum council plans the evaluation of the curriculum. It studies results of student assessment and proposes changes based on the data gathered. The council studies the educational needs of the community and implements programs to meet legitimate needs. The council seeks solutions to short-range curricular problems while also establishing and refining long-range plans.

The council is both proactive and reactive in its manner of operating. Whereas it may react to proposals presented by both the principal and the faculty, it also generates its own proposals and solutions to curricular problems.

At the time of a pending school evaluation by a regional accreditation team, the curriculum council may act as a steering committee and assign specific tasks to various committees. The council coordinates an intensive self-study prior to the visit of an accrediting team.

The council must ensure articulation between and among the various grades and departments of the school, making certain that teachers are following agreed-upon sequences and meeting minimal prescribed objectives. Requests from higher levels and various sectors for the school's cooperation on curriculum projects are routed to the curriculum council.

The local school curriculum council occupies a strategic position and fulfills a key role in the process of curriculum development. Of all groups at all levels and sectors of planning, the school-wide curriculum council is in the position to make the most significant contributions to curriculum improvement.

The School District Level

None of the previously discussed levels—classroom, team/grade/department, or individual school—can work as isolated units. They function within the context of the school district under the direction of the duly elected school board and its administrative officer, the superintendent. Their efforts must be coordinated among themselves and with the central district office. Goals and objectives of the subordinate units must mesh with those of the district level. Consequently, the superintendent must provide a mechanism whereby district-level curriculum planning may be conducted.

Curriculum planning on a district-wide level is often conducted through the district curriculum council composed of teachers, administrators, supervisors, lay persons, and, in some cases, students. The size of the district curriculum council and the extent of its representation depend upon the size of the school district. Representatives may be either elected by members of their respective groups or appointed by district-level administrators, frequently on the recommendation of school principals.

Decisions and Organizational Patterns. District-wide committees meet to consider problems such as these:

- □ adding new programs for the district
- □ abandoning district-wide programs
- □ reviewing student achievement in the various schools and recommending ways to improve programs of deficient schools, if any
- □ writing or reviewing proposals for state and federal grants
- □ gathering data on student achievement for presentation to parent groups and lay advisory councils
- □ supervising district compliance with state mandates and federal legislation
- □ evaluating programs on a district-wide basis
- □ articulating programs between levels

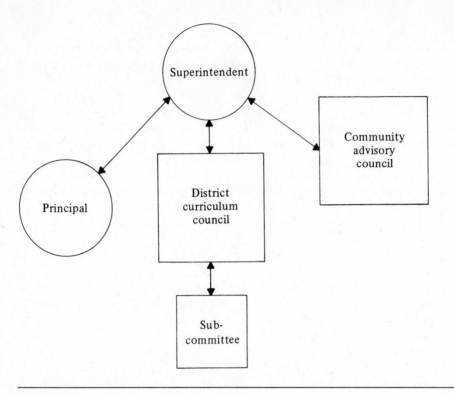

PATTERN B1   Small school district

The patterns that follow show typical organizational arrangements for curriculum development at the district level. The patterns increase in complexity as the size of the school district increases. The district represented in Pattern B1 uses a curriculum council composed of professionals only—administrators and supervisors named by the superintendent and teachers selected by their principals or elected by their faculties to represent them on the council. Subcommittees of professionals from anywhere in the school system are appointed by the curriculum council to conduct specific phases of curriculum development. The community advisory council serves in an advisory capacity to the superintendent and may or may not consider curriculum matters. Subordinate school units are responsible to the superintendent through the principals. Pattern B2 is essentially like Pattern B1 except that this school district extends membership on the curriculum council to students and lay persons.

Pattern B3 charts the organizational structure for curriculum development in a large county system broken down into four administrative areas or subdistricts, each of which is placed under the control of an area superintendent. The area superintendents report on matters of curriculum and instruction to the assistant superintendent for curriculum and instruction who, in turn, is re-

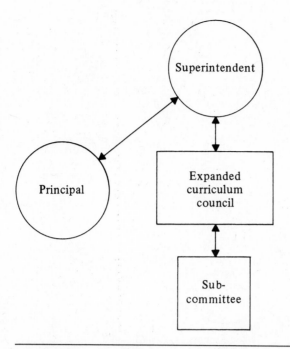

PATTERN B2   Small school district with expanded curriculum council composed of administrators, teachers, students, and lay people

sponsible to the superintendent. Each area superintendent charges a director of instruction (actually curriculum *and* instruction) or a director of elementary and secondary schools with the job of leadership in curriculum development. In each of the four areas, a curriculum council made up of administrators, supervisors, and teachers representative of the area works with the director of instruction in the vital task of improving the curriculum in their subdivision of the district. Subcommittees are appointed by the curriculum councils as they are needed in their areas. Principals are supervised by the directors of instruction. In some cases the directors of instruction supervise only in curriculum and instruction; in other cases, they supervise in all areas, including administrative matters. The area superintendents enlist the aid of community advisory councils, which counsel them on curricular and other matters. To maintain coordination among the four areas of the district, the assistant superintendent has established a district-wide curriculum coordinating council.

Decisions made at the area level, which is a subdistrict of the larger school district, affect all the schools within that area, whereas decisions made at the district level are binding on all schools of the entire system. The district curriculum council serves in a coordinating capacity. It acts on proposals from

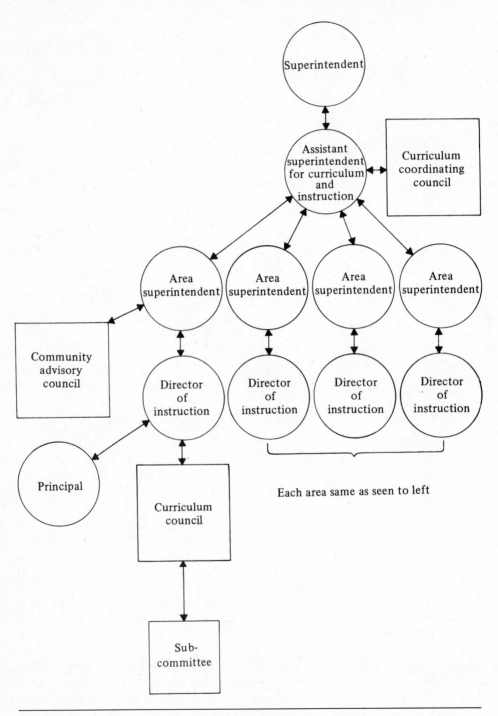

PATTERN B3   Large county school district with four district subordinate areas (subdistricts)

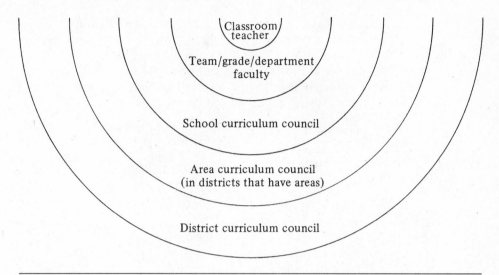

Classroom teacher

Team/grade/department faculty

School curriculum council

Area curriculum council (in districts that have areas)

District curriculum council

FIGURE 3–4   Sequence of decision making

subordinate levels; develops or causes to be developed statements of district philosophy, goals, and objectives; and establishes minimal competencies to be achieved by all students in the entire district. It makes recommendations concerning district-wide programs and projects, develops plans to secure federal moneys, and reviews district efforts to cooperate with state, regional, national, and other outside agencies on curriculum matters. The district curriculum committees, such as the curriculum coordinating council of Pattern B3, can be extremely influential groups; they, in the last analysis, make recommendations about the curriculum that the chief administrator may, if he or she approves, take to the public's representatives—the school board—for action.

Sequence for Decision Making.   We might visualize the sequence for decision making by the curriculum groups at the various levels within a school system in the form of waves starting in the individual teacher's classroom and terminating with the district curriculum coordinating council, as pictured in Figure 3–4. Teachers new to a school system should be informed, perhaps through a faculty handbook, of the district's structures for curriculum development. Teachers should be aware not only of the process of curriculum development in the district but also of the opportunities for curricular leadership.

Each level receives information, ideas, and proposals from the lower levels and, in turn, sends information, ideas, and proposals to them. Each level acts within the limitations of its own "territory." Councils at any level may initiate action as well as react to suggestions made to them. Councils must be responsive to both subordinate and higher levels. If a council wishes to initiate a plan that affects lower levels, it must involve persons from those levels from the earliest planning stage. If a council wishes to initiate or endorse a plan that goes beyond its "territory" or that might be likely to create repercussions anywhere in the system, it must seek approval at higher levels.

Before we discuss curriculum development at the next level—the state level—we should consider the following observations about the previously discussed organizational patterns for curriculum development:

☐ Although administrators—the principal or superintendent—have been shown at the top of each model, the patterns should not be considered simply administrative models in which orders are given by the administrator to his or her subordinates. The arrows at both ends of the lines from administrator to curriculum committees signify that exchange is a two-way rather than a one-way process. The administrator is shown in the patterns because, like Everest, he or she is there. The administrator holds the power for final decision making and must take the consequences if decisions prove to be wrong. The administrator's presence at the top of each pattern does not in itself make the pattern undemocratic.

The key difference between a democratic and an undemocratic process is the involvement of people. No administrator worth his or her keep can turn over the decision-making process completely to others, yet every administrator can seek to obtain the widest possible participation of people in that process.

☐ The patterns presented are rather typical arrangements that permit the work of curriculum development to be carried out by the professionals in the school system and by others whose aid they solicit. Other patterns also exist. Zais, for example, analyzed a number of existing and proposed models of curriculum development.[20]

☐ Realistically, we must admit that a significant amount of curriculum change is brought about *outside* of the established structure. Individual teachers and small committees often effect changes that are well received and disseminated through the school system and sometimes beyond. B. Frank Brown pointed out that a few teachers, by their example, may be instrumental in bringing about curriculum revision, a process he referred to as "spinning out."[21] The public and teachers' organizations are often ahead of the designated curriculum leaders.[22]

☐ The patterns described in this chapter are models of structure—the organizational arrangements whereby the professionals and those who assist them may apply their knowledge and skills to curriculum improvement. We should distinguish these organizational patterns from models for the process of curriculum development, which we will consider in Chapter 5.

---

[20] Zais, *Curriculum,* Chapter 19.

[21] B. Frank Brown, *The Nongraded High School* (Englewood Cliffs, N.J.: Prentice-Hall, 1963), pp. 209–210.

[22] See Peter F. Oliva, "In Search of the Curriculum Leader," *FASCD Journal,* no. 2 (February 1980): 29–33.

The State Level

Curriculum development beyond the boundaries of the school district seems like a remote undertaking to most school personnel. Administrators, teachers, and others are aware, sometimes painfully, that curriculum development does go on outside the school district and that it has an impact on schools of the district. Although state involvement in curricular and instructional development has increased over the years, relatively few school personnel in proportion to the number of employees are actively involved in curriculum making outside the district and then rarely on a sustaining basis.

As we move further and further away from the district level, the percentage of school personnel actively and continuously participating in curriculum development shrinks in size. Were the state not in a superordinate position over the local school districts and were the state not directly responsible for the educational system within its borders, we should classify the state as a sector rather than as a level. Clearly, however, under the Tenth Amendment to the U.S. Constitution and under the state constitutions, the state holds the primary power over education.

Channels Within Education. The state operates in the arena of curriculum development through a number of channels within the education profession. The state department of education and school people from the various districts of the state who are called on to assist the state department of education constitute the professional channel for curriculum development under the aegis of the state.

State Departments of Education. The state department of education, often a large bureaucracy, exercises direct responsibility over the curriculum of the schools of the state. Led by a chief state school officer (superintendent or commissioner of education), the state department of education—an agency of the executive branch of the state government—consists of a number of assistant superintendents, heads of branches, curriculum specialists, and other staff members. The state department of education provides general leadership to the schools; it interprets, enforces, and monitors legislated regulations as well as its own regulations that attain the force of law.

The state department of education wields great power over the districts of the state. In curriculum matters it accredits and monitors school programs, disburses state and federal-through-state moneys for specific programs, enforces standards for high school graduation, and sets specifications for amounts of time to be devoted to specific content areas. The state department of education develops statewide statements of philosophy, goals, and objectives. Additionally, the state department of education makes available a limited amount of consultant help to the individual schools and districts and conducts evaluations of school programs.

At times, decisions are made on the state level without advance consultation with the local school personnel of the state. At other times, however, the state department of education seeks advice and assistance from individuals and from ad hoc committees that they create for the purpose of studying specific problems and recommending solutions. Administrators and teachers are often asked to participate in organizing, conducting, or attending conferences and workshops held throughout the state on specific topics—for example, drug abuse, programs for the handicapped, eliminating sexism, writing curriculum guides, conducting research studies, identifying teacher competencies, specifying minimal competencies that students should be expected to achieve at each grade level, and selecting textbooks for state adoption.

The state department of education takes a leadership role in disseminating information regarding curriculum innovations and practices among the schools of the state. It issues both regular and periodic bulletins, monographs, and newsletters, frequently containing articles written by persons from local school districts, to keep local school personnel up to date on recent developments in curriculum, instruction, and other matters.

The state's presence in all school matters is a commanding one. Yet, bureaucratic as it may be, local school personnel do find limited opportunity to participate in curriculum decision making through established state channels.

State Professional Organizations. In a less formal way curriculum workers find opportunities for curriculum planning and consideration of curriculum problems through activities of the state professional organizations. Conference programs of such organizations as the state chapters of the National Council for the Social Studies, the National Council of Teachers of English, and the Association for Supervision and Curriculum Development customarily focus on curriculum concerns. Although the participants may engage in curriculum planning in only the most rudimentary and often passive way, the sharing of curriculum ideas often lays groundwork for subsequent curriculum planning. This type of curriculum activity cannot, of course, be equated with more structured efforts under the state department of education. Nor can we truly label the examination of curriculum problems by state professional organizations as a level of planning since no element of authority exists in this type of voluntary activity. More appropriately, the state professional organizations constitute a state sector that seeks to effect curriculum change through example and persuasion. Nevertheless, we would be remiss if we did not credit state professional organizations for the influence they often have in bringing about changes in the curriculum of the local school systems of the state.

Channels Outside of Education.   Other departments of the executive branch, the state legislature, and the state judicial branch form channels outside the profession of education that have an impact on the curriculum of all the schools of the state. Within the executive branch the governor and state board of education wield tremendous power over the state educational system. The governor presents a budget to the legislature in which he or she recommends supporting or curtailing programs. The state board sets policies that bind all the schools of the state.

Legislative Decisions. State legislatures throughout the country consistently demonstrate a penchant for curriculum making. The legislature of the state of Florida is an excellent case, as the following statute reveals:

Members of the instructional staff of the public schools, subject to the rules and regulations of the state board and of the school board, shall teach efficiently and faithfully, using the books and materials required, following the prescribed courses of study, and employing approved methods of instruction the following: The essentials of the United States Constitution, flag education, including proper flag display and flag salute, the elements of civil government, the elementary principles of agriculture, the true effects of all alcoholic and intoxicating liquors and beverages and narcotics upon the human body and mind, kindness to animals, the history of the state, conservation of natural resources, and such additional materials, subjects, courses, or fields in such grades as may be prescribed by law or by regulations of the state board and the school board. . . . [23]

The legislature became very specific when it required a high school course in Americanism versus Communism, making the following stipulations:

The public high schools shall each teach a complete course of not less than 30 hours, to all students enrolled in said public high schools entitled "Americanism versus Communism."

The course shall provide adequate instruction in the history, doctrines, objectives and techniques of Communism and shall be for the primary purpose of instilling in the mind of the students a greater appreciation of the democratic processes, freedom under law, and the will to preserve that freedom.

The course . . . shall emphasize the free-enterprise-competitive economy of the United States as the one which produces higher wages, higher standards of living, greater personal freedom and liberty than any other system of economics on earth.

The course shall lay particular emphasis upon the dangers of Communism, the ways to fight Communism, the evils of Communism, the fallacies of Communism, and the false doctrines of Communism. [24]

Perhaps even more sweeping is the statute of the Florida legislature directing the commissioner (state superintendent) to

Develop and administer in the public schools a uniform, statewide program of assessment to determine, periodically, educational status and progress and the degree of achievement of approved minimum performance standards. The uniform statewide program shall consist of testing in grades 3, 5, 8, and 11; however, the test of standards established for grade 11 may be administered after March 15 in grade 10. The uniform, statewide program may include the testing of additional grades and skill areas as specified by the commissioner. [25]

---

[23] Florida Statute 233.061, *Florida School Laws* (1985), p. 123.
[24] Florida Statute 233.064, *Florida School Laws,* p. 124.
[25] Florida Statute 229.57, *Florida School Laws,* p. 30. Florida modified its assessment program in 1990–91.

Although some legislation is a result of grassroots movements within the state and some statutes evolve from recommendations made by the state superintendent and the state department of education, many acts of the state legislature stem from the personal beliefs and desires of the legislators themselves. Even the state judicial branch finds itself entangled in curriculum decision making from time to time. Two famous cases may serve to illustrate involvement of the state courts in curriculum making.

The Supreme Court of Michigan ruled in 1874 in a case brought against the school district of Kalamazoo by a taxpayer of that community that the school board of Kalamazoo could, indeed, spend public funds to provide a secondary school education for youth of their district.[26]

In 1927 the Supreme Court of Tennessee replied to the appeal of the defense attorneys of John Thomas Scopes of the world famous "monkey trial" by upholding the constitutionality of the Tennessee law that forbade teaching in the public schools any theory that denied human creation by a Divine Being.[27] Periodically, state legislatures have attempted to mandate the teaching of "scientific creationism" in the public schools as a counterbalance to the theory of evolution. The scientific creationism/evolution issue, to which we will return in Chapter 14, continues to surface in some state legislatures.

SECTORS BEYOND THE STATE

When curriculum planners leave the state level and move onto the broader scene, they work in quite a different context. Participation in planning in the regional, national, and international sectors is ordinarily a voluntary activity. Except in the case of federal legislation, information sharing and persuasion rather than statutory power are the tools of the regional, national, and international sectors. No assurance of any kind exists that curriculum decisions reached in these sectors will or can be put into operation in the schools.

Although fewer opportunities exist for curriculum workers to engage in planning in the regional, national, and international sectors, the opportunities that do arise can be exciting for the participants.

The Regional Sector

Participation in planning in the regional, national, and international sectors is not comparable to that in the previously described levels. On occasion curriculum specialists of a particular region of the United States, from around the nation, or even from a number of foreign countries may assemble and develop curriculum materials that they will then disseminate or try out in their own schools. The most notable illustrations of this type of cooperative

---

[26]*Stuart v. School District No. 1, Village of Kalamazoo,* 30 Mich. 69 (1874).

[27]See Lyon Sprague de Camp, *The Great Monkey Trial* (Garden City, N.Y.: Doubleday, 1968).

endeavor were the efforts of the scholars from various parts of the country who in the late 1950s developed the so-called "new math" and "new science" programs.

As a general rule, curriculum activities in the regional, national, and international sectors are more likely to consist of sharing problems, exchanging practices, reporting research, and gathering information. Conferences of the professional organizations—for example, the South Atlantic Modern Language Association—are the most common vehicle whereby school personnel participate in regional curriculum study.

With considerable frequency teachers, administrators, and curriculum specialists are invited to take part in the activities of the regional associations (New England, Middle States, Southern, North Central, Northwest, and Western) that accredit schools and colleges. This participation consists of three types. First, school personnel are invited to serve on various committees and commissions of the associations—for example, the Commission on Elementary Schools, the Commission on Secondary Schools, and the regional association's state committees. Second, committees of professionals review, revise, and write for each subject area the criteria that schools follow in evaluating their programs. The third and most extensive of the three types of participation is service on accreditation visiting committees that go into schools in the region to discover the strengths and weaknesses of the school's programs and to make recommendations for improvements and accreditation of the schools.

Much of the participation in which school personnel take part in the regional sector falls into the category of curriculum evaluation in contrast to planning or implementation of the curriculum.

The National Sector

U.S. Department of Education. The national scene is peppered with a variety of public, private, and professional curriculum activities, and school personnel from the state level and below play key roles in some of these activities. In the public governmental sector, the Department of Education exercises a strong influence. Called the United States Office of Education until education was separated from the U.S. Department of Health, Education, and Welfare in 1980, the Department of Education with its large bureaucracy gathers data, disseminates information, provides consultant assistance, sponsors and conducts research, funds projects, and disburses money appropriated by Congress. Local school people find the opportunity to participate in national curriculum efforts by writing and submitting proposals for grants to conduct curricular research or to put particular programs into operation in their school systems.

Federal Funding. To choose recipients of funds for proposals awarded competitively, the Department of Education calls in readers who are specialists in the particular fields in which grants are being given, such as bilingual education. These readers evaluate and make recommendations on proposals to be awarded by the specific office within the Department of Education. Several persons from all over the United States journey to Washington (or sometimes to other sites) to read proposals. In so doing, they grow professionally and bring back new ideas for curriculum development in their own communities.

Federal funding permits numerous committees to carry out curriculum projects that the U.S. Congress deems significant; for example, Title I of the Elementary and Secondary Education Act of 1965 (which later became Chapter 1 of the Education Consolidation and Improvement Act of 1981) provided for programs to aid the culturally disadvantaged.

Grants from the federal government over the years have enabled national study groups to prepare curriculum materials, some of which (as in foreign languages, mathematics, and science) have been used extensively.

Federal aid has stimulated and resulted in the involvement of curriculum workers both directly as participants and indirectly as consumers of products and services of the Educational Resources Information Center (ERIC), the National Diffusion Network, the Regional Educational Laboratories, and the National Research and Development Centers.[28]

In the late 1960s, the publicly funded National Science Foundation joined with the U.S. Office of Education to assist social studies and humanities specialists led by Jerome S. Bruner[29] to develop *Man: A Course of Study,* a multimedia curriculum for elementary school pupils.[30] Heralded by many, *Man: A Course of Study* presents an interesting case of problems of curriculum development on a national scale. Imbued with the ambitious goal of analyzing the human condition, *Man: A Course of Study* became controversial subject matter by contrasting life in the United States with life among members of an Eskimo tribe.

John D. McNeil pointed out that criticisms of *Man: A Course of Study* (MACOS) came from different curricular concerns—from the humanists who "criticized Bruner for failing to recognize the potential of MACOS for fostering emotional growth," from "social reconstructionists opposed [to] MACOS on the ground that it was created by a scholarly elite," and from the U.S. Congress, where a congressman "said the material was full of references to adultery, cannibalism, killing of female babies and old people, trial marriage, wife-swapping, and violent murders."[31]

Local schools in various regions of the country have participated in curriculum evaluation on a national scale through the National Assessment of Educational Progress, which is funded by the Office for Educational Research and Improvement of the U.S. Department of Education. Under the direction of the National Assessment of Educational Progress (NAEP), objectives have been

---

[28]For current lists of these centers and laboratories, see Appendices B, C, D, and E.

[29]Author of *The Process of Education* (Cambridge, Mass.: Harvard University Press, 1960).

[30]*Man: A Course of Study* (Washington, D.C.: Curriculum Development Associates, 1970).

[31]John D. McNeil, *Curriculum: A Comprehensive Introduction,* 4th ed. (Glenview, Ill.: Scott, Foresman/Little, Brown, 1990) p. 77.

specified, criterion-referenced measurement instruments have been created, and assessments have been conducted in a number of subject areas.[32] From these data curriculum developers in the local school systems can draw inferences about appropriate objectives of the areas tested, achievements of pupils in their region as compared to other regions, and their own state and local assessment programs.

Historically, the U.S. Department of Education has exercised a degree of leadership in curriculum development for the schools of the nation.

In this discussion of curriculum efforts on a national scale I have mentioned the executive branch of the U.S. government (the Department of Education) and the legislative branch (the U.S. Congress). We should not neglect to note that on occasion the judicial branch of the federal government assumes the role of curriculum maker. For example, the U.S. Supreme Court has ruled that public schools may not conduct sectarian practices,[33] that released time for religious instruction under certain conditions is permissible,[34] that the theory of evolution may be taught,[35] that special instruction in English must be given to non-English-speaking pupils,[36] and that prayer in the public schools is a violation of the First Amendment of the U.S. Constitution.[37] The U.S. Supreme Court justices do not seek the role of curriculum specialists but by virtue of the cases that come before them sometimes find themselves in that role.

Professional Education Associations.   The professional education associations afford opportunities for educators to engage in curriculum deliberations. The National Education Association (NEA) has repeatedly called together influential groups to evaluate purposes and programs of the schools. The NEA's Committee of Ten issued a report in 1893 that recommended the same courses (foreign languages, history, mathematics, and science) and the same allotment of time for each course for both college-bound and non-college-bound students.[38] Gerald R. Firth and Richard D. Kimpston commented on the influence of the Committee of Ten's report:

> The recommendations of courses to be taught, coupled with a statement that the courses should be offered in the same manner to both the college-bound and the noncollege-bound, became a powerful force influencing the secondary school curriculum well into the 20th century.[39]

---

[32]See pp. 462–465 of this text for additional details about the National Assessment of Educational Progress.

[33]*Illinois ex rel McCollum* v. *Board of Education,* 333 US 203, 68 S. Ct. 461 (1948).

[34]*Zorach* v. *Clauson,* 343 US 306, 72 S. Ct. 679 (1952).

[35]*Epperson* v. *Arkansas,* 393 US 97, 89 S. Ct. 266 (1968).

[36]*Lau* v. *Nichols,* 414 US 663 (1974).

[37]*School District of Abington Township, Pa.* v. *Schemp & Murray* v. *Curlett,* 374 US 203, 83 S. Ct. 1560 (1963).

[38]National Education Association, *Report of the Committee of Ten on Secondary School Studies* (New York: American Book, 1894).

[39]Gerald R. Firth and Richard D. Kimpston, *The Curricular Continuum in Perspective* (Itasca, Ill.: F. E. Peacock, 1973), p. 70.

One of the more significant attempts at curriculum decision making at the national level was the appointment of the Commission on the Reorganization of Secondary Education following World War I. In 1918 this commission stated the purposes of secondary education in the United States in the form of Seven Cardinal Principles.[40] These principles were

1. health
2. command of fundamental processes (currently known as the basic skills)
3. worthy home membership
4. vocation
5. citizenship
6. worthy use of leisure
7. ethical character

The commission's report, possessing no authority other than its persuasiveness, was widely received and accepted as a valid statement of goals for secondary education of its time. Many high schools have attempted to implement the commission's Cardinal Principles. Many educators feel that this statement of the purposes of secondary education is as relevant today as it was when first issued so many years ago.[41]

Between 1938 and 1961 the prestigious Educational Policies Commission of the National Education Association formulated statements of the purposes of education. Three of these statements have had an enduring effect on American education. In 1938 the Educational Policies Commission defined the purposes of education as fourfold: self-realization, human relationship, economic efficiency, and civic responsibility.[42] Six years later, in the midst of World War II, the Educational Policies Commission released its report on *Education for All American Youth,* which set forth ten imperative educational needs of American youth.[43]

Refining the earlier Seven Cardinal Principles, the Educational Policies Commission in 1944 saw the purposes of secondary education as follows:

1. All youth need to develop salable skills.
2. All youth need to develop and maintain good health, physical fitness, and mental health.
3. All youth need to understand the rights and duties of the citizen of a democratic society.
4. All youth need to understand the significance of the family.
5. All youth need to know how to purchase and use goods and services intelligently.

---

[40]Commission on the Reorganization of Secondary Education, *Cardinal Principles of Secondary Education* (Washington, D.C.: United States Office of Education, Bulletin no. 35, 1918).

[41]For recent criticism of the Seven Cardinal Principles, see Chapter 9 of this text.

[42]Educational Policies Commission, *The Purposes of Education in American Democracy* (Washington, D.C.: National Education Association, 1938).

[43]Educational Policies Commission, *Education for All American Youth* (Washington, D.C.: National Education Association, 1944).

6. All youth need to understand the methods of science.
7. All youth need opportunities to develop their capacities to appreciate beauty in literature, art, music, and nature.
8. All youth need to be able to use their leisure time well.
9. All youth need to develop respect for other people, to grow in their insight into ethical values and principles, to be able to live and work cooperatively with others, and to grow in the moral and spiritual values of life.
10. All youth need to grow in their ability to think rationally, to express their thoughts clearly, and to read and listen with understanding.[44]

Once again, this time in 1961, the Educational Policies Commission turned its attention to the purposes of education and decided that the central purpose of American education was to develop the ability to think.[45]

On the current scene, the Association for Supervision and Curriculum Development (ASCD), a professional association with a special interest in curriculum improvement, engages its members and others in numerous curriculum studies. It disseminates the results of studies through its journal, *Educational Leadership,* its yearbooks, and its monographs. Of special help to persons interested in the curriculum field are the ASCD's National Curriculum Study Institutes in which participants under the leadership of recognized experts focus on particular curriculum problems.

Development of curricula in specialized fields has been made possible by the National Science Foundation in cooperation with professional associations. The National Science Foundation, the American Mathematical Society, the National Council of Teachers of Mathematics, and the Mathematical Association of America joined forces in the 1950s to produce the School Mathematics Study Group (SMSG) program for grades 4 through 12. Involved in the production of this program were mathematicians, mathematics educators, and high school teachers. At about the same time and through a similar collaborative effort, the American Institute of Biological Sciences, with financial backing by the National Science Foundation, brought forth the Biological Sciences Curriculum Study (BSCS) programs (in three versions) for high school biology.

Professional education organizations have made and continue to make significant contributions to the curriculum field.

Private Foundations. Several private foundations, notably the Ford and Kellogg Foundations, have demonstrated a keen interest in supporting projects designed to improve education in the United States. Ford has given generous backing to experimentation with novel staff patterns in the schools and the use of educational television, whereas Kellogg has zeroed in on studies of educational administration. As examples of foundations' interest in the curriculum of the schools we might mention the Carnegie Corporation's support in the field

---

[44]Educational Policies Commission, *American Youth,* pp. 225–226. Adapted with permission.
[45]Educational Policies Commission, *The Central Purpose of American Education* (Washington, D.C.: National Education Association, 1961).

of mathematics and the Alfred P. Sloan Foundation's aid in the field of science. In the early 1950s the Carnegie Corporation financially backed professors in arts and sciences, education, and engineering at the University of Illinois to develop a school mathematics program for grades 9 through 12, which has become known as the University of Illinois Committee on School Mathematics (UICSM) math. Shortly thereafter, in the late 1950s, the Carnegie Corporation funded another mathematics project: the development of a program for grades seven and eight by teachers of mathematics, mathematicians, and mathematics educators at the University of Maryland.

The Alfred P. Sloan Foundation entered into curriculum development in the late 1950s by supporting, along with the National Science Foundation and the Ford Foundation's Fund for the Advancement of Education, the production of a new program for high school physics known as Physical Science Study Committee (PSSC) physics.

Several observations can be made about these illustrations of national curriculum development in mathematics and science. First, these programs were developed through the collaboration of scholars and practitioners, professors and teachers, combinations that have been tried with rather low frequency, unfortunately. Second, all these undertakings took considerable effort and cost a significant amount of money. Without the largesse of the federal government, public and private foundations, and professional organizations, these materials would most probably have never seen the light of day. Third, as you may have already noted, all these developments occurred in the decade of the 1950s and continued into the early 1960s. The 1950s were a time when there was great ferment in education and money flowed into educational pursuits as if from the proverbial horn of plenty. As a response to Soviet technology and in the name of national defense, the availability of funds for educational projects and research made the 1950s a heady time for educators. No such concerted collaborative activity on such a broad scale has occurred since, and we may well ponder whether it is ever likely to occur again. Finally and most significantly, in spite of the curriculum fervor of the 1950s (Could it be *because* of the fervor of the 1950s?), some of the "new math" and the "new science" programs have gone into eclipse, causing us to muse with François Villon, "Where are the snows of yesteryear?"

In recent years the Carnegie Corporation with the Atlantic Richfield Foundation funded the study of American high schools directed by Ernest L. Boyer, president of the Carnegie Foundation for the Advancement of Teaching.[46] Six philanthropic foundations—the Charles E. Culpeper Foundation, the Carnegie Corporation, the Commonwealth Fund, the Esther A. and Joseph Klingenstein Fund, the Gates Foundation, and the Edward John Noble Foundation—supported Theodore R. Sizer's study of the American high school. Cosponsors

---

[46]Ernest L. Boyer, *High School: A Report on Secondary Education in America* (New York: Harper & Row, 1983).

of Sizer's study were the National Association of Secondary School Principals and the National Association of Independent Schools.[47]

Funds for John Goodlad's study of schooling in America were provided by 11 foundations, including the Danforth Foundation, the Ford Foundation, the International Paper Company Foundation, the JDR[3rd] Fund, the Martha Holden Jennings Foundation, the Charles F. Kettering Foundation, the Lilly Endowment, the Charles Stewart Mott Foundation, the Needmor Fund, the Rockefeller Foundation, and the Spencer Foundation; funding was also provided by Pedamorphosis, Inc., the National Institute of Education, and the U.S. Office of Education.[48]

The Danforth Foundation, which long concerned itself with the professional growth and development of secondary school administrators, has over the years also taken an interest in promoting international education in the schools. The John D. and Catherine T. MacArthur Foundation aided the Paideia Group, which issued the *Paideia Proposal,* calling for the same course of study for all students in the 12 years of basic schooling, the only exception being the choice of a second language.[49]

It can be readily seen that private foundations play a significant role in promoting change in the school's curriculum.

Other Influential Voices.   In 1990, President George Bush and the National Governors Association set forth six national educational goals. We will examine these goals and their significance in Chapter 6.

Tests and Texts.   Before we leave the national sector, we should mention an aspect of curriculum development that has evoked considerable discussion. Standardized tests of achievement and textbooks used in the schools have played a great part in molding the contemporary curriculum. Combined with the movement toward specification of minimal competencies for high school graduation, achievement tests profoundly affect what is being taught and how it is being taught. Under these conditions, curriculum decisions have been, in effect, put into the hands of the test makers and the textbook writers. Some curriculum experts see the reliance on tests and textbooks marketed throughout the country as constituting a "national curriculum."[50] Elliot W. Eisner expressed concern about the influence of the testing movement:

> One may wax eloquent about the life of the mind and the grand purposes of education, but must face up to the fact that school programs are shaped by other factors, as well. Communities led to believe that the quality of education is represented by the reading and math scores students receive come

---

[47]Theodore R. Sizer, *Horace's Compromise: The Dilemma of the American High School* (Boston: Houghton Mifflin, 1984).

[48]Goodlad, *A Place Called School.*

[49]Mortimer J. Adler, *The Paideia Proposal: An Educational Manifesto* (New York: Macmillan, 1982).

[50]Other educators identify federal aid for specific categories as creating types of national curricula.

to demand that those areas of the curriculum be given highest priority. When this happens, teachers begin to define their own priorities in terms of test performance. Indeed, I do not believe it an exaggeration to say that test scores function as one of the most powerful controls on the character of educational practice.[51]

Considerable activity in planning, implementing, and evaluating curriculum transpires in the national sector. Although curriculum activities on the national scene are many and diverse, opportunities for personal involvement in planning are rather limited for the rank-and-file teacher and curriculum specialist. Their roles are more often as recipients of curriculum plans developed by others, implementors of plans, and sometimes evaluators.

The International Sector

International Professional Associations.   Involvement of American curriculum workers on the international scene is made possible through membership in international professional associations, primarily those based in the United States. The International Reading Association, for example, attracts reading specialists from around the world but primarily from the United States and Canada. The World Council for Gifted and Talented Children holds conferences in various parts of the world. One of the more pertinent international organizations for those interested in curricular acitivies on an international scale is the World Council for Curriculum and Instruction (WCCI), which is open to all educators who have an interest in "global fellowship."[52] This organization, comprising members from more than 70 countries, provides advice and assistance on curricular matters, carries out transnational projects, and sponsors triennial conferences in various locations throughout the world.

If teachers and administrators are willing to spend a period of time abroad, they can become intimately involved in curriculum development overseas by accepting employment in the U.S. Department of Defense Schools or in the private American Community/International Schools whose curricula are mainly those offered stateside. Or they may become active in developing curricula of national schools through employment with the Peace Corps or the Agency for International Development.

The United Nations Educational, Scientific, and Cultural Organization (UNESCO), with headquarters in Paris, affords opportunities for curriculum study, research, teaching, and technical assistance to educators from the members of the United Nations.[53] The Institute of International Education in New

---

[51]Elliot W. Eisner, *The Educational Imagination: On the Design and Evaluation of School Programs,* 2nd ed. (New York: Macmillan, 1985), p. 4.

[52]World Council for Curriculum and Instruction Secretariat, Box 171, Teachers College, Columbia University, New York, N.Y. 10027.

[53]Objecting to some of UNESCO's policies, the United States, at the time of the writing of this text, is not a member of UNESCO.

York City directs an international exchange of students and teachers supported in part by Fulbright funds. The Council for International Exchange of Scholars in Washington, D.C., administers Fulbright grants that enable faculty from institutions of higher education to conduct research and teach in foreign countries.

Opportunities for firsthand participation in actual curriculum construction on a cross-national basis are rare, and this dearth of opportunity is, perhaps, to be expected. The curricular needs and goals of education in various countries are so divergent as to make impractical the building of a particular curriculum that will fit the requirements of the educational system of every country.

Comparative Studies of Student Achievement.   Significant efforts primarily in the realm of assessment of student achievement should be noted. Studies comparing achievement of students in a number of countries and in a variety of disciplines have been conducted by the International Association for the Evaluation of Educational Achievement (IEA) and the International Assessment of Educational Progress (IAEP). You will find discussion of international comparative studies in Chapter 12 of this text.

U.S.-USSR Textbook-Study Project.   One of the more interesting international curriculum studies of recent years was the U.S.-USSR Textbook-Study Project sponsored by the National Council for the Social Studies, the Council of Chief State School Officers, the Association of American Publishers, the Association for the Advancement of Slavic Studies, and the Soviet Union's Ministry of Education.[54] Begun in 1977 as a phase of cultural exchange agreements between the two countries, the project ceased functioning after the Soviet march into Afghanistan in 1979. The project resumed operation in 1985, drafted a report in 1987, and presented a subsequent report on the conclusion of a seminar in Moscow in June 1989.

Educators from both countries examined history and geography textbooks used in the secondary schools of each country to ascertain what one nation's students were taught about the other nation. These educators searched for errors of fact and distortions in the textbooks. Project efforts pointed to the need for textbooks published in each country to present a more accurate picture of the other country. This exciting approach to international curriculum study could well furnish a model that the United States could replicate with other countries.

Global Awareness   To this point we have concentrated on opportunities for collaborative cross-cultural curriculum research and development. A somewhat different curriculum activity was the funding by the U.S. Department of Education of programs in the schools for the development of global awareness among American children and youth. In spite of international tensions, American commitment to the development of students' and teachers' understanding of foreign

---

[54]Robert Rothman, "Americans, Soviets Critique Texts," *Education Week* 7, no. 12 (November 25, 1987): 5 and Oliva's correspondence from the National Council for the Social Studies, dated December 4, 1990.

nations remains high. Recommendations of such groups as the President's Commission on Foreign Languages and International Studies have helped stimulate study of foreign languages and cultures.[55] Among the many recommendations of the President's Commission were these:

- □ regional centers for upgrading competencies for foreign language teachers
- □ summer institutes abroad for foreign language teachers and others
- □ reinstatement of foreign language requirements in schools and colleges
- □ the integration of international studies throughout the school curricula
- □ expansion of international exchanges of students, teachers, administrators, and policymakers
- □ requirement of two to three courses in international studies for all bachelor's degree candidates
- □ establishment of regional international studies centers at colleges and universities

The National Commission on Excellence in Education included foreign language study among its recommendations. According to the commission's report:

> Achieving proficiency in *foreign language* ordinarily requires from 4 to 6 years of study and should, therefore, be started in the elementary grades. We believe it is desirable that students achieve such proficiency because study of a foreign language introduces students to non-English speaking cultures, heightens awareness and comprehension of one's native tongue, and serves the Nation's needs in commerce, diplomacy, defense, and education.[56]

A rationale for global education is the focus of the 1991 Yearbook of the Association for Supervision and Curriculum Development. The yearbook includes descriptions of ways to introduce global studies into the curriculum.[57]

Although opportunities for actual curriculum development on the international scene are limited, many opportunities exist for school personnel to study and compare curricula of the world's nations. Professional organizations like Phi Delta Kappa and the Comparative and International Education Society conduct frequent study tours for those interested in examining firsthand the curricula of other countries and meeting educational leaders of those countries. Many teachers have taken advantage of opportunities to serve as leaders of educational study tours abroad. Furthermore, development of both awareness and understanding of other cultures (both within and outside of our borders) remains a high priority of our elementary and secondary curricula.

---

[55]See Malcolm G. Scully, "Require Foreign-Language Studies, Presidential Panel Urges Colleges," *The Chronicle of Higher Education* 19, no. 11 (November 13, 1979): 1 ff.

[56]National Commission on Excellence in Education, *A Nation at Risk: The Imperative for Educational Reform* (Washington, D.C.: U.S. Government Printing Office, 1983), p. 26.

[57]Kenneth A. Tye, ed., *Global Education: From Thought to Action*, 1991 Yearbook (Alexandria, Va.: Association for Supervision and Curriculum Development, 1990).

SUMMARY

Curriculum planning is viewed as occurring on five levels: classroom, team/grade/department, individual school, school district, and state. Each level in ascending order exercises authority over levels below it.

In addition, planning takes place in regional, national, and world sectors. Sectors are distinguished from levels because powers of the sectors over the five levels are either nonexistent or limited.

Teachers and curriculum specialists will find their most frequent opportunities to participate actively in curriculum development at the first four levels. Some curriculum workers are called on by the state to serve on curriculum projects. A limited number of school-based persons take part in a variety of curriculum efforts sponsored by regional, national, and international organizations and agencies.

This chapter diagrams a variety of organizational patterns for carrying out curriculum development activities in the individual school and school district. A teacher or curriculum specialist may be requested to serve on a number of curriculum committees and councils within a school system.

Forces outside the schools also influence curriculum decision making. Curriculum development is perceived as a multilevel, multisector process and as a collaborative effort.

QUESTIONS FOR DISCUSSION

1. To what degree should teachers be involved in curriculum planning at the individual school level? At the district level?
2. What are the strengths and limitations of the concept of levels of planning?
3. What are the strengths and limitations of the concept of sectors of planning?
4. What do you believe is the best way for organizing a curriculum council on the individual school level?
5. What do you believe is the best way for organizing a curriculum council on the school district level?

SUPPLEMENTARY EXERCISES

1. Chart the organizational pattern for curriculum development in your school and district.
2. Write a short paper describing the extent to which the organizational patterns operating in your school system can be called participatory.
3. Tell how curriculum committees and councils are selected and constituted in your school district.
4. Account for any program changes in the last three years that resulted from curriculum development activities in the school district.

5. Describe activities of the faculty of a team, grade, or department in the area of curriculum development.
6. Describe the roles and powers of (a) the state superintendent, (b) the state board of education, and (c) the state department of education in curricular and instructional matters within your state.
7. Study an organizational chart of your state department of education and identify those offices that are charged with providing curricular and instructional leadership in the state. Describe some of the services of these offices.
8. Report on several programs that have come about or been affected as a result of state legislation.
9. Describe any curriculum developments that have come about as a result of regional activities.
10. Report on the purposes and activities of the accrediting associations of your region.
11. Report on several programs that have come about or been affected as a result of federal legislation.
12. Report on any national curriculum studies that you would call significant.
13. Report on at least two state and two federal court decisions that have had an impact on the curriculum of your school system.
14. Describe any curriculum development in your school system that might be attributed to international influences.
15. Report on the purposes and recent activities of at least two state, two national, and two international professional organizations concerned with curriculum development.
16. Write a description of the processes by which textbooks are selected in your state or district.
17. If you work in a private school and if your school is accredited by an association or associations other than the regional accrediting association, describe the purpose and activities of that association or associations.
18. In Chapter 11 of his book, John D. McNeil (see bibliography) discusses the politics of curriculum making. Report several ways in which curriculum making is a political process.

BIBLIOGRAPHY

Beauchamp, George A. *Curriculum Theory*, 4th ed. Itasca, Ill.: F. E. Peacock, 1981.

Bruner, Jerome S. *The Process of Education*. Cambridge, Mass.: Harvard University Press, 1960. Carroll, Joseph M. "The Copernican Plan: Restructuring the Ameri-can High School." *Phi Delta Kappan* 71, no. 5 (January 1990): 358–365.

Commission on the Reorganization of Secondary Education. *Cardinal Principles of Secondary Education*. Washington, D.C.: United States Office of Education, Bulletin no. 35, 1918.

Doll, Ronald C. *Curriculum Improvement: Decision Making and Process.* 7th ed. Boston: Allyn and Bacon, 1989.

Educational Policies Commission. *The Central Purpose of American Education.* Washington, D.C.: National Education Association, 1961.

———. *Education for All American Youth.* Washington, D.C.: National Education Association, 1944.

———. *The Purposes of Education in American Democracy.* Washington, D.C.: National Education Association, 1938.

Eisner, Elliot W. *Confronting Curriculum Reform.* Boston: Little, Brown, 1971.

———. *The Educational Imagination: On the Design and Evaluation of School Programs,* 2nd ed. New York: Macmillan, 1985.

Featherstone, Joseph. "Measuring What Schools Achieve." *Phi Delta Kappan* 55, no. 7 (March 1974): 448–450.

Firth, Gerald R. and Kimpston, Richard D. *The Curricular Continuum in Perspective.* Itasca, Ill.: F. E. Peacock, 1973.

Frymier, Jack R. and Hawn, Horace C. *Curriculum Improvement for Better Schools.* Worthington, Ohio: Charles A. Jones, 1970.

Gomez, Joseph J., "The Path to School-based Management Isn't Smooth, but We're Scaling the Obstacles One by One," *The American School Board Journal* 176, no. 10 (October 1989): 20–22.

Hass, Glen, ed. *Curriculum Planning: A New Approach,* 5th ed. Boston: Allyn and Bacon, 1987.

Kimbrough, Ralph B. and Nunnery, Michael Y. *Educational Administration: An Introduction,* 3rd ed. New York: Macmillan, 1988.

McNeil, John D. *Curriculum: A Comprehensive Introduction,* 4th ed. Glenview, Ill.: Scott, Foresman/Little, Brown, 1990.

Mendez, Roy. "The Curriculum Council: One Way to Develop the Instructional Leadership Role." *NASSP Bulletin* 67, no. 464 (September 1983): 18–21.

Oliva, Peter F. *The Secondary School Today,* 2nd ed. New York: Harper & Row, 1972.

Oliver, Albert I. *Curriculum Improvement: A Guide to Problems, Principles, and Process,* 2nd ed. New York: Harper & Row, 1977.

Prasch, John. *How to Organize for School-Based Management.* Alexandria, VA: Association for Supervision and Curriculum Development, 1990.

"Restructuring Schools to Match a Changing Society." *Educational Leadership* 45, no. 5 (February 1988): 3–79.

Rubin, Louis, ed. *Curriculum Handbook: The Disciplines, Current Movements, and Instructional Methodology.* Boston: Allyn and Bacon, 1977.

Saylor, J. Galen, Alexander, William M., and Lewis, Arthur J. *Curriculum Planning for Better Teaching and Learning,* 4th ed. New York: Holt, Rinehart and Winston 1981.

Shanker, Albert. "The End of the Traditional Model of Schooling—and a Proposal for Using Incentives to Restructure Our Public Schools." *Phi Delta Kappan* 71, no. 5 (January 1990): 344-357.

Tye, Kenneth A., ed. *Global Education from Thought to Action,* 1991 Yearbook. Alexandria, VA: Association for Supervision and Curriculum Development, 1990.

Walberg, Herbert J., Bakalis, Michael J., Bast, Joseph L., and Baer, Steven "Reconstructing the Nation's Worst Schools," *Phi Delta Kappan* 70, no. 10 (June 1989): 802–805.

Zais, Robert S. *Curriculum: Principles and Foundations.* New York: Harper & Row, 1976.

CHAPTER FOUR

Curriculum Planning: The Human Dimension

After studying this chapter you should be able to:

1. Describe the roles of (a) the principal, (b) the curriculum leader, (c) the teachers, (d) the students, and (e) the parents and other citizens in curriculum development.

2. Describe the knowledge and skills needed by the curriculum leader.

THE SCHOOL AS A UNIQUE BLEND

Let us for a few moments step into the shoes of the superintendent of a hypothetical school district. It is mid-May. The school year is almost over and summer school plans are ready to be implemented. The superintendent has just concluded a meeting with his principals on the budget and staffing needs for next year. In 30 minutes he will meet with an assistant superintendent and one of the principals of the district, who intend to bring charges of insubordination against one of the teachers in the principal's school. For a half hour the superintendent muses on what improvements in curriculum and instruction have been accomplished in the school district this year. Since his energies have been channeled into public relations, budgeting, personnel problems, transportation, new buildings, and other administrative matters, he has delegated responsibility for curriculum and instruction in the school district to the assistant superintendent for curriculum and instruction. He holds in his hands a report updating developments in the district this year.

The superintendent is struck by the large amount of time and effort that the school district is expending toward improving curriculum and instruction. He is impressed by the sizable number of people involved in this activity. He notes that most teams of teachers meet practically daily; most grade faculties or departments meet as groups regularly, some of them on a weekly basis; every school has its own curriculum council, which meets at least once a month; and a number of curriculum committees meet at various times on district-wide problems of curriculum and instruction. The superintendent certainly cannot fault the quantity of effort expended by the professionals in curriculum development.

As to quality he is less certain. He reviews some of the accomplishments to date and is struck by the unevenness of developments from school to school. The accomplishments of some schools far outshine those of others. Several innovative programs are in experimental stages in some schools. Other schools have defined their philosophies, goals, and objectives. Some have conducted thorough reexaminations of their curricula, whereas others have been content with the status quo. Several groups of teachers have revised their particular curricula. Other groups have developed some new curriculum guides. Some schools have responded to previously unmet curricular needs of their students, and others have failed to come up with solutions to some of their more pressing curricular problems. The superintendent is surprised (though he realizes that he should not be) that a few schools obviously surpass the others in both quantity and quality of curriculum efforts. A few schools have tackled curriculum development with a vigor that has effected significant change. He finds repeated references in the assistant superintendent's report to positive changes made by a few schools. He concludes that some schools are imbued with the spirit of change and are willing to move forward and out, while others find the established ways of operating more comfortable. The superintendent wonders why such great variations in curriculum development exist from school to school. Whom should he credit in those schools that seem to be engaged in productive curriculum efforts? The principals? The teachers? The curriculum leaders, whoever they are? The students? The parents? The signs of the zodiac? Just plain luck? Or a combination of all these factors?

The superintendent is aware that schools differ considerably from one another. Their physical facilities, resources, and locales all differ. Yet these more or less tangible factors do not explain the great differences in strides made by schools in curriculum and instruction. Yes, we may say that schools differ in many ways, but schools are only brick, concrete, mortar, steel, wood, glass, and a host of other building materials. It is not the schools that differ but the people who either support them or operate within them. The superintendent must credit not the schools in the abstract but the people who make them function. In his short period of reflection, the superintendent reinforces a long-held, verified belief—that curriculum development is a "people" process, a human endeavor. Curriculum development is a process in which the human players accept and carry out mutually reinforcing roles. Given a predisposition to change and a subtle blending of skills and knowledge, a faculty can achieve significant successes in curriculum improvement even in a substandard physical environment. The "people" setting far outweighs the physical setting.

Differences Among Faculty

Let's leave the meditating superintendent and focus our attention on another place, another time. It is early in the school year. The principal of a medium size secondary school is presiding over the initial organizational meeting of the school's curriculum council. Representatives of the nine departments of the school are about to elect their chairperson. With freshness, high spirits, and a modicum of levity, the curriculum council is getting under way. The principal wonders what progress the school will make this year in curriculum improvement. She realizes as she looks around the room that success in improving the curriculum depends largely on human differences among individual curriculum workers and between curriculum groups.

Each school is characterized by its own unique blend of persons, each with different skills, knowledge, experience, and personality. The principal mentally lists some of the ways individuals within the curriculum council, which represents the faculty, differ. Certainly, the philosophical beliefs of the various council members diverge greatly. It will take considerable effort to reach some kind of consensus on the goals of this school, let alone the general goals of education. The council members differ in their knowledge about and ability to apply learning theory. Some are outstanding instructors, others only passable. Variations exist in the members' knowledge of curriculum history and theory and in experience in curriculum development.

Some younger members, new to teaching and the particular school, are less knowledgeable about children in general and in this setting than older teachers who have taught several years, many of them in this school. As soon as the council settles down to work it becomes apparent that there are great differences in individuals' skills in interacting with others, in the leadership skills of the various council members, in followership skills, in organizational skills, in writing skills, and in oral skills.

Some of the council members will show themselves as being more perceptive of parental roles and the needs of the community. Personal traits like friendliness, reliability, motivation, sense of humor, enthusiasm, and frustration level are significant differences among individuals that contribute to the success or failure of group efforts like curriculum development. Outside commitments, family obligations, and allocations of time differ from person to person and can affect the process of curriculum planning.

The human variables in the process are many and complex. Success or failure will depend to a great extent on how the council members relate to one another, on how each member relates to other teachers on the faculty, and how they, in turn, relate to one another. The way the council and faculty interact with parents, others in the community, and the students can make or break curriculum efforts.

Dependent Variables

The differences among individuals and groups participating in curriculum development are dependent rather than independent variables. The presence or absence of a particular skill or trait and the degree to which an individual possesses it have an impact on all other individuals who take part in the process. Not only are the leaders' leadership skills and the followers' followership skills significant in themselves, but the manner in which they come together is even more important. Competence in leadership must ideally be met with competence in followership. Whether in military service, industry, or education, a superb leader is going nowhere without committed followers. In the same manner superb followers are going nowhere without competent leadership.

In accounting for success or failure in a cooperative enterprise, we should also look to differences among groups as well as individuals. It is trite but pertinent to say that the whole is greater than the sum of its parts. A group is not simply the addition of each individual member to make a sum but something more than the sum, something special created by an inexplicable meshing of the human elements. Working together, members of a group must become unified as they move toward common goals in a spirit of mutual respect. Thus a curriculum council *as a group* can demonstrate leadership skills and a faculty *as a group* can demonstrate competence in leadership. Success in curriculum development is more likely to be achieved when the leadership skills of the council interface with those of the faculty, resulting in a total team approach to the solution of curriculum problems. When we compare schools' achievements in curriculum improvement, we quickly discover great variations in the leadership skills of (1) the person or persons directing the curriculum study, (2) the curriculum committees or councils, (3) the total faculty, and (4) the preceding three entities working together. The contributions to curriculum improvement that may be made by students, parents, and others from the community enhance the work of the professionals.

THE CAST OF PLAYERS

We would not be far off the mark if we perceived the process of curriculum development as a continuing theatrical production in which actors play specific roles. Some of these roles are determined by society and the force of law; others are set by players themselves. Some roles are mandated, whereas others spring out of the personalities of the players themselves.

When discussing roles of various groups, J. Galen Saylor and William M. Alexander applied the analogy of drama to the process of curriculum planning:

> In addition to leading roles of students and teachers in the curriculum planning drama, important supporting actors include the members of lay advisory groups, curriculum councils and committees, teacher teams, and curriculum development units. . . . all of these roles are affected by their interaction with various groups and agencies outside the curriculum theatre.[1]

Although the metaphor of curriculum planning as drama can be overworked, we must admit that a good deal of role-playing does occur, much of it unconsciously, in the group process itself. For the moment, let's talk about the conscious roles the curriculum participants are called on to play. For purposes of analysis we will focus our attention on roles of constituent groups (administrators, students, lay people, curriculum workers-teachers, curriculum consultants, and supervisors). To achieve clarity we will focus on the individual school level.

Role of the Administrator

Whether the chief administrator of the school, the principal, serves actively as curriculum leader or passively by delegating leadership responsibilities to subordinates, curriculum development is doomed to failure without his or her support. In these times the role of the administrator is in a period of transition. Although some school administrators take the position that they are trying to be instructional leaders, others admit that they are primarily managers.

---

[1]Excerpts from *Planning Curriculum for Schools,* p. 59, by J. G. Saylor and W. M. Alexander, copyright©1974 by Holt, Rinehart and Winston, Inc., reprinted by permission of the publisher.

More than 30 years ago the Southern States Cooperative Program in Educational Administration listed the tasks of educational administration. Sponsored by the W. K. Kellogg Foundation this study group specified the following as critical tasks for administrators:

1. instruction and curriculum development
2. pupil personnel
3. community-school leadership
4. staff personnel
5. school plant
6. school transportation
7. organization and structure
8. school finance and business management[2]

You will note that instructional and curriculum development headed this list. Although the role of the principal as instructional leader is a current and growing emphasis, instructional and curriculum development do not head the list of priorities of many school principals. Thelbert L. Drake and William H. Roe observed that the principal is torn between his or her desired role as instructional leader and his or her actual role as administrator and manager:

> By reading the literature, attending state and national meetings, and discussing the position with incumbents, one gained a mental picture of a professional person being torn apart, on the one hand by an intense interest and desire to lead in instruction and learning, and on the other hand by the responsibility "to keep school," the latter being the proper administration and management of "things," as expected by the central administration. In this little drama an eternal struggle seemed to take place, and in the end, the strong instructional leadership role had to be set aside because of the immediacy and press of everyday administrative duties.[3]

The reasons for the low priority assigned by principals to what used to be their main raison d'être are found both within the personality of the principal and in the pressure from outside forces. Some of the factors that lead principals away from spending time on instructional leadership are the priority that the higher officers place on efficiency of operation, limitations placed on principals' fields of operation by teachers' organizations, and preservice programs for administrators that stress business and personnel management, minimizing curriculum and instructional development.

Perceptions of Parents.   The managerial direction in administration apparently opposes the perceptions of parents about the manner in which the principal should be occupying his or her time. Drake and Roe reported a 1978

---

[2]Southern States Cooperative Program in Educational Administration, *Better Teaching in School Administration* (Nashville, Tenn.: McQuiddy, 1955), pp. 125–177.

[3]Thelbert L. Drake and William H. Roe, *The Principalship,* 3rd ed. (New York: Macmillan, 1986), p. 17.

study sponsored by the Indiana Congress of Parents and Teachers that cited priorities parents set on the duties of principals. They rated as top priorities the following:

1. Initiate improvements in teaching techniques and methods.
2. Make certain that curricula fit the needs of students.
3. Direct teachers to motivate students to learn at their optimal levels.
4. Afford teachers the opportunity to individualize programs.
5. Direct teachers to coordinate and articulate the subject matter taught on each grade level.[4]

Glenys G. Unruh observed that training programs for administrators may be at least partially at fault for the lower priority placed on curriculum and instruction by some principals.[5]

With growing emphasis on the individual school as the locus of change, on public demand for improvement in students' achievement, and on the assessment of teacher performance, there are hopeful signs that the principals' priorities are shifting. Professional associations for administrators are stressing the importance of instructional leadership. Preservice and in-service education programs for school administrators are incorporating training in the technical, supervisory, and human relations skills and knowledge needed by the instructional leader. Thus the principal may more and more play a direct, central role in curriculum development. In the near future instructional leadership may top the list of tasks actually performed by most principals.

Whether the principal plays a direct or indirect role, his or her presence is always keenly felt by all the players. The participants are aware that the principal by both tradition and law is charged with responsibility for running all the affairs of the school and for decision making in that school. In that sense, all curriculum groups and subgroups of the school are advisory to the principal.

"Theory X" and "Theory Y."   Through management style the principal exerts a force on all operations within the school. The success of the curriculum developers may depend to some extent on whether the principal is a "Theory X" or a "Theory Y" person. Douglas McGregor has classified two sets of assumptions that he believes managers have about people into the categories Theory X and Theory Y.[6] These theories are widely quoted in the literature on management. According to McGregor, managers following Theory X believe the following:

☐ The average person dislikes work and tries to avoid it.
☐ Most people must be forced to work and threatened with punishment to get them to work.

---

[4]Ibid., p. 153.
[5]Glenys G. Unruh, "Curriculum Politics," in Fenwick W. English, ed., *Fundamental Curriculum Decisions,* 1983 Yearbook (Alexandria, Va.: Association for Supervision and Curriculum Development, 1983), p. 109.
[6]Douglas M. McGregor, *The Human Side of Enterprise* (New York: McGraw-Hill, 1960).

□ The average person lacks ambition and avoids responsibility.

□ The average person must be directed.

□ The need for security is the chief motivation of the average person.

Authority, control, task maintenance, and product orientation dominate the thinking of the Theory X administrator. On the other hand, the administrator who subscribes to Theory Y follows a human relations approach, for he or she holds these beliefs:

□ The average person welcomes work.

□ The average person seeks responsibility.

□ Most people will demonstrate self-reliance when they share a commitment to the realization of common objectives.

□ The average person will be committed to an organization's objectives if he or she is rewarded for that commitment.

□ Creativity in problem solving is a trait found rather widely among people.

Whereas the typical administrator will be more inclined toward one theory, he or she will manifest behavior that will at times lean toward the other. There are occasions, for example, when the Theory Y administrator must exercise authority and follow Theory X principles. Nevertheless, the position among current specialists in curriculum development, supervision, and administration counsels a human relations approach. Thomas J. Sergiovanni and Fred D. Carver expressed this position well: "In our view, the unique role of the school as a humanizing and self-actualizing institution requires that school executives adopt the assumptions and behavior manifestations of Theory Y."[7]

The human-relations–oriented principal nurtures the curriculum development process by establishing a climate in which the planners feel valued and in which they can satisfy, to use Abraham Maslow's term, "the need for self-actualization."[8] The principal must encourage and facilitate the process. Since he or she holds the power for final decision making within the school, the principal must give serious consideration to recommendations made by the school's curriculum study groups. Further, the principal must always demonstrate sincere interest in the curriculum development process. Personal traits such as a negative attitude or indifference by the school's chief administrator will effectively block progress in improving the school's curriculum. The principal's personality may, indeed, be a more powerful determinant of progress than his or her training, knowledge, or conscious intentions.

Theory Y principals might well find compatible with their views of administration some of the principles of Theory Z organizations.[9] Based on practices

---

[7]Thomas J. Sergiovanni and Fred D. Carver, *The New School Executive: A Theory of Administration,* 2nd ed. (New York: Harper & Row, 1980), p. 49.

[8]Abraham H. Maslow, *Motivation and Personality,* 2nd ed. (New York: Harper & Row, 1970), p. 46.

[9]See William G. Ouchi, *Theory Z: How American Businesses Can Meet the Japanese Challenge* (Reading, Mass.: Addison-Wesley, 1981).

followed by Japanese business and industry, Theory Z organizations emphasize collective decision making and responsibility over individual decision making and responsibility. Theory Z organizations welcome the establishment of "quality control circles," or simply "quality circles," small groups of employees whose task it is to study and propose ways of solving problems and improving the effectiveness of the organization.[10]

Regardless of their style or approach—and here we may generalize to all levels of the school system—administrators and their assistants must assume responsibility for providing leadership in many areas. They must establish the organizational framework so that curriculum development may proceed, secure facilities and needed resources, coordinate efforts of the various groups, offer consultative help, keep the groups on task, resolve conflicts, communicate school needs to all groups, maintain a harmonious working climate, assure collection of needed data, provide for communication among groups, advise groups on latest developments in education, and make final decisions for their particular level.

Role of Students

Before turning our attention to the main participants in the curriculum development process (the curriculum leaders and their fellow workers), let's briefly consider the roles of two supporting groups—the students and the adult citizens from the community. With increasing frequency, students, depending upon their maturity, are participating both directly and indirectly in the task of improving the curriculum. In some cases, notably at the high school level (and above), students are accorded membership on curriculum councils. More commonly, student input is sought in a more indirect fashion. There are still many administrators and teachers who take a dim view of sharing decision making with the student clientele of the school. On the other hand, it is becoming increasingly more common for administrators and faculties to solicit student reactions to the curriculum. Surveys are conducted to obtain student perceptions of their programs; individual students and groups are interviewed. Suggestions for improvement in the curriculum and for ways of meeting their perceived needs are actively sought.

The recipient of the program—the student—is often in the best position to provide feedback about the product—the curriculum. Advice from the student constituency of the school may well provide clues for intelligent curriculum decision making.

Some schools seek information and advice from the chosen student leaders—the student government—whereas others look toward a wider sam-

---

[10]Ibid., pp. 261–268; see also the videotape *Quality Circles: Problem-Solving Tool for Educators,* Association for Supervision and Curriculum Development, 1984. For a view of the negative side of Japanese management see Joel Kotkin and Yoriko Kishimoto, "Theory F," *Inc.* 8, no. 4 (April 1986): 53–60.

pling of opinion about programs. Even in those schools in which student input is not actively sought and in which channels have not been established for gathering data from students, the learners speak loudly by their achievements in class. When standardized and state assessment test scores are consistently below level in a given school, the faculty can conclude that some adjustments are necessary in respect to either the curriculum or instruction. When diagnostic tests reveal deficiencies on the part of learners, something is being conveyed about the school's program.

John McNeil pointed out how students can silently make an impact on the curriculum:

> Informally, however, students have much influence over what is taught. Often they can "vote with their feet" by refusing to enroll in courses that feature the curriculum of academic specialists. The failure of students to respond to the Physical Science Study Committee's "physics" was an argument for curriculum change. Alternative schools and underground newspapers are other instances of student power.[11]

In Chapter 7 we will consider the student as a source of the curriculum. Here we are primarily concerned with the student's role as a participant in curriculum development.

Student Involvement.   Student involvement in curriculum improvement has been connected with the growing movements toward student rights and the stress on humanism in the schools.[12] Ronald Doll spoke of the connection between student participation in curriculum development and the student rights movement as follows:

> Changes have occurred in the role of pupils, especially at secondary school level, in planning the curriculum. The revolutionary movement in colleges of the sixties had almost immediate effect on many high schools and indeed on some elementary schools. Student rights came to include the right to participate with adults in planning the uses to which pupils' time in schools was to be put. Though this right had existed in some better-known schools for many years and had been advocated to a limited extent by authors in the curriculum field, it now meant permission to speak freely and at length in curriculum meetings, often on a footing equal to that of experienced adults. To some teachers and principals, pupils' newly acquired status represented a refreshing view of human potential and a deserved position in the educational hierarchy; to others it seemed an especially time-consuming and plaguing form of contemporary insanity.[13]

---

[11]John D. McNeil, *Curriculum: A Comprehensive Introduction,* 4th ed. (Glenview, Ill.: Scott, Foresman/Little, Brown, 1990), p. 271.

[12]See, for example, Albert J. Oliver, *Curriculum Improvement: A Guide to Problems, Principles and Process,* 2nd ed. (New York: Harper & Row, 1977), p. 46.

[13]From Ronald C. Doll, *Curriculum Improvement: Decision Making and Process,* Seventh edition, p. 392. Copyright ©1989 by Allyn & Bacon. Reprinted with permission.

Students can help out greatly by indicating to the professional curriculum planners how they perceive a new proposal or program. They can provide input from the standpoint of the recipients of the program, the persons for whom the program was designed. The more alert students can point out pitfalls that the professional planners might be able to avoid. The students can communicate to the professional planners reactions of their peers, and they can further communicate the nature and purpose of curricular changes to their parents and other citizens of the community. Students can excel in relating to the professional planners how they perceive a development and how they feel about it.

The degree to which students may participate and the quality of that participation depend on a number of variables such as intelligence, motivation, and knowledge. The most significant variable is the student's maturity. For that reason students in senior high schools and in higher education find more opportunities for participating in curriculum development than students in elementary, middle, and junior high schools.

A particularly valuable contribution to curriculum improvement that students can make is to evaluate the teacher's instruction. Although some teachers resist student evaluations of their performance—as one senior high school principal was heard to comment, "Students have no business evaluating teachers"—evaluations done anonymously by the learners can provide valuable clues for modifying a curriculum and improving methods of instruction.

Although students do enter actively into the process of curriculum development in some school systems, their involvement by and large still tends to be sporadic and ancillary.

Role of the Adult Citizens of the Community

The roles of parents and other members of the community in the affairs of the school have changed considerably over the years. Originally, the community *was* the school. Parents tutored their young at home for lack of or in preference to a formal school; the well-to-do imported tutors from Europe to live in their homes and to instruct their children. The church provided instruction in its religious precepts, and young men learned trades as apprentices on the job. Women in colonial America would bring youngsters into their homes and, for a small payment from each of their families, teach them the three R's.[14]

As formal schools evolved, the community turned the task of educating the young (for many years only the young white males) over to the school. A rift developed between the community and the school. Both the community and the institution it established developed the attitude that the community should get on with its business and leave teaching to those who know how to do it best—the school personnel. An invisible wall was erected between community and school, resembling the one between church and school.

---

[14]This practice is commonly referred to in the literature on educational history as the "dame school" or "kitchen school."

Some parents with their state's consent have turned in recent years to instructing their children at home. The home-school movement, while small, is significant enough to be of concern to the public schools.

Erosion of the Wall Between School and Community. Although some school administrators prefer to cling to an outmoded concept of community/school relationships, the wall separating school from community has crumbled. The process of erosion began slowly and has accelerated in recent years. The involvement of parents and other community members can be readily observed in school affairs today. The literature on professional education is filled with discussions of the necessity for involving the community in the educational process.

For the greater part of the twentieth century, community involvement was interpreted as passive support to the schools. The school would send bulletins and notices home to inform parents about issues and activities. The Parent-Teacher Association (PTA) would meet and discuss educational issues, hear about the school's achievements, and plan a rummage sale to raise funds for some school improvement. The school would conduct a "Back to School Night" with much fanfare, which brought parents in record numbers. Booster clubs would raise money for athletics and the band. During this period the community rarely participated in decision making even of an advisory nature. The old sentiment still prevailed that school matters were best left to the school people. The community's role was to support and strengthen decisions made by the school.

Erosion of the wall between school and community was hastened when administrators and teachers began to realize that parents might supply them with certain types of information that might aid in decision making. Consequently, still resorting to a somewhat passive technique, the school sent home questionnaires for parents to fill out and return. While the school and community were taking careful, modest steps toward reparing the rift, American society in the twentieth century was bubbling. First the sociologists and then the educators began to subject the American community to intense study, identifying networks of influential persons who are referred to in the literature as "the power structure."[15] Educators started to give attention to the politics of education as they realized that the school was as much a part of the total political structure as other social institutions. The astute school administrator became intensely conscious of public relations and sought to involve community members in support of the school. Some might say that the educators' attention to community concerns was more effect than cause as discontent, anxiety, and pressure

---

[15]See the following: Robert S. Lynd, *Middletown: A Study in American Culture* (New York: Harcourt Brace Jovanovich, 1929) and Robert S. Lynd and Helen M. Lynd, *Middletown in Transition: A Study in Cultural Conflicts* (New York: Harcourt Brace Jovanovich, 1937).

Ralph B. Kimbrough, *Community Power Structure and Analysis* (Englewood Cliffs, N.J.: Prentice-Hall, 1964).

Ralph B. Kimbrough and Michael Y. Nunnery, *Educational Administration: An Introduction,* 3rd ed. (New York: Macmillan, 1988), Chapter 13.

on educators from outside the schools had been growing and increasing in intensity for several decades.

Social Problems.   Four major wars, several revolutions, a number of sociological movements, and an ailing economy changed the tapestry of twentieth-century America. The technological revolution, the sexual revolution, the heightened divorce rate, the change in family structure, the equal rights movement, the student rights movement, the declaration of unconstitutionality of segregation, and a period of severe inflation all created problems for the schools, problems that they could no longer solve by themselves. With America's social and economic problems came a disenchantment with the programs of the school and the achievement of the pupils. From this dissatisfaction arose the concept of accountability of school personnel for the success or failure of their students.

Today, community involvement in school activities is widespread, encouraged, and valued. Members of the community aid in curriculum development in a variety of ways. Parents and other citizens serve on numerous advisory committees. Schools frequently call on parents and other citizens to serve as resource persons and volunteer aides. Across the country, especially in urban areas, local businesses have entered into partnerships with the schools, supplementing and enriching the schools' curricula by providing expertise, materials, and funds.

It is always a dilemma for a school principal to decide how lay people should be involved and who these people should be. Some principals seek the participation of parents of children in their own schools. Some try to involve a representative stratum of the community, including parents and nonparents and representatives from all socioeconomic levels of the area served by the schools. Some limit participation by plan or by default to parents who happen to be available to attend meetings during the day. The chief participants under this condition tend to be middle-class housewives. Some principals seek out the community decision makers from among the citizens who make up the power structure.

State and National Initiatives.   State and national efforts have supplemented local initiatives to involve the community in school affairs. Roald F. Campbell, Luvern L. Cunningham, Raphael O. Nystrand, and Michael D. Usdan described a number of organizations that advocate the participation of citizens in the affairs of the school.[16] In 1976 the Florida legislature not only established school advisory councils but also charged the principal of every public school in the state with the responsibility of publishing by November 1 of each year an annual report of school progress that must be distributed to the parent or guardian of each student in the school.[17]

---

[16]Roald F. Campbell, Luvern L. Cunningham, Raphael O. Nystrand, and Michael D. Usdan, *The Organization and Control of American Schools,* 6th ed. (Columbus, Ohio: Charles E. Merrill, 1990), pp. 329–342.

[17]Florida Statute 229.575 (3), *Florida School Laws,* 1979, pp. 19–20.

Campbell and his coauthors noted the impact of federal legislation on citizen involvement in the affairs of the local schools:

> Most federal legislation enacted since the early 1970's required citizen consulting and advisory mechanisms. The number of federally mandated advisory councils was staggering: there were approximately 14,000 district-wide Title I Parent Advisory Committees and 44,000 building-level committees with a total of nearly 900,000 members; another 150,000 persons served on Head Start, Follow Through, and other district and building-level groups.[18]

Thus local, state, and federal initiatives have promoted the involvement of members of the community in affairs of the school. The universal use of program advisory groups in connection with federally funded vocational education programs, for example, has exerted a significant influence on the curriculum of local school systems.

Looking to the future, Campbell and his coauthors identified community groups with which administrators must be concerned and made the following prediction:

> Interest groups representing blacks, American Indians, and other ethnic groups will continue to focus on the schools as a major mechanism for equalizing educational, social, and economic opportunities for their constituencies.
>
> Taxpayer groups, concerned about periodic inflation, recession, and energy shortages in an uncertain economy, will continue to scrutinize school expenditures.[19]

They also observed, "Hispanics are the nation's most rapidly growing population group and their political influence certainly will continue to expand in the decades ahead as they are projected to become the largest racial ethnic group by the end of the century."[20]

The wise administrator realizes that strong community support can make his or her job much simpler and for that reason devotes considerable time to building that support. Some schools have been turned into community schools in which the resources of the school are shared with the community and vice versa.

Models for citizen participation in school affairs differ widely from community to community. In some communities citizens play a purely advisory role; in others they share directly in the decision-making process. In some localities members of the community serve on standing committees that meet regularly; in other locations they serve on ad hoc groups that undertake a specific task and are then disbanded. In some school districts parents and others are invited to address themselves to any and all problems of the schools, whereas in other communities their areas of responsibility are clearly delimited.

---

[18]Campbell et al., *Organization and Control*, p. 166.
[19]Ibid., p. 380.
[20]Ibid., p. 359.

Community Involvement. J. Galen Saylor, William M. Alexander, and Arthur J. Lewis envisioned persons from the community as helping in four stages of curriculum planning: goal setting, designing, implementing, and evaluating.[21] As examples of community participation at the goal-setting stage, they pointed to

- ☐ groups of community representatives appointed by the school board to advise on educational goals
- ☐ groups appointed by the school board to advise on a particular area of the curriculum
- ☐ Parent-Teacher Association committees at the local school
- ☐ homeroom parents' organizations
- ☐ dads' clubs

Members of the community are consulted in the curriculum designing stage to arrange for work-experience programs. Saylor, Alexander, and Lewis suggested the possible need for councils to coordinate the educational experiences that take place outside the school and with the cooperation of persons in the community.

At the implementation stage citizens of the community are called on to serve as resource persons, volunteer tutors, and school aides. The resources of individuals, businesses, institutions, and other agencies are tapped to enhance the learning experiences of the students.

With guidance from the school, parents can assist their children in their studies at home. They are able to describe the effect of new programs on their children and can be very specific in telling teachers about problems their children are experiencing.

Parents and others share in curriculum development by responding to surveys sent out by the school. They can serve as resource persons and voluntary aides to the teachers. They may invite children to their places of work and thereby contribute to the children's knowledge of the world around them. They may supervise student work experiences in the community.

Parents and others can inform the professional planners about potential conflicts that are likely to arise in the community over the teaching of controversial topics and programs. They can help the school authorities review instructional materials and books for bias and distortion. Parents and other citizens of the community are often able to suggest programs that would help meet certain educational needs in the community. By actively seeking citizen participation, the principal is able to develop a reservoir of good will toward the school, which will stand him or her in good stead when problems inevitably develop. The principal is more readily able to gain support for new programs and to defuse potential controversies if parents and others perceive the school as their institution and as a place where their voices may be heard and their opinions

---

[21]J. Galen Saylor, William M. Alexander, and Arthur J. Lewis, *Curriculum Planning for Better Teaching and Learning,* 4th ed. (New York: Holt, Rinehart and Winston, 1981), pp. 103–105.

valued. Community participation in curriculum development is a natural consequence of the public's legal power over education in a democratic society.[22] With
the current move toward local control, active parental participation in the operation of the school is growing, and this growth may be expected to continue.

Role of the Curriculum Workers

Primary responsibility for curriculum development is assigned to teachers and
their elected or appointed leaders, both of whom we will refer to as "curriculum
workers." This group of persons working together carries the heaviest burden in
seeking to improve the curriculum. In Chapter 3 I pointed out that curriculum
groups function at several levels and in several sectors. To make the following
discussion clearer, however, let's conceptualize the curriculum council of a
particular school. Let's choose an elementary school with grades K through
6 that is fortunate enough to have a full-time curriculum coordinator on its
staff. By agreement of the total faculty, the grade coordinators (seven of them)
join with the curriculum coordinator (appointed by the principal) to form the
school's curriculum council. In our hypothetical school, by tacit understanding
between the principal and the faculty, the coordinator serves as chairperson or
leader of the council.

Let's imagine that we are neutral observers watching this council at its
first session of the year. We watch the group get organized; we listen to its
discussion; we study the faces of the council members; we observe the inter-
play between the coordinator and the council members and among the council
members themselves. We cannot help speculating about whether this curriculum group will have a productive year. The question crosses our mind, "What
conditions make for a productive year in curriculum development?" We wonder,
"Could we predict whether a curriculum council is likely to be productive?"

After a great deal of thought, we might conclude that success in terms of
productivity is more likely to come about if the group

- ☐ sets its goals at the beginning of its work
- ☐ is made up of compatible personalities
- ☐ has members who bring to the task expertise, knowledge, and technical competence
- ☐ is composed of persons who are motivated and willing to expend time and energy
- ☐ accepts its appropriate leadership and followership roles
- ☐ has persons who can communicate with each other
- ☐ has developed skills in decision making
- ☐ has members who keep their own personal agendas in appropriate relation-ship to the groups' goals

[22]For discussion of limitations on the state's power to compel school attendance, you may
wish to read *Teach Your Own: A Hopeful Path for Education* (New York: Delacorte Press/Seymour
Lawrence, 1981) by John Holt, an advocate of home schooling. also pp. 531–533 of this text.

What are the roles, we may ask, of those persons whom we call curriculum workers? How do teachers function in curriculum development? What role does the curriculum leader play?

Role of the Teachers

Throughout this text teachers are repeatedly seen as the primary group in curriculum development. Numerous examples are given of teacher involvement in curriculum development. The teachers constitute either the majority or the totality of the membership of curriculum committees and councils. Teachers participate at all stages in curriculum development. They initiate proposals and carry them out in their classrooms. They review proposals, gather data, conduct research, make contact with parents and other lay people, write and create curriculum materials, evaluate resources, try out new ideas, obtain feedback from learners, and evaluate programs. Teachers serve on committees mainly at the classroom, team/grade/department, school, and district levels or sectors and on occasion may serve at other levels or sectors.

New teachers typically view themselves primarily as instructors and are often scarcely aware of the responsibilities that are likely to be expected of them in the curriculum area. Beginning teachers' lack of awareness of their professional obligations in curriculum development is not surprising given that preservice teacher education programs, as a rule and understandably, emphasize the mastery of instructional skills over curriculum development competencies.

At the very least, preservice teachers should be oriented to the obligations and opportunities they will encounter in curriculum development. Becoming aware that they will serve on various councils and committees, that curriculum development takes place in many levels and sectors, and that instruction and curriculum are different domains, both worthy of involvement, should be part of their training. Thus the teachers, in cooperation with the administrators and other professionals, can bring appropriate knowledge and skills to bear in efforts to improve the curriculum. *Only* the teachers, by being at the classroom level, can assure that curricular plans are carried out.

Assumption of a primary role by teachers not only in curriculum development but also in the general affairs of the school is the goal of current efforts at "empowerment," which permits teachers as professionals to take part in the decision-making process.[23] The empowerment movement of the 1980s and 1990s seeks to raise the status of teachers and thereby improve the school's program and effectiveness.

Conducted by the Carnegie Foundation for the Advancement of Teaching, a 1990 survey of more than 21,000 public elementary and sec-

---

[23]See Gene Maeroff, *The Empowerment of Teachers: Overcoming the Crisis of Confidence* (New York: Teachers College Press, 1988).

ondary school teachers revealed that teachers are not very happy with their lot.[24] The Carnegie study found that more than half (61 percent) of the teachers rated the morale of their school as fair or poor. Forty-five percent of the teachers were dissatisfied with the control they have over their professional life as a teacher. Eighty-two percent gave a grade of "C" or below to school reform efforts of recent years.

Significant to the issue of empowerment is the finding that many teachers feel left out of the decision-making process. You might conjecture that if teachers are involved in decision making at all, they would most likely participate in the areas of curriculum, instruction, and staff development. Although a large majority (79 percent) said they participated to a moderate or great extent in selecting textbooks and materials, 21 percent said they participated slightly or not at all. A surprising 35 percent indicated that they were only involved slightly or not at all in shaping the curriculum, and a majority (57 percent) reported that they participated slightly or not at all in the design of staff development or in-service education programs. Teacher participation in curriculum development showed but a small (2 percent) drop among those involved only slightly or not at all compared to that reported in an earlier Carnegie survey, and the percentage of teachers involved only slightly or not at all in planning staff development activities remained at the same level.[25]

You would expect that in-service education programs that are designed for teachers would be chosen and planned with their cooperation. Apparently, the fine 1970s example of teacher empowerment in the area of staff development— the teacher education center—has waned instead of waxed.[26]

Although critics of empowerment argue that teacher involvement in decision making is an unnecessary demand on their time, an inappropriate role, or an infringement on administrative authority, industrial research of the 1930's and the success of Japanese quality circles in recent years have revealed that meaningful involvement in decision making enhances worker morale and consequently increases production.[27] John Naisbitt stated the principle succinctly when he said, "People whose lives are affected by a decision must be part of the process of arriving at that decision."[28] Translated into school terms, the

---

[24]Carnegie Foundation for the Advancement of Teaching, *The Condition of Teaching: A State-by-State Analysis, 1990* (Princeton, N.J.: Carnegie Foundation for the Advancement of Teaching, 1990). See also John Godar, *Teacher Talk* (Macomb, Ill.: Glenbridge Publishing Ltd., 1990).

[25]Carnegie Foundation for the Advancement of Teaching, *The Condition of Teaching: A State-by-State Analysis, 1988* (Princeton, N.J.: Carnegie Foundation for the Advancement of Teaching, 1988).

[26]See Peter F. Oliva, *Supervision for Today's Schools,* 3rd ed. (White Plains, N.Y.: Longman, 1989), pp. 370–372 for discussion of teacher education centers.

[27]See F. J. Roethlisberger and William J. Dickson, *Management and the Worker* (Cambridge, Mass.: Harvard University Press, 1939); see also William G. Ouchi; footnote 9 of this chapter.

[28]John Naisbitt, *Megatrends* (New York: Warner, 1982), p. 159. Reprinted with permission.

principle indicates that when teachers find themselves to be valued professionals whose opinions carry some weight, they will be more satisfied with their profession. This improvement in teacher morale, in turn, will increase school productivity—that is, student achievement.

Role of the Curriculum Leader

As we consider the complexities in carrying out curriculum development we become keenly aware of the curriculum leader's responsibility for the success or failure of the work of a curriculum committee or council. The curriculum leader most often is a member of the faculty but can be an outsider. It is perhaps inaccurate here to refer to a curriculum leader as *the* curriculum leader. A person may serve as a leader for a period of time and then give way to another leader for any number of sound reasons. Some teachers may serve as leaders at one level, such as the grade, whereas others may serve as leaders at another level, such as the school. In a democratic organization individuals serve as either leaders or followers as the situation demands.

The curriculum leader (coordinator) may also come from outside the teacher group, as in the case of central office supervisors, curriculum consultants, directors of instruction, and assistant principals for curriculum. Perhaps even in these cases it would be useful to think of the teachers and leaders from outside the faculty as constituting the "extended family," for they are all colleagues, albeit with different functions and duties. The leadership position is filled either by appointment by an administrator or supervisor, election by the group's members, or self-selection from the group.

The principles we will now discuss apply to all curriculum leaders regardless of whether they come from inside or outside the teacher group. We may begin to look at the role of the curriculum leader by asking ourselves what special knowledge and skills he or she must bring to the task. The curriculum coordinator must

☐ possess a good general education
☐ have good knowledge of both general and specific curricula
☐ be knowledgeable about resources for curriculum development
☐ be skilled in research and knowledgeable about locating pertinent research studies
☐ be knowledgeable about the needs of learners, the community, and the society
☐ be a bit of a philosopher, sociologist, and psychologist
☐ know and appreciate the individual characteristics of his or her participating colleagues

Most significantly, the curriculum coordinator must be a specialist in the group process, possessing a unique set of skills. Many treatises on the functioning of groups reveal that managing groups effectively is not a trivial task.

It is an enormously complicated effort that brings into play all the subtleties of environment and personality. Curriculum development is an exercise in group process, a human endeavor that leads to both joy and frustration.

Success in curriculum improvement depends, of course, on the concerted effort of both group members and leaders. We will focus our attention, however, on the curriculum leader; no matter how well-intentioned, motivated, and skilled the followers of a group are, group effort cannot succeed without competent leadership.

THE CURRICULUM LEADER AND GROUP PROCESS

Neither technical expertise nor knowledge about curriculum theory can substitute for a curriculum leader's knowledge of and aptitude for group process. What, then, might we ask, are some basic principles from the research on group process that would help those who take a leadership role in curriculum development? What skills and knowledge about group process are essential to the job? Four sets or clusters of skills and knowledge appear to be of particular significance:

1. *The change process.* The leader must be knowledgeable about the process of effecting change and be able to implement that knowledge with the group. He or she must demonstrate effective decision-making skills and be able to lead group members in demonstrating them.
2. *Interpersonal relations.* The leader must be knowledgeable about group dynamics. He or she must exhibit a high degree of human relations skills, be able to develop interpersonal skills among members of the group, and be able to establish a harmonious working climate.
3. *Leadership skills.* The leader must demonstrate leadership skills, including organizational skills and the ability to manage the process. He or she must help members of the group to develop leadership skills so that they may assume leadership roles when necessary.
4. *Communication skills.* The leader must communicate effectively and be able to lead members of the group in communicating effectively. He or she must be a proficient discussion leader.

The Change Process

Axiom 1 in Chapter 2 presented the proposition that change is both inevitable and desirable. Human institutions, like human beings, must change if they are to continue growing and developing. Institutions, however, tend to preserve the status quo.

Gail McCutcheon cited the ease and comparative safety of the status quo, the requirements of time and effort, the lack of rewards, established school policies, and routines as impediments to change.[29] Nevertheless, neither the status quo nor regression to outmoded practices is a defensible position for living institutions like the schools. They must constantly seek to better themselves.

Curriculum development is the planned effort of a duly organized group (or groups) that seeks to make intelligent decisions in order to effect planned change in the curriculum. Planned change, far different from trial and error or natural evolution, implies a systematic process to be followed by all participants. Let's begin our examination of the change process by looking at the variables that exist within organizations and that have an impact upon that process.

Four Variables.   Harold J. Leavitt and Homa Bahrami identified four organizational variables: "structure," "information and control methods (i.e., the technology of managing)," "people," and "task."[30]

Every organization establishes its own *structure*. In Chapter 3 we considered some of the organizational patterns that schools have adopted to carry out curriculum development. As already mentioned, structures differ considerably among school systems and among individual schools. "It is the structure that gives an organization order, system, and many of its distinctive characteristics," said Robert G. Owens.[31] Organizational structures are shaped not only by the tasks to be accomplished but also by the idiosyncrasies of administrators, supervisors, and teachers. No single organizational structure will satisfy the personal and professional needs of participants in every school system. Determination of the appropriate organizational structure is one of the prior decisions that the curriculum developers must make.

Owens spoke of information and control methods when he defined *technology* in organizations as follows:

> The organization must have *technological resources* or, in other words, the "tools of its trade." Technology, used in this sense, does not only include such typical hardware items as computers, milling machines, textbooks and chalk, and electron microscopes. Technology may also include program inventions: systematic procedures, the sequencing of activities, or other procedural inventions designed to solve problems that stand in the way of organizational task achievement.[32]

The human element—the *people*—sets the operation in motion and carries out the task. The differences in people make each school's efforts at curriculum development a unique undertaking. The persons essential to the curriculum

[29]Gail McCutcheon, "Curriculum Theory/Curriculum Practice: A Gap or the Grand Canyon?" in Alex Molnar, ed., *Current Thought on Curriculum*, 1985 Yearbook (Alexandria, Va.: Association for Supervision and Curriculum Development, 1985), p. 46.

[30]Harold J. Leavitt and Homa Bahrami, *Managerial Psychology: Managing Behavior in Organizations,* 5th ed. (Chicago: University of Chicago Press, 1988), pp. 246–256.

[31]Robert G. Owens, *Organizational Behavior in Education,* 3rd ed. ©1987, p. 76. Reprinted by permission of Prentice-Hall, Englewood Cliffs, New Jersey.

[32]Robert G. Owens, *Organizational Behavior in Education,* 3rd ed. ©1987, p. 76. Reprinted by permission of Prentice-Hall, Englewood Cliffs, New Jersey.

development process have been discussed. Experts in the social science of human behavior refer to the main characters in the change process as *the change agent* and *the client system.* In their language a change agent is a person trained in the behavioral sciences who helps an organization change. The client system consists of those persons in the organization with whom the change agent works and who may, themselves, undergo change. This point reinforces Axiom 4 in Chapter 2, which postulates that curriculum change results from changes in people.

Behavioral scientists argue whether the change agent must come from within or without the system. In practical terms schools will ordinarily use their own personnel for developing the curriculum. William H. Lucio and John D. McNeil attested that personnel from within the system are charged with the responsibility for bringing about change.[33]

Robert J. Alfonso, Gerald R. Firth, and Richard F. Neville identified change theory as one of four theoretical fields assumed to have implications for the behavior of instructional supervisors.[34] John T. Lovell devoted a chapter in a text on supervision to demonstrating that coordinating and facilitating change are important responsibilities of the instructional supervisor.[35]

Alfonso, Firth, and Neville clearly showed that the supervisor from within the system must serve as a change agent:

> If change is to occur, a school system must value it enough to give some person or group the responsibility for it, and not leave it to chance occurrence. Supervisors, if they desire change, must make this a priority, or else it will not occur. They should not expect to be agents of change unless they devote a significant amount of time, effort, and creative thought to the change process.[36]

Even when the services of an outside change agent are sought, Alfonso, Firth, and Neville gave this advise:

> If a supervisor wishes to use the services of an outside change agent or consultant, the external agent must be perceived as enhancing the work of the supervisor. If such linkage can take place, or if, in fact, the external agent can be at least temporarily joined to the system, the total change effort will be more successful. Simply "importing" a change agent will not assist the supervisor markedly unless teachers perceive such a person as connected to the system or to the supervisor in some acceptable way.[37]

---

[33] See William H. Lucio and John D. McNeil, *Supervision: A Synthesis of Thought and Action,* 2nd ed. (New York: McGraw-Hill, 1969), p. 208.

[34] See Robert J. Alfonso, Gerald R. Firth, and Richard F. Neville, *Instructional Supervision: A Behavior System,* 2nd ed. (Boston: Allyn and Bacon, 1981), Chapter 8.

[35] See John T. Lovell and Kimball Wiles, *Supervision for Better Schools,* 5th ed. (Englewood Cliffs, N.J.: Prentice-Hall, 1983), Chapter 6. Kimball Wiles, *Supervision for Better Schools,* 3rd ed., was revised by John T. Lovell for the 4th and 5th editions.

[36] Alfonso, Firth, and Neville, *Instructional Supervision,* p. 283.

[37] Ibid., p. 284.

What are the typical functions of a change agent? Warren G. Bennis listed the following normative goals of change agents:

- □ improving interpersonal competence of managers;
- □ effecting a change in values so that human factors and feelings come to be considered legitimate;
- □ developing increased understanding among and within working groups to reduce tensions;
- □ developing "team management";
- □ developing better methods of "conflict resolution" than suppression, denial, and the use of unprincipled power;
- □ viewing the organization as an organic system of relationships marked by mutual trust, interdependence, multi-group membership, shared responsibility, and conflict resolution through training and problem solving.[38]

Regarding *task,* Owens addressed the purpose of organizations:

By definition, an organization exists for the purpose of achieving something: reaching some goal or set of goals. It seeks to do this by accomplishing certain *tasks.* . . . There are numerous tasks that the school district must organize internally in order to achieve its goals.[39]

The school performs many tasks in a number of curriculum development areas and provides a vital service—the education of the young. Although the school is not engaged in the tasks of manufacturing and selling products for profit, it does turn out products—a quite different kind of product—the learners themselves, human beings whose behavior is modified as a result of exposure to the school curriculum.

Owens perceived the interdependence of these four variables as the key factor in choosing strategies for change in organizations:

These four internal organization factors—*task, structure, technology,* and *people*—are variables that differ from time to time and from one organization to the next. Within a given organization these four factors are highly interactive, each tending to shape and mold the others. As in any system, the interdependence of the variable factors means that a significant change in one will result in some adaptation on the part of the other factors.[40]

Leadership calls for the judicious integration of these four variables.

Kurt Lewin viewed organizations as being in a state of balance or equilibrium when forces of change (driving forces) and forces of resistance (restraining

---

[38]Reprinted with permission from NTL Institute, "Theory and Method in Applying Behavioral Science to Planned Organizational Change," by Warren G. Bennis, pp. 347–348, *Journal of Applied Behavioral Science,* Vol. 1, No. 4, copyright 1988.

[39]Robert G. Owens, *Organizational Behavior in Education,* 3rd ed. ©1987, p. 75. Reprinted by permission of Prentice-Hall, Englewood Cliffs, New Jersey.

[40]Robert G. Owens, *Organizational Behavior in Education,* 3rd ed. ©1987, p. 76. Reprinted by permission of Prentice-Hall, Englewood Cliffs, New Jersey.

forces) are equal in strength.[41] Changes occur when the organization is forced into a state of disequilibrium. This state of imbalance may be accomplished by augmenting the driving forces or by reducing the restraining forces—either action breaks the force field that maintains the organization in equilibrium.

Following his concept of the force field, Lewin proposed a simple strategy consisting of three steps. Or was it so simple? Lewin suggested that existing targets of change be unfrozen, then changes or innovations made, and finally the new structures refrozen until the start of a new cycle.

How shall we go about unfreezing old programs and practices—in effect, changing old habits? How would we move, for example, from the junior high school, to the middle school, from independent to cooperative learning, from discrete linguistic concepts to whole language, from exclusive stress on cognitive learning to provision for cognitive, affective, and psychomotor learning, from emphasis on convergent thinking to more on divergent thinking, or from rote learning to critical thinking? How do we thaw out old patterns?

When we identify the barriers or impediments to change and eliminate those barriers, we can set the organization into disequilibrium. Table 4–1 lists several commonly encountered barriers and suggests tactics for overcoming them.

Decision Making.   Axiom 6 of Chapter 2 takes the position that curriculum development is basically a decision-making process. A lack of skills in decision making on the part of a curriculum leader and group can be a formidable barrier to change. Are there any principles of decision making that could be helpful to curriculum study groups? Let's turn to Daniel L. Stufflebeam and the Phi Delta Kappa National Study Committee on Evaluation, which Stufflebeam chaired, for guidance on the process of decision making.[42]

Stufflebeam and his committee ventured that the process of decision making consists of four stages—awareness, design, choice, and action—during which four kinds of decisions must be made—planning, structuring, implementing, and recycling.

Planning decisions are made "to determine objectives." They "specify *major changes that are needed in a program.*" Structuring decisions are made "to design procedures." They "specify the *means to achieve the ends* established as a result of planning decisions." Implementing decisions are made "to utilize, control and refine procedures." Decisions on implementation are "those involved in *carrying through the action plan.*" Recycling decisions are made "to judge and react to attainments." "These are decisions used in determining the relationship of attainments to objectives and whether to continue, terminate, evolve, or drastically modify the activity."[43]

---

[41] See Kurt Lewin, *Field Theory in Social Science* (New York: Harper Torchbooks, 1951). Also in Kurt Lewin, "Frontiers in Group Dynamics," *Human Relations* 1 (1947): 5–41.

[42] Daniel L. Stufflebeam et al., *Educational Evaluation and Decision Making* (Itasca, Ill.: F. E. Peacock, 1971), especially Chapter 3. Reprinted with permission.

[43] Ibid., pp. 80–84.

TABLE 4–1   Common barriers to change

BARRIERS	TACTICS
Fear of change on the part of those likely to be affected	The group should proceed slowly. Leader gives repeated reassurance to those affected by change. Involvement of those affected in decision making. The changed status must be made more attractive than the old pattern.
Lack of clear goals	The group must set clear goals before proceeding further.
Lack of competent leadership	Superiors must appoint or peers must elect persons as leaders who are most qualified. Leaders who prove to be incompetent should be removed.
Lack of ability of group members to function as a group	Training in group process should be conducted.
Lack of research on problems before the group	The leader should have the ability to conduct research, to locate pertinent research data, and to interpret research studies to the group.
A history of unsuccessful curriculum efforts	The group must be made to feel that progress is being made continuously.
Lack of evaluation of previous curriculum efforts	Efforts should be made to evaluate previous efforts, and an evaluation plan for current efforts must be designed.
Negative attitudes from the community	School personnel must call parents and citizens in for discussion, involve them in the process, and try to change their attitudes.
Lack of resources	Adequate resources both to carry out curriculum planning and to implement plans decided upon must be available. Personnel needed must be available.
External pressures such as state and federal legislation, regional accreditation, and regulations of the state department of education	Efforts must be made to work within the framework of laws and regulations or to try to get the laws and regulations changed. Responses to laws and regulations, which are broad and general, may vary from school to school.
Lack of experience or knowledge about a particular curricular problem	The group may call in consultants for assistance, or the school may provide training for its personnel.

From the time a perceptive staff member in a school first starts to feel uneasy about a program and senses that something is not right and change is needed, decisions must be made constantly. Since decision making never ends, skills in the process need to be developed.

Creative Individuals. Although the literature on change stresses the necessity of group involvement, change can be and often is brought about by creative individuals and small groups of individuals working independently. Many of our great inventors, for example, have been individualists.

What sometimes happens is that an individual experiments with a new idea; a few others who like the idea adopt it; success with the idea builds on success and the idea is widely translated into practice. Creative individual enterprise should be encouraged by administrators and faculty as long as the implications of the activity do not invade areas outside the individual's own sphere. When creative endeavor begins to force demands on others without their sanction or involvement, independence must give way to cooperation.

In summary, curriculum leaders guide cooperating workers in bringing about change. In so doing they must exhibit skill in directing the change process. Both leaders and followers must have skill in decision making if positive curricular changes are to be effected.

Interpersonal Relations

The principal's reminder, "faculty meeting today at 3:30 P.M.," is normally greeted with less than enthusiasm. The typical teacher responses are likely to be "Oh, no, not again!", "I hope it's short," and "Faculty meetings are such a waste of time." At best these group meetings are received with a quiet resignation. Why does a group effort like a faculty meeting, which should be such a potent instrument for group deliberation, provoke such widespread dissatisfaction?

Let's try to answer that question by picturing a typical faculty meeting of a secondary school. Some 50 faculty members shuffle into a classroom and take their seats while the principal stands at the desk at the front of the room. We observe the faculty meeting in session and take some notes:

- ☐ The classroom is crowded and the pupils' desks are uncomfortable for some of the faculty, particularly the heavier teachers.
- ☐ The straight rows are not conducive to group discussion.
- ☐ No refreshments were provided to help set a pleasant tone for the meeting.
- ☐ It is difficult to understand the purpose of the meeting. Is it information-giving on the part of the principal? A sermon from the principal on responsibilities? An effort to gain faculty approval of policies? An attempt to get faculty opinion on an issue?
- ☐ One teacher in the back was reading the daily newspaper.
- ☐ One teacher by the window was grading papers.

- ☐ Two teachers were talking about an incident that took place in one of the teacher's classrooms that day.
- ☐ One teacher, tired, sat with her eyes closed during the meeting.
- ☐ The football coaches were absent.
- ☐ The principal spoke for 30 of the 45 minutes of the meeting.
- ☐ A couple of teachers spoke repeatedly, whereas the majority remained silent.
- ☐ Several teachers watched the clock on the wall.
- ☐ The principal became visibly annoyed with the comment of one teacher.
- ☐ A restlessness among the teachers was apparent after the first 30 minutes.
- ☐ The group rushed out of the room as soon as the meeting ended.

None of the behaviors at this hypothetical meeting was unusual. The behaviors were quite predictable and to a great extent preventable. The general faculty meeting is but one of many group configurations in which teachers and administrators will participate. If the administrator fosters a collegial approach to administration, teachers will find themselves working on a number of committees for a variety of purposes, including curriculum development.

Most new teachers do not fully realize the extent to which teaching is a group-oriented career. Training in group process, for example, is conspicuous by its absence in preservice programs. The mind-set that novice teachers have developed about teaching pictures the teacher as an *individual* planner, presenter, evaluator, and curriculum developer. When they begin teaching, they are unaware of the degree to which these activities are group tasks in which responsibilities should be shared.

Whereas beginning teachers realize from student teaching that they work with groups of children, they are often not ready to work cooperatively with their professional colleagues. A preparation program for teachers should seek to develop an appreciation of the necessity of working in groups, an attitude of willingness to work cooperatively, an understanding of the working or dynamics of a group, and skills as group members. If these cognitive and affective objectives are not achieved in preservice teacher education, their attainment should be sought in in-service education programs.

Let's try to improve our understanding of the composition and functioning of groups by examining some of the salient characteristics of group dynamics. We shall not belabor the question of defining *group* but will call two or more persons working together for a mutual purpose a group. In all human institutions, of which the school is one example, we find both formal and informal groups.

Formal groups are established to carry out tasks officially designated by the organization. Created by the administrative structure, they are usually shown in the institution's table of organization. The faculty as a body, curriculum councils, departments, advisory committees, teams, and cabinets are illustrations of formal groups.

Informal groups are self-constituted, ad hoc, and impromptu collections of individuals who gather together for some immediate purpose and later disband. Protest groups and cliques of teachers are illustrations of informal groups. Although we are primarily concerned with the functioning of formally constituted groups, we should not overlook the possible impact of informal groups. It is quite possible, for example, for the formal and informal groups within a school to be working at cross purposes. The wise curriculum leader seeks to identify informal groups that may have an impact on curriculum development efforts and to channel their energies into the deliberations of the formal structure.

Recall that in the illustration of the hypothetical secondary school faculty meeting, the sense of purpose was unclear. Both the general purpose and the specific goals of the group must be known. Groups are organized most frequently for the following purposes:

□ To receive instructions or information. Faculty meetings are often used for this purpose.

□ To help individuals develop personally or professionally. Sensitivity groups, study groups, and workshops in pedagogy are examples of groups with this purpose.

□ To recommend solutions to problems. Making such recommendations is a major purpose of curriculum improvement groups.

□ To produce something. Curriculum committees, for example, may be charged with the task of creating new programs or writing curriculum guides.

□ To resolve conflicts. Curriculum development efforts sometimes result in disagreements among factions, necessitating new groups to resolve these differences.

To some extent all these purposes operate in curriculum development. However, the latter three are the primary purposes, which make curriculum committees action- or task-oriented groups rather than ego- or process-oriented groups. In all human groups we find individuals who are there to serve the social needs of the organization—that is, the fulfillment of the group's task—and others who are there to satisfy their own ego needs.

One of the great difficulties for the curriculum leader is keeping a group "on task." Challenging this goal are the many individuals who are impelled to satisfy their own personal needs in a group setting, behavior referred to as "processing." Some processing is essential in any group, particularly early in the group's activity when individuals are getting to know each other and trying to analyze the task. The leader must ensure some balance between "task orientation" and "process orientation." He or she must see to it that a group moves on with its task while permitting individuals to achieve personal satisfaction as members of the group. Excessive stress on either approach can lead to frustration and withdrawal.

The curriculum leader, who is, of course, a key—or the key—member of a curriculum planning group, must be aware of the presence of three types of behavior within a group. First, each group is composed of individuals who bring their own individual behaviors to the group. Some will maintain these behaviors, sometimes consciously and other times subconsciously, regardless of the group setting. Thus the teacher who is habitually punctual, conscientious, confident, or complaining is likely to bring those traits into the group setting. Some traits have a positive impact on the group, others a negative one.

Individuals bring their motivations, often covert, into group efforts—their personal desires, feelings, or goals, commonly referred to as the "hidden agenda." Individuals may react negatively to a curriculum proposal, for example, not because they object to the proposal per se but because they dislike the person who made the proposal. Individuals may attack a proposal because they feel their ideas have not been adequately considered. Individuals may strive to ask a group member embarrassing questions because they perceive that person as a potential rival for a leadership position. The curriculum leader must constantly attempt to channel negative behaviors into constructive paths or to eliminate them where possible. He or she must often act as mediator to ensure that the individuals' hidden agendas do not sabotage the official agenda.

Second, individuals in groups often behave in ways that are quite different from their individual behaviors. We have only to turn to studies of mob psychology to demonstrate that individuals change their behavior in group situations. Have we never observed, for example, a group of otherwise sweet, innocent elementary school youngsters taunting a fellow classmate? Have we never seen an otherwise cautious adolescent driver become reckless when driving a car filled with friends? The presence of fellow human beings who read and evaluate an individual's behavior causes that individual to behave in a way in which he or she perceives the group members wish him or her to act.

We see great contrasts in behavior between the individual who relies on his or her own inner resources (the inner-directed personality) and the individual who takes cues from those around him or her (the outer-directed personality). Although few individuals are immune from outer-direction in our society, some individuals are more adept than others at weighing external influences before acting on them. Some individuals are aware when they are being manipulated by others, whereas others are highly subject to suggestion. Not only do personal behaviors sometimes change in a group setting, but individuals assume, as we shall soon see, special roles that they do not or cannot perform in isolation.

Third, the group itself assumes a personality of its own. We already noted the cliché, "The whole is greater than the sum of its parts," and that the functioning of the group is more than the sum of the functioning of each of the individuals who make up the group. The individuals interact with and reinforce each other, creating a unique blend. In this respect some departments of a school are perceived as being more productive (pick your own word: creative, enthusiastic, reactionary, innovative, obstreperous) than others, just as schools are perceived as being different from one another.

The curriculum leader must try to develop pride in the group as a team organization by promoting group morale and by helping the group feel a sense of accomplishment. The group concept is fostered when

☐ interaction among group members is frequent, on a high professional level, friendly, and harmonious

☐ personal conflicts among group members are infrequent or nonexistent

☐ leadership is allowed to develop from within the group so that the group capitalizes on the strengths of its members

☐ constructive dissent is encouraged

☐ the group realizes that it is making progress toward meeting its goals, which points out again the necessity for clearly specifying the goals the group expects to attain

☐ the group feels some sense of reward for accomplishment

Perhaps the most satisfying reward for a group is to see its recommendations translated into practice. A word of appreciation from the administrator also goes a long way in securing the continuous motivation of teachers to participate in curriculum development.

Roles Played by Group Members.   Many years ago Kenneth D. Benne and Paul Sheats developed a classification system for identifying functional roles of group members.[44] They organized their classification system into three categories: group task roles, group building and maintenance roles, and individual roles. Group members take on task roles when they seek to move the group toward attaining its goals and solving its problems. Group members play group building and maintenance roles when they are concerned with the functioning of the group. Group members indulge in individual roles to satisfy personal needs.

Since the Benne-Sheats classification system stands as one of the most creative and comprehensive expositions of roles played by group members, its categories and roles are reproduced:

GROUP TASK ROLES

a. Initiator-contributor. Suggests ideas, ways of solving problems, or procedures.

b. Information seeker. Seeks facts.

c. Opinion seeker. Asks for opinions about the values of suggestions made by members of the group.

d. Information giver. Supplies facts as he/she sees them.

e. Opinion giver. Presents his/her own opinions about the subject under discussion.

f. Elaborator. States implications of suggestions and describes how suggestions might work out if adopted.

g. Coordinator. Tries to synthesize suggestions.

h. Orienter. Lets group know when it is off task.

---

[44]Kenneth D. Benne and Paul Sheats, "Functional Roles of Group Members," *Journal of Social Issues* 4, no. 2 (Spring 1948): 43–46. Reprinted with permission.

  i. Evaluator-critic. Evaluates suggestions made by group members as to criteria which he/see feels important.

  j. Energizer. Spurs the group to activity.

  k. Procedural technician. Performs the routine tasks which have to be done such as distributing materials.

  l. Recorder. Keeps the group's record.

GROUP BUILDING AND MAINTENANCE ROLES

  a. Encourager. Praises people for their suggestions.

  b. Harmonizer. Settles disagreements among members.

  c. Compromiser. Modifies his/her position in the interests of group progress.

  d. Gate keeper. Tries to ensure that everybody has a chance to contribute to the discussion.

  e. Standard setter or ego ideal. Urges the group to live up to high standards.

  f. Group-observer and commentator. Records and reports on the functioning of the group.

  g. Follower. Accepts suggestions of others.

INDIVIDUAL ROLES

  a. Aggressor. Attacks others or their ideas.

  b. Blocker. Opposes suggestions and group decisions.

  c. Recognition-seeker. Seeks personal attention.

  d. Self-confessor. Expresses personal feelings not applicable to the group's efforts.

  e. Playboy. Refrains from getting involved in the group's work with sometimes disturbing behavior.

  f. Dominator. Interrupts others and tries to assert own superiority.

  g. Help-seeker. Tries to elicit sympathy for himself/herself.

  h. Special interest pleader. Reinforces his/her position by claiming to speak for others not represented in the group.[45]

A group will be more effective if the individual and negative roles are minimized or eliminated. Groups can be helped by the leader or by an outside consultant by exposing them to group dynamics theory and a classification system such as the Benne-Sheats model. Help of a more personal nature can be achieved through group interaction that permits feedback to its members. This feedback could be in the form of simple analysis of interaction skills by the various members, or it could be derived from sensitivity training or encounter sessions. Certainly, a group will be more productive if its members already possess a high degree of interaction skill. If, however, a group appears to lack skills in interaction or human relations, it may be advisable to depart from the group's task long enough to seek to develop some fundamental interpersonal skills.

A trained observer who records the performance of individuals participating in a group can provide valuable feedback. In the first edition of their

---

[45] Ibid.

book on supervision, Thomas J. Sergiovanni and Robert J. Starratt suggested an observation sheet that used the Benne-Sheats roles.[46] On the observation sheet (shown in Figure 4–1 in a form expanded by this author), the observer would record the frequency of role performance by the members of the group. After the observation period members would be furnished feedback about their performance.

The observer must exercise great tact in how he or she presents the information. Some of the individual roles are particularly unflattering, and it will be difficult for some individuals to accept that they behave in this way. Therefore, negative feedback should be supplied to individuals only on request and in confidence.

Task-Oriented Groups. Curriculum development groups are or should be essentially task-oriented groups. They are given a specific job to do, carry it out, and then either accept another job or cease to function. Their productivity should be measured first in the quality of improvement that takes place in the curriculum and second in the personal and professional growth of the participants.

Curriculum development consists of a continuing series of interpersonal experiences. Both leaders and followers are obligated to study the process of group decision making and of working together to make the process successful. With a modicum of training professional persons should be able to bury their hidden agendas and to eliminate or suppress negative behaviors that disrupt the group's effort. Fortunately, some human beings have learned during their formative years to demonstrate human relations skills like warmth, empathy, valuing of others' opinions and beliefs, intellectual honesty, patience, mutual assistance, and respect for others as persons. They have learned to accept responsibility and to refrain from blaming others for their own deficiencies. They have learned to put aside their own ego needs in deference to the needs of the group. They have learned to enjoy and take pride in group accomplishments. Others who demonstrate a low level of performance in these skills should be encouraged to participate in a human relations training program to improve their interpersonal skills.

Remember that curriculum development is ordinarily a voluntary undertaking. Curriculum workers might ask themselves what motivated them to agree to serve in a group devoted to curriculum improvement. They might uncover motives like the following:

☐ a desire to please the administrator
☐ a desire to work with certain colleagues
☐ a desire to be where the action is
☐ a desire to grow professionally

---

[46]From *Emerging Patterns of Supervision: Human Perspectives*, p. 199, by Thomas J. Sergiovanni and Robert J. Starratt. Copyright©1971 by McGraw-Hill. Used with permission of McGraw-Hill Book Company.

	Members								
	A	B	C	D	E	F	G	H	I
Task roles									
Initiator-contributor									
Information seeker									
Opinion seeker									
Information giver									
Opinion giver									
Elaborator									
Coordinator									
Orienter									
Evaluator-critic									
Energizer									
Procedural technician									
Recorder									
Building/maintenance roles									
Encourager									
Harmonizer									
Compromiser									
Gate keeper									
Standard setter									
Group-observer									
Follower									
Individual roles									
Aggressor									
Blocker									
Recognition-seeker									
Self-confessor									
Playboy									
Dominator									
Help-seeker									
Special interest pleader									

FIGURE 4–1   Record of behavior of individuals in groups. From Thomas J. Sergiovanni and Robert J. Starratt, *Emerging Patterns of Supervision: Human Perspectives* (New York: McGraw-Hill, 1971), p. 199. Reprinted by permission.

☐ a desire to make a professional contribution to the school system

☐ a desire to make use of one's skills and talents

☐ a desire for a new experience

☐ a desire to socialize

☐ a desire to use the group as a sounding board for personal beliefs and values.

The reasons why individuals agree to participate in group activity are many and varied, sometimes verbalized but often not; sometimes valid in terms of the group's goals, sometimes not. Individuals who are motivated and possess the necessary personal and professional skills should be encouraged to take part in curriculum development.

Characteristics of Productive Groups. From examining the wealth of literature on group dynamics and group process, how might we summarize the characteristics that make for group effectiveness or productivity? We have already noted in Chapter 1 that research conducted in the Hawthorne plant of the Western Electric Company in Chicago produced evidence that involvement of workers in planning and carrying out a project led to greater productivity. Research by Kurt Lewin, Ronald Lippitt, and Ralph K. White on groups of 11-year-old children showed their productivity to be greater in a democratic group climate than in an authoritarian or laissez-faire one.[47] Rensis Likert saw a supportive environment, mutual confidence and trust among group members, and sharing of common goals as contributing to group effectiveness.[48] Ned A. Flanders's studies of classroom verbal interaction led users of his instrument for observing this process to conclude that group leaders need to decrease their own verbal behavior and stimulate members of the group to interact more.[49] John Dewey[50] and Daniel L. Stufflebeam[51] wrote of the importance of the skill of problem solving or decision making. Warren G. Bennis, Kenneth D. Benne, and Robert Chin advocated skill in planning for change.[52] Fred E. Fiedler concentrated on the effectiveness of the leader,[53] and Kimball Wiles gave attention to skill in communication[54] as essential to group effectiveness. These latter two sets of skills will be discussed in the next section, but first, based on the foregoing principles, we might conclude that a group is effective when

---

[47] Kurt Lewin, Ronald Lippitt, and Ralph K. White, "Patterns of Aggressive Behavior in Experimentally Created Social Climates," *Journal of Social Psychology* 10 (May 1939): 271–299.

[48] Rensis Likert, *New Patterns of Management* (New York: McGraw-Hill, 1961).

[49] Ned A. Flanders, *Analyzing Teacher Behavior* (Reading, Mass.: Addison-Wesley, 1970).

[50] John Dewey, *How We Think,* rev. ed. (Lexington, Mass.: D. C. Heath, 1933).

[51] Stufflebeam et al., *Educational Evaluation.*

[52] Warren G. Bennis, Kenneth D. Benne, and Robert Chin, eds. *The Planning of Change,* 4th ed. (New York: Holt, Rinehart and Winston, 1985).

[53] Fred E. Fiedler, *A Theory of Leadership Effectiveness* (New York: McGraw-Hill, 1967).

[54] Kimball Wiles, *Supervision for Better Schools,* 3rd ed. (Englewood Cliffs, N.J.: Prentice-Hall, 1967). Also Lovell and Wiles, *Supervision for Better Schools.*

□ leaders and members support each other
□ trust is apparent among members
□ goals are understood and mutually accepted
□ adequate opportunity exists for members to express their own feelings and perceptions
□ roles played by group members are essentially positive
□ hidden agendas of members do not disrupt the group
□ leadership is competent and appropriate to the group
□ members possess the necessary expertise
□ members have the necessary resources
□ members share in all decision making
□ communication is at a high level
□ leadership is encouraged from within the group
□ progress in accomplishing the task is noticeable and significant
□ the group activity satisfies members' personal needs
□ leaders seek to release potential of the members
□ the group manages its time wisely

Leadership Skills

Let's attend the meeting of a school's curriculum committee as guest of the curriculum coordinator who is serving as chairperson. It is early in the year. We take a seat in the back of the room and in the course of less than an hour we observe the following behaviors:

□ Two teachers are discussing an action of the principal.
□ Each person speaks as long as he or she wishes, sometimes going on at length.
□ The coordinator engages in dialogue with one individual, ignoring the group.
□ Several members ask whether this discussion is in keeping with the group's purposes.
□ The coordinator pushes his ideas and is visibly annoyed when someone disagrees with him.
□ Two teachers become involved in arguing.
□ The coordinator steers the group toward a proposal that he has offered.
□ The meeting breaks up without closure and without identifying next steps.

We might conclude that this session of the curriculum committee was less than productive. Would we attribute this lack of productivity to deficiencies on the part of the group members? To lack of leadership skills on the part of the coordinator? To both? Certainly, group productivity arises from a harmonious blend of skills by group members and the group leader, yet a heavy burden for the productivity of the group rests with the leader. This person has been chosen to set the pace, to provide expertise, and to channel the skills of others.

The skilled leader would have been able to avoid and resolve some of the unproductive situations that developed in this curriculum committee.

Traits of Leaders. When asking ourselves and others what traits a leader should possess, we would probably garner the following responses:

- □ intelligent
- □ experienced
- □ assertive
- □ articulate
- □ innovative
- □ dynamic
- □ charismatic

Some would say, "You must be in the right place at the right time." Others, perhaps more cynical, would say a leader must be

- □ a politician
- □ a climber
- □ a friend of a person in power

Like Laurence J. Peter, Jr., some people would observe that persons rise to their level of incompetence.[55]

What the research has found, however, is that it is almost impossible to ascribe any single set of traits to all persons in positions of leadership. Ralph B. Kimbrough and Michael Y. Nunnery offers four generalizations about leaders and leadership that they believe to be reasonably valid:

1. Leaders tend to be slightly higher in intelligence than the average of the group led and have the administrative skills and technical competence appropriate to the situation.
2. Leaders tend to be emotionally mature, to exhibit self-confidence, to be goal oriented, to initiate action, to be dependable in exercising responsibilities, to have insight into problems faced by the group, and to have a strong continuing drive to succeed.
3. Leaders realize that people are essential for goal achievement. Therefore they attempt to communicate with others, tend to be sociable, show consideration for people, and seek cooperation of others.
4. The presence of such traits and characteristics does not guarantee effective performance as a leader, nor does their absence preclude effective performance; rather, the presence of these traits and characteristics enhances the probability of effective performance as a leader.[56]

Two Approaches. Leaders tend to lean toward one of two basic approaches to administration: the bureaucratic approach or the collegial approach. The

---

[55] See Laurence J. Peter, Jr., and Raymond Hull, *The Peter Principle: Why Things Always Go Wrong* (New York: William Morrow, 1969).

[56] Kimbrough and Nunnery, *Educational Administration,* p. 347.

first approach has been labeled autocratic; the second, democratic. Edgar L. Morphet, Roe L. Johns, and Theodore L. Reller discussed the assumptions that underlie these two approaches. According to these authors, leaders who follow what they term the traditional, monocratic, bureaucratic approach hold the following beliefs:

- Leadership is confined to those holding positions in the power echelon.
- Good human relations are necessary in order that followers accept decisions of superordinates.
- Authority and power can be delegated but responsibility cannot be shared.
- Final responsibility for all matters is placed in the administrator at the top of the power echelon.
- The individual finds security in a climate in which the superordinates protect the interests of subordinates in the organization.
- Unity of purpose is obtained through loyalty to the administrator.
- The image of the executive is that of a superman.
- Maximum production is attained in a climate of competition.
- The line-and-staff plan of organization should be utilized to formulate goals, policies, and programs as well as to execute policies and programs.
- Authority is the right and privilege of a person holding a hierarchical position.
- The individual in the organization is expendable.
- Evaluation is the prerogative of superordinates.[57]

On the other hand, according to Morphet, Johns, and Reller, leaders who follow what they call the emerging, pluralistic, collegial approach believe the following:

- Leadership is not confined to those holding status position in the power echelon.
- Good human relations are essential to group production and to meeting the needs of the individual members of the group.
- Responsibility, as well as power and authority, can be shared.
- Those affected by a program or policy should share in decision making with respect to that program or policy.
- The individual finds security in a dynamic climate in which responsibility for decision making is shared.
- Unity of purpose is secured through consensus and group loyalty.
- Maximum production is attained in a threat-free climate.
- The line-and-staff organizations should be used exclusively for the purpose of dividing labor and implementing policies and programs developed by the total group affected.
- Laws and regulations legitimatizing authority recognize that need for authority arises from the situation.

---

[57]Edgar L. Morphet, Roe L. Johns, and Theodore L. Reller. From *Educational Organization and Administration: Concepts, Practices, and Issues*, 4th ed., ©1982, pp. 77–79. Reprinted by permission of Prentice-Hall, Inc., Englewood Cliffs, New Jersey.

□ The individual in the organization is not expendable.
□ Evaluation is a group responsibility.[58]

In contrasting these two approaches to administration Morphet, Johns, and Reller noted that the traditional approach operates in a closed climate, whereas the democratic approach functions in an open climate. The traditional approach relies on centralized authority with a fixed line-and-staff structure. Authority is spread out and shared under the pluralistic approach; the structure, while sometimes more complex than the traditional structure, is more flexible to allow for maximum participation of members of the organization. The flow of communication is much different under these two approaches. The autocratic or authoritarian approach is imbued with the philosophy of going through channels. Messages may originate from the top of the echelon, which is most common, or from the bottom. Messages from the top down pass through intermediate echelons but may not be stopped by these echelons. On the other hand, messages originating from the bottom proceed through intermediate echelons and may be stopped by any echelon. Subordinates are required to conduct business through channels and may not with impunity "go over the head" of their immediate superior. Under a pluralistic approach communications may flow in any direction—up, down, circularly, or horizontally. They may skip echelons and may be referred to persons outside the immediate chain of command. The pluralistic administrator is not "hung up" on channels and personal status. It is the traditional approach that begets the "organization man."

Morphet, Johns, and Reller cautioned, in comparing these two approaches, "It should not be inferred, however, that democratic administration is *ipso facto* good and that authoritarian administration is *ipso facto* bad. History provides numerous examples of successful and unsuccessful democratic administration and successful and unsuccessful authoritarian administration."[59] They noted, however, that some studies reveal monocratic organizations to be less innovative than pluralistic ones.

Some people would identify the traditional leader as an adherent to Theory X; they would classify the pluralistic leader as a follower of Theory Y. Leaders in organizations of the Theory Z type are largely Theory Y practitioners who structure their organizations to secure maximum involvement and commitment from the workers. The pluralistic assumption that the individual is not expendable, for example, is interpreted in Japanese Theory Z organizations as a guarantee of lifetime employment in the organization in return for full commitment to that organization in the realization of its goals.[60]

---

[58] Edgar L. Morphet, Roe L. Johns, and Theodore L. Reller. From *Educational Organization and Administration: Concepts, Practices, and Issues,* 4th ed., ©1982, pp. 80–82. Reprinted by permission of Prentice-Hall, Inc., Englewood Cliffs, New Jersey.

[59] Edgar L. Morphet, Roe L. Johns, and Theodore L. Reller. From *Educational Organization and Administration: Concepts, Practices, and Issues,* 4th ed., ©1982, p. 85. Reprinted by permission of Prentice-Hall, Inc., Englewood Cliffs, New Jersey.

[60] See Ouchi, *Theory Z.*

Leadership style is a potent factor in the productivity of groups. A classic study of the impact of leadership is the previously mentioned research conducted by Lewin, Lippitt, and White, who studied the effects of three different styles of adult leadership on four groups of 11-year-old children. They examined the effects of "authoritarian" "democratic," and "laissez-faire" leadership.

> Under the authoritarian leadership, the children were more dependent upon the leader, more discontent, made more demands for attention, were less friendly, produced less work-minded conversation than under the democratic leadership. There was no group initiative in the authoritarian group climate.

> The laissez-faire atmosphere produced more dependence on the leader, more discontent, less friendliness, fewer group-minded suggestions, less work-minded conversation than under the democratic climate. In the absence of the laissez-faire leader, work was unproductive. The laissez-faire group was extremely dependent upon the leader for information.

> The converse of these situations was true for the democratic group climate. In addition, relations among the individuals in the democratic leadership atmosphere were friendlier. Those under the democratic leadership sought more attention and approval from fellow club members. They depended upon each other for recognition as opposed to recognition by the leader under the authoritarian and laissez-faire systems. Further, in the absence of the leader the democratic groups proceeded at their work in productive fashion.[61]

Thus, if a curriculum leader seeks commitment from a group, the authoritarian and laissez-faire approaches are not likely to be effective. The curriculum leader's power (what little there is) is conferred by the group, especially if the leadership is encouraged from *within* the group. The democratic approach is, indeed, the only viable approach open to the curriculum leader who is a staff and not a line person propped up by an external authority.

Task- and Relationship-Oriented Leaders. Fred E. Fiedler studied the age-old question of whether successful leadership results from personal style or from the circumstances of the situation in which the leader finds himself or herself.[62] Fiedler spoke of the need for an appropriate match between the leader's style and the group situation in which he or she must exercise leadership. Developing what is called a "contingency model," Fiedler classified leaders as task-oriented or relationship-oriented. We might substitute human-relations–oriented for the latter term. In some respects this classification resembles the dichotomy between the autocratic and democratic leader. The task-oriented leader keeps the goals of the organization always in front of him or her and the group. The needs of the organization take precedence over the needs of individuals. The superordinate-subordinate relationship is always clear. The relationship-oriented leader is less task-oriented and more

---

[61]Lewin, Lippitt, and White, "Patterns of Aggressive Behavior." Quoted from Peter F. Oliva, "High School Discipline in American Society," *NASSP Bulletin* 40, no. 26 (January 1956): 7–8. Reprinted with permission.

[62]See Fiedler, *Theory of Leadership*. Also, "Style or Circumstance: The Leadership Enigma," *Psychology Today* 2, No. 10 (March 1969): 38–43.

concerned with building harmonious relationships among the members of the organization. He or she possesses a high degree of human relations skill and is less conscious of status.

Persons exhibiting either of these two styles may find themselves in organizations that are either structured or unstructured, or in mixed situations possessing elements of both structure and lack of structure. Successful leadership depends upon the fortuitous combination of both style and circumstance. Fiedler found that task-oriented leaders perform better than relationship-oriented leaders at both ends of the continuum from structure to lack of structure. They perform well in structured situations where they possess authority and influence and in unstructured situations where they lack authority and influence. Relationship-oriented persons function best in mixed situations in which they possess moderate authority and influence.

Leadership, then, arises from the exigencies of a situation. Stephen J. Knezevich, for example, espoused a situational view of leadership when he said:

> A person is selected to perform the leadership role because of possessing a set of sensitivities, insights, or personal qualities the group may require for realization of group objectives and decisions. . . . The leader is selected and followed because of being capable to achieve what the followers need or want. A leader successful in one community with a unique set of educational needs may not experience similar success when moved to another with a markedly different set of educational problems, personnel, and value orientations. Changing the situation, or group's nature and purposes, results in a significant variation in leader characteristics desired that upsets all but the broadest interpretations of personal attributes.[63]

When a group member who has been in the role of follower assumes the role of leader, that person is then expected to demonstrate democratic behaviors associated with his or her new status of leadership. If the original leader remains a part of the group, he or she then assumes the role of follower. Some status leaders find it difficult to surrender power and are compelled to be constantly on center stage. Such behavior will effectively prevent leadership from developing within the group and is likely to impede its progress. When the original leader resists being replaced, the leader's superior with executive power may have to correct the situation by urging changes in the original leader's behavior or by removing him or her from the scene.

The research on leadership thus suggests that the leader in curriculum development should

- □ seek to develop a democratic approach
- □ seek to develop a relationship-oriented style

---

[63] Stephen J. Knezevich, *Administration of Public Education,* 4th ed. (New York: Harper & Row, 1984), p. 66.

□ move between a task-oriented and relationship-oriented style as the situation demands (Jacob W. Getzels, James M. Lipham, and Roald F. Campbell called this flexible style "transactional.")[64]

□ keep the group on task and avoid excessive processing

□ avoid a laissez-faire approach

□ encourage the development of leadership from within the group

□ maintain openness and avoid a defensive posture

□ fulfill his or her role as a change agent by serving as

advisor	interpreter
expert	reinforcer
mediator	spokesperson
organizer	intermediary
explainer	summarizer
discussion leader	team builder

Even with the best leadership some groups experience great difficulties in moving toward accomplishment of their goals. Without effective leadership little can be expected of groups in terms of productivity.

Communication Skills

Curriculum development is primarily an exercise in verbal behavior—to some degree written but to a greater degree oral. Through the miraculous gift of language one human being is able to communicate his or her thoughts and feelings to another. Much of the world's business—particularly in a democratic society—is transacted through group discussions. Sometimes it seems as if most administrators, including school personnel, spend the majority of their hours participating in groups, for the standard response to callers is "Sorry, he's [she's] in a meeting."

Thoughts are communicated verbally in the form of oral activity and handwritten and printed documents; visually in the form of pictures, diagrams, charts, and the like; and nonverbally in the form of gestures and actions. Styles of oral communication and writing differ from individual to individual and from group to group. Styles vary among ethnic, regional, and national groups.

The choice of words, the loudness or softness of speech, and the rapidity of the spoken language differ from person to person and from group to group. We find differences in "accent" and in tone or intonation. The flexibility of language, both a strength and a problem, can be seen in a simple example. By using the same words but by varying the intonation or stress pattern, a speaker can convey different meanings, as follows:

---

[64]Jacob W. Getzels, James M. Lipham, and Roald F. Campbell, *Educational Administration as a Social Process* (New York: Harper & Row, 1968).

- □ *They* said that.
- □ They *said* that.
- □ They said *that*.
- □ They said *that?*

Individuals from some cultures are said to "talk with their hands," indicating frequent use of nonverbal behavior, whereas individuals from other cultures are taught not to be so expressive. Proficiency in communication skills by both the leader and the group members is essential to successful curriculum development. They must demonstrate proficiency in both oral and written communication. At the same time, they must be aware of their own nonverbal behavior and be skilled at reading other people's.

The leader must demonstrate proficiency in two ways: he or she must possess a high degree of communication skill and must also be able to help group members to increase their proficiency in communicating.

For purposes of our discussion, we will assume that the school or district curriculum committees, in which we are most interested, operate through the medium of the English language and that, although they represent a variety of ethnic groups and national origins, they possess at least average proficiency in English language usage. What we have to say about communication goes beyond the mere mechanics of grammar, syntax, spelling, vocabulary, and sentence structure. Deficiencies in the linguistic aspects of communication can be remedied perhaps more easily than some of the more complex psychological, social, and cultural aspects.

It is safe to conjecture that even in a group in which all members possess an excellent command of the language, communication leaves something to be desired. Have you ever sat in, for example, on group meetings where

- □ two people talk at the same time?
- □ one member consistently finishes sentences for people?
- □ one member jumps into the discussion without recognition from the chair, elevates his or her voice, and continues to do so until he or she has forced others to be silent?
- □ one member, angered with the way the discussion is going, gets up and stomps out of the room?
- □ members snicker and make snide remarks whenever a particular member of the group speaks?
- □ one member drones on ad infinitum?
- □ one member cannot resist displaying his or her advanced knowledge of the subject under discussion?
- □ one member becomes sullen when another disagrees with his or her ideas?
- □ the leader has to explain a point three times before all group members seem to understand?

Do you recognize any of these people? Some of them are, of course, playing the group roles discussed earlier. It is possible that many, even most, of the members thought they were communicating something to the group while they were speaking. It is highly probably that what they were communicating was much different from what they thought they were.

Two people vying for the floor may communicate that they both are individuals who demand attention. Or shall we say that they possess a trait, lauded by some, called "assertiveness"? The member who finishes others' sentences may communicate that it is necessary for him or her to think for others. The member who stomps out of the room might attempt to convey that he or she is a person who sticks to his or her principles. More likely, in rejecting the group, this person will be perceived as a "sore loser." We communicate not only through words but through our actions as well.

Common Misunderstandings.   We should clear up some common misunderstandings about communication. First, skill in speaking is sometimes mistaken for communication. The ability to respond quickly and fully—to "think on one's feet"—is an attribute desired, some say required, of a leader. However, facility in speaking does not ensure that a message is getting across. One need only listen to some political leaders to make the distinction between the ability to articulate and the ability to communicate. People place great stress on oral skills, often to such an extent that they do not realize they are accepting form in place of substance. A soft answer turneth away wrath, but a glib tongue may also obfuscate a topic under discussion. A speaker should strive to be both articulate and communicative.

Second, group interaction is sometimes mistaken for communication. Comments like "We had a lively discussion" are meaningless unless we know whether the discussion led to understanding and decision making. Processing, the sharing of personal feelings and opinions, is sometimes equated with communication. Interaction for interaction's sake cannot be accepted as a legitimate activity for work in curriculum development.

Third, the assumption that communication is full, clear, and completely understood is often made without sufficient evidence. Alfonso, Firth, and Neville advised supervisors against making such an assumption: "Communication will always be inaccurate because sender and receiver can never share common perceptions. Supervisors often operate on the assumption that communication is perfect. Instead, they should function on the basis that communication is imperfect and must always be so."[65]

How many times have we heard the words of a speaker, understood them all, yet not comprehended what the speaker was saying? How many times have we heard a member of a group tell another, "I hear you," but mean, "Even though I hear you, I do not know what you are saying"?

What are some common problems people experience in trying to communicate and what can be done to solve them? Let's create three categories: (1) problems with oral communications or those that oral and written communica-

---

[65]Alfonso, Firth, and Neville, *Instructional Supervision*, p. 175.

tion share, (2) problems with written communication, and (3) problems brought about by nonverbal behavior or the absence thereof.

Oral Communication. Difficulties in oral communication can arise in the following situations:

1. *Members of the group either unintentionally or deliberately fail to come to the point.* They talk "around" instead of "to" an issue. Sometimes they engage in avoidance behavior—that is, they resist coming to grips with the issue. The curriculum leader must help group members to address the issues and to come to the point. When some group members prattle on, others in the group become bored and frustrated. The burden of keeping the group's attention on the issues falls on the group leader.

2. *Members of the group use fuzzy, imprecise language.* They use words with many interpretations, like "relevance," without defining them. They use "psychobabble," like "Tell me where you're coming from" and "I'm into behavioral objectives." They employ words of low frequency, like "nomothetic," "synergy," and "androgogy," that some members of the group may not understand. They lapse into pedagese, like "Each child must develop his or her personal curriculum," without venturing how this may be done. They borrow Madison Avenue jargon, like "Let's run it up the flagpole," or turn to sports analogies, like "It's in your court now" and "What's the game plan?" The group leader must be alert to difficulties members may have in following a discussion. He or she must ask speakers to repeat and clarify statements and questions as necessary. The leader must keep in mind that some members hesitate to ask for clarifications themselves, feeling that in so doing they may expose their own ignorance.

3. *Members of the group select out of a discussion those things that they wish to hear.* It is a well-known fact that we hear and see selectively. We hear and see things that we wish to hear and see and reject those that we do not want to hear or see. The leader must help group members to see all facets of a problem, calling attention to points they may have missed.

4. *Members fail to express themselves, particularly if they disagree with what has been said.* Some persons hold back their views from a sense of insecurity. They feel that their opinions are not worthwhile, or they fear embarrassment or ridicule. They may not wish to seem in disagreement with status persons who are in a position to reward or punish them. The group leader must assure members that dissent is possible and encouraged. The leader must foster a climate in which each person can express himself or herself without fear.

5. *Members fail to follow an orderly process of discussion.* Communication is impossible when group members are unwilling to discipline themselves and do not take turns in discussing, listen to each other, and respect each other's views. The group leader must enforce order during the discussion process to ensure that everyone who wishes to be heard has an opportunity.

6. *Discussion is shut off and the group presses for a premature vote.* The group should be striving to reach consensus on issues. The goal is commitment of as many persons as possible. The group leader should keep the goal of consensus in front of the group. Close votes on issues should be reexamined, if possible.

7. *Sessions break up without some sort of closure.* If next steps are not clear, members leave the group sessions confused and frustrated. The leader has the responsibility for seeking closure on issues when possible, for summarizing the group's work, and for calling the group's attention to next steps.

8. *The communication flow is primarily from leader to members.* The leader should resist the temptation to dominate a discussion and to foist his or her views on the group. He or she should ensure that communication is initiated by members of the group to the leader and to each other as well as from the leader to group members.

9. *Acrimony, hostility, and disharmony exist within a group.* When these conditions occur, the leader must spend time developing a pleasant, harmonious group climate before positive communication can take place among members. Members must learn to work together in an atmosphere of trust and mutual respect. The leader should seek to promote a relaxed threat-free atmosphere.

Written Communication. In the course of a group's activity there will be occasions on which the leader and members of the group will wish and need to communicate in written form between group sessions. They will also need to communicate in writing with persons outside the work group. Difficulties arise with this form of communication when the following situations occur:

1. *The writer cannot sense the impact of his or her words in a written communication.* Extra care needs to be taken when structuring a written message. Writers of memos must weigh their choice of words and manner of phrasing their thoughts. Some messages are unintentionally blunt or curt and cause negative responses in the receivers. A message when put in writing may give a far different impression from what the writer intended. The writer should review any written communication in the light of the impact it would have on him or her if he or she were the recipient.

2. *Written communications are excessive in number.* Some persons indulge in memorandum writing with almost the same frequency as some individuals write letters to the editor of a newspaper. Some vent their own frustrations in memo after memo. Some people believe that every thought, word, and deed must be committed to writing in order to (1) preserve them for posterity, (2) maintain an ongoing record for current use, or (3) cover one's posterior, as is crudely suggested. Some recipients—or intended recipients—will not take any action unless they have word in written form. In some organizations we have almost immobilized ourselves with the ubiquitous memo to

the point where we have many communiqués but little communication. The leader should encourage the use of memoranda and other written communications as needed and discourage their excessive use. Courtesy, clarity, and brevity should be earmarks of written communications.

3. *The use of English is poor.* Many memoranda, particularly from professional people, lose their impact because of poor English. Inaccurate spelling and improper grammar can detract from the message contained in the memoranda and can subject the writers to unnecessary criticism.

The writing of intelligible memoranda that do not create negative responses on the part of recipients is an art that, at least in a cooperative activity like curriculum development, should serve only to supplement, not replace, oral communication.

Face-to-face communication is ordinarily—barring the need for complex or technical data—a far more effective means of conveying ideas among members of small groups of peers such as a typical curriculum development group. Even in the case of complex or technical data presented in written form, follow-up discussion is usually necessary.

Nonverbal Behavior. Human beings communicate with each other without the use of words. A smile, a frown, a wave, and a wink all say something to the recipient. Who among those watching the television set at that historic time can forget the former premier of the Soviet Union, Nikita Khrushchev, seated at a meeting of the United Nations in New York, banging the top of his desk with his shoe! Did Mario Puzo's *Godfather* convey any message when he planted the kiss of death on the cheek of his formerly trusted associate? Does the behavior of children and adolescents change when they detect pleasant aromas emanating from the school cafeteria?

Nonverbal behavior is shaped both biologically and culturally. Most human beings start out life with basically the same physiological equipment—two eyes, arms, legs, and so on. But what they do with that equipment is shaped by the culture in which they grow and develop. Thus it is possible for every human being to smile, but some individuals within a single culture are more prone to smile than others, and members of a particular culture are more prone to smile than members of another. South American Indians, for example, are much more stoic and reserved than the more expressive Latinos of Spanish origin.

Nonverbal behavior is less studied and less understood than verbal behavior. We have great need in our teacher education programs for training in understanding differences in nonverbal behavior between members of the U.S. culture and foreign cultures; among members of diverse cultures in the United States; and among members of a single culture in the United States.

In our pluralistic society many social and work groups are composed of persons from varying subcultures: white, black, Hispanic, Native American, and Asian, among others. Every individual brings to a group his or her culturally determined ways of behaving. While some cultures prize assertiveness, others stress deference. Signs of respect are accorded to age, status, and experience more often in some cultures than in others. Attitudes of both males and females toward children and of one sex toward the other vary among cultures, and these attitudes are shown in both verbal and nonverbal behavior.

Some cultures value physical closeness among individuals and gregariousness. Other cultures strive to maintain distance among individuals both physically and socially.

We need to learn to perceive what our colleagues are trying to communicate to us by the expressions on their faces, by the look in their eyes, by the way they hold their mouths or their heads, by the movement of their hands, and by the fidgeting of their legs. A group leader should be able to detect fatigue, boredom, hostility, and sensitivity on the part of members of the organization. He or she should be able to sense when one individual is stepping on another's toes and turn the discussion to constructive paths. He or she should strive to effect more signs of pleasure than pain among members of the group. The leader must be especially cautious of the nonverbal signals he or she gives and must make every effort to ensure that those signals are positive. Finally, for successful curriculum development both the leader and group members must exhibit a high degree of skill in all modes of communication.[66]

SUMMARY

This chapter focused on the roles played by various persons and groups participating in curriculum development at the individual school level. Some principals perceive themselves as instructional leaders and take an active part in curriculum development, whereas others delegate that responsibility. A Theory X administrator emphasizes authority and control, whereas a Theory Y administrator follows a human relations approach. Theory Y leaders may adopt Theory Z principles.

Students in some schools, depending on their maturity, participate in curriculum improvement by serving on committees and by providing data about their own learning experiences.

Parents and other citizens participate in curriculum work by serving on advisory committees, responding to surveys, providing data about their children, and serving as resource persons in school and out.

---

[66]For interesting analyses of some aspects of nonverbal behavior see Edward T. Hall, *The Silent Language* (Garden City, N.Y.: Doubleday, 1959); Julius Fast, *Body Language* (New York: M. Evans, 1970); and Desmond Morris, Peter Collett, Peter Marsh, and Marie O'Shaughnessy, *Gestures: Their Origin and Distribution* (New York: Stein and Day, 1979).

The professional personnel—teachers and specialists—share the greatest responsibility for curriculum development.[67] Both leaders and followers need to develop skills in group process. Among the competencies necessary for the curriculum leader are skills in producing change, in decision making, in interpersonal relationships, in leading groups, and in communicating.

QUESTIONS FOR DISCUSSION

1. What evidence is there that today's principals either are or are not instructional leaders?
2. What are some community groups with which school administrators and supervisors should be concerned?
3. What impact does America's multicultural diversity have on the public schools?
4. Do you agree that teachers should be the primary group in curriculum development? Why?
5. How would you as a curriculum leader proceed to bring about change in the curriculum?

SUPPLEMENTARY EXERCISES

1. Write a paper stating the pros and cons and showing your position on the role of the principal as instructional leader.
2. List qualities and qualifications needed by a curriculum leader.
3. Explain what is meant by Theory X, Theory Y, and Theory Z, and draw implications of these theories for curriculum development.
4. Write a paper on developing a Theory Z school.
5. Report on ways pupils are involved in curriculum development in a school district with which you are familiar.
6. Report on ways parents and others from the community are involved in curriculum development in a school district with which you are familiar.
7. Explain the meaning of the term "power structure," and draw implications of the power structure for curriculum development.
8. Analyze the power structure of a community that you know well.

---

[67]This textbook focuses on the roles of the various constituencies of the school in relationship to *curriculum development*. However, concerning one of those constituencies—the teachers—you may wish to read the informative books by John I. Goodlad et al. on the role, responsibilities, and preparation of teachers. All three books are from Jossey-Bass, San Francisco, 1990: *The Moral Dimensions of Teaching, Places Where Teachers are Taught,* and *Teachers for Our Nation's Schools.* See also John Goodlad's article in *Phi Delta Kappan* vol. 70, no. 3, November 1990, pp. 185–194, entitled "Better Teachers for Our Nation's Schools," a summary of the findings of the Study of the Education of Educators.

9. Write an essay on the curriculum leader as change agent.
10. Write a brief paper on ways to unfreeze an existing curricular pattern.
11. Identify roles played by group members and how the curriculum leader copes with each. You should make an effort to describe roles in addition to those mentioned in this chapter.
12. Describe common barriers to educational change and suggest ways the curriculum leader may work to eliminate them.
13. List steps in the decision-making process.
14. Observe a discussion group in action and apply the observation chart based on the Benne-Sheats classification system discussed in this chapter. (You might want to try this chart on a school board meeting.)
15. Observe a discussion group in action and record evidence of task orientation and process orientation. Conjecture on hidden agendas present in the group.
16. Observe a discussion group in action and evaluate the effectiveness of the leader, using criteria discussed in this chapter.
17. Report on the meaning of gestures used within a particular culture.
18. Analyze the gestures you use, if any.
19. Explain the ten kinds of human activity which Edward T. Hall labeled Primary Message Systems (see bibliography).
20. Explain and demonstrate examples of body language as described by Julius Fast (see bibliography).
21. Report on the home-school movement and its impact on compulsory school attendance. (See John Holt reference in bibliography.)
22. Prepare a written oral report on the Concerns-Based Adoption Model (CBAM) developed by the University of Texas Research and Development Center for determining stages of teacher concerns about an innovation and levels of teacher use of innovations. See references to Gene E. Hall and Susan Loucks and to Hall, Loucks, Rutherford, and Newlove in the bibliography. See also description of this model in John P. Miller and Wayne Seller (see bibliography).

BIBLIOGRAPHY

Alfonso, Robert J., Firth, Gerald R., and Neville, Richard F. *Instructional Supervision: A Behavior System,* 2nd ed. Boston: Allyn and Bacon, 1981.

Benne, Kenneth D. and Sheats, Paul. "Functional Roles of Group Members," *Journal of Social Issues* 4, no. 2 (Spring 1948): 43–46.

Bennis, Warren G., Benne, Kenneth D., and Chin, Robert, eds. *The Planning of Change,* 4th ed. New York: Holt, Rinehart and Winston, 1985.

Berman, Louise M. and Roderick, Jessie A. *Curriculum: Teaching the What, How, and Why of Living.* Columbus, Ohio: Charles E. Merrill, 1977.

Brubaker, Dale. L. *Curriculum Planning: The Dynamics of Theory and Practice.* Glenview, Ill.: Scott, Foresman, 1982.

Campbell, Roald F., Cunningham, Luvern L., Nystrand, Raphael O., and Usdan, Michael D. *The Organization and Control of American Schools,* 6th ed. Columbus Ohio: Charles E. Merrill, 1990.

Carnegie Foundation for the Advancement of Teaching. *The Condition of Teaching: A State-by-State Analysis, 1990.* Princeton, N.J.: Carnegie Foundation for the Advancement of Teaching, 1990.

Connelly, F. Michael and Clandinin, D. Jean. *Teachers as Curriculum Planners: Narratives of Experience.* New York: Teachers College Press, 1988.

Doll, Ronald C. *Curriculum Improvement: Decision Making and Process,* 7th ed. Boston: Allyn and Bacon, 1989.

Drake, Thelbert L. and Roe, William H. *The Principalship* 3rd ed. New York: Macmillan, 1986.

Fast, Julius. *Body Language.* New York: M. Evans, 1970.

Fiedler, Fred E. *A Theory of Leadership Effectiveness.* New York: McGraw-Hill, 1967.

Galloway, Charles. *Silent Language in the Classroom.* Bloomington, Ind.: Phi Delta Kappa Educational Foundation, 1976.

George, Paul S. *The Theory Z School: Beyond Effectiveness.* Columbus, Ohio: National Middle School Association, 1983.

Getzels, Jacob W., Lipham, James M., and Campbell, Roald F. *Educational Administration as a Social Process.* New York: Harper & Row, 1968.

Glatthorn, Allan A. *Curriculum Leadership.* Glenview, Ill.: Scott, Foresman, 1987.

Good, Thomas L. and Brophy, Jere E. "School Effects." In Merlin C. Wittrock, ed., *Handbook of Research on Teaching,* 3rd ed., 570–602. New York: Macmillan, 1986.

Goodlad, John I. *The Dynamics of Educational Change: Toward Responsive Schools.* New York: McGraw-Hill, 1975.

Haiman, Franklyn S. *Group Leadership and Democratic Action.* Boston: Houghton Mifflin, 1951.

Hall, Edward T. *The Silent Language.* Garden City, N.Y.: Doubleday, 1959.

Hall, Gene E. and Loucks, Susan "Teacher Concerns as a Basis for Facilitating and Personalizing Staff Development." *Teachers College Record* 80, no. 1 (September 1978): 36–53.

Hall, Gene E., Loucks, Susan F., Rutherford, William L., and Newlove, Beaulah W. "Levels of Use of the Innovation: A Framework for Analyzing Innovation Adoption." *Journal of Teacher Education* 26, no. 1 (Spring 1975): 52–56.

Herriott, Robert E. and Gross, Neal, eds. *The Dynamics of Planned Educational Change.* Berkeley, Calif.: McCutchan, 1979.

Holt, John. *Teach Your Own: A Hopeful Path for Education.* New York: Delacorte Press/Seymour Lawrence, 1981.

Hord, Shirley M., Rutherford, William L., Huling-Austin, Leslie, and Hall, Gene E. *Taking Charge of Change.* Alexandria, Va.: Association for Supervision and Curriculum Development, 1987.

Kimbrough, Ralph B. and Nunnery, Michael Y. *Educational Administration: An Introduction,* 3rd ed. New York: Macmillan, 1988.

Knezevich, Stephen J. *Administration of Public Education,* 4th ed. New York: Harper & Row, 1984.

Krug, Edward A., Babcock, Chester D., Fowlkes, John Guy, and James, H. T. *Administering Curriculum Planning.* New York: Harper & Brothers, 1956.

Leavitt, Harold J. and Bahrami, Homa. *Managerial Psychology: Managing Behavior in Organizations,* 5th ed. Chicago: University of Chicago Press, 1988.

Leese, Joseph. *The Teacher in Curriculum Making.* New York: Harper & Row, 1961.

Lewin, Kurt. *Field Theory in Social Science: Selected Theoretical Papers,* edited by Dorwin Cartwright. New York: Harper Torchbooks, 1951.

Lewin, Kurt, Lippitt, Ronald, and White, Ralph K. "Patterns of Aggressive Behavior in Experimentally Created Social Climates." *Journal of Social Psychology* 10 (May 1939): 271–299.

Lovell, John T. and Wiles, Kimball. *Supervision for Better Schools,* 5th ed. Englewood Cliffs, N.J.: Prentice-Hall, 1983.

Lucio, William H. and McNeil, John D. *Supervision: A Synthesis of Thought and Action,* 2nd ed. New York: McGraw-Hill, 1969.

Lynd, Robert S. *Middletown: A Study in American Culture.* New York: Harcourt Brace Jovanovich, 1929.

Lynd, Robert S. and Lynd, Helen M. *Middletown in Transition: A Study in Cultural Conflicts.* New York: Harcourt Brace Jovanovich, 1937.

McCutcheon, Gail. "Curriculum Theory/Curriculum Practice: A Gap or the Grand Canyon?" In Alex Molnar, ed., *Current Thought on Curriculum,* 1985 Yearbook, 45–52. Alexandria, Va.: Association for Supervision and Curriculum Development, 1985.

McGregor, Douglas M. *The Human Side of Enterprise.* New York: McGraw-Hill, 1960.

McNeil, John D. *Curriculum: A Comprehensive Introduction.* 4th ed. Boston: Scott, Foresman/Little, Brown, 1990.

Madeja, Stanley S. "Where Have All the Disciplines Gone?" *Educational Leadership* 38, no. 8 (May 1981): 602–604.

Maeroff, Gene I. *The Empowerment of Teachers: Overcoming the Crisis of Confidence.* New York: Teachers College Press, 1988.

Martin, David S. *Curriculum Leadership: Case Studies for Program Practitioners.* Alexandria, Va.: Association for Supervision and Curriculum Development, 1989.

Maslow, Abraham H. *Motivation and Personality,* 2nd ed. New York: Harper & Row, 1970.

Miel, Alice. *Changing the Curriculum: A Social Process.* New York: Appleton-Century-Crofts, 1946.

Miller, John P. and Seller, Wayne. *Curriculum: Perspectives and Practice.* White Plains, N.Y.: Longman, 1985.

Morphet, Edgar L., Johns, Roe L., and Reller, Theodore L. *Educational Organization and Administration: Concepts, Practices, and Issues,* 4th ed. Englewood Cliffs, N.J.: Prentice-Hall, 1982.

Morris, Desmond, Collett, Peter, Marsh, Peter, and O'Shaughnessy, Marie. *Gestures: Their Origin and Distribution.* New York: Stein and Day, 1979.

Myers, Donald A. *Decision Making in Curriculum and Instruction.* Dayton, Ohio: Institute for Development of Educational Activities, 1970.

Oliver, Albert I. *Curriculum Improvement: A Guide to Problems, Principles, and Process,* 2nd ed. New York: Harper & Row, 1977.

Ouchi, William G. *Theory Z: How American Businesses Can Meet the Japanese Challenge.* Reading, Mass.: Addison-Wesley, 1981.

Owens, Robert G. *Organizational Behavior in Education,* 3rd ed. Englewood Cliffs, N.J.: Prentice-Hall, 1987.

Peter, Laurence J. *The Peter Prescription.* New York: William Morrow, 1972.

———. *Why Things Go Wrong; Or, the Peter Principle Revisited.* New York: William Morrow, 1985.

Peter, Laurence J. and Hull, Raymond. *The Peter Principle: Why Things Always Go Wrong.* New York: William Morrow, 1969.

Roethlisberger, F. J. and Dickson, William J. *Management and the Worker.* Cambridge, Mass.: Harvard University Press, 1939.

Saylor, J. Galen, Alexander, William M., and Lewis, Arthur J. *Curriculum Planning for Better Teaching and Learning,* 4th ed. New York: Holt, Rinehart and Winston, 1981.

Sergiovanni, Thomas J. and Carver, Fred D. *The New School Executive: A Theory of Administration,* 2nd ed. New York: Harper & Row, 1980.

Sergiovanni, Thomas J. and Starratt, Robert J. *Supervision: Human Perspectives,* 4th ed. New York: McGraw-Hill, 1988.

"Strengthening Partnerships with Parents and Community." *Educational Leadership* 47, no. 2 (October 1989): 3–67.

Stufflebeam, Daniel L. et al. *Educational Evaluation and Decision Making.* Itasca, Ill.: F. E. Peacock, 1971.

Toffler, Alvin. *Future Shock.* New York: Random House, 1970.

————. *The Third Wave.* New York: William Morrow, 1980.

Unruh, Glenys G. "Curriculum Politics." In Fenwick W. English, ed., *Fundamental Curriculum Decisions,* 1983 Yearbook, 99–111. Alexandria Va.: Association for Supervision and Curriculum Development, 1983.

Wiles, Jon and Bondi, Joseph C. *Curriculum Development: A Guide to Practice,* 2nd ed. Columbus, Ohio: Charles E. Merrill, 1984.

————. *Supervision: A Guide to Practice,* 2nd ed. Columbus, Ohio: Charles E. Merrill, 1986.

Wiles, Kimball. *Supervision for Better Schools,* 3rd ed. Englewood Cliffs, N.J.: Prentice-Hall, 1967.

Zenger, Weldon F. and Zenger, Sharon K. *Curriculum Planning: A Ten-Step Process.* Palto Alto, Calif.: R & E Research Associates, 1982.

FILMS

Leadership: Style or Circumstance? 30 min. color. 1975. CRM/McGraw-Hill Films, Del Mar, Calif. 92014. Identifies and differentiates two types of leaders: the relationship-oriented and the task-oriented leader. Shows how each type of leader can work effectively depending on the job situation.

Putting the Group Process to Work. 28 min. black and white. 1969. University of Georgia Film Library, Georgia Center for Continuing Education, Athens, Ga. 30602. Describes how teachers can be democratic group leaders.

Theory X and Theory Y: Work of Douglas McGregor, 25 min. color. 1969. BNA Communications, Inc., 9401 Decoverly Hall Rd., Rockville, Md. 20850. Two basic sets of assumptions about human nature that characterize management style.

VIDEOTAPES

Association for Supervision and Curriculum Development, 1250 N. Pitt Street, Alexandria, Va. 22314:

The Principal as Instructional Leader: Reflections on Effectiveness. Approx. 1 hour. 1984. Dr. Gordon Cawelti, executive director of the Association for Supervision and Curriculum Development, narrates; the tape examines the behavior patterns of four elementary, middle, and high school principals.

Quality Circles: Problem-Solving Tool for Educators. 30 min. color. 1984. Jim Bellanca, director of the Illinois Renewal Institute, Inc., Arlington Heights, Ill., describes the four-part quality-circle process: problem selection, problem analysis, solutions selection, and presentation to management.

Selecting Appropriate Leadership Styles for Instructional Improvement. 30 min. color. 1978. Dr. Gordon Cawelti, executive director of the Association for Supervision and Curriculum Development, narrates this taped program that synthesizes studies on leader behavior and develops the Situational Leadership Model of Philip E. Gates, Kenneth H. Blanchard, and Paul Hersey.

PART III

Curriculum Development: Components of the Process

CHAPTER FIVE

Models for Curriculum Development

After studying this chapter you should be able to:

1. Analyze each model for curriculum development in this chapter and to decide which models, if any, meet the necessary criteria for such a model.

2. Choose one model and carry out one or more of its components in your school.

3. Distinguish between deductive and inductive models for curriculum development.

4. Distinguish between linear and nonlinear models for curriculum development.

5. Distinguish between prescriptive and descriptive models for curriculum development.

SELECTING MODELS

The current literature of education is replete with discussions of "modeling." Models, which are essentially patterns serving as guidelines to action, can be found for almost every form of educational activity. The profession has models of instruction, of administration, of evaluation, of supervision, and others. By one count, there were some 99 models of observational analysis.[1] We can even find models of *curriculum* as opposed to models of *curriculum development*.[2]

Unfortunately, the term "model" rates with "scenario" as one of the most abused words in current English usage. While a scenario may turn out to be any plan or series of events, a model may be a tried or untried scheme. It may be a proposed solution to a piece of a problem; an attempt at a solution to a specific problem; a microcosmic pattern proposed for replication on a grander scale.

Some faculties have been "modeling" for years. They have been devising their own patterns for solving educational problems or establishing procedures, though they may not have labeled their activity as "modeling."

Variation in Models

Some of the models found in the literature are simple; others are very complex. The more complex ones border on computer science, with charts that consist of squares, boxes, circles, rectangles, arrows, and so on. Within a given area of specialization (such as administration, instruction, supervision, or curriculum development), models may differ but bear great similarities. The similarities may outweigh the differences. Individual models are often refinements or revisions (frequently major, often minor) of already existing models.

Practitioners to whom a model is directed, therefore, have the heavy responsibility of selecting a model in their particular field from the often bewildering variety in the literature. If the practitioners are not disposed to apply models they discover, they may either design their own, by no means a rare event, or may reject all models that prescribe order and sequence. They may thus proceed intuitively without the apparent limitations imposed by a model. After proceeding intuitively, the practitioners may then "put it all together" and come out with a working model at the end of the process instead of starting with a model at the beginning.

Four models of curriculum development are presented in this chapter, one of which is my own. I believe that using a model in such an activity as curriculum development can result in greater efficiency and productivity.

---

[1]See Anita Simon and E. Gil Boyer, *Mirror for Behavior III: An Anthology of Observation Instruments* (Philadelphia: Research for Better Schools, 1974).

[2]For a model of *curriculum,* see Mauritz Johnson, Jr., "Definitions and Models in Curriculum Theory," *Educational Theory* 17, no. 2 (April 1967): 127–140.

By examining models for curriculum development, we can analyze the phases their originators conceived as essential to the process. The purpose in presenting four models is to acquaint the reader with some of the thinking that has gone on or is going on in the field. Three of the chosen models were conceived by persons well known in the curriculum field: Hilda Taba;[3] J. Galen Saylor, William M. Alexander, and Arthur J. Lewis;[4] and Ralph W. Tyler.[5] My own model is presented as an effort to tie together essential components in the process of curriculum development. The supplementary exercises at the end of this chapter will direct you to additional models.

Three of the models (Saylor, Alexander, and Lewis's; Tyler's; and mine) are deductive. They proceed from the general (examining the needs of society, for example) to the specific (specifying instructional objectives, for example). On the other hand, Taba's model is inductive, starting with the actual development of curriculum materials and leading to generalization.

The four models described in this chapter are linear; that is, they propose a certain order or sequence of progression through the various steps. A nonlinear approach would permit planners to enter at various points of the model, skip components, reverse the order, and work on two or more components simultaneously. You might say that the ultimate in a nonlinear approach is the absence of a model when curriculum planners operate intuitively.

The four models presented in this chapter are prescriptive rather than descriptive. They suggest what ought to be done (and what is done by many curriculum developers). A descriptive model takes a different approach. Proposing a descriptive model that he termed "naturalistic," Decker F. Walker included three major elements: platform, deliberation, and design.[6] By *platform* he meant the beliefs or principles that guided the curriculum developers. Platform principles lead to *deliberation,* the process of making decisions from among the alternatives available. From the deliberation comes the curriculum *design.* Walker contrasted his naturalistic or descriptive model with the classical or prescriptive model as follows:

> This model is primarily descriptive, whereas the classical model is prescriptive. This model is basically a temporal one; it postulates a beginning (the platform), an end (the design), and a process (deliberation) by means of which the beginning progresses to the end. In contrast, the classical model is a means-end model; it postulates a desired end (the objective), a means for attaining this end (the learning experience), and a process (evaluation) for determining whether the means does indeed bring about the end. The two

[3]Hilda Taba, *Curriculum Development: Theory and Practice* (New York: Harcourt Brace Jovanovich, 1962).

[4]J. Galen Saylor, William M. Alexander, and Arthur J. Lewis, *Curriculum Planning for Better Teaching and Learning,* 4th ed. (New York: Holt, Rinehart and Winston, 1981).

[5]Ralph W. Tyler, *Basic Principles of Curriculum and Instruction* (Chicago: University of Chicago Press, 1949).

[6]Decker F. Walker, "A Naturalistic Model for Curriculum Development," *School Review* 80, no. 1 (November 1971): 51–67.

models differ radically in the roles they assign to objectives and to evaluation in the process of curriculum development.

In the classical model objectives are essential. . . . In the naturalistic model, on the other hand, objectives are only one means among others for guiding our search for better educational programs. . . .

Evaluation in the classical model is a self-corrective process for determining whether learning experiences lead to the attainment of given objectives. . . . In the naturalistic model this kind of evaluation is not *logically* necessary. Design decisions *can* be justified by reference to the platform only. . . . in the naturalistic model evaluation is a useful tool for justifying design decisions, even though it is quite possible and not nonsensical (although probably unwise) for a curriculum developer to neglect systematic formal evaluation. [7]

All of these models specify or depict major phases and a sequence for carrying out these phases. The models, including mine, show *phases* or *components,* not *people*. The various individuals and groups involved in each phase are not included in the models per se. To do so would require a most cumbersome diagram, for we would have to show the persons involved in every component. For example, if we showed the people involved in the component "specification of curriculum goals," we would need to chart a progression of steps from departmental committee to school faculty curriculum committee or extended school committee to principal to district curriculum committee to superintendent to school board. The roles of individuals and groups in the process are discussed elsewhere in this text.

MODELS OF CURRICULUM DEVELOPMENT

Curriculum development is seen here as the process for making programmatic decisions and for revising the products of those decisions on the basis of continuous and subsequent evaluation.

A model can give order to the process. As Taba stated, "If one conceives of curriculum development as a task requiring orderly thinking, one needs to examine both the order in which decisions are made and the way in which they are made to make sure that all relevant considerations are brought to bear on these decisions." [8]

The Taba Model

Taba took what is known as a grass-roots approach to curriculum development. She believed that the curriculum should be designed by the teachers rather than handed down by higher authority. Further, she felt that teachers should begin the process by creating specific teaching-learning units for their students in their

---

[7]Ibid., pp. 58–59. Reprinted with permission.

[8]Excerpts from *Curriculum Development: Theory and Practice*, pp. 11–12, by Hilda Taba, copyright ©1962 by Harcourt Brace Jovanovich, Inc. and renewed 1990 by Margaret J. Spalding, reprinted by permission of the publisher.

schools rather than by engaging initially in creating a general curriculum design. Taba, therefore, advocated an inductive approach to curriculum development, starting with specifics and building up to a general design as opposed to the more traditional deductive approach of starting with the general design and working down to the specifics.

Five-Step Sequence. Eschewing graphic exposition of her model, Taba listed a five-step sequence for accomplishing curriculum change, as follows: [9]

1. *Producing pilot units* representative of the grade level or subject area. Taba saw this step as linking theory and practice. She proposed the following eight-step sequence for curriculum developers who are producing pilot units.[10]

   a. *Diagnosis of needs.* The curriculum developer begins by determining the needs of the students for whom the curriculum is being planned. Taba directed the curriculum worker to diagnose the "gaps, deficiencies, and variations in [students'] backgrounds."[11]

   b. *Formulation of objectives.* After student needs have been diagnosed, the curriculum planner specifies objectives to be accomplished. Taba used the terms "goals" and "objectives" interchangeably, a point to which we will return later.

   c. *Selection of content.* The subject matter or topics to be studied stem directly from the objectives. Taba pointed out that not only must the objectives be considered in selecting content but also the "validity and significance." of the content chosen.[12]

   d. *Organization of content.* With the selection of content goes the task of deciding at what levels and in what sequences the subject matter will be placed. Maturity of learners, their readiness to confront the subject matter, and their levels of academic achievement are factors to be considered in the appropriate placement of content.

   e. *Selection of learning experiences.* The methodologies or strategies by which the learners become involved with the content must be chosen by the curriculum planners. Pupils internalize the content through the learning activities selected by the planner-teacher.

   f. *Organization of learning activities.* The teacher decides how to package the learning activities and in what combinations and sequences they will be utilized. At this stage the teacher adapts the strategies to the particular students for whom he or she has responsibility.

   g. *Determination of what to evaluate and of the ways and means of doing it.* The planner must decide whether objectives have been accom-

---

[9]Ibid., pp. 456–459.

[10]Ibid., pp. 345–379. On page 12 of her book Taba lists the first seven steps. See Chapter 11 of this text for a discussion of the creation of units.

[11]Taba, *Curriculum Development,* p. 12.

[12]Ibid.

plished. The instructor selects from a variety of techniques appropriate means for assessing achievement of students and for determining whether the objectives of the curriculum have been met.

   h. *Checking for balance and sequence.* Taba counseled curriculum workers to look for consistency among the various parts of the teacher-learning units, for proper flow of the learning experiences, and for balance in the types of learning and forms of expression.

2. *Testing experimental units.* Since the goal of this process is to create a curriculum encompassing one or more grade levels or subject areas and since teachers have written their pilot units with their own classrooms in mind, the units must now be tested "to establish their validity and teachability and to set their upper and lower limits of required abilities."[13]

3. *Revising and consolidating.* The units are modified to conform to variations in student needs and abilities, available resources, and different styles of teaching so that the curriculum may suit all types of classrooms. Taba would charge supervisors, the coordinators of curricula, and the curriculum specialists with the task of "stating the principles and theoretical considerations on which the structure of the units and the selection of content and learning activities are based and suggesting the limits within which modifications in the classroom can take place."[14] Taba recommended that such "considerations and suggestions might be assembled in a handbook explaining the use of the units."[15]

4. *Developing a framework.* After a number of units have been constructed, the curriculum planners must examine them as to adequacy of scope and appropriateness of sequence. The curriculum specialist would assume the responsibility of drafting a rationale for the curriculum that has been developed through this process.

5. *Installing and disseminating new units.* Taba called on administrators to arrange appropriate in-service training so that teachers may effectively put the teaching-learning units into operation in their classrooms.

Taba's inductive model may not appeal to curriculum developers who prefer to consider the more global aspects of the curriculum before proceeding to specifics. Some planners might wish to see a model that includes steps both in diagnosing the needs of society and culture and in deriving needs from subject matter, philosophy, and learning theory. Taba, however, elaborated on these points in her text.[16]

Other planners may prefer to follow a deductive approach, starting with the general—specification of philosophy, aims, and goals—and moving to the specific—objectives, instructional techniques, and evaluation. The remaining models described in this chapter are deductive.

---

[13]Ibid., p. 458.
[14]Ibid.
[15]Ibid., pp. 458–459.
[16]Ibid., Part 1.

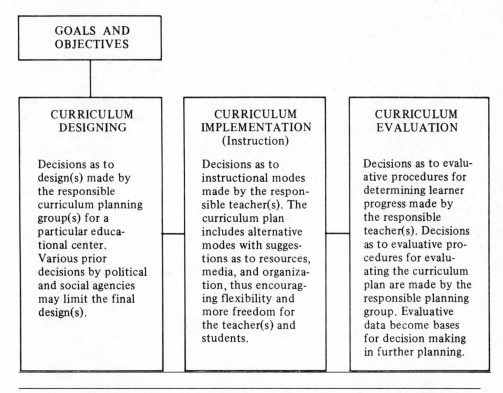

FIGURE 5–1   Saylor, Alexander, and Lewis's conception of the curriculum planning process. From J. Galen Saylor, William M. Alexander, and Arthur J. Lewis, *Curriculum Planning for Better Teaching and Learning,* 4th ed. (New York: Holt, Rinehart and Winston, 1981),p. 30. Reprinted by permission.

The Saylor, Alexander, and Lewis Model

Saylor, Alexander, and Lewis conceptualized the *curriculum planning process* in the model shown in Figure 5–1.[17] To understand this model we must first analyze their concepts of "curriculum" and "curriculum plan." Earlier in this text you encountered their definition of curriculum: "a plan for providing sets of learning opportunities for persons to be educated."[18] However, the curriculum plan is not to be conceived as a single document but rather as "many smaller plans for particular portions of the curriculum."[19]

Goals, Objectives, and Domains.   The model indicates that the curriculum planners begin by specifying the major educational goals and specific objec-

---

[17]Excerpts from *Curriculum Planning for Better Teaching and Learning*, p. 30, by J. G. Saylor and W. M. Alexander, copyright ©1954 by Holt, Rinehart and Winston, Inc. and renewed 1982 by J. G. Saylor and W. M. Alexander, reprinted by permission of the publisher.
[18]Ibid., p. 8.
[19]Ibid., p. 28.

tives they wish to be accomplished. Saylor, Alexander, and Lewis classified sets of broad goals into four domains under which many learning experiences take place: personal development, social competence, continued learning skills, and specialization.[20] Once the goals, objectives, and domains have been established, the planners move into the process of designing the curriculum. The curriculum workers decide on the appropriate learning opportunities for each domain and how and when these opportunities will be provided. For example, will the curriculum be designed along the lines of academic disciplines, according to a pattern of social institutions, or in relation to student needs and interests?

Instructional Modes. After the designs have been created—and there may be more than one—all teachers affected by a given part of the curriculum plan must create the instructional plans. They select the methods through which the curriculum will be related to the learners.[21] At this point in the model it would be helpful to introduce the term "instructional objectives." Teachers would then specify the instructional objectives before selecting the strategies or modes of presentation.

Evaluation. Finally, the curriculum planners and teachers engage in evaluation. They must choose from a wide variety of evaluation techniques. Saylor, Alexander, and Lewis proposed a design that would permit (1) evaluation of the total educational program of the school, including goals, subgoals, and objectives; the effectiveness of instruction; and the achievement of learners in specific segments of the program, as well as (2) evaluation of the evaluation program itself.[22] The evaluation processes allow curriculum planners to determine whether or not the goals of the school and the objectives of instruction have been met.

Saylor, Alexander, and Lewis supplemented their model of the curriculum planning process with companion models depicting the elements of the curriculum system, the process of defining the goals and objectives of educational institutions, and curriculum evaluation.[23] Curriculum planners might find some synthesis of the model of the curriculum planning process with its companion models desirable. We will look at the Saylor, Alexander, and Lewis model of curriculum evaluation in Chapter 13.

The Tyler Model

Perhaps the best or one of the best known models for curriculum development with special attention to the planning phases is Ralph W. Tyler's in his classic little book, *Basic Principles of Curriculum and Instruction*.[24] "The Tyler Ra-

---

[20] Ibid.
[21] Ibid., Chapter 6.
[22] Ibid., Chapter 7.
[23] Ibid., pp. 29, 165, 334.
[24] Tyler, *Basic Principles,* p. 3.

tionale," a process for selecting educational objectives, is widely known and practiced in curriculum circles. Although Tyler proposed a rather comprehensive model for curriculum development, the first part of his model (the selection of objectives) received the greatest attention from other educators.

Tyler recommended that curriculum planners identify general objectives by gathering data from three sources: the learners, contemporary life outside the school, and the subject matter. After identifying numerous general objectives, the planners refine them by filtering them through two screens: the educational and social philosophy of the school and the psychology of learning. The general objectives that successfully pass through the two screens become specific instructional objectives. In describing general objectives Tyler referred to them as "goals," "educational objectives," and "educational purposes."[25]

Student as Source.   The curriculum worker begins his or her search for educational objectives by gathering and analyzing data relevant to student needs and interests. The total range of needs—educational, social, occupational, physical, psychological, and recreational—is studied. Tyler recommended observations by teachers, interviews with students, interviews with parents, questionnaires, and tests as techniques for collecting data about students.[26] By examining the needs and interests of students, the curriculum developer identifies a set of potential objectives.

Society as Source.   Analysis of contemporary life in both the local community and in society at large is the next step in the process of formulating general objectives. Tyler suggested that curriculum planners develop a classification scheme that divides life into various aspects such as health, family, recreation, vocation, religion, consumption, and civic roles.[27] From the needs of society flow many potential educational objectives. The curriculum worker must be somewhat of a sociologist to make an intelligent analysis of needs of social institutions. After considering this second source, the curriculum worker has lengthened his or her set of objectives.

Subject Matter as Source.   For a third source the curriculum planner turns to the subject matter, the disciplines themselves. Many of the curricular innovations of the 1950s—the new math, audio-lingual foreign language programs, and the plethora of science programs—came from the subject matter specialists. From the three aforementioned sources curriculum planners derive general or broad objectives that lack precision and that I would prefer to call instructional goals. These goals may be pertinent to specific disciplines or may cut across disciplines.

Johnson held a different perspective about these sources. He commented that the "only possible source [of the curriculum] is the total available cul-

---

[25]Ibid.
[26]Ibid., pp. 12–13.
[27]Ibid., pp. 19–20.

ture" and that only organized subject matter—that is, the disciplines, not the needs and interests of learners or the values and problems of society—can be considered a source of curriculum items.[28]

Once this array of possibly applicable objectives is determined, a screening process is necessary, according to Tyler's model, to eliminate unimportant and contradictory objectives. He advised the use of the school's educational and social philosophy as the first screen for these goals.

Philosophical Screen.   Tyler advised teachers of a particular school to formulate an educational and social philosophy. He urged them to outline their values and illustrated this task by emphasizing four democratic goals:

☐ the recognition of the importance of every individual human being as a human being regardless of his race, national, social or economic status;
☐ opportunity for wide participation in all phases of activities in the social groups in the society;
☐ encouragement of variability rather than demanding a single type of personality;
☐ faith in intelligence as a method of dealing with important problems rather than depending upon the authority of an autocratic or aristocratic group.[29]

In his discussion about the formulation of an educational and social philosophy, Tyler personified the school. He talked about "the educational and social philosophy to which the school is committed," "when a school accepts these values," "many schools are likely to state," and "if the school believes."[30] Thus Tyler made of the school a dynamic, living entity. The curriculum worker will review the list of general objectives and omit those that are not in keeping with the faculty's agreed-upon philosophy.

Psychological Screen.   The application of the psychological screen is the next step in the Tyler model. To apply the screen, teachers must clarify the principles of learning that they believe to be sound. "A psychology of learning," said Tyler, "not only includes specific and definite findings but it also involves a unified formulation of a theory of learning which helps to outline the nature of the learning process, how it takes place, under what conditions, what sort of mechanisms operate and the like."[31] Effective application of this screen presupposes adequate training in educational psychology and in human growth and development by those charged with the task of curriculum development.

---

[28]Johnson, "Definitions and Models," p. 132.
[29]Tyler, *Basic Principles,* p. 34. Reprinted with permission.
[30]Ibid., pp. 33–36.
[31]Ibid., p. 41.

Tyler explained the significance of the psychological screen:

☐ A knowledge of the psychology of learning enables us to distinguish changes in human beings that can be expected to result from a learning process from those that cannot.

☐ A knowledge of the psychology of learning enables us to distinguish goals that are feasible from those that are likely to take a very long time or are almost impossible of attainment at the age level contemplated.

☐ Psychology of learning gives us some idea of the length of time required to attain an objective and the age levels at which the effort is most efficiently employed.[32]

After the curriculum planner has applied this second screen, his or her list of general objectives will be reduced, leaving those that are the most significant and feasible. Care is then taken to state the objectives in behavioral terms, which turns them into instructional, classroom objectives. We will return to the writing of behavioral objectives in Chapters 7, 8, and 10.

Tyler did not make use of a diagram in describing the process he recommended. However, W. James Popham and Eva L. Baker cast the model into the illustration shown in Figure 5–2.[33]

For some reason, discussions of the Tyler model often stop after examining the first part of his model—the rationale for selecting educational objectives. Actually, Tyler's model goes beyond this process to describe three more steps in curriculum planning: selection, organization, and evaluation of learning experiences. He defined learning experiences as "the interaction between the learner and the external conditions in the environment to which he can react."[34] He suggested teachers give attention to learning experiences

☐ that will "develop skill in thinking"
☐ that will be "helpful in acquiring information"
☐ that will be "helpful in developing social attitudes"
☐ that will be "helpful in developing interests."[35]

He explained how to organize the experiences into units and described various evaluation procedures.[36] Although Tyler did not devote a chapter to a phase called direction of learning experiences (or implementation of instruction), we can infer that instruction must take place between the selection and organization of the learning experiences and the evaluation of student achievement of these experiences.

---

[32]Ibid., pp. 38–39.
[33]W. James Popham and Eva L. Baker, *Establishing Instructional Goals* (Englewood Cliffs, N.J.: Prentice-Hall, 1970), p. 87.
[34]Tyler, *Basic Principles,* p. 63. Reprinted with permission.
[35]Ibid., Chapter 2.
[36]Ibid., Chapters 3 and 4.

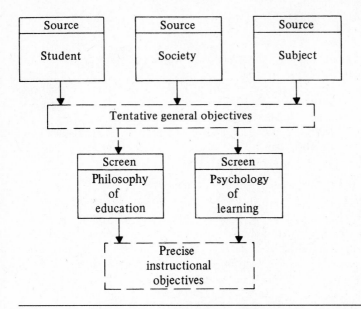

FIGURE 5–2   Tyler's curriculum rationale. Figure from W. James Popham and Eva L. Baker, *Establishing Instructional Goals* (Englewood Cliffs, N.J.: Prentice-Hall, 1970), p. 87. Based on the work of Ralph W. Tyler, *Basic Principles of Curriculum and Instruction* (Chicago: The University of Chicago Press, 1950), pp. 3–85. Reprinted by permission.

Expanded Model.   We could, therefore, modify the diagram of Tyler's model by expanding it to include steps in the planning process after specifying the instructional objectives. Figure 5–3 shows how such an expanded model might appear.

In discussing the Tyler rationale, Daniel and Laurel Tanner pointed out, "The key elements embodied in the Tyler rationale were derived from progressive educational thought during the early decades of the twentieth century."[37] One of the difficulties in the Tyler rationale, in the Tanners' view, is that Tyler presented the three sources as separate entities, not showing their interaction. If curriculum planners consider the components to be separate and fail to understand the interaction among the sources, curriculum development can become too mechanical a process. The Tanners did note, however, "To this day, Tyler's formulation is widely discussed by curriculum scholars and occupies a focal position in the field of curriculum theory."[38]

---

[37]Reprinted by permission of Macmillan Publishing Company from *Curriculum Development: Theory into Practice*, 2nd ed., p. 84, by Daniel Tanner and Laurel N. Tanner. Copyright© 1980 by MacMillan Publishing Company.

[38]Ibid.

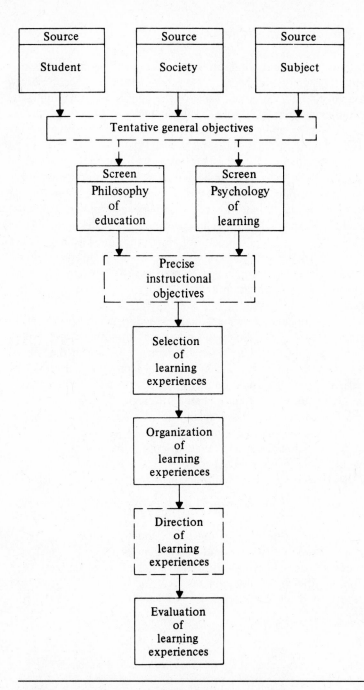

FIGURE 5–3   Tyler's curriculum rationale (expanded).

Similarities and Differences Among Models

The models discussed reveal both similarities and differences. Taba and Tyler outlined a sequence of steps to be taken in curriculum development. Saylor, Alexander, and Lewis charted the components of the curriculum development process (design, implementation, and evaluation) as opposed to actions taken by the curriculum workers (diagnosis of needs, formulation of objectives, and the like). Tyler's concepts of sources and screens stand out in his model.

Models are inevitably incomplete; they do not and cannot show every detail and every nuance of a process as complicated as curriculum development. In one sense the originator of a model is saying, sometimes in graphic form, "These are the features you should not forget." To depict every detail of the curriculum development process would require an exceedingly complex drawing or several models. One task in building a model for curriculum improvement is to determine what the most salient components in the process are—no easy task—and to limit the model to those components. Model builders find themselves between the Scylla of oversimplification and the Charybdis of complexity to the point of confusion.

In looking at various models we cannot say that any one model is inherently superior to all other models. For example, some curriculum planners have followed the Tyler model for years with considerable success. On the other hand, this success does not mean that the Tyler model represents the ultimate in models for curriculum improvement or that all educators are satisfied with it.[39] As you continue to study the complex nature of curriculum development, you will note that refinements of earlier models can be made.

Before choosing a model or designing a new model—certainly a viable alternative—curriculum planners might attempt to outline the criteria or characteristics they would look for in a model for curriculum improvement. They might agree that this model should show the following:

1. major components of the process, including stages of planning, implementation, and evaluation
2. customary, but not inflexible, "beginning" and "ending" points
3. the relationship between curriculum and instruction
4. distinctions between curricular and instructional goals and objectives
5. reciprocal relationships among components
6. a cyclical rather than a linear pattern
7. feedback lines

[39]See "Is the Tyler Rationale a suitable basis for current curriculum development?" *ASCD Update* 22, no. 6 (December 1980): 4–5. Replies to the question from Fenwick English, Dwayne Huebner, Rodgers Lewis, James Macdonald, Laurel Tanner, and Marilyn Winters. See also Herbert M. Kliebard, "Reappraisal: The Tyler Rationale," in William Pinar, ed., *Curriculum Theorizing: The Reconceptualists* (Berkeley, Calif.: McCutchan, 1975), pp. 70–83, and Herbert M. Kliebard, "The Tyler Rationale," in Arno Bellack and Herbert M. Kliebard, eds. *Curriculum and Evaluation* (Berkeley, Calif.: McCutchan, 1977), pp. 56–67. See also Walker, "Naturalistic Model."

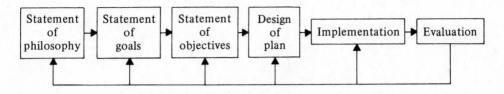

FIGURE 5–4   A model for curriculum development (Oliva, 1976)

8. the possibility of entry at any point in the cycle
9. an internal consistency and logic
10. enough simplicity to be intelligible and feasible
11. components in the form of a diagram or chart

I would agree that these are reasonable criteria to follow, and to this end, I will now propose a model incorporating these guidelines. The model will accomplish two purposes: (1) to suggest a system that curriculum planners might wish to follow and (2) to serve as the framework for explanations of phases or components of the process for curriculum improvement.

The model is not presented as the be-all and end-all of models of curriculum development but rather as an attempt to implement the aforementioned guidelines. The proposed model may be acceptable in its present form to curriculum planners, especially those who agree with a deductive, linear, and prescriptive approach. It may, at the same time, stimulate them to improve the model or to create another that would better reflect their goals, needs, and beliefs.

The Oliva Model

Some years ago I set out to chart a model for curriculum development that met three criteria: the model had to be simple, comprehensive, and systematic. The design is shown in Figure 5–4.[40] Although this model represents the most essential components, it can be readily expanded into an extended model that provides additional detail and shows some processes that the simplified model assumes. In this chapter we will look at an extended model and briefly describe its components. The subsequent chapters of Part III elaborate on each component. The extended model appears in Figure 5–5.

The Twelve Components.   The model charted in Figure 5–5 illustrates a comprehensive, step-by-step process that takes the curriculum planner from the sources of the curriculum to evaluation. In chapters 6 through 13, we will examine each part of the model. Each component (designated by Roman numerals

---

[40]Peter F. Oliva, *Supervision of Today's Schools* (New York: Harper & Row, 1976)., p. 232. Reprinted with permission.

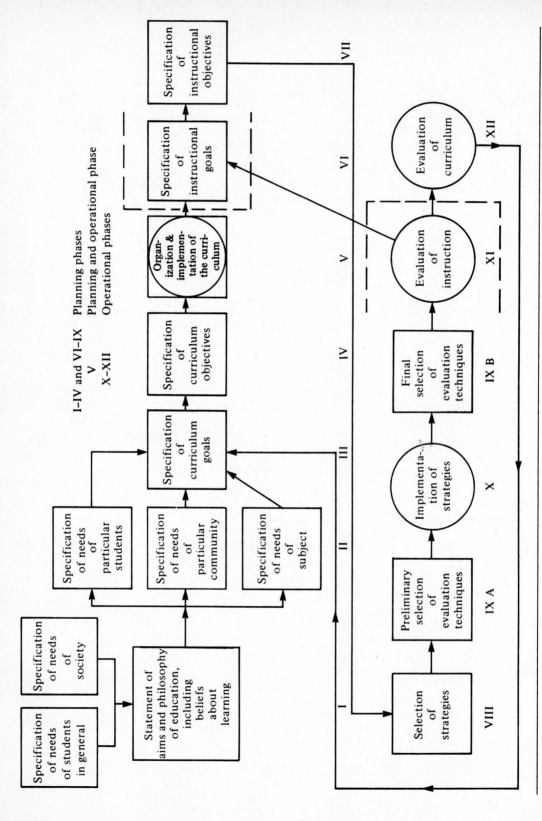

FIGURE 5–5   The Oliva model for curriculum development

I through XII) will be described, and illustrations will be given to guide curriculum planners and their co-workers. Let us now undertake a cursory overview of the model.

You will note that both squares and circles are used in the model. The squares are used to represent planning phases; the circles, operational phases. The process starts with component I, at which time the curriculum developers state the aims of education and their philosophical and psychological principles. These aims are beliefs that are derived from the needs of our society and the needs of individuals living in our society. This component incorporates concepts similar to Tyler's "screens."

Component II requires an analysis of the needs of the community in which the school is located, the needs of students served in that community, and the exigencies of the subject matter that will be taught in the given school. Sources of the curriculum are seen as cutting across components I and II. Whereas component I treats the needs of students and society in a more general sense, component II introduces the concepts of needs of particular students in particular localities because the needs of students in particular communities are not always the same as the general needs of students throughout our society.

Components III and IV call for specifying curricular goals and objectives based on the aims, beliefs, and needs specified in components I and II. A distinction that will be clarified later with examples is drawn between goals and objectives. The tasks of component V are to organize and implement the curriculum and to formulate and establish the structure by which the curriculum will be organized.

In components VI and VII an increasing level of specification is sought. Instructional goals and objectives are stated for each level and subject. Once again we will distinguish between goals and objectives and will show by illustration how the two differ.

After specifying instructional objectives, the curriculum worker moves to component VIII, at which point he or she chooses instructional strategies for use with students in the classroom. Simultaneously, the curriculum worker initiates preliminary selection of evaluation techniques, phase A of component IX. At this stage the curriculum planner thinks ahead and begins to consider ways he or she will assess student achievement. The implementation of instructional strategies—component X—follows.

After the students have been provided appropriate opportunity to learn (component X), the planner returns to the problem of selecting techniques for evaluating student achievement and the effectiveness of the instructor. Component IX, then, is separated into two phases: the first *precedes* the actual implementation of instruction (IX A) and the second *follows* the implementation (IX B). The instructional phase (component X) provides the planner with the opportunity to refine, add to, and complete the selection of means to evaluate pupil performance.

Component XI is the stage when evaluating instruction is carried out. Component XII completes the cycle with evaluation not of the student or the teacher but rather of the curricular program. In this model components I–IV and VI–IX are planning phases, whereas components X–XII are operational phases. Component V is both a planning and operational phase.

Like some other models, this model combines both a scheme for curriculum development (components I–V and XII) and a design for instruction (components VI–XI).

Important features of the model are the feedback lines that cycle back from the evaluation of the curriculum to the curriculum goals and from the evaluation of instruction to the instructional goals. These lines indicate the necessity of continuous revision of the components of their respective sub-cycles.

Use of the Model.   The model can be used in a variety of ways. First, the model offers a process for the complete development of a school's curriculum. The faculty of each special area—for example, language arts—can, by following the model, fashion a plan for the curriculum of that area and design ways in which it will be carried out through instruction, or the faculty may develop school-wide, interdisciplinary programs that cut across areas of specialization such as career education, guidance, and extraclass activities.

Second, a faculty may focus on the curricular components of the model (components I–V and XII) to make programmatic decisions. Third, a faculty may concentrate on the instructional components (VI–XI).

Two Submodels.   This 12-phase model integrates a general model for curriculum development with a general model for instruction. Components I–V and XII constitute a curriculum development submodel which I will refer to as the curriculum submodel. Components VI–XI constitute an instructional submodel. To distinguish between the curricular and instructional components, I have enclosed the instructional submodel within broken lines.

When the curricular submodel is followed, the curriculum planners must keep in mind that the task has not been completed until the curricular goals and objectives are subsequently translated by them or others into instruction. Furthermore, when the instructional submodel is followed, the instructional planners must be aware of the curriculum goals and objectives of the school as a whole or of a given subject area or areas.

In order to keep the model as uncluttered as possible at this point I have not attempted to show all the nuances of the model. At several places in subsequent chapters certain refinements and embellishments of the model will be described.

For those who prefer a model in the form of steps instead of a diagram, I have provided a listing of the steps in Figure 5–5. The model recommends the following steps:

1. Specify the needs of students in general.
2. Specify the needs of society.

3. Write a statement of philosophy and aims of education.
4. Specify the needs of students in your school.
5. Specify the needs of the particular community.
6. Specify the needs of the subject matter.
7. Specify the curriculum goals of your school.
8. Specify the curricular objectives of your school.
9. Organize and implement the curriculum.
10. Specify instructional goals.
11. Specify instructional objectives.
12. Select instructional strategies.
13. Begin selection of evaluation strategies.
14. Implement instructional strategies.
15. Make final selection of evaluation strategies.
16. Evaluate instruction and modify instructional components.
17. Evaluate the curriculum and modify curricular components.

Steps 1–9 and 17 constitute a curriculum submodel; steps 10–16, an instructional submodel.

SUMMARY

Four models of curriculum development are presented in this chapter. Models can help us to conceptualize a process by showing certain principles and procedures. Whereas some models are in the form of diagrams, others are lists of steps that are recommended to curriculum workers. Some models are linear, step-by-step approaches; others allow for departure from a fixed sequence of steps. Some models offer an inductive approach, and others follow a deductive approach. Some are prescriptive; others, descriptive.

Those who take leadership in curriculum development are encouraged to become familiar with various models, to try them out, and to select or develop the model that is most understandable and feasible to them and to the persons with whom they are working.

I have presented for consideration a model consisting of 12 components. This model is comprehensive in nature, encompassing both curricular and instructional development.

QUESTIONS FOR DISCUSSION

1. On what bases would you choose a model for curriculum development?
2. Who should decide which model for curriculum development to follow?

3. In your opinion which is better: an inductive or a deductive model for curriculum development?

4. What are the strengths and limitations of a linear model for curriculum development?

5. In your opinion which is better: a prescriptive or descriptive model for curriculum development?

SUPPLEMENTARY EXERCISES

1. Define "sources" and "screens" as used by Ralph W. Tyler.

2. Explain why Tyler's model has been referred to as "linear" in nature and identify the presence or absence of linearity in each of the other models.

3. Write a brief position paper, giving reasons for your position, on the question: "Is the Tyler Rationale a suitable basis for current curriculum development?"

4. Cast Taba's steps for curriculum development into a diagrammed model.

5. Identify one or more domains in addition to the four suggested by Saylor, Alexander, and Lewis, or, alternatively, design your own pattern of domains.

6. Explain the meaning of the broken lines in the diagram of the Oliva model.

7. Explain why components X, XI, and XII of the Oliva model are shown as circles whereas the other components, except for component V, are shown as squares. Explain why component V is depicted with both a square and a circle.

8. Describe the four models of curriculum planning found in Geneva Gay's chapter in the 1980 Yearbook of the Association for Supervision and Curriculum Development (see bibliography). These models are the academic model, the experiential model, the technical model, and the pragmatic model.

9. Summarize George A. Beauchamp's concept of curriculum engineering (see bibliography).

10. Find or design a nonlinear model for curriculum development. For one example, see Mario Leyton Soto and Ralph W. Tyler, *Planeamiento Educacional* (listed in bibliography). This model is discussed in Peter F. Oliva, *Developing the Curriculum*, Little, Brown and Company, 1982, pp. 159, 161–162.

11. Define curriculum engineering as used by Robert S. Zais (see bibliography) and report on one of the following models for curriculum engineering discussed by Zais:
    a. The Administrative (Line-Staff) Model
    b. The Grass-Roots Model

    c. The Demonstration Model

    d. George Beauchamp's System

    e. Carl Rogers' Interpersonal Relations Model

12. Robert M. Gagné maintains that there is no such step in curriculum development as "selection of content" (see bibliography). State whether you agree and give reasons, citing quotes from the literature that support your position.

13. Describe the model of curricular and instructional planning and evaluation proposed by Mauritz Johnson, Jr., in *Intentionality in Education* (see bibliography).

14. Describe the Generic Curriculum Planning Model presented by Arthur W. Steller (see bibliography).

15. Describe the curriculum development models presented by Jerry J. Bellon and Janet R. Handler; H. H. Giles, S. P. McCutchen, and A. N. Zechiel; Francis P. Hunkins; George J. Posner and Alan N. Rudnitsky; David Pratt; and Decker F. Walker (see bibliography).

16. Report on any model for curriculum development described by John P. Miller and Wayne Seller that is different from the models described in this chapter (see bibliography).

17. Report on the curriculum planning model described by Weldon F. Zenger and Sharon K. Zenger (see bibliography) and tell how it differs from the models described in this chapter.

BIBLIOGRAPHY

Beauchamp, George A. *Curriculum Theory,* 4th ed. Itasca, Ill.: F. E. Peacock, 1981.

Bellon, Jerry J. and Handler, Janet R. *Curriculum Development and Evaluation: A Design for Improvement.* Dubuque, Iowa: Kendall/Hunt, 1982.

Bloom, Benjamin S., ed. *Taxonomy of Educational Objectives: The Classification of Educational Goals: Handbook I: Cognitive Domain.* New York: Longman, 1956.

Foshay, Arthur W., ed. *Considered Action for Curriculum Improvement,* 1980 Yearbook. Alexandria, Va.: Association for Supervision and Curriculum Development, 1980.

Gagné, Robert M. "Curriculum Research and the Promotion of Learning." *Per-spectives of Curriculum Evaluation,* AERA Monograph Series on Evaluation, no. 1, 19–23. Chicago: Rand McNally, 1967.

Gay, Geneva. "Conceptual Models of the Curriculum-Planning Process." In *Considered Action for Curriculum Improvement,* 1980 Yearbook, 120–143. Alexandria, Va.: Association for Supervision and Curriculum Development, 1980.

Giles, H. H., McCutchen, S. P., and Zechiel, A. N. *Exploring the Curriculum.* New York: Harper, 1942.

Golby, Michael, Greenwald, Jane, and West, Ruth, eds. *Curriculum Design.* London: Croom Helm in association with the Open University Press, 1965.

Herrick, Virgil E. and Tyler, Ralph W., eds. *Toward Improved Curriculum Theory.* Papers presented at the Conference on Curriculum Theory, University of Chicago, 1947. Chicago: University of Chicago Press, 1950.

Hunkins, Francis P. *Curriculum Improvement: Program Improvement.* Columbus, Ohio: Charles E. Merrill, 1980.

Johnson, Mauritz, Jr. "Definitions and Models in Curriculum Theory," *Educational Theory* 17, no. 2 (April 1967): 127–140.

———. *Intentionality in Education.* Albany, N.Y.: Center for Curriculum Research and Services, 1977.

Krathwohl, David R., Bloom, Benjamin S., and Masia, Bertram B. *Taxonomy of Educational Objectives: The Classification of Educational Goals: Handbook II: Affective Domain.* New York: Longman, 1964.

Leyton Soto, Mario and Tyler, Ralph W. *Planeamiento Educacional.* Santiago, Chile: Editorial Universitaria, 1969.

McNeil, John D. *Curriculum Administration: Principles and Techniques of Curriculum Development.* New York: Macmillan, 1965.

———. *Designing Curriculum: Self-Instructional Modules.* Boston: Little, Brown, 1976.

Miller, John P. and Seller, Wayne. *Curriculum: Perspectives and Practice,* Chapter 9. White Plains, N.Y.: Longman, 1985.

Nicholls, Audrey and Nicholls, S. Howard. *Developing a Curriculum: A Practical Guide,* 2nd ed. London: George Allen & Unwin, 1978.

Oliva, Peter F. *Supervision for Today's Schools,* Part 3. 1st ed., New York: Harper & Row, 1976; 3rd ed., White Plains, N.Y.: Longman, 1989.

Popham, W. James. *Evaluating Instruction.* Englewood Cliffs, N.J.: Prentice-Hall, 1973.

Posner, George J. and Rudnitsky, Alan N. *Course Design: A Guide to Curriculum Development for Teachers,* 3rd ed. White Plains, N.Y.: Longman, 1986.

Pratt, David. *Curriculum Design and Development.* New York: Harcourt Brace Jovanovich, 1980.

Saylor, J. Galen, Alexander, William M., and Lewis, Arthur J. *Curriculum Planning for Better Teaching and Learning,* 4th ed. New York: Holt, Rinehart and Winston, 1981.

Schaffarzick, Jon and Hampson, David H., eds. *Strategies for Curriculum Development.* Berkeley, Calif.: McCutchan, 1975.

Steller, Arthur W., "Curriculum Planning," in Fenwick W. English, ed., *Fundamental Curriculum Decisions,* 1983 Yearbook, 68–89. Alexandria, Va.: Association for Supervision and Curriculum Development, 1983.

Taba, Hilda. *Curriculum Development: Theory and Practice.* New York: Harcourt Brace Jovanovich, 1962.

Tanner, Daniel and Tanner, Laurel N. *Curriculum Development: Theory into Practice,* 2nd ed. New York: Macmillan, 1980.

Tyler, Ralph W. *Basic Principles of Curriculum and Instruction.* Chicago: University of Chicago Press, 1949.

Unruh, Glenys G. *Responsive Curriculum: Theory and Action.* Berkeley, Calif.: McCutchan, 1975.

Walker, Decker F. "A Naturalistic Model for Curriculum Development." *School Review* 80, no. 1 (November 1971): 51–67.

Zais, Robert S. *Curriculum: Principles and Foundations,* Chapter 19. New York: Harper & Row, 1976.

Zenger, Weldon F. and Zenger, Sharon K. "Planning for Curriculum Development: A Model for Administrators." *NASSP Bulletin* 68, no. 471 (April 1984): 17–28.

FILMSTRIP–AUDIOTAPE PROGRAM

A Curriculum Rationale. 1969. Vimcet Associates, P.O. Box 24714, Los Angeles, Calif. 90024.

CHAPTER SIX

Philosophy and Aims of Education

After studying this chapter you should be able to:

1. Explain how aims of education are derived.
2. Cite commonly voiced statements of the aims of education.
3. Write statements of the aims of education.
4. Outline major beliefs of four well-known schools of philosophy.
5. Draft a school philosophy that could be submitted to a school faculty for discussion.

USING THE PROPOSED MODEL

A comprehensive model for the process of curriculum development, consisting of twelve phases of components, was presented in Chapter 5. For a moment, let's take another look at it (see Figure 5–5, p. 172), and then I'll underscore some of its characteristics.

Examining the model reveals the following special characteristics:

1. *The model flows from the most general (aims of education) to the most specific (evaluation techniques).* Beginning here and in the remaining chapters of Part III, I will describe each component and define its terms in such a way as to show this flow.

2. *The model can be followed by curriculum planning groups (or even to some extent by individuals) in whole or in part.* The model allows for a comprehensive, holistic study of the curriculum. Given the many demands on the time of teachers, administrators, and others, it is likely that a complete look at the curriculum from the aims of education (component I) to evaluation of the curriculum (component XII) will be carried out only periodically. Although somewhat arbitrary, reassessment and revision of the various phases might be considered on the following schedule:

BOX 6–1

SUGGESTED SCHEDULE FOR REASSESSING CURRICULUM DEVELOPMENT COMPONENTS

Aims of education	In depth: Limited:	every 10 years every 5 years
Assessment of needs	In depth: Limited:	every 3 years every year
Curriculum goals	In depth: Limited:	every 2 years every year
Curriculum objectives	In depth: Limited:	every 2 years every year
Instructional goals	In depth: Limited:	every year continuously
Instructional objectives	In depth: Limited:	every year continuously
Organization and implementation of the curriculum	In depth: Limited:	every 10 years every year
Other components	Continuously	

Faculties may wish to set their own schedules for considering the various components. Those components that are closest to the faculty, involve fewer persons, are more easily manageable, and are less costly in time and money might be reassessed with greater frequency than those components that are more remote, involve many persons, are more difficult to manage, and are more costly.

3. *A single curriculum group, like the curriculum committee of an individual school, department, or grade, will not carry out all phases of the model by itself.* Various groups, subgroups, and individuals will assume responsibility for different parts of the model. One group (for example, the school's curriculum council) may work on the first component, the aims of education. A subgroup may conduct a needs assessment and study the derivation of curricular needs. The school's curriculum council may attempt to define school-wide curriculum goals and objectives while committees within the various disciplines identify curriculum goals and objectives within particular fields. Individual faculty members and groups in various grades and departments will be engaged in specifying instructional goals and objectives. Decisions at any phase that have relevance to the entire school may be presented to the total faculty for its information and support or rejection. Throughout the process, decisions made by any of the subgroups must be shared so that relationships among the various components are clearly understood. In this respect the curriculum council of the school will serve as a coordinating body.

4. *With modifications, the model can be followed at any level or sector of curriculum planning.* Parts of the model may also be applied at the various levels and sectors that were discussed in Chapter 3.

AIMS OF EDUCATION

Proliferation of Terms

The educational literature uses a proliferation of terms, rather loosely and often interchangeably, to signify terminal expectations of education. Educators speak of "outcomes," "aims," "ends," "purposes," "functions," "goals," and "objectives." Although these terms may be used synonymously in common language, it is helpful if distinctions are made in pedagogical language.

In this book the term "outcome" applies to terminal expectations generally. "Aims" are equated with "ends," "purposes," "functions," and "universal goals." The aims of education are the very broad, general statements of the purposes of education; they are meant to give general direction to education throughout the country.

In this text "curriculum goals," "curriculum objectives," "instructional goals," and "instructional objectives" are separate entities of special relevance to the local school or school system. Curriculum goals are defined as general, programmatic expectations without criteria of achievement or mastery, whereas curriculum objectives are specific, programmatic targets with criteria of achievement and, therefore, are measurable. The curriculum objectives stem from the curriculum goals.[1] Both curriculum goals and curriculum objectives trace their sources to the school's philosophy and the statement of aims of education.

Instructional goals are statements of instructional targets in general, nonobservable terms without criteria of achievement, whereas instructional objectives are expected learner behaviors formulated, with possible exceptions for those in the affective domain, in measurable and observable terms.[2] Instructional objectives are derived from instructional goals, and both instructional goals and instructional objectives originate from the curriculum goals and objectives.

The aims of education have special relevance to the nation as a whole. We will talk about aims of our educational system, society, and country. Presumably, in former days we could have set forth regional aims for the North, South, Midwest, and West. In the fast-approaching twenty-first century, however, it would seem an anachronism to promote regional aims as if the broad purposes of education in California, for example, were different from those in New York.

GLOBAL AIMS

It is possible, even desirable, to define aims of education on a global scale, and sometimes such definitions are attempted. The United Nations Educational, Scientific, and Cultural Organization (UNESCO) is the foremost exponent of attempts on a worldwide scale to state aims of education for humanity. Among the aims of education that UNESCO seeks to promote are these:

☐ fostering international understanding among all peoples of the world
☐ improving the standard of living of people in the various countries
☐ solving continuing problems that plague humanity, such as war, disease, hunger, and unemployment.

Similar organizations, such as the Organization of American States, are also concerned with the aims of education on an international scale. The few Americans who participate in such organizations find some opportunity for expressing aims of education that can apply across national boundaries. More common are statements of aims of education by the respective nations of the world to guide the development of their own educational systems.

[1]See Chapter 8 for discussion of curriculum goals and objectives.
[2]See Chapter 10 for discussion of instructional goals and objectives.

In any discipline, the field of curriculum notwithstanding, the specialist seeks to find or develop generalizations or rules that apply in most situations. On the other hand, the specialist must always be aware that exceptions may be found to most rules. Although we may hold to the view that curriculum development is a group process and is more effective as a result of that process, we must admit that individuals can carry out any of the components of the suggested model of curriculum development. It would seem at first sight, for example, that defining aims of education to which the entire country might subscribe would certainly be a group project. However, as we will see, several significant statements of aims of education have been made over the years by prominent individuals. When statements are generated by individuals instead of groups, members of the social structure for which the aims were intended become, in effect, consumers and interpreters of the ideas of the individuals— certainly a tenable procedure.

That statements of aims, goals, and objectives may originate from individuals rather than groups should not invalidate them. It might be said that "While individuals propose, the group will dispose." Groups should react to coherent statements in a deliberative manner. The model of curriculum development should not be construed to eliminate spontaneous, individual efforts at curriculum development. Some of the most successful innovations in schools have been effected as the result of the work of independently motivated mavericks on the school's staff.

STATEMENTS OF PURPOSES

We are confronted with aims of education when we read various societies' statements of purposes:

- □ to inculcate adult values in the behavior of the young
- □ to prepare youth to fit into a planned society
- □ to promote free enterprise
- □ to further the glorious revolution
- □ to create citizens who will serve the fatherland
- □ to prepare an enlightened citizenry
- □ to nurture the Islamic heritage
- □ to correct social ills
- □ to promote the Judeo-Christian heritage

We encounter aims of education in a descriptive form when someone makes declarations like the following:

- □ Education is life, not preparation for life.
- □ Education is the molding of the young to the values of the old.
- □ Education is the transmission of the cultural heritage.
- □ Education is vocational training.

☐ Education is the liberal arts.
☐ Education is training in socialization.
☐ Education is intellectual development.
☐ Education is personal development.

We can even find implied aims of education in slogans like these:

☐ If you think education is expensive, try ignorance.
☐ If you can read this sign, thank a teacher.

Presumably ever since primitive peoples discovered that the flint axe was more effective for killing game than a wooden club, that animal skins protected their bodies against the elements, and that roast boar was superior to raw, they continually discussed what training they must provide their Neanderthal young so that they could cope with their environment. In their own primitive way they must have dealt with the heady topic of the purposes of education in Neanderthal land.

Today, many thousand years later, people still affirm coping with the environment as a central purpose of education. The common term to express this purpose is "survival skills." Instead of learning survival skills like stalking a gazelle, frightening a tiger, and spearing a fish, today's children and youth must master the basic skills, learn to conserve resources, learn to live on a more densely populated planet, and know how to earn a legitimate living. Sometimes, as has been the case throughout the history of humankind, the martial arts become survival skills. Not only do the martial arts become a priority when a nation is confronted by an enemy from beyond its borders, but it is an unfortunate commentary on today's civilization that many children (along with their parents) are flocking to self-defense classes so that they can protect themselves from predators on the streets of many urban areas.

Derivation of Aims

The aims of education are derived from examining the needs of children and youth in our American society, from analyzing our culture, and from studying the various needs of our society. Given the historic development of nations with their own institutions, mores, and values, and often their own language, no two countries exhibit exactly the same needs. One does not have to be an anthropologist to recognize that the needs of Japanese, Chinese, Russian, English, Mexican, or Tahitian youngsters are not identical to those of American youth. The automobile, for example, has become a "need" of American high school youth if we judge by the school parking lots crammed with vehicles of students. A high school student, when asked how he could continue to afford the rising cost of gasoline, averred that he would buy it no matter what the cost because the automobile was a part of his "lifestyle."

Few countries have such a heterogeneous population as the United States. A comment often heard about people in the Sun Belt cities of America, "Everybody here is from someplace else," might be extended to America in toto. We are a nation of immigrants who have brought, as some say, both the best and worst traits of the societies that we left. We cannot even claim the American Indians, who were here first, as indigenous to America, for theory holds that they themselves migrated out of Asia across the Bering Strait.

Such heterogeneity makes it extremely difficult to reach consensus on aims of education and particularly on values central to aims. Many years ago the National Education Association attempted to identify moral and spiritual values that it believed should be taught in the public schools.[3] They listed the following ten values:

1. human personality
2. moral responsibility
3. institutions as the servants of men
4. common consent
5. devotion to truth
6. respect of excellence
7. moral equality
8. brotherhood
9. the pursuit of happiness
10. spiritual enrichment

The assumption was made that these are common values held by a majority of the people of the society at that particular time. On how many of these values could we still reach consensus? In 1991 James Patterson and Peter Kim surveyed the current status of Americans' adherence to moral values and found a pronounced absence of consensus on values. Some of the beliefs and behaviors revealed by this study run counter to the more traditional conception of moral and spiritual values.[4] The specter of indoctrination has loomed so large that educators are often hesitant to identify broad-based, common, secular values to which Americans as a whole can subscribe. Less concerned about indoctrination than about the absence of moral education, the National Conference of Catholic Bishops and the Synagogue Council of America issued a joint report in the spring of 1990 in which they advocated a new effort on the part of the public schools to teach shared moral values.[5]

Salad Bowl Versus Melting Pot. As our heterogeneous population reveals plural rather than common values, the "salad bowl" concept now challenges

---

[3]Educational Policies Commission, *Moral and Spiritual Values in the Public Schools* (Washington, D.C.: National Education Association, 1951), pp. 17–34. Adapted with permission.

[4]James Patterson and Peter Kim, *The Day America Told the Truth: What People Really Think About Everthing That Really Matters* (New York: Prentice-Hall Press, 1991).

[5]See press report, *The New York Times*, June 20, 1990: A12.

the old "melting pot" idea. Some people argue that since few, if any, common values exist in our society, we should no longer strive to assimilate values but should collect and assemble the diverse values in a saladlike concoction that preserves the essence of each (like a tasty fruit salad, for example).[6] If we make this dilemma an either/or question, we create a false dichotomy. We need the salad bowl concept to preserve the values on which Americans are divided, such as materialistic versus nonmaterialistic goals, pro-choice versus "right to life," pro-ERA versus anti-ERA, and sectarian versus secular goals. On the other hand, we need the melting pot concept to preserve fundamental, overarching values that promote the welfare of all.[7]

In recent years the salad bowl/melting pot controversy has intensified. Whether to promote multicultural values or common values of American society is a highly charged contemporary issue both in public schools and on college campuses. We will return to this issue in chapter 14. As we examine statements of aims of education, we soon discover that these statements are, in effect, philosophical positions based on some set of values and are derived from an analysis of society and its children and youth.

Statements by Prominent Individuals and Groups

To gain a perception of statements of educational aims, let's sample a few of the better known ones proffered by various individuals and groups over the years. In 1916 John Dewey described the functions of education in a number of ways, including its socialization of the child and its facilitation of personal growth.[8] Putting these concepts into the form of aims of education, we could say that, according to Dewey, the aims of education are (1) to socialize the young, thereby transforming both the young and the society, and (2) to develop the individual in all his or her physical, mental, moral, and emotional capacities.

Dewey made it clear that the school is an agency for socializing the child:

> I believe that all education proceeds by the participation of the individual in the social consciousness of the race . . . the only true education comes through the stimulation of the child's powers by the demands of the social situations in which he finds himself. . . . this educational process has two sides— one psychological and one sociological—and that neither can be subordinated to the other, or neglected, without evil results following. Of these two sides, the psychological is the basis . . . knowledge of social conditions, of the present state of civilization, is necessary in order properly to interpret the child's pow-

---

[6]See Theodore R. Sizer, "Education and Assimilation: A Fresh Plea for Pluralism," *Phi Delta Kappan* 58, no. 1 (September 1976): 31–35.

[7]See Richard Mitchell, *The Leaning Tower of Babel and Other Affronts by the Underground Grammarian* (Boston: Little, Brown, 1984), pp. 113–116.

[8]John Dewey, *Democracy and Education: An Introduction to the Philosophy of Education* (New York: Macmillan, 1916; New York: Free Press, 1966), Chapters 2 and 4.

ers. . . . In sum, I believe that the individual who is to be educated is a social individual, and that society is an organic union of individuals. . . . I believe that the school is primarily a social institution.[9]

Dewey elaborated on his conception of education as growth in the following terms:

> One net conclusion is that life is development, and that developing, growing, is life. Translated into its educational equivalents, that means (*i*) that the educational process has no end beyond itself; it is its own end; and that (*ii*) the educational process is one of continual reorganizing, reconstructing, transforming. . . . Normal child and normal adult alike, in other words, are engaged in growing. . . . Since in reality there is nothing to which growth is relative save more growth, there is nothing to which education is subordinate save more education.[10]

The National Education Association's Commission on the Reorganization of Secondary Education in 1918 spoke to the role of education in our democratic society in this way: "Education in a democracy, both within and without the school, should develop in each individual the knowledge, interests, ideals, habits, and powers whereby he will find his place and use that place to shape both himself and society toward even nobler ends."[11]

The Educational Policies Commission of the National Education Association in 1937 related the aim of education to democracy as follows:

> In any realistic definition of education for the United States, therefore, must appear the whole philosophy and practice of democracy. Education cherishes and inculcates its moral values, disseminates knowledge necessary to its functioning, spreads information relevant to its institutions and economy, keeps alive the creative and sustaining spirit without which the letter is dead.[12]

In 1943—in the midst of the Second World War—James B. Conant, president of Harvard University, appointed a committee of professors from the fields of education and the liberal arts and sciences to examine the place of general (i.e., required, liberal) education in American society. The Harvard Committee on General Education took the position that the aim of education was "to prepare an individual to become an expert both in some particular vocation or art and in the general art of the free man and the citizen."[13] To accomplish this aim the Harvard committee recommended a prescribed set of subjects, in-

---

[9]John Dewey, *My Pedagogic Creed* (Washington, D.C.: Progressive Education Association, 1929), pp. 3–6.

[10]Dewey, *Democracy and Education,* pp. 59–60.

[11]Commission on the Reorganization of Secondary Education, *Cardinal Principles of Secondary Education* (Washington, D.C.: United States Office of Education, Bulletin 35, 1918), p. 9.

[12]Educational Policies Commission, *The Unique Function of Education in American Democracy* (Washington, D.C.: National Education Association, 1937), p. 89.

[13]Harvard Committee on General Education, *General Education in a Free Society* (Cambridge, Mass.: Harvard University Press, 1945), p. 54.

cluding English, science, mathematics, and the social studies for all secondary school pupils.[14]

Statements of aims of education repeatedly address great themes like democracy and the progress of humanity. In 1961 the National Education Association's Educational Policies Commission elaborated on the role of education in solving the problems of humanity:

> Many profound changes are occurring in the world today, but there is a fundamental force contributing to all of them. That force is the expanding role accorded in modern life to the rational powers of man. By using these powers to increase his knowledge, man is attempting to solve the riddles of life, space, and time which have long intrigued him.[15]

Before the Committee on Appropriations of the United States House of Representatives of the Eighty-Seventh Congress in 1962, Vice-Admiral Hyman G. Rickover, generally acknowledged as the father of the nuclear submarine, testified on distinctions between American and British educational systems and formulated for the committee the aims of education as he saw them:

> The school's major objective should be to send its graduates into the world equipped with the knowledge they will need to live successfully, hence happily. . . . A school system performs its proper task when it does a first-rate job of equipping children with the requisite knowledge and intellectual skill for successful living in a complex modern society. . . . There is general agreement abroad that a school must accomplish three difficult tasks: First, it must transmit to the pupil a substantial body of knowledge; second, it must develop in him the necessary intellectual skill to apply this knowledge to the problems he will encounter in adult life; and third, it must inculcate in him the habit of judging issues on the basis of verified fact and logical reasoning.[16]

Mortimer J. Adler expressed the aims of education and schooling as follows: "The ultimate goal of the educational process is to help human beings become educated persons. Schooling is the preparatory stage; it forms the habit of learning and provides the means for continuing to learn after all schooling is completed."[17]

John I. Goodlad addressed the themes of social purposes served by the schools, educational goals and aims, and school goals. He divided the school goals into four categories: academic, vocational, social and civic, and personal. He and his colleagues analyzed approximately a hundred goals from various

---

[14]Ibid., pp 99–100.

[15]Educational Policies Commission, *The Central Purpose of American Education* (Washington, D.C.: National Education Association, 1961), p. 89.

[16]H. G. Rickover, *Education for All Children: What We Can Learn From England: Hearings Before the Committee on Appropriations, House of Representatives, Eighty-Seventh Congress, Second Session* (Washington, D.C.: U.S. Government Printing Office, 1962), pp. 14, 17, 18.

[17]Mortimer J. Adler, *The Paideia Proposal: An Educational Manifesto* (New York: Macmillan, 1982), p. 10.

sources and refined them into a list of 12 which they saw as generally accepted goals for schooling in the United States. These are as follows:

GOALS FOR SCHOOLING IN THE U.S.

A. Academic Goals
  1. Mastery of basic skills and fundamental processes
    1.1 Learn to read, write, and handle basic arithmetical operations.
    1.2 Learn to acquire ideas through reading and listening.
    1.3 Learn to communicate ideas through writing and speaking.
    1.4 Learn to utilize mathematical concepts.
    1.5 Develop the ability to utilize available sources of information.
  2. Intellectual development
    2.1 Develop the ability to think rationally, including problem-solving skills, application of principles of logic, and skill in using different modes of inquiry.
    2.2 Develop the ability to use and evaluate knowledge, i.e., critical and independent thinking that enables one to make judgments and decisions in a wide variety of life roles—citizen, consumer, worker, etc.—as well as in intellectual activities.
    2.3 Accumulate a general fund of knowledge, including information and concepts in mathematics, literature, natural science, and social science.
    2.4 Develop positive attitudes toward intellectual activity, including curiosity and a desire for further learning.
    2.5 Develop an understanding of change in society.

B. Vocational Goals
  3. Career education-vocational education:
    3.1 Learn how to select an occupation that will be personally satisfying and suitable to one's skills and interests.
    3.2 Learn to make decisions based on an awareness and knowledge of career options.
    3.3 Learn salable skills and specialized knowledge that will prepare one to become economically independent.
    3.4 Learn habits and attitudes, such as pride in good workmanship, that will make one a productive participant in economic life.
    3.5 Learn positive attitudes toward work, including acceptance of the necessity of making a living and an appreciation of the social value and dignity of work.

C. Social, Civic, and Cultural Goals
  4. Interpersonal understandings
    4.1 Develop a knowledge of opposing value systems and their influence on the individual and society.
    4.2 Develop an understanding of how members of a family function under different family patterns as well as within one's own family.
    4.3 Develop skill in communicating effectively in groups.
    4.4 Develop the ability to identify with and advance the goals and concerns of others.

4.5   Learn to form productive and satisfying relations with others based on respect, trust, cooperation, consideration, and caring.
4.6   Develop a concern for humanity and an understanding of international relations.
4.7   Develop an understanding and appreciation of cultures different from one's own.

5. Citizenship participation
5.1   Develop historical perspective.
5.2   Develop knowledge of the basic workings of the government.
5.3   Develop a willingness to participate in the political life of the nation and the community.
5.4   Develop a commitment to the values of liberty, government by consent of the governed, representational government, and one's responsibility for the welfare of all.
5.5   Develop an understanding of the interrelationships among complex organizations and agencies in a modern society, and learn to act in accordance with it.
5.6   Exercise the democratic right to dissent in accordance with personal conscience.
5.7   Develop economic and consumer skills necessary for making informed choices that enhance one's quality of life.
5.8   Develop an understanding of the basic interdependence of the biological and physical resources of the environment.
5.9   Develop the ability to act in light of this understanding of interdependence.

6. Enculturation
6.1   Develop insight into the values and characteristics, including language, of the civilization of which one is a member.
6.2   Develop an awareness and understanding of one's cultural heritage and become familiar with the achievements of the past that have inspired and influenced humanity.
6.3   Develop understanding of the manner in which traditions from the past are operative today and influence the direction and values of society.
6.4   Understand and adopt the norms, values, and traditions of the groups of which one is a member.
6.5   Learn how to apply the basic principles and concepts of the fine arts and humanities to the appreciation of the aesthetic contributions of other cultures.

7. Moral and ethical character
7.1   Develop the judgment to evaluate events and phenomena as good or evil.
7.2   Develop a commitment to truth and values.
7.3   Learn to utilize values in making choices.
7.4   Develop moral integrity.
7.5   Develop an understanding of the necessity for moral conduct.

D. Personal Goals

8. Emotional and physical well-being

    8.1 Develop the willingness to receive emotional impressions and to expand one's affective sensitivity.

    8.2 Develop the competence and skills for continuous adjustment and emotional stability, including coping with social change.

    8.3 Develop a knowledge of one's own body and adopt health practices that support and sustain it, including avoiding the consumption of harmful or addictive substances.

    8.4 Learn to use leisure time effectively.

    8.5 Develop physical fitness and recreational skills.

    8.6 Develop the ability to engage in constructive self-criticism.

9. Creativity and aesthetic expression

    9.1 Develop the ability to deal with problems in original ways.

    9.2 Develop the ability to be tolerant of new ideas.

    9.3 Develop the ability to be flexible and to consider different points of view.

    9.4 Develop the ability to experience and enjoy different forms of creative expression.

    9.5 Develop the ability to evaluate various forms of aesthetic expression.

    9.6 Develop the willingness and ability to communicate through creative work in an active way.

    9.7 Seek to contribute to cultural and social life through one's artistic, vocational, and avocational interests.

10. Self-realization

    10.1 Learn to search for meaning in one's activities, and develop a philosophy of life.

    10.2 Develop the self-confidence necessary for knowing and confronting one's self.

    10.3 Learn to assess realistically and live with one's limitations and strengths.

    10.4 Recognize that one's self-concept is developed in interaction with other people.

    10.5 Develop skill in making decisions with purpose.

    10.6 Learn to plan and organize the environment in order to realize one's goals.

    10.7 Develop willingness to accept responsibility for one's own decisions and their consequences.

    10.8 Develop skill in selecting some personal, life-long learning goals and the means to attain them.[18]

---

[18]From *A Place Called School: Prospects for the Future* by John I. Goodlad. Copyright©1984 by McGraw-Hill. Used with the permission of McGraw-Hill Book Company. An earlier version of "Goals for Schooling in the U.S." appeared in John I. Goodlad, *What Schools Are For* (Bloomington, Ind.: Phi Delta Kappa Educational Foundation, 1979), pp. 46–52.

In Chapter 9 you will encounter additional beliefs about the aims of education when we examine some of the recommendations made during the 1980s for reform of the schools.

Perhaps the most influential recent statement of aims was issued by President George Bush and the National Governors' Association. In September 1989 at the University of Virginia, the president and the governors' association developed a statement of six performance goals. The president presented this statement to the nation in his State of the Union address in January 1990. The six goals postulated that by the year 2000:

- All American children will start school ready to learn.
- The high school graduation rate will increase to at least 90 percent.
- American students will leave grades four, eight, and twelve having demonstrated competency in challenging subject matter including English, mathematics, science, history, and geography; and every school in America will ensure that all students learn to use their minds well, so they may be prepared for responsible citizenship, further learning, and productive employment in our modern economy.
- U.S. students will be first in the world in science and mathematics achievement.
- Every adult American will be literate and will possess the knowledge and skills necessary to compete in a global economy and exercise the rights and responsibilities of citizenship.
- Every school in America will be free of drugs and violence and will offer a disciplined environment conducive to learning.[19]

In the spring of 1991 President Bush announced proposals for implementing the six national goals. Known as "America 2000," the proposals—promoted by the U.S. Department of Education under the leadership of Lamar Alexander, U.S. Secretary of Education—included the creation of 535 experimental schools (one in each congressional district) for the purpose of demonstrating effective curricula and instructional techniques, voluntary national examinations in English, mathematics, science, history, and geography at the fourth-, eighth-, and twelfth-grade levels, and parental choice of school.

These proposals have met with varying reactions from educators around the country. Many educators would welcome realization of these noble goals, but some wonder whether the goals can be realized, especially in the short time until the year 2000. Educators have expressed concern about the lack of sufficient federal funding to implement the proposals, the effects of parental choice on the public schools, the expenditure of over 500 million dollars for experimental schools, and the burden of new national examinations.

Although at the present time the National Assessment of Educational Progress assesses student achievement in thirty-seven states, the new exam-

---

[19]U.S. Department of Education, *National Goals for Education* (Washington,D.C.: U.S. Department of Education, July 1990).

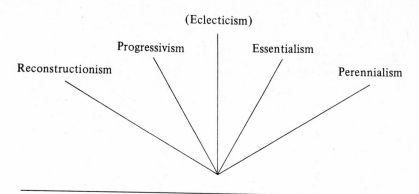

FIGURE 6–1   Four philosophies of education. In the middle is eclecticism, the borrowing of beliefs from more than one school of philosophy.

inations would purportedly concentrate more on thinking skills in the various disciplines.[20] National assessment tests, however, may lead to a national standardized curriculum, a possibility that some educators find unacceptable. These educators fear that national examinations will dictate the curriculum rather than vice versa. They also believe that a national curriculum would prevent schools from tailoring the curriculum to local needs.

You will note that the statements of aims of education cited in this chapter vary from advocacy of cognitive competencies alone to concern for the development of cognitive, affective, and psychomotor competencies.

PHILOSOPHIES OF EDUCATION

Statements of aims of education are positions taken that are based on a set of beliefs—a philosophy—of education. Clearly, the authors of the illustrations of aims cited in the preceding section held certain assumptions about education, society, and how young people learn. An aim of education, then, is a statement of belief central to the author's philosophical creed that is directed to the mission of the school.

We will now examine four major philosophies of education that have demanded the attention of educators, only two of which appear to have large followings in today's schools. Although these philosophies are known by various names and there are schools of philosophy within schools, we shall refer to these four philosophies as reconstructionism, progressivism, essentialism, and perennialism.

The four philosophies could be charted from most liberal to most conservative as shown in Figure 6–1. At the far left is the most liberal of these four philosophies, reconstructionism, and at the far right, the most conserva-

_____

[20] See Chapter 12 for further discussion of the National Assessment of Educational Progress.

tive, perennialism. Although essentialism and progressivism have been widely accepted and practiced by educators, neither reconstructionism nor perennialism has found widespread endorsement in the schools. The American public appears to be far too conservative to espouse reconstructionism, and at the same time far too liberal to accept perennialism as a prevailing philosophy. Since reconstructionism and perennialism have had less impact on the schools than the two other philosophies, we will discuss them first and then come back to the two more pervasive philosophies: essentialism and progressivism.

Reconstructionism

Hilda Taba pointed out that John Dewey "consistently saw the function of the school in both psychological and social terms."[21] She explained:

> A flowering of the idea that education is a social process, the primary and the most effective instrument of social reconstruction, came with the work and the writings of Dewey and his followers. The main thesis of this group was that the school is not merely a residual institution to maintain things as they are: education has a creative function to play in the shaping of individuals and through them in the shaping of the culture. . . . In subsequent development one fork of this dual orientation of Dewey on the function of education matured into an elaboration of the social responsibilities of the school, while the other centered more emphatically on individual development.[22]

Branching out from Dewey's philosophy, the reconstructionists followed a path that led them to propose using the school to achieve what they considered to be improvements in society. George S. Counts, in his much-discussed book *Dare the School Build a New Social Order?*, challenged educators to reconsider the role of schools in our society.[23] In essence, reconstructionism holds that the school should not simply transmit the cultural heritage or simply study social problems but should become an agency for solving political and social problems. The subject mater to which all youngsters should be exposed consists of the unsolved, often controversial, problems of the day such as unemployment, health needs, housing needs, and ethnic problems. Group consensus is the methodology by which solutions to the problems are sought.

Theodore Brameld made clear the values of the reconstructionists. Most people want the following things:

    a. sufficient nourishment

    b. adequate dress

    c. shelter and privacy

    d. erotic expression and celebration

---

[21] Excerpts from *Curriculum Development: Theory and Practice*, p. 23, by Hilda Taba, copyright©1962 by Harcourt Brace Jovanovich, Inc. and renewed by Margaret J. Spalding, reprinted by permission of the publisher.

[22] Ibid.

[23] George S. Counts, *Dare the School Build a New Social Order?* (New York: John Day, 1932).

    e. physiological and mental health

    f. steady work, steady income

    g. companionship, mutual devotion, belongingness

    h. recognition, appreciation, status

    i. novelty, curiosity, variation, recreation, adventure, growth, creativity

    j. literacy, skill, information

    k. participation, sharing

    l. fairly immediate meaning, significance, order, direction[24]

Some educators agree that young people should consider pressing social, economic, and political problems and even attempt to reach consensus on possible solutions. They do take exception when teachers propose their own specific solutions.

With its heavy emphasis on controversial social issues and its major premise to make the school a primary agency for social change, reconstructionism has not made great inroads into the largely middle-class, centrist schools of the United States.

Perennialism

In the tradition of Plato, Aristotle, and the scholasticism of the Catholic thinker, St. Thomas Aquinas, the contemporary perennialist sees the aims of education as the disciplining of the mind, the development of the ability to reason, and the pursuit of truth. Unlike progressivists who, as we shall see later, hold that truth is relative and changing, the perennialists believe that truth is eternal, everlasting, and unchanging. In their pursuit of truth the secular perennialists joined hands with the sectarian perennialists. The secular perennialists advocated a highly academic curriculum with emphasis on grammar, rhetoric, logic, classical and modern languages, mathematics, and—at the heart of the perennialist curriculum—the great books of the Western world. In the great books of the past, one could find truth, which in perennialist thinking is the same today as it was then and always shall be. To these academic disciplines the sectarian perennialists would add study of the Bible and theological writings.

Robert M. Hutchins, former president of the University of Chicago, was perhaps the best known exponent of the philosophy of perennialism in America. Hutchins and other perennialists eschewed immediate needs of the learners, specialized education, and vocational training. Hutchins made these points clear when he stated: "The ideal education is not an ad hoc education, not an education directed to immediate needs; it is not a specialized education, or a preprofessional education; it is not a utilitarian education. It is an education calculated to develop the mind."[25]

---

[24]Excerpts from *Patterns of Educational Philosophy: Divergence and Convergence in Culturological Perspective,* p. 148, Theodore Brameld, copyright©1971 by Holt, Rinehart and Winston, Inc., reprinted by permission of the publisher.

[25]Robert M. Hutchins, *On Education* (Santa Barbara, Calif.: Center for the Study of Democratic Institutions, 1963), p. 18.

The perennialist agrees with the essentialist that education is preparation for life but opposes the progressivist who holds that education *is* life. If taken seriously, perennialism would afford an education suitable to that small percentage of students who possess high verbal and academic aptitude.

The perennialist looks backward for the answers to social problems. We must wonder, for example, how useful Lucretius's *De Rerum Natura* is in helping twentieth-century men and women solve environmental problems. One criticism that appears to be overlooked in most critiques of perennialism is its ethnocentricity. The perennialist showcase features the great books of the Western world, considered by some as the greatest works of all humanity. Excluded are great books of the Middle East, Egypt, China, India, and Japan—those of the Eastern world of which many of us are abysmally ignorant. An outstanding curriculum project would bring together, perhaps under the auspices of UNESCO, a group of world scholars who would draw up a set of great books of the world. East and West would undoubtedly have something to say to each other.

In conclusion, perennialism has not proved an attractive philosophy for our educational system.

Essentialism

Historically, essentialism and progressivism succeeded in commanding the allegiance of the American public. Both have been and remain potent contenders for public and professional support. In longevity and durability, essentialism is clearly the victor. With only slight inaccuracies, we can mark the periods of supremacy of one school over another. From 1635 with the establishment of Boston Latin School to 1896 with the creation of John Dewey's Laboratory School at the University of Chicago—a period of 261 years—the doctrines of essentialism (with a patina of sectarian perennialism from 1635 to the advent of the English High School in 1824) held sway. Starting in 1896, moving slowly, and gathering steam in the 1930s and 1940s until 1957 (the year of Sputnik), progressivism emerged for a short time as the more popular educational philosophy. Its path was somewhat rocky, however, strewn as it was with the loss of the Progressive Education Association and essentialist criticisms from sources like the Council on Basic Education, Arthur Bestor, Max Rafferty, John Keats, Albert Lynd, and Mortimer Smith. Since 1957 essentialism has reclaimed its predominant position.

The aim of education according to essentialistic tenets is the transmission of the cultural heritage. Unlike the reconstructionists who would actively change society, the essentialists seek to preserve it. Again, unlike the reconstructionists who would seek to adjust society to its populace, the essentialists seek to adjust men and women to society.

Cognitive Goals.   The goals of the essentialist are primarily cognitive and intellectual. Organized courses are the vehicle for transmitting the culture, and emphasis is placed on mental discipline. The three R's and the "hard" (i.e., academic) subjects form the core of the essentialist curriculum. In one sense the essentialist tailors the child to the curriculum, whereas the progressivist tailors the curriculum to the child.

The subject matter curriculum, which we will examine in Chapter 9, is an essentialist plan for curriculum organization, and the techniques of Assign-Study-Recite-Test are the principal methods. Erudition, the ability to reproduce that which has been learned, is highly valued, and education is perceived as preparation for some future purpose—for college, vocation, life.

In spite of the mitigating influence of Jean-Jacques Rousseau, Johann Pestalozzi, and Friedrich Froebel, essentialism has for generations dominated European education and all the areas of the globe to which it has been exported. Essentialist thinking fits in well with centralized administrative structures as represented in the European and most colonial ministries of education. The ministries, following essentialist concepts, can select, promote, and control the content to which their young people are exposed. They can promote and reward the young in respect to their mastery of subject matter. They can screen youth for the universities on the basis of stringent examinations that call for recapitulation of subject matter.

William C. Bagley, one of the foremost advocates of essentialistic philosophy, strongly criticized the child-centered approach and urged teachers to follow essentialistic principles.[26] James B. Conant, in a series of reports on the junior and senior high school conducted in the late 1950s and mid-1960s, revealed an essentialist outlook in his major recommendations.[27] Conant championed stress on the academic disciplines.[28]

Behavioristic Principles.   The essentialists found the principles of the behaviorist school of psychology to be particularly harmonious with their philosophical beliefs. V. T. Thayer called attention to the urbanization of America and immigration taking place in the late 1800s and early 1900s and explained the reason for the essentialists' espousal of behavioristic principles:

> The changes in American society to which we have drawn attention affected education on all levels. But the contrast between programs of education keyed, on the one hand, to the inner nature of the young person and, on the other, to the demands of society were most obvious on the junior high school level. Here genetic psychology was emphasizing the dynamic and distinctive potentialities of the young person, with the clear implication that nature was to be followed; whereas life outside the school, in the home and community, in business and industry, stressed the importance of education for adjustment, one that would give specific and detailed attention to the formation of desirable habits and skills and techniques. Confronted with this necessity of

---

[26] See William C. Bagley, "An Essentialist's Platform for the Advancement of American Education," *Educational Administration and Supervision* 24, no. 4 (April 1938): 251–252.

[27] See James B. Conant, *The American High School Today* (New York: McGraw-Hill, 1959); Conant, *Recommendations for Education in the Junior High School Years* (Princeton, N.J.: Educational Testing Service, 1960); Conant, *The Comprehensive High School* (New York: McGraw-Hill, 1967).

[28] See Chapter 9 for further discussion of the Conant reports.

choice, educators turned to a psychology that would further education for adjustment.[29]

Behaviorism casts the learner in a passive role as the recipient of the many stimuli to which he or she must respond. Known in its variants as connectionism, association, S-R (Stimulus-Response) bond, and conditioning, behaviorism brought into the classroom drill, programmed instruction, teaching machines, standardized testing, and, of course, behavioral objectives. The whole current competencies movement in both general and teacher education owes a debt to the behaviorists. Selection of content by the adult for the immature learner and reinforcement, preferably immediate and positive, are central to behaviorist thought. Noted among the behaviorists are Ivan Pavlov, the Russian scientist who performed the classic experiment in which a dog was taught to salivate at the ringing of a bell; John B. Watson, who maintained that with the right stimuli he could shape a child into whatever he wished; Edward L. Thorndike, who is considered by many to be the father of the controversial standardized test; and B. F. Skinner, who popularized teaching machines.

Teachers of the behaviorist-essentialist school fragment content into logical, sequential pieces and prescribe the pieces the learner will study. Typically, they begin instruction by giving the learners a rule, concept, or model (for example, the formula for finding the area of a rectangle) and then provide many opportunities to practice (drill) using this guide. With adequate practice the learner can presumably use the rule, concept, or model whenever he or she needs it. The learning has become a habitual part of the individual's behavior. Though human beings are prone to forget content not used regularly, the behaviorists and essentialists maintain that if the content has been thoroughly mastered, it can be easily retrieved.

Current emphasis on the basic skills clearly derives from the essentialists. Thus present educational programs and practices maintain a strong essentialistic orientation.

Progressivism

In the late nineteenth and early twentieth centuries progressivism, also known as pragmatism, swept through the educational structure of America challenging the time-honored doctrines of essentialism. Led by John Dewey, William H. Kilpatrick, John Childs, and Boyd Bode, the progressivists maintained that it was time to subordinate subject matter to the learner. Borrowing from some European philosophers like Rousseau, who advocated rearing a child in a relaxed environment without forcing learning, the progressivists created the child-centered school. Its prototype was the University of Chicago Laboratory School. Moving east from Chicago to New York, John Dewey formulated progressive beliefs in a series of publications that included *Democracy and Ed-*

---

[29]V. T. Thayer, *The Role of the School in American Society* (New York: Dodd, Mead, 1960), pp. 251–252.

ucation,[30] *Experience and Education,*[31] *How We Think,*[32] and *My Pedagogic Creed.*[33] By insisting that the needs and interests of learners must be considered and by recognizing that learners bring their bodies, emotions, and spirits to school with their minds, progressivism captured the attention and allegiance of educators for a time.

Dewey clearly stated the differences between the essentialist and the progressive curriculum:

> The fundamental factors in the educative process are an immature, under-developed being; and certain social aims, meanings, values incarnate in the matured experience of the adult. The educative process is the due interaction of these forces. . . . From these elements of conflict grow up different educational sects. One school fixes its attention upon the importance of the subject-matter of the curriculum as compared with the contents of the child's own experience. . . . Hence the moral: ignore and minimize the child's individual peculiarities, whims, and experiences. . . . As educators our work is precisely to substitute for these superficial and casual affairs stable and well-ordered realities; and these are found in studies and lessons.
>
> Subdivide each topic into studies; each study into lessons; each lesson into specific facts and formulae. Let the child proceed step by step to master each one of these separate parts, and at last he will have covered the entire ground. . . . Problems of instruction are problems of procuring texts giving logical parts and sequences, and of presenting these portions in class in a similar definite and graded way. Subject matter furnishes the end, and it determines method. The child is simply the immature being who is to be matured; he is the superficial being who is to be deepened; his is narrow experience which is to be widened. It is his to receive, to accept. . . .
>
> Not so, says the other sect. The child is the starting-point, the center, and the end. His development, his growth, is the ideal. It alone furnishes the standard. To the growth of the child all studies are subservient; they are instruments valued as they serve the needs of growth. Personality, character, is more than subject matter. Not knowledge or information, but self-realization, is the goal. . . . Moreover, subject matter never can be got into the child from without. Learning is active. It involves reaching out of the mind. It involves organic assimilation starting from within. . . . It is he and not the subject matter which determines both quality and quantity of learning.
>
> The only significant method is the method of the mind as it reaches out and assimilates. Subject matter is but spiritual food, possible nutritive material. It cannot digest itself; it cannot of its own accord turn into bone and muscle and blood. The source of whatever is dead, mechanical, and formal in schools is found precisely in the subordination of the life and experience of the child to the curriculum. It is because of this that "study" has become a synonym for what is irksome, and a "lesson" identical with a task.[34]

---

[30]Macmillan, 1916.

[31]Macmillan, 1938.

[32]D. C. Heath, 1933.

[33]Progressive Education Association, 1929.

[34]John Dewey, *The Child and the Curriculum* (Chicago: University of Chicago Press, 1902), pp. 7–14. Reprinted with permission.

To the progressivists then, education is not a product to be learned—for example, facts and motor skills—but a process that continues as long as one lives. To their way of thinking a child learns best when actively experiencing his or her world as opposed to passively absorbing preselected content. If experiences in school are designed to meet the needs and interests of individual learners, it follows that no single pattern of subject matter can be appropriate for all learners. Brameld explained this point of view held by progressivists like Dewey and Rugg:[35]

> The proper subject matter of a curriculum is any experience that is educative. This means that the good school is concerned with every kind of learning that helps students, young and old, to grow. No single body of content, no system of courses, no universal method of teaching is inappropriate. For, like experience itself, the needs and interests of individuals and groups vary from place to place, from time to time, from culture to culture.[36]

The progressivist position that the child should undergo educative experiences in the here and now has led to the clichélike indicators of progressive philosophy: "education is life" and "learn by doing." The progressivists urged schools to provide for learners' individual differences in the broadest sense of the word, encompassing mental, physical, emotional, spiritual, social, and cultural differences.

At the heart of progressive thinking is an abiding faith in democracy. Hence the progressivists see little place for authoritarian practices in the classroom and the school. They do not hold with the essentialists that the learners are immature subjects of adult preceptors and administrators but rather consider them partners in the educational process. Teachers influenced by progressive thinking see themselves as counselors to pupils and facilitators of learning rather than expounders of subject matter. Cooperation is fostered in the classroom rather than competition. Individual growth in relationship to one's ability is considered more important than growth in comparison to others.

A concern for the many unresolved problems of democracy led to a split in the progressive camp with reconstructionists advocating that the schools become the instrument for building a new social order. It has been mentioned that the perennialist considers truth to be absolute, enduring, and found in the wisdom of the past; the essentialist presents the cultural heritage as truth, whereas the progressive pragmatist regards truth as relative, changing, and in many cases as yet to be discovered. For the pragmatist, education is a continuing search for the truth utilizing whatever sources are needed to discover that truth.

Scientific Method. The scientific method, known also as reflective thinking, problem solving, and practical intelligence, became both a goal and a technique

---

[35]Harold Rugg et al., *Foundations for American Education* (Yonkers, N.Y.: World Book Company, 1947).

[36]Excerpts from *Patterns of Educational Philosophy: Divergence and Convergence in Culturological Perspective,* p. 133, by Theodore Brameld, copyright©1971 by Holt, Rinehart and Winston, Inc., reprinted by permission of the publisher.

in the progressive school. The scientific method was both a skill to be achieved and a means of finding solutions to problems. In its simplest elements the scientific method consists of five steps:

- identifying a problem
- forming an hypothesis or hypotheses
- gathering data
- analyzing the data
- drawing conclusions

The progressivists proposed the scientific method as a general methodology to be applied in any area of human endeavor. It is generally accepted for both unsophisticated problem solving and for sophisticated research. Taba offered a very legitimate caution about accepting this methodology of problem solving as complete training in the ability to think:

> But to maintain that all aspects of thinking are involved in problem solving or in the process of inquiry is one thing. To assume that following these steps also provides sufficient training in all elements of thinking is something else. For training purposes it is important both to master the various aspects of elements of thinking—such as generalizing, concept formation, analysis of assumptions, application of principle—and to use these processes in an organized sequence of problem solving. . . . If these elements are not consciously recognized and mastered, problem solving can turn into a ritualistic process of defining any kind of question, collecting any kind of data, hypothesizing any variety of solutions, and so on.
>
> Subsuming all reflective thinking under the category of problem solving has also caused certain elements of thinking to be neglected, especially those which, although involved in problem solving, are not fully attended to *while* solving problems. Among these are such mental processes as concept formation, abstracting, and various methods of induction.[37]

Experimentalist Psychology.   In behaviorism the essentialists found learning theories compatible with their philosophy. The progressivists didn't have to look far for theories of learning compatible with their views on education. They found a wealth of ideas in the experimentalist psychology of Charles S. Pierce and William James; in the field (gestalt) psychology of Max Wertheimer, Wolfgang Köhler, Kurt Koffka, and Kurt Lewin; and in the perceptual psychology of Earl Kelley, Donald Snygg, Arthur Combs, Abraham Maslow, and Carl Rogers.

The experimentalists encourage the active involvement of the learner in all his or her capacities in the educational process. Brameld credited James's efforts to promote experimentalist-progressive thought:

> The influence of James has, of course, been very great throughout the twentieth century. His famous *Principles of Psychology* is still, in various

---

[37]Excerpts from *Curriculum Development: Theory and Practice,* p. 184, by Hilda Taba, copyright©1962 by Harcourt Brace Jovanovich, Inc. and renewed 1990 by Margaret J. Spalding, reprinted by permission of the publisher.

respects, the foremost single achievement in this field by any American scholar-scientist. . . . the dominant point of view is one of living organisms that function through experience, action, flowing feelings, habit patterns. Concern is nearly always with the total self viewed in a range of overlapping perspectives—spiritual, emotional, bodily.[38]

Gestalt Psychology.　In contrast to the behaviorist's presentation of subject matter in parts, the gestaltists concentrated on wholes, "the big picture," so to speak. They advised teachers to organize subject matter in such a way that learners could see the relationships among the various parts. This advice fit in perfectly with the progressivist's concern for "the whole child." The unit method of teaching in which content from all pertinent areas is organized into a holistic plan in order to study a particular topic or problem became a popular and enduring instructional technique. It is common now to find teachers writing unit plans. For example, the topic of the Victorian Era provides a unifying theme for the study of the history, philosophy, government, literature, science, and fine arts of the period.

The gestaltists pointed out that the learners achieve insight when they discern relationships among elements in a given situation. The gestaltists encourage inquiry or discovery learning in order to sharpen the skill of insight. Both the experimentalists and gestaltists agree that the closer content to be mastered is to real-life situations and the closer problems are to the previous experiences of the learner, the more likelihood there is for successful mastery of the material.

Perceptual Psychology.　Of more recent vintage, perceptual psychology focused on the development of the learner's self-concept. The goal of the perceptualists is the development of the "self-actualizing" or "fully functioning" personality. Abraham H. Maslow defined self-actualization as follows:

> Self-actualization is defined in various ways, but a solid core of agreement is perceptible. All definitions accept or imply: (a) acceptance and expression of the inner core or self, i.e., actualization of these latent capacities and potentialities, "full functioning," availability of the human and personal essence; and (b) minimal presence of ill health, neurosis, psychosis, or loss or diminution of the basic human and personal capacities.[39]

The perceptualists concentrate their efforts on developing persons who are adequate. Arthur W. Combs listed the following "four characteristics of the perceptual field which always seem to underlie the behavior of truly ade-

---

[38]Excerpts from *Patterns of Educational Philosophy: Divergence and Convergence in Culturological Perspective,* pp. 96–97, by Theodore Brameld, copyright©1971 by Holt, Rinehart and Winston, Inc. reprinted by permission of the publisher.

[39]Abraham H. Maslow, "Some Basic Propositions of a Growth and Self-Actualization Psychology," in *Perceiving, Behaving, Becoming,* 1962 Yearbook (Alexandria, Va.: Association for Supervision and Curriculum Development, 1962), p. 36. Reprinted with permission of the Association for Supervision and Curriculum Development and A. H. Maslow. Copyright©1962 by the Association for Supervision and Curriculum Development. All rights reserved.

quate persons"[40]: (a) a positive view of self, (b) identification with others, (c) openness to experience and acceptance, and (d) possession of a rich field of perceptions gained from both formal schooling and informal sources.[41]

According to the perceptual psychologists, teachers must help young people to develop an adequate concept of themselves and must be willing to deal both with their perceptions of the world and the world as it is. The perceptualist maintains that it is more important to know how the learner perceives the facts than what the facts of a given situation are. It is known that we all have a tendency to selectively perceive our environment. We recognize familiar faces before we pay attention to unfamiliar persons. We pick out words we know and ignore those that we do not know. We are sure that our version of the truth of any situation is the right one, for that is the way we perceive it. The perceptualists emphasize dealing with people's perceptions of the world around them.

An individual's feeling of adequacy or inadequacy can often be attributed to other people's perceptions. If a child is told by a parent that he or she is a weakling, the child may agree that this is so. If a child is told by teachers that he or she has an artistic talent, the child may seek to develop that ability. If a child is told that he or she is a poor reader, lacks aptitude for mathematics, or is short on musical talent, the child may accept these perceptions and internalize them. The child is exemplifying then what is referred to in the literature as the self-fulfilling prophecy. We are not only what we eat, as health food devotees tell us—we are what others have made us, as the perceptual psychologists maintain. Combs described how the self-concept is learned in the following passage:

> People *learn* who they are and what they are from the ways in which they have been treated by those who surround them in the process of their growing up. . . . People discover their self-concepts from the kinds of experiences they have had with life; not from telling, but from experience. People develop feelings that they are liked, wanted, acceptable and able from *having been* liked, wanted, accepted and from *having been* successful. One learns that he is these things, not from being told so, but only through the experience of *being treated as though he were so.* Here is the key to what must be done to produce more adequate people. To produce a positive self, it is necessary to provide experiences that teach individuals they are positive people.[42]

The perceptualists attacked the notion that children must experience failure. Said Combs, "Actually, the best guarantee we have that a person will be able to deal with the future effectively is that he has been successful in the past. People learn that they are able, not from failure, but from success."[43]

---

[40]Arthur W. Combs, "A Perceptual View of the Adequate Personality," in *Perceiving, Behaving, Becoming,* 1962 Yearbook (Alexandria, Va.: Association for Supervision and Curriculum Development, 1962), p. 51. Reprinted with permission of the Association for Supervision and Curriculum Development and Arthur W. Combs. Copyright©1962 by the Association for Supervision and Curriculum Development. All rights reserved.

[41]Ibid., pp. 51–62.

[42]Ibid., p. 53.

[43]Ibid.

The progressive philosophers identified readily with the experimentalist, gestalt, and perceptual schools of psychology. Their combined efforts to humanize education captured the imagination of educators, particularly those in teacher education, flourished for a relatively brief period, peaked, but left an indelible mark on our educational system. Because of progressivism, essentialism will never be the same.

The Eight-Year Study.   The cause of the progressives was boosted by the Eight-Year Study, conducted by the Progressive Education Association between 1933 and 1941. Many educators recognize this study as one of the most significant pieces of educational research ever conducted in the United States. There have been few longitudinal studies that followed subjects over a period of years. Few studies have been as sweeping or have involved as many people. Students, high school teachers and administrators, curriculum consultants, researchers, and college professors all played significant roles in the study.

The Progressive Education Association was disenchanted with the typical high school college preparatory curriculum with its customary prescribed constants required for college admission. The Association wanted to see more flexibility in the secondary school curriculum but realized that such a change would not be possible as long as the colleges demanded a prescribed set of courses. It therefore enlisted the cooperation of more than 300 colleges and universities that agreed to accept graduates from a limited number of high schools without regard to the usual college entrance requirements. Obtaining the cooperation of so many colleges and universities for an experiment of this nature, which might shatter traditional notions of what is needed to succeed in college, was a feat in itself. Wilford M. Aikin, H. H. Giles, S. P. McCutchen, Ralph W. Tyler, and A. N. Zechiel brought it about and were instrumental in the conduct of the study.[44]

The colleges and universities consented to admit graduates from 30 public and private schools regardless of their programs for a five-year period, from 1936 to 1941. Beginning in 1933 these 30 experimental schools were able to modify their programs in any way they saw fit.

Once admitted to cooperating colleges or universities, graduates of the experimental schools were matched with counterparts in the same institution who came from conventional high schools, and their performance in college was analyzed. More than 1,400 matched pairs of students were involved in this study. The findings of the Eight-Year Study are summarized as follows:

> The graduates of the experimental schools, as it turned out, did as well as or better than their counterparts in college in all subjects except foreign languages. The graduates of the experimental schools excelled their counterparts in scholastic honors, leadership positions, study habits, intellectual curiosity,

---

[44]See Wilford M. Aikin, *The Story of the Eight-Year Study* (New York: Harper & Row, 1942).

and extraclass activities. The Eight-Year Study showed rather conclusively that a single pattern of required courses is not essential for success in college.[45]

The Eight-Year Study gave impetus to novel curriculum experiments like the core curriculum, which along with the progressivist experience curriculum will be discussed in Chapter 9.

Decline of Progressivism.   In spite of its contributions—placing the child at the center of the educational process, treating the whole child, appealing to children's needs and interests, providing for individual differences, and emphasizing reflective thinking—progressivism has declined in acceptance by both the public and educators. It is probably not too far from the truth to maintain that the public was never completely enamored of progressive doctrines.

It was not Sputnik per se followed by the panicky rush to the "substantive" courses—science, mathematics, and foreign languages—that caused the turn away from progressivism. Trouble had been brewing for a number of years prior to the Soviet achievement in space.

The essentialist curriculum has always been the easiest to understand and the simplest to organize and administer. It appears clear-cut and can be readily preplanned by teachers and administrators drawing on their knowledge of the adult world. We must not overlook the force that tradition plays in our society. The essentialist curriculum has been the one to which most Americans have been exposed and which, therefore, they know best and wish to retain.

There can be no doubt that some of the so-called progressive schools went to extremes in catering to the needs and interests of children. The high school graduate who must write in block printing because he or she was not required to master cursive writing raised eyebrows among the American public. Appealing to the child's immediate needs and interests, some of the progressive schools seemed to sacrifice long-range needs and interests of which the immature learner was scarcely aware.

A feeling developed that the graduates of progressive schools were not learning the basic skills or the elements of the nation's cultural heritage. The public was uncomfortable with assertions from educators such as "The child should be taught to read only after he or she expresses a felt need for reading" (even if the child does not express that need until high school) or "There's no need to memorize the multiplication tables, you can always look them up or [today] use a calculator."

Compared to the apparent tidiness of the essentialist curriculum and the relative ease of measuring achievement of subject matter, the progressivist curriculum appeared at times disorganized and impossible to evaluate. In attempting to deal with the whole child, the progressive school seemed to many parents to be usurping some of the functions of the home, and many harried teachers agreed with them.

---

[45]Peter F. Oliva, *The Secondary School Today,* 2nd ed. (New York: Harper & Row, 1972), p. 120.

Some of the more zealous progressivists led even Dewey to warn:

> Apart from the question of the future, continually to appeal even in child-
> hood to the principle of interest is eternally to excite, that is, distract, the child.
> Continuity of activity is destroyed. Everything is made play, amusement. This
> means overstimulation; it means dissipation of energy. Will is never called into
> action. The reliance is upon external attractions and amusements. Everything
> is sugar-coated for the child, and he soon learns to turn from everything that
> is not artificially surrounded with diverting circumstances.[46]

Mass education alone has contributed to the decline of progressive practices. What might work in a class of 25 will not necessarily work in classes of
35 and above. No one has yet demonstrated satisfactorily how a high school
English teacher can provide for the cognitive differences among 150 pupils per
day, let alone the affective. As long ago as 1959 James B. Conant was advocating a maximum of 100 pupils per high school English teacher—a standard
yet to be realized in many schools.[47]

Criticisms of progressive education by the essentialists, the behaviorists, and
the scholastics converged to restore essentialism to its currently strong position.

The numerous reports on educational reform in the 1970s and 1980s, some
of which will be discussed in Chapter 9, reveal dissatisfaction with the present
essentialistic curriculum. Dissatisfaction emanates also from a small group of
curriculum theorists known as the reconceptualists. John D. McNeil attributed
the term "reconceptualist" to James B. Macdonald, "who sensed a need for
reconceiving the fundamental concerns, questions, and priorities that give direction to curriculum as a field of inquiry."[48]

This group of theorists, for the most part college professors of curriculum,
has expressed concern about the hidden curriculum, the values that are not
directly taught but that children nevertheless experience in school. These values
include the rules students live by, their relationships with peers and adults in
the school, and the values embedded in the content of their studies.

The reconceptualists argue for fundamental changes in curriculum and instruction. They draw support for their position from the humanities, especially
history, philosophy, and literary criticism. William Pinar explained the interests
of this group of theorists:

> The reconceptualists tend to concern themselves with the internal and
> existential experience of the public world. They tend to study not "change
> in behavior" or "decision making in the classroom," but matters of temporal-
> ity, transcendence, consciousness, and politics. In brief, the reconceptualist
> attempts to understand the nature of educational experience.[49]

---

[46]John Dewey, *Interest and Effort in Education* (Boston: Houghton Mifflin, 1913), pp. 4–5.
Reprinted with the permission of the Center for Dewey Studies, Southern Illinois University at
Carbondale.

[47]Conant, *American High School,* p. 51.

[48]John D. McNeil, *Curriculum: A Comprehensive Introduction,* 4th ed. (Boston: Scott,
Foresman/Little, Brown, 1990), p. 402.

[49]William Pinar, ed., *Curriculum Theorizing: The Reconceptualists* (Berkeley, Calif.: Mc-
Cutchan, 1975), pp. xii–xiii.

Pinar noted in 1975 that the reconceptualists constituted 3 to 5 percent of all curriculum theorists. Another 60 to 80 percent were what Pinar called "traditionalists" whose primary mission is guiding practitioners in the schools. The others were "conceptual empiricists" whose interests lie in the behavioral sciences, of which the curriculum is one.[50]

FORMULATING A PHILOSOPHY

In a holistic approach to curriculum development, the curriculum committee designated to lead the process examines statements of aims of education, chooses those that appear most significant, and tries its skill at fashioning its own statements.

The curriculum committee should be cognizant of the major principles of the leading schools of philosophy, particularly essentialism and progressivism. They should know where they stand as individuals and as a group in the philosophical spectrum. They may discover that they have adopted, as have perhaps a majority of educators, an eclectic approach to philosophy, choosing the best from several philosophies. They may find that there is no such thing as a pure essentialist or a pure progressivist but rather, more commonly, one is an essentialist who leans toward progressive thinking (a progressive essentialist) or, conversely, a progressivist who leans toward essentialist ideas (an essentialistic progressivist).

Curriculum workers should take the time to think through their own philosophies and to formulate them into some kind of coherent statement. The formulation of philosophy is not an activity that most Americans—pragmatists as they are—engage in with either zeal or frequency. Unlike European schools that include the study of philosophy at the secondary level, in our secondary schools philosophy is conspicuous by its absence. Even on the college level philosophy professors rarely have to beat off hordes of students clamoring at their doors.

Educators should reexamine their beliefs periodically to see if they reflect changes in society and the continuous expansion of knowledge. Schools would do well to draw up a statement of philosophy, review and revise it every five years, and thoroughly reexamine and revise it every ten years. This recommendation follows the requirements for schools that wish to achieve and maintain accreditation by the regional associations of colleges and schools.[51] Whether or not a school seeks regional accreditation, it should formulate a school philosophy to establish a framework for the practices of that school. A school's philosophy should always be the result of cooperative efforts by teachers and administrators and preferably with the additional help of parents and students. Statements of philosophy are often written and promulgated by a school administrator as the philosophy of that school. Such

---

[50]Ibid., p. xii.
[51]See Chapters 7 and 13 of this text for discussion of the criteria used for this purpose.

an activity might be engaged in to meet the terms for a report to the accreditation association, yet it misses the spirit of the exercise. The writing of a school philosophy should be an effort to gain consensus among divergent thinkers and to find out what aims and values the group holds in common. For this reason even a statement of philosophy drawn up by a faculty committee should be presented to the total faculty for acceptance, rejection, or modification. In a very real sense, the faculty's statement of philosophy becomes a manifesto signifying "This is what we believe" or "This is where we stand" as of now.

Value in Writing a Philosophy

Some hold that writing statements of philosophy is a waste of time, that such an effort takes up too much valuable time that could be better spent in other ways, and that most efforts wind up with empty platitudes. It is true that philosophical statements *can* become meaningless slogans, but they do not *have* to be. Should we call the following phrases of political philosophy from the Declaration of Independence—"all men are created equal" and "they are endowed by their Creator with certain unalienable Rights," including "Life, Liberty, and the pursuit of Happiness"—empty platitudes? Why, we might ask, did our forebears not just sever relations between the motherland and the colonies instead of prattling about unalienable rights? Perhaps they recognized that they must set the stage and provide a rationale around which other like-minded persons might rally.

A school's philosophy is not of the same order or in the same class as the Declaration of Independence, yet it does set the stage and does offer a rationale that calls for the allegiance of the school's faculty. If a statement of philosophy is to serve this purpose, it must be a truthful one and not simply platitudinous window dressing. If a school faculty believes that the major purpose of its school is to develop cognitive skills, to preserve the social status quo, or to direct the growth and development of the gifted and academically talented, it should say so. A frank statement of philosophical beliefs is much more defensible than a sanctimonious statement of platitudes that many faculty may not support and that many teachers do not translate into classroom practice.

As curriculum workers we must disabuse ourselves of the notions that it is somehow indecent to expose our beliefs and that we must feel either silly or guilty when setting forth ideals. The formulation of a school philosophy can be a valuable in-service educational experience, giving teachers and administrators a chance to exchange views and to find a common meeting ground.

A school's philosophy should include statements of belief about the purposes of education, society, the learner, and the role of the teacher. Statements of philosophy written by school personnel will soon be presented. These statements are typical of philosophies written by faculties throughout the United States. They speak about democracy, the individual, and the learning process. Some of the statements are brief; others are lengthy. The statements of some a school's schools also include goals and objectives. Here we are concerned primarily with philosophy. In Chapter 8 we will discuss the writing of curriculum goals and objectives and will provide examples of these.

These statements of philosophy reveal the schools of thought to which the faculties subscribe. In spite of the essentialistic turn in American education, progressive beliefs are still strong. Despite the current stress on developing the intellect, these examples show concern for the whole child. In spite of the increased emphasis on the development of cognitive abilities, the examples provided give attention to the affect.

Problems in Developing and Implementing a Philosophy

Before examining the examples of school philosophies, we should mention that curriculum workers often encounter two sets of problems in developing and implementing a school's philosophy. First, those who are charged with drafting a statement usually enter into the process with differing assumptions, sometimes unexpressed, about the learning process, the needs of society, and the roles of individuals in that society. The various participating individuals may well espouse differing and conflicting philosophies of life, which color their beliefs about education. Somehow the differing views need to be aired and reconciled. If consensus cannot be reached, perhaps no statement of philosophy can be drafted or that which is drafted will be so inconsequential as to be useless.

A second set of problems arises from the statement of philosophical beliefs in rather general, often vague, terms that permit varying interpretations. When a statement of philosophy has been completed and, presumably, consensus has been reached on the *wording,* curriculum leaders will experience the continuing problem of striving to achieve consensus (sometimes even among those who drafted the statement) on *interpretations* of the wording.

EXAMPLES OF SCHOOL PHILOSOPHIES

Let's now look at a small sampling of school philosophies. A district-wide statement (Omaha Public Schools) is shown in Box 6–2, and a school statement (Seawell School, Chapel Hill, North Carolina) is given in Box 6–3. You will notice references to democratic concepts, to respect for the individual, and to the necessity of providing programs to develop the pupil in all his or her capacities. Although some may fault the style or prose of a given school philosophy, what we have to keep in mind is the purpose of the statement—to communicate to professionals and the public the beliefs held by the personnel of a school or a school system. A philosophy serves its purpose when significant beliefs are successfully communicated.

From our beliefs about education, schooling, learning, and society, we can proceed to subsequent steps of the curriculum development process. Component I of the suggested model for curriculum development calls for a statement of

BOX 6–2

STATEMENT OF PHILOSOPHY OF THE SCHOOL DISTRICT OF OMAHA

The Board of Education of the Omaha Public School is responsible for meeting the challenge of providing a comprehensive educational program in an atmosphere that is open, concerned, and responsive to the needs of students and the community. To this end, the Board of Education establishes policies that are translated into practices and procedures by the Superintendent and staff to maintain and improve the quality of teaching and learning in the Omaha Public Schools. The following statements express the philosophy that guided the school district in formation of its goals and objectives:

WE BELIEVE

☐ all students have an inherent right to an education that will enable them to reach their highest possible intellectual, social, physical, and ethical development.

☐ education must concentrate on the complete development of students as individuals and as citizens.

☐ quality education programs and a committed staff provide learners with the knowledge and skills necessary for full participation in our changing society.

☐ the responsibility of education in a democracy is to make it possible for all citizens to understand themselves and the world about them, so that they can live effectively in the world of expanding experiences and constant change.

☐ education requires systematic and sustained effort by students, staff, parents, and community.

☐ education is a life-long process.

SOURCE: School District of Omaha, Nebraska, May 11, 1984. Reprinted with permission.

---

educational aims and philosophy. In respect to aims of education, curriculum workers should

☐ be aware that educational aims are derived from and are a part of one's educational philosophy

☐ be cognizant of national statements of aims of education made by prominent individuals and groups

☐ evaluate national statements and select from those statements, revising as they deem necessary, the aims of education that they find acceptable

☐ draw up a statement of educational aims to which they subscribe or, alternately, incorporate the aims they have selected into a statement of philosophy

In respect to the philosophical dimension of component I, curriculum workers should be able to

☐ identify principal beliefs of leading schools of educational philosophy

☐ analyze statements of philosophy and identify the schools to which they belong

□ analyze and clarify their own educational philosophies
□ write a statement of philosophy for their schools

SUMMARY

A holistic approach to curriculum development begins with an examination of the aims of education in society. Aims are perceived as the broad purposes of education that are national and, on occasion, international in scope.

Over the years a number of prominent individuals and groups expressed their positions on the appropriate aims of education for America. The curriculum worker should be able not only to formulate his or her own statement of aims but should also be knowledgeable about historic and significant statements of aims.

In this chapter we examined four philosophies of education—reconstructionism, progressivism, essentialism, and perennialism—two of which, essentialism and progressivism, are deemed to have special significance for our schools.

Essentialism, with its emphasis on subject matter, has been the prevailing philosophy of education throughout most of our country's history. Progressivism, however, with its emphasis on the child's needs and interests, has had a profound impact on educational programs and practices. Curriculum workers are urged to clarify their own philosophies and to draw up a statement of their school's philosophy that can be communicated to other professionals and to the public. Samples of school philosophies are included in this chapter not as models of content—that is, statements to be borrowed—but rather as examples of process. Curriculum developers should put together their own statement of beliefs in their own words. It is very likely that their statements will be eclectic in nature, borrowing from both essentialism and progressivism.

The development of a statement of aims of education and a school philosophy is seen as the first phase or component of a comprehensive model for curriculum development.

QUESTIONS FOR DISCUSSION

1. Why has the essentialistic philosophy of education been so enduring?
2. What value is there in having a faculty state its philosophy?
3. How can you keep a statement of philosophy from becoming mere verbalism?
4. Is truth relative or absolute? Explain?
5. From what sources are aims of education derived?

BOX 6–3

THE PHILOSOPHY OF SEAWELL SCHOOL

The Seawell staff believes that public education should provide learning experiences which will enable students to behave responsibly in accordance and balance with the needs of themselves, others and future generations for a harmonious existence in this world.

We feel that these goals can be reached by:

- ☐ Providing the child with a positive atmosphere where he or she learns self acceptance and experiences mutual respect and understanding from peers and adults.

- ☐ Providing many opportunities for student participation in decision making relative to daily learning activities and the operation of the pod and school.

- ☐ Including in the curriculum direct opportunities for students and teachers to increase their skills within the affective domain.

- ☐ Providing opportunities for students and teachers to interact in sharing the responsibility and excitement of learning experiences.

We further believe that:

- ☐ Every child is capable of intellectual growth, that children display natural exploratory behavior, that they learn at their own rate and in their own style, and that learning is best facilitated when based on the child's interests.

- ☐ The uniqueness of the individual deserves to be respected and encouraged.

- ☐ Interpersonal relationships should be characterized by acceptance of each individual on his or her own merit, that these relationships require patience, tolerance, understanding and open-mindedness, and that they should be based on mutual trust.

- ☐ The school should foster the development of a positive self concept.

- ☐ Student behavior guidelines should be based on fairness, be mutually agreed upon by all in the school community and lead toward the ultimate goal of self-control.

- ☐ It is the school's responsibility to foster the development of individual values and ethics and that this development is enhanced by an atmosphere of mutual trust and respect.

- ☐ Education is a continuous life process and it is our responsibility to help each individual develop to the fullest potential.

BOX 6–3   continued

- ☐ There should be equal educational opportunities for all students and that these opportunities are provided when the needs of the individual learners are met; we believe that resources should be allowed in sufficient quantity and dispensed in such a manner as to insure these opportunities.

- ☐ The curriculum followed in accordance with state and local guidelines should be directed toward meeting the needs of the students.

- ☐ We should be responsible for encouraging students to want to learn, teaching them how to learn, encouraging them to develop the ability to apply what is learned, and to develop the capacity for self evaluation.

- ☐ Optimal learning occurs in an atmosphere where there is inquiry and discovery, the right to make decisions and mistakes, and that the behavior and input of the child has a direct effect on the child's own success as a learner.

- ☐ The school has the responsibility to provide an atmosphere conducive to the development of creativity and individual initiative.

- ☐ The school should strive to develop those basic competencies and qualities of citizenship in each individual necessary for functioning successful in a changing society.

- ☐ Evaluation should be a continuous process involving student and teacher with follow-up involving parents; the evaluations of each student should be on an individual basis and not on a comparative basis with other students. We also believe that evaluation should be a constructive integral part of the learning process.

- ☐ The school should utilize the specialty services of external agencies in an ongoing developmental program.

- ☐ The relationships between the school and the community should be characterized by a two-way flow of communication and by involvement of the community in school activities.

- ☐ Continuous efforts must be made to improve the educational program through continuous planning, implementation and evaluation of improvements.

Seawell's philosophy is further reflected by contracts for multi-leveled groups of students, individualized and small group instruction and team teaching. Individual conferences, PTA meetings and parent group meetings continually reshape the program to meet the needs of the members of the school community and promote optimal emotional, social and intellectual growth of students.

SOURCE: Seawell School, Chapel Hill, North Carolina. Reprinted with permission.

SUPPLEMENTARY EXERCISES

1. Compare, citing appropriate references, aims of education in a democratic society with those of a totalitarian society.
2. State at least three premises of each of the following schools of philosophy:
   a. reconstructionism
   b. progressivism
   c. perennialism
   d. essentialism
3. Write a report, using appropriate references, contrasting essentialism and progressivism.
4. Search the literature and prepare a report on the research or beliefs of one (or more) of the following people, citing quotations from one or more of that person's works:

Jean Anyon	Kurt Lewin
Michael W. Apple	Sarah Lawrence Lightfoot
William C. Bagley	Gail McCutcheon
Louise M. Berman	James B. Macdonald
Theodore Brameld	Abraham H. Maslow
Jerome S. Bruner	Alice Miel
John Childs	Maria Montessori
Arthur W. Combs	Jeannie Oakes
James B. Conant	Ivan Pavlov
George S. Counts	Johann Pestalozzi
John Dewey	Philip Phenix
Friedrich Froebel	Jean Piaget
Henry Giroux	William Pinar
Maxine Greene	Charles S. Pierce
Madeleine Grumet	Hyman G. Rickover
Georg W. F. Hegel	Carl Rogers
Johann F. Herbart	Jean-Jacques Rousseau
Dwayne Huebner	Harold Rugg
Robert M. Hutchins	B. F. Skinner
William James	Donald Snygg
Immanuel Kant	Herbert Spencer
Earl Kelley	Florence B. Stratemeyer
William H. Kilpatrick	Edward L. Thorndike
Herbert M. Kliebard	John B. Watson
Kurt Koffka	Max Wertheimer
Wolfgang Köhler	

5. Identify several practices in the schools that follow behavioristic principles.
6. Identify several practices in the schools that follow (a) experimentalist principles, (b) gestaltist principles, and (c) principles of perceptual psychology.

7. Demonstrate with appropriate references how particular learning theories are related to certain schools of philosophy.
8. Write a short paper with appropriate references on the place and use of memorization in the classroom.
9. Write a paper on reflective thinking and show how it can be applied in the field of specialization you know best.
10. Write a report summarizing the findings of the Eight-Year Study.
11. Locate in the literature any curriculum proposals within the past five years that you would label either perennialist or reconstructionist.
12. Summarize the major beliefs of the following schools of philosophy and draw implications, if any, for the curriculum:
    a. existentialism
    b. idealism
    c. realism
    d. scholasticism
    Identify by name at least one philosopher from each school.
13. Write an analysis of beliefs of the reconceptualists. (See William Pinar reference in bibliography.)

BIBLIOGRAPHY

Adler, Mortimer J. *The Paideia Proposal: An Educational Manifesto.* New York: Macmillan, 1982.

Aikin, Wilford M. *The Story of the Eight-Year Study.* New York: Harper & Row, 1942.

Apple, Michael W. *Ideology and Curriculum,* 2nd ed. New York: Routledge, 1990.

———. "The Politics of Curriculum and Teaching." *NASSP Bulletin* 75, no. 532, (February 1991): 39–50.

Aronowitz, Stanley and Giroux, Henry A. *Education Under Siege: The Conservative, Liberal, and Radical Debate over Schooling.* South Hadley, Mass. Bergin & Garvey, 1985.

Association for Supervision and Curriculum Development, Committee on Research and Theory. *Measuring and Attaining the Goals of Education.* Alexandria, Va.: Association for Supervision and Curriculum Development, 1980.

Bagley, William C. "An Essentialist's Platform for the Advancement of American Education." *Educational Administration and Supervision,* 24, no. 4 (April 1938); 241–256.

Bode, Boyd H. *How We Learn.* Boston: D.C. Heath, 1940.

———. "Pragmatism in Education." *New Republic* 121, no. 16 (October 17, 1949): 15–18.

Bossing, Nelson L. *Principles of Secondary Education.* Englewood Cliffs, N.J.: Prentice-Hall, 1949.

Brameld, Theodore. *Patterns of Educational Philosophy: A Democratic Interpretation.* Yonkers, N.Y.: World Book Company, 1950.

———. *Patterns of Educational Philosophy: Divergence and Convergence in Culturological Perspective.* New York: Holt, Rinehart and Winston, 1971.

Combs, Arthur W. "A Perceptual View of the Adequate Personality." In *Perceiving, Behaving, Becoming,* 1962 Yearbook, 50–64. Alexandria, Va.: Association for Supervision and Curriculum Development, 1962.

Combs, Arthur W. and Snygg, Donald. *Individual Behavior: A Perceptual Ap-*

proach to Behavior, rev. ed. New York: Harper & Row, 1959.

Commission on the Reorganization of Secondary Education. *Cardinal Principles of Secondary Education.* Washington, D.C.: United States Office of Education, Bulletin 35, 1918.

Conant, James B. *The American High School Today.* New York: McGraw-Hill, 1959.

———. *The Comprehensive High School.* New York: McGraw-Hill, 1967.

———. *Recommendations for Education in the Junior High School Years.* Princeton, N.J.: Educational Testing Service, 1960.

Counts, George S. *Dare the School Build a New Social Order?* New York: John Day, 1932.

Cremin, Lawrence A. *The Transformation of the School: Progressivism in American Education, 1876–1975.* New York: Alfred A. Knopf, 1961.

Dewey, John. *The Child and the Curriculum.* Chicago: University of Chicago Press, 1902.

———. *Democracy and Education: An Introduction to the Philosophy of Education.* New York: Macmillan, 1916; New York: Free Press, 1966.

———. *Interest and Effort in Education.* Boston: Houghton Mifflin, 1913.

———. *My Pedagogic Creed.* Washington, D.C.: Progressive Education Association, 1929.

Ebel, Robert L. "What Are Schools For?" *Phi Delta Kappan* 54, no. 1 (September 1972): 3–7.

Educational Policies Commission. *Moral and Spiritual Values in the Public Schools.* Washington, D.C.: National Education Association, 1951.

———. *The Unique Function of Education in American Democracy.* Washington, D.C.: National Education Association, 1937.

Eisner, Elliot W. and Vallance, Elizabeth, eds. *Conflicting Conceptions of Curriculum.* Berkeley, Calif.: McCutchan, 1974.

Giroux, Henry A. "Curriculum Planning, Public Schooling, and Democratic Struggle." *NASSP Bulletin* 75, no. 532 (February 1991): 12–25.

———. *Teachers as Intellectuals: Toward a Critical Pedagogy of Learning.* Granby, Mass.: Bergin & Garvey, 1988.

———. *Theory and Resistance in Education: A Pedagogy for the Opposition.* South Hadley, Mass: Bergin & Garvey, 1983.

Giroux, Henry A. and Purpel, David, eds. *The Hidden Curriculum and Moral Education: Deception or Discovery?* Berkeley, Calif.: McCutchan, 1983.

Goodlad, John I. *A Place Called School: Prospects for the Future.* New York: McGraw-Hill, 1984.

Greene, Maxine. *Landscapes of Learning.* New York: Teachers College Press, 1970.

Harvard Committee on General Education. *General Education in a Free Society.* Cambridge, Mass.: Harvard University Press, 1945.

Hutchins, Robert M. *The Higher Learning in America.* New Haven, Conn.: Yale University Press, 1936.

———. *On Education.* Santa Barbara, Calif.: Center for the Study of Democratic Institutions, 1963.

Jelinek, James John, ed. *Improving the Human Condition: A Curricular Response to Critical Realities,* 1978 Yearbook, Alexandria, Va.: Association for Supervision and Curriculum Development, 1978.

Johnson, Harold T. *Foundations of Curriculum.* Columbus, Ohio: Charles E. Merrill, 1968.

Kilpatrick, William H., ed. *The Educational Frontier.* New York: Appleton-Century-Crofts, 1933.

Kliebard, Herbert M. *The Struggle for the American Curriculum 1898–1958.* Boston: Routledge & Kegan Paul, 1986.

McNeil, John D. "Philosophical Models." In *Designing Curriculum: Self-Instructional Modules,* 85–100. Boston: Little, Brown, 1976.

Maslow, Abraham H. "Some Basic Propositions of a Growth and Self-Actualization Psychology." In *Perceiving, Behaving, Becoming*, 1962 Yearbook, 34–49. Alexandria, Va.: Association for Supervision and Curriculum Development, 1962.

———. *Toward a Psychology of Being*, 2nd ed. New York: Van Nostrand Reinhold, 1968.

Miller, John P. and Seller, Wayne. *Curriculum: Perspectives and Practice*. White Plains, N.Y.: Longman, 1985.

Molnar, Alex, ed. *Current Thought on Curriculum*, 1985 Yearbook. Alexandria, Va.: Association for Supervision and Curriculum Development, 1985.

Myers, Donald A. *Decision Making in Curriculum and Instruction*. Dayton, Ohio: Institute for Development of Educational Activities, 1970.

"National Goals: Let Us Count the Ways," *The Education Digest 56*, no. 2 (October 1990): 8–26.

"The National Goals—Putting Education Back on the Road." *Phi Delta Kappan* 72, no. 4 (December 1990): 259–314.

National Governors' Association. *Educating America: State Strategies for Achieving the National Education Goals*. Washington, D.C.: National Governors' Association, 1990.

———. *Time for Results: The Governors' 1991 Report on Education*. Washington, D.C.: National Governors' Association, 1990.

Ornstein, Allan C. and Hunkins, Francis P. *Curriculum: Foundations, Principles, and Issues*. Englewood Cliffs, N.J.: Prentice-Hall, 1988.

Ornstein, Allan, C. and Levine, Daniel U. *An Introduction to the Foundations of Education*, 3rd ed. Boston: Houghton Mifflin, 1985.

Patterson, James and Kim, Peter. *The Day America Told the Truth: What People Really Believe About Everything that Really Matters*. New York: Prentice-Hall, 1991.

Pinar, William, ed. *Curriculum Theorizing: The Reconceptualists*. Berkeley, Calif.: McCutchan, 1975.

Rickover, Hyman G. *Education for All Children: What We Can Learn From England: Hearings Before the Committee on Appropriations, House of Representatives, Eighty-Seventh Congress, Second Session*. Washington, D.C.: U.S. Government Printing Office, 1962.

Rugg, Harold et al. *The Foundations and Technique of Curriculum-Construction*, 26th Yearbook of the National Society for the Study of Education. Part 2, *The Foundations of Curriculum-Making*, ed. Guy Montrose Whipple. Bloomington, Ill.: Public School Publishing Company, 1927; New York: Arno Press and *The New York Times*, 1969.

———. *Foundations for American Education*. Yonkers, N.Y.: World Book Company, 1947.

Schiro, Michael. *Curriculum for Better Schools: The Great Ideological Debate*. Englewood Cliffs, N.J.: Educational Technology Publications, 1978.

Sizer, Theodore R. "Education and Assimilation: A Fresh Plea for Pluralism." *Phi Delta Kappan* 58, no. 1 (September 1976): 31–35.

Taba, Hilda, *Curriculum Development: Theory and Practice*. New York: Harcourt Brace Jovanovich, 1962.

Tanner, Daniel and Tanner, Laurel N. *Curriculum Development: Theory into Practice*, 2nd ed. New York: Macmillan. 1980.

———*History of the School Curriculum*. New York: Macmillan, 1990.

Thayer, V. T. *The Role of the School in American Society*. New York: Dodd Mead, 1960.

U.S. Department of Education. *National Goals for Education*. Washington, D.C.: U.S. Department of Education, 1990.

Walker, Decker F. and Soltis, Jonas F. *Curriculum and Aims*. New York: Teachers College Press, 1986.

"What Schools Should Teach." *Educational Leadership* 46, no. 1 (September 1988): 2–60.

Wiles, Jon and Bondi, Joseph C. *Curriculum Development: A Guide to Practice*, 2nd ed, Chapter 3. Columbus, Ohio: Charles E. Merrill, 1984.

CHAPTER SEVEN

Needs Assessment

After studying this chapter you should be able to:

1. Identify and describe major sources of curriculum content.
2. Outline levels and types of needs of students.
3. Outline levels and types of needs of society.
4. Show how needs are derived from the structure of a discipline.
5. Describe the steps in conducting a needs assessment.
6. Construct an instrument for conducting a curricular needs assessment.

CATEGORIES OF NEEDS

In the 1990s the following items of content among thousands of items were being taught at specified grades somewhere in the United States:

- ☐ Kindergarten: Identification of the primary and secondary colors.
- ☐ First grade: Identification of U.S. coins.
- ☐ Second grade: Demonstration of ability to use period, comma, question mark, and quotation marks correctly.
- ☐ Third grade: Distinguishing between a solid, liquid, and gas.
- ☐ Fourth grade: Identification of common musical instruments.
- ☐ Fifth grade: Demonstration of skill in administering first aid to victims of accidents.
- ☐ Sixth grade: Performance of selected calisthenic drills.
- ☐ Seventh grade: Demonstration of use of library reference works.
- ☐ Eighth grade: Tracing historical development of own state.
- ☐ Ninth grade: Using a circular saw properly.
- ☐ Tenth grade: Describing preparation needed for selected careers.
- ☐ Eleventh grade: Demonstrating skill in using microcomputer for data and word processing.
- ☐ Twelfth grade: Writing a research paper.

We could have listed hundreds of items that young people are called on to master in the course of their education from elementary through secondary school. For the moment, these 12 items will suffice for our purpose.

In reviewing these and other items, we could raise a number of questions. How did these particular items of content get there? Did they come about by tradition, by a superintendent's or faculty's decision, or by a school board's or state legislature's mandate? Are they there because the current textbooks contain these items?

We should also ask: Are these items the same as last year or the year before? Will they be the same next year, the year after, or forever? What needs do the items fulfill? Have the right items been selected? What has been omitted that should have been included, and what might be eliminated from the curriculum? How do we find out whether an item is filling a need? Which needs are being met satisfactorily and which are not being met? What kinds of needs are there to which curriculum planners must pay attention?

The first section of this chapter discusses needs of students and society, classified by levels and types, and needs derived from the subject matter. The second section describes a process for conducting a curriculum needs assessment. When carrying out this process, curriculum planners study the needs of learners, society, and subject matter. With the help of the community, students, teachers, and administrators they identify and place in order of priority programmatic needs that the school must address.

In the preceding chapter we saw that statements of educational aims and philosophy are based upon needs of students in general and needs of society. Needs of both students and society are evident in the following phrases drawn from statements of aims and philosophy:

- □ to promote the Judeo-Christian heritage
- □ to promote free enterprise
- □ to develop a well-rounded individual
- □ to develop a skilled worker
- □ to promote the pursuit of happiness
- □ to enrich the spirit
- □ to develop the ability to use the basic skills
- □ to develop the ability to think
- □ to develop a knowledgeable citizen
- □ to develop communication skills
- □ to develop respect for others
- □ to develop ethical values

Statements of aims and philosophy point to common needs of students and society and set a general framework within which a school or school system will function. In formulating curriculum goals and objectives for a particular school or school system, curriculum developers must give their attention not only to (1) the needs of students in general and (2) the needs of society but also to (3) the needs of particular students, (4) the needs of the particular community, and (5) the needs derived from the subject matter. You will recall that Ralph W. Tyler, in a similar vein, listed three sources from which tentative general objectives are derived: student, society, and subject.[1]

We can expand upon the needs of both students and society in a greater level of detail than is shown in the model for curriculum development. We may classify the needs of students and society into two broad categories—levels and types—thereby emphasizing points that curriculum planners should consider.

A Classification Scheme

To focus our thinking, let's take a look at the following four-part classification scheme:

- □ needs of students by level
- □ needs of students by type
- □ needs of society by level
- □ needs of society by type

Before analyzing each category, I must stress that the needs of the student cannot be completely divorced from those of society or vice versa. The needs of one are intimately linked to those of the other. True, the two sets of needs

---

[1]See p. 165.

sometimes conflict. For example, an individual's need may be contrary to society's when he or she shouts "Fire" to gain attention in a crowded theatre when there is no fire. An individual's desire to keep an appointment may result in his or her speeding on the highway and thereby endangering the lives of other members of society. In these two examples, the apparent needs of the person and those of society are antithetical.

The needs of the person and the needs of society are, fortunately, often in harmony. An individual's desire to amass wealth, if carried out legally and fairly, is compatible with a democratic, productive society. The wealth may benefit society in the form of investment or taxes. An individual's need for physical fitness is congruent with society's demand for physically fit people. The literate citizen is as much a need of society as literacy is a need of the individual. Consequently, it is sometimes difficult to categorize a particular need as specifically a need of the person or of society. That degree of refinement is not necessary. As long as the curriculum planner recognizes the need, its classification is a secondary matter.

As stated earlier, curriculum goals and objectives are derived from five sources (components I and II of the model for curriculum development).[2] Lest there be a misunderstanding, the needs of the particular student do not completely differ from those of students in general but do vary from those of other students who share the same general needs. Students manifest not only their own particular needs but also the needs of young people generally in our society. The needs of a particular community do not completely vary from those of society in general but do differ from those of other communities that share the same general societal needs. The thousands of communities in the United States are, in spite of local distinctions of needs, resources, and cultural idiosyncrasies, parts of the total culture linked by mass media and transportation.

Interests and Wants

Before proceeding with a discussion of needs of students, I should say a word about the place of student *interests* and *wants* in curriculum development. *Interest* refers to attitudes of predisposition toward something (for example, auto mechanics, history, dramatics, or basketball). *Want* includes wishes, desires, or longings for something, such as the want for an automobile, spending money, or stylish clothes.

None of the models of curriculum development in Chapter 5 builds into it either the interests or wants of students. The reasons why interests and wants of students are not shown in the proposed model for curriculum development are the following:

1. The model would become unduly complex and burdensome were these facets of student behavior to be incorporated as well as needs.

---

[2] See pp. 172–173.

2. Interests and wants can be immediate or long-range, serious or ephemeral. Immediate and ephemeral interests and wants have less relevance than long-range and serious interests and wants.
3. Both interests and wants may actually be the bases of needs. For example, an interest in the opposite sex, which may be derived from a basic human drive, may indicate a need for curriculum responses in the areas of human and social relationships. A want may actually be a need. The *want* to be accepted, for example, is, in fact, the psychological *need* to be accepted. Alternatively, the want for a pair of expensive, brand-name jeans, though some may possibly argue, is not a need. If, then, interests and wants can be the bases for needs and are sometimes needs themselves, it would be redundant for them to be shown separately in a model for curriculum improvement.
4. Needs are given higher priority in the grand scheme of curriculum development than interests and wants. The curriculum worker is on more solid ground when he or she seeks to give closer attention to needs than to interests or wants.

Curriculum workers and instructional personnel know full well, of course, that they cannot ignore interests and wants of students, for these can be powerful motivators. Certainly, as far as interests go, the literature is filled with admonitions for educators to be concerned with student needs and interests to the point where the three words seem to be one, and the two concepts, needs and interests, are one blended concept, needs-and-interests.

Interests and wants of students must be continuously considered and sifted in the processes of both curriculum development and instruction. Although curriculum developers cannot cater to whimsical interests and wants of students, they cannot ignore legitimate and substantial interests and wants.

NEEDS OF STUDENTS: LEVELS

The levels of student needs of concern to the curriculum planner may be identified as (1) human, (2) national, (3) state or regional, (4) community, (5) school, and (6) individual.

Human

It is helpful for curriculum planners to ask themselves what the needs of students are as members of the human race and what the common needs are of all human beings on this globe. As examples of universal human needs, we might mention food, clothing, shelter, and good health.

In his state of the union address to the U.S. Congress in 1941, Franklin D. Roosevelt iterated four universal needs of humanity, widely known as the Four

Freedoms. These freedoms are freedom from want, freedom from fear, freedom to worship God in one's own way, and freedom of speech and expression. The American student shares in common with brothers and sisters all over the world certain fundamental human needs. The democratic revolutions in the former Communist countries attest to the human need for freedom. The curriculum planner must be a student of anthropology in order to recognize fundamental human needs.

National

At the national level, the general needs of students in American society are assessed. Chapter 6 already presented efforts to identify nationwide needs of students through statements of aims of education. We might identify as needs of students throughout the nation development of the ability to think, mastery of basic skills, preparation for a vocation or college, the ability to drive a car, consumer knowledge and skills, and a broad general knowledge. Some of the national needs we might identify are ones held in common by inhabitants of all nations. For example, few would argue that literacy education is not essential to the development and growth of any nation. In that sense literacy education is a worldwide but not a human need because men and women do not need to read or write to exist. Human beings, however, cannot exist without food and water or with overexposure to the elements.

To become aware of nationwide needs of students, the curriculum planner must be well read, and it is helpful for him or her to be well traveled. The curriculum planner should recognize changing needs of our country's youth. For example, contemporary young people must learn to live with the computer, to conserve dwindling natural resources, to protect the environment, and to change some basic attitudes to survive in twenty-first-century America.

State or Regional

Curriculum planners should determine whether students have needs particular to a state or region. Whereas preparing for a vocation is a common need of all students in American society, preparing for specific vocations may be more appropriate in a particular community, state, or region. General knowledge and specialized training in certain fields, such as secretarial science, auto mechanics, woodworking, computer programming, and data processing, may be applied throughout the country. However, states or regions may require students to be equipped with specific knowledge and skills for their industrial and agricultural specializations. Construction workers may be needed, for example, in growing areas of the Sun Belt and not in states or regions that are losing population.

Community

The curriculum developer studies the community served by the school or school system and asks what students' needs are in this particular community. Students growing up in a mining town in West Virginia have some demands that differ from those of students living among the cherry orchards of Michigan. In some urban communities with their mélange of races, creeds, colors, and national origins, one of the greatest needs of students may be to learn to get along with one another. Students who finish school and choose to remain in their communities will need knowledge and skills sufficient for them to earn a livelihood in those communities.

School

The curriculum planner typically probes and excels at analyzing the needs of students in a particular school. These needs command the attention of curriculum workers to such an extent that sometimes the demands of the individual student are obscured. The need for remedial reading and mathematics is obvious in schools where test scores reveal deficiencies. The need for the English language may be pressing in a school with a large percentage of children with another native language. Recently integrated or multiethnic school populations show, as a rule, the need for opening communication among groups. Some schools (especially magnet schools specializing, for example, in science, the performing arts, or the building trades) reflect the built-in needs of their student body.[3]

Individual

Finally, the needs of individual students in a particular school must be examined. Can it be that the needs of individual students go unattended while focus is on the needs of the many? Has the school addressed the needs of the average, the gifted, the academically talented, the slow, the retarded, the diabetic, the hyperactive, the withdrawn, the aggressive, the antisocial, and the creative pupil (to mention but a few categories of individual behavior)? We must ask to what extent the philosophical pledges to serve the needs of individuals are being carried out.

Each level of student needs builds upon the preceding level and makes, in effect, a cumulative set. Thus the individual student presents needs that emanate from his or her (1) individuality, (2) membership in the school, (3) residence in the community, (4) living in the state or region, (5) residing in the United States, and (6) belonging to the human race.

---

[3]For discussion of magnet schools see Chapter 9.

NEEDS OF STUDENTS: TYPES

Another dimension is added when the curriculum planner analyzes the needs of students by types. Four broad types of needs can be established: physical, sociopsychological, educational, and developmental tasks.

Physical

Biologically determined, the physical needs of young people are common within the culture and generally constant across cultures. Students need movement, exercise, rest, proper nutrition, and adequate medical attention. On leaving the childhood years, students need help with the transition from puberty to adolescence. In the adolescent years they must learn to cope with their developing sexuality. Providing for the physically handicapped is a growing concern in our society. A sound curriculum aids students to understand and meet their physical needs not only during the years of schooling but into adulthood as well.

Sociopsychological

Some curriculum developers might divide this category into social and psychological needs, yet it is often difficult to distinguish between the two. For example, an individual's need for affection is certainly a psychological need. Affection, however, is sought from other individuals and in that context becomes a social need. At first glance, self-esteem seems a purely psychological need. If we believe perceptual psychologists like Earl C. Kelley, however, the self is formed through relationships with others:[4] "The self consists, in part at least, of the accumulated experiential background, or backlog, of the individual. . . . This self is built almost entirely, if not entirely, in relationship to others. . . . Since the self is achieved through social contact, it has to be understood in terms of others."[5]

Among the common sociopsychological needs are affection, acceptance and approval, belonging, success, and security. Furthermore, each individual, both in school and out, needs to be engaged in meaningful work. The lack of significant work may well account, at least in part, for the notorious inefficiency of some nations' bloated governmental bureaucracies.

The needs of the mentally and emotionally exceptional child fit more clearly into the psychological category. Attention must be paid to the wide range of exceptionalities: the gifted, the creative, the emotionally disturbed, the mildly

---

[4]See pp. 202–203.

[5]Earl C. Kelley, "The Fully Functioning Self," *Perceiving, Behaving, Becoming,* 1962 Yearbook (Alexandria, Va.: Association for Supervision and Curriculum Development, 1962), pp. 9, 13. Reprinted with permission of the Association for Supervision and Curriculum Development and Earl C. Kelley. Copyright©1962 by the Association for Supervision and Curriculum Development. All rights reserved.

retarded, and the severely retarded. Curriculum workers must be able to identify sociopsychological needs of students and to incorporate ways to meet these needs into the curriculum.

Educational

Curriculum planners view their task of providing for the educational needs of students as a primary concern. The educational needs of students shift as society changes and as more is learned about the physical and sociopsychological aspects of child growth and development. Historically, schools have gone from emphasizing a classical and theocratic education to a vocational and secular education. They have sought to meet the educational needs of young people through general education, sometimes interpreted as the liberal arts and sciences and sometimes as the study of contemporary problems of students and/or society. "Life adjustment" courses and career education have been featured in our educational history. The basic skills and academic disciplines are currently proffered as the curricular pièce de résistance. The curriculum worker should keep in mind that educational needs do not exist outside the context of students' other needs and society's needs.

Developmental Tasks

Robert J. Havighurst made popular the concept of a "developmental task," which he viewed as a task that had to be completed by an individual at a particular time in his or her development if that individual is to experience success with later tasks.[6] He traced the developmental tasks of individuals in our society from infancy through later maturity and described the biological, psychological, and cultural bases as well as the eduational implications of each task.

Found between individual needs and societal demands, developmental tasks do not fall neatly into the schemes developed in this chapter for classifying the needs of students and the needs of society. These tasks are, in effect, personal-social needs that arise at a particular stage of life and that must be met at that stage. In middle childhood, for example, youngsters must learn to live, work, and play harmoniously with each other. In adolescence, individuals must learn to become independent, responsible citizens.

Havighurst addressed the question of the usefulness of the concept of developmental tasks in the following way:

> There are two reasons why the concept of developmental tasks is useful to educators. First, it helps in discovering and stating the purposes of education in the schools. Education may be conceived as the effort of society, through the school, to help the individual achieve certain of his developmental tasks.

---

[6]See Robert J. Havighurst, *Developmental Tasks and Education*, 3rd ed. (New York: Longman, 1972).

The second use of the concept is in the timing of educational efforts. When the body is ripe, and society requires, and the self is ready to achieve a certain task, the teachable moment has come. Efforts at teaching which would have been largely wasted if they had come earlier, give gratifying results when they come at the *teachable moment*, when the task should be learned.[7]

NEEDS OF SOCIETY: LEVELS

The curriculum worker not only looks at the needs of students in relation to society but also at the needs of society in relation to students. These two levels of needs sometimes converge, diverge, or mirror each other. When we make the needs of students the focal point, we gain a perspective that may differ from that accorded us in studying the needs of society. In analyzing the needs of society, the curriculum planner must bring a different set of skills to the task. Grounding in the behavioral sciences is especially important for the analysis of the needs of the individual, whereas training in the social sciences is pivotal to the analysis of the needs of society.

As we did in the case of assessing students' needs, let's construct two simple taxonomies of the needs of society: first, as to level, and second, as to type. We can classify the levels of needs of society from the broadest to the narrowest: human, international, national, state, community, and neighborhood.

Human

What needs, we might ask, do human beings throughout the world have as a result of their membership in the human race? Humans as a species possess the same needs as individual human beings—food, clothing, and shelter. Collectively, humankind has a need for freedom from want, from disease, and from fear. As a civilized society, presumably thousands of years removed from the Stone Age, human beings have the need to live in a state of peace. Human society, by virtue of its position at the pinnacle of evolutionary development, has a continuing need to maintain control over subordinate species of the animal kingdom. When we see the devastation wrought by earthquakes, volcanoes, floods, tornadoes, and drought, we are repeatedly reminded of the need for humankind to strive to understand and control the forces of nature. Some of the needs—or demands, if you will—of society are common to the human race.

International

Curriculum developers should consider needs that cut across national boundaries and exist not so much because they are basic needs of humanity but be-

---

[7]Robert J. Havighurst, *Developmental Tasks and Education*, 1st ed. (Chicago: University of Chicago Press, 1948), p. 8.

cause they arise from our loose confederation of nations. The study of foreign languages, for example, is a response to the need for peoples to communicate with each other. The nations of the world need to improve the flow of trade across their borders. They need to work out more effective means of solving mutual problems and conflicts. They need to develop better means of sharing expertise and discoveries for the benefit of all nations. The more fortunate nations can assist the less fortunate to meet their developmental needs by sharing the fruits of their good fortune. The people of each nation continually need to try to understand more about the culture of other nations.

Many years ago I attempted to define a number of understandings that appeared to be essential for American youth to know about the world.[8] Few of these understandings have changed significantly with the passing of time. With the possible exception of the last item in the following list, the same understandings are relevant to the people of every nation, not only Americans.

All American youth need to understand that

1. the world's population is rapidly outstripping its resources.
2. there is more poverty in the world than riches.
3. more than one-third of the world's population is illiterate.
4. there are more "colored" people in the world than white.
5. there are more non-Christians in the world than Christians.
6. our actions at home are sources of propaganda abroad.
7. nationalism is on the march as never before.
8. most of the nations of the world are struggling for technical advances.
9. you can reach by air any point on the globe within 36 hours.
10. in spite of our problems at home, thousands of foreigners abroad want to migrate to the land of the free and the home of the brave.

Thus contemporary curriculum development takes into consideration international needs.

National

The curriculum planner must be able to define the needs of the nation with some degree of lucidity. Certainly, our form of government rests upon the presence of an educated and informed citizenry. Education in citizenship is to a great extent the function of the school. One means of identifying national needs is to examine the social and economic problems faced by the country. The United States has an urgent need, for example, to solve the problem of unemployment. One solution is to train or retrain persons in occupations that appear to be growing rather than declining. The curriculum planner must be cognizant of careers that are subject to growth and decline.

---

[8] Peter F. Oliva, "Essential Understandings for the World Citizen," *Social Education* 23, no. 6 (October 1959): 266–268.

Between 1988 and 2000, opportunities for employment will vary from occupation to occupation. Some will experience an increase; others, a decrease. Shelley J. Davis summarized U.S. Department of Labor projections. [9] Among occupations projected to grow at a faster than average rate are technical and related services such as paralegals, computer programmers, science technicians; professional specialty occupations such as engineers, lawyers, teachers; executive, administrative, and managerial jobs; service occupations such as food and beverage workers, medical assistants, nursing aides, prison guards; and marketing and sales workers. Occupations that are projected for average growth include clerical services; mechanical occupations; construction; and transportation occupations such as truck and bus drivers. No growth or decline is anticipated for jobs in agriculture, forestry, fishing, water and railroad transportation, production occupations, and laborers.

Ronald E. Kutscher pointed out that "the projections indicate that the occupations that require the most education will generally grow faster than occupations with the lowest educational requirements."[10] Barring some calamity like war, severe recession, or depression, college graduates have cause to be hopeful about employment opportunities. Regarding opportunities for college graduates, Jon Sargent and Janet Pfleeger commented:

> On average, about 92 percent of the graduates who enter the labor force over the 1988–2000 period are expected to find college-level jobs—the same proportion as over the 1983–88 period. The near balance of college level entrants and job openings should mean that moderate competition in the job market for college graduates will continue. Nevertheless, it represents a significantly more favorable job market than that experienced by college graduates during the 1970's.[11]

Of course, a nation's employment needs change from time to time as the economy changes and as new technologies appear. A curriculum worker must stay tuned to changing needs. An excellent illustration of changing national need is the current demand for teachers. When the first edition of this book appeared, openings for teachers in the elementary and secondary schools were limited except in certain fields such as vocational education, mathematics, science, and special education. However, increased pupil enrollments had been predicted, and a general shortage of teachers came to pass. The decrease in enrollments in teacher education programs for a variety of reasons over the past decade further exacerbated the problem. At the present time the job market for teachers has improved somewhat. Although impeded by recession, improvements in teacher salaries, working conditions, and teacher education programs are making teaching more attractive as a career, completing a cycle of change.

---

[9]Shelley J. Davis, "The 1990-91 Job Outlook in Brief," *Occupational Outlook Quarterly* 34, no. 1 (Spring 1990): 8–14.

[10]Ronald E. Kutscher, "Outlook 2000: The Major Trends," *Occupational Outlook Quarterly* 34, no. 1 (Spring 1990): 6.

[11]Jon Sargent and Janet Pfleeger, "The Job Outlook for College Graduates for the Year 2000: A 1990 Update," *Occupational Outlook Quarterly* 34, no. 2 (Summer 1990): 3.

As the nation strives to achieve full employment, it needs employees who feel secure in their work and who do not fear that the competitive free enterprise system will force them into the ranks of the unemployed. In Japan the workers feel a close identity with their company and are protected against arbitrary dismissals. To a far greater extent than in America, the Japanese workers are retained in their jobs on a lifelong basis. Could the collective feeling of security among Japanese workers account at least in part for the phenomenal success of Japanese industry throughout the world? Does this feeling of security contribute to a feeling of pride in the organization that, in turn, translates into efficiency and quality performance?

The United States Congress responded to a national need—and caused the schools to respond as well—by enacting Public Law 94–142, the Education for All Handicapped Children Act of 1975. Through this and similar legislation, the Congress said that the country could not afford to waste the talents of a sizable segment of the population. The presence of programs in basic skills; citizenship; consumer, global, career, computer, and sex education in schools across the country is indicative of curriculum planners' responding to national needs.

The United States has many needs, from improving its educational system to solving its ethnic problems to providing for full employment to meeting the health needs of its population to maintaining its strength as a world power. The curriculum worker must be a student of history, sociology, political science, economics, and current events to perceive the needs of the nation.

State

States also have special needs. When the sale of automobiles declines, the state of Michigan experiences special difficulties. When the oil industry goes into recession, Texas suffers. When drought parches the corn or wheat belt, the producers of corn and wheat in mid-America suffer. When frost strikes the citrus crop, Florida's economy is hurt. When whole industries move from the cold and expensive Northeast to sunnier climes where labor and other costs are lower, the abandoned states feel the loss.

The continuing movement of population from the North and Midwest to the South, Southwest, and West has brought with it an array of needs not only in the states that people are deserting but also in the states whose populations are growing. Migratory waves of citizens—including those from Puerto Rico—and of noncitizens from Cuba, Vietnam, Mexico, and Haiti have had a great impact on some states and, of course, on the nation as a whole.

State needs are made apparent when pupils in schools of some states consistently score below the median of national norms on standardized tests of achievement. Consequently, many states have begun to require students to pass tests of minimal competence for receipt of the high school diploma.

Job opportunities, needs for training of specialized workers, and types of schooling needed differ from state to state and pose areas of concern for curriculum workers.

Community

Curriculum workers are more frequently able to identify the needs of a community because they are usually aware of significant changes in its major businesses and industries. They know very well, as a rule, whether the community's economy is stagnant, depressed, or booming. On the other hand, changes are sometimes so gradual that schools neglect to adapt their programs to changing community needs. For example, it is possible to find schools that offer programs in agriculture although their communities have shifted to small business and light industry, or we find schools training pupils for particular manufacturing occupations when the type of manufacturing in the area has changed or factories have been converted to automation. More subtle and more difficult to respond to are needs produced by the impersonality of large urban areas and their deteriorating quality of life. Urban dwellers need to break through the facade of impersonality and to develop a sense of mutual respect. They also need to become aware of possible contributions they can make to improve life in the big city.

Shifts of population within a state create problems for communities—there may be a population movement from the city to the suburbs or the country, followed later by another population shift from the suburbs or the country back to the city. During the 1970s, as disenchanted city dwellers sought a higher quality of life in the country, rural areas experienced significant growth. However, U.S. Census Bureau figures show that in the 1980s many Americans became dissatisfied with the rural areas and once again gravitated to the metropolitan areas.[12]

Shifts in population create problems for the schools just as the tax base, on which schools rely for partial support, affects the quality of education in a community. School staffs know full well the differences in communities' abilities to raise taxes to support public education. As the *Serrano* v. *Priest* decision of the California Supreme Court in 1971 and the *Edgewood* v. *Kirby* decision of the Texas Supreme Court in 1989 clearly demonstrated, wealthier communities with the ability to raise funds through taxes on property can provide a higher quality of education than can communities with a poorer tax base.[13] In this respect community need becomes a state need because education,

---

[12]Donald E. Starsinic, *Patterns of Metropolitan Area and County Population Growth, 1980–1984,* Current Population Reports, Population Estimates and Projections, Series P–25, No. 976, U.S. Department of Commerce, Bureau of the Census (Washington, D.C.: U.S. Government Printing Office, October 1985).

[13]*Serrano* v. *Priest,* 5 Cal. 3rd 584, 487 P. 2nd 1241 (1971) and *Edgewood Independent School District et al.* v. *William Kirby et al.* S.W. Texas 777 S.W. 2d 391 (Tex. 1989).

through the Tenth Amendment to the U.S. Constitution, is a power reserved to the states.

Schools cannot, of course, solve these societal problems by themselves. Communities must turn primarily to their state legislatures for help in equalizing educational opportunities throughout the state. On the other hand, schools can make—and cannot avoid the obligation to make—an impact on the future citizens of the community whom they are educating by making them aware of the problems and equipping them with skills and knowledge that will help them resolve some of the problems.

Neighborhood

Are there needs, the curriculum developer must ask, peculiar to the neighborhood served by the school? The answer is obvious in most urban areas. The people of the inner city have needs of which the people of the comfortable suburbs are scarcely aware except through the press and television. Crime and use of drugs are more common in some neighborhoods than in others. The needs of people in areas that house migrant workers are much different from those of people in areas where executives, physicians, and lawyers reside. Children in lower socioeconomic levels often achieve less in their neighborhood schools than more affluent children do in theirs. A notable and heartwarming exception is Jaime Escalante's success in teaching calculus to inner-city students at Garfield High School in Los Angeles.[14] As a rule, families of children in the more fortunate schools are able to afford cultural experiences that children in the less fortunate schools seldom encounter.

The curriculum worker must be perceptive of changes in neighborhoods. For example, city dwellers who moved to suburbia in search of the good life are finding—after some years in a housing development, often a tract variety with a sameness of architectural design, and after countless hours of commuting—that the good life has eluded them. They have become disenchanted with wall-to-wall housing (which some sociologists predict as our future) and with block after block of shopping centers. Grass, trees, and unpolluted air have given way to the bulldozer, the cement mixer, and, in spite of the development of unleaded fuel, an overabundance of air-polluting automobiles.

Some of the suburban settlements have joined the central city in experiencing blight and decay and the host of problems that accompany these conditions. On the other hand, we have begun to see a small reversal in the movement of people within the metropolitan areas. A few suburban dwellers have been returning to the central city where properties are depressed and therefore cheap. Renovation of old homes promises to make some formerly depressed central city locations once again choice, even expensive, places to inhabit.

---

[14]See the Warner Brothers movie *Stand and Deliver,* Burbank, Calif.: Warner Home Video, 1988, starring James Edward Olmos.

Worth watching are housing developments designed to create a congenial small-town atmosphere in a suburban setting. These new planned communities employ the concept of a community center surrounded by a mixture of single-family and multi-family residences and apartments. Schools and commercial and recreational facilities are planned to be within easy walking distance of the homes. Mass transit will link suburbs and nearby urban centers, reducing dependence upon the automobile. Sites near Sacramento, California, Tacoma, Washington, Tampa, Florida and in Brevard County, Florida have been mentioned as locales for development of the small-town center concept. Perhaps in the twenty-first century not all of America's population will be living in the beehive dwellings predicted by some futurists.

The curriculum specialist must develop plans that show an understanding of the needs of society on all of the foregoing levels.

NEEDS OF SOCIETY: TYPES

The curriculum planner must additionally look at the needs of society from the standpoint of types. For example, each of the following types of societal needs has implications for the curriculum:

□ political
□ social
□ economic
□ educational
□ environmental
□ defense
□ health
□ moral and spiritual

A curriculum council studying the needs of society would be well advised to try to generate its own system for classifying societal needs. It might then compare its classification system with some of those found in the literature. The Seven Cardinal Principles and the Ten Imperative Needs, mentioned in Chapter 3, were efforts to identify needs of students as a function of the needs of society.

Social Processes

Numerous attempts have been made throughout the years to identify societal needs or demands under the rubrics of social processes, social functions, life activities, or social institutions. As we review several of the better known efforts to specify these needs, we should recall the student-society duality of needs. "Making a home," for example, is both a societal and a personal need. The person has a need for the skills of making a home while society has a need for persons who possess homemaking skills. Curriculum specialists who seek to delineate social processes or functions do so in order to identify individual needs that have social origins. It might be argued, parenthetically, that all personal needs (except purely biological ones) are social in origin.

Robert S. Zais credited Herbert Spencer for the beginning of the practice of studying society empirically.[15] In 1859 Spencer recommended that students be prepared for "the leading kinds of activity which constitute human life."[16] He classified these activities in order of importance as follows:

1. those activities which directly minister to self-preservation.
2. those activities which, by securing the necessaries of life, indirectly minister to self-preservation.
3. those activities which have for their end the rearing and discipline of offspring.
4. those activities which are involved in the maintenance of proper social and political relations.
5. those miscellaneous activities which make up the leisure part of life, devoted to the gratification of the tastes and feelings.[17]

The 1934 Virginia State Curriculum Program has been identified as one of the better known attempts to organize a curriculum around life processes.[18] O. I. Frederick and Lucile J. Farquear reported the following nine areas of human activity that the state of Virginia incorporated into the curriculum of its schools:

1. Protecting life and health
2. Getting a living
3. Making a home
4. Expressing religious impulses
5. Satisfying the desire for beauty
6. Securing education
7. Cooperating in social and civic action
8. Engaging in recreation
9. Improving material conditions.[19]

The Wisconsin State Department of Public Instruction's *Guide to Curriculum Building* has been highly regarded for its social functions approach. The Wisconsin State Department of Public Instruction listed the following social

---

[15]Robert S. Zais, *Curriculum: Principles and Foundations* (New York: Harper & Row, 1976), p. 301.
[16]Herbert Spencer, "What Knowledge Is of Most Worth?" in *Education: Intellectual, Moral, and Physical* (New York: John B. Alden, 1885). Quotations are from 1963 ed. (Paterson, N.J.: Littlefield, Adams), p. 32.
[17]Ibid.
[18]Hilda Taba, *Curriculum Development: Theory and Practice* (New York: Harcourt Brace Jovanovich, 1962), p. 398.
[19]O. I. Frederick and Lucile J. Farquear. "Areas of Human Activity," *Journal of Educational Research* 30, no. 9 (May 1937): 672–679.

functions in its guide for a core curriculum[20] at the junior high school level:

☐ To keep the population healthy.
☐ To provide physical protection and guarantee against war.
☐ To conserve and wisely utilize natural resources.
☐ To provide opportunity for people to make a living.
☐ To rear and educate the young.
☐ To provide wholesome and adequate recreation.
☐ To enable the population to satisfy aesthetic and spiritual values.
☐ To provide sufficient social cement to guarantee social integration.
☐ To organize and govern in harmony with beliefs and aspirations.[21]

Florence B. Stratemeyer, Hamden L. Forkner, Margaret G. McKim, and A. Harry Passow proposed a plan for organizing curriculum experiences around activities of human beings, as shown in the following list:

Situations Calling for Growth in Individual Capacities:
Health
    A. Satisfying physiological needs
    B. Satisfying emotional and social needs
    C. Avoiding and caring for illness and injury
Intellectual power
    A. Making ideas clear
    B. Understanding the ideas of others
    C. Dealing with quantitative relationships
    D. Using effective methods of work
Moral choices
    A. Determining the nature and extent of individual freedom
    B. Determining responsibility to self and others
Aesthetic expression and appreciation
    A. Finding sources of aesthetic satisfaction in oneself
    B. Achieving aesthetic satisfactions through the environment

Situations Calling for Growth in Social Participation:
Person-to-person relationships
    A. Establishing effective social relations with others
    B. Establishing effective working relations with others
Group membership
    A. Deciding when to join a group
    B. Participating as a group member
    C. Taking leadership responsibilities
Intergroup relationships
    A. Working with racial, religious, and national groups
    B. Working with socioeconomic groups
    C. Dealing with groups organized for specific action

---

[20] For discussion of the core curriculum see Chapter 9.
[21] Wisconsin State Department of Public Instruction, *Guide to Curriculum Building,* Bulletin No. 8 (Madison, Wis.: State Department of Public Instruction, January 1950), p. 74. Reprinted with permission.

Situations Calling for Growth in Ability to Deal with Environment Factors and Forces:

  Natural phenomena
    A. Dealing with physical phenomena
    B. Dealing with plant, animal, and insect life
    C. Using physical and chemical forces
  Technological resources
    A. Using technological resources
    B. Contributing to technological advance
  Economic-social-political structures and forces
    A. Earning a living
    B. Securing goods and services
    C. Providing for social welfare
    D. Molding public opinion
    E. Participating in local and national government[22]

Taba pointed out the strength of the Stratemeyer, Forkner, McKim, and Passow scheme:

> This . . . scheme seems to be an effort to correct one deficiency of the social-process approach, the disregard for the learner. In effect this approach combines the concepts of common activities, needs, and life situations with an awareness of the learner as a factor in curriculum design and uses both to find a unifying scheme.[23]

In sum, the curriculum worker must analyze both the needs of learners and of society. The study of both "sources," as they are called by Ralph Tyler, provides clues for curricular implementation and organization.

NEEDS DERIVED FROM THE SUBJECT MATTER

One major source of curriculum objectives remains for us to consider—needs as derived from the subject matter or, as Jerome S. Bruner and others would say, from the "structure of a subject."[24] Bruner refers to the structure of a subject as the "basic ideas"[25] or "fundamental principles."[26] "Grasping the structure of a subject," said Bruner, "is understanding it in such a way that permits many other things to be related to it meaningfully. To learn structure, in short, is to learn how things are related."[27]

---

[22]Reprinted by permission of the publisher from Stratemeyer, Forkner, McKim and Passow, *Developing a Curriculum for Modern Living,* 2nd. edition. NY: Teachers College Press, Columbia University. All rights reserved. pp. 146–172.

[23]Excerpts from *Curriculum Development: Theory and Practice,* p. 399, by Hilda Taba, copyright©1962 by Harcourt Brace Jovanovich, Inc. and renewed 1990 by Margaret J. Spalding, reprinted by the permission of the publisher.

[24]Jerome S. Bruner, *The Process of Education* (Cambridge, Mass.: Harvard University Press, 1960), p. 6.

[25]Ibid., pp. 12–13.

[26]Ibid., p. 25.

[27]Ibid., p. 7.

As examples of elements of the structure of disciplines, Bruner mentioned tropism in the field of biology; commutation, distribution, and association in mathematics; and linguistic patterns in the field of language.[28] Each subject contains certain essential areas or topics (the bases for determining the scope of a course) that, if the learner is to achieve mastery of the field, must be taught at certain times and in a logically prescribed order (sequence). The sequence could be determined by increasing complexity (as in mathematics, foreign languages, English grammar, science), by logic (as in social studies programs that begin with the child's immediate environment—the home and school—and expand to the community, state, nation, and world), or by psychological means (as in vocational education programs that start with immediate interests of learners and proceed to more remote ones).

New Programs in the Disciplines

The subject matter areas remained essentially the same (except for updating) until the 1950s with the advent of the "new math," the "new science," the "new linguistics," and the widespread development of the audio-lingual method of teaching foreign languages. The scholarly ferment of the 1950s, propelled by National Defense Education Act funds, produced such new definitions of the structures of the disciplines as the three versions of a course in biology (blue, green, and yellow) developed by the Biological Sciences Curriculum Study (BSCS). Each version presented principles of biology with a different central focus and organization. The structure of this field of science as prescribed in the green version, considered the easiest of the three, centered around the topics of evolution and ecology. The blue version, considered the most difficult, stressed biochemistry and physiology, and the yellow version concentrated on genetics and the development of organisms.

Two additional projects illustrate the type of planning going on in the field of science in the mid-1950s and early 1960s. The Physical Sciences Study Committee—which began its work in 1956, just three years before the Biological Sciences Curriculum Study was initiated—unified a high school course in physics under the following four topics:

1. the universe, which includes time, space, matter, and motion.
2. optics and waves, which involves a study of optical phenomena.
3. mechanics, which concerns dynamics, momentum, energy, and the laws of conservation.
4. electricity, which includes electricity, magnetism, and the structure of the atom.[29]

---

[28] Ibid., pp. 7–8.
[29] Peter F. Oliva, *The Secondary School Today,* 2nd ed. (New York: Harper & Row, 1972), p. 151.

In the early 1960s the Earth Science Curriculum Project developed an earth-science course with the following ten unifying themes:

1. Science as inquiry
2. Comprehension of scale
3. Prediction
4. Universality of change
5. Flow of energy in the universe
6. Adjustment to environmental change
7. Conservation of mass and energy in the universe
8. Earth systems in time and space
9. Uniformity of process
10. Historical development and presentation[30]

While the scientists were overhauling the curriculum of their specialties, the foreign language curriculum workers were breaking out of the mold of the old reading-translation objectives that dominated foreign language study for generations. Calling attention to the change in objectives of foreign language study, I wrote:

> The objectives, in order of priority, among foreign language teachers are: (a) aural comprehension, (b) speaking, (c) reading, and (d) writing. . . . The four above-mentioned linguistic objectives are integrated with the general cultural objective, understanding of the foreign customs and foreign peoples.[31]

Foreign language study provides an excellent illustration of a sequenced structure because language students will learn a foreign language more readily when, for example, the concept of singular is presented before the concept of plural, when regular verbs are taught before irregular verbs, when the first person singular is mastered before other persons, when the present tense is perfected before other tenses, when simple tenses come before compound, and when the indicative mood is taught before the subjunctive.

Many state departments and/or local school districts have published syllabi, courses of study, and curriculum guides developed by teacher-specialists in the particular fields.[32] These publications outline the structure of a subject, the appropriate grade level for each topic, and often the order of presentation (sequence) of topics. For example, in preparing its systemwide objectives and standards the Chicago Public Schools has integrated Illinois State Goals for Learning in the various disciplines.[33] Chicago has used the state's seven goals for learning in mathematics and has created a list of performance objectives for

---

[30]Ibid., p. 152.

[31]Peter F. Oliva, *The Teaching of Foreign Languages* (Englewood Cliffs, N.J.: Prentice-Hall, 1969), p. 11.

[32]For discussion of curriculum products, see Chapter 15 of this text.

[33]Selected from instructional program objectives in *Systemwide Objectives and Standards, Grades 9–12, 1990.* Reprinted with permission of the Board of Education of the City of Chicago.

each goal based on the state's sample learning objectives (SLO)[34] and standards of the National Council of Teachers of Mathematics (NCTM).[35]

To illustrate this integration, we will examine the fourth goal for learning in mathematics:

> As a result of their schooling, students will be able to identify, analyze, and solve problems using algebraic equations, inequalities, functions, and their graphs.[36]

To meet this state goal Chicago has identified the following performance objectives, which students are expected to master during their algebra courses.

OBJECTIVES

Apply the rules for order of operations to evaluate expressions involving integers and powers. (SLO)

Relate situations that involve variable quantities to expressions, equations, and inequalities. (NCTM)

Define and use function notation and terminology. (SLO)

Solve linear equations. (SLO)

Solve one-step inequalities. (SLO)

Interpret solutions to an equation or inequality in terms of the situation they represent. (SLO)

Solve equations and inequalities resulting from situations that occur in everyday life. (SLO)

Recognize all real numbers whose squares are given numbers. (SLO)

Compare different powers of the same number or the same power of different numbers. (SLO)

Judge the appropriateness of particular values for a variable in a formula. (SLO)

Apply formulas with and without the use of a calculator. (SLO)

Recognize and determine equivalent forms of a formula. (SLO)

Determine values in a sequence when given a formula for the next term. (SLO)

Cite the rule by which the next term in a given sequence may be obtained. (SLO)

Model real-world phenomena by using a variety of functions. (NCTM)

Operate on expressions and solve equations and inequalities. (NCTM)

Use an equation or a rule and graph a simple function. (SLO)

---

[34] Illinois State Board of Education, *State Goals for Learning and Sample Learning Objectives, Mathematics* (Springfield, Ill.: Illinois State Board of Education, n.d.).

[35] National Council of Teachers of Mathematics, *Curriculum and Evaluation Standards for School Mathematics* (Reston, Va.: The Council, 1989). Reprinted with permission.

[36] Illinois State Board of Education, *State Goals*, as cited in Chicago Public Schools, *Systemwide Objectives*, p. 34.

Identify the slope of a line that is determined by two points. (SLO)

Use the graph of a function to interpret rates of change. (SLO)

Identify the solutions to a system of equations from a graph on a coordinate plane. (SLO)

Solve a simple system of equations in two variables by using graphing, algebraic techniques, or technology. (SLO)

Test solutions to systems of equations. (SLO)

Compare values of two or more functions represented on a graph or in a table. (SLO)

Add and subtract polynomials. (SLO)

Factor common monomial factors out of algebraic expressions. (SLO)

Multiply binomials. (SLO)

Make a table of values for a simple polynomial function by using a given domain. (SLO)

Represent and analyze relationships by using tables, verbal rules, equations, and graphs. (NCTM)

Analyze a graph to determine when a function has a given value. (SLO)

Translate tabular, symbolic, and graphical representations of functions. (NCTM)

Analyze the effects of parameter changes on the graphs of functions. (NCTM)

Use tables and graphs as tools to analyze and interpret expressions, equations, and inequalities. (NCTM)

Read maximum and minimum values of a function from the graph of the function. (SLO)[37]

Essential Skills/Minimal Competencies

Curriculum planners have traditionally conveyed the fundamentals of subject matter to the learners by outlining topics or identifying unifying themes. In more recent years the structures of the disciplines have been communicated to learners in terms of essential skills or minimal competencies written in the form of objectives to be accomplished at various grade levels and before high school graduation. The state of Arizona, for example, has developed an extensive list of eighth- and twelfth-grade skills in seven subject areas. Eighty-seven skills have been identified in the area of health for eighth-grade students. The first ten skills from this list may serve as examples:

1. Identifies personal care practices. Example: washing hands before eating, brushing teeth.
2. Communicates symptoms of his/her physical illness.

---

[37]Selected from instructional program objectives in *Systemwide Objectives and Standards, Grades 9–12, 1990*, pp. 34–36. Reprinted with permission of the Board of Education of the City of Chicago.

3. Lists some of the ways communicable diseases are transmitted.
4. Identifies and describes a variety of foods.
5. States the importance of eating breakfast and describes a healthful breakfast.
6. Explains that medicines are never taken except when given by parents, guardians, doctors, or nurses.
7. Describes the dangers of taking unknown substances.
8. Names common safety hazards and rules for preventing home, school, and transportation accidents.
9. Identifies major body parts. Example: arms, legs, ears, and eyes.
10. Describes how people in a community work together to keep the neighborhood clean.[38]

The state of Georgia has identified essential concepts and skills for ten subject areas as well as thinking skills and study skills. It has specified the level (K–4, 5–8, 9–12) at which each concept or skill is introduced (I), developed (D), or reinforced (R). Following the Bloom taxonomy of the cognitive domain, Georgia's list of thinking skills (shown in Table 7–1) furnishes an illustration of a procedure that identifies and classifies essential concepts and skills.[39]

The state of Florida has established minimum performance standards in reading, writing, and mathematics for students completing grades 3, 5, 8, and 11. As an illustration of attempts to set forth the structure of a discipline in the form of performance standards—that is, competencies—Table 7–2 shows two of Florida's ten minimal performance standards in writing, the specific basic skills to be demonstrated, and the designated grade level.[40]

Some people would refer to the standards presented in the Florida document as competencies or objectives and the basic skills as subcompetencies, subobjectives, enablers (or enabling activities), or indicators. Note that both standards and basic skills are behaviorally stated.

Curriculum workers who are specialists in a field may either attempt to define the structure of a discipline as they view it or make use of studies of the discipline that have already been done. Some of the studies that identify the elements of a discipline have benefited from the talents of recognized experts in a subject area. Consequently, the use of predetermined national, regional, and state analyses of structure may prove a wiser course of action for curriculum planners than the creation of their own analyses.

The purpose of the discussion of needs to this point is to direct the curriculum developers to consider three major sources of needs—the learner, the

---

[38] Arizona Department of Education, *Essential Skills List* (Phoenix: Arizona Department of Education, June 1984), p. 1. Reprinted by permission.

[39] Georgia Department of Education, *Essential Skills for Georgia Schools* (Atlanta: Division of Curriculum Services, Georgia Department of Education, 1980), pp. 87–88.

[40] Florida Department of Education, *Minimum Student Performance Standards for Florida Schools, 1985–86, 1986–87, 1987–88, 1988–89, 1989–90: Beginning Grades 3, 5, 8, and 11: Reading Writing, and Mathematics* (Tallahassee: Florida Department of Education, 1982), pp. 17, 22.

TABLE 7–1   Georgia's list of thinking skills

TOPIC	CONCEPT/SKILL	K–4	5–8	9–12
A. Recall	The learner will			
	recognize information previously encountered such as facts, concepts or specific elements in a subject area.	ID	DR	R
1. Identification	ascertain the origin, nature or definitive characteristics of an item.	ID	DR	R
2. Observation	obtain information by noting, perceiving, noticing and describing. Observation may involve looking, listening, touching, feeling, smelling or tasting.	ID	DR	R
3. Perception	become aware of objects through using the senses, especially seeing or hearing.	ID	DR	R
B. Comprehension	The learner will			
	understand information that has been communicated.	ID	D	R
1. Translation	change information from one form to another, maintaining accuracy of the original communication.	ID	DR	DR
2. Analogy Recognition	infer that if two things are known to be alike in some respects then they may be alike in others.	ID	DR	DR
C. Hypothesizing	The learner will			
	assume, making a tentative explanation.	I	DR	DR
1. Prediction	tell or declare beforehand.	I	DR	DR
2. Imagination	form a mental image of, represent or picture to oneself.	I	DR	DR
D. Application	The learner will			
	put information to use.	I	DR	DR
1. Clarification	make something easier to understand.		ID	DR
2. Hypothesis Testing	try out ideas for possible solutions.	I	ID	DR
3. Operational Definition	order ideas into a step by step plan.		ID	DR
4. Decision-making	choose the best or most desirable alternative.	I	ID	DR
5. Consequence Projection	define further steps toward probable solutions or identify cause/effect relationships.	I	ID	DR
E. Analysis	The learner will			
	break down a concept, problem, pattern or whole into its component parts, systematically or sequentially, so that the relations between parts are expressed explicitly.		ID	DR

TABLE 7–1   continued

TOPIC	CONCEPT/SKILL	K–4	5–8	9–12
1. Comparison	determine similarities and differences on the basis of given criteria.	ID	DR	R
2. Classification	place elements into arbitrarily established systems of groupings and subgroupings on the basis of common characteristics.	ID	DR	R
3. Selection	choose an element from a set of elements on the basis of given criteria.	ID	DR	R
4. Association	relate elements either given or as they come to mind.	ID	DR	R
5. Inference	draw a conclusion based on facts or evidence.	I	ID	DR
6. Interpretation	express meaning of or reaction to an experience.	I	ID	DR
7. Qualification	describe by enumerating characteristics.	I	ID	R
F. Synthesis	The learner will			
	arrange and combine elements to form a structure, pattern or product.	I	ID	DR
1. Summarization	express a brief or concise restatement.	I	ID	DR
2. Generalization	formulate or derive from specifics (to make universally applicable) a class, form or statement.	I	ID	DR
3. Formulation of Concepts	originate or express ideas.		ID	DR
4. Integration	form into a whole and unite information.		ID	DR
G. Evaluation	The learner will			
	make judgments regarding quantity and quality on the basis of given criteria.		ID	DR
1. Justification	show adequate reason(s) for something done.	I	ID	DR
2. Imposition of Standards	assure equal comparison with established criteria.		ID	DR
3. Judgment	form an idea or opinion about any matter.		ID	DR
4. Internal Consistency	understand that all the parts of a process fit together.		ID	DR
5. Value	establish worth or esteem.	I	ID	DR

SOURCE: Georgia Department of Education, *Essential Skills for Georgia Schools* (Atlanta: Division of Curriculum Services, Georgia Department of Education, 1980), pp. 87–88. Reprinted by permission.

TABLE 7–2   Partial list of Florida's minimal performance standards in writing

STANDARDS	BASIC SKILLS— THE STUDENT WILL:	GRADE LEVEL(S)			
#A THE STUDENT WILL COMPOSE GRAMMATICALLY CORRECT SENTENCES.	1. Dictate grammatically correct sentences.	3			
	2. Write the plural form of nouns by adding "s" or "es" to the base word.		5		
	3. Complete sentences with the appropriate singular and/or plural forms of nouns.		5	8	
	4. Complete sentences with the appropriate forms of regular verbs.		5		
	5. Write simple declarative sentences using appropriate English word order.		5		
	6. Write simple interrogative sentences using appropriate English word order.		5		
	7. Write the plural forms of nouns correctly.			8	11
	8. Use the appropriate forms of common regular verbs in writing.			8	
	9. Write declarative sentences having compound subjects and/or verbs.			8	11
	10. Make subjects and verbs agree.			8	11
	11. Use the appropriate forms of common irregular verbs in writing.			8	11
	12. Write compound declarative sentences using appropriate English word order.			8	11

TABLE 7–2   continued

STANDARDS	BASIC SKILLS— THE STUDENT WILL:	GRADE LEVEL(S)			
#H THE STUDENT WILL PUNCTUATE COR- RECTLY.	62. Use a period or question mark to punctuate simple declara- tive or interrogative sentences, respectively.	3	5	8	11
	63. Use a period to complete abbre- viations of common titles used as proper nouns (Mr., Mrs., Dr.).		5	8	11
	64. Use a comma between names of cities and states and between the day of the month and the year.		5	8	11
	65. Use the comma after the greet- ing and after the closing of a friendly letter.		5	8	11
	66. Use an apostrophe to form contractions.		5	8	11
	67. Use the comma to separate words in a series.			8	11
	68. Use the comma to set off proper names in direct address.			8	11
	69. Use an apostrophe and "s" to show the possessive of singu- lar and plural nouns which do not end in "s."				11

SOURCE: Florida Department of Education, *Minimum Student Performance Standards for Florida Schools, 1985–86, 1986–87, 1987–88, 1988–89, 1989–90: Beginning Grades 3,5,8, and 11: Reading, Writing, and Mathematics* (Tallahassee: Florida Department of Education, 1982), pp. 17,22. The standards have been extended through 1993–94, after which revised standards will be in effect. Reprinted by permission.

society, and the subject matter. Although Ralph Tyler discusses these three sets of needs as sources from which tentative general objectives are derived[41] — a sound procedure—they are examined and illustrated here as a preface to a systematic procedure for studying needs and identifying those not met by the school's curriculum. Such a procedure is usually referred to in the literature as a needs assessment.

CONDUCTING A NEEDS ASSESSMENT

In its simplest definition a *curriculum needs assessment* is a process for identifying programmatic needs that must be addressed by curriculum planners. Fenwick W. English and Roger A. Kaufman offered several interpretations of the term "needs assessment." They described the process in the following ways:

> Needs assessment is a process of defining the desired end (or outcome, product, or result) of a given sequence of curriculum development. . . .
>
> Needs assessment is a process of making specific, in some intelligible manner, what schooling should be about and how it can be assessed. Needs assessment is not by itself a curricular innovation, it is a method for determining if innovation is necessary and/or desirable.
>
> Needs assessment is an empirical process for defining the outcomes of education, and as such it is then a set of criteria by which curricula may be developed and compared. . . .
>
> Needs assessment is a process for determining the validity of behavioral objectives and if standardized tests and/or criterion-referenced tests are appropriate and under what conditions.
>
> Needs assessment is a logical problem-solving tool by which a variety of means may be selected and related to each other in the development of curriculum.
>
> Needs assessment is a tool which formally harvests the gaps between current results (or outcomes, products) and required or desired results, places these gaps in priority order, and selects those gaps (needs) of the highest priority for action, usually through the implementation of a new or existing curriculum or management process.[42]

The objectives of a needs assessment are twofold: (1) to identify needs of the learners not being met by the existing curriculum and (2) to form a basis for revising the curriculum in such a way as to fulfill as many unmet needs as possible. The conduct of a needs assessment is not a single, one-time operation but a continuing and periodic activity. Some curriculum workers perceive a needs assessment as a task to be accomplished at the beginning

---

[41] See p. 165.

[42] Fenwick W. English and Roger A. Kaufman, *Needs Assessment: A Focus for Curriculum Development* (Alexandria, Va.: Association for Supervision and Curriculum Development, 1975), pp. 3–4. Reprinted with permission of the Association for Supervision and Curriculum Development and Fenwick W. English and Roger A. Kaufman. Copyright©1975 by the Association for Supervision and Curriculum Development. All rights reserved.

of an extensive study of the curriculum. Once the results are obtained from this initiatory needs assessment, these planners believe that further probing is unnecessary for a number of years.

Since the needs of students, society, and the subject matter change over the years and since no curriculum has reached a state of perfection in which it ministers to all the educational needs of young people, a thorough needs assessment should be conducted periodically—at least every five years—with at least minor updating annually.

A needs assessment is also not time-specific in that it takes place only at the beginning of a comprehensive study of the curriculum. A needs assessment is a continuing activity that takes place (a) before specification of curricular goals and objectives, (b) after identification of curricular goals and objectives, (c) after evaluation of instruction, and (d) after evaluation of the curriculum.[43] English and Kaufman pointed out that most school systems require six months to two years to complete a full-scale needs assessment.[44] Not all school systems, of course, conduct full-scale needs assessments. The scope of assessments varies from simple studies of perceived needs to thorough analyses using extensive data.

Perceived Needs Approach

Some schools limit the process of assessing needs to a survey of the needs of learners as perceived by (1) teachers, (2) students, and (3) parents. Instead of turning to objective data, curriculum planners in these schools pose questions that seek opinions from one or more of these groups. Parents, for example, are asked questions like these:

- □ How well do you feel your child is doing in school?
- □ Is your child experiencing any difficulty in school? If so, please explain.
- □ What content or programs do you believe the school should offer that are not now being offered?
- □ What suggestions do you have for improving the school's program?
- □ Are you satisfied with the programs that the school is offering your child? If you are dissatisfied with any programs, please specify which ones and your reasons.

Teachers and students may be asked to respond to similar questions in order to gain their perceptions of the school's curriculum and of needed improvements. The perceived needs approach, however, is but the first stage of the process. It is advantageous in that it is a simple process, requires relatively little time and effort, and is relatively inexpensive to conduct. It also provides an opportunity for the various groups to express their views about what is needed in the curriculum. The perceived needs approach becomes an effective

---

[43] See components of the suggested model for curriculum development, Figure 5-5, p. 172.
[44] English and Kaufman, *Needs Assessment*, p. 14.

public relations device when it is used with parents; it says, in effect, that the school cares to know what parents think about the school's programs and wants their suggestions. As a first step, the perceived needs approach is worthwhile.

On the other hand, the perceived needs approach is limited. By its very nature, it is concerned with perceptions rather than facts. Although the curriculum planner must learn the perceptions of various groups, he or she must also know what the facts are. The needs of learners as perceived by the various groups may be quite different from needs as shown by more objective data. Consequently, the needs assessment must be carried beyond the gathering of perceptions of needs.

Data Collection

Those charged with conducting a needs assessment should gather data about the school and its programs from whatever sources of data are available. Necessary data include background information about the community, the student body, and the staff. Curriculum planners will need information on programs offered and available facilities. They must have access to all test data on the achievement of students in the school. Data may be obtained from various sources, including student records; school district files; surveys of attitudes of students, teachers, and parents; classroom observations; and examination of instructional materials. English described a process for collecting data in a school through examination of appropriate documents and practices, which he referred to as a "curriculum audit."[45]

Adequate data are necessary for making decisions about the selection of fields and topics to be encountered by the students and for specifying the goals of the curriculum. The data will provide clues as to the necessity for curriculum change. All these data should be put together in a coherent fashion so that they can be analyzed and decisions can be made about revising the curriculum.[46]

A needs assessment is customarily carried out when pressure is felt by personnel in schools seeking accreditation by their regional accrediting association. Schools seeking regional accreditation must conduct a full-scale self-study and be visited by a full committee every ten years; they must also conduct an interim study every five years. The standards used, entitled *Evaluative Criteria*, provide for a comprehensive needs assessment. These criteria call for a statement of the school's philosophy and objectives, a report on the school and community, data on each staff member, information on school facilities, and evaluations of all phases of the school's curriculum.[47]

---

[45]Fenwick W. English, *Curriculum Auditing* (Lancaster, Penn.: Technomic Publishing Company, 1988), p. 33.

[46]See Jon Wiles and Joseph C. Bondi, *Curriculum Development: A Guide to Practice,* 2nd ed. (Columbus, Ohio: Charles E. Merrill, 1984), pp. 106, 108-109, for a suggested outline of needs assessment data.

[47]National Study of School Evaluation, *Evaluative Criteria* (Falls Church, Va.: National Study of School Evaluation). Periodically. Separate criteria for elementary, junior high/middle school, and secondary schools.

Steps in Conducting a Needs Assessment

English and Kaufman proposed one of the most detailed plans for conducting a needs assessment. Their plan included 14 generic and seven post-needs-assessment steps.[48] Following each step is a brief explanation in my own words.

Generic Steps of Needs Assessment

1. *Planning to plan: charting means and ends*—Preparations need to be made for the needs assessment, including decisions about time allotted, resources available, who will be participating, and so on.
2. *Goal derivation*—Knowledgeable persons are asked to state outcomes of education that they feel to be desirable.
3. *Goal validation*—Face validity is determined by asking citizens, both educators and noneducators, whether the goals are appropriate.
4. *Goal prioritization*—A large sampling of citizens, including students, educators, and school board members, is asked to rank the goals in order of importance.
5. *Goal translation*—Statements of goals are converted into measurable performance standards.
6. *Validation of performance objectives*—The groups that validated the goals now validate the performance standards (objectives) as to the accuracy of translating the goals into performance objectives and as to whether all the necessary objectives have been specified.
7. *Goal reprioritization*—Goals are reconsidered in light of a second sampling of students, staff, and community that repeats step 2. Step 3 and following steps may also be repeated, if desired.
8. *Futuristic input in goal ranking*—Future-oriented objectives are included. The Delphi Technique, in which informed persons are asked to predict future directions (in this case for education), may be used to generate and validate educational goals from which performance objectives may then be derived.[49]
9. *Rerank goals*—Goals are reranked using research and predictive studies such as the Delphi Technique.
10. *Select testing instruments or evaluative strategies for assessing the current state*—Testing instruments are selected and administered to ascertain current levels of student performance, to learn whether student achievement meets the desired defined levels.
11. *Collate data gathered*—Collected data must be put into tables, charts, graphs, and the like. English and Kaufman reminded us that "a needs assessment is the process of formulating gaps or discrepancies between two

[48] English and Kaufman, *Needs Assessment,* pp. 12–48.
[49] For discussion of the Delphi Technique see Olaf Helmer, "Analysis of the Future: The Delphi Method," in James R. Bright, ed., *Technological Forecasting for Industry and Government: Methods and Applications* (Englewood Cliffs, N.J.: Prentice-Hall, 1968), pp. 116–122.

sets of criteria, a list of future desired conditions and results, and a list of current, existing (not necessarily desired) conditions and results."[50] Thus in presenting the data "the most detailed information should be provided to those by whom decisions must ultimately be made about what to do with the 'gaps' as the primary consideration."[51]

12. *Develop initial gap or "need statements"*—A list of needs—gaps in student performance between what is desired and what is performed—is drawn up.
13. *Prioritize gap statements according to step four*—Gaps are clustered around the educational goals to which they relate and are ranked by the degree of difference between desired levels of student achievement and actual performance.
14. *Publish list of gap statements*—At this point the needs assessment is complete.

Post-Needs-Assessment Steps

1. *Interpolate gaps by program and level*—Needs that are identified—the gaps—are located by program and level.
2. *Conduct diagnostic/planning sessions to develop implementation strategies to meet identified needs*—The responsible curriculum group tries to find out the reasons for the gaps and makes plans for closing them.
3. *Budget for implementation strategies*—The cost of each implementation strategy is calculated and budgeted.
4. *Fund strategies*—Depending on availability of funds, all strategies or only top strategies are funded.
5. *Implement strategies*—Strategies are put into operation either in existing or new programs.
6. *Reassess gap via feedback*—Both formative and summative data are gathered and analyzed to see if the gaps have actually been closed.
7. *Repeat steps of needs assessment process*—English and Kaufman recommended that generic steps 1 through 9 be repeated periodically and generic steps 10 through 14 continually.[52]

The process recommended by English and Kaufman goes beyond a simple needs assessment, incorporating the generation of goals and performance objectives as well as implementation and evaluation phases.

We can see that a thorough needs assessment is more than a "quick-and-dirty" survey of perceived needs. When done properly, it is a time-consuming process that requires the commitment of human and material resources sufficient to accomplish the job. A systematic process for discovering unmet needs of learners is an essential step in curriculum improvement.

---

[50]English and Kaufman, *Needs Assessment,* p. 35. Reprinted with permission.
[51]Ibid., p. 39.
[52]Ibid., p. 47.

SUMMARY

Curriculum planners must attend to the needs of students and society. These needs may be classified as to level and type. Various attempts have been made to identify the social processes, functions, and institutions that have import for the curriculum.

Each discipline has its own unique set of elements or structure that affects decisions about scope and sequence. The structure of a subject is shown by exposition of the basic ideas, fundamental principles, broad generalizable topics, competencies, or performance objectives.

In addition to studying empirically the needs of students, society, and the disciplines, curriculum workers should conduct systematic needs assessments to identify gaps—discrepancies between desired and actual student performance. Identified unmet needs should play a major role in curriculum revision.

A curriculum needs assessment permits school systems to discover deficiencies in their curricula. In addition, it creates a vehicle for school and community cooperation, builds community understanding of the school's programs and support for the school's efforts to fill in the gaps, and forces decisions on priorities.

QUESTIONS FOR DISCUSSION

1. What is the relationship between (1) needs of learners, society, and subject matter and (2) a curriculum needs assessment?
2. What is the appropriate role of the community in a curriculum needs assessment?
3. What is the appropriate role of students in a curriculum needs assessment?
4. What is the appropriate role of teachers in a curriculum needs assessment?
5. What is the appropriate role of administrators and supervisors in a curriculum needs assessment?

SUPPLEMENTARY EXERCISES

1. Give an illustration of at least one need of students at the following levels:
   human
   national
   state or regional
   community
   school
   individual
2. Give an illustration of at least one student need of the following types:
   physical
   sociopsychological
   educational

3. Analyze Robert J. Havighurst's developmental tasks of middle childhood or adolescence (see bibliography) and judge whether you feel each task is still relevant. Give reasons for your position on each task that you feel is no longer relevant.

4. Confer with appropriate personnel in a school system you know well and see if the school system has conducted a curriculum needs assessment in recent years. Report on instrumentation and results if a needs assessment has been conducted.

5. Conduct a simple study using the Delphi Technique. (See Olaf Helmer reference in the bibliography.)

6. Describe the process of goal validation as explained by English and Kaufman (see bibliography).

7. Examine the report of the school-and-community committee of a school that has undergone regional accreditation and summarize the data contained therein.

8. Identify needs that the following content is supposed to fulfill:

     income tax
     Jacksonian democracy
     principle of leverage
     Beowulf
     adding mixed fractions
     Latin declensions
     building cabinets
     typing

9. Read and report in detail on Henry C. Morrison's description of social institutions (see bibliography).

10. Create your own list of social processes or functions and compare this list with one found in the professional literature.

11. Read and report on Herbert Spencer's description of life activities (see bibliography).

12. Explain how you would go about identifying needs of students.

13. Explain how you would go about identifying needs of society.

14. Identify several of the basic ideas (structure) of a discipline you know well.

15. Explain how one of the needs assessment models discussed in this chapter might be implemented in your community.

BIBLIOGRAPHY

Association for Supervision and Curriculum Development. *What Are the Sources of the Curriculum? A Symposium.* Alexandria, Va.: Association for Supervision and Curriculum Development, 1962.

Banathy, Bela H. *Instructional Systems.* Belmont, Calif.: Fearon, 1968.

Bruner, Jerome S. *The Process of Education.* Cambridge, Mass.: Harvard University Press, 1960.

Combs, Arthur W., ed. *Perceiving, Behaving, Becoming* 1962 Yearbook. Alexandria, Va.: Association for Supervision and Curriculum Development, 1962.

English, Fenwick W. *Curriculum Auditing.* Lancaster, Penn.: Technomic Publishing Company, 1988.

English, Femwick W. and Kaufman, Roger A. *Needs Assessment: A Focus for Curriculum Development.* Alexandria, Va.: Association for Supervision and Curriculum Development, 1975.

Erikson, Erik. *Identity, Youth, and Crisis.* New York: W. W. Norton, 1968.

Frederick, O. I. and Farquear, Lucile J. "Areas of Human Activity." *Journal of Educational Research* 30 (May 1937): 672–679.

Goodlad, John I. *Curriculum Inquiry: The Study of Curriculum Practice.* New York: McGraw-Hill, 1979.

Harap, Henry, ed. *The Changing Curriculum.* New York: Appleton-Century-Crofts, 1937.

Havighurst, Robert J. *Developmental Tasks and Education,* 3rd ed. New York: Longman, 1972.

Helmer, Olaf. "Analysis of the Future: The Delphi Method." In *Technological Forecasting for Industry and Government: Methods and Applications,* ed. James R. Bright, 116–122. Englewood Cliffs, N.J.: Prentice-Hall, 1968.

Kaplan B. A. *Needs Assessment for Education: A Planning Handbook for School Districts.* Trenton, N.J.: New Jersey Department of Education, Bureau of Planning, February 1974. ERIC: ED 089 405.

Kaufman, Roger A. "Needs Assessment." In Fenwick W. English, ed., *Fundamental Curriculum Decisions,* 1983 Yearbook. Alexandria, Va.: Association for Supervision and Curriculum Development, 1983.

———. *Planning Educational Systems.* Englewood Cliffs, N.J.: Prentice-Hall, 1988.

Kaufman, Roger and English, Fenwick W. *Needs Assessment: Concept and Application.* Englewood Cliffs, N.J.: Educational Technology Publications, 1979.

———. *Needs Assessment: A Guide to Improve School District Management.*

Arlington, Va.: American Association of School Administrators, 1976.

Kaufman, Roger and Stakenas, Robert G. "Needs Assessment and Holistic Planning." *Educational Leadership* 38, no. 8 (May 1981): 612–616.

Kaufman, Roger and Thomas, Susan. *Evaluation Without Fear.* New York: Franklin Watts, 1980.

Kelley, Earl C. "The Fully Functioning Self." *Perceiving, Behaving, Becoming,* 1962 Yearbook, 9–20. Alexandria, Va.: Association for Supervision and Curriculum Development, 1962.

Kimmel, W. A. *Needs Assessment: A Critical Perspective.* Washington, D.C.: U.S. Department of Education, 1977.

McNeil, John D. "The Needs Assessment Approach to Selecting Educational Objectives." *Designing Curriculum: Self-Instructional Modules,* 79–84. Boston: Little, Brown, 1976.

Molnar, Alex and Zahorik, John A., eds. *Curriculum Theory: Selected Papers from the Milwaukee Curriculum Theory Conference.* Alexandria, Va.: Association for Supervision and Curriculum Development, 1977.

Morrison, Henry C. *The Curriculum of the Common School.* Chicago: University of Chicago Press, 1940.

National Study of School Evaluation. *Elementary School Evaluative Criteria,* 2nd ed. Falls Church, Va.: National Study of School Evaluation, 1981.

———. *Evaluative Criteria,* 6th ed. Falls Church, Va.: National Study of School Evaluation, 1987.

———. *Middle School/Junior High School Evaluative Criteria.* Falls Church, Va.: National Study of School Evaluation, 1979.

New Orleans Public Schools, *Guidelines for Mathematics Grades 7–9.* New Orleans, La.: Division of Instruction, New Orleans Public Schools, 1969.

Oliva, Peter F. *The Secondary School Today,* 2nd ed. New York: Harper & Row, 1972.

Smith, B. Othanel, Stanley, William O., and Shores, J. Harlan. *Fundamentals of Curriculum Development,* rev. ed. New York: Harcourt Brace Jovanovich, 1957.

Spencer, Herbert. *Education: Intellectual, Moral, and Physical.* New York: John B. Alden, 1885; Paterson, N.J.: Littlefield, Adams, 1963.

Stratemeyer, Florence B., Forkner, Hamden L., McKim, Margaret G., and Passow, A. Harry. *Developing a Curriculum for Modern Living,* 2nd ed. New York: Bureau of Publications, Teachers College Press, Columbia University, 1957.

Taba, Hilda. *Curriculum Development: Theory and Practice.* New York: Harcourt Brace Jovanovich, 1962.

Tyler, Ralph W. *Basic Principles of Curriculum and Instruction.* Chicago: University of Chicago Press, 1949.

Wiles, Jon and Bondi, Joseph C. *Curriculum Development: A Guide to Practice,* 2nd ed. Columbus, Ohio: Charles E. Merrill, 1984.

Wisconsin State Department of Public Instruction. *Guide to Curriculum Building,* Bulletin No. 8. Madison, Wis.: State Department of Public Instruction, January 1950.

Witkin, B. R. *An Analysis of Needs Assessment Techniques for Educational Planning at State, Intermediate, and District Levels,* May 1975. ERIC: ED 108 370.

Zais, Robert S. *Curriculum: Principles and Foundations.* New York: Harper & Row, 1976.

Zenger, Weldon F. and Zenger, Sharon K. *Curriculum Planning: A Ten-Step Process.* Palo Alto, Calif.: R & E Research Associates, 1982.

FILM

Stand and Deliver. 103 min. 1988. Warner Bros. Jaime Escalante teaches calculus to inner-city students in Los Angeles.

FILMSTRIP-AUDIOTAPE PROGRAM

Deciding on Defensible Goals via Educational Needs Assessment. 1971. Vimcet Associates, P.O. Box 24714, Los Angeles, Calif. 90024.

CHAPTER EIGHT

Curriculum Goals and Objectives

After studying this chapter, you should be able to:

1. Distinguish between goals and objectives.

2. Distinguish between aims of education and curriculum goals and objectives.

3. Distinguish between curriculum goals and objectives and instructional goals and objectives.

4. Specify and write curriculum goals.

5. Specify and write curriculum objectives.

HIERARCHY OF OUTCOMES

Following the model for curriculum improvement suggested in Chapter 5, let's see how far we have come. We have

- ☐ analyzed needs of students in general in society
- ☐ analyzed needs of American society
- ☐ reviewed aims of education and affirmed those with which we are in agreement
- ☐ written a philosophy of education
- ☐ initiated a needs assessment by surveying needs of students in the community and school and by surveying needs of the community
- ☐ conducted a needs assessment and identified unmet needs

All of these steps are a prelude to the next phase. They provide a framework; they set the stage. They furnish data that are vital to making curricular decisions. The planning of the curriculum is now about to begin.

In Chapter 6 you encountered the terms "aims of education," "curriculum goals," "curriculum objectives," "instructional goals," and "instructional objectives" as used in this text. We discussed a hierarchy of purposes of education from the broadest to the narrowest. Let's review that hierarchy; it is essential both to this chapter on curriculum goals and objectives and to Chapter 10 on instructional goals and objectives. We might chart this hierarchy as shown in Figure 8–1.[1]

It sometimes seems that the educational literature is surfeited with discussions of goals and objectives. In spite of these many commentaries, I have included three chapters in this text (Chapters 6, 8, and 10) on aims, goals, and objectives for the following reasons:

1. They are essential components in a comprehensive model for curriculum improvement.
2. These various terms for purpose are used loosely and interchangeably in some of the literature, leading to possible confusion.
3. Some of the recommendations in the literature on the writing of goals and objectives are helpful; other recommendations seem less helpful.

Aims, Goals, and Objectives

Several problems can be found if we research the literature on aims, goals, and objectives. First, aims of education are often equated with goals, and in

---

[1] For a different hierarchy of goals see Ronald S. Brandt and Ralph W. Tyler, in Fenwick W. English, ed., *Fundamental Curriculum Decisions,* 1983 Yearbook (Alexandria, Va.: Association for Supervision and Curriculum Development, 1983), pp. 40–52.

FIGURE 8–1   Hierarchy of outcomes

a lexical sense, of course, they are the same. John W. Gardner in *Goals for Americans* was describing aims of education when he wrote:

> Our deepest convictions impel us to foster individual fulfillment. We wish each one to achieve the promise that is in him. We wish each one to be worthy of a free society, and capable of strengthening a free society. . . . Ultimately, education serves all of our purposes—liberty, justice, and all our other aims— but the one it serves most directly is equality of opportunity.
>
> [The] . . . tasks of producing certain specially needed kinds of educated talent . . . should not crowd out the great basic goals of our educational system: to foster individual fulfillment and to nurture the free, rational and responsible men and women without whom our kind of society cannot endure. Our schools must prepare *all* young people, whatever their talents, for the serious business of being free men and women.[2]

In this case the problem of equating aims of education with goals is minor because Gardner communicates to the reader that he is consistently discussing broad goals or aims. The problem arises when discussions of aims, curriculum goals and objectives, and instructional goals and objectives are intermingled. There is little difficulty when a single meaning for a term is used in a single context or when an author clearly defines how he or she uses a term. That, however, does not always happen.

---

[2]John W. Gardner, "National Goals in Education," in *Goals for Americans: Programs for Action in the Sixties*, Report of the President's Commission on National Goals, Henry M. Wriston, Chairman (New York: The American Assembly, Columbia University, 1960), pp. 81, 100.

Second, the terms "educational goals" and "educational objectives" are used in the profession with varying meanings. Some use these terms in the same way other people speak of aims of education or educational aims. Some perceive educational goals as curriculum goals and educational objectives as curriculum objectives. Some substitute educational goals for instructional goals and educational objectives for instructional objectives.

Third, as we shall see in examples of school statements of goals and objectives, goals are equated with objectives, and the terms are used synonymously. However, if we believe what we read, there are two entities—one called goals and another, objectives—for numerous schools have prepared statements of both goals and objectives.

Some writers have used the terms "goals" and "objectives" interchangeably. W. James Popham and Eva L. Baker, for example, wrote: "We have given considerable attention to the topic of instructional objectives because they represent one of the most important tools available to the teacher. . . . There is undoubtedly a positive relationship between a teacher's clarity of instructional goals and the quality of his teaching."[3] Robert F. Mager in his popular work on instructional objectives commented:

> An instructor . . . must then select procedures, content, and methods that . . . measure or evaluate the student's performance according to the objectives or goals originally selected. . . . Another important reason for stating objectives sharply relates to the evaluation of the degree to which the learner is able to perform in the manner desired. . . . Unless goals are clearly and firmly fixed in the minds of both parties, tests are at best misleading.[4]

Two widely followed taxonomies of educational objectives bear the subtitle *The Classification of Educational Goals*.[5] In some of the literature goals *are* objectives and vice versa.

Fourth, some curriculum specialists do not distinguish curriculum goals and objectives from instructional goals and objectives, or they use these two sets of terms synonymously. If curriculum and instruction are two different entities—the position taken in this text—then curriculum goals and objectives are different from instructional goals and objectives. Only if we choose a curriculum-instruction model in which the two are mirror images can curriculum goals and objectives be identical to instructional goals and objectives. This text, however, presents the view that the two are separate but related entities.

---

[3]W. James Popham and Eva L. Baker, *Systematic Instruction* (Englewood Cliffs, N.J.: Prentice-Hall, 1970), p. 43.

[4]Robert F. Mager, *Preparing Instructional Objectives* (Belmont, Calif.: Fearon, 1962), pp. 1, 3–4.

[5]Benjamin S. Bloom, ed., *Taxonomy of Educational Objectives: The Classification of Educational Goals: Handbook I: Cognitive Domain* (New York: Longman, 1956) and David R. Krathwohl, Benjamin S. Bloom, and Bertram B. Masia, *Taxonomy of Educational Objectives: The Classification of Educational Goals: Handbook II: Affective Domain* (New York: Longman, 1964).

These observations are not meant to criticize the positions, definitions, or approaches of other curriculum specialists nor to hold that the definitions given in this text are the "right" or only ones. As Decker F. Walker aptly stated in an enlightened discussion of writings on curriculum:

> Curriculum is clearly an iffy subject. It belongs to Aristotle's "region of the many and variable" where certain knowledge is not possible, only opinion—multiple and various, more or less considered, more or less adequate, but never clearly true or false.[6]

Mary M. McCaslin spoke in a similar vein when she said:

> We all live in glass houses. None of us can afford glib dismissal of alternative conceptions any more than we can afford to be noncritical or nonreflective about our own work.[7]

My remarks about the differences in use of curriculum terms convey, as mentioned in Chapter 1, that the language of curriculum is somewhat imprecise and can lead to confusion. Curriculum specialists, unfortunately, do not agree among themselves on terminology. As a result, the practitioner who seeks to carry out curriculum development following principles established by the experts must first understand these terms and the contexts within which they appear.

In this text I have made distinctions between curriculum goals and objectives and instructional goals and objectives in order to help practitioners facilitate the natural flow of curriculum development from general aims of education to precise instructional objectives. Specifying curriculum goals and objectives, then, is viewed as an intermediate planning step between these two poles. I will first define the terms curriculum goals and objectives, present some examples, and then develop some guidelines for writing them.

DEFINING GOALS AND OBJECTIVES

Curriculum Goals

A *curriculum goal* is a purpose or end stated in general terms without criteria of achievement. Curriculum planners wish students to accomplish it as a result of exposure to segments or all of a program of a particular school or school system. For example, the following statement meets this definition of a curriculum goal: "Students will demonstrate responsible behavior as citizens of our school, community, state, nation, and world."

---

[6]Decker F. Walker, "A Barnstorming Tour of Writing on Curriculum," in Arthur W. Foshay, ed., *Considered Action for Curriculum Improvement,* 1980 Yearbook (Alexandria, Va.: Association for Supervision and Curriculum Development, 1980), p. 81.

[7]Mary M. McCaslin, "Commentary: Whole Language—Theory, Instruction, and Future Implementation", *The Elementary School Journal* 90, no. 2 (November 1989): 227.

We have already seen examples of curriculum goals in Chapter 3. The Seven Cardinal Principles—health, command of fundamental processes, worthy home membership, vocation, citizenship, worthy use of leisure, and ethical character—are examples of curriculum goals, albeit in a form of shorthand. [8] The Commission on the Reorganization of Secondary Education could have expanded these principles into forms like the following:

- ☐ The school will promote the physical and mental health of the students.
- ☐ Students will achieve a command of the fundamental processes.
- ☐ A goal of the school is to foster worthy home membership.

The Ten Imperative Needs of Youth, listed by the Educational Policies Commission, is a set of curriculum goals that, as noted earlier, included such statements as these:

> All youth need to develop salable skills.
> All youth need to develop and maintain good health, physical fitness, and mental health.
> All youth need to grow in their ability to think rationally, to express their thoughts clearly, and to read and listen with understanding. [9]

The Educational Policies Commission pointed to four purposes or aims of education in American democracy. It identified these aims as self-realization, human relationships, economic efficiency, and civic responsibility.[10] These purposes might be modified by a particular school or school system and turned into curricular goals, stated in a variety of ways, as follows:

- ☐ The school's program provides experiences leading to self-realization.
- ☐ Our school seeks to promote human relationships.
- ☐ A goal of the school is development of skills of learners that will lead to their country's and their own economic efficiency.
- ☐ Students will develop a sense of civic responsibility.

Many variations are used for expressing these four purposes. This chapter will later present a preferred form for writing goals and objectives. For now, these four goals are shown only as examples of substance, not of form.

Aims of education can become curriculum goals when applied to a particular school or school system. The distinction drawn between aims of education and curriculum goals is one of generality (or looking at it from the other end of the telescope, specificity). "To transmit the cultural heritage" and "to overcome ignorance" are aims of all school programs. No single program or school can accomplish these extremely broad purposes. A school can, of course, contribute to transmitting the cultural heritage and to overcoming ignorance;

---

[8]Commission on the Reorganization of Secondary Education, *Cardinal Principles of Secondary Education* (Washington, D.C.: United States Office of Education, Bulletin No. 35, 1918).

[9]Educational Policies Commission, *Education for All American Youth* (Washington, D.C.: National Education Association, 1944), pp. 225–226.

[10]Educational Policies Commission, *The Purposes of Education in American Democracy* (Washington, D.C.: National Education Association, 1938).

stated with those qualifications, educational aims can become curriculum goals. The expression "to contribute to the physical development of the individual" can be both an educational aim of society and a curriculum goal of a particular school or school system.

Curriculum Objectives

Curriculum goals are derived from a statement of philosophy, defined aims of education, and assessment of needs. From curriculum goals, we derive curriculum objectives. We may define a curriculum objective in the following manner: A *curriculum objective* is a purpose or end stated in specific, measurable terms. Curriculum planners wish students to accomplish it as a result of exposure to segments or all of a program of the particular school or school system.

The following example of a curriculum goal has already been presented: "Students will demonstrate responsible behavior as citizens of our school, community, state, nation, and world." From that curriculum goal the following curriculum objectives are among those which could be derived:

- □ During the election of student government officers, 90 percent of the student body will cast ballots.
- □ 100 percent of the students will make some kind of positive contribution to the community's clean-up, fix-up campaign.
- □ 90 percent of the students will be able to name the candidates running for the state senate and the state assembly from their district. They will be able to identify the candidates for the principal state executive offices. They will also identify the political parties of the candidates.
- □ 90 percent of the students will be able to identify their current U.S. senators and their representative to the U.S. House of Representatives. They will also identify the political parties of these officeholders.
- □ 90 percent of the students will participate in some project that can increase international understanding, such as contributing coins to UNICEF, donating food or clothing to victims of some natural disaster abroad, writing to pen pals overseas, or taking part in other school or community projects of an international nature.

Note how the curriculum objectives refine the curriculum goal. Many curriculum objectives can emanate from the same curriculum goal.

LOCUS OF CURRICULUM GOALS AND OBJECTIVES

As the statements of the Seven Cardinal Principles and the Ten Imperative Needs of Youth demonstrated, curriculum goals are infrequently written on a national basis by individuals and groups as proposals for consideration by schools throughout the country. However, curriculum objectives, as just defined, are too specific to emanate from national sources.

Curriculum goals and objectives are regularly written at the state, school-district, and individual school level with the expectation that they will be followed within the jurisdiction of each level. State pronouncements apply to all public schools in the state; school-district statements apply district-wide; and individual school specifications, school-wide.

For the most part, curriculum goals and objectives developed at any level cut across disciplines. A school's statement, for example, applies generally throughout the school. It is possible, however, for grades and departments to develop curriculum goals and objectives that do not apply generally throughout the school but to a particular group of students—that is, those within a particular grade or subject area.

Let us suppose, by way of example, that the following statement is a curriculum goal of the school: "All children need to develop skill in working with numbers." The fourth-grade teachers could create a grade level goal by simply reiterating the school goal as "Fourth-graders need to develop skill in working with numbers." On the other hand, the fourth-grade teachers might choose to interpret the school's curriculum goal and create a grade level curriculum objective, as follows: "This year's fourth-graders will excel last year's by an average of five percentile points on the same standardized test of arithmetic."

Another example of a school-wide curriculum goal is "Students will improve their scores on state assessment tests." One of the school's curriculum objectives derived from this goal might be "At least 85 percent of the students will achieve passing scores on the statewide assessment tests." The eleventh-grade faculty might set as its objective: "90 percent of the juniors will pass the state assessment test this year."

We encounter a similar case with a twelfth-grade faculty when the school seeks to accomplish the following curriculum goal: "Students will develop self-discipline and self-reliance." A twelfth-grade faculty might spell out the following curriculum goal: "Seniors will demonstrate skills of independent study." The twelfth-grade teachers might be more specific by following up this curriculum goal with a curriculum objective, as follows: "At least 70 percent of the seniors will seek to improve their self-discipline, self-reliance, and self-study techniques by engaging in independent research projects at least one hour of the school day three hours a week."

Teachers of foreign language may furnish us with an example of curriculum goals and objectives found within a discipline. They might, for example, consider the school's curriculum goal: "Students will develop the ability to relate to ethnic and national groups different from their own." The foreign language teachers might also note one of the school's curriculum objectives, in this case applying to all the students in general but aimed at a particular field: "75 percent of the student body will elect a foreign language."

The foreign language teachers might decide on the following curriculum goal: "Students will initiate a number of requests for advanced courses in a foreign language." They might identify as a curriculum objective: "50 percent of the students who are taking or who have taken a foreign language will enroll in a second foreign language."

In all cases, the grade or departmental level's and the school's curriculum goals and objectives must relate to one another. In the same manner, a school's curriculum goals and objectives must be compatible with the district's, and both an individual school's and the district's curriculum goals and objectives must be coordinated with those of the state.

State Curriculum Goals and Objectives

The state, through either its board or department of education, may exert curriculum leadership by promulgating a statement of curriculum goals and, in some cases, curriculum objectives for all its schools. The state of Florida, for example, has identified seven goals of education and one major curriculum objective, as shown in Box 8–1. Goal 1 is a curriculum goal primarily for the public schools. Goals 2 through 5 are curriculum goals for both the public school and postsecondary levels. Goal 6 is more of an administrative goal, although it has curricular implications. Goal 7 is both an administrative and curricular goal. Florida's aim to raise educational attainment of its students in the public schools to the upper quartile of states within five years can be termed a curriculum objective for the entire state.

In an earlier document the state of Florida offered some useful advice on how to conceptualize educational goals:

> The goals of education can be conceived in terms of the life activities of human adults in modern society. These activities may generally be placed in three categories: occupational, citizenship, and self-fulfillment. By constructing such a framework, it becomes possible to state the kinds of performance which should equip adults to function effectively in society—the *objectives* of education.[11]

The foregoing quotation recalls the method described in Chapter 7 of analyzing society's needs by spelling out social processes, functions, or life activities.

This same document helped curriculum planners by summarizing the characteristics of goals as follows:

1. Goals are statements of ultimate desired outcomes; they specify conditions desired for the population in general.
2. Goals are timeless, in the sense that no time is specified by which the goals must be reached.
3. Goals do not specify criteria for achievement, but provide a direction for system improvement.

---

[11] Florida Department of Education, *Goals for Education in Florida* (Tallahassee, Fla.: State Department of Education, 1972), p. 4.

BOX 8–1

FLORIDA'S GOALS OF EDUCATION

1. *Basic Skills.* All Floridians must have every opportunity, including remedial education, to master the basic skills for communication and computation (listening, speaking, reading, writing, and arithmetic). Basic skills are fundamental to success and mastery shall be developed through basic programs in the following areas of learning: language arts, mathematics, problem solving, art, music, physical education, science, and social studies.

2. *General Education.* All Floridians shall have the opportunity to acquire the general education fundamental to career and personal development and necessary for participation in a democratic society, including an emphasis on the arts. This includes skills, attitudes and knowledge for general problem solving and survival, human relations and citizenship, moral and ethical conduct, mental and physical health, aesthetic, scientific and cultural appreciation, and environmental and economic understanding.

3. *Vocational Competencies.* All Floridians shall have the opportunity to master vocational competencies necessary for entry level employment by the time they leave full-time education. For persons who continue formal education through advanced or professional programs, vocational competencies will be in areas of professional employment, including the arts. Vocational education shall be continuously reviewed to assure that Florida's needs for workers are met and that individuals can secure further training needed for career advancement.

4. *Professional Competencies.* Floridians with demonstrated interest, academic background, and aptitude shall have the opportunity to acquire professional competencies necessary for employment in a profession and to update their competencies

---

4. Goals are not permanent. Feedback from the entire evaluation/decision-making process is used to assess progress in the direction specified by the goals, and goals may be modified wherever necessary or desirable.
5. Goals are of equal importance.[12]
6. Goals are stated broadly enough to be accepted at any level of the educational enterprise: state, district, or local school. They thus represent the conceptual framework upon which the education enterprise depends.[13]

The Florida document on educational goals commented: "While it is necessary to know current status in order to specify educational needs and to assign priorities for satisfaction of these needs, the statements of desired outcomes are logically a prerequisite to establishing needs.[14] In Chapter 7, I made the following comment on timing of needs assessment and goal specification: "A needs

---

[12]Some may question this point.
[13]Florida Department of Education, *Goals for Education,* pp. 5–6.
[14]Ibid., p. 5.

BOX 8–1   continued

periodically. Programs of professional studies, including the arts, shall be organized to assure that Florida's and society's needs for professionals are met.

5. *Advanced Knowledge and Skills.* Floridians with demonstrated interest, academic background, and aptitude shall have the opportunity to acquire advanced knowledge and skills in the academic disciplines or other specialized fields of study and to update their knowledge and skills periodically. Programs of advanced academic training shall be organized to meet Florida's and society's needs for highly trained specialists.

6. *Research and Development.* The public education network shall seek solutions to local, regional, state, and national problems through organized research and development. Research and development shall be organized to solve pressing problems and to expand the store of knowledge in all areas of human endeavor, including education.

7. *Recreation and Leisure Skills.* Floridians shall have the opportunity to pursue recreation and leisure skills which satisfy the recreational and cultural needs of individuals in areas outside of general education.

On a statewide average, educational achievement in the State of Florida will equal that of the upper quartile of states within five years, as indicated by commonly accepted criteria of attainment. (S B E 1/20/81)

SOURCE: Goals 1–7: Florida State Board of Education, March 1975, amended May 6, 1980. (See also Ralph D. Turlington, *Focus on Public Education in Florida: The Annual Report of the Commissioner of Education* [Tallahassee, Fla.: State Department of Education, 1978], p. 16.) Unnumbered objective: Florida State Board of Education, January 20, 1981. Reprinted with permission.

assessment is a continuing activity that takes place (a) before specification of curricular goals and objectives, (b) after identification of curricular goals and objectives, (c) after evaluation of instruction, and (d) after evaluation of the curriculum."[15] To clarify the sequence of goal writing and needs assessment, we may refer to Figure 8–2.

Once curriculum goals and objectives have been spelled out, the needs assessment process proceeds to determine unmet needs. Once identified, these needs will result in the creation of more curriculum goals and objectives or a modification of those already specified.

In summary, a state may formulate both broad aims and curriculum goals (and also in some cases curriculum objectives, instructional goals, and instructional objectives as well) for all schools and all students in that state.

---

[15]See p. 247.

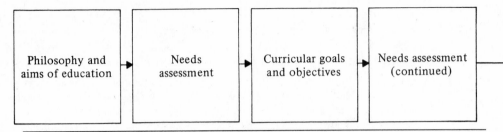

FIGURE 8–2   The sequence of goal specification and needs assessment

School-District Curriculum Goals and Objectives

in practice, school districts and individual schools may accept the state's formulation of goals and objectives verbatim or, if the state permits, may independently develop their own statements. In either case, however, the statements of
the school districts and individual schools must be in harmony with the state's.
Let's examine the statement of goals of the Dade County Public Schools, a large
urban school district with a multiethnic population. Borrowed from an earlier
pronouncement of the state of Florida and amended slightly by the school
district, this statement, "Goals for Student Development," is shown in Box
8–2.[16] The statement, which appeared in an earlier edition of Dade County's
District Comprehensive Educational Plan, is still retained in the district's board
policies.

In a more recent comprehensive plan, the Dade County public schools
focused on a particular curriculum goal with four subgoals, as follows:

> Prepare students for their life's work by providing germane curricula;
> methods by which students can address the basic issues of their own lives and
> interpersonal relationships; by rewarding creativity; and by instilling motiva-
> tion for excellence.

> □ Provide all students with the opportunity and encouragement to become
> bilingual, including special help for those students whose native language
> is not English.
> □ Improve students' thinking skills including, but not limited to, analysis,
> reasoning, and logic.
> □ Provide students those computer experiences and skills needed to function
> in a technical age.
> □ Provide a free and appropriate education to each handicapped student,
> directly utilizing school system programs and personnel when possible.[17]

---

[16]Dade County Public Schools, *District Comprehensive Educational Plan, 1974–79* (Miami,
Fla.: Dade County Public Schools, 1974), pp. 8–11. Reprinted with permission.

[17]Dade County Public Schools, *Preliminary District Comprehensive Plan, 1986–87 to 1990–
91* (Miami, Fla.: Office of Educational Accountability, Dade County Public Schools, March 1986),
p. B–1. Reprinted with permission.

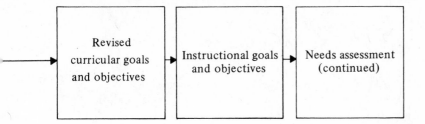

Individual School Curriculum Goals and Objectives

Not only do the states and school districts establish curriculum goals and objectives, but the individual schools also enter into the process by specifying their own goals and objectives. Box 8–3 (Philosophy and Goals of Lafayette Middle School) furnishes an example of a middle school's statement of both its philosophy and goals.

In order to show the relationships between the state's, the school district's, and the individual school's statements of goals and objectives, I have reproduced in Box 8–4 the statement of philosophy and objectives (which in the context of this chapter would be called goals) of Miami Palmetto Senior High School, which is in the same school district cited earlier in this chapter (Dade County).

The School Improvement Plan of the Hephzibah Middle School (Georgia) demonstrates how a school takes a curriculum goal of the school district and from it specifies its own curriculum objectives. One of the district's goals and the school's objectives derived from it are as follows:

> System Goal: To increase student mastery of academic skills as evidenced by improved test scores.
> Objectives:
>
> □ To exceed the state scores on the Criterion-Referenced Test for all objectives for both reading and mathematics and to have 80% of all students at grade level for the Iowa Tests of Basic Skills.
> □ To implement the new reading series throughout the school.
> □ To increase the number of students participating in the curriculum fair, science fair, literary fairs.
> □ To increase student use of the media center and to improve students' media and research skills (as outlined by the state's Quality Basic Education Act).[18]

Although the illustrations of curriculum goals and objectives cited in this chapter follow different formats, they serve as examples of the step in the planning process that calls for specification of curriculum goals and objectives.

---

[18]*School Improvement Plan, 1986–87,* Hephzibah Middle School, Hephzibah, Georgia. Reprinted with permission.

BOX 8–2

GOALS FOR STUDENT DEVELOPMENT

Goal Area I:

Communication and Learning Skills. Students shall acquire, to the extent of their individual physical, mental, and emotional capacities, a mastery of the basic skills required in obtaining and expressing ideas through the effective use of words, numerals, and other symbols.

a) Students shall achieve a working knowledge of reading, writing, speaking, and arithmetic during the elementary school years, accompanied by gradual progress into the broader fields of mathematics, natural science, language arts, and the humanities.

b) Students shall develop and use skills in the logical processes of search, analysis, evaluation and problem-solving, in critical thinking, and in the use of symbolism.

c) Students shall develop competence and motivation for continuing self-evaluation, self-instruction, and adaptation to a changing environment.

d) Students shall have the opportunity during the elementary school years to develop and use the skills of speaking and understanding a foreign language in order to communicate effectively in the language for future personal or vocational achievements.

Goal Area II:

Citizenship Education. Students shall acquire and continually improve the habits and attitudes necessary for responsible citizenship.

a) Students shall acquire knowledge of various political systems with emphasis on democratic institutions, the heritage of the United States, the contributions of our diverse cultural backgrounds, and the responsibilities and privileges of citizenship.

b) Students shall develop the skills required for participation in the political processes of our country and for influencing decisions made by political organizations.

c) Students shall develop the competence and desire to become informed and critical participants in the electoral process of this county.

d) Students shall acquire those attributes necessary for functioning, on a daily basis, as good citizens in their own school and community settings.

Goal Area III:

Career and Occupational Education. Students shall acquire a knowledge and understanding of the opportunities open to them for preparing for a productive life, and shall develop those skills and abilities which will enable them to take full advantage of those opportunities—including a positive attitude toward work and respect for the dignity of all honorable occupations.

a) Students shall acquire knowledge of and develop an understanding of the fundamental structure and processes of America's economic system, together with an

BOX 8–2   continued

understanding of the opportunities and requirements for individual participation and success in this changing system.

b) Students shall develop occupational competencies, consistent with their interests, aptitudes, and abilities, which are necessary for entry and advancement in the economic system; they shall develop those academic competencies necessary for the acquisition of technical or professional skills through post–high school training.

c) Students shall develop competence in the application of economic knowledge to practical economic functions: such as, planning and budgeting for the investment of personal income, calculating tax obligations, financing major purchases, and obtaining desirable employment.

d) Students shall develop an awareness of the relevance of the curriculum to the world of work and our social existence.

Goal Area IV:

Mental and Physical Health. Students shall acquire good health habits and an understanding of the conditions necessary for the maintenance of physical, emotional, and social well-being.

a) Students shall develop an understanding of the requirements of personal hygiene, adequate nutrition and leisure time activities essential to the maintenance of physical health, and a knowledge of the dangers to mental and physical health from addiction and other aversive practices.

b) Students shall develop skills in sports and other forms of recreation which will provide for life-long enjoyment of participation according to their own preferences and abilities.

c) Students shall develop competence in recognizing and preventing environmental health problems.

d) Students shall acquire a knowledge of basic psychological and sociological factors affecting human behavior and mental health, and shall develop competence for adjusting to changes in personal status and social patterns.

Goal Area V:

Home and Family Relationships. Students shall develop an appreciation of the family as a social institution.

a) Students shall develop an understanding of their roles and the roles of others as members of a family, together with a knowledge of the requirements for successful participation in family living.

b) Students shall develop an understanding of the role of the family as a basic unit in the society.

c) Students shall develop an awareness of the diversity of family patterns and the value of the contributions of the individuals to family and community living.

(continued)

BOX 8–2   continued

Goal Area VI:

Aesthetic and Cultural Appreciations. Students shall develop understanding and appreciation of human achievement in the natural sciences, the humanities and the arts.

a) Students shall acquire a knowledge of and an appreciation for major arts, music, literary, and drama forms, and their place in the cultural heritage.

b) Students shall acquire a knowledge of the natural, physical and social sciences and their relationships to human and social development.

c) Students shall develop skills for creative use of leisure time and shall develop an interest in becoming active in one or more areas of creative endeavor.

d) Students shall develop discrimination skills in the critical evaluation of cultural offerings and opportunities.

Goal Area VII:

Human Relations. Students shall develop a concern for moral, ethical, and spiritual values and for the application of such values to life situations.

a) Students shall acquire the greatest possible understanding and appreciation of themselves as well as of persons belonging to social, cultural, and ethnic groups different from their own, and of the worthiness of all persons as members of society.

b) Students shall develop those skills and attitudes necessary for positive interpersonal and group relationship and shall recognize the importance of and need for ethical and moral standards of behavior.

c) Students shall recognize the value of that level of group discipline and self-discipline that promotes a sense of worth of the individual while contributing to the collective benefit of all involved.

SOURCE: Dade County Public Schools, *District Comprehensive Educational Plan, 1974–79* (Miami, Fla.: Dade County Public Schools, 1974), pp. 8–11. Reprinted with permission.

CONSTRUCTING STATEMENTS OF CURRICULUM GOALS

The examples of curriculum goals suggest a variety of forms of expression. Some schools phrase their goals in a way that stresses the role of the curriculum or of the school, like the following examples:

☐ To teach students to express themselves clearly and correctly in written and oral English.

☐ To develop the students' abilities to purchase goods and services wisely.

☐ To expose students to cultures other than their own.

Although an expression that stresses the role of the school is common, an alternate form that focuses on the student seems preferable for a number of reasons:

1. Philosophically, this form is more in keeping with progressive doctrine that places the pupil at the center of learning—a sound principle.
2. It is in keeping with modern instructional design that focuses on the achievements of the learner rather than the performance of the teacher or school.
3. It parallels common practice, as we shall see in Chapter 10, in writing instructional goals and objectives. Thus curriculum goals may be better understood and the process of curriculum development better integrated.
4. It is easier to design evaluation processes when we know what is expected of students as opposed to what is expected of the teacher or school.

Writing curriculum goals in a form that starts with the students, we might revise the previous illustrations in the following manner:

□ Students will express themselves clearly and correctly in written and oral English.
□ Students will demonstrate the ability to purchase goods and services wisely.
□ Students will show interest in and understanding of cultures other than their own.

Characteristics of Curriculum Goals

The characteristics of curriculum goals as conceptualized in this text may be summarized as follows:

1. They relate to the educational aims and philosophy.
2. They are programmatic. Although they speak to one or more areas of the curriculum, they do not delineate specific courses or specific items of content.
3. They refer to the accomplishment of groups (all students, students in general, most students) rather than the achievement of individual students.
4. They are stated in general terms that provide directions for curriculum development.
5. They are broad enough to lead to specific curriculum objectives.

CONSTRUCTING STATEMENTS OF CURRICULUM OBJECTIVES

Like curriculum goals, curriculum objectives relate to the educational aims and philosophy, are programmatic in nature, and refer to accomplishments of groups. Unlike curriculum goals, curriculum objectives are stated in specific and measurable terms.

BOX 8–3

PHILOSOPHY AND GOALS OF LAFAYETTE MIDDLE SCHOOL

The middle school is an organization designed to answer the needs of boys and girls in their pre- and early adolescent years, who through common physiological changes and through common interests typical to these years form a homogeneous unit in the community. By the grouping together of students of common age and with common interests, the middle school provides better opportunities for meeting the needs of this age group.

The school must provide an appropriate balance among opportunities for emotional, intellectual, and social aspects of growth of the students. This aim should be achieved by emphasis upon the following goals:

1. Provide opportunities for intellectual growth toward eventual mastery of skills and abilities.

   Skill in the application of such fundamental tools of knowledge as reading, writing, and arithmetic is necessary to enable each pupil to go beyond his knowledge and to meet the needs of life situations. Because of the extremely uneven development in these skill areas, pupils must be allowed to progress at their own optimal rates.

2. Help all students to gain the fundamental background, concepts, and understanding of the various subject matter areas.

   An emphasis on unique modes of inquiry and teaching of basic structural elements, rather than on the fragmented learning of facts, can help bring order and depth of understanding to the learner.

Characteristics of Curriculum Objectives

Curriculum objectives are refinements of the curriculum goals. They specify the performance standards for the students for whom the curriculum is designed. We can turn a curriculum goal into a curriculum objective by adding the following three elements, which we will see again when discussing instructional objectives:

□ performance or behavioral terms—that is, those skills and knowledge that students are expected to be able to demonstrate
□ the degree of mastery desired by the curriculum planners
□ conditions under which the performance will take place, if not readily understood

Let's analyze the following curriculum objective for these three elements: "On completion of the first testing, 75 percent of the eleventh graders will have successfully passed the state's minimal competencies test; by com-

BOX 8–3 continued

---

3. Give as many opportunities as possible for the exploration of interests and abilities.

   Exploration as a concept derives from the purposes of initiative of the individual pupil rather than from the purposes of society. As such, it is crucial among the educational purpose of the middle school.

4. Provide through these investigations of unique needs, desires, and purposes a basis upon which students, with their parents, will be enabled to make wiser choices in the educational and vocational offerings of their later educational experiences.

5. Provide opportunities for healthful living, both mental and physical.

   The possession of mental resources for the use of leisure, the appreciation of beauty, the skillful maintenance of a healthful home and community, and the ability to function both as a participant and a spectator in many sports and pastimes are valid goals for all courses.

6. Provide opportunities for development, understanding, and appreciation of the democratic way of living.

   Educational practices that show a concern for the orderly structure of society, as well as for the individual, can strengthen loyalty to democratic ideals. Furthermore, giving students experience in management of their own school activities and helping them to strengthen their study skills will enable them to adjust more readily to the independence required by the high school program.

7. Throughout this program, continue to make available an effective counseling service which will aid pupils in their educational, social, and occupational problems.

   SOURCE: Lafayette Middle School, Lafayette, Louisiana. Reprinted with permission.

---

pletion of the second testing, 90 percent will have passed." Are all three elements present in this two-part objective? Yes, they are. The performance expected is successfully passing the state's minimal competencies test. The degrees of mastery desired are 75 and 90 percent. Completion of the first and second testings is the condition.

To accomplish the transition from curriculum goal to curriculum objective, you may find it helpful to jot down several indicators of student performance that will serve as guides for writing the objectives. Let's take another look at the illustrative curriculum goal mentioned earlier: "Students shall demonstrate responsible behavior as citizens of our school, community, state, nation, and world." What are some indicators of learner performance that would reveal evidence of students' accomplishment of this goal? We might look for such behaviors as the following:

☐ care of school building and grounds
☐ less fighting among students
☐ orderliness in school assemblies

BOX 8–4

PHILOSOPHY AND OBJECTIVES OF THE
MIAMI PALMETTO SENIOR HIGH SCHOOL

Miami Palmetto Senior High School provides opportunities for all students to become mature, thinking, skilled young people, well equipped for education, career, personal, and life-long growth. The staff seeks to create an atmosphere conducive to the learning process and one which enables students to develop a positive self-image. These factors combine to enable students to develop as responsible citizens.

As educators, we are committed to the following philosophical principles:

1. To foster a knowledge of self and of the world in which the individual lives.

2. To encourage understanding and respect for the rights of others.

3. To stimulate critical, constructive, and creative thinking.

4. To assist in the development of a set of values meaningful to the individual and worthwhile to society.

5. To assist in the development of functional skills necessary for an individual to be a contributing member of society.

6. To provide experiences which will enrich career education and career choices.

7. To provide a positive and challenging experience for all students.

In order to fulfill the previous statements, the faculty seeks to meet the objectives stated below:

1. To offer a flexible curriculum ranging from instruction in basic through college-level courses.

2. To instruct students in learning processes which will provide them with methods of inquiry applicable to the future, as well as present, learning situations.

3. To encourage students to practice courtesy, friendliness, and cooperation as a way of life.

4. To motivate students in the development and maintenance of sound mental, emotional, and physical health.

5. To provide experiences which will enable students to develop an appreciation and an understanding of their own culture as well as the culture of others.

6. To provide students with instruction and materials which are appropriate to their ability and maturity level.

7. To guide students to think logically and creatively, to express ideas clearly in speaking and writing, and to listen and view critically.

     □ participation in community youth organizations such as church groups, scout groups, and the like

     □ contribution of labor or money to some worthy cause

     □ keeping informed on current events

     □ refraining from littering the school and community

BOX 8–4   continued

8. To help students learn to discuss and to see the relationship between cause and effect.

9. To enable students to distinguish facts from unstated opinions, conclusions, and inferences.

10. To strengthen pupils' computational skills and to provide for those who operate at the concept level in mathematics.

11. To provide all students instruction in reading skills.

12. To encourage students to read widely both for their own intellectual growth and for their own enjoyment.

13. To assist students in the discovery of scientific principles through the study of factual and experimental evidence.

14. To help students acquire an understanding of the principles and processes of the American free-enterprise system.

15. To involve students in school and community resources.

16. To promote in students an appreciation and understanding of those factors conducive to successful family living.

17. To orient students in the effective use of print and nonprint materials in the Media Center.

18. To provide opportunities for interested students to develop manual skills.

19. To provide students with vocational information and the opportunity to develop occupational skills.

20. To provide students with co-curricular activities which will develop interest, cooperativeness, pride, and satisfaction.

21. To foster a positive educational experience for the potential dropout.

22. To encourage female students to enroll in high level math and science courses.

23. To encourage minority students with potential to enroll in courses which will challenge their abilities.

24. To encourage students to maximize their potential by enrolling in courses which will challenge them.

SOURCE: Miami Palmetto Senior High School, Miami, Florida. Reprinted with permission.

☐ serving on committees of the school
☐ observing highway speed limits
☐ taking an interest in local, state, and national elections
☐ engaging in discussions on ways to reduce international tensions

We could turn the first performance indicator—care of school building and grounds—into a curriculum objective in the following manner: "By the end of April students will have demonstrated care of the building to the extent that there will be a 95 percent reduction in the number of graffiti on the walls." From this one curriculum goal on good citizenship we can generate many curriculum objectives, and from the first performance indicator alone we can create a number of objectives.

The generation of curriculum goals and objectives is a highly creative exercise. The curriculum goals and objectives set the direction for the subsequent organization and development of the curriculum. The curriculum goals and objectives determine the activities that will take place in the many classrooms of the school.

VALIDATING AND DETERMINING PRIORITY OF GOALS AND OBJECTIVES

As stated earlier, the assessment of curriculum needs is a continuing process that starts after a school formulates its philosophy and clarifies its aims of education. The needs of society, of students in general, and of the particular students, community, and subject matter give rise to initial statements of curriculum goals and objectives. After these goals and objectives have been identified, the needs assessment process is continued to determine if any needs have not been met. When unmet needs are exposed, a revised list of curriculum goals and objectives is prepared. These goals and objectives require validation and placing in order of priority.

Validation is the process of determining whether the goals and objectives are accepted as appropriate or "right" for the school system proposing them. *Determining priority* is the placing of the goals and objectives in order of relative importance in the school system. Groups concerned with the progress of the school should be enlisted to help identify suitable goals and objectives and to set priorities.

Some school systems seek to validate both goals and objectives; others limit the process to validating goals on the presumption that once the goals are identified, a representative committee can handle the task of making the goals specific—that is, turning them into objectives.

Function of Curriculum Committee

The validation process, whether carried out by the state, district, or school, assumes the formation of a curriculum committee or council charged with the task. The curriculum committee will submit the goals by means of a questionnaire or opinionnaire to groups who are concerned with the progress of the school(s).

Submitting curriculum goals and any already identified curriculum objectives to a broad sampling of groups—lay persons (including parents), students, teachers, administrators, and curriculum experts (on the staffs of public school systems or on the faculties of teacher education institutions)—is good practice. The effort should be made to learn whether there is widespread acceptance of the goals formulated by the curriculum planners and what the groups' priorities will be. Curriculum objectives that are developed after a broad sampling of opinion has been gathered can be submitted to either a more limited sampling of the same groups or to the curriculum committee for validation and ranking.

Data should be gathered and interpreted, preferably by a curriculum committee representative of the various groups polled. Such a committee will be called on to make judgments that will tax its collective wisdom. It cannot treat the data in a simplistic fashion, tallying responses from all groups, and simply following the majority's opinions. It needs to analyze discrepancies of opinion, if any, among the various groups surveyed and discuss the discrepancies among themselves and with members of the various groups.

Weighting Opinions. As a general rule, the wishes of students, for example, should not hold the same priority as the beliefs of parents and other lay people. The opinions of groups small in number, like curriculum specialists or college professors, cannot be treated in the same light as the attitudes of large numbers of residents of the community. For that matter, the opinions of a few school administrators should not be given, simply because of their status, as great a weight as those of large numbers of teachers and parents.

Since the committee interpreting the data may not find consensus on goals and objectives among the various groups, it has the heavy responsibility of reconciling differing positions and reaching consensus among its own members. Drawing on the opinions of the groups that have been polled, the curriculum committee must decide which goals are valid and which should be assigned priority. To set priorities is to say that some goals are more important than others and deserve more time, attention, and emphasis in the curriculum.

It is clear that the goals of a state, district, or school should be submitted for validation and ranking by sizable numbers of educators and noneducators. It is debatable, however, whether curriculum goals and objectives of grades or departments need or should be submitted to persons beyond the school or school-district personnel. It would be somewhat impractical, redundant, expensive, and time-consuming for curriculum goals and objectives of the grades and departments to be submitted to significant numbers of the school system's constituents. The faculties of the grade and departmental levels may satisfy their responsibilities for validation and ranking of goals and objectives by submitting their statements to the curriculum committee and to experts in the field for review and endorsement.

The process of validation and determining priorities may be repeated as often as the curriculum committee finds necessary, with modifications and repeated ranking made as a result of each survey and prior to a subsequent survey. After the curriculum goals and objectives have been validated and placed in rank order, the curriculum planners turn to the next phase in the curriculum development process—putting the goals and objectives into operation.

SUMMARY

State school systems, school districts, and individual schools engage in the task of specifying curriculum goals and objectives. Curriculum goals and objectives are derived from the developers' philosophy and educational aims.

Curriculum goals are programmatic statements of expected outcomes without criteria of achievement. They apply to students as a group and are often interdisciplinary or multidisciplinary.

Curriculum objectives are specific, measurable, programmatic statements of outcomes to be achieved by students as a group in the school or school system.

Curriculum goals and objectives are essential for

1. conducting a complete needs assessment to identify unmet needs
2. carrying out subsequent phases of the suggested model for curriculum improvement
3. generating instructional goals and objectives
4. providing a basis for evaluating the curriculum
5. giving direction to the program

It is recommended that curriculum goals and objectives be phrased in terms of anticipated accomplishments of students. Curriculum objectives, which are more specific than curriculum goals, should stipulate expected degrees of mastery and the conditions under which students can master the desired behaviors. Curriculum goals and objectives should be validated and put in order of priority by the school's curriculum committee after review by representatives of the various constituencies that the school serves.

QUESTIONS FOR DISCUSSION

1. How do you go about specifying curriculum goals and objectives? Who does the specifying?
2. Which comes first: a curriculum needs assessment or the specification of curriculum goals and objectives? Why?
3. Can you have curriculum goals and objectives both across disciplines and within disciplines? If the answer is yes, give examples.
4. Can you have curriculum goals without curriculum objectives? Explain.
5. Can you have curriculum objectives without curriculum goals? Explain.

SUPPLEMENTARY EXERCISES

1. Define and give *two* examples of
   a. aims of education
   b. curriculum goals
   c. curriculum objectives
2. Following definitions in this text, explain both the relationship and difference between
   a. an aim of education and a curriculum goal
   b. a curriculum goal and a curriculum objective
3. Explain the relationship of curriculum goals and objectives to needs assessment.
4. Respond to the following questions, showing your position on each:
   a. Is it necessary to write an educational philosophy in order to specify curriculum goals and objectives?
   b. Is it necessary to list educational aims to specify curriculum goals and objectives?
   c. Is it necessary to specify both educational aims and curriculum goals and objectives?
   d. Is it necessary to specify curriculum goals to identify curriculum objectives?
5. Locate and report on illustrations of curriculum goals either in education textbooks or in curriculum materials of any school or school system in the United States.
6. Locate and report on illustrations of curriculum objectives either in education textbooks or in curriculum materials of any school or school system in the United States.
7. Obtain and, following principles advocated in this chapter, critique the statement of
   a. curriculum goals of a school that you know well
   b. curriculum objectives of a school that you know well
   c. curriculum goals and objectives of a school district that you know well
   d. curriculum goals and/or objectives of one of the 50 states
8. Write as many curriculum objectives as you can for each of the following curriculum goals:
   a. Students will maintain good health and physical fitness.
   b. Students will demonstrate skill in writing.
   c. Students will develop an appreciation for the free enterprise system.
   d. Students will exhibit positive attitudes toward each other regardless of differences in sex, religion, or ethnic origin.
   You may wish to do this exercise in small groups.
9. Write a comparative analysis of the author's position on the separateness of curricular and instructional objectives and that of another curriculum specialist who takes a different position.

10. Describe the hierarchy of goals discussed by Ronald S. Brandt and Ralph W. Tyler (see bibliography) and give examples of each type.

BIBLIOGRAPHY

Berman, Louise M., and Roderick, Jessie A. *Curriculum: Teaching the What, How, and Why of Living*. Columbus, Ohio: Charles E. Merrill, 1977.

Bloom, Benjamin S., ed. *Taxonomy of Educational Objectives: The Classification of Educational Goals: Handbook I: Cognitive Domain*. New York: Longman, 1956.

Brandt, Ronald S., ed. *Content of the Curriculum*. 1988 Yearbook. Alexandria, Va.: Association for Supervision and Curriculum Development., 1988.

Brandt, Ronald S. and Tyler, Ralph W. "Goals and Objectives." In Fenwick W. English, ed., *Fundamental Curriculum Decisions*, 1983 Yearbook, 40–52. Alexandria, Va.: Association for Supervision and Curriculum Development, 1983.

Commission on the Reorganization of Secondary Education. *Cardinal Principles of Secondary Education*. Washington, D.C.: United States Office of Education, Bulletin No. 35, 1918.

Czajkowski, Theodore J., and Patterson, Jerry L. *School District Needs Assessment: Practical Models for Increasing Involvement in Curriculum Decisions*. Madison, Wis.: Madison Public Schools, 1976.

Doherty, Victor W., and Peters, Linda B. "Goals and Objectives in Educational Planning and Evaluation." *Educational Leadership* 38, no. 8 (May 1981): 606–611.

Doll, Ronald C. *Curriculum Improvement: Decision Making and Process,* 7th ed. Boston: Allyn and Bacon, 1989.

Educational Policies Commission. *Education for All American Youth*. Washington, D.C.: National Educational Association, 1944.

————. *The Purposes of Education in American Democracy*. Washington, D.C.: National Education Association, 1938.

English, Fenwick W., ed. *Fundamental Curriculum Decisions,* 1983 Yearbook. Alexandria, Va.: Association for Supervision and Curriculum Development, 1983.

Florida Department of Education. *Goals for Education in Florida*. Tallahassee, Fla.: State Department of Education, 1972.

Foshay, Arthur W., ed. *Considered Action for Curriculum Improvement,* 1980 Yearbook. Alexandria, Va.: Association for Supervision and Curriculum Development, 1980.

Fraser, Dorothy M. *Deciding What to Teach*. Washington, D.C.: Project on the Instructional Program of the Public Schools, National Education Association, 1963.

Krathwohl, David R., Bloom, Benjamin S., and Masia, Bertram B. *Taxonomy of Educational Objectives: The Classification of Educational Goals: Handbook II: Affective Domain*. New York: Longman, 1964.

Mager, Robert F. *Preparing Instructional Objectives*. Belmont, Calif.: Fearon, 1962; 2nd ed., Belmont, Calif.: Pitman Learning, 1975.

Myers, Donald A. *Decision Making in Curriculum and Instruction*. Dayton, Ohio: Institute for Development of Educational Activities, 1970.

Popham, W. James, and Baker, Eva L. *Establishing Instructional Goals*. Englewood Cliffs, N.J.: Prentice-Hall, 1970.

————. *Systematic Instruction*. Englewood Cliffs, N.J.: Prentice-Hall, 1970.

Pratt, David. *Curriculum: Design and Development*. New York: Harcourt Brace Jovanovich, 1980.

Saylor, J. Galen, Alexander, William M., and Lewis, Arthur J. *Curriculum Planning for Better Teaching and Learning,* 4th ed. New York: Holt, Rinehart and Winston, 1981.

Tyler, Ralph W. *Basic Principles of Curriculum and Instruction*. Chicago: University of Chicago Press, 1949.

Unruh, Glenys G. and Unruh, Adolph. *Curriculum Development; Problems, Processes, and Progress*. Berkeley, Calif.: McCutchan, 1984.

Wiles, Jon, and Bondi, Joseph C. *Curriculum Development: A Guide to Practice*, 2nd ed. Columbus, Ohio: Charles E. Merrill, 1984.

FILMSTRIP-AUDIOTAPE PROGRAMS

Vimcet Associates, P.O. Box 24714, Los Angeles, Calif. 90024:

#1 Educational Objectives. 1967.

#3 Selecting Appropriate Educational Objectives. 1967.

#25 Deciding on Defensible Goals via Educational Needs Assessment. 1971.

VIDEOTAPE

Planning Curriculum with a Futures Perspective. 1982. 21 min. Willis Harman, Arthur Lewis, Don Glines, Robert Bundy, and Sherry Shiller analyze trends and ways schools can help students prepare for the future. Association for Supervision and Curriculum Development, 1250 North Pitt Street, Alexandria, Va. 22314.

CHAPTER NINE

Organizing and Implementing the Curriculum

After studying this chapter you should be able to:

1. Describe and state strengths and weaknesses of various plans and proposals for organizing and implementing the curriculum.

2. Relate each organizational arrangement discussed in this chapter to (a) the psychological and sociological circumstances of the public school and (b) the achievement of one or more aims of education or curriculum goals at each of the three school levels: elementary, middle, and senior high.

3. Specify several curriculum goals for the elementary, middle school, or senior high school level; choose or design and defend a curriculum organization plan that you believe will most satisfactorily result in accomplishment of these goals.

NECESSARY DECISIONS

A Hypothetical Setting

Imagine, if you will, a building complex of three schools—an elementary school of five grades plus kindergarten, a middle (formerly junior high) school of three grades, and a senior high school of four grades—constructed in the early days of Franklin D. Roosevelt's presidency and situated on a large tract of land. We could place this complex in a small town in any state where the three schools serve all the children of a particular school district, or we could locate it in a sector of a large urban area where the three schools are a part of the local school system.

Let's create in our own minds the administrative offices of the superintendent (or area superintendent) and school board across the street from this complex. From a second floor conference room we can look out on the children at play in the elementary school yard, we can see awkward teeny-boppers of the middle school up the street to our right, and we can observe the senior high school Harrys and Janes spinning out in their gasoline chariots from the parking lot in the background.

On a particular day in September a group of curriculum planners has gathered in the conference room. It is 4:00 P.M., and for a moment they stand at the window looking over the complex across the way. Activity at the elementary school has virtually ceased for the day, has just about tapered off at the middle school, and continues apace at the senior high school. Only two cars remain in the elementary school parking lot—the principal's and the custodian's.

Making up the curriculum group are the district supervisor (director of curriculum) and the chairpersons of the district curriculum steering committee and the curriculum councils of each of the three schools. In front of them—in finished form, neatly typed and packaged—are (1) the report of the needs assessment that revealed gaps in the school district's curricula and (2) a set of both district and individual school curriculum goals and objectives that they laboriously hammered out with the help of many faculty members, students, administrators, supervisors, and lay citizens.

Hypothetical Steps

The task of this curriculum group now is to decide on next steps. What do they do with the curriculum goals and objectives now that they are finished? Shall they duplicate, distribute, and then forget them? Shall they take the position that the process of defining the goals and objectives was sufficient, or that the process should lead to further action? Shall they file the goals and objectives with the superintendent and principals, to be pulled out on special occasions such as visits of parent groups, accrediting committees, or others? How shall they meet the discrepancies shown by the needs assessment and the curriculum goals and objectives developed as a result of that assessment?

The curriculum planners of the district, whose leadership is represented by this committee, must decide how to put the goals and operations into effect and how to organize the curriculum in such a way that the goals and objectives can be achieved. They must decide what structure will be the most conducive to successfully accomplishing the goals and objectives and to fulfilling learner needs. They must ask themselves and their colleagues how best to go about implementing the curriculum decisions that they have made up to this point.

Assessing Curriculum Organization

The question is often posed to curriculum workers: "How shall we go about organizing the curriculum?" The literature on curriculum organization often appears to make one of two assumptions: (1) Curriculum planners regularly have the opportunity to initiate a curriculum in a brand new school (or perhaps in a deserted old school) for which no curriculum patterns yet exist; or (2) curriculum developers automatically have the freedom to discard that which now exists and replace it with patterns of their own choosing.

Both assumptions are likely to be erroneous. Curriculum planners do not frequently experience the responsibility for developing an original curriculum for a brand new school (or more accurately, for an upcoming new school, since planning must precede construction). It is true, of course, that new schools are built to meet growths and shifts in population and to replace decrepit structures, which, like old soldiers, slowly fade away. The development of a curriculum for a brand new school does provide an opportunity for curriculum planning from the ground floor, so to speak. But even that planning must be carried out within certain boundaries, including local traditions, state and district mandates, and the curricula of other schools of the district. The programs of the new school must be compatible with others in the district.

Curriculum planners cannot expect simply to substitute as they wish new patterns of curriculum organization for old. Again we face certain parameters: student needs, teacher preferences, administrators' values, community sentiment, physical restrictions, and financial resources.

Our fictitious curriculum group is talking about possible ways of reorganizing the curriculum to meet pupil needs and to provide the best possible structure for attaining the district's and each school's curriculum goals and objectives. The group decides that one way of approaching this task is to consider the schools' past, present, and future ideas for curriculum organization. They will identify patterns that have been tried and those that might be feasible or successful in the immediate and distant future.

The committee decides to clarify at this meeting what they mean by curriculum organization. They agree to talk with their colleagues on their schools' curriculum councils and others and come to the next meeting of this group prepared to trace the historical development of the curricular organizations of the three schools. Each will provide an overview of the more significant patterns of curriculum organization that have been studied and implemented, studied and rejected, and considered for future implementation.

Before adjourning this meeting, the committee agrees on what they will include under the rubric of curriculum organization. They define curriculum organization as those patterns of both a curricular and administrative nature by which students encounter learning experiences and subject matter. Thus it includes not only broad plans for programmatic offerings, such as the subject matter curriculum, but also delivery systems, which possess an administrative dimension, such as team teaching.

Several weeks later when the committee reassembles, exhilarated by its research on the history of curriculum developments in their schools, it expresses a newfound admiration for previous curriculum planners. Whereas the aging facades of the buildings might convey to the outside world that "the more things change, the more they stay the same," inside, innovation and change have been key words. The committee spends several sessions sharing its discoveries and studying what the experts say about the structures it uncovered. The committee is sure that by examining past patterns, projecting future arrangements, and comparing both past practices and future possibilities with present structures, it can create more effective ways of implementing the curriculum.

This hypothetical committee's discoveries are significant enough to be shared with you. Our discussion will be organized into three major parts: the past (Where We've Been), the present (Where We Are), and the future (Where We're Going). For each period some major plans in school and curriculum organization at each of three levels—elementary, junior high/middle school, and senior high school—are described.

Remember that Axiom 3 in Chapter 2 postulates that changes do not, as a rule, start and stop abruptly but overlap. Axiom 3 applies to our hypothetical community as it does elsewhere. Consequently, when I discuss the graded school, for example, as a place where we have been, I do not imply that it has necessarily disappeared from the present or that it will not exist in the future. When I discuss the middle school, I do not suggest that its predecessor, the junior high school, no longer exists.

Nor are curricular arrangements always confined to one level. The subject matter curriculum, the graded school, the nongraded school, team teaching, and flexible scheduling exist or have existed at more than one level. By placing a curricular arrangement at a particular level, I am not saying that it could not be found or could not have been found either at the same time or at another time at other levels even in the hypothetical community used for illustrative purposes. However, you would tire if, for example, discussion of the subject matter

TABLE 9–1   Arrangements and recommendations of the past, present, and future

LEVEL	WHERE WE'VE BEEN (PAST)	WHERE WE ARE (PRESENT)	WHERE WE'RE GOING (FUTURE)
Elementary	Graded school Activity curriculum Nongraded elementary school Open education and open space	Basic skills Teaching thinking skills Provision for students with special needs	Continuation of traditional modes Cooperative learning Whole language
Junior high/ middle	The school in between: the junior high school Conant's recommendations ASCD proposals Core curriculum	Middle school	Universality of the middle school
Senior high	Subject matter curriculum Conant's proposals Broad fields curriculum Team teaching and differentiated staffing Flexible and modular scheduling Nongraded high school	Comprehensive high school Alternative (including magnet) schools Higher requirements for graduation	Recommendations of recent studies, including Mortimer J. Adler, David P. Gardner (National Commission on Excellence in Education), Ernest L. Boyer, John I. Goodlad, Theodore R. Sizer Community service

curriculum were repeated at each of the three levels. Therefore, I have placed the arrangements, perhaps arbitrarily, at levels where the arrangements were particularly strong, significant, or common. Unless a curricular arrangement had particular significance for more than one level and possessed distinctive characteristics for each level, as in the case of the nongraded elementary school and the nongraded high school, a particular plan is discussed at only one level.

Table 9–1 shows various curricular and organizational arrangements and recommendations tried in the past or present and proposals for future change. You will be directed to other chapters for discussion of several of the arrangements cited in Table 9–1.

WHERE WE'VE BEEN: CURRICULUM PAST

THE ELEMENTARY SCHOOL

The Graded School

Historians tell us that the concept of the graded school started in Prussia, a land famed for discipline and regimentation, and migrated across the ocean to the New World.[1] The Quincy Grammar School of Boston, which opened in 1848, is credited as the first school in the United States to become completely graded. With enough youngsters for several groups, it took not a quantum leap but a simple bit of ingenuity to reason that youngsters might be taught more efficiently if they were sorted and graded. Instead of being mixed, they could be divided largely on the basis of chronological age.

The graded school has become the standard model not only for the United States but for the world. As our country steadily grew in population, expanded westward, and became industrialized, the number of grades provided for children by the numerous school districts of the nation increased in proportion.

By the early twentieth century 12 grades were made available and were considered sufficient for most American boys and girls. School systems grew, providing the opportunity for young people to receive not ten, not 11, but 12 full years of education at public expense. For one reason or another many children and youth in early days (and to a decreasing extent today) were not able to complete the 12 grades of elementary and secondary education even in communities that offer 12 grades. We could add in passing that both public and private community junior colleges and senior institutions have been established to offer youth opportunities for further learning, but that's another story in itself.

Twelve Years As Norm.   Administrators, curriculum experts, teachers, and the public have accepted the 12 years as a norm for most of our young people and have adjusted the component levels as the situation seemed to demand. Thus until rather recently the most common organizational plan for schools across the country was the eight-four plan (eight years of elementary school and four of secondary school). Under this plan grades seven and eight were considered as parts of the elementary rather than the secondary school. As the junior high school began to emerge after the first decade of the twentieth century, the six-two-four plan (six elementary, two junior high, and four senior high grades) offered a variant to the eight-four.

Communities of moderate size showed a fondness for the six-six plan (six elementary, six secondary), which, although it clearly attaches junior high school to secondary education, also buries its identity in that of the senior high school. Larger communities expressed a preference for the six-three-three plan with three years of junior high school between the elementary and senior high

---

[1]William J. Shearer, *The Grading of Schools* (New York: H. P. Smith, 1898).

school. The three-year junior high school combining grades seven, eight, and nine replicated the structure of the first junior high schools that came into existence in 1910 in Berkeley, California, and Columbus, Ohio. Other variations have been suggested such as the six-three-five plan and the six-three-three-two plan, which would extend public secondary education through grades 13 and 14. Those last two years, however, have clearly become identified with college age. As it is, grades 11 and 12 are normally beyond the age of 16, the usual limit for compulsory school attendance. The rearrangement of the 12 years of public schooling has continued to the present, as we shall see later when we discuss the development of the middle school.

The concomitant outgrowth of the graded school was the self-contained classroom—a heterogeneous group of youngsters of approximately the same age, in multiples of 25 to 35, under the direction of one teacher. Primary school teachers of the graded school were no longer required to master all disciplines of all grades like their counterparts in the one-room school but only to master all disciplines at the particular grade level. The group of children assigned to a teacher in a self-contained, graded elementary school spent the entire day under the watchful eye of that teacher. It has taken militant action of teacher organizations in recent years to pry loose some breathing time for elementary school teachers during the school day.

The concept of the graded school, aided by the measurement movement in education, has firmly established the principle that certain learnings should be accomplished by pupils not at certain periods of growth and development but by the end of certain grade levels. Syllabi, courses of study, and, lately, minimal competencies have been determined for each grade level. In the graded school, material is tailored to fit the confines of fixed times during the customary ten months of the school year. Thus, by means of a standardized test of reading, for example, we can state that a third-grade child in April (the eighth month of the school year) whose test score placed him or her at the grade norm of 3.2 (second month of the third-grade year) was reading at a level six months below the norm for that grade.

When we speak of the self-contained classroom, we normally think of the elementary school. We sometimes forget that the self-contained classroom has been the prevailing pattern in the secondary school except for a brief period of popularity of core programs, which we shall discuss later.

Like the junior and senior high school, the elementary school adopted an organizational framework that stressed the mastery of subject matter. This framework, commonly referred to as the subject matter curriculum, will be examined shortly.

Typical Schedule.   A typical week in a self-contained, subject-oriented elementary school calls for separate subjects scheduled at specific and regular times during the day. Little or no effort is made to integrate these diverse areas. Some elementary schools, of course, have never departed from this model, whereas others departed for a time and then swung back in recent years.

In the late 1920s, through the 1930s, and into the 1940s, many elementary schools, warmed by the glow of the progressive movement that championed the child over subject matter, abandoned the subject matter curriculum for the activity or experience curriculum.

The Activity Curriculum

The activity (or experience) curriculum was an attempt by educators to break away from the rigidity of the graded school. It is of historical interest that the activity curriculum was a contribution of two of the better known laboratory schools—the Laboratory School founded by John Dewey at the University of Chicago and the University Elementary School directed by J. L. Meriam at the University of Missouri. The activity curriculum came about as an effort to translate progressive beliefs into the curriculum. As such, it captured the imaginations of elementary school educators in the first quarter of the twentieth century.

Disenchanted with the subject matter curriculum promoted by the essentialist philosophers and curriculum makers, Dewey and others sought to free the learner from the confines of a subject-centered curriculum and to create an environment that catered to learner needs and interests.

Human Impulses. B. Othanel Smith, William O. Stanley, and J. Harlan Shores observed that Dewey's Laboratory School curriculum was based on the following four human impulses, which Dewey referred to as "uninvested capital":

> the *social impulse,* which is shown in the child's desire to share his experiences with the people around him; the *constructive impulse,* which is manifested at first in play, in rhythmic movement, in make-believe, and then in more advanced form in the shaping of raw materials into useful objects; the *impulse to investigate and experiment,* to find out things, as revealed in the tendency of the child to do things just to see what will happen; and the *expressive or artistic impulse,* which seems to be a refinement and further expression of the communicative and constructive interests.[2]

Dewey's curriculum eschewed the usual subject organizers and focused on occupations in which all men and women engaged—carpentry, cooking, and sewing.

Human Activities. The University Elementary School at the University of Missouri followed principles advocated by Junius L. Meriam and structured its program not around subjects but around human activities of observation, play, stories, and handwork.[3] The California State Curriculum Commission

---

[2] Excerpts from *Fundamentals of Curriculum Development,* Revised Edition, p. 265, by B. O. Smith, W. O. Stanley, and J. Harlan Shores, copyright ©1957 by Harcourt Brace Jovanovich, Inc. and renewed 1985 by B. O. Smith, W. O. Stanley, and J. Harlan Shores, reprinted by permission of the publisher.

[3] See Junius L. Meriam, *Child Life and the Curriculum* (Yonkers, N.Y.: World Book Company, 1920), p. 382.

outlined a daily program for an activity curriculum as shown in Table 9–2. As these two examples reveal, the content of the activity curriculum is centered on projects or experiences that are of immediate interest to the learners. The various subjects, including the basic skills, are used as a means of promoting learning rather than as ends or centers of learning for themselves.

Subject Matter from Child's World.   Here the curriculum is developed by the teacher in cooperation with the pupils. The subject matter evolves from the child's world rather than from the adult world. Although the teacher can suggest activities or problems to the learners, the children's interests become the dominant factor. William H. Kilpatrick advocated pupil activities that he referred to as projects (ergo, the "project method") and took the position that the child should do his or her own thinking and planning.[4]

Problem solving—Dewey's "reflective thinking"—is the instructional method par excellence. Experience in the process of problem solving is perceived by those who espouse progressive thought as more important than attaining the solutions to the problems. A great effort is made to integrate subject matter, using any and all content as needed without regard to discipline boundaries, for the solution of problems or carrying out of projects.

By its very nature, the activity curriculum cannot be fully planned in advance. Consequently, the activity curriculum can be described only after it has been completed, for the teacher cannot be sure in advance where the interests of the students will lead them.

The unit method of organizing instruction (a unit of work centered on a single topic or problem) lends itself well to the goal of problem solving. Units are designed by the teacher in cooperation with the pupils to include a sufficient variety of activities to provide for individual differences among pupils. A series of units can provide a skeletal framework for a given grade level.

Drill, if needed, is carried out in meaningful terms, not in isolated rote fashion. With the social orientation of the progressivists, the activity curriculum calls for the socialization of the learners and the use of the community as a learning laboratory.

Scheduling is flexible with time allotments variable depending on the activities under way. Pupils are grouped according to interests and abilities, obviating the need for fixed grade levels. Some schools tossed out marks, report cards, and the assumption that certain learnings have to be mastered at each grade level.

The teacher of the activity curriculum finds his or her role not as subject matter specialist and expert-in-residence but rather as a guide and facilitator of

---

[4]See William H. Kilpatrick, "The Project Method," *Teachers College Record* 19, no. 4 (September 1918): 319–335.

TABLE 9–2   Schedule for an activity curriculum

TIME	MONDAY	TUESDAY	WEDNESDAY	THURSDAY	FRIDAY
9:00	Informal greetings, reports, observations, rhymes, music, events of current interest, informal activities designed to create a mental set conducive to a happy, profitable day.				
	Arithmetical Enterprises				
9:15	Playstores, banking activities, handling of school supplies, etc. Although rich in arithmetical content through which the child is trained in skills and abilities, such units also yield abundantly in group and individual situations which develop initiative, responsibility, and cooperation. The flexible period provides opportunity for individual instruction.				
	Healthful Living Enterprises				
10:00	Physical education enterprises, free play, the nutrition program, and adequate relief periods are provided for daily; units of work such as: "the study of milk," "a balanced meal," etc., provide enterprises which have healthful living as a center of interest but provide situations developmental of social and civic attitudes as well.				
	Language Arts				
10:50	Oral and written composition, spelling and writing develop from activities rich in opportunities for expression, as the writing of a play to be presented in the auditorium period, puppet shows, the school newspaper, etc. The period should provide opportunity for literary discrimination and original expression; the long period provides for concentration of effort and attention according to individual interest and need.				
12:00	Lunch, Rest and Directed Playground Activities.				
	Avocational Activities				
1:00	Music; activities, music appreciation, rhythm, harmonica, band, orchestra, etc.	Nature Club, school museum, aquarium, gardens, terrarium.	Creative art and constructive activities in pottery, weaving, painting, drawing.	Use of auditorium for music, dancing, dramatics, projects, stagecraft, related to class activities.	Civics Club Committees responsible for various phases of school life.
1:50	Recreation and Rest				
	Reading Groups: Library Activities				
2:00	Group organization on the basis of reading ability provides opportunity for remedial work with children having reading deficiencies and library guidance to superior readers. The quiet reading period may contribute to the development of information needed in the class activities related to social science, avocational, or health or other interests.				
2:50	Recreation and Rest				
3:00	Social studies activities	Social studies activities	Free creative work period	Social studies activities	Shop enterprises

SOURCE: Ruth Manning Hockett, ed., *Teachers' Guide to Child Development: Manual for Kindergarten and Primary Teachers* (Sacramento, Calif.: California Department of Education, 1930), pp. 355–356. Reprinted by permission.

learning. Key concepts that the progressivists wove into the activity curriculum are the active rather than the passive role of the learner and the sharing of students' experiences with the teacher and each other.

The activity curriculum, like progressive education itself, left its indelible imprint on American education. Flexible scheduling, unit teaching, problem solving, project method, nongraded schools, and open education owe a debt to the activity curriculum. Nevertheless, the activity curriculum lost popularity and died out as a viable organizational pattern for the public elementary school. There are a number of reasons for its demise.

With the activity curriculum the needs of society and the needs of the adult world took a back seat to the needs of immature youngsters. Progressive—that is, activity-oriented—schools, projected an unfavorable image to the public who felt that subject matter learning was being neglected and too much stress was being placed on the immediate interests of immature learners.

Excesses on the part of some progressive schools led to cynical jokes, such as the joke in which the teacher asks, "Is the earth round or flat?" and the pupil answers, "I don't know; let's vote on it." Another one tells that, during a unit on redbirds, the primary school teacher used every device possible to work redbirds into English, science, mathematics, social studies, and so on. At the end of a hard day something struck the outside of the classroom window. The teacher, startled, asked, "What was that?" A pupil in the back responded, "Aw, it was just that damn redbird." Then there is a classic put-down of the progressive school: The teacher enters the room in the morning and asks the class, "O.K., kids, what do you want to learn today?" and the children complain, "Do we have to do what we want to do today?"

It was not commonly understood that teachers of the activity curriculum had to be more knowledgeable and better trained not only in subject matter but also in techniques of guiding learning. The activity curriculum also required for its success resources and facilities that exceeded those of the typical elementary school. Further, more flexible administrators and teachers were needed for successful operation of a program of this type. The secondary schools also complained when they received students who were products of the activity curriculum who had a great range of knowledge and skills and glaring gaps in their education.

The Nongraded Elementary School

The nongraded elementary school, following plans that permit continuous progress, evolved as an alternative to the graded school. The nongraded or continuous progress school was a reaction to increasing rigidity of the graded school, which was an innovation designed to provide a more efficient education for children.

Persons unfamiliar with the concept of the nongraded school are sometimes confused by the term and interpret it to signify a school without a formal marking system. When we speak of the nongraded school, we refer to schools that have abandoned grade level designations rather than marks.

In a nongraded school, typical grade levels and standards for those levels are absent. Children are grouped for instruction according to their particular needs and progress through the program at their own speed. Effort is made to individualize—some say personalize—instruction. The nongraded concept has made its greatest headway at the elementary school level. However, as we shall see when we discuss developments in secondary education later in this chapter, nongradedness is possible in the high school as well.

John I. Goodlad and Robert H. Anderson, proponents of the nongraded elementary school, saw nongradedness as a reaction to the Procrustean bed of the graded school.[5] "The realities of child development defy the rigorous ordering of childrens' abilities and attainments into conventional graded structures," observed Goodlad and Anderson.[6]

Herbert I. Von Haden and Jean Marie King explained some of the principles underlying the nongraded school in the following way:

> Nongrading is a philosophy of teaching and learning which recognizes that children learn at different rates and in different ways and allows them to progress as individuals rather than classes. Such designations as grade one or grade three are eliminated. Flexible groupings allow the pupil to proceed from one level of work to another whenever he is ready. Thus, the child's progress is not dependent upon that of others in the room. His own readiness, interest, and capacity set the pace for each pupil. . . . Flexible grouping permits each child to move ahead with other children of approximately the same level of ability. Groupings are different for each subject area and can be changed at any time. Failure, retention, and skipping of grades are replaced by continuous progress as the pupil proceeds at his own rate. Slower children are not forced to go on with the class group before they are ready. Faster workers are not compelled to wait for the others. Individualization and continuous progress are the key elements of nongrading.[7]

Growth of Nongraded Schools. The nongraded movement began in earnest in the 1930s, grew in intensity through the 1940s and 1950s, and leveled off in the 1960s. Among the nongraded schools of the 1930s and 1940s were those in Western Springs, Illinois; Richmond, Virginia; Athens, Georgia; Youngstown, Ohio; and Milwaukee, Wisconsin.[8] In the 1950s and 1960s nongraded schools were started in Bellevue, Washington; Appleton, Wisconsin; Chicago, Illinois; and Southern Humboldt Unified School District, California.[9]

---

[5]John I. Goodlad and Robert H. Anderson, *The Nongraded Elementary School,* rev. ed. (New York: Teachers College Press, 1987), p. 1.

[6]Ibid., p. 3.

[7]Herbert I. Von Haden and Jean Marie King, *Educational Innovator's Guide* (Worthington, Ohio: Charles A. Jones, 1974), pp. 30–31. Reprinted with permission.

[8]Ibid., p. 33. See also p. 38 for list of schools where nongraded plans were tried.

[9]David W. Beggs III and Edward G. Buffie, eds., *Nongraded Schools in Action: Bold New Venture* (Bloomington: Indiana University Press, 1967).

TABLE 9–3   Comparison of the graded and continuous progress schools

GRADED STRUCTURE	CONTINUOUS PROGRESS
1. It is assumed that all children of the same chronological age will develop to the same extent in a given period of time.	1. It is assumed that each child has his own pattern and rate of growth and that children of the same age will vary greatly in their ability and rate of growth.
2. A child who does not measure up to certain predetermined standards of what should be accomplished in nine months is called a failure.	2. No child is ever considered a failure. If he does not achieve in proportion to his ability, we study the cause and adjust his program to fits his needs and problems.
3. If a child fails, he is required to repeat the grade in which he did not meet the standards.	3. A child never repeats. He may progress more slowly than others in the group, but individual records of progress make it possible to keep his growth continuous.
4. A decision as to grade placement must be made after each nine months.	4. Decisions as to group placement can be made at any time during the three-year period (for social or emotional adjustment, an additional year if needed, etc.).
5. Grade placements are based too largely upon academic achievement.	5. Group placement is flexible, based upon physical, mental, social, and emotional maturity.
6. Fixed standards of achievement within a set time put pressures upon teachers and children which cause emotional tensions and inhibit learning.	6. Elimination of pressures produces a relaxed learning situation conducive to good mental health.

SOURCE: Royce E. Kurtz and James N. Reston, "Continuous Progress in Appleton, Wisconsin," in David W. Beggs Ill and Edward G. Buffie, eds., *Nongraded Schools in Action: Bold New Venture* (Bloomington: Indiana University Press, 1967), p. 139. Reprinted by permission.

School personnel of Appleton, Wisconsin, compared the graded school with the continuous progress school, as shown in Table 9–3. The nongraded school seeks to eliminate failure and retention by permitting children to proceed through the program at their own pace. Programs of the nongraded school are organized primarily around reading levels and to a lesser extent around mathematics levels rather than around the traditional chronological age-grade levels.

Reading is used as the nucleus for grouping of youngsters in the nongraded school. Maurie H. Hillson explained:

> The present-day nongraded elementary schools, for the most part, rely on levels of accomplishment in reading as the bases for advancement and assignment in a program of vertical progression through the six years of the elementary school organization. Current nongraded plans, with some rare but exciting departures, accept the format of an attempted homogeneous grouping based on factors attendant to reading achievement.[10]

To form reading groups instructors pay attention to many factors, including intelligence, achievement, motivation, readiness, and maturity.

Hillson elaborated on the salient features of nongraded plans:

> Briefly, then, many of the present nongraded schools are ones in which grades are replaced by levels which a child accomplishes at his own speed. No grade designators are used. These levels of experience are clearly described and without the fear of retention or, conversely, without the fear of encroachment upon material reserved for a next higher grade, the child progresses through them as competency is achieved. . . . The rapid learner may accomplish a three-year nongraded program in two years. . . . The slow learner may take four years to accomplish three.[11]

Problems Encountered.   Nongraded plans encountered problems that led to a tapering off in their popularity. Nongraded programs are much more complex than the traditional, graded organization. They require continuous flexibility, more time by the faculty, greater resources, and a style of teaching different from that in typical graded schools. Careful diagnosis must be made of the learners' needs.

Nongraded schools could become as inflexible as the graded school if teachers and administrators merely substituted reading levels for chronological grades. Continuous progress plans concentrated to a great degree on reading and to a much lesser degree on mathematics, generally leaving the other subjects in the curriculum much as they were before—traditionally organized without well-planned sequencing of levels.

Nongraded plans excelled in vertical organization of the reading curriculum and sometimes the mathematics curriculum but failed to work out relationships at any level among the various disciplines. Further, the transition from a continuous progress elementary school to a graded junior high school could be rather abrupt for the learners when the junior high school was less concerned with personalized learning.

---

[10]Maurie H. Hillson, "The Nongraded School: A Dynamic Concept," in David W. Beggs III and Edward G. Buffie, eds., *Nongraded Schools in Action: Bold New Venture* (Bloomington: Indiana University Press, 1967), p. 34. Reprinted with permission.

[11]Ibid., p. 45.

Daniel Tanner and Laurel N. Tanner spoke of the shortcomings of the nongraded school as follows:

> Although the proponents of nongrading claimed that it provided for pupil differences and fostered a longitudinal concept of curriculum, or vertical curriculum articulation, the nongraded approach presented its own difficulties. For example, many nongraded schools had replaced the so-called graded lockstep with mechanical criteria for establishing the level of pupil placement in their studies, namely, standardized achievement test scores. Moreover, although it was claimed that the nongraded approach allowed for greater attention being given to vertical curriculum articulation, it also tended to mitigate against horizontal curriculum articulation or the interrelationships between the various studies that constitute the total curriculum.
>
> Finally, the claim that nongraded arrangements provide for superior pupil achievement over graded patterns has not been substantiated by research.[12]

That advocacy of the nongraded elementary school is still alive can be seen in the recent publication of a revised edition of *The Nongraded Elementary School* by Goodlad and Anderson.[13]

Open Education and Open Space

Several years ago the hypothetical elementary school created at the beginning of this chapter caught on to the tail-end of a movement known as the open-space school. The interior walls between classrooms came tumbling down—or as many walls as possible in a building constructed as a graded school many years ago. The purpose in eliminating barriers between classes was to permit innovative approaches such as flexible grouping, individualized instruction, nongradedness, and team teaching.

Open-space or *open-area education* is an architectural response to a broader philosophical and organizational concept called open education, the open classroom, or, simply, the open school. In practice, the terms are often interchanged. An *open classroom,* for example, might signal a classroom operated according to principles of *open education.* At the same time, this classroom might be an *open area,* although open space is not a prerequisite to open education. An *open school* might be a school that implements the open-education concept, or it might be an open-space school in which all classrooms are without walls.

C. M. Charles and others commented: "Many people think that open space and open education are synonymous. They are not. In fact they can be (but don't

---

[12]Reprinted by permission of Macmillan Publishing Company from *Curriculum Development: Theory Into Practice,* 2nd ed., p. 453, by Daniel Tanner and Laurel N. Tanner. Copyright ©1980 by Macmillan Publishing Company.

[13]Goodlad and Anderson, *The Nongraded Elementary School.*

have to be) quite opposite."[14] Charles and others defined an open school not as an open-space school but as a school with several open classrooms following principles of open education.[15] Open-space schools normally subscribe to at least some of the principles of open education, whereas open schools, as defined by Charles and co-workers, may or may not be open-space schools.

In the ensuing discussion I will use the terms "open school," "open classroom," and "open education" when speaking of the broad concept and "open space" or "open area" when talking about the architectural arrangement of classrooms without walls.[16] The open-space concept was illustrated in Chapter 3 by Patterns 1 and 2 of team/grade-level organization.

Imported from Great Britain, the open-classroom concept was designed as a curricular and organizational response to formal, traditional schools. Charles and others briefly described open education as follows:

> Open education refers to organization and management that allow much student choice and self-direction. The teacher helps, but dominates neither the planning nor the learning activities. Instead, the teacher "facilitates" student learning. This facilitation is done through talking, exploring, suggesting options, helping find resources, and deciding on ways of working that suit the group. Emphasis falls continually on maintaining relationships, interacting positively with others, fostering a sense of personal and group worth, and providing for the development of individual potential.[17]

Louis Rubin described the philosophical basis for the open classroom as follows:

> The basic ideology is rooted in the notion that children have a natural interest and desire in learning. Thus, when there is a conducive environment, and when the learning structure does not inhibit individuality, good education invariably will occur. What we have come to call relevance, as a result, is built into the fundamental philosophy itself; the curriculum, in short, is derived almost entirely from student interests and needs.[18]

---

[14]From Charles, C. M., Gast, David K., Servey, Richard E., and Burnside, Houston M.: *Schooling, Teaching, and Learning: American Education,* p. 118, St. Louis, 1978, The C. V. Mosby Co.

[15]Ibid., pp. 118–119.

[16]To complicate the matter further, classrooms without walls are not the same as schools without walls. Schools without walls operate without their own school buildings, sending their students wherever they need to be sent in the area to receive the education they need. Thus the students may be studying in agencies of the community or may be enrolled in other schools.

[17]From Charles, C. M., Gast, David K., Servey, Richard E., and Burnside, Houston M.: *Schooling, Teaching, and Learning: American Education,* p. 119, St. Louis, 1978, The C. V. Mosby Co.

[18]Louis Rubin, "Open Education: A Short Critique," in Louis Rubin, ed., *Curriculum Handbook: The Disciplines, Current Movements, and Instructional Methodology* (Boston: Allyn and Bacon, 1977), p. 375. Reprinted with permission.

Rubin went on to contrast the traditional and open classrooms:

> The critical distinctions between open and traditional education are that the goals are different, their means of attainment vary, and different outputs are yielded by each. A traditional program, for example, requires that a prescribed course of study be followed, leaving little leeway for accommodation to individual student interests. Its chief virtue, therefore, is that we can determine in advance, to a very sizable extent, what the child will and will not learn. But in the open education climate precisely the opposite condition prevails; since the child's own intellectual interests serve as the educational point of departure, predetermined objectives must defer to individual whim, and specified learning outcomes cannot be guaranteed.[19]

Common sights in the open-area school are large expanses of classroom space, groups of 100 or more pupils spread out and engaged in a variety of activities at many stations within the areas, and teams of teachers working with individuals, small groups, and large groups of learners.

Beliefs Underlying Open-Space Schools.   Proponents of the open classroom stress active learning and the affective domain. John H. Proctor and Kathryn Smith stated six beliefs to which the faculty and administration of Oliver Ellsworth School (Windsor, Connecticut), a modified open-area elementary school, subscribed:

1. We believe learning should be an active process; therefore, both the children and the teacher are actively involved in learning and teaching.
2. We believe children develop at different rates and have different strengths and weaknesses; therefore, different assignments and groupings are used by the teachers and students to meet these needs.
3. We believe children learn best what they are interested in; therefore, a wide variety of activities is provided.
4. We believe that children should learn to function as cooperative members of a group; therefore, we provide for constant group interaction.
5. We believe children function best under conditions of trust, support, encouragement, and success; therefore, we emphasize the positive aspects of behavior and work, rather than the coercive, negative factors.
6. We believe children should learn how to learn and make decisions; therefore we emphasize both skills and processes.[20]

"The primary advantage of open space," said Proctor and Smith, "is the increased communication and interaction of teacher to teacher, teacher to student, and student to student."[21] Significant features of the open-space concept are the flexibility of grouping and the use of concrete materials that appeal to

---

[19]Ibid., pp. 375–376.
[20]John H. Proctor and Kathryn Smith, "IGE and Open Education: Are They Compatible?" *Phi Delta Kappan* 55, no. 8 (April 1974): 564. Reprinted with permission.
[21]Ibid., p. 565.

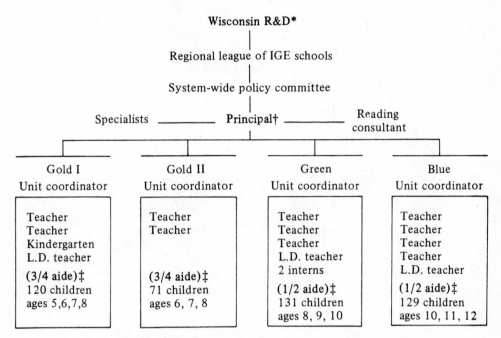

Wisconsin R&D*

|

Regional league of IGE schools

|

System-wide policy committee

|

Specialists ————— Principal† ————— Reading
consultant

Gold I	Gold II	Green	Blue
Unit coordinator	Unit coordinator	Unit coordinator	Unit coordinator
Teacher	Teacher	Teacher	Teacher
Teacher	Teacher	Teacher	Teacher
Kindergarten		Teacher	Teacher
L.D. teacher		L.D. teacher	Teacher
(3/4 aide)‡	(3/4 aide)‡	2 interns	L.D. teacher
120 children	71 children	(1/2 aide)‡	(1/2 aide)‡
ages 5,6,7,8	ages 6, 7, 8	131 children	129 children
		ages 8, 9, 10	ages 10, 11, 12

*Center for Cognitive Learning, Madison, Wisconsin.
†The principal and unit coordinators make up the Instructional Improvement Committee.
‡All units use parent volunteers.

FIGURE 9–1   Organization chart for Oliver Ellsworth School. From John H. Proctor and Kathryn Smith, "IGE and Open Education: Are They Compatible?" *Phi Delta Kappan* 55, no. 8 (April 1974), p. 565. Reprinted by permission.

the interests and maturity level of the learners. Whereas many open elementary schools are organized into clusters or teams of a single grade level (e.g., first grade), others, like Oliver Ellsworth School, are nongraded and organized into multiunits. The pattern for this school with its four units or teams is shown in Figure 9–1.[22]

The open-education/open-space movements have crested. Many schools that removed or built walls just for an open-area model have reinstalled walls or partitions to recreate smaller, self-contained units. What happened to this seemingly promising movement within the short space of some ten years?

David Pratt offered one reason for difficulties incurred by the open-space school when he observed:

The attempt to transplant the architectural aspect (of open-area schools in England) to North America has not been universally successful. Frequently, the innovation consisted of building schools with fewer interior walls, an en-

[22]Ibid.

vironment into which teachers were introduced who had neither participated in, approved of, or been trained for the open environment. Continuing to teach in a conventional way, they found the absence of walls merely an audible and visible distraction. Bookcases, screens, and miniature palm trees were quickly turned into makeshift barriers between the teaching areas. Small wonder that the research evidence shows, at best, disappointing performance by students in open classrooms, not only in academic subjects but also in creativity, and an increased anxiety level.[23]

The audible and visual distractions have been, in my judgment, erroneously minimized. Visits to open classrooms rather consistently reveal a noise level that is not conducive to learning. Harried teachers must consistently elevate their voices to make themselves understood. When ardent proponents of the open classroom are questioned about the noise, their response is often: "What noise?" or "Some noise is necessary for learning to take place." Perhaps we can attribute some of the fault for these distractions to the lack of fit between program and architecture.

Rubin pointed out that, contrary to the claims of some advocates of open education, traditional education is not necessarily as bad as some people painted it:

> In fairness, it must be acknowledged that the proponents of open education have sometimes built their case upon a straw man. Traditional education—although formalized and structured—need not be depressing nor debilitating of the learner's spirit. In point of fact, there is abundant reason to believe that some learners thrive better in a traditional setting than in an open one. To wit, children sometimes find a lack of structure uncomfortable and large doses of freedom anxiety provoking. Similarly, provisions for the affective components of education, for the emotional feelings of students, can be made in both a traditional and an open format. As a result, one cannot in good conscience claim that an unstructured, open curriculum is necessarily more "humanistic" than a structured, traditional one.
>
> Nor, to extend the point further, can one claim that an open curriculum automatically teaches the child to think more than a traditional one, or that multiage grouping cannot exist in either situation, or that prescribed programs of instruction must, inevitably, prohibit individualization. Put another way, a large number of benefits habitually claimed by champions of one approach or the other can, in reality, be used with equal effectiveness in both.[24]

In regard to the success of open-space and open-education plans, Charles and co-workers observed: "In many cases, open space has not produced the results that were hoped for.... There is little evidence, however, to support open education on the grounds of academic achievement."[25]

---

[23]David Pratt, *Curriculum: Design and Development* (New York: Harcourt Brace Jovanovich, 1980), p. 384.

[24]Rubin, "Open Education," p. 376. Reprinted with permission.

[25]From Charles, C. M., Gast, David K., Servey, Richard E., and Burnside, Houston M.: *Schooling, Teaching, and Learning: American Education*, pp. 118–119, St. Louis, 1978, The C. V. Mosby Co.

THE JUNIOR HIGH SCHOOL

The School in Between

Educators and behavioral scientists of the late nineteenth century and early twentieth century recognized the necessity for a type of educational program and institution that would provide special attention to the needs of youngsters between childhood and adolescence. Out of this concern grew the junior high school. From its inception the junior high school was an institution in search of an identity. The junior high school that came into existence at Berkeley, California, and Columbus, Ohio, in 1910 encompassed grades seven, eight, and nine. Prior to the separation of these grades to form their own institution, grades seven and eight were normally considered an integral part of the elementary school; grades 9 through 12 formed the secondary school. Early schools, if they did not house all grades in one classroom, grouped their pupils in self-contained seventh- and eighth-grade classrooms. Not until the advent of the junior high as an institution did departmentalization come to the schooling of the 12- to 14-year-olds.

With the appearance of the junior high school, children entering adolescence found an institution created specifically for them. It bore the trappings of both the primary school below it and the secondary school above it. Offering both a basic general education and exploratory experiences, the junior high school spread rapidly through the first half of the twentieth century. School systems adopted either the seven–eight–nine pattern or a seven–eight model that maintained the ninth grade in the senior high school.

Educators' perceptions of the role of the junior high school have varied considerably. Is it an upward projection of the elementary school? Is it a downward extension of the senior high school? Is its purpose mainly exploratory, serving learners in a transition period between puberty and adolescence, or is it a preparatory school for the senior high? Should it be housed in the same building with the senior high school or located in a separate building?

In spite of varying perceptions of its role the junior high school serves as an example of the self-fulfilling prophecy. Established as a unique institution, the junior high school began to live up to its label, "junior." The junior high school quickly came to be identified as a part of secondary education, resulting in the K–6, 7–12 dichotomy that to some extent still exists. Although at first it was somewhat experimental in nature with block-time scheduling and core curricula, as the years rolled by the junior high school became more and more like its higher-level companion with complete departmentalization of courses, senior-high scheduling patterns, and a subject matter curriculum.

Conant's Recommendations. In Chapter 6 we discussed the studies of the junior and senior high school conducted by James B. Conant. Since Conant's recommendations were so favorably received, we should be remiss not to examine some and to discern their nature. Among Conant's 14 recommendations for the junior high school are the following:

REQUIRED SUBJECTS FOR ALL PUPILS IN GRADES 7 AND 8.
The following subjects should be required of all pupils in grades 7 and 8: English (including heavy emphasis on reading skills and composition), social studies (including emphasis on history and geography), mathematics (arithmetic except as noted . . .) and science.

   In addition, all pupils should receive instruction in art, music, and physical education. All girls should receive instruction in home economics and all boys instruction in industrial arts. . . .

NEW DEVELOPMENTS IN MATHEMATICS AND FOREIGN LANGUAGES.
A small fraction of pupils should start algebra (or one of the new brands of mathematics) in grade 8. Some, if not all, pupils should start the study of a modern foreign language on a conversational basis with a bilingual teacher in grade 7.

BASIC SKILLS.
Instruction in the basic skills begun in the elementary school should be continued as long as pupils can gain from the instruction. This statement applies particularly to reading and arithmetic. Pupils with average ability should read at or above grade level; superior pupils considerably above grade level. By the end of grade 9 even the poorest readers (except the mentally retarded) should read at least at the sixth-grade level.

BLOCK-TIME AND DEPARTMENTALIZATION.
Provisions should be made to assure a smooth transition for the young adolescent from the elementary to the secondary school.

FLEXIBILITY IN SCHEDULE.
The daily class schedule should be sufficiently flexible to avoid the necessity for pupils to make choices between, for example, science and foreign languages.

PROGRAM IN GRADE 9.
In the ninth grade, the curriculum should provide for the usual sequential elective program as well as the continuation of the required courses in general education.

COORDINATION OF SUBJECT-MATTER INSTRUCTION.
Whatever the organization of a school system, there should be careful coordination in each one of the subject areas in grades K–12.[26]

Many schools reviewed, reaffirmed, or modified their curricula in light of the Conant recommendations, and our hypothetical junior high school was no exception.

---

[26]James B. Conant, *Recommendations for Education in the Junior High School Years* (Princeton, N.J.: Educational Testing Service, 1960), pp. 16–33. Reprinted by permission of Educational Testing Service.

ASCD Proposals.   At about the same time Conant was recommending in-creased emphasis on the academics, the Commission on the Education of Adolescents of the Association for Supervision and Curriculum Development (ASCD) was presenting a different point of view on the function and programs of the junior high school.[27] Writing for the ASCD, Jean D. Grambs and others, acknowledging that the junior high school was under pressure, advocated varia-tions in lengths of class periods, programs planned explicitly for the junior high school years, ungraded programs, and a block-of-time program offered each year for the three years of junior high school. As we will see, a block-of-time program usually runs for two or three hours of a school day.

Whereas Conant's proposals for the school in the middle were more subject-centered, the ASCD proposals were more learner-centered. However, propo-nents of both points of view agree on the necessity for adequate facilities and resources, a professionally trained staff, a moderate and manageable size of school, and ample guidance.

The Core Curriculum

Basic education, common learnings, core curriculum, and general education are terms, like goals and objectives, that are tossed about rather loosely in the profession. These terms are used by educators to describe programs that are almost at opposite poles. To some, basic education, common learnings, and general education signal a set of courses or subjects that are required of all students—the earmark of the subject matter curriculum, grounded in essential-istic philosophy. In this vein, the Harvard Committee stated its interpretation of general education:

> Clearly, general education has somewhat the meaning of liberal education [p. 52]. . . . General education, we repeat, must consciously aim at these abili-ties: at effective thinking, communication, the making of relevant judgments, and the discrimination of values [p. 72]. . . . It therefore remains only to draw the scheme of general education that follows from these premises. At the cen-ter of it . . . would be the three inevitable areas of man's life and knowledge . . . : the physical world, man's corporate life, his inner visions and standards [p. 98]. . . . In school, in our opinion, general education in these three areas should form a continuing core for all, taking up at least half a student's time [p. 99]. . . . Accepting the course-unit system as established, at least for the present, despite its grave weaknesses dwelt on earlier, that would amount to some eight units, preferably spaced by means of half-courses over the four years of school rather than compressed into two or three. The common and desirable division within these eight units would probably be three in English,

---

[27]Jean D. Grambs, Clarence G. Noyce, Franklin Patterson, and John Robertson, *The Junior High School We Need* (Alexandria, Va.: Association for Supervision and Curriculum Develop-ment, 1961).

three in science and mathematics, and two in the social studies. But—and this is the important point—this half of the schoolwork to be spent on general education would seem the barest minimum, either for those not going on to college or for those who are [p. 100].[28]

James B. Conant, president of Harvard University at the time the Harvard Committee issued its report, took a similar position when he recommended general education programs consisting of required courses at both the junior and senior high school levels. In keeping with the spirit of the 1894 Report of the Committee of Ten, the 1945 Report of the Harvard Committee, and several national reports of the 1980s, high schools today designate a "core" or set of required subjects for graduation. In the section which follows I have used the terms "core" and "core curriculum" to describe a unique organizational structure in the secondary school, not required courses.

The essentialists championed—and still advocate—the set of required courses as their model for general education in the high school. At the other end of the spectrum, from the camps of the pragmatic and reconstructionist philosophers, come those who hold a quite different conception of general education. They frequently refer to their plans for common learnings or general education as a "core curriculum." Unlike the "continuing core for all" recommended by the Harvard Committee, the core curriculum at its inception was a radically new departure in curriculum organization. John H. Lounsbury and Gordon F. Vars noted that many curriculum specialists regarded core as a truly innovative development.[29]

What is the core curriculum? Lounsbury and Vars defined core—short for core curriculum—as follows: "Specifically, core is a form of curriculum organization, usually operating within an extended block of time in the daily schedule, in which learning experiences are focused directly on problems of significance to students."[30]

Unification of Subject Matter.   The core curriculum gained momentum in the 1930s and 1940s, but its roots go back to the nineteenth century. In a presentation made by Emerson E. White to the National Department of Superintendents in 1896, White discussed one of the basic principles of core: the unification of subject matter.

> Complete unification is the blending of all subjects and branches of study into one whole, and the teaching of the same in successive groups or lessons or sections. When this union is effected by making one group or branch of

---

[28]Harvard Committee, *General Education in a Free Society* (Cambridge, Mass.: Harvard University Press, 1945), pp. 52–100.

[29]See John H. Lounsbury and Gordon F. Vars, *A Curriculum for the Middle School Years* (New York: Harper & Row, 1978), p. 57.

[30]Excerpts from *A Curriculum for the Middle Years,* p. 56, by John H. Lounsbury and Gordon F. Vars. Copyright ©1978 by John H. Lounsbury and Gordon F. Vars. Reprinted by permission of HarperCollins Publishers.

study in the course the center or core, and subordinating all other subjects to it, the process is properly called the concentration of studies.[31]

Smith, Stanley, and Shores credited Ziller, founder of the Herbartian school at the University of Leipzig, and Colonel Francis W. Parker, superintendent of schools, Quincy, Massachusetts, in 1875 and later principal of the Cook County (Chicago) Normal School, as proponents of the principle of unification of subject matter.[32]

The core concept received a significant boost in the 1930s when the curriculum committees of a number of states sought to plan a curriculum around social functions of living and turned for assistance to Hollis L. Caswell, then of George Peabody College for Teachers and later of Teachers College, Columbia University. The Virginia State Curriculum Program pioneered in establishing the core curriculum—the content of which centered on societal functions.[33]

The core curriculum is in philosophy and intent the secondary school counterpart of the activity curriculum of the elementary school. Espoused as a concept for both the junior and senior high schools, the core curriculum made its greatest inroads at the junior high school level. The core concept was especially popular in the state of Maryland. However, Lounsbury and Vars pointed out that core, like many programs that are different, did not meet with universal acceptance even at the junior high school level.[34]

Characteristics of Core.   Although varying in structure and focus, core curricula, as described in this chapter, possess the following characteristics:

1. They constitute a portion of the curriculum that is required for all students.
2. They unify or fuse subject matter, usually English and social studies.
3. Their content centers on problems that cut across the disciplines; the primary method of learning is problem solving, using all applicable subject matter.
4. They are organized into blocks of time, usually two to three periods under a "core" teacher (with possible use of additional teachers and others as resource persons).
5. They encourage teachers to plan with students.
6. They provide pupil guidance.

---

[31]Emerson E. White, "Isolation and Unification as Bases of Courses of Study," *Second Yearbook of the National Herbart Society for the Scientific Study of Teaching* (now the National Society for the Study of Education) (Bloomington, Ill.: Pantograph Printing and Stationery Co., 1896), pp. 12–13.

[32]Smith, Stanley, and Shores, *Fundamentals of Curriculum Development*, pp. 312–313.

[33]State of Virginia, *Tentative Course of Study for the Core Curriculum of Virginia Secondary Schools* (Richmond, Va.: State Board of Education, 1934).

[34]Lounsbury and Vars, *Curriculum for Middle School*, p. 57.

Types of Core.   Harold B. Alberty and Elsie J. Alberty distinguished five types of core.[35] The first two are core in the sense that subjects are required of all; as such these two types fall into the classification of the subject matter curriculum. Writing in 1962, Alberty and Alberty classified types of core as follows:

☐ Type 1: A set of subjects ("constants") is required for all students. Subjects are taught separately with little or no effort to relate them to each other. This type of organizational plan is predominant in high schools today.

☐ Type 2: Two or more subjects are correlated. Although subjects remain discrete and are taught separately, effort is made to relate one to the other. The history teacher, for example, may work with the English teacher to show students relationships between topics that they happen to be studying in the two courses.

☐ Type 3: Two or more subjects are fused. The majority of core programs in schools fall into this classification. English and social studies are fused or integrated and scheduled in a block of time, usually two to three periods. Not a complete departure from traditional subject matter organization, this type of core organizes content around contemporary social problems or around historic or cultural epochs. Several experimental schools of the Eight-Year Study of the Progressive Education Association used Types 2 and 3 cores.[36]

☐ Type 4: A block of time is established to study adolescent and/or social problems, such as school living, family life, economic problems, communication, multicultural relationships, health, international problems, conservation, and understanding the self. This type of core requires a complete departure from the typical subject matter curriculum and a thorough reorganization of the curriculum.

☐ Type 5: Learning activities are developed cooperatively by teachers and students, who are free to pursue whatever interests or problem areas they desire. This core program resembles the unstructured experience curriculum of the elementary school.

Core curricula tend to consume a block of time consisting of two to three periods of the school day. The remaining periods are devoted to specialized interests of students. "Block-time classes" is a term sometimes equated with "core." However, block-time classes may or may not be core classes.[37] They

---

[35]Harold B. Alberty and Elsie J. Alberty, *Reorganizing the High-School Curriculum,* 3rd ed. (New York: Macmillan, 1962), pp. 199–233. It is of interest to note that in previous editions Alberty and Alberty distinguished six types of core. They included a type of correlation related to Type 2, in which teachers of separate courses agreed on a joint theme to be taught in their respective courses.

[36]See Wilford M. Aikin, *The Story of the Eight-Year Study* (New York: Harper & Row, 1942).

[37]See William Van Til, Gordon F. Vars, and John H. Lounsbury, *Modern Education for the Junior High School Years,* 2nd ed. (Indianapolis: Bobbs-Merrill, 1967), pp. 181–182.

may simply be subjects scheduled in a block of time but taught separately, as in the cases of Types 1 and 2 of the Alberty and Alberty classification. Block-time classes can be core classes, however, if they meet the characteristics of a core as just outlined.

Reporting in 1958 on a survey of block-time classes and core programs in junior high schools, Grace S. Wright listed four types of programs in block-time classes as follows:

> *Type A*—Each subject retains its identity in the block-time class, that is, separate subjects are taught (1) with consciously planned correlation, (2) with no planned correlation.
>
> *Type B*—Subjects included in the block-time class are unified or fused around a central theme or units of work or problems stemming from one or more of the subject fields in the block-time class.
>
> *Type C*—Predetermined problem areas based upon the personal-social needs of adolescents—both needs that adolescents themselves have identified and needs as society sees them determine the scope of the core program. Subject matter is brought in as needed in working on the problems. Pupils may or may not have a choice from among several of these problem areas; they will, however, have some responsibility for suggesting and choosing activities in developing units of study.
>
> *Type D*—The scope of the core program is not predetermined. Pupils and teacher are free to select the problems upon which they wish to work. Subject matter content is brought in as needed to develop or to help solve the problems.[38]

Note the points of agreement between the Wright and the Alberty and Alberty classifications.

Illustrative Schedule.[39]   The organizational plan of the core and its relationship to other subject areas are illustrated by the plan for grades 7 through 12 shown in Figure 9–2. In a six-period day a block of four periods is devoted to core in the seventh grade, three periods in the eighth, and two periods each succeeding year.

Although a few core programs may still be found, those that were in existence have generally been discontinued. They have never been fully understood by the public. "What is core?" asks the average citizen. What does an "A" in core mean to parents, to college admissions officers? Informed persons will admit that the ripples caused by the Eight-Year Study, which allowed for innovative plans like the core, generally lost their force, and colleges went back to demanding high school credit in subjects they understood.

---

[38]Grace S. Wright, *Block-Time Classes and the Core Program in the Junior High School*, Bulletin 1958, no. 6 (Washington, D.C.: U.S. Office of Education, 1958), p. 9.

[39]For a widely cited theoretical model of a senior high school schedule with a "common learnings" core, see Educational Policies Commission, *Education for All American Youth* (Washington, D.C.: National Education Association, 1944), p. 244.

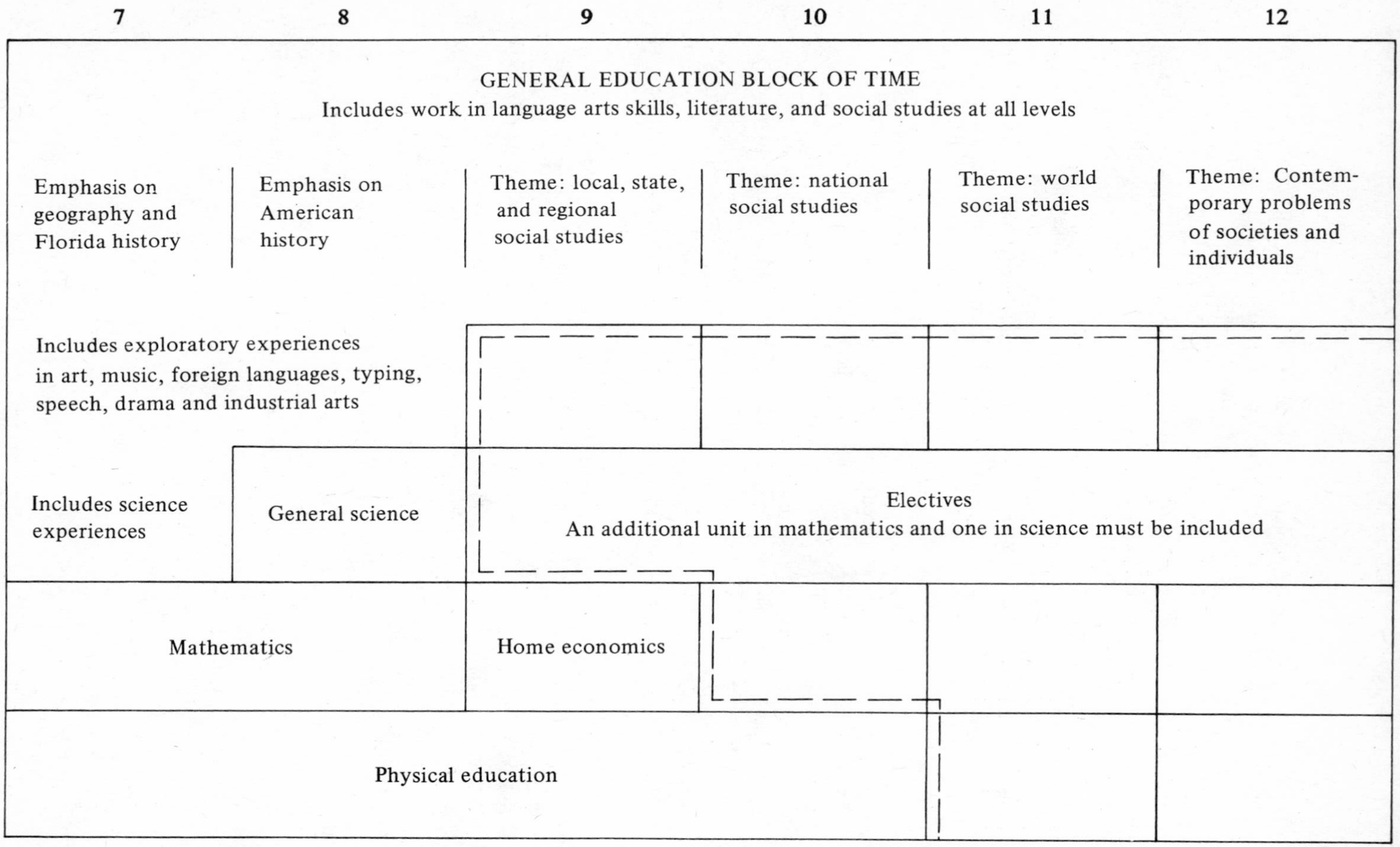

GENERAL EDUCATION BLOCK OF TIME

Includes work in language arts skills, literature, and social studies at all levels

7	8	9	10	11	12
Emphasis on geography and Florida history	Emphasis on American history	Theme: local, state, and regional social studies	Theme: national social studies	Theme: world social studies	Theme: Contemporary problems of societies and individuals

Includes exploratory experiences in art, music, foreign languages, typing, speech, drama and industrial arts

Includes science experiences

General science

Electives

An additional unit in mathematics and one in science must be included

Home economics

Mathematics

Physical education

FIGURE 9–2   Plan of a core curriculum. This plan existed for many years at the P.K. Yonge Laboratory School, University of Florida, Gainesville, Florida. Reprinted by permission.

Core teaching is a demanding task requiring skills that take special training. Teachers' colleges, by and large, neglected the preparation of core teachers. The perceived threat from the Russians in 1957 renewed demand for the "hard" subjects—science, mathematics, and foreign language—and brought about negative reactions to unusual programs like core.

Conant, who commanded a considerable audience, was less than ecstatic about core. He recommended that core be limited to a block of time (two to three periods) in grade seven only. Even in that block of time Conant took the position that instruction need not be integrated:

> To my mind, there should be a block of time set aside, at least in grade 7, in which one teacher has the same pupils for two or more periods, generally in English and social studies. Otherwise, grades 7, 8, and 9 should be departmentalized; that is to say, pupils should have specialist teachers in each of the subject-matter fields. . . . The block-time teaching I am discussing need not break down subject-matter lines.[40]

Tanner and Tanner assessed the core curriculum:

> The core idea never gained the widespread acceptance that was expected of it by progressive educators. Not only was it countered by the discipline-centered curriculum reforms of the 1950's and 1960's but it has met with other difficulties over the years. . . . teachers are products of discipline-centered curricula in the colleges and universities, and so they tend to be oriented toward the subject curriculum. Textbooks and other curriculum materials are geared to the subject curriculum. . . . Without extensive resource materials the core class is unable to attack problems in any great breadth and depth of treatment. The core curriculum requires enormous teacher resourcefulness. . . . The core curriculum requires teachers to have considerable breadth and depth of background in general education. Yet, the colleges have been largely allowing their own curricula in general education to erode in favor of specialism and special-interest studies.
>
> Perhaps the most serious problem, aside from the national trend toward disciplinary studies over a period of almost two decades, was the unrealistic expectation that teachers should develop their own curriculum materials under conditions where resources are lacking.[41]

In the mid- and late twentieth century, the junior high school underwent a metamorphosis, developing into a new institution designed to better meet the needs of the preadolescent. This innovative concept, the middle school, is discussed later in this chapter.

---

[40]Conant, *Recommendations for Junior High,* pp. 22–23. Reprinted by permission of Educational Testing Service.

[41]Reprinted by permission of Macmillan Publishing Company from *Curriculum Development: Theory into Practice,* 2nd ed., p. 485, Daniel Tanner and Laurel N. Tanner. Copyright ©1980 by Macmillan Publishing Company.

THE SENIOR HIGH SCHOOL

The Subject Matter Curriculum

The subject matter curriculum has been the most prevalent form of curriculum organization at all levels of education ever since the Boston Latin School, the first Latin Grammar School in the United States, opened in 1635. The subject matter curriculum remains the most common pattern of organization throughout most of the world. Although other forms of curriculum organization have asserted themselves in the United States from time to time, the subject matter curriculum has continued strong and has gained renewed strength in recent years with the stress placed on the academics and basic skills. The subject matter curriculum has existed at all levels of schooling but has been particularly entrenched at the senior high and college levels.

Smith, Stanley, and Shores pointed out in the following passages that the subject matter curriculum dates back to antiquity:

> The subject is the oldest and most widely accepted form of curriculum organization. Perhaps the earliest example of this organization is the Seven Liberal Arts, which were present in an incipient form in the schools of ancient Greece and Rome, and which were offered in a more advanced stage of development in the monastery and cathedral schools of the Middle Ages. The Seven Liberal Arts consisted of two divisions: the trivium, which was comprised of grammar, rhetoric, and dialectic (logic); and the quadrivium, which consisted of arithmetic, geometry, astronomy, and music. . . . In the modern period the trivium was further divided to include literature and history as distinct subjects; and the quadrivium, to include algebra, trigonometry, geography, botany, zoology, physics, and chemistry. In the last half century the number of subjects offered in the public schools increased by leaps and bounds, so that by 1930 there were over three hundred distinct subjects of instruction. Despite this enormous multiplication of subjects the Seven Liberal Arts are still the nucleus of the subject curriculum, as a casual survey of required courses will reveal.[42]

As the name implies, the subject matter curriculum is an organizational pattern that breaks the school's program into discrete subjects or disciplines. The seventeenth-century Latin Grammar School stressed classical subjects, including Greek, Latin, Hebrew, mathematics, history, and the Bible. Notably absent from this early school were English and science, which were considered too functional or too frivolous for scholars of this period. With the opening of Benjamin Franklin's Philadelphia Academy and Charitable School in 1751, English, science, and modern languages were added to the curriculum. Today's secondary schools offer a potpourri—some say smorgasbord—of courses.

---

[42]Excerpts from *Fundamentals of Curriculum Development,* Revised Edition, pp. 229–230, by B. O. Smith, W. O. Stanley, and J. Harlan Shores, copyright ©1957 by Harcourt Brace Jovanovich, Inc. and renewed 1985 by B. O. Smith, W. O. Stanley, and J. Harlan Shores, reprinted by permission of the publisher.

Essentialistic in outlook, the subject matter curriculum seeks to transmit the cultural heritage. The subjects or disciplines organize knowledge from the adult world in such a way that it can be transmitted to the immature learner.

As we saw in Chapter 6 when we discussed the philosophy of essentialism, the subject matter curriculum has not been at a loss for spokespersons. Max Rafferty left no doubt of his position regarding the subject matter curriculum when he said, "What *is* significant for the children—what the people want for their children and mean to get—is subject matter that is systematic, organized, and disciplined and that is taught effectively and interestingly as subject matter. . . . Stress subject matter, *all* subject matter."[43]

Although the subject matter curriculum is found at both the elementary and second school levels, it has had its greatest impact at the secondary level. Elementary school faculties have been more prone to experiment and to try out new patterns of organization that depart from subject matter emphasis. Secondary school teachers and administrators have consistently tended to be more subject-centered than their counterparts at the elementary school level.

Advantages. The subject matter curriculum presents to its followers certain distinct advantages. It is the easiest organizational pattern to structure. On the elementary school level, it is simply a matter of allocating a certain number of minutes for each subject during the course of the day. On the secondary school level, subject matter is organized into "courses" that are designated as either required subjects (constants) or electives. Every subject of the secondary school is typically scheduled for the same amount of time. The recommendations of two well-known groups helped to imprint the model of equal time for each subject in the secondary schools.

At the tail end of the nineteenth century the National Education Association's Committee of Ten proposed:

> Every subject which is taught at all in a secondary school should be taught in the same way and to the same extent to every pupil so long as he pursues it, no matter what the probable destination of the pupil may be, or at what point his education is to cease. Thus, for all pupils who study Latin, or history, or algebra, for example, the allotment of time and the method of instruction in a given school should be the same year by year. Not that all pupils should pursue every subject for the same number of years; but so long as they do pursue it, they should all be treated alike.[44]

A few years later, in 1906, the Carnegie Foundation for the Advancement of Teaching created the Carnegie unit, which for purposes of college admission standardized the amount of time to be spent in each subject in high school. To

[43] Max Rafferty, *What They Are Doing to Your Children* (New York: New American Library, 1964), pp. 43–44.

[44] National Education Association, *Report of the Committee of Ten on Secondary School Studies* (New York: American Book Company, 1894), p. 17.

most people today the concept is known simply as a "unit," the Carnegie modi-fier having been lost over time. The Carnegie Foundation for the Advancement of Teaching defined a unit as satisfactory completion of a subject that met five days per week, a minimum of 40 minutes per period, and a minimum of 120 clock hours for the school year. In addition, the Carnegie Foundation stipulated that a secondary school pupil should amass a total of 16 units for graduation. These two recommendations were universally adopted by American secondary schools and have continued in force with infrequent modifications up to the present. In today's educational environment, states have moved well past the Carnegie Foundation's recommendation of 16 units for high school graduation, as we shall see later in this chapter.

The content of the subject matter curriculum, unlike that of the experience curriculum, is planned in advance by the teacher or, more accurately, by the writers of the textbooks or curriculum guides that the teacher follows. The needs and interests of learners play little part in the curriculum that is organized around the disciplines.

Unlike the activity or experience curriculum and the core curriculum dis-cussed earlier in this chapter, the subject matter curriculum is well understood by the public, students, and the profession and for the most part has met with general favor. The methodology followed in the subject matter curriculum is rather straightforward. The teacher is the expert in the field and is likely to pursue a set of procedures that some instructional specialists refer to as the "assign-study-recite-test" method. William H. Burton succinctly described these procedures:

> The learning situation is organized around materials and experiences which are assigned by the teacher. The pupils then study in various ways. The results of their studying are presented and shared during a recitation pe-riod. Testing of results occurs at the conclusion of a series of assignments and may occur at stated times within the sequence.[45]

Writing in 1962, Burton stated, "The assign-study-recite-test formula will be used for many years to come."[46] What he might have said is that the assign-study-recite-test formula has been used for generations and is likely to continue for generations to come. This approach is what many people both within and without the profession call "teaching."

Cognitive Emphasis.   The subject matter curriculum, which in days of old was imbedded in faculty psychology or mental discipline, has found behavior-istic psychology compatible with its objectives. Student achievement is rather easily assessed, since evaluation is limited to measuring cognitive objectives

---

[45]William H. Burton. From *The Guidance of Learning Activities: A Summary of the Prin-ciples of Teaching Based on the Growth of the Learner,* 3rd ed., © 1962, p. 289. Reprinted by permission of Prentice-Hall, Inc., Englewood Cliffs, NJ.

[46]Ibid.

by teacher-made or standardized tests. Some effort is made to measure performance in the psychomotor domain, but the perceptual motor skills are treated more or less as appendages to the cognitive domain. For example, in high schools that have separate tracks of curricula—such as general, commercial, industrial, and college preparatory—the most cognitive, the college preparatory track, is usually regarded as the most prestigious.

In the subject matter curriculum little effort is made to gauge student performance in the affective domain. Not only is evaluation of feelings and values extremely difficult, but also proponents of the subject matter curriculum, essentialist as they are, do not accept the affective domain as a primary concern of the school. Robert L. Ebel expressed this position forcefully when he said:

> Feelings are essentially unteachable.... Nor do they need to be taught .... The kind of learning on which schools should concentrate most of their efforts is cognitive competence.... Affective dispositions are important by-products of the human experience, but they seldom are or should be the principal targets of our educational efforts.[47]

The approach to individual differences and needs of students in the subject matter curriculum lies more in the provision of elective or special interest subjects from among which the students may choose. The breadth or scope of the subject matter curriculum and its sequence are revealed in the textbooks that are adopted for use in the classroom.

Conant's Proposals. Conant's studies of both the American high and junior high schools strengthened advocates of the subject matter curriculum. So that you may sense the overall impact of the Conant report on the high school, which preceded the report on the junior high, I will cite several of his 21 recommendations.

One wonders if the titles of Conant's two reports have political significance. His 1959 report on the high school was labeled "a first report to interested citizens," whereas his 1960 junior high school report was subtitled "a memorandum to school boards." Among Conant's proposals for the high school were the following:

REQUIRED PROGRAMS FOR ALL.

A. General Education.

The requirements for graduation for all students should be as follows: four years of English, three or four years of social studies—including two years of history (one of which should be American history) and a senior course in American problems or American government—one year of mathematics in the ninth grade (algebra or general mathematics), and at least one year of science in the ninth or tenth grade, which might well be biology or general physical science. By a year, I mean that a

---

[47]Robert L. Ebel, "What Are Schools For?" *Phi Delta Kappan* 54, no. 1 (September 1972): pp. 4, 7.

course is given five periods a week throughout the academic year or an equivalent amount of time. This academic program of general education involves nine or ten courses with homework to be taken in four years and occupies more than half the time of most students, whatever their elective programs.

B. The Elective Program.

The other requirement for graduation should be successful completion of at least seven more courses, not including physical education. *All students should be urged to include art and music in their elective programs.* All students should be advised to have as the central core of their elective programs significant sequences of courses, either those leading to the development of a marketable skill or those of an academic nature.

C. Standards for Pass and Failure.

. . . the teachers of the advanced academic *elective* courses—foreign languages, mathematics, and science—should be urged to maintain high standards. They should be told not to hesitate to fail a student who does not meet the minimum level of performance they judge necessary for mastery of the subject in question. . . . On the other hand, for the *required* courses another standard should be applied. Since these courses are required of all, irrespective of ability, a student may be given a passing grade if he has worked to full capacity whether or not a certain level of achievement has been reached. . . .

ABILITY GROUPING.

In the required subjects and those elected by students with a wide range of ability, the students should be grouped according to ability, subject by subject. . . . This type of grouping is not to be confused with across-the-board grouping according to which a given student is placed in a particular section in *all* courses. . . .

ENGLISH COMPOSITION.

The time devoted to English composition during the four years should occupy about half the total time devoted to the study of English. Each student should be required to write an average of one theme a week. Themes should be corrected by the teacher . . . no English teacher should be responsible for more than one hundred pupils.

To test the ability of each student in English composition, a schoolwide composition test should be given in every grade; in the ninth and eleventh grades, these composition tests should be graded not only by the teacher but by a committee of the entire school. Those students who do not obtain a grade on the eleventh-grade composition test commensurate with their ability as measured by an aptitude test should be required to take a special course in English composition in the twelfth grade. . . .

DIVERSIFIED PROGRAMS FOR THE DEVELOPMENT OF MARKETABLE SKILLS.

Programs should be available for girls interested in developing skills in typing, stenography, the use of clerical machines, home economics. . . . Distributive education should be available. . . . If the community is rural, vocational agriculture should be included. . . . For boys, depending on the community, trade and industrial programs should be available. Half a day is required in the eleventh and twelfth grades for this vocational work. . . .

SPECIAL CONSIDERATION FOR THE VERY SLOW READERS.
Those in the ninth grade of the school who read at a level of the sixth grade or below should be given special consideration. These pupils should be instructed in English and the required social studies by special teachers. . . . Remedial reading should be part of the work, and special types of textbooks should be provided. The elective programs of these pupils should be directed toward simple vocational work. . . .

THE PROGRAMS OF THE ACADEMICALLY TALENTED.
. . . the elective programs of academically talented boys and girls [the top 15 percent] should [include] . . . as a minimum:
Four years of mathematics, four years of one foreign language, three years of science, in addition to the required four years of English and three years of social studies; a total of eighteen courses with homework to be taken in four years. This program will require at least fifteen hours of homework each week. . . .

HIGHLY GIFTED PUPILS.
For the highly gifted pupils [the top 3 percent] some type of special arrangement should be made. . . . If enough students are available to provide a special class, these students should take in the twelfth grade one or more courses which are part of the Advanced Placement Program. . . .

ORGANIZATION OF THE SCHOOL DAY.
The school day should be so organized that there are at least six periods in addition to the required physical education and driver education. . . . A seven- or eight-period day may be organized with periods as short as forty-five minutes . . . laboratory periods as well as industrial arts should involve double periods. . . . [48]

The thrust of the Conant recommendations for the high school reaffirmed the subject matter curriculum and placed special emphasis on the needs of the academically talented. As such, albeit in more modern dress, it reinforced and expanded the Harvard Report that had preceded it by almost 15 years. Whereas many secondary schools rushed to implement some of Conant's recommendations, particularly those for the academically talented, they gave up on others. English teachers still wistfully hope for a maximum of 100 pupils. School personnel still dream of a full-time counselor for every 250 to 300 pupils; the normal ratio is often one counselor to 500 or more. Finally, although the recommendation to group students by ability has been implemented widely, it remains enmeshed in controversy.

The subject matter curriculum has been popular with many curriculum planners because it lends itself well to a mechanical type of curriculum development: dropping, adding, or splitting courses, rearranging or extending sequences, updating topics, and changing textbooks.

---

[48] James B. Conant, *The American High School Today* (New York: McGraw-Hill, 1959), pp. 47–65. Reprinted with permission.

Broad-Fields Curriculum

In the early part of the twentieth century a pattern of curriculum organization appeared that became—on the surface at least—a standard feature of both elementary and secondary schools. Called the broad-fields curriculum, this form of curriculum organization is a modification of the strict subject matter curriculum. Effort is made to unify and integrate content of related disciplines around broad themes or principles. For example, history A (ancient), history B (modern) and history C (American), as existed in the secondary school curriculum of New York State schools well into the 1930s, were converted into broad fields and designated simply tenth-grade social studies, eleventh-grade social studies, and twelfth-grade social studies.

"In the broad-fields approach," said Tanner and Tanner, "the attempt is made to develop some degree of synthesis or unity for an entire branch of knowledge.... it may even go so far as to synthesize two or more branches of knowledge into a new field. Ecology represents such a synthesis."[49] "Courses in the broad-fields curriculum," explained Smith, Stanley, and Shores, "have various appellations.... In the college, they are called 'survey' or 'comprehensive' courses, and sometimes 'general courses.' At the high school level they are called 'fusion courses' or 'general courses,' or else they are simply designated by course titles as in the elementary school."[50]

Thus we find the various elements of English (reading, writing, grammar, literature, speech, etc.) brought together under the rubric of language arts. The various social science fields (history, political science, government, economics, anthropology, sociology, etc.) were combined to become the social studies. Art, music, architecture, and literature became the humanities. Principles of physical and natural science were unified into a course in general science. The industrial arts tied together various aspects of vocational education. Physical education included health and safety. General mathematics offered knowledge and skills drawn from arithmetic, algebra, geometry, and so on.

Robert S. Zais spoke about the advantages of the broad-fields curriculum as follows:

> Two main advantages are claimed for the broad-fields design. First, because it is ultimately based on the separate subjects, it provides for an orderly and systematic exposure to the cultural heritage. This advantage it shares with the subject curriculum. But it also integrates separate subjects, thereby enabling learners to see relationships among various elements in the curricu-

---

[49]Reprinted by permission of Macmillan Publishing Company from *Curriculum Development: Theory into Practice,* 2nd ed., p. 257, by Daniel Tanner and Laurel N. Tanner. Copyright ©1980 by Macmillan Publishing Company.

[50]Excerpts from *Fundamentals of Curriculum Development,* Revised Edition p. 257 by B. O. Smith, W. O. Stanley, and J. Harlan Shores, copyright ©1957 by Harcourt Brace Jovanovich, Inc. and renewed 1985 by B. O. Smith, W. O. Stanley, and J. Harlan Shores, reprinted by permission of the publisher.

lum. This second advantage is the special strength that the broad-fields design claims over the subject curriculum.[51]

He warned, however, "With respect to the integration claimed for the broad-fields design, it is worth noting that in practice, combining subjects into a broad field often amounts to little more than the compression of several separate subjects into a single course with little actual unification taking place."[52]

In a true broad-fields approach, teachers select certain general themes or principles to be studied at each year of the sequence of a discipline, such as social studies. Obviously, not all curricula labeled broad fields are truly of that genre.

Common criticisms of the broad-fields curriculum focus on its lack of depth as opposed to breadth, its lack of appeal to student needs and interests, and its emphasis on covering content, which excludes other important goals of education.[53]

Proponents of the broad-fields curriculum would respond to these criticisms by saying that if the curriculum were properly planned and carried out, these deficiencies would be overcome. What appears to have happened in many schools is that the rubric of broad fields has been retained but the curricula themselves have reverted to the separate disciplines of the subject matter curriculum.

The majority of boys and girls in American schools, both elementary and secondary, have been and continue to be educated under some form of the subject matter curriculum. Admittedly, some modifications have been made, but by and large the subject matter curriculum has proved to be a comfortable plan that is widely accepted in American culture. The subject matter curriculum at the senior high school level has been favored by college admissions officers and regional accrediting associations, for it is much easier to understand and evaluate than more experimental types of curricula. We must also add that the subject matter curriculum has met with considerable success.

Team Teaching

While Conant was conducting his surveys of the American high and junior high schools, the National Association of Secondary School Principals in 1956 was seeking ways to cope with increased enrollments in the schools, a teacher shortage, and the introduction of new curricula in various disciplines. Under the leadership of J. Lloyd Trump, associate secretary of the National Association of Secondary School Principals, the Commission on Curriculum Planning and Development was launched to develop a proposal for new ways of using staff through teaming of faculty.

---

[51] Excerpts from *Curriculum: Principles and Foundations,* p. 407, by Robert S. Zais. Copyright ©1976 by Harper & Row, Publishers, Inc. Reprinted by permission of HarperCollins Publishers.

[52] Ibid.

[53] See Zais, pp. 407–408, for criticisms of the broad-fields curriculum.

Supported by the Ford Foundation's Fund for the Advancement of Education, team teaching enjoyed a brief flurry of popularity across the nation from Newton, Massachusetts, to Evanston, Illinois, to San Diego, California. The National Association of Secondary School Principals proceeded to appoint the Commission on the Experimental Study of the Utilization of the Staff in the Secondary School (with J. Lloyd Trump as its director) and to charge it with the task of promoting the cause of team teaching. Harvard University's Graduate School of Education and Claremont Graduate School (California) took a special interest in this innovative organizational plan.

J. Lloyd Trump and Delmas F. Miller defined team teaching as follows:

> The term "team teaching" applies to an arrangement in which two or more teachers and their assistants, taking advantage of their respective competencies, plan, instruct, and evaluate in one or more subject areas a group of elementary or secondary students equivalent in size to two or more conventional classes, using a variety of technical aids to teaching and learning through large-group instruction, small-group discussion, and independent study.[54]

Ira J. Singer described team teaching in this way:

> Team teaching may be defined as an arrangement whereby two or more teachers, with or without teacher aides, cooperatively plan, instruct, and evaluate one or more class groups in an appropriate instructional space and given length of time, so as to take advantage of the special competencies of the team members.[55]

Singer pointed out that the major factors in a team teaching plan are

- cooperative planning, instruction, and evaluation.
- student grouping for special purposes (large group instruction, small group discussion, independent study).
- flexible daily schedule.
- use of teacher aides.
- recognition and utilization of individual teacher talents.
- use of space and media appropriate to the purpose and content of instruction.[56]

The purpose of team teaching was to capitalize on the strengths of teachers, using their varying expertise in different ways. Teams were organized within subject areas and across subject fields.

A particular variant of team teaching came to be known as the Trump Plan. J. Lloyd Trump and Dorsey Baynham postulated three ingredients for an effective organizational structure that would capitalize on teacher assets and

[54]J. Lloyd Trump and Delmas F. Miller. From *Secondary School Curriculum Improvement: Meeting Challenges of the Times,* 3rd ed. (Boston: Allyn & Bacon, 1979), p. 410. Reprinted by permission of Allyn & Bacon, Inc.
[55]Ira J. Singer, "What Team Teaching Really Is," in David W. Beggs III, ed., *Team Teaching: Bold New Venture* (Bloomington: Indiana University Press, 1964), p. 16. Reprinted with permission.
[56]Ibid.

provide better opportunities for the learners. The school week, according to Trump and Baynham, should provide opportunities for pupils to attend large-group instruction, to interact in small groups, and to carry out independent study. Prophesied Trump and Baynham:

> The school of the future will schedule students in class groups an average of only 18 hours a week. The average student at the level of today's tenth grade will spend about 12 of the 18 hours in *large-group instruction* and six in *small-group discussion*.
>
> In addition, students will spend, on an average, 12 hours each week in school in individual *independent study*.[57]

These figures convert to 40 percent of a student's time in large-group instruction, 20 percent in small-group discussion, and 40 percent in independent study.

Singer contrasted schedules of two history teachers under a conventional plan and under a team teaching plan that incorporates the three ingredients: large-group instruction (LG), small-group discussion (SG), and independent study (IS) (see Table 9–4).

Differentiated Staffing. Team teaching offered a creative answer to the problem of using limited faculty and resources more effectively. More elaborate school-wide staffing patterns were developed that incorporated the principle of differentiated assignment. In the early 1970s the North Miami Beach Senior High School (Florida), for example, developed a set of categories of personnel for its differentiated staffing plan.[58] These included in addition to a principal, vice-principal, and business manager the following positions:

- □ *Community Relations Specialist.* Coordinates activities involving school and community.
- □ *Human Relations Specialist.* Seeks to create harmonious climate within the school.
- □ *In-service Coordinator.* Coordinates the training and development program of the professional and paraprofessional staff.
- □ *Psychologist.* Counsels students on emotional problems.
- □ *School Social Worker.* Helps students to function adequately in school; a behavioral consultant.
- □ *Media Specialist.* Supervises and develops media program.
- □ *Media Technician.* Provides skilled technical assistance to staff and students.
- □ *Coordinating Librarian.* Supervises library resources.
- □ *Teaching Designer.* Assists teachers in improving instruction and evaluating effectiveness.
- □ *Teaching Prescriber.* Provides assessment, diagnosis, and prescription for each student's program through observation, testing, and individual and/or group conferences.

---

[57] J. Lloyd Trump and Dorsey Baynham, *Focus on Change: Guide to Better Schools* (Chicago: Rand McNally, 1961), p. 41.

[58] North Miami Beach Senior High School, Dade County, Florida Public Schools.

TABLE 9–4 Comparison of two types of schedules

(a) CONVENTIONAL SCHEDULE

TIME	MONDAY	TUESDAY	WEDNESDAY	THURSDAY	FRIDAY
8:00- 8:50	Hist.10A Hist.10B	Hist.10A Hist.10B	Hist.10A Hist.10B	Hist.10A Hist.10B	Hist.10A Hist.10B

(b) SINGLE-DISCIPLINE TEAM SCHEDULE

TIME	MONDAY	TUESDAY	WEDNESDAY	THURSDAY	FRIDAY
8:00– 8:50	History 10AB (LG)	History 10AB1* (SG) History 10AB2 (SG) History 10AB3 (SG)	History 10AB (LG)	History 10AB1* (SG) History 10AB2 (SG) History 10AB3 (SG)	History 10AB (IS) Project work in library, laboratory, music room, art studio, etc.

(60 students, 2 teachers, 1 instruction assistant)
*One History 10AB-SG can be supervised by an instruction assistant, student teacher or student leader.
LG = large group, SG = small group, IS = independent study.
SOURCE: Ira J. Singer, "What Team Teaching Really Is," in David W. Beggs III, ed., *Team Teaching: Bold New Venture* (Bloomington: Indiana University Press, 1964), p. 17. Reprinted by permission.

☐ *Resource Specialist.* Gathers, coordinates, and disseminates materials for helping solve specific learning situations.
☐ *Facilitating Teacher.* Guides students through learning; teaches specific courses.
☐ *Instructional Intern.* Assists a directing teacher; a college junior, senior, or graduate student who serves for a full school year in the high school.
☐ *Instructional Aide.* Assists by performing paraprofessional responsibilities.
☐ *Clerical Aide.* Performs clerical duties.

In recent years secondary schools have turned away from the concepts of team teaching and differentiated staffing. However, team teaching is a prominent feature of most plans for middle and open-space schools. Results were not always as anticipated. In some cases teachers found themselves incompatible, unable to cooperate effectively. Cooperative planning requires a high degree of interpersonal skill that some team members lacked.

Some administrators favored the large-group instruction aspect of team teaching for the convenience and economy of scheduling large numbers of students; they omitted the important companion features of small-group discussion and independent study. Large-group instruction by itself deprives students of interaction with the teacher and with each other. When these techniques were coupled with instructional television, also attempted at this period, students became inattentive and bored.

Schools experienced varying degrees of success with independent study. Plans for large-group instruction, small-group discussion, and independent study call for special facilities and resources that were missing in some schools that attempted this type of organization.

The very complexity of staffing and scheduling under team teaching patterns confused parents, teachers, and students. Tradition, therefore, caused them to prefer uniform time blocks, completely supervised study, and individual assignments.

Flexible and Modular Scheduling

With but a few significant departures from traditional practice, high schools have continued to schedule subjects in the conventional mode, one period per day, five days per week. The Carnegie unit, Conant's recommendations that each course meet five times a week for the academic year, and customary standards of the regional accrediting associations have added to the pressure to maintain traditional scheduling.

However, it is difficult to find a logical reason why all subjects must be taught for the same period of time. Some disciplines are by their very nature more difficult than others and require more time for mastery. Some courses are most effectively taught when accompanied by a laboratory that requires extra time. Some subject matter is simply not as relevant as other subject matter and, therefore, should be accorded less time.

Nor is there a logical reason why equal amounts of time must be allotted to every subject every day of the week. Some days and some weeks more time is needed to explore a topic in depth. Some days it is apparent to the teacher that youngsters have not comprehended the lesson and need to spend more time on the lesson or undergo remedial work.

There is also not sufficient reason why the instructional mode must be standardized every period of every day. Variation should be possible for lecture, mediated instruction, laboratories, seminars, field trips, independent study, and other modes.

Efforts were made in the 1960s to break out of the mold of the standard schedule. These efforts are subsumed in a movement referred to as flexible scheduling. Donald C. Manlove and David W. Beggs III described the concept of flexible scheduling as follows:

> The flexible schedule is an organization for instruction which:
>
> 1. calls for classes of varying size within and between courses. (Students sometimes may meet in large assembly classes, and at other times in small inquiry classes. In addition, part of the day will be spent in individual or independent study.)
> 2. provides for instructional groups which meet at varying frequencies for varying lengths. (Some classes may meet every day of the week, others will not. Some instructional sessions will be for a short duration, others for an extended period of time.)
> 3. makes team teaching possible in any content area or for any group of students in the school. (The use of a teaching team, two or more teachers working with a given group of students on a common instructional problem, is suggested in this model.)
> 4. requires countless professional decisions by teachers about students, content, and teaching methods.[59]

Types of Schedules. Flexible schedules have taken varying forms; some are minor departures from traditional plans, others radical changes. Among the varieties of flexible scheduling are the following:

1. Two or more periods are simply combined, as in the case of core classes.
2. Subjects are scheduled for both double and single periods in the same week. For example, some classes may meet two periods on Monday and Thursday, other classes two periods on Tuesday and Friday, but all only one period on Wednesday. Teachers can thus use the larger blocks of time in ways not permitted by the constraints of the single-period schedule.
3. Classes are rotated during the week. Trump and Miller supplied diagrams of rotating schedules with standard periods and with periods varying in length (see Table 9–5).
4. Instead of typical 45 to 55 minute periods, the schedule is broken into modules, which, by faculty agreement, may be multiples of 15, 20, 30, or more minutes. Modular scheduling was described as follows:

> Modular scheduling, or flexible-modular scheduling . . . requires complete abandonment of the division of the school schedule into equal amounts of time for each course. . . . Some subjects are scheduled for two or three modules (conceivably, even for a single module) per day. Those which require a great deal of time are scheduled in multiple modules. . . .
>
> The duration of the module is purely a matter for decision, ordinarily made by the faculty of the school at the time a modular schedule is introduced.

---

[59]Donald C. Manlove and David W. Beggs III, *Flexible Scheduling: Bold New Venture* (Bloomington: Indiana University Press, 1965), pp. 22–23. Reprinted with permission.

TABLE 9–5   Rotating schedules

ROTATION OF CLASSES—STANDARD PERIODS

TIME	MONDAY	TUESDAY	WEDNESDAY	THURSDAY	FRIDAY
8:00	1	1	1	1	2
9:00	2	2	2	3	3
10:00	3	3	4	4	4
11:00	4	5	5	5	5
12:00			Lunch		
12:30	6	6	6	6	7
1:30	7	7	7	Special	Special

ROTATION OF CLASSES—PERIODS VARY IN LENGTH

TIME	MONDAY	TUESDAY	WEDNESDAY	THURSDAY	FRIDAY
8:55–10:26	1	2	4	5	6
10:36–11:26	2	4	5	6	1
11:30–12:26	3	3	3	3	3
12:26–1:04			Lunch		
1:04–2:30	4	5	6	1	2
2:34–3:30	5	6	1	2	4

NOTE: Numbers indicate different subjects.
SOURCE: J. Lloyd Trump and Delmas F. Miller, From *Secondary School Curriculum Improvement: Meeting Challenges of the Times,* 3rd ed. (Boston: Allyn & Bacon, Inc. 1979), p. 400. Reprinted by permission of Allyn & Bacon, Inc.

Fifteen-minute modules are common. A school day based on fifteen-minute modules would encompass approximately twenty-five modules. Schools which follow the Stanford School Scheduling System use modules of twenty-two minutes; twenty modules make up the day. The Indiana Flexible Schedule uses fifteen modules per day of thirty minutes each. Ridgewood High School, Norridge–Harwood Heights, Illinois (as one example) has a school day made up of twenty modules of twenty minutes plus an additional ten-minute module for homeroom period.[60]

Trump and Miller provided an illustration of a modular schedule using 15-minute modules, as shown in Table 9–6.

---

[60] Peter F. Oliva, *The Secondary School Today,* 2nd ed. (New York: Harper & Row, 1972), p. 196.

TABLE 9–6   Fifteen-minute modules—same schedule every day

TIME	SUBJECT
8:00	
8:15	Mathematics
8:30	
8:45	
9:00	Speech correction
9:15	
9:30	
9:45	Science
10:00	
10:15	
10:30	
10:45	Music
11:00	
11:15	Spanish
11:30	
11:45	Music practice
12:00	Lunch
etc.	

SOURCE: J. Lloyd Trump and Delmas F. Miller, From *Secondary School Curriculum Improvement: Meeting Challenges of the Times,* 3rd ed. (Boston: Allyn & Bacon, Inc. 1979), p. 398. Reprinted by permission of Allyn & Bacon, Inc.

5. Class schedules are set frequently, even daily. This "scheduling on demand" is the ultimate goal of flexible scheduling. As J. Lloyd Trump observed, it allows teachers and students the greatest possible latitude in determining their instruction and learning. Trump told how this process was accomplished at the Brookhurst Junior High School in Anaheim, California:

Individual members of teaching teams determine three days in advance what students they want to teach, in what size groups, for what length of time, in what places, and with what technological aids. Teacher job-specification forms containing this information are turned in to their team leaders. The team leaders then assemble to make a master schedule for the day, a procedure that takes approximately twenty minutes each day. The master schedule is then duplicated and made available to the students and their counselors. In a daily 20-minute meeting, with the advice and consent of their counselor (twenty minutes to a counselor), each student makes his schedule. A student noting, for example, that the schedule calls for a large-group presentation on a given subject and deciding that he already knows that material, may elect rather to spend his time in independent study in the art room or library or some place

TABLE 9–7   Characteristics of traditional and flexible schedules

ELEMENT	TRADITIONAL SCHEDULE	FLEXIBLE SCHEDULE
Content	Assumes each course is equivalent in requirements for mastery to all others	Assumes requirements for mastery of content vary from course to course
Facilities	Use is set by schedule	Use is determined sometimes by student needs
Groups	All class groups are nearly equal size	Class groups differ in size depending on instructional task
Scheduling unit	The day; each day in the week has the same order as every other day	The week; each day in the week has a different order
Students	Students should be in a class group or supervised study	Students may be in a class group or working independently
Teachers	All have equal numbers of classes or assignments and demands on their time	Number of classes varies from teacher to teacher and demands on time vary
Time	Usually equal for all subjects	Usually different for various subjects

SOURCE: Donald C. Manlove and David W. Beggs III, *Flexible Scheduling: Bold New Venture* (Bloomington: Indiana University Press, 1965), p. 26. Reprinted by permission.

else. The counselor either approves or rejects this decision. Then the student makes out his own schedule for the day in quadruplicate. One copy is for himself, one for the office, one for the counselor, and one for his parents.[61]

Traditional Versus Flexible Scheduling.   Flexible scheduling is an essential aspect of plans for curriculum organization such as team teaching, which calls for large-group instruction, small-group instruction, and independent study. Traditional schedules have forced teachers to use the same amounts of time for all activities.

Manlove and Beggs contrasted the traditional and the flexible schedule in Table 9–7. They summarized the advantages and disadvantages of flexible scheduling to teachers, making the comparisons shown in Table 9–8.

Trump and Miller also warned of a danger inherent in modular scheduling— or in any innovation, for that matter—"once a change is made, the new schedule

---

[61]J. Loyd Trump, "Flexible Scheduling—Fad or Fundamental?" *Phi Delta Kappan* 44, no. 8 (May, 1963): 370. Reprinted with permission.

TABLE 9–8   Advantages and disadvantages of flexible scheduling

ADVANTAGES FOR TEACHERS	DISADVANTAGES FOR TEACHERS
1. Provides a mean for pacing the instruction to an individual student's needs	1. Danger of not giving enough time to one subject
2. Allows teachers to make decisions about the length and frequency of learning activities	2. Requires more time and cooperative effort of teachers in making the schedule
3. Gives teachers time to work with small groups and individuals	3. Possibility of too little identification of a student with his teachers
4. Takes unnecessary repetition out of the teacher's day	4. Is difficult to schedule
5. Places increased responsibility on students for learning	5. Requires teachers to change their teaching patterns
6. Provides the opportunity to use resource experts for a large group of students in an economical way for the resource person	6. Is not understood by the public or even by all teachers

SOURCE: Donald C. Manlove and David W. Beggs III, *Flexible Scheduling: Bold New Venture* (Bloomington: Indiana University Press, 1965), p. 67. Reprinted by permission.

can become almost as rigid as the one it replaced."[62] The complexity of operation, a structure that shifts from day to day, the high degree of planning required on the part of students, teachers, and administrators, and the decline in popularity of the team teaching concept have militated against flexible scheduling and caused some schools to return to more traditional and more commonly understood forms of scheduling.

Rotating schedules are not necessarily practices of the past. The Tuskawilla Middle School (Oviedo, Florida), for example, employs rotation of its six periods on a six-week cycle. Table 9–9 shows the seventh-grade team's schedule. Every six weeks, the class in the last time slot moves to the first time slot, and the other classes move accordingly. This system of rotation allows for distribution of classes over the mornings and afternoons during the school year, thus averaging out the effect of the hour of the day on students' learning.

The Nongraded High School

During the 1960s when the elementary schools were experimenting with continuous progress plans and eliminating grades as we know them, several high

---

[62]J. Lloyd Trump and Delmas F. Miller. From *Secondary School Curriculum Improvement: Meeting Challenges of the Times*, 3rd ed. (Boston: Allyn & Bacon, 1979), p. 398. Reprinted by permission of Allyn & Bacon, Inc.

TABLE 9–9   Rotating schedule, 7th grade. Tuskawilla Middle School, Oviedo, Florida, 1990–91. Reprinted by permission.

	ROTATING PERIODS					
	9:34 a.m.	10:30 a.m.	11:26 a.m.	12:22 a.m.	1:48 p.m.	2:44 p.m.
First six weeks	1	2	3	4	5	6
Second six weeks	6	1	2	3	4	5
Third six weeks	5	6	1	2	3	4
Fourth six weeks	4	5	6	1	2	3
Fifth six weeks	3	4	5	6	1	2
Sixth six weeks	2	3	4	5	6	1

NOTE: The planning period is indicated by "2." Lunch for the 7th grade team is 1:14–1:44 P.M.

schools were attempting to develop ungraded patterns of organization. Prominent among these high schools were Nova High School (Broward County, Florida) and Melbourne High School (Brevard County, Florida).

In the mid-1960s Nova High School and Melbourne High School were the epitome of innovation. Nova High School was established amid what was at that time a semirural tract of now populous Broward County (Fort Lauderdale) as the first facility in a projected complex that eventually included elementary schools, a junior high, and a junior college as well as the high school—all publicly supported. A private institution of higher learning, Nova University, is nearby.

Nova High School made use of teaching teams complete with clerical assistants and teacher aides. Organized on a trimester plan, Nova High School incorporated closed circuit television, a photographic laboratory, data processing equipment, and learning resource centers equipped with tape recorders, microfilm readers, and teaching machines.

A daily schedule was devised that consisted of five periods of 80 minutes each and an optional sixth period of one hour's duration. Speaking about the nongraded feature of Nova High School, Arthur B. Wolfe, Director of the K–12 Center at that time, set forth the Nova Plan in these terms:

> The Nova Plan will eliminate grade designation and will establish a far wider range of learning levels through which each student may progress at a rate commensurate with his interests and abilities. Each of the established levels will be only slightly advanced over the level below, thereby enabling the student to move from one level to the next at any given time during the school year. This process will be applicable to the program of each student and to each separate subject area, thereby placing a realistic evaluation on each student's progress on an individual basis, one not entirely related to the sum total of his progress. . . .
>
> Following the enrollment of new students, records will be examined and a series of tests will be administered. The faculty will place students in an achievement group that will provide a smooth transition to a new learning environment. This process will be followed for each of the subject areas in which students may be enrolled. It will be necessary in some cases to move students forward or back until an achievement level has been found in which they will feel comfortable.[63]

Nova, like Melbourne, sought to put into action some of the more significant innovations of the day.

Situated in the stimulating setting of the space-oriented Brevard County, with Cape Canaveral practically in its backyard, Melbourne High School (under its principal, B. Frank Brown) achieved widespread recognition in both the professional and lay periodicals. As its stationery proclaimed, Melbourne High School was the school "where the library is bigger than the gymnasium." Melbourne High was host to so many visitors from all over the country that at one time it set up monthly briefing sessions.

Like Nova High School, Melbourne High School ventured to try out many new ideas. Its emphasis on the academics was evidenced by its library with carrels, which resembled a college library, by its six foreign languages (including Russian and Chinese), and by its stress on independent study, particularly for the academically talented. Melbourne's chief claim to fame lay in its nongraded organizational plan. In the Melbourne Plan students are grouped not by ability as measured by tests of intelligence or scholastic aptitude but on the basis of achievement tests, subject by subject. A tenth-grade student, therefore, might be enrolled in Algebra 1, Phase 2 and English, Phase 4. Some subjects, such as typing and physical education, are neither graded nor

---

[63] Arthur B. Wolfe, *The Nova Plan for Instruction* (Fort Lauderdale, Fla.: Broward County Board of Public Instruction, 1962), pp. 14–15. Reprinted with permission.

phased. Melbourne's schedule of course offerings described each of its seven phases:

- Phase 1: Subjects are designed for students who need special assistance in small classes.
- Phase 2: Subjects are designed for students who need more emphasis on the basic skills.
- Phase 3: Courses are designed for students who have an average background of achievement.
- Phase 4: Subject matter is designed for extremely well prepared students desiring education in depth.
- Phase 5: Courses are available to students who are willing to assume responsibility for their own learning and pursue college level courses while still in high school.
- Phase Q: Students whose creative talents are well developed should give consideration to the Quest phase of the curriculum. This is an important dimension of the phased organization designed to give thrust in the direction of individual fulfillment. In this phase a student may research an area in which he is deeply and broadly curious either to develop creative powers or in quest of knowledge.
- Phase X: Subjects which do not accommodate student mobility; e.g., typing, physical education, are ungraded but unphased.[64]

A recent schedule, reproduced in Figure 9–3, shows the full scope of the phased organizational plan of Melbourne High School. More recently, Melbourne's schedule has been recast in a different format. For example, the 1990–91 schedule of science courses appears as shown in Figure 9–4. The last digit of the eight-number designation denotes the phase level.

Brown referred to the ungraded concept implemented at Melbourne High School not only as the nongraded school[65] but also the multiphased school.[66] Brown gave particular attention to the independent study or quest phase of the program. He referred to the quest phase as both "Education by Appointment"[67] because students see their teachers by appointment in the tutorial fashion and "Education by Agreement" because he recommended that schools emulate the Dalton plan by drawing up an agreement form or contract specifying the independent study that a student plans to do.[68]

---

[64]Melbourne High School, Brevard County, Florida Public Schools. Reprinted with permission.

[65]B. Frank Brown, *The Nongraded High School* (Englewood Cliffs, N.J.: Prentice-Hall, 1963).

[66]B. Frank Brown, *The Appropriate Placement School: A Sophisticated Nongraded Curriculum* (West Nyack, N.Y.: Parker, 1965).

[67]B. Frank Brown, *Education by Appointment: New Approaches to Independent Study* (West Nyack, N.Y.: Parker, 1968), p. 61.

[68]For information on the Dalton (Massachusetts) Plan see Helen Parkhurst, *Education on the Dalton Plan* (New York: E. P. Dutton, 1922).

FIGURE 9–3 Schedule of course offerings at Melbourne High School, Florida, 1986–87. Donald L. Beggs, principal. Reprinted by permission.

MELBOURNE HIGH SCHOOL
SCHEDULE OF COURSE OFFERINGS

DEPARTMENT	PERIOD 1 7:15 - 8:05	PHASE	PERIOD 2 8:10 - 9:00	PHASE	PERIOD 3 9:05 - 9:55	PHASE
ENGLISH Recommendation: Phase 3-5, 10th year students take American Literature All students must take one English class each semester. ★ Means Semester Only	English II Hon. 1001350	5	English II Hon. 1001350	5	A.P. Literature 1001430	5
	English III Hon. 1001380	5	Speech 1007300	3/4		
			English II Hon. 1001350	4	English II Hon. 1001350	4
	English III 1001370	3	English III 1001370	3	English IV 1001400	3
	English III Hon. 1001380	4	Drama I 0400310	3/4	Drama I 0400310	3/4
	English Skills 3 1001360	2			English III 1001370	3
	English IV Hon. 1001410	4	Writing I ★ 1009300	4	English IV Hon. 1001410	4
	English II 1001340	3			English II 1001340	3
			English III Hon. 1001380	4	English III Hon. 1001380	4
			English IV Hon. 1001410	4		
	English IV 1001400	3	English IV 1001400	3		
	Latin I & III	3/4	Latin II	3/4		
	English IV 1001400	3			English IV 1001400	3
			English Skills II 1001330	2	English III 1001370	3
			English III 1001370	3	English II 1001340	3
			English II Hon. 1001350	3	English II 1001340	3
	English Skills 4 1001390	2			English Skills 4 1001390	2
MATHEMATICS 3 credits required (Grades 9 through 12). ★ Means Semester Only	Computer Prog. Basic 0201330	3			Computer Prog. Basic 0201330	4
	Trigonometry ★ 1211300	4	A.P. Calculus 1202310	5		
	General Math III 1205360	2	General Math III 1205360	2	Algebra I 1200310	3
			Algebra II 1200340	4	Algebra II 1200340	5
	Algebra II 1200330	3			Algebra II 1200330	3
	Comp. Ed. Pullout		Comp. Ed. Pullout			
	Geometry 1206320	4				
	Algebra I 1200310	3	Geometry 1206310	3		
			Algebra I 1200310	3	Geometry 1206310	3
			Consumer Math 1205370		Consumer Math 1205370	3
	Comp. Ed. Math 1601300	X	Comp. Ed. Math 1601300	X	Comp. Ed. Math 1601300	X
	Computer App. 0200310	2-4	Introduction to Computers 0200300	2-4	Introduction to Computers 0200300	2-4
SCIENCE 3 credits required (Grades 9 through 12).	Biology I Hon. 2000320	4	Biology I Hon. 2000320	4	Science Res. 1700300/1700310	0
	Biology I 2000310	3	Biology I 2000310	3		
			Chemistry I 2003340	3		
	Chemistry I Hon. 2003350	5	Chemistry I Hon. 2003350	4	Chemistry I. Hon. 2003350	5
	Oceanography 2001370	3	Oceanography 2001370	4/5	Oceanography 2001370	3
	Chemistry I Hon. 2003350	4			Chemistry I 2003340	3
			Physics I 2003380	3	Physics I 2003380	3
			Introduction to Biology 2000300	2	Introduction to Biology 2000300	2
	Science Daily Liv. 2002300	2	Biology I 2000310	3	Biology I 2000310	3
SOCIAL STUDIES See Graduation Requirements above. ★ Means Semester Only	Adv. World History 2109320	4/5			American Government ★ 2106320	4/5
			Adv. American Govt. 2106320	4/5	Psychology ★ 2107300	4
	Adv. American History 2100320	5	Adv. American History 2100320	4	Adv. American History 2100320	4
	Economics ★ 2102310		Economics ★ 2102320	4		
					Economics ★ 2102320	4
	American Government ★ 2106310	3	World History 2109310	3		
	American History 2100310	3	American History 2100310	3	American History 2100310	3
	American History 2100320	4	American Government ★ 2106310	3		
	Economics ★ 2102310	3	Economics ★ 2102310	3	Intro. American History 2100300	2

(continued)

FIGURE 9–3 continued

PERIOD 4 10:00 - 11:20		PHASE	PERIOD 5 11:25 - 12:15		PHASE	PERIOD 6 12:20 - 1:10		PHASE	PERIOD 7 1:15 - 2:05		PHASE
			A.P. Literature	1001430	5	English II Hon.	1001350	5			
English III Hon.	1001380	5	English III Hon.	1001380	4				English III Hon.	1001380	4
German I		3/4				German II		3/4	English II Hon.	1001350	4
English III	1001370	3							English IV	1001400	3
English III Hon.	1001380	4				Drama II & III	0400320/30	3/4			
			English Skills 3	1001360	2	English III	1001370	3	English III	1001370	3
			English IV Hon.	1001410	4				English IV Hon.	1001410	5
			English III	1001370	3	English II	1001340	3	English III	1001370	3
Journalism I	1006300	3/4	Journalism II	1006310/20	3/4	English III Hon.	1001380	4			
English IV Hon.	1001410	4	English IV Hon.	1001410	4	English II	1001340	3	English IV	1001410	4
English IV Hon.	1001410	4	English IV	1001400	3	English IV	1001400	3			
English II Hon.	1001350	4	English II Hon.	1001350	4				Latin I		3/5
English II	1001340	3	English II	1001340	3				English II	1001340	3
			English Skills 2	1001330	2	English III Hon.	1001380	4	English III Hon.	1001380	4
English III	1001370	3									
Writing I ★	1009300	3	English II Hon.	1001350	4	English II Hon.	1001350	4			
English III	1001370	3	English III	1001370	3	English III	1001370	3			
			Algebra II	1200330	3	Algebra II	1200330	3	Algebra II	1200330	3
Calculus	1202300	4/5	Calculus	1202300	4/5	Trigonometry ★	1211300	4			
Algebra I	1200310	3				Algebra I	1200310	3			
Apply Basic Skills	1205310	2	Apply Basic Skills	1205310	2				Algebra II	1200340	4
			Trigonometry ★	1211300	3	Trigonometry ★	1211300	3	Trigonometry ★	1211300	3
Geometry	1206320	4/5	Algebra II	1200340	4	Algebra II	1200340	4	Trigonometry ★	1211300	5
Algebra II	1200330	3	Geometry	1206310	3				Algebra I	1200310	3
			Algebra I	1200310	3	Geometry	1206310	3	Geometry	1206310	3
Intro. to Computers	0200300	2-4	Business Math	1205380	3	Consumer Math	1205370	3	Business Math	1205380	3
Comp. Ed. Math	1601300	X				Comp. Ed. Math	1601300	X			
			Computer App.	0200310	2-4						
Biology I Hon.	2000320	4				Biology I Hon.	200320	5			
Biology I	2000310	3	Physical Science	2003310	3				Biology I	2000310	3
Anat. & Physio.	2000360	3-5	Chemistry I	2003340	3	Chemistry I	2003340	3	Anat. & Physio.	2000360	3-5
			Chemistry I Hon.	2003350	4				A.P. Chemistry	2003370	5
			Oceanography	2001370	4/5				Oceanography	2001370	3
Chemistry I	2003340	3				Chemistry I Hon.	2003350	4	Chemistry I	2003340	3
			Physics I	2003390	4/5	Physics I	2003390	4/5	Physics I	2003390	4/5
Oceanography	2001370	3				Oceanography	2001370	3	Introduction to Biology	2000300	2
			Biology I	2000310	3	Biology I	2000310	3			
			American Government ★	2106320	4/5	American Government ★	2106320	4/5	Intro. to World History	2109300	2
American History	2100310	3				American History	2100310	3	Psychology	2107300	4
			Adv. American History	2100320	4				Adv. American History	2100320	4
Intro. to Economics ★	2102300	2				Economics ★	2102320	4	Economics	2102310	3
Psychology ★	2107300	3	Economics ★	2102320	4	Psychology	2107300	3	Law Studies	2106350	3/4
Intro. Amer. Govt. ★	2106300	2	World History	2109310	3				American Government ★	2106310	3
American History	2100310	3				A.P. American History	2100330	5			
			American History	2100310	3	American Government ★	2106310	3	American History	2100310	3
Economics ★	2102310	3				Intro. American History	2100300	2			

(continued)

FIGURE 9–3 continued

DEPARTMENT	PERIOD 1 7:15 - 8:05	PHASE	PERIOD 2 8:10 - 9:00	PHASE	PERIOD 3 9:05 - 9:55	PHASE
FOREIGN LANGUAGES	Latin I & III 0706300/20	3-5	Latin II 0706310	3-5		
			Spanish I 0708340	3	Spanish I 0708340	3
			English II Hon. 1001350	4	English II Hon. 1001350	4
	French IV 0701350	3/4			French II 0701330	3
	Spanish III 0708360	4			Spanish II 0708350	4/5
	Spanish II 0708350	3	Spanish I 0708340	4/5	French I 0701320	3
			French III 0701340	3/4		
PHYSICAL EDUCATION ★ *Means Semester Only*	Adv. Weight Training ★ 1501360	X	Beg. Weight Training ★ 1501340	X	Personal Fitness ★ 1501300	X
			Dance I 0300300	X	Team Sports ★ 1503350	X
	Life Management ★ 0800300	X	Life Management ★ 0800300	X		
	Dance I 0300300	X			Dance 3 0300330	X
DRIVER EDUCATION ★ *Means Semester Only*	Driver Education ★ 1900310	X			Driver Education ★ 1900310	X
AIR FORCE ROTC	Aero Science I 1800300	X	Aero Science II 1800310	X		
HUMANITIES			Humanities I 0900310	3	Search 1700340	Q
TV PRODUCTION	Library/Media		Library/Media		Library/Media	
LIBRARY SERVICE	Library/Media		Library/Media		Library/Media	
AV MEDIA						
EXCEPTIONAL ED. EH/SLD/EMH	SLD Math Daily Living 7912310	E	SLD Math Daily Living 7912310	E	SLD Math Daily Living 7912310	E
	SLD Language Arts 7910310	E			SLD Language Arts 7910310	E
			SLD Funct. Economics 7921310	E	SLD Funct. Economics 7921310	E
	SLD Health & Safety 7920320	E	SLD Health & Safety 7920320	E	SLD Health & Safety 7920320	E
			SLD Life Management 7960020	E		
	SLD Employment Skills 7980110	E			SLD Employment Skills 7980110	E
	EH Math Daily Living 7912310	E			EH Math Daily Living 7912310	E
	EH Social & Per. Skills 7963070	E	EH Social & Per. Skills 7963070	E		
			EH Math 1205360	E	EH Employment Skills 7980110	E
					Ex. Ed. Voc. Ag. 7980033	E
BUSINESS EDUCATION ★ *Means Semester Only*	Accounting I 8203010	X			Practical Bus. Skills ★ 8209000	X
	Typing I 8209010	X	Typing I 8209010	X		
HOME ECONOMICS ★ *Means Semester Only*	Family Living ★ 8500340	X	Family Living ★ 8500340	X		
TRADE AND INDUSTRIAL ★ *Means Semester Only*	Intro. to Drafting 8600810	X			Intro. to Drafting 8600810	X
			Basic Auto Mechanics I 8709110	X	Basic Auto Mechanics II 8709120	X
	Drafting I 8724010	X				
	Comp Ed. Pullout		Comp Ed. Pullout		Intro. to Electronics 8600910	X
	Commercial Art I 8718010	X			Commercial Art 2-6 8718020	X
	Ex. Ed. Voc. Construction 7980030	E	Brick & Block II 8721220	X		
FINE ARTS ★ *Means Semester Only*	Inst. Tech. I 1302420	X			Band 2 1302310/11/12	X
	English III Hon. 1001380	4	Drama I 0400310	3/4	Drama I 0400310	3/4
	Art 3/D I ★ 0101330	X	Art 2/D I ★ 0101300	X		
	Commercial Art I 8718010	X			Commercial Art 2-6 8718020	X
	Chorus I 1303300	X	Chorus 2 & 3 1303310/20	X	Chorus I 1303300	X
DCT	DCT 8300990	X	DCT 83300990	X	DCT 8300990	X
	DCT 8300990	X	DCT 8300990	X	DCT 8300990	X
ALTERNATIVE ED.	By Assignment Only		By Assignment Only		By Assignment Only	

(continued)

FIGURE 9–3   continued

PERIOD 4 10:00 - 11:20		PHASE	PERIOD 5 11:25 - 12:15		PHASE	PERIOD 6 12:20 - 1:10		PHASE	PERIOD 7 1:15 - 2:05		PHASE
English II Hon.	1001350	4	English II Hon.	1001350	4				Latin I	0706300	4/5
Spanish I	0708340	3	Spanish I	0708340	3				Spanish III	0708360	3
German I	0702320	3/5				German II	0702330	3/4	English II Hon.	1001350	4
French II	0701330	4/5				Spanish I	0708340	4	Spanish I	0708340	4
			Spanish IV & V	0708370/300	4/5	Spanish III	0708360	4	Spanish II	0708350	4/5
Spanish I	0708340	3	French I	0701320	4	Spanish II	0708350	3			
French I	0701320	3									
Personal Fitness ★	1501300	I				Intermed. Wt. Train ★	1501350	I			
			Team Sports ★	1503350	I	Team Sports ★	1503350	I	Personal Fitness ★	1501300	I
Life Management ★	0800300	I	Beg. Wt. Train ★	1501340	I				Beg. Swim ★	1502330	I
Dance	0300330	I				Dance Chor. Per.	0300380	I	Dance I	0300300	I
Driver Education ★	1900310	I	Driver Education ★	1900310	I				Driver Education ★	1900310	I
Aero Science 3 & 4	1800320/30	I				Aero Science II	1800310	I	Aero Science I	1800300	I
Humanities I	0900310	4/5									
TV Production	1100300	4	Library/Media			Library/Media			Library/Media		
Library/Media			Library/Media			Library/Media			Library/Media		
			SLD Health & Safety	7920320	E	SLD Health & Safety	7920320	E			
SLD Reading	7910360	E				SLD Language Arts	7910310	E	SLD Language Arts	7910310	E
SLD Funct. Economics	7921310	E	SLD Funct. Economics	7921310	E				SLD Funct. Economics	7921310	E
SLD Health & Safety	7920320	E				SLD English Skills III	1001360	E			
SLD Math Daily Liv.	7912310	E	SLD Math Daily Liv.	7912310	E	SLD Gen. Math III	1205360	E	SLD Life Management	7960020	E
SLD Employment Skills	7980110	E	SLD Employment Skills	7980110	E				SLD Employment Skills	7980110	E
			EH Cons. Econ.	7921310	E	EH Health & Safety	7920320	E	EH Health & Safety	7920320	E
EH Cons. Econ.	7921310	E	EH Language Arts	7910300	E				EH Language Arts	7910300	E
EH Employment Skills	7980110	E									
			Pract. Bus. Skills ★	8209000	I	Pract. Bus. Skills ★	8209000	I	Typing I	8209010	I
Typing II	8209020	I				Typing II	8209020	I	Office Procedures	8209220	I
Home & Family Manage.	8500320	I	Ex. Ed. Foods	7980030	I	Ex. Ed. Voc. Foods	7980030	I	Ex. Ed. Voc. Foods	7980030	I
Interm. Drafting	8600820	I	Intro. to Drafting	8600810	I	Draft. Indepen. Study	8600830	I			
Ex. Ed. Voc. Trade	7980031	E	Auto Mech. 3 - 6	8709130/40/50/60	I	Auto Mech 3 - 6	8709130/40/50/60	I	Basic Auto Mech. I	8709110	I
Drafting II	8724020	I	Drafting 3 - 6	8724030/40/50/60	I	Drafting 3 - 6	8724030/40/50/60	I	Drafting I	8724010	I
			Elect. Ind. St./Inter. Elect.	8600930/20	I	Introduction to Electronics	8600910				
Commercial Art 2-6	8718020	I	Art 2/D I ★	0101300	I				Art 2/D I ★	0101300	I
Brick & Block I	8721210	I				Br & Block 3-6	8721230/40/50/60	I	Br & Block 3-6	8721230/40/50/60	I
Band 3	1302320/21/22	I				Inst. Tech 3 & 4	1302440/50	I	Jazz Ensemble	1302500	I
English III Hon.	1001380	4				Drama II	0400320	3-5			
Draw & Paint II	0104330	I	Draw & Paint II	0104330	I	Art 3/D I ★	0101330	I			
Commercial Art 2-6	8718020	I	Art 2/D I ★	0101300	I				Art 2/D I ★	0101300	I
			Am. Mus. Theater	1300390	I				Vocal Ensemble	1302440	I
			Work Exp.	8300991	I	Work Exp.	8300991	I			
			Work Exp.	8300991	I				Work Exp.	8300991	I
By Assignment Only			By Assignment Only			By Assignment Only			By Assignment Only		

SOURCE: Reprinted by permission.

NOTE: To conserve space, names of faculty, room assignment, and other descriptive material have been omitted from this reproduction.

FIGURE 9–4　Partial schedule, Melbourne High School, Florida, 1990–91. Reprinted by permission.

FILE: SCIENCE I

	1	2	3	4	5	6	7
Campbell Room 63	AP Bio. 10 20003405			Physics Hon 40 20033904 20033905	Physics Hon 50 20033904 20033905	Physics 60 20033803	Research I, II, III 70 1700300Q 1700310Q/20Q
Colona Room 48	Biology 11 20003103	Biology 21 20003103		Biology 41 20003103		Biology 61 20003103	Biology 71 20003103
Johnson, ML Room 75		An. Phy Hon 22 20003503 20003604	Biology I 32 20003103	Biology I 42 20003103		Biology I 62 20003103	An. Phy Hon 72 20003503 20003604
Vanderveer Room 74	Oceanogr 13 20013703 20013704	Oceanogr 23 20013703 20013704			Oceanogr 53 20013703 20013704	Oceanogr 63 20013704 20013703	Oceanogr 73 20013703 20013704
Lube Room 64	Chem I 18 20033403	Chem I 28 20033403		Chem I 48 20033403	Chem Hon I 58 20033504 20033505	Chem I 68 20033403	
McCormick Room-Float	Fnd Bio 14 20003002 Rm. 76	Fnd Gen Sci 24 20023002 Rm. 76		Fnd Phys & Phy Sc Rm 50 45 20033002 20033103	Dr. Ed 54 1900310X Rm. Port	Dr. Ed 64 1900310X Rm. Port	
Kasimier Room-Float					Bio. I 58 20003103 Rm. 48	Bio. I Hon 68 20003204 20003205 Rm. 47	Bio. I 78 20003103 Rm. 47
Wiles Room 47	Bio Hon I 17 20003204 20003205		Bio Hon I 37 20003205 20003204	Bio Hon I 47 20003204 20003205	Bio Hon I 57 20003205 20003204	Weight Tr. 67 1501360X 1501350X	
Wells Room 49	Env Sci 16 20013403 20013404		Oceanogr Oceanogr 36 20013703 20013704	Oceanogr 46 20013704 20013703	Env Sci 56 20013404 20013403		Env Sci 76 20013403 20013404
Donovan Room 76			Chem Hon I 39 20033505 20033504	Chem Hon I 49 20033505 20033504	Chem I 59 20033403		

Although a noble experiment in curriculum reorganization, nongradedness has not reached the goal that Brown predicted—namely, that within a few years after its inception "every intellectually respectable high school will have some degree of nongraded education."[69]

Over the decades a number of curricular arrangements have been tried with varying degrees of success in both our hypothetical community and elsewhere.

WHERE WE ARE: CURRICULUM PRESENT

THE ELEMENTARY SCHOOL

Basic Skills

Schools at all levels are engaged in massive efforts to raise student achievement in the subject areas. Nowhere are these efforts more apparent than in the elementary school, where an all-out attack is being made to improve students' mastery of the basic skills.

Concerned about students' low achievement and public dissatisfaction, schools at all levels have taken strong and sometimes controversial measures for improving student achievement and restoring public confidence. Among the measures are the following:

□ Implementation of measures resulting from the effective schools research documented by Ronald R. Edmonds, Wilbur Brookover, Lawrence Lezotte, and others.[70] This body of research has led teachers to such practices as stressing basic skills, keeping students on task, holding learners to high expectations, and monitoring pupil achievement.

□ Implementation of research on instruction conducted by David C. Berliner, N. L. Gage, Donald M. Medley, Barak V. Rosenshine, and others, whose research attributed such factors as time on task (academic engaged time) and direct instruction to effective teachers.[71]

□ Emphasis—what some people might call overemphasis—on testing. Student progress is monitored by a plethora of local, state, and national tests and is measured not only by local and state criterion-referenced tests but also by national norm-referenced tests.

□ Detailed planning and demand for implementation of the curriculum on a district-wide and sometimes statewide basis, sometimes referred to as

---

[69] Brown, *Nongraded High School*, p. 44.

[70] See *Phi Delta Kappan* 64, no. 10 (June 1983): 679–702; bibliography, p. 694. Note articles both supportive and critical of the effective schools research.

[71] See Penelope L. Peterson and Herbert J. Wahlberg, eds., *Research on Teaching: Concepts, Findings, and Implications* (Berkeley, Calif.: McCutchan, 1979).

"curriculum alignment." Curriculum coordinators and teachers strive for curriculum uniformity by specifying pupil performance objectives in targeted subject areas for every grade level. School personnel choose or prepare teaching materials, learning activities, and tests that fit the specified objectives. Those objectives that are tested by state and national tests are included and coded by test. Some school systems specify objectives and administer tests for each marking period in the designated disciplines. Principals', teachers', and—ipso facto—the schools' successes are measured by pupils' mastery of the objectives.

The schools are making a strenuous effort to develop students' mastery of the basic skills. We will return to this topic in Chapter 14 when we discuss current curriculum problems.

Teaching Thinking Skills

More than 40 years ago (1944) the Educational Policies Commission identified the ability to think rationally as one of the Ten Imperative Needs of Youth.[72] Seventeen years later the Educational Policies Commission set forth the premise that the central purpose of American education was the development of the student's ability to think.[73] About the same time the influential National Committee of the National Education Association Project on Instruction included among its priorities for improving the instructional program of the schools "ways of creative and disciplined thinking, including methods of inquiry and application of knowledge."[74]

In the 1980s we witnessed a resurgence of interest in the teaching of thinking skills. Prominent national organizations called for renewed and increased emphasis on the development of thinking skills. Among these associations are the National Council of Teachers of Mathematics;[75] the National Council of Teachers of English;[76] the National Science Board Commission on Pre-College Education in Mathematics, Science, and Technology;[77] and the Association for Supervision and Curriculum Development.[78]

A new body of literature defines thinking skills and suggests strategies for teaching those skills. Discussion has moved away from the general declared

---

[72] See pp. 92–93.

[73] See p. 93.

[74] Dorothy M. Fraser, *Deciding What to Teach* (Washington, D.C.: Project on the Instructional Program of the Public Schools, National Education Association, 1963), p. 222.

[75] *An Agenda for Action* (Reston, Va.: National Council of Teachers of Mathematics, 1980).

[76] *Essentials of English* (Urbana, Ill.: National Council of Teachers of English, 1982).

[77] *Educating Americans for the 21st Century* (Washington, D.C.: National Science Board Commission on Pre-College Education in Mathematics, Science, and Technology, 1983).

[78] Association for Supervision and Curriculum Development, "1984 Resolutions," *ASCD Update* 26, no. 4 (May 1984), insert.

goal of teaching young people to think to identification of thinking skills and prescribed methods for achieving those skills.[79] Students are learning, for example, how to attack problems, make decisions, analyze issues, and think critically and creatively.

As with some other terms in education, there are differing definitions of thinking skills. Barry K. Beyer pointed out that some people use the term "critical thinking" to signify all forms of thinking. Beyer felt that it was a mistake to equate critical thinking with inquiry, decision making, problem solving, and other thinking skills. Said Beyer, "Critical thinking is, instead, the process of determining the authenticity, accuracy, and worth of information or knowledge claims."[80]

Where the experts do agree, however, is that thinking skills are fundamental, the most basic of the basic skills.

Provision for Students with Special Needs

Schools are struggling to meet the needs of many special groups — exceptionalities of all types of students, including the physically handicapped, emotionally disturbed, mentally retarded, and those with behavior disorders. Bolstered by federal legislation and dollars and by state mandates and funding, special education is a fundamental part of today's curriculum. To care for the needs of the many exceptionalities, special education teachers, psychometrists, and school psychologists have been in demand.

One of the groups with special needs — the so-called "students-at-risk" — has received considerable attention in recent years. "Students-at-risk" may be narrowly defined as those students most likely to drop out of school or broadly defined as those most likely to emerge from school with insufficient education, unprepared to play a productive role in society.

Students-at-risk tend to come from low-income environments and to perform poorly in the basic skills. Proposals for meeting the needs of students-at-risk suggest modification of instructional strategies, such as offering compensatory education and increasing student motivation; staff development to enable teachers to understand the special needs of these students; increased use of positive disciplinary practices; encouraging participation in extraclass activi-

---

[79] See Arthur L. Costa, ed., *Developing Minds: A Resource Book for Teaching Thinking* (Alexandria, Va.: Association for Supervision and Curriculum Development, 1985); Edward de Bono, "The Direct Teaching of Thinking As a Skill," *Phi Delta Kappan* 64, no. 10 (June 1983): 703–708; Jerry L. Brown, "On Teaching Thinking Skills in the Elementary and Middle School," *Phi Delta Kappan* 64, no. 10 (June 1983): 709–714; and Bruce Joyce, "Models for Teaching Thinking," *Educational Leadership* 42, no. 8 (May 1985): 4–7. See also Chapter 7 of this text.

[80] Barry K. Beyer, "Critical Thinking: What Is It?" *Social Education* 49, no. 4 (April 1985): 276.

ties; working with parents; addressing community problems; and abandonment of the graded school structure.

Increasingly, a cyclically neglected group—the gifted—are receiving attention through classes and other means that are designed for their particular intellectual capacities. Bilingual education programs are provided for those pupils for whom English is not their native language. In Chapter 14 we will examine some of the issues involved in educating the handicapped and speakers of languages other than English.

THE MIDDLE SCHOOL

A New Institution

Until five years ago our hypothetical school district maintained a traditional organizational plan for six years of elementary school, three years of junior high school, and three years of senior high school. Dissatisfaction with that organizational structure had been brewing for a long time. As our school staff studied the literature and watched innovations at other school districts, they began to realize that the junior high school as they knew it was rapidly disappearing. A new institution—the middle school—was rising to the forefront, creating an organizational structure that was more suited to its time.

As it became clear to the personnel of our hypothetical school district that the needs of a special group of youngsters—early adolescents or, as Donald H. Eichhorn called them, "transescents"[81]—were not being met by the existing junior high school structure, they implemented dramatic and substantial changes which had an impact on all levels of the educational ladder of that district. The elementary school lost a grade, and the senior high school regained a grade that it had lost years ago to the junior high school. The junior high school was transformed into a middle school that consisted of three grades (six through eight) for preadolescents—the children in the middle.

Special Needs of Students.   Some other countries have recognized the needs of middle students for a long time, as in Germany with its *Mittelschule*. Boys and girls of the pre- and early adolescent years ages ten to fourteen as a rule are too mature to be treated as primary school children and too immature to be considered high schoolers. They evidence a host of physical, social, and emotional growth needs as well as educational demands. Their career and life interests are just beginning to take shape. They need time to explore, to adjust, and to socialize as well as to study.

As a result, the junior high school spun off from the other levels as a separate institution and mushroomed. From the two identified separate junior

---

[81]Donald H. Eichhorn, *The Middle School* (New York: Center for Applied Research in Education, 1966), p. 3.

high schools with grades seven, eight, and nine in 1910, the junior highs grew to approximately 6,000.

Lounsbury and Vars characterized the junior high school as a significantly successful development in American education.[82] Although the seven-eight-nine pattern was the most common for the junior high school, other relatively common patterns were seven-eight, six-seven-eight, seven through ten, and eight through ten. Despite this variety, as the years passed dissatisfaction with the junior high school began to set in. It was argued that this intermediate school had become a carbon copy of the senior high school with all the trappings—interscholastic athletics, band, high school subjects, and so on.

Junior high school students were changing not only physically but also socially in response to new, unexpected social values. L. J. Chamberlin and R. Girona described the more recent drives that affect early adolescents:

> Today's young child is motivated by drives that a few years ago affected only youths ten years his or her senior. Traits such as straining against parental authority, desire for greater freedom, and extreme loyalty to peer groups that once characterized the late teen years, now are often encountered in much younger children.[83]

As a result of these changes and of society's new demands on adolescents, the program for these years was revised and updated. A new organizational pattern grouped grades five or six through eight into a middle school with its own unique program, and a four-four-four system or five-three-four system began to emerge. Although the ninth grade is generally considered as "belonging" to the high school, there is some uncertainty amongst middle-school specialists as to whether the fifth grade should be attached to the elementary school or to the middle school.

Phenomenal Growth. The middle school has experienced phenomenal growth. In 1965 the Educational Research Service of the National Education Association conducted a nationwide survey and found 63 middle schools.[84] In a 1967–68 survey William M. Alexander reported 1,101 middle schools, and Mary F. Compton accounted for 3,723 middle schools in 1974.[85] Kenneth Brooks identified 4,060 middle schools operating in 1978.[86] By the mid-1980s figures showed close to 7,000 middle schools in existence.[87] A National

---

[82]See Lounsbury and Vars, *Curriculum for Middle School*, p. 15.

[83]L. J. Chamberlin and R. Girona, "Our Children Are Changing," *Educational Leadership* 33, no. 4 (January 1976): 303. Reprinted with permission of the Association for Supervision and Curriculum Development and L. J. Chamberlin and R. Girona. Copyright ©1976 by the Association for Supervision and Curriculum Development. All rights reserved.

[84]Lounsbury and Vars, *Curriculum for Middle School*, pp. 22–23.

[85]Ibid.

[86]Kenneth Brooks, "The Middle Schools—A National Survey," *Middle School Journal* 9, no. 1 (February 1978): 6–7.

[87]Valena White Plisko and Joyce D. Stern, *The Condition of Education,* 1985 Edition, Statistical Report of the National Center for Education Statistics (Washington, D.C.: U.S. Government Printing Office, 1985), p. 28.

Education Association publication in 1988 projected a figure of over 12,000 of these schools by 1992.[88] Although junior high schools still exist in many communities throughout the United States, their number is declining as they undergo the metamorphosis from junior high to middle school.

William M. Alexander and others saw the middle school as an emerging institution and defined it in the following manner:

> To us, it is *a school providing a program planned for a range of older children, preadolescents, and early adolescents that builds upon the elementary school program for older childhood and in turn is built upon by the high school's program for adolescence.*[89]

They perceived the middle school as a distinct phase of schooling between elementary and secondary school levels.

Somewhat later Alexander in writing with Paul S. George offered a briefer definition:

> We define a middle school as a school *of some three to five years between elementary and high school focused on the educational needs of students in these in-between years and designed to promote continuous educational progress for all concerned.*[90]

Transformation of the junior high school into a middle school should not be perceived as a reorganization of but one level of the school system. Alexander and others observed that the change from junior high to middle school is a reorganization of the entire grade structure.[91]

Recommendations for the Middle School. Thomas E. Gatewood and Charles A. Dilg, speaking for the Association for Supervision and Curriculum Development's Working Group on the Emerging Adolescent Learner, made a series of recommendations for the middle school.[92] Let's examine a few. Speaking of the physical characteristics of transescents, they recommended

> A program for the emerging adolescent that is adapted to the ever-changing physical needs of this learner. . . .

---

[88]Sylvester Kohut, Jr., *The Middle School: A Bridge Between Elementary and High Schools,* 2nd ed. (Washington, D.C.: National Education Association, 1988), p. 7.

[89]William M. Alexander et al., *The Emergent Middle School,* 2nd enl. ed. (New York: Holt, Rinehart and Winston, 1969), p. 5.

[90]William M. Alexander and Paul S. George, *The Exemplary Middle School* (New York: Holt, Rinehart and Winston, 1981), p. 3.

[91]Alexander et al., *Emergent Middle School,* p. 4.

[92]Thomas E. Gatewood and Charles A. Dilg, *The Middle School We Need* (Alexandria, Va.: Association for Supervision and Curriculum Development, 1975). Reprinted with permission of the Association for Supervision and Curriculum Development and Thomas E. Gatewood and Charles A. Dilg. Copyright ©1975 by the Association for Supervision and Curriculum Development. All rights reserved.

Instruction related to growth of the body so that one can better understand changes in himself or herself and in others and be prepared for future changes and problems.[93]

Speaking of mental and intellectual growth, Gatewood and Dilg made the following recommendations:

Learning experiences for transescents at their own intellectual levels, relating to immediate rather than remote academic goals.

A wide variety of cognitive learning experiences to account for the full range of students who are at many different levels of concrete and formal operations. . . .

Opportunities for the development of problem-solving skills, reflective-thinking processes, and awareness for the order of the student's environment.

Cognitive learning experiences so structured that students can progress in an individualized manner. However, within the structure of an individualized learning program, students can interact with one another. . . .

A common program in which areas of learning are combined and integrated to break down artificial and irrelevant divisions of curriculum content. . . .

Methods of instruction involving open and individually directed learning experiences. The role of the teacher should be more that of a personal guide and facilitator of learning than of a purveyor of knowledge.[94]

Speaking of personality development characteristics, Gatewood and Dilg recommended

Administrative arrangements to ensure that personality development has continuity both in breadth and in depth. Thus continuous, cooperative curriculum planning is essential among elementary, middle, and secondary school personnel.

A comprehensive, integrated series of learning encounters to assist learners to develop a self which they realize, accept, and approve. . . .

Classroom instruction, counseling, and extra-class activities that take into account the social-emotional needs of transescents.

An approach in working with emerging adolescents that will have consistency with basic democratic principles.[95]

Gatewood and Dilg have called attention to the broad range of physical, intellectual, and personal characteristics of middle school students. In their recommendations they have presented guidelines for meeting various needs of the emerging adolescent.

---

[93] Ibid., p. 8.
[94] Ibid., pp. 11–12.
[95] Ibid., p. 16.

Proposed Design.   Lounsbury and Vars proposed a curriculum design for the middle school that consists of three main components: core, continuous progress (nongraded learning experiences), and variable. [96]

Core in their conception is "a problem-centered block-time program." [97] The continuous progress (nongraded) component consists of "those skills and concepts that have a genuine sequential organization." [98] Science, for example, may overlap with the core along with its placement in the nongraded component. The variable component is comprised of "the activities and programs that have proven their worth in schools . . . neither so highly sequential as to be placed exclusively in the nongraded component nor so essentially problem-centered as to fit entirely within the core." [99] The middle-school curriculum as proposed by Lounsbury and Vars is shown schematically in Figure 9–5.[100] Note that this proposal incorporates some earlier principles of the core curriculum and nongradedness.

Our hypothetical junior high school has changed to a pattern that has been in successful operation throughout the United States for over 20 years. The new middle school in our hypothetical school district is part of a promising development in education for the preadolescent years.

THE SENIOR HIGH SCHOOL

A Comprehensive High School

The academics? Students from this school regularly achieve high scores on national standardized tests of achievement in the subject areas; graduates are placed in colleges and universities without difficulty; students master computer skills; science students yearly win recognition at the science fairs; foreign language students bring home prizes from state competitions in their field; many students are enrolled in advanced placement courses; the student body as a whole is well above the norm in reading and mathematics.

Marching band? They can put on a razzle-dazzle spectacular at half-time and compete with the best. They have been invited to participate in parades of the major bowls in the United States.

Football? Basketball? Try baseball, golf, and tennis. The showcase in front of the principal's office is crammed with shiny trophies won by students of this

---

[96]Lounsbury and Vars, *Curriculum for Middle School,* pp. 45–48.

[97]Ibid., p. 46.

[98]Ibid., p. 47.

[99]Ibid.

[100]Gordon F. Vars, "New Knowledge of the Learner and His Cultural Milieu: Implications for Schooling in the Middle Years." Paper presented at the Conference on the Middle School Idea, College of Education, University of Toledo, November 1967. ERIC Document No. ED 016 267 CG 901400, p. 14. See also Lounsbury and Vars, *Curriculum for Middle School,* p. 45.

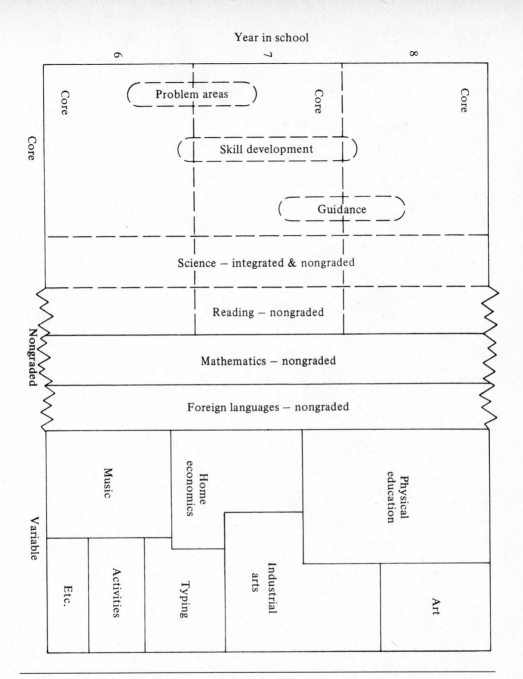

FIGURE 9–5   A junior high/middle school program. Note that core classes are scheduled back-to-back in order to facilitate cross-graded grouping on a temporary basis whenever appropriate. From Gordon F. Vars, "New Knowledge of the Learner and His Cultural Milieu: Implications for Schooling in the Middle Years." Paper presented at the Conference on the Middle School Idea, College of Education, University of Toledo, November 1967. Reprinted by permission. ERIC Document No. ED016267CG901400, p. 14. See also John H. Lounsbury and Gordon F. Vars, *A Curriculum for the Middle School Years* (New York: Harper & Row, 1978), p. 45.

school. School officials are moving rapidly to eliminate gender discrimination in athletics and proudly display trophies won by both the boys' and the girls' teams.

Business education? Students are mastering the use of computers, electronic typewriters, and fax machines. Students in all programs are encouraged to develop skill in typing and word processing.

Art? Come to the annual art show put on by the school's art students to appreciate the excellence of their work.

Vocational education? Wood shop, metals shop, electricity, and auto mechanics are all available. Each shop has ample space and is well equipped.

What we are describing here is a high-quality, traditional, comprehensive high school. As such, it meets the definition of a comprehensive high school given by James B. Conant, who saw it as "a high school whose programs correspond to the educational needs of *all* youth in the community."[101] Personnel of this school concur with the Association for Supervision and Curriculum Development (ASCD) and with Conant as to the objectives of the school. The ASCD maintained:

> The secondary school should be a comprehensive school. If a major task of the public school system in America is to develop the basic values of a free society, and mutual respect for the range of persons and groups within our diverse culture, students must have an opportunity to live and work together. The comprehensive secondary school is an essential element in the development of a common viewpoint sufficiently strong to hold our nation together.[102]

Conant cited three main objectives of a comprehensive high school:

> *First,* to provide a general education for all the future citizens; *second,* to provide good elective programs for those who wish to use their acquired skills immediately on graduation; *third,* to provide satisfactory programs for those whose vocations will depend on their subsequent education in a college or university.[103]

This school performs well on criteria suggested by both Conant and the ASCD. Conant listed the following points to be considered in evaluating a comprehensive school:

A. Adequacy of general education for all as judged by:
    1. Offerings in English and American literature and composition
    2. Social studies, including American history
    3. Ability grouping in required courses

---

[101]Conant, *American High School,* p. 12. Reprinted with permission.

[102]Kimball Wiles and Franklin Patterson, *The High School We Need* (Alexandria, Va.: Association for Supervision and Curriculum Development, 1959), pp. 5–6. Reprinted with permission of the Association for Supervision and Curriculum Development and Kimball Wiles and Franklin Patterson. Copyright ©1959 by the Association for Supervision and Curriculum Development. All rights reserved.

[103]Conant, *American High School,* p. 17. Reprinted with permission.

B. Adequacy of nonacademic elective program as judged by:
  4. The vocational programs for boys and commercial programs for girls
  5. Opportunities for supervised work experience
  6. Special provisions for very slow readers
C. Special arrangements for the academically talented students:
  7. Special provisions for challenging the highly gifted
  8. Special instruction in developing reading skills
  9. Summer sessions from which able students may profit
  10. Individualized programs (absence of tracks or rigid programs)
  11. School day organized into seven or more instructional periods
D. Other features:
  12. Adequacy of the guidance services
  13. Student morale
  14. Well-organized homerooms
  15. The success of the school in promoting an understanding between students with widely different academic abilities and vocational goals (effective social interaction among students)[104]

ASCD Recommendations. Our hypothetical secondary school would meet not only the criteria set forth by Conant but also the standards recommended by the Association for Supervision and Curriculum Development. Writing for the ASCD's Commission on the Education of Adolescents, Kimball Wiles and Franklin Patterson made recommendations for the comprehensive high school, some of which are cited here:

> Certain types of growth must be promoted in all youth who attend the secondary school. Each youth should develop increased understanding of self and his responsibilities in society, commitment to democratic values, economic understanding, political acumen, and ability to think. . . .
>
> The program for each individual must contain general education and specialized education. . . . One-third to one-half of each student's program should be devoted to general education . . . the required courses and activities . . . essential for competent citizenship. . . . One-half to two-thirds of each student's program should be used to develop his talents and to further his personal goals within the framework that the community is willing and able to support. . . .
>
> Choices among the various offerings of the curriculum should be made jointly by the pupil, parents, and staff members of the school in terms of the pupil's purposes, aptitude and level of achievement. . . .
>
> Each student should have one staff member who guides him throughout his high school career. . . .
>
> Each high school student should be a member of at least one home base group with which he has a continuing relationship. . . .
>
> Students should be grouped in various ways in different phases of their high school experience . . . the general education phase of an individual's schedule should be in classes that are heterogeneously grouped. . . . In the

---

[104]Ibid., pp. 19–20.

portion of the student's program that is elective, the grouping should be homogeneous in terms of two factors: the pupil's intensity of purpose and his level of achievement.[105]

When Conant came out with his follow-up study, officials of our hypothetical senior high school were pleased that their school compared favorably with the better comprehensive high schools. They surely enrolled more than 750 pupils; they graduated at least 100 pupils each year; they offered calculus and four years of a modern foreign language (two languages, to be exact); their ratio of counselors to students was within the recommended range of 250 to 300; their students were grouped homogeneously in the elective subjects and heterogeneously in the required courses; and they offered a full range of courses in the academic disciplines, business education, home economics, and industrial arts.[106] This school met the tests of comprehensiveness well.

Some Alternatives

The comprehensive high school was conceived as a unique American response to the needs of youth. Every young person would find in this institution programs necessary to his or her present and future success in society. The comprehensive high school was a reaction to specialized high schools that cared for specific segments of the student population. This institution would accommodate boys and girls from every social stratum and ethnic group. They would study, work, and play together, thus breaking down barriers between them. The comprehensive high school was a democratic response to education in a democratic society.

The comprehensive high school, however, has not been free of criticism. The National Panel on High Schools and Adolescent Education claimed that the comprehensive high school reinforced social-class and race stratification rather than diminished it.[107] The comprehensive high school was criticized for a number of reasons. Some felt it deemphasized the academics; others felt the opposite and claimed it deemphasized the affective domain. Some believed it was too structured; others, that it was not structured enough. Some maintained it was taking on too many responsibilities; some, that it was not assuming enough. Some accused the comprehensive high school of slighting career education; others were not satisfied with the students' achievement in the cognitive domain.

Call for Reform.   In recent years we have heard the clarion cry for "reform" in secondary education. John Henry Martin, author of *The Education of Adolescents* —the report of the National Panel on High Schools and Adolescent

---

[105]Wiles and Patterson, *High School We Need,* pp. 6–17.

[106]See James B. Conant, *The Comprehensive High School* (New York: McGraw-Hill, 1967).

[107]See John Henry Martin, *The Education of Adolescents,* Report of the National Panel on High Schools and Adolescent Education (Washington, D.C.: U.S. Office of Education, 1976).

Education of the United States Office of Education—expressed the belief that the Seven Cardinal Principles were too inclusive and were "inflated statements of purpose."[108] He argued that the Seven Cardinal Principles were much too broad, stating, "Among the unfortunate consequences of the sweeping language of the Seven Cardinal Principles has been our assumption that the schools could reform all of society's ills. Schools have undertaken burdens that they have neither the resources nor the talents to overcome."[109] The excessive offerings and services of some high schools have caused Arthur G. Powell, Eleanor Farrar, and David K. Cohen to apply the label "Shopping Mall High School."[110]

Richard Mitchell challenged the Seven Cardinal Principles as antiintellectual, labeling them "The Seven Deadly Principles" proposed by "The Gang of Twenty-Seven" (i.e., the NEA's Commission on the Reorganization of Secondary Education appointed in 1913). Mitchell was favorably disposed toward the NEA's Committee of Ten, which was formed in 1892 and made up "largely of scholars."[111]

Martin took the position that schools cannot be responsible for all aspects of life, that goals of the school (that is, the high school) must be redefined, and that aims more modest than those of the Seven Cardinal Principles must be set. Theodore R. Sizer, however, observed that Americans have agreed for decades on the goals set forth by the Seven Cardinal Principles.[112]

Martin perceived the community as sharing responsibility for the education of youth. He advised as follows:

> Redefining the goals of schools and building new relationships between youth and adults requires that the comprehensive high school be replaced with a comprehensive program of community-based education. Such a design for the education of adolescents should delineate those purposes of education that would remain the primary responsibility of the high school, those that might better be shifted to other and new community agencies, and those that would be served by a cooperative sharing of resources.[113]

A. Harry Passow discussed proposals of five national groups looking at secondary education.[114] In addition to the reports of the National Panel on

---

[108] John Henry Martin, "Reconsidering the Goals of High School Education," *Educational Leadership* 37, no. 4 (January 1980): 280. Reprinted with permission of the Association for Supervision and Curriculum Development and John Henry Martin. Copyright ©1980 by the Association for Supervision and Curriculum Development. All rights reserved.

[109] Ibid., p. 279.

[110] Arthur G. Powell, Eleanor Farrar, and David K. Cohen, *The Shopping Mall High School: Winners and Losers in the Educational Marketplace* (Boston: Houghton Mifflin, 1985).

[111] Richard Mitchell, *The Graves of Academe* (Boston: Little, Brown, 1981), pp. 69–70.

[112] Theodore R. Sizer, *Horace's Compromise: The Dilemma of the American High School* (Boston: Houghton Mifflin, 1984), p. 78.

[113] Martin, "Reconsidering Goals," p. 281. See also "High School Goals: Responses to John Henry Martin," *Educational Leadership* 37, no. 4 (January 1980): 286–298.

[114] A. Harry Passow, "Reforming America's High Schools," *Phi Delta Kappan* 56, no. 9 (May 1975): 587–590.

High Schools and Adolescent Education, the American public has received reports from the National Association of Secondary School Principals,[115] the National Commission on the Reform of Secondary Education (referred to as the Kettering Commission),[116] the Panel on Youth of the President's Science Advisory Committee,[117] and Educational Facilities Laboratories and I/D/E/A.[118]

Among the proposals coming out of these national groups were calls for

- □ a reduced school day with more time being spent in work experience programs in the community
- □ educational options—that is, alternative forms of schooling to be selected by students and parents
- □ a lowering of the age of compulsory attendance to 14 years of age
- □ establishment of specialized high schools in the European tradition
- □ an emphasis on career education
- □ restriction of the function of the high school to cognitive learning

It is clear that if some of these proposals were seriously considered and adopted, the comprehensive high school—which Tanner and Tanner described as "the institutional ideal of the American social conscience"[119]—would be greatly altered or might even disappear. It is an anomaly that some of America's educators advocate alternative and specialized schools as a response to the democratization of education, whereas England's planners, for example, long experienced with separate schools, have looked to comprehensive secondary schools to keep their people unified.

Alternative Schools.   Some of the current criticisms of public education have resulted in an increase in alternative schools at both the elementary and secondary levels. Alternative education is also known as education by choice or educational options.

Let's briefly consider the rationale for developing and supporting alternative public secondary education. Some young people, perhaps many, cannot profit from the established high school; they cannot learn effectively in a structured setting. The impact of agencies outside the school—families, peer groups,

---

[115]National Association of Secondary School Principals, National Committee on Secondary Education, *American Youth in the Mid-Seventies* (Reston, Va.: National Association of Secondary School Principals, 1972).

[116]National Commission on the Reform of Secondary Education, *The Reform of Secondary Education: A Report to the Public and the Profession* (New York: McGraw-Hill, 1973).

[117]James S. Coleman, chairman, Panel on Youth of the President's Science Advisory Committee, *Youth: Transition to Adulthood* (Washington, D.C.: Superintendent of Documents, U.S. Government Printing Office, 1973; Chicago: University of Chicago Press, 1974).

[118]Ruth Weinstock, *The Greening of the High School* (New York: Educational Facilities Laboratories, 1973).

[119]Reprinted by permission of Macmillan Publishing Company from *Curriculum Development: Theory into Practice,* 2nd ed., p. 605, by Daniel Tanner and Laurel N. Tanner. Copyright ©1980 by Macmillan Publishing Company.

churches, businesses, and industries—on learners is far greater than that of the school; these agencies should therefore be tapped. In a democratic society families should have a choice as to the type of education they wish their children to receive. Unless the public schools make changes from within, young people will either drop out physically, stay in and drop out mentally, or transfer to private schools.

What, we may ask, is an alternative school? The National Consortium for Options in Public Education defined an alternative school as "any school (or minischool) within a community that provides alternative learning experiences to the conventional school program and is available by choice to every family within the community at no extra cost."[120]

Some school systems have established what are called "alternative schools" for young people with behavior problems who cannot function well in regular schools. However, these schools are not alternative schools in the true sense because they are not available by choice. Students are assigned to these schools by the school system and must remain until their behavior improves sufficiently for them to return to their regular schools. (In the case of some alternative schools, however, choice by parents and students must necessarily be restricted by admission requirements and examinations, especially when demand for enrollment exceeds the capacity of the school.)

Free schools, street academies, storefront schools, and schools without walls are examples of alternative education. Among the better known options are the Parkway Program in Philadelphia, which dates back to 1969, and Metro High School in Chicago, which began its program in 1970. In programs of this type, the community, in effect, becomes the school. The school system enlists the cooperation of business, cultural, educational, industrial, and social institutions to serve in the education of young people. The school system draws on the talents of knowledgeable and experienced persons in the community to serve as instructors.

However, education by choice is possible in the more typical school *with* walls. Parents may be accorded the option of placing their children in open-space schools, bilingual schools, or even traditional basic skills schools. In many communities, particularly in urban centers, parents may choose to send their children to a magnet school, an institution that offers high-quality specialized programs around a central theme designed to attract students from all parts of the school district. Developed as a means of fostering racial integration, magnet schools offer strong academic or vocational programs in specialties that appeal to young people from all ethnic groups and that are not adequately provided, if at all, in the traditional schools.

The Boston Latin School, Detroit's Cass Technical School, the Bronx High School of Science, New York's High School for the Performing Arts, Brooklyn

---

[120]National Consortium for Options in Public Education, *The Directory of Alternative Public Schools,* ed. Robert D. Barr (Bloomington, Ind.: Educational Alternatives Project, Indiana University, 1975), p. 2. The 1975 directory is out of print and no longer available.

Tech, Stuyvestant High School in New York City, Lane Technical School in Chicago, Central High School in Philadelphia, and Lowell High School in San Francisco, all still in existence, are examples of specialized schools that were forerunners of today's magnet schools. Since attendance at a magnet school is by choice rather than by assignment according to neighborhood boundaries, magnet schools often produce higher student motivation and achievement.

Magnet schools have grown in number in recent years. Figures for the year 1981–82 showed 1,018 magnet schools: 601 elementary, 173 junior high and middle, and 244 secondary.[121] Dallas, Texas, furnishes an example of the rapid growth of magnet schools; since 1976 that community has established seven magnet schools in addition to the already existing Skyline Center: the Arts Magnet High School, the Business and Management Center, the Health Professions High School, the Human Services Center, the Law and Public Administration High School, the Transportation Institute, and the Multiple Careers Center for special education students.

Extending the magnet school concept on a statewide basis, some states have established or plan to create residential public secondary schools. Opened in 1980, the prototype of such schools in the United States, the School of Science and Mathematics in Durham, North Carolina, admits juniors and seniors from around the state on a competitive basis and offers them a highly intensive program.

The concept of choice in education is certainly appealing and is in the best democratic tradition. Obviously, growth in alternative schools will have an inevitable impact on the neighborhood and comprehensive schools, illustrating once again the change process in operation.

The American public—concerned that children achieve the fundamentals, that they have access to higher education, and that economy of operation is maintained—is unlikely to support radical departures from the established forms of schooling. The public is not likely to heed proposals for deschooling or for turning loose 14-year-olds on the precarious job market. On the other hand, it may well support reasonable alternatives within the existing framework. We will examine some of the more recent and controversial aspects of alternatives in education in Chapter 14.

Requirements for Graduation

In the mid-1900s, 16 Carnegie units were the minimum required for graduation from the four-year high school. Only the academically talented carried

[121]Denis Doyle and Marsha Levine, "Magnet Schools: Choice and Quality in Public Education," *Phi Delta Kappan* 66, no. 4 (December 1984): 267–268. See also Robert D. Barr, "Magnet Schools: An Attractive Alternative," *Principal* 61, no. 3 (January 1982): 37–40; and Jane Powers, "Magnet Schools: Are They the Answer?" *Today's Education* 68, no. 3 (September/October 1979): 68–70.

five or more units per year. Twenty or more units are rapidly becoming the norm throughout the United States, with ten or more "solid" subjects required for the regular diploma.

Idaho, for example, in 1988 increased its requirements for the regular diploma from 40 semester credits (20 units) to 42 (21). Of the 42 credits (21 units), thirty (15) are required. In 1986–87, Kentucky increased its requirement from 18 to 20 units, with 13 units required. Missouri has set 22 units with 12 required. Oklahoma mandates 20, requiring 10 of them. Tennessee, too, places its requirement at 20, with 11 subjects specified.[122]

College-bound students exceed these minimal requirements. They are finding more of their high school program required and less elective as the number of subjects and credits that they must present for admission to college rises. States are mandating a set (called a "core" by some people) of subjects that students must pass to earn the high school diploma. Some states have added the passing of a test to the requirements for the diploma. Tennessee, for example, administers a proficiency test consisting of four subtests on reading, language, spelling, and mathematics. Florida and Georgia require satisfactory performance on a test of basic skills.

The movement toward raising requirements for graduation from high school is very much in line with repeated reports on reform that have been issued over the years. They bring to fruition reports of the Committee of Ten (1894), the Harvard Committee (1945), James B. Conant (1959), and several reports of the 1970s and 1980s.

High schools of the future will generally follow current moves to increasing the number of required courses, decreasing the number of electives, raising the score considered passing in the various subjects, deemphasis of extraclass activities, coverage of more content, more effective use of instructional time, passing of local and/or state tests as a requirement for the diploma, and improved teaching techniques, including the use of computers and other forms of technology.

An Encouraging Note.   Amid the many studies of the high school in the 1980s (some of which are discussed in the following section of this chapter) is the study carried out by Sara Lawrence Lightfoot.[123] Lightfoot deliberately chose schools that teachers, lay people, and others considered "good." Unlike some studies, Lightfoot's work focused on the positive aspects of the schools that she studied rather than their deficiencies, Painting word "portraits" of six high schools, both public and private, she concentrated on the good features of each institution.

She found faculties and administrators who cared for their students, sought to motivate them, and took pride in their achievements. She discovered imper-

---

[122]Figures from the various state departments of education.

[123]Sara Lawrence Lightfoot, *The Good High School* (New York: Basic Books, 1983).

fect institutions struggling to achieve and making carefully considered changes. Though demonstrating quite different and contrasting styles, the leaders of these schools set the tone for the schools. Teachers played a central and dominant role; administrators treated them with respect as persons and professionals. In these schools Lightfoot observed a high degree of rapport between teachers and students. Students and adults felt a sense of community arising from clear codes of behavior, a secure environment, and positive interrelationships.

Lightfoot's study demonstrated that, contrary to impressions some people hold of high schools, it is possible without too much difficulty to find goodness in high schools *today*.

WHERE WE'RE GOING: CURRICULUM FUTURE

THE ELEMENTARY SCHOOL

Continuation of Traditional Modes

With the accountability movement still strong, we find the elementary school maintaining its emphasis on the basic skills. The public, through its state legislatures, has given its strong endorsement to programs of state assessment—the testing of youngsters in a number of subject areas, but especially in reading and mathematics.

Until the public begins to feel that schools have gone too far with testing programs, we will see the continuation of state testing to determine whether pupils will move on to higher grade levels and, in high school, whether they will receive a diploma. States have even tested kindergartners to decide whether the pupils will be promoted to the first grade. If testing plans are fully implemented throughout the country, we may anticipate more retentions with all the accompanying problems of motivation, provision for remediation, staffing, and facilities.

Our hypothetical elementary school is restoring its walls as rapidly as possible, reverting to the self-contained classroom model. The broad-fields approach will continue to predominate, but teachers will give more attention to preplanning. Minimal competencies in the various disciplines will be spelled out by the school, district, or state so that the direction of the school's program will be more evident. The elementary school will attempt to curb the flight of pupils to private, home, and parochial schools by emphasizing the academics.

For the immediate future it is possible that less attention rather than more attention will be given to individual differences among students. Mastery of the same minimal competencies will be expected of all. There is the real danger that those competencies that are labeled "minimal" will become maximal as well. Teachers may be so preoccupied with helping students to achieve minimal competencies and pass the tests that measure attainment of the competencies that they will allow little time to go beyond the minimum. Findings to the effect that students sometimes demonstrate higher achievement when taught as a total group lend support for pedagogical techniques that minimize individual differences.[124]

In the long run we may expect to see a swing away from subject-centeredness toward child-centeredness. Once schools have satisfied the public's desire for higher test scores and once the schools have demonstrated that pupils have mastered basic and survival skills, they may pay greater attention to the affective domain with its concern for attitudes, feelings, and values. We may find greater interest in individual students, in their learning styles, and in their special learning capacities. A growing body of research that reveals differences in learning strategies of students will affect teaching strategies.[125] We will find greater efforts on the part of administrators to match teachers' instructional styles with pupils' learning styles.[126]

Some schools, particularly elementary schools, may move into year-round schooling. One plan assigns different vacation periods to different groups of students throughout the year so that the whole student body is not in school at the same time. The concept of year-round schooling has been talked about for years and has been, and is being, tried. Advocates of year-round schooling claim that schools cannot afford to allow their facilities to lie idle during the summer months. This idea holds appeal for residents of heavily populated regions where construction is expensive and property taxes are high, particularly in times of inflation when the cost of living is also high. Schools are experimenting with both multi-track and single-track year-round plans. However, it is too early to determine whether year-round schooling will become a definite, nationwide trend.

On the other hand, the 23rd Annual Gallup Poll on the public's attitudes toward the public schools revealed that the public might eventually endorse a longer school day and a longer school year. In 1991, 46 percent of those polled favored extending the school day by one hour (up from 37 percent in 1982) and 51 percent favored extending the school year from 180 to 210 days (up from 37 percent in 1982).[127]

---

[124]See Donald M. Medley, "The Effectiveness of Teachers," in Penelope L. Peterson and Herbert J. Wahlberg, eds., *Research on Teaching: Concepts, Findings, and Implications* (Berkeley, Calif.: McCutchan, 1979), p. 24.

[125]See Ned Herrman, "The Creative Brain," *NASSP Bulletin* 66, no. 455 (September 1982): 31–46.

[126]See Rita S. Dunn and Kenneth J. Dunn, *Teaching Students Through Their Individual Learning Styles: A Practical Approach* (Reston, Va.: Reston Publishing Company, 1978).

[127]Stanley M. Elam, Lowell C. Rose, and Alec M. Gallup, "The 23rd Annual Gallup Poll of the Public's Attitudes Toward the Public Schools," *Phi Delta Kappan* 73, no. 1 (September 1991): 45.

Cooperative Learning

The strategy of organizing people into small groups with the intended purpose of helping each other to learn has blossomed into a full-blown movement, commonly referred to as cooperative learning. Cooperative learning will be discussed in greater depth in Chapter 11. As an observer of curriculum developments for many years, I cannot help being awed at how rapidly some innovations flower into movements with a body of literature, recognized experts, a network of like-minded people, how-to textbooks and other media on the subject, and both preservice and in-service educational activities on the topic. Cooperative learning—as well as whole language, another recent development—fits this pattern well. Both cooperative learning and whole language are active contenders for attention in the 1990s.

Whole Language

Many elementary schools are rapidly espousing the concept of whole language. Basically, whole language involves the use of real ("authentic") materials for teaching reading and writing, concentration on pupils' needs and interests, and integration of language skills with other subject matter. The whole language movement has given rise to controversy and will be more fully discussed in Chapter 14.

The elementary school of the immediate future will be a sophisticated version of the school of the past, essentialistic in character but with progressive overtones.

THE MIDDLE SCHOOL

Universality of the Middle School

The junior high school is fast fading from the scene. Existing junior high schools will continue to be converted into middle schools, in concept if not in name. Just as some senior high schools still cherish the name "academy," some newly converted middle schools may continue to call themselves "junior high schools." However, they will have all the characteristics of the modern middle school as described earlier in this chapter. New schools for transescents will be specifically built as middle schools and will be referred to as "middle schools" for "middle school students."

You may very well take the position that before the middle school reaches 100 percent universality it may evolve into another institution, as yet undefined. To support your position you can reiterate the axioms cited in Chapter 2: Change is both inevitable and necessary, for it is through change that life forms grow and develop; a school curriculum not only reflects but is a product of its time;

and curriculum changes made at an earlier period of time can exist concurrently with newer curriculum changes at a later period of time.

THE SENIOR HIGH SCHOOL

Recent Studies and Reform Efforts

Movements of accountability, emphasis on cognitive skills and minimal competencies, expansion of content, an increase in academic engaged time, continuous testing, and the raising of marking standards have affected the high school as well as the levels below it. During the 1980s the high school was examined and reexamined in a series of studies that produced numerous recommendations.[128]

Among the many studies were the following:

☐ *The Paideia Proposal: An Educational Manifesto* by Mortimer J. Adler for the Paideia Group (1982)[129]

☐ *A Nation at Risk: The Imperative for Educational Reform* by David P. Gardner for the National Commission on Excellence in Education (1983)[130]

☐ *High School: A Report on Secondary Education in America* by Ernest J. Boyer, president of the Carnegie Foundation for the Advancement of Teaching (1983)[131]

☐ *A Place Called School: Prospects for the Future* by John I. Goodlad (1984)[132]

☐ *Horace's Compromise: The Dilemma of the American High School* by Theodore R. Sizer (1984)[133]

Three of the studies (Adler, Gardner, and Goodlad) addressed schools at both the elementary and secondary levels. To help grasp the essence of these studies, we might chart their major curricular recommendations for the high school, as in Table 9–10.

---

[128] See "A Compilation of Brief Descriptions of Study Projects," *Wingspread* (Racine, Wis.: Johnson Foundation, November 1982); *Almanac of National Reports,* wall chart (Reston, Va.: National Association of Secondary School Principals, 1983); *An Analysis of Reports on the Status of Education in America* (Tyler, Tex.: Tyler Independent School District, 1983); A. Harry Passow, "Tackling the Reform Reports of the 1980's," *Phi Delta Kappan* 65, no. 10 (June 1984): 674–683.

[129] Mortimer J. Adler, *The Paideia Proposal: An Educational Manifesto* (New York: Macmillan, 1982).

[130] National Commission on Excellence in Education, David P. Gardner, chairman, *A Nation at Risk: The Imperative for Educational Reform* (Washington, D.C.: U.S. Government Printing Office, 1983).

[131] Boyer, Ernest L. *High School: A Report on Secondary Education in America* (New York: Harper & Row, 1983).

[132] John I. Goodlad, *A Place Called School: Prospects for the Future* (New York: McGraw-Hill, 1984).

[133] Sizer, *Horace's Compromise*.

TABLE 9–10   Major curricular recommendations for the high school

ADLER (1982)	BOYER (1983)	GARDNER (1983)*	GOODLAD (1984)	SIZER (1984)
One track with same objectives for all	Centrality of language (English proficiency)	Five new basics to be required for graduation:	Five fingers of knowledge and experience:	Skills
No electives except in choice of foreign language	Required core (a half to a third of total units required for graduation):	Four years of English	Up to 18% literature and language (English and foreign)	Reading
No specialized training for jobs	Literature	Three years of math		Writing
	U.S. history (one year)	Three years of science	Up to 18% mathematics and science	Speaking
Areas of subject matter:	Western civilization	Three years of social studies		Listening
Acquisition of organized knowledge	Non-Western civilization (one semester)	Two years of foreign language for college-bound	Up to 15% society and social studies	Measuring
Development of intellectual skills	Science and the natural world (two years)		Up to 15% the arts	Estimating
Enlarged understanding of ideas and values	Technology	Better use of time	Up to 15% the vocations	Calculating
	Mathematics (two years)	Longer school day or longer school year (seven-hour school day; 200- to 220-day school year)	Up to 10% physical education	Seeing
	Foreign language (two years for all students)		No more than 90% from the above categories	Knowledge:
	The arts		At least 10% electives, as high as 20% to pursue special interests	No universal body of subject matter
	Civics			Vocational training
	Health		Common required core: common concepts, principles, skills, and ways of knowing, not common topics	Start where the student is
	Work (one semester)			
	Senior independent project		About two-thirds of program in each of five domains of knowledge will be common to all students	Understanding:
	First two years devoted to the core			Development of powers of discrimination and judgment
	Last two years devoted to elective clusters		Opposed to ability grouping and tracking	Discovery-values-character education:
	Requirement of one unit of service in the community or at school			Fairness
				Generosity
				Tolerance

* For the National Commission on Excellence in Education

Having reviewed past developments and evaluated present programs of the high school, our hypothetical curriculum committee—like those in other school systems throughout the country—is studying the many, sometimes conflicting, recommendations for change in the high school.

Predicting the impact of these studies in the years ahead is difficult. Will school systems lean toward Adler's recommendations? Boyer's? Gardner's? Goodlad's? Sizer's? Will they return to early proposals of Conant and the ASCD? Will they go even further back to the Committee of Ten, the Commission on the Reorganization of Secondary Education, and the Educational Policies Commission? What we are most likely to see will be a synthesis of the many recommendations with variations determined by local school districts and the states. No single standardized model of secondary education—nor of elementary or middle schools, for that matter—is likely to be acceptable to all the school systems in the United States. Certainly, as the trends toward greater local autonomy over the school's program and toward the empowerment of teachers gain momentum, diversity of models may be anticipated.

We have to take notice of the cyclical nature of curricular recommendations. The Committee of Ten (1894) recommended the same program for all high school students. Almost 100 years later the Paideia Group (1982) was proposing a single track for all students during their 12 years of schooling. Conant (1959) recommended a year of calculus in high school, as did the Paideia Group (1982). In 1959 Conant advocated foreign languages for the academically talented (four years of one foreign language), in 1983 the National Commission on Excellence in Education recommended two years of a foreign language for the college-bound, and in that same year Boyer advocated beginning foreign language study in the elementary school and requiring two years of all high school pupils. Conant (1959) pointed to the need for more guidance counselors, as did Boyer (1983). Goodlad (1984) accepted the broad categories of human knowledge and organized experiences of the Harvard Committee on General Education (1945).

We can already see that it has become more difficult for high school students to earn a diploma—a fact that may satisfy a long-held wish of both the public and the profession to make the high school diploma a symbol of a reasonable standard of academic achievement.

Once minimal competencies have been comfortably mastered by students, faculties will seek ways of enriching the program and responding to individual differences. Efforts to create voucher plans, proposals for tuition tax credits, and competition from private schools have contributed to forcing the public schools to reassess their programs. Although schools are now on a necessary cognitive swing, they are not likely to abandon the psychomotor domain nor eliminate affective learnings from the curriculum. Two generations of progressive doctrine, with its concern for the whole child instead of solely the intellect, cannot be—nor should it be—lightly discarded.

Despite the intensity of reform efforts in recent years, gains in student achievement have been very limited. In a 1989 report, the Center for Policy Research in Education noted two waves of reform efforts. The first occurred from about 1982 to 1986 with state mandates for minimum competency standards. The second, beginning in 1986 and continuing into the present, saw efforts in some localities to restructure schooling at the local level. The Center observed that state policies are still more characteristic of first wave reform efforts than of the second wave's implementation of restructuring at the local level.[134]

Sizer has sought to stimulate reform through the Coalition of Essential Schools, which was formed in 1984. Working with 52 schools Sizer has attempted to combat the "shopping mall" concept of the high school by encouraging schools to reduce the amount of subject matter covered and to emphasize depth rather than breadth. Sizer's efforts have encountered difficulties including financing; faculty resistance, cynicism, and inertia; parental concern over deemphasis of extracurricular activities within the context of the school day; and student objections to a more demanding, academically oriented curriculum.

Among reported successes of the coalition schools ("essential schools"-within-a-school) are improved reading scores, a rise in the number of graduates going on to college, and a decrease in the dropout rate. Emphasis on the academics for all students, a coaching model of instruction, smaller classes, depth of content as opposed to breadth, and local faculty control are central to Sizer's efforts.[135]

Donald C. Orlich took a critical view of recent reform efforts in general when he observed:

> This nation has wasted billions of dollars on poorly conceived but politically popular reform movements that have sapped the energies of schoolpeople. We need a national moratorium on reforms so that educators and local policy makers can analyze their own problems. This could lead to a new concept: *local system analysis*. Each local school district would systematically study its own cultures—yes, *cultures*—and *then* implement a carefully researched, well-coordinated, and well-funded plan for specific improvements.[136]

---

[134]William A. Firestone, Susan H. Fuhrman, and Michael W. Kirst, *The Progress of Reform: An Appraisal of State Education Initiatives* (New Brunswick, N.J.: Center for Policy Research in Education, Eagleton Institute of Politics, Rutgers, The State University of New Jersey, 1989), p. 13.

[135]See Thomas Toch and Matthew Cooper, "Lessons from the Trenches," *U.S. News and World Report* 108, no. 8 (February 26, 1990): 50–55.

[136]Donald C. Orlich. From "Educational Reforms: Mistakes, Misconceptions, Miscues," *Phi Delta Kappan* 70, no. 7 (March 1989): 517. Adapted from Donald C. Orlich, *Staff Development: Enhancing Human Potential*. Copyright © 1989 by Allyn & Bacon.

Community Service

Opportunities exist in many high schools for students to participate in community service projects. A recent Carnegie study reported that youth service is becoming a trend in our high schools.[137] Service to the community, a concept promoted by the Carnegie Foundation for the Advancement of Teaching as "The New Carnegie Unit," is increasingly popular throughout the nation's schools. The Carnegie study found that, out of 1,000 public high schools responding to its survey, 70 percent offered community service programs, and 20 percent of these schools had made community service a requirement.

Atlanta, Detroit, and Washington, D.C. provide examples of this trend in the secondary school curriculum. The Atlanta Public Schools offer a course, "Duties to the Community," that requires students to perform 75 hours of unpaid volunteer work and to write a follow-up report on their experiences. Through this service students can earn $\frac{1}{2}$ credit toward graduation. The Detroit public schools provide ten hours of credit toward graduation for "Outside of Class Learning Experience," which requires each pupil to work 200 clock hours of paid or voluntary service. Banneker High School, a magnet school in Washington, D.C., requires completion of a community laboratory project— during all four years, students spend one afternoon a week performing voluntary service. For this experience they earn $1\frac{1}{2}$ units of credit.

In keeping with society's demands for high school graduates who can demonstrate civic competence, programs that enable students to learn to serve the community can also help them develop positive social attitudes. At the same time students can acquire vocational and interpersonal skills and can make a contribution to the improvement of the community.

WHAT IS IN THE DISTANT FUTURE?

A growing number of individuals both inside and outside of the academic world are identified by the rather ambiguous label of "futurist." One of the better known persons in this group is Alvin Toffler, whose books, *Future Shock* and *The Third Wave,* provoked many of us to contemplate problems of the future and to begin considering ways to solve them.[138] High on the agenda of any futurist are problems like population control, health needs, preservation of the environment, housing needs, adequate food supplies, demands for energy, and the use of technology.

The futurists' scenario inevitably calls our attention to the invention of tiny semiconductor chips that have made possible new electronic marvels for leisure

---

[137]Charles H. Harris, *Student Service: The New Carnegie Unit* (Princeton, N.J.: The Carnegie Foundation for the Advancement of Teaching, 1987).

[138]Alvin Toffler, *Future Shock* (New York: Random House, 1970); *The Third Wave* (New York: William Morrow, 1980).

(home video equipment, electronic games) and for business (microcomputers, data banks). Futurists who concern themselves with educational problems see computer literacy as a needed basic skill.

Some educational futurists view the new technology as aiding the teacher and administrator to provide a more effective education within the school setting. Others predict what amounts to a type of deschooling. Peter Sleight, for example, reported on the type of deschooling that might be effected by the computer age:

> It may be that children won't attend schools at all, but attend classes in their own homes, taking lessons through the computer, with the teacher talking to them through a video image.
>
> Through the same network, the teacher will know whether a student is tuned in and can take "attendance" in the old-fashioned sense.
>
> Homework for the children will also be changed. No longer will they be bringing home textbooks and doing assignments on paper. Instead, they may plug into the school data base to receive their assignments, execute them on the computer screen at home and "send" it to their teacher via the computer hook-up.[139]

When or if this day comes, what will happen to the notion of interactive learning—that is, interaction between teacher and students and between student and student? How will students learn to socialize with each other? What will happen to multicultural, multiethnic education? How will boys and girls learn to live in a pluralistic society? Perhaps we might wish to conceptualize this type of computerized schooling as consuming only a portion of the day, with alternative forms of education in the community filling the remaining portion. At any rate, you may be safe in postulating that the elementary, middle, and senior high school as we know them today and as we will know them in the immediate future may well evolve into decidedly different kinds of institutions in the distant future. What do you suppose as yet unborn authors will be including in their as yet unwritten curriculum textbooks or yet-to-be-produced alternative media in the remote future?

SUMMARY

Before curriculum planners can proceed with their task of developing the curriculum, they must decide on the organizational structure within which programs will be implemented. At the beginning of this chapter we visualized as illustrative examples three schools—elementary, middle, and senior high. Like their actual counterparts, our hypothetical schools have undergone numerous internal changes.

---

[139]Peter Sleight, "Information Services: Possibilities Are Endless," *Fort Lauderdale News and Sun-Sentinel,* July 27, 1980, Section H, p. 3. Reprinted with permission.

This chapter traced some of the past organizational patterns at each level, described current organizational structures, and discussed possible and probable future developments. On the elementary level we reviewed the graded school, the activity curriculum, continuous progress plans, and open-education/open-space plans. At the middle school level we looked at its predecessor, the junior high school, and at a variety of proposals for that level, including the core curriculum. We studied several organizational plans at the senior high school level, including the subject matter curriculum, the broad-fields curriculum, team teaching, differentiated staffing, flexible and modular scheduling, and the nongraded high school.

The elementary school currently emphasizes teaching basic and thinking skills and providing for students with special needs. The middle school presently offers programs that have been adapted to meet the needs of preadolescents. The senior high school is involved in efforts to establish a quality comprehensive model, to furnish a number of alternatives both within and outside the school system, and to reinforce higher requirements for graduation.

In the near future the elementary school will most likely continue its traditional, subject-centered, basic-skills emphasis, although it will maintain some of the fundamental overtones of child-centeredness. At this level we noted trends toward the cooperative learning and whole language concepts. The middle school is well on its way to becoming the universal model for the education of preadolescents. The comprehensive high school will meet demands for the reform of secondary education by continuing the emphasis on subject matter and adopting some of the recommendations of recent national studies and organizations. Community service may become a common feature of the high school curriculum.

The ubiquitous computers, videocassette recorders, and laser videodiscs could conceivably revolutionize education at all levels. Curricula could be expected to respond substantively—and perhaps organizationally—to emerging social problems of growing concern to the American people.

QUESTIONS FOR DISCUSSION

1. What are some ways of organizing and implementing the curriculum that have been repeated through American educational history?
2. Why have the graded school and the subject matter curriculum been so enduring?
3. Which of the present curriculum programs and practices do you believe are only temporary and will disappear in the future? Why?
4. How can curriculum planners reconcile conflicting proposals for reform of the high school?

5. What programs and practices would you add to the second and third sections of this chapter, "Where We Are: Curriculum Present" and "Where We're Going: Curriculum Future"?

SUPPLEMENTARY EXERCISES

1. Explain what is meant by the activity curriculum. Critique this approach.
2. Describe advantages and disadvantages of the nongraded elementary school.
3. Prepare a written report on British open schools.
4. Write a paper summarizing some of the research on the achievement of learners in open-space schools.
5. Look up the Eight-Year Study and write a report summarizing its methodology and findings.
6. Describe one or more core programs from either the professional literature or from a school with which you have had firsthand experience.
7. Prepare a paper on the topic: "Shall We Group Pupils?" If so, how? Whether the answer is yes or no, reasons must be stated.
8. Describe advantages and disadvantages of the nongraded high school.
9. Describe one or more plans for team teaching and show its advantages and disadvantages.
10. Write a paper, citing at least three references, that accounts for the current emphasis on the basic skills.
11. Write a paper on the question of the placement of fifth grade in the educational system—in elementary school or middle school?
12. Write a paper on the question of the placement of ninth grade in the educational system—in middle school or high school?
13. From the literature or from firsthand knowledge, describe several options in education—that is, alternative forms of schooling.
14. State pros and cons of specialized versus comprehensive high schools and show your position.
15. Write a paper on the topic "Junior High School or Middle School—Which?"
16. Explain what is meant by a broad-fields curriculum. Critique this approach.
17. Write a paper on the question "Why did the decade from 1955 to 1965 produce so many curricular innovations?"
18. Read and summarize one of the national reports of the 1980s on reform of the high school.
19. Read and summarize one of the national reports of the 1980s on reform of the elementary school.
20. State whether you believe the school (any level) should limit itself to cognitive learning. Give reasons for the position taken.

21. Explain what is meant by differentiated staffing and show its advantages and disadvantages.
22. Distinguish between traditional, flexible, and modular scheduling and state the purposes of each.
23. Write a position paper on the topic "Teaching Values in the Public Schools."
24. Write a paper on how you would teach thinking skills.
25. Describe ways in which schools are providing for students in special education, gifted students, or students-at-risk.
26. Define "magnet school," state its purposes, and report on one successful example of such a school.
27. Find out if there is a residential public secondary school in your state. If there is, describe its program, its student body, its admission requirements, and its costs of operation.
28. Play the role of futurist and predict what may happen in curriculum organization and implementation 15 years hence.
29. Write a paper on the application of the computer in education.
30. Assign two students—one to argue the pro side and one to argue the con side—to each of the following issues:
    a. Using school buildings for year-round schooling.
    b. Extending the school day by one hour (you may separate the various levels if you wish).
    c. Extending the school year by 30 days—from 180 to 210 days (you may separate the various levels if you wish).

BIBLIOGRAPHY

Adler, Mortimer J. *Paideia: Problems and Possibilities*. New York: Macmillan, 1983.

———. *The Paideia Program: An Educational Syllabus*. New York: Macmillan, 1984.

———. *The Paideia Proposal: An Educational Manifesto*. New York: Macmillan, 1982.

Aikin, Wilford M. *The Story of the Eight-Year Study*. New York: Harper & Row, 1942.

Alberty, Harold B. and Alberty, Elsie J. *Reorganizing the High-School Curriculum*, 3rd ed. New York: Macmillan, 1962.

Alexander, William M. and George, Paul S. *The Exemplary Middle School*. New York: Holt, Rinehart and Winston, 1981.

Alexander, William M. et al. *The Emergent Middle School*, 2nd enl. ed. New York: Holt, Rinehart and Winston, 1969.

———. "Guidelines for the Middle Schools We Need Now." *The National Elementary School Principal* 51, no. 3 (November 1971): 79–89.

Association for Supervision and Curriculum Development. *Effective Schools and School Improvement*. Alexandria, Va.:

Association for Supervision and Curriculum Development, 1989.

———. *Teaching Thinking*. Alexandria, Va.: Association for Supervision and Curriculum Development, 1989.

Beggs, David W., III, ed. *Team Teaching: Bold New Venture*. Bloomington: Indiana University Press, 1964.

Beggs, David W., III, and Buffie, Edward G., eds., *Nongraded Schools in Action: Bold New Venture*. Bloomington: Indiana University Press, 1967.

Boyer, Ernest L. *High School: A Report on Secondary Education in America*. New York: Harper & Row, 1983.

Brandt, Ronald S., ed. *Content of the Curriculum*. 1988 Yearbook. Alexandria, Va.: Association for Supervision and Curriculum Development, 1988.

Brooks, Kenneth. "The Middle Schools—A National Survey." *Middle School Journal* 9, no. 1 (February 1978): 6–7.

Brown, B. Frank. *The Appropriate Placement School: A Sophisticated Nongraded Curriculum*. West Nyack, N.Y.: Parker, 1965.

———. *Education by Appointment: New Approaches to Independent Study*. West Nyack, N.Y.: Parker, 1968.

———. *The Nongraded High School*. Englewood Cliffs, N.J.: Prentice-Hall, 1963.

Buffie, Edward G. and Jenkins, John M. *Curriculum Development in Nongraded Schools: Bold New Venture*. Bloomington: Indiana University Press, 1971.

Burton, William H. *The Guidance of Learning Activities,* 3rd ed. New York: Appleton-Century-Crofts, 1962.

Bush, Robert N. and Allen, Dwight W. *A New Design for High School Education: Assuming a Flexible Schedule*. New York: McGraw-Hill, 1964.

Caine, Renate Nummela and Caine, Geoffrey. *Making Connections: Teaching and the Human Brain*. Alexandria, Va.: Association for Supervision and Curriculum Development, 1991.

Calvin, Allen D., ed. *Programmed Instruction: Bold New Venture*. Bloomington: Indiana University Press, 1969.

Chamberlin, L. J. and Girona, R. "Our Children Are Changing." *Educational Leadership* 33, no. 4 (January 1976): 301–305.

Coleman, James S., chairman, Panel on Youth of the President's Science Advisory Committee. *Youth: Transition to Adulthood*. Washington, D.C.: Superintendent of Documents, U.S. Government Printing Office, 1973; Chicago: University of Chicago Press, 1974.

Commission on the Reorganization of Secondary Education. *Cardinal Principles of Secondary Education*. Bulletin 35. Washington, D.C.: U.S. Office of Education, 1918.

Conant, James B. *The American High School Today*. New York: McGraw-Hill, 1959.

———. *The Comprehensive High School*. New York: McGraw-Hill, 1967.

———. *Recommendations for Education in the Junior High School Years*. Princeton, N.J.: Educational Testing Service, 1960.

Costa, Arthur L., ed. *Developing Minds: A Resource Book for Teaching Thinking*. Alexandria, Va.: Association for Supervision and Curriculum Development, 1985.

Costa, Arthur L. and Lowery, Lawrence. *Techniques for Teaching Thinking*. Pacific Grove, Calif.: Midwest Publications Critical Thinking Press, 1990.

Costello, Lawrence F. and Gordon, George H. *Teach with Television*. New York: Hastings House, 1961.

Cuban, Larry. "At-Risk Students: What Teachers and Principals Can Do." *Educational Leadership* 70, no. 6 (February 1989): 29–32.

"Curriculum Development in the U.S. and the World." *Educational Leadership* 44, no. 4 (December 1986–January 1987): 3–79.

Doyle, Denis and Levine, Marsha. "Magnet Schools: Choice and Quality in Public Education." *Phi Delta Kappan* 66, no. 4 (December 1984): 265–270.

Dunn, Rita S. and Dunn, Kenneth J. *Teaching Students Through Their Individual Learning Styles: A Practical Approach.* Reston, Va.: Reston Publishing Company, 1978.

Educational Policies Commission. *Education for All American Youth.* Washington, D.C.: National Education Association, 1944.

Eichhorn, Donald H. *The Middle School.* New York: Center for Applied Research in Education, 1966.

Elam, Stanley M., Rose, Lowell C., and Gallup, Alec M. "The 23rd Annual Gallup Poll of the Public's Attitudes Toward the Public Schools." *Phi Delta Kappan* 73, no. 1 (September 1991): 41–56.

Eurich, Alvin C., ed. *High School 1980.* New York: Pitman, 1970.

Fantini, Mario, ed. *Alternative Education: A Source Book for Parents, Teachers, and Administrators.* Garden City, N.Y.: Anchor Books, 1976.

Fantini, Mario. "Alternatives within Public Schools." *Phi Delta Kappan* 54, no. 7 (March 1973): 444–448.

———. *Public Schools of Choice: Alternatives in Education.* New York: Simon and Schuster, 1973.

———. "The What, Why, and Where of the Alternatives Movement." *The National Elementary Principal* 52, no. 6 (April 1973): 14–22.

Faunce, Roland C. and Bossing, Nelson L. *Developing the Core Curriculum.* Englewood Cliffs, N.J.: Prentice-Hall, 1951.

Foshay, Arthur W. *Curriculum for the 70's: An Agenda for Invention.* Washington, D.C.: National Education Association, Center for the Study of Instruction, 1970.

Fry, Edward B. *Teaching Machines and Programmed Instruction: An Introduction.* New York: McGraw-Hill, 1963.

Frymier, Jack. *A Study of Students at Risk: Collaborating To Do Research.* Bloomington, Ind.: Phi Delta Kappa, 1989.

Frymier, Jack and Gansneder, Bruce. "The Phi Delta Kappa Study of Students at Risk." *Phi Delta Kappan* 71, no. 2 (October 1989): 142–146.

Gatewood, Thomas E. and Dilg, Charles A. *The Middle School We Need.* Alexandria, Va.: Association for Supervision and Curriculum Development, 1975.

George, Paul S. and Lawrence, Gordon. *Handbook for Middle School Teaching.* Glenview, Ill.: Scott, Foresman, 1982.

Gibbons, Maurice, chairman, Phi Delta Kappa Task Force on Compulsory Education and Transitions for Youth. *The New Secondary Education: Task Force Report.* Bloomington, Ind.: Phi Delta Kappa, 1976.

Giroux, Henry A. "Rethinking Education Reform in the Age of George Bush." *Phi Delta Kappan* 70, no. 9 (May 1989): 728–730.

Glasser, William. *Schools Without Failure.* New York: Harper & Row, 1969.

Goodlad, John I. *A Place Called School: Prospects for the Future.* New York: McGraw-Hill, 1984.

Goodlad, John I. and Anderson, Robert H. *The Nongraded Elementary School,* rev. ed. New York: Teachers College Press, 1987.

Grambs, Jean D., Noyce, Clarence G., Patterson, Franklin, and Robertson, John. *The Junior High School We Need.* Alexandria, Va.: Association for Supervision and Curriculum Development, 1961.

Hansen, John H. and Hearn, Arthur C. *The Middle School Program.* Chicago: Rand McNally, 1971.

Harrison, Charles H. *Student Service: The New Carnegie Unit.* Princeton, N.J.: The Carnegie Foundation for the Advancement of Teaching, 1987.

Harvard Committee. *General Education in a Free Society.* Cambridge, Mass.: Harvard University Press, 1945.

Hass, Glen. *Curriculum Planning: A New Approach,* 5th ed. Boston: Allyn and Bacon, 1987.

Hassett, Joseph D. and Weisberg, Arline. *Open Education: Alternatives Within Our Tradition.* Englewood Cliffs, N.J.: Prentice-Hall, 1972.

Hillson, Maurie and Bongo, Joseph. *Continuous-Progress Education: A Practical Approach.* Palo Alto, Calif.: Science Research Associates, 1971.

Hunkins, Francis P. *Curriculum Development: Program Planning and Improvement.* Columbus, Ohio: Charles E. Merrill, 1980.

Illich, Ivan. *Deschooling Society.* New York: Harper & Row, 1971.

"Improving Learning Conditions for Students at Risk." *Educational Leadership* 44, no. 6 (March 1987): 3–80.

Jacobson, Stephen L. and Conway, James A., eds. *Educational Leadership in an Age of Reform.* White Plains, N.Y.: Longman, 1990.

Kilpatrick, William H. *Foundations of Method: Informal Talks on Teaching.* New York: Macmillan, 1925.

Kindred, Leslie W., Wolotkiewicz, Rita J., Mickelson, John M., and Coplein, Leonard E. *The Middle School Curriculum,* 2nd ed. Boston: Allyn and Bacon, 1981.

Kohl, Herbert R. *The Open Classroom: A Practical Guide to a New Way of Teaching.* New York: New York Review, distributed by Random House, 1969.

Kohut, Sylvester, Jr. *The Middle School: A Bridge Between Elementary and High Schools,* 2nd ed. Washington, D.C.: National Education Association, 1988.

Lehr, Judy Brown and Harris, Hazel Wiggins. *At Risk, Low Achieving Students in the Classroom.* Washington, D.C.: National Education Association, 1988.

Lewis, Arthur J. "Educational Basics to Serve Citizens in the Future." *The FASCD Journal* 1, no. 1 (February 1979): 1–8.

Lightfoot, Sara Lawrence. *The Good High School.* New York: Basic Books, 1983.

Link, Frances R., ed. *Essays on the Intellect.* Alexandria, Va.: Association for Supervision and Curriculum Development, 1985.

Lounsbury, John H. *Middle School Education as I See It.* Columbus, Ohio: National Middle School Association, 1984.

Lounsbury, John H. and Vars, Gordon F. *A Curriculum for the Middle School Years.* New York: Harper & Row, 1978.

Lowery, Lawrence. *Thinking and Learning.* Pacific Grove, Calif.: Midwest Publications Critical Thinking Press, 1990.

McDaniel, Thomas R. "Demilitarizing Public Education: School Reform in the Era of George Bush." *Phi Delta Kappan* 71, no. 1 (September 1989): 15–18.

McNeil, John D. *Curriculum Administration: Principles and Techniques of Curriculum Development.* New York: Macmillan, 1965.

Manlove, Donald C. and Beggs, David W., III. *Flexible Scheduling: Bold New Venture.* Bloomington: Indiana University Press, 1965.

Martin, John Henry. *The Education of Adolescents.* Report of the National Panel on High Schools and Adolescent Education. Washington, D.C.: United States Office of Education, 1976.

Marzano, Robert et al. *Dimensions of Thinking: A Framework for Curriculum and Instruction.* Alexandria, Va.: Association for Supervision and Curriculum Development, 1988.

Meriam, Junius L. *Child Life and the Curriculum.* Yonkers, N.Y.: World Book Company, 1920.

Michaels, Kenneth G. "A Statement on Behalf of Education by Choice." *The FASCD Journal* 1, no. 1 (February 1979): 16–20.

Miller, John P. and Seller, Wayne. *Curriculum: Perspectives and Practice.* White Plains, N.Y.: Longman, 1985.

Miller, John W. "Ten Reform Reports That Can Change Your School." *Principal* 66, no. 2 (November 1986): 26–28.

Miller, Richard I., ed. *The Nongraded School: Analysis and Study.* New York: Harper & Row, 1967.

Mitchell, Richard. *The Graves of Academe.* Boston: Little, Brown, 1981.

Morris, Robert C., ed. "At-Risk Youth." *Thresholds in Education* 16, no. 2 (May 1990): 1–33.

Moss, Theodore C. *Middle School.* Boston: Houghton Mifflin, 1969.

Murray, Evelyn M. and Wilhour, Jane R. *The Flexible Elementary School: Practical Guidelines for Developing a Nongraded Program.* West Nyack, N.Y.: Parker, 1971.

National Association for Core Curriculum. *Core Today: Rationale and Implications.* Kent, Ohio: National Association for Core Curriculum, 1973.

National Association of Secondary School Principals, National Committee on Secondary Education. *American Youth in the Mid-Seventies.* Reston, Va.: National Association of Secondary School Principals, 1972.

National Commission on Excellence in Education, David P. Gardner, chairman. *A Nation at Risk: The Imperative for Educational Reform.* Washington, D.C.: U.S. Government Printing Office, 1983.

National Commission on the Reform of Secondary Education. *The Reform of Secondary Education: A Report to the Public and the Profession.* New York: McGraw-Hill, 1973.

National Consortium for Options in Public Education. *The Directory of Alternative Public Schools.* Bloomington, Ind.: Educational Alternatives Project, Indiana University, 1975.

National Education Association. *Report of the Committee of Ten on Secondary School Studies.* New York: American Book Company, 1894.

National Middle School Association. *Perspectives: Middle School Education, 1964–1984.* Columbus, Ohio: National Middle School Association, 1984.

Norris, Stephen and Ennis, Robert. *Evaluating Critical Thinking.* Pacific Grove, Calif.: Midwest Publications Critical Thinking Press, 1990.

Ogden, Evelyn and Germinario, Vito. *The At-Risk Student: Answers for Educators.* Lancaster, Pa.: Technomic Publishing Company, 1988.

Oliva, Peter F. *The Secondary School Today,* 2nd ed. New York: Harper & Row, 1972.

Orlich, Donald C. "Education Reforms: Mistakes, Misconceptions, Miscues." *Phi Delta Kappan* 70, no. 7 (March 1989): 512–517.

Parkhurst, Helen. *Education on the Dalton Plan.* New York: E. P. Dutton, 1922.

Passow, A. Harry, ed. *Curriculum Crossroads.* New York: Teachers College, Columbia University, 1962.

Passow, A. Henry. "Reforming America's High Schools." *Phi Delta Kappan* 56, no. 9 (May 1975): 587–596.

———. "Tackling the Reform Reports of the 1980's." *Phi Delta Kappan* 65, no. 10 (June 1984): 674–683.

Paul, Robert. *Critical Thinking: What Every Person Needs to Survive in a Rapidly Changing World.* Rohnert Park, Calif.: Center for Critical Thinking and Moral Critique, Sonoma State University, 1990.

Phenix, Philip H. *Realms of Meaning: A Philosophy of the Curriculum for General Education.* New York: McGraw-Hill, 1964.

Popper, Samuel H. *The American Middle School: An Organizational Analysis.* Waltham, Mass.: Blaisdell, 1967.

Powell, Arthur G., Farrar, Eleanor, and Cohen, David K. *The Shopping Mall High School: Winners and Losers in the Educational Marketplace*. Boston: Houghton Mifflin, 1985.

Pratt, David. *Curriculum: Design and Development*. New York: Harcourt Brace Jovanovich, 1980.

Proctor, John H. and Smith, Kathryn. "IGE and Open Education: Are They Compatible?" *Phi Delta Kappan* 55, no. 8 (April 1974): 564–566.

"The Quest for Higher Standards." *Educational Leadership* 48, no. 5 (February 1991): 3–69.

Rafferty, Max. *What They Are Doing to Your Children*. New York: New American Library, 1964.

Resnick, Lauren B. and Klopfer, Leopold E., eds. *Toward the Thinking Curriculum: Current Cognitive Research*. 1989 Yearbook. Alexandria, Va.: Association for Supervision and Curriculum Development, 1989.

"Restructuring Schools: What's Really Happening?" *Educational Leadership* 48, no. 8 (May 1991): 3–76.

Roberts, Arthur D. and Cawelti, Gordon. *Redefining General Education in the American High School*. Alexandria, Va.: Association for Supervision and Curriculum Development, 1984.

Rogers, Vincent R. "English and American Primary Schools." *Phi Delta Kappan* 51, no. 2 (October 1969): 71–75.

Rollins, Sidney P. *Developing Nongraded Schools*. Itasca, Ill.: F. E. Peacock, 1968.

Rubin, Louis, ed. *Current Movements and Instructional Technology*. Boston: Allyn and Bacon, 1977.

"The School in the Middle," *NASSP Bulletin* 67, no. 463 (May 1983): 1–82.

Shane, Harold G. *Curriculum Change Toward the 21st Century*. Washington, D.C.: National Education Association, 1977.

Shanker, Albert. "The End of the Traditional Model of Schooling—and a Proposal for Using Incentives to Restructure Our Public Schools." *Phi Delta Kappan* 71, no. 5 (January 1990): 344–357.

Shearer, William J. *The Grading of Schools*. New York: H. P. Smith, 1898.

Sizer, Theodore R. *Horace's Compromise: The Dilemma of the American High School*. Boston: Houghton Mifflin, 1984.

Slavin, Robert E., Karweit, Nancy L., and Madden, Nancy A. *Effective Programs for Students at Risk*. Needham Heights, Mass.: Allyn and Bacon, 1989.

Slavin, Robert E. and Madden, Nancy A. "What Works for Students at Risk: A Research Synthesis" *Educational Leadership* 70, no. 6 (February 1989): 4–13.

Smith, B. Othanel, Stanley, William O., and Shores, J. Harlan. *Fundamentals of Curriculum Development*, rev. ed. New York: Harcourt Brace Jovanovich, 1957.

A special section on middle schools. *Phi Delta Kappan* 71, no. 6 (February 1990): 436–469.

"A Special Section on Youth Service." *Phi Delta Kappan* 72, no. 10 (June 1991): 738–773.

Stephens, Lillian S. *The Teacher's Guide to Open Education*. New York: Holt, Rinehart and Winston, 1974.

Swartz, Robert and Perkins, David. *Teaching Thinking: Issues & Approaches*. Pacific Grove, Calif.: Midwest Publications Critical Thinking Press, 1990.

Tanner, Daniel and Tanner, Laurel N. *Curriculum Development: Theory into Practice*, 2nd ed. New York: Macmillan, 1980.

"Teaching Thinking Skills in the Curriculum." *Educational Leadership* 39, no. 1 (October 1981): 6–54.

"Teaching Thinking Throughout the Curriculum." *Educational Leadership* 45, no. 7 (April 1988): 3–30.

"Thinking Skills in the Curriculum." *Educational Leadership* 42, no. 1 (September 1984): 3–87.

Timar, Thomas B. and Kirp, David L. "Education Reform in the 1980s: Lessons from the States," *Educational Leadership* 70, no. 7 (March 1989): 504–511.

Toch, Thomas. *In the Name of Excellence: The Struggle to Reform the Nation's Schools, Why It's Failing and What Should Be Done*. New York: Oxford University Press, 1991.

Toch, Thomas with Litton, Nancy and Cooper, Matthew. "Schools that Work." *U.S. News & World Report* 110, no. 20 (May 27, 1991): 58–66.

Toffler, Alvin. *Future Shock*. New York: Random House, 1970.

———. *The Third Wave*. New York: William Morrow, 1980.

Trump, J. Lloyd. "Flexible Scheduling—Fad or Fundamental?" *Phi Delta Kappan* 44, no. 8 (May 1963): 370.

Trump, J. Lloyd and Baynham, Dorsey. *Focus on Change: Guide to Better Schools*. Chicago: Rand McNally, 1961.

Trump, J. Lloyd and Miller, Delmas F. *Secondary School Curriculum Improvement: Meeting Challenges of the Times*, 3rd ed. Boston: Allyn and Bacon, 1979.

Tyler, Ralph W. "Curriculum Development Since 1900," *Educational Leadership* 38, no. 8 (May 1981): 598–601.

Van Til, William, Vars, Gordon F., and Lounsbury, John H. *Modern Education for the Junior High School Years*, 2nd ed. Indianapolis, Ind.: Bobbs-Merrill, 1967.

Vars, Gordon F., ed. *Common Learnings: Core and Interdisciplinary Team Approaches*. Scranton, Pa.: International Textbook Company, 1969.

Von Haden, Herbert I. and King, Jean Marie. *Educational Innovator's Guide*. Worthington, Ohio: Charles A. Jones, 1974.

Weeks, Ruth Mary. *A Correlated Curriculum: A Report of the Committee on Correlation of the National Council of Teachers of English*. New York: D. Appleton-Century, 1936.

Weinstock, Ruth. *The Greening of the High School*. New York: Educational Facilities Laboratories, 1973.

"When Teachers Tackle Thinking Skills." *Educational Leadership* 42, no. 3 (November 1984): 3–72.

Wiles, Kimball. *The Changing Curriculum of the American High School*. Englewood Cliffs, N.J.: Prentice-Hall, 1963.

Wiles, Kimball and Patterson, Franklin. *The High School We Need*. Alexandria, Va.: Association for Supervision and Curriculum Development, 1959.

Wolfe, Arthur B. *The Nova Plan for Instruction*. Fort Lauderdale, Fla.: Broward County Board of Public Instruction, 1962.

Wright, Grace S. *Block-Time Classes and the Core Program in the Junior High School*, Bulletin 1958, no. 6. Washington, D.C.: U.S. Office of Education, 1958.

Zais, Robert S. *Curriculum: Principles and Foundations*. New York: Harper & Row, 1976.

AUDIOTAPES

The following are available from the Association for Supervision and Curriculum Development, 1250 N. Pitt Street, Alexandria, Va. 22314.

Children in Crisis: The Learning Styles of At-Risk, Drop-Out, and Multicultural Underachievers—and How to Increase Their Achievement. 1990. (Rita Dunn).

Curriculum Planning. (Arthur Roberts).

Dimensions of Thinking: A New Framework for Curriculum and Instruction. (Robert Marzano et al.).

Districtwide Programs for At-Risk Youth. Five tapes. 1988:

Curriculum in At-Risk Schools. (Larry Cuban).

The Dropout and the Public Investment. (Richard Green).

Dropouts in America. (Jacqueline Danzberger).

Expanding Learning Opportunities for the Educationally Disadvantaged. (Floretta McKenzie).

Meeting the Needs of Students at Risk in a Large School District. (Victor Herbert).

Hear Arthur Costa! Three one-hour tapes:

Classroom Conditions that Encourage Student Thinking, 1985.

Teaching Thinking: Who's Really Doing It, 1988.

What Human Beings Do When They Behave Intelligently, 1987.

Restructuring Schools for Results. Seven audiotapes:

Organizing Schools for Change Based on the Teacher's Role. (Albert Shanker).

Reshaping the Teaching Profession Through Agency Cooperation. (Phillip Schlechty).

Restructuring High Schools. (Ted Sizer).

Roles Administrators Play in Supporting and Initiating Restructuring. (Marian Leibowitz).

School Illustrations of Restructuring. Two tapes. (Robert McClure, Patricia Schaefer, David Wallace, and Gerald Dreyfuss).

What Restructuring the Teaching Profession Means. (Ann Lieberman).

Rethinking the Curriculum for the Next Decade. Six one-hour audiotapes, 1990:

Curriculum and Citizenship. (Maxine Greene).

Curriculum Deliberations in Hard Times. (Walter Parker).

Curriculum for the 1990s. (Graham Down).

Direct Instruction Reconsidered. (Barak Rosenshine).

Falling Between the Cracks. (Grant Wiggins).

Where Have We Been and Where Are We Going? (Ralph Tyler).

Talks on Teaching Thinking. Ten audiotapes, 1984 and 1985. Titles include:

Practice Is Not Enough. (Barry Beyer).

Survey of Thinking Skills. (Sandra Black).

Approaches to Teaching Thinking. (Ron Brandt).

Classroom Conditions That Encourage Student Thinking. (Arthur Costa).

Teaching for Intelligent Behavior. (Arthur Costa).

Thinking as a Skill. (Edward de Bono).

Knowledge as Design. (David Perkins).

Beyond the Three R's—Reasoning and Responsibility. (Jane Stallings).

Teaching for Problem Solving in the Real World. (Robert Sternberg).

Training Intellectual Skills—A Triarchic Model. (Robert Sternberg).

Teaching Thinking in Elementary Schools. Five audiotapes, 1987:

Analyzing Approaches to Teaching Thinking. (Ron Brandt and David Perkins).

Critical Thinking in Elementary School. (Richard Paul).

The Development of Children's Thinking and Teaching. (Esther Fusco and John Barell).

Planning a Thinking Skills Program. (Barry Beyer).

What Human Beings Do When They Behave Intelligently. (Arthur Costa).

FILMS

And No Bells Ring, parts 1 and 2. Total time: 57 min. black and white. Reston, Va.: National Association of Secondary School Principals, 1960. Hugh Downs narrates this film on team teaching. Film depicts large-group instruction, small-group discussion, and independent study. J. Lloyd Trump is shown in the film.

A Conversation with James B. Conant. 28 min. black and white. New York: N.Y.: National Broadcasting Service, 1960. Dr. Conant talks about his report on the American high school.

A Conversation with B. F. Skinner. 28 min. color. Del Mar, Calif.: CRM Educational Films, 1972. Dr. Skinner talks about behaviorism and his book *Beyond Freedom and Dignity*.

Education by Choice. 29 min. color. Wilmette, Ill.: Films, Inc., 1975. Shows the seven separate schools of the Education by Choice program of the Quincy (Illinois) High School.

High School Team Teaching: The Ferris Story. 26 min. color. Spokane, Wash.: Crown Films, 1966. Shows team teaching and modular/flexible scheduling at Ferris High School, Spokane, Washington.

How Good Are Our Schools? Dr. Conant Reports. 29 min. black and white. Washington, D.C.: National Education Association, 1959. Ralph Bellamy narrates this film on the 1959 Conant report on the American high school.

Make a Mighty Reach. 28 min. color. Melbourne, Fla.: Institute for Development of Educational Activities, 1967. Shows a variety of innovations, including ungraded programs, flexible scheduling, and computer-assisted instruction.

The National Reports. 58 min. color. Menomonie, Wis.: University of Wisconsin–Stout, 1984. Dr. Ernest Boyer, Dr. Anne Campbell, and Dr. Robert Stout discuss the national reports on American education.

Teaching Machines and Programmed Learning. 29 min. black and white. Washington, D.C.: U.S. Office of Education, 1960. Dr. Robert Glaser, Dr. Arthur A. Lumsdaine, and Dr. B. F. Skinner discuss teaching machines and programmed instruction.

Team Teaching in the Elementary School. 23 min. color. Dayton, Ohio: Institute for Development of Educational Activities, 1969. Describes a team teaching program on the elementary school level in Cypress, Texas.

What's New at School? 47 min. color. New York: Carousel Films, 1972. Discussion of the open school.

FILMSTRIP-AUDIOTAPE PROGRAM

Opening Classroom Structure. Vimcet Associates, P.O. Box 24714, Los Angeles, Calif. 90024.

FILMSTRIP/RECORD

Focus on Change, 23 min. Washington, D.C.: National Education Association, 1962. Howard K. Smith narrates this recording on large-group instruction, small-group discussion, and independent study. Filmstrip in color.

MULTI-MEDIA

Tactics for Thinking. Association for Supervision and Curriculum Development, 1250 N. Pitt Street, Alexandria, Va. 22314.

Includes eight hours of videotape identifying 22 tactics for thinking, a trainer's manual, a teacher's manual, and student activities blackline masters. Features Robert Marzano and Daisy Arredondo.

VIDEOTAPES

Association for Supervision and Curriculum Development, 1250 N. Pitt Street, Alexandria, Va. 22314.

Improving the Quality of Student Thinking. 20 min. 1986. Illustrates ways teachers can improve student thinking skills.

Teacher and School Effectiveness. 21 min. 1981. Barak K. Rosenshine, Ronald Edmonds, and Peter Mortimore discuss ways of improving teacher and school effectiveness.

Teaching Skillful Thinking. 103 min. 1986. Four videotapes featuring Ernest Boyer, Arthur Costa, Matthew Lippman, David Perkins, and Robert Sternberg; leader's guide. Titles are:

> *Issues in Teaching Thinking*.
> *The Skillful Thinker*.
> *Teaching for Thinking*.
> *Teaching of and About Thinking*.

Center for Critical Thinking and Moral Critique, Sonoma State University, Rohnert Park, Calif. 94928.

Critical Thinking Forum 1990: Educational Reform for the Year 2000 and Beyond. A series of eight one-hour videotapes originally broadcast by the Adult Learning Satellite Service of PBS. Titles include:

Critical Thinking and the Human Emotions.

Critical Thinking and Mathematical Problem Solving.

Infusing Critical Thinking into Community College Instruction.

Infusing Critical Thinking into Instruction at Four-Year Colleges and Universities.

Critical Thinking: The Thinking that Masters the Content.

Transforming Critical Thinking Principles into Teaching Strategies.

Remodeling Lessons and Redesigning Instruction to Infuse Critical Thinking.

The Greensboro Plan: Long-Term Critical Thinking Staff Development in an Urban Multi-Racial School District.

CHAPTER TEN

Instructional Goals and Objectives

After studying this chapter you should be able to:

1. Identify the three major domains of learning.

2. List the major categories of learnings from one taxonomy of each of the three domains.

3. Explain the relationships between curriculum goals and objectives and instructional goals and objectives.

4. Distinguish between instructional goals and instructional objectives.

5. Be able to identify and write instructional goals in each of the three domains.

6. Be able to identify and write instructional objectives in each of the three domains.

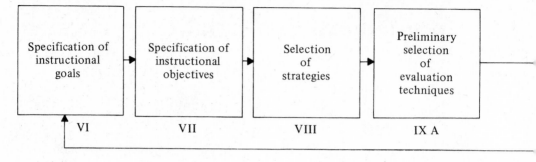

Specification of instructional goals	Specification of instructional objectives	Selection of strategies	Preliminary selection of evaluation techniques
VI	VII	VIII	IX A

VI–IX Planning phases
X–XI Operational phases

FIGURE 10–1   The instructional model

PLANNING FOR INSTRUCTION

With the curriculum decisions made, the broad territory known as instruction looms before us. In some ways it is a familiar land whose landmarks—lesson plans, teaching strategies, and tests—are recognized by administrators, teachers, students, and parents. As we enter the area of instruction, decision making remains a major responsibility, only this time the responsibility falls directly on the classroom teacher. Up to this point persons identified as curriculum planners, among whose number are classroom teachers, have been engaged in making decisions of a programmatic nature. Now classroom teachers will become occupied in making decisions of a methodological nature. They will be answering questions like these:

□ What are the objectives to be accomplished as a result of instruction?
□ What topics will we cover?
□ What procedures are best for directing the learning?
□ How do we evaluate instruction?

At this stage the teacher must decide whether to designate topics or specify competencies, whether to feature the teacher's objectives or the pupils', whether to seek mastery of content or simply exposure to the material, and whether to aim instruction at groups or at individuals.

Planning for instruction includes specifying instructional goals and objectives (discussed in this chapter), selecting instructional strategies (considered in Chapter 11), and choosing techniques to evaluate instruction (treated in Chapter 12).

To put our next task in perspective, let's review the steps we have taken so far. We have

□ surveyed needs of students in general
□ surveyed needs of society

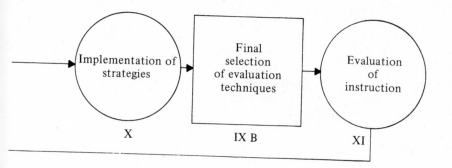

- clarified our philosophy of education and stated general aims
- identified curriculum goals and objectives
- determined needs of students in the school, needs of the community, and needs as shown by the subject matter
- reaffirmed plans for organizing the curriculum or selected and implemented plans for reorganizing the curriculum

Having completed these steps, we are ready to undertake planning, presenting, and evaluating instruction. The instructional phases of the curriculum-instruction continuum are shown as a subset of the model for curriculum development suggested in Chapter 5.[1] The subset consists of six components (VI, VII, VIII, IX A and B, X, XI), shown in Figure 10–1. In Chapter 5, we diagrammed these instructional components in such a way that they could be removed from the overall model for curriculum development. However, in Chapter 1 we posited an intimate relationship between curriculum and instruction, concluding that the two could be separated for purposes of analysis but that the existence of one could not be meaningful without the other.

The Instructional Model

Figure 10–1 represents a model of instruction that, for simplicity, we will refer to as the Instructional Model. This Instructional Model is broken into two major phases: planning and operational. The operational phase is divided into two parts: the implementation or presentation of instruction and the evaluation of instruction.

The planning phase of the Instructional Model consists of four components: component VI—the identification of instructional goals; component VII—the specification of instructional objectives; component VIII—the teacher's plans for instructional strategies; and component IX—which consists of both a preliminary and a final phase of planning for the evaluation of instruction.

---

[1]See Figure 5–5, p 172.

Then where and how does the teacher begin to plan for instruction? Let's look at several approaches to planning for instruction. Teacher A comes into the class without a preconceived notion of what he or she will cover and pulls a theme out of the air as the spirit moves him or her. Given the profession's penchant for turning rubrics into seeming substance, some might call this approach instantaneous planning. Others, less kind, might term it nonplanning.

Teacher B takes the textbook, divides the number of chapters by the number of weeks in the school year, lists the topics of each chapter by week, and from there takes any one of a number of directions. For each topic in its turn the teacher might

- jot down some questions for class discussion
- prepare notes for a lecture
- design individual and group assignments for clarifying points in the chapters

Teacher C selects topics for study during the year, using all kinds of materials related to the topic—including the textbook—and creates a succession of units of work for the class.

Teacher B's most likely course of action is the assign-study-recite-test approach, mentioned in the preceding chapter. Teacher C will follow what is commonly called the unit method of teaching, a problem-solving approach.

All three teachers may or may not relate their plans to the predetermined curriculum goals and objectives. All three may or may not specify the instructional goals and objectives that pupils are expected to accomplish. It is my position that both of these actions should be taken by teachers.

Of course, these three illustrations of types of teachers are exaggerated. Eclectic as teachers are, they are not likely to fall into any one consistent mold. These are but three illustrations of an almost infinite variety of teacher models, yet the illustrations are general enough to represent a significant number of teachers. The thesis of this chapter is that, regardless of the teacher's model or style of teaching, curriculum goals and objectives are more likely to be accomplished and students more likely to demonstrate mastery of learning if instructional goals and objectives are specified before starting instruction.

INSTRUCTIONAL GOALS AND OBJECTIVES DEFINED

Before we tackle the central mission of this chapter—selecting and writing instructional goals and objectives—let's see where instructional goals and objectives come in the curriculum development process. First, however, we should review the hierarchy of outcomes discussed in Chapter 8. At the top of the hierarchy are aims of education from which the school's curriculum goals and objectives are derived. In turn, the curriculum goals and objectives serve as sources of the instructional goals and objectives. Aims are stated by prominent individuals and groups for national, and sometimes even international, consider-

BOX 10–1   Illustration of the hierarchy of outcomes

□ *Aim:* Students will develop knowledge and skills necessary for living in a technological society.
□ *Curriculum goal:* Students will recognize the influence of the computer on our
lives.
□ *Curriculum objective:* By the end of the senior year, at least ninety percent of
the students will have taken a computer literacy course either in this school or
elsewhere.
□ *Instructional goal:* The student will become familiar with personal computers.
□ *Instructional objective:* The student will demonstrate skills in word processing
using his or her assigned computer by writing a one-page paper with ninety percent
accuracy.

ation. Curriculum goals and objectives are formulated by individual school and
school-system curriculum groups. Instructional goals and objectives are specified by the classroom teacher, who is sometimes assisted by other teachers and
local curriculum groups.

To put these various aims, goals, and objectives in perspective, let's look
at a simple example of outcomes in their hierarchical order (Box 10–1).

From the broad aim of education, we have moved to the specific instructional objective. Now let's examine instructional goals and objectives more
closely.

An *instructional goal* is a statement of performance expected of each student in a class, phrased in general terms without criteria of achievement. The
term "instructional goal" is used in this text like Norman E. Gronlund's *general instructional objective*[2] and Tyler's term *tentative general objective*.[3] "The
student will show an understanding of the stock market" is an example of an
instructional goal. It indicates the performance expected of the learner, but the
performance is not stated in such a fashion that its attainment can be readily
measured. As a curriculum goal points the direction to curriculum objectives,
so an instructional goal points the way to instructional objectives.

An *instructional objective* is a statement of performance to be demonstrated
by each student in the class, derived from an instructional goal and phrased in
measurable and observable terms. We may equate this term with Gronlund's
specific learning outcome and Tyler's *precise instructional objective*. The following statement is an example of an instructional objective: "The student will
convert the following fractions to percentages with 100 percent accuracy: $\frac{1}{4}$,
$\frac{1}{3}$, $\frac{1}{2}$, $\frac{2}{3}$, $\frac{3}{4}$." Instructional objectives are also known as behavioral objectives,
performance objectives, or competencies.

---

[2]Norman E. Gronlund, *Stating Objectives for Classroom Instruction*, 2nd ed. (New York:
Macmillan, 1978).
[3]Ralph W. Tyler, *Basic Principles of Curriculum and Instruction* (Chicago: University of
Chicago Press, 1949).

Stating Objectives

Tyler discussed four ways that instructors state objectives. Objectives are

1. things that the instructor will do. Tyler gave them examples, "to present the theory of evolution," "to demonstrate the nature of inductive proof," "to present the Romantic poets," and "to introduce four-part harmony."
2. topics, concepts, generalizations, or other elements of content that are to be dealt with in the course or courses. Tyler's examples are "the Colonial period" and "matter can be neither created nor destroyed."
3. generalized patterns of behavior that fail to indicate more specifically the area of life or the content to which the behavior applies. Tyler identified illustrations of this type of objective: "to develop critical thinking," "to develop appreciation," and "to develop social attitudes."
4. terms that identify both the kind of behavior to be developed in the student and the content or area of life in which this behavior is to operate. Tyler's examples are "to write clear and well-organized reports of social studies projects" and "to develop an appreciation of the modern novel."[4]

Of the four types of objectives outlined by Tyler, the fourth is preferable. As the next section reveals, current methodology advocates specifying instructional objectives in terms of expected, specific student behavior, not as actions of the teacher, as topics, or as generalized patterns of behavior.

THE USE OF BEHAVIORAL OBJECTIVES

Whether to use behavioral objectives or not is a debate that has raged among educators for years. Supporters of behavioral objectives argue that this approach to instruction

☐ forces the teacher to be precise about what is to be accomplished
☐ enables the teacher to communicate to pupils what they must achieve
☐ simplifies evaluation
☐ makes accountability possible
☐ makes sequencing easier

W. James Popham, in support of behavioral objectives, wrote:

> Measurable instructional objectives are designed to counteract what is to me the most serious deficit in American education today, namely, a preoccupation with the process without assessment of consequences. . . . There are at least three realms in which measurable objectives have considerable potential dividends: in curriculum (what goals are selected); in instruction (how to accomplish those goals); and in evaluation (determining whether objectives of the instructional sequences have been realized). . . . It is perhaps because I am

---

[4]Ibid., pp. 44–47. Reprinted with permission.

a convert to this position that I feel viscerally, as well as believe rationally, that measurable objectives have been the most significant instructional advance in the past 10 years.[5]

The opponents of behavioral objectives hold that writing behavioral objectives

☐ is a waste of time
☐ is dehumanizing
☐ restricts creativity
☐ leads to trivial competencies

James D. Raths voiced his opposition to behavioral objectives as follows:

> Consider the long range implications a teacher and his students must accept once it has been decided that all students are to acquire a specific instructional objective. The teacher's task becomes at once difficult and tedious. He must inform his students of the objective to which they are expected to aspire; he must convince them of the relevance of this objective to their lives; he must give his students the opportunity to practice the behavior being taught; he must diagnose individual differences encountered by members of his group; he must make prescriptions of assignments based on his diagnosis and repeat the cycle again and again. . . . Yet even if all programs could be set up on the basis of behavioral objectives and even if strict training paradigms could be established to meet the objectives, who could argue that such a program would be other than tedious and ultimately stultifying?[6]

Problems with Behavioral Objectives

While the yea-sayers and naysayers argued with each other, the behavioral objectives camp itself added to the difficulty of convincing teachers to use behavioral objectives. Some, perhaps overenthusiastic about the behavioral objectives movement, turned off teachers by

1. assuming a rather dogmatic approach that seemed to rule out all other methods. Although I am favorably disposed toward the use of behavioral objectives, I would be hard-pressed to come up with solid experimental data to show that students exposed to a behavioral-objectives approach consistently show higher achievement than students whose instruction has been guided by other approaches.

    What some of the research reveals is that behavioral objectives can be useful as preinstructional strategies, that objectives work better if they

---

[5]W. James Popham, "Practical Ways of Improving Curriculum via Measurable Objectives," *Bulletin of the National Association of Secondary School Principals* 55, no. 355 (May 1971): 76. Reprinted with permission.

[6]James D. Raths, "Teaching Without Specific Objectives," *Educational Leadership* 28, no. 7 (April 1971): 715. Reprinted with permission of the Association for Supervision and Curriculum Development and James D. Raths. Copyright ©1971 by the Association for Supervision and Curriculum. All rights reserved.

pertain to the particular instructional task, that objectives are more effective with certain kinds of instruction than with others, that objectives are useful in accomplishing learning at higher levels of the cognitive taxonomy, and that students of average ability, male students of high socioeconomic background, and both the more independent and less conscientious students benefit from behavioral objectives.[7]

2. resorting to formulas, which tended to make the writing of behavioral objectives mechanical rather than creative—for example, "Given the _____, the student will _____ in _____ minutes with a score of _____."

3. downplaying affective objectives—a primary concern among opponents of behavioral objectives—and sometimes implying that it is as easy to write behavioral objectives in the affective domain as in the cognitive and psychomotor domains.

In spite of the hubbub over behavioral objectives, I believe that, with a reasoned approach, the practice of identifying and writing both instructional goals and objectives has considerable merit. Whether the regular classroom teacher specifies behavioral objectives or not, those who write individualized education programs (IEPs) for handicapped students must state both goals that students are to achieve by the end of the year and behavioral objectives for accomplishing the goals.

The writing of instructional objectives forces the teacher to identify the outcomes he or she seeks. The specification of instructional objectives simplifies the selection of instructional strategies and resources. When stated in behavioral terms, instructional objectives provide a basis for assessment, and they communicate to all—students, parents, and other professionals—exactly what it is students are expected to demonstrate.[8]

GUIDELINES FOR PREPARING INSTRUCTIONAL GOALS AND OBJECTIVES

To pursue the task of selecting and writing instructional goals and objectives, we will find it helpful to establish several guidelines to be followed. Instructional goals and objectives should

☐ relate to the already specified curriculum goals and objectives

☐ be specified for three domains of learning—the cognitive, affective, and psychomotor—whenever applicable

---

[7]See James Hartley and Ivor K. Davies, "Preinstructional Strategies: The Role of Pretests, Behavioral Objectives, Overviews, and Advance Organizers," *Review of Educational Research* 46, no. 2 (Spring 1976); 239–265.

[8]Leslie J. Briggs cited 21 reasons for writing instructional objectives in *Handbook of Procedures for the Design of Instruction* (Washington, D.C.: American Institutes for Research, 1970), pp. 17–18.

> □ be identified at both low and high levels of learning with greater emphasis on the higher
> □ follow a few simple rules for writing

We shall consider each of these guidelines.

Relationship to Curriculum Goals and Objectives

Instructional goals and objectives should relate to curriculum goals and objectives. Unless the classroom teacher participated in drafting the curriculum goals and objectives, he or she must become familiar with them. The instructional goals and objectives are derived from the curriculum goals and objectives. Let's show this relationship by choosing a *curriculum goal* for the fifth grade: During the course of the year students will appreciably improve their skills in reading. From this general goal we may deduce the following *curriculum objectives:* (1) By the end of the eighth month, 75 percent of the students will have increased their ability to comprehend a selected set of English words by 25 percent, and (2) By the end of the academic year, all students will have met or exceeded the grade norm of 5.9 in reading comprehension.

The curriculum objectives are derived from the curriculum goals, are applied to the program and to groups of students, and are stated in measurable terms. The formulation of *instructional goals* follows and bears a direct relationship to the curriculum goals and objectives, as seen in the following examples: (1) The student will demonstrate his or her ability to read new material silently without great difficulty, and (2) The student will demonstrate his or her ability to read new material orally without difficulty.

Both of the foregoing statements are expectations of each pupil. The statements are couched in general terms and include no criteria of mastery. For each of the instructional goals we may create *instructional objectives*. To promote the goal of reading silently, for example, the teacher might design the following objectives: (1) The student will read silently a passage from the fifth-grade reader and then summarize orally without appreciable error in comprehension each of its four major points, and (2) The student will read silently a passage from the fifth-grade reader and then will write correct responses to eight out of ten written questions provided by the teacher.

To further the goal of reading orally, the teacher might identify the following objectives: (1) The student will read orally from a classroom library book and make no more than four mistakes in pronunciation in a passage of about 100 words, and (2) The student will read orally a passage from a classroom library book and then orally summarize each of the three main points of the passage without appreciable error in comprehension.

Unless an instructional objective is differentiated for a particular sub-group of students—for example, bright, slow, or handicapped—it is expected that every student will master the objective. When instructional objectives are aimed at all students in a given class, they may be called minimal competencies.

State testing programs are designed to assess students' mastery of the minimal competencies—for example, competencies to be achieved in all or selected disciplines at the end of, say, fourth, eighth, or eleventh grade.

Some confusion may exist between curriculum and instructional goals and objectives, for in one sense they both may be designed for all students. The curriculum goals and objectives are broader in nature, are aimed at all students as a group or groups, frequently jump across grade boundaries, often cut across disciplines, and many times are relevant to more than one teacher either within a discipline or among disciplines.

However, there are times when a curriculum objective may be congruent with an instructional objective or, put another way, an instructional objective may repeat a curriculum objective. When we as curriculum planners designate as a curriculum objective improving the scores of all students on a standardized achievement test in mathematics by ten percentile points, we will be pleased that the mathematics curriculum (program) is functioning to that degree. When we as classroom teachers stipulate that all of our pupils score ten percentile points higher on a standardized test of mathematics, we will be pleased with each student who functions that well and may refer to our own instruction as effective if many students achieve that objective.

Though we may state them slightly differently, curriculum and instructional goals and objectives may converge. One is the alter ego of the other, so to speak. Conversely, curriculum and instructional goals and objectives may diverge. When we as curriculum planners desire that 80 percent (even 100 percent) of the seniors with quantitative aptitude test scores at the 75th percentile elect calculus, we are talking about program, not instruction.

The distinctions between curriculum and instructional goals and objectives matter only to the extent that neither of the two sets is overlooked. If an instructional objective repeats a curriculum objective, so be it; it is a perfect fit. On the other hand, instructional objectives by their very nature tend to be more specific than the curriculum goals and objectives, focus on what takes place in the classroom, and come to pass as a result of the individual instructor's efforts. Whatever the degree of congruence, there is a direct and natural progression from curriculum goal to instructional objective.

Domains of Learning

The instructional goals and objectives should be specified for three domains of learning—the cognitive, the affective, and the psychomotor—whenever applicable. Note these three illustrations of different types of learning:

- knowledge of the system of election primaries
- enjoyment in reading
- skill in laying bricks

These examples are illustrative of the three major areas (domains) of learning. Knowledge of the primary system falls into the cognitive domain, enjoyment in reading in the affective domain, and skill in laying bricks in the psychomotor domain.

Cognitive Domain.   Speaking for a committee of college and university examiners, Benjamin S. Bloom defined the cognitive domain as including objectives that "deal with the recall or recognition of knowledge and the development of intellectual abilities and skills."[9] Cognitive learnings, which involve the mental processes, range from memorization to the ability to think and solve problems.

Affective Domain.   David R. Krathwohl, Benjamin S. Bloom, and Bertram B. Masia defined the affective domain as including objectives that "emphasize a feeling tone, an emotion, or a degree of acceptance or rejection."[10] Affective learnings encompass the emotions, feelings, beliefs, attitudes, and values.

Psychomotor Domain.   Robert J. Armstrong, Terry D. Cornell, Robert E. Kraner, and E. Wayne Roberson defined the psychomotor domain as including behaviors that "place primary emphasis on neuromuscular or physical skills and involve different degrees of physical dexterity."[11] Sometimes referred to as "perceptual-motor skills," psychomotor learnings include bodily movements and muscular coordination.

Ordinarily, schools assume responsibility for student achievement in all three broad areas. Although we might visualize the three horses—Cognitive, Affective, and Psychomotor—in the form of a Russian troika, racing three abreast, they are hitched more like a lead horse followed by two abreast. More often than not, Cognitive is in the forefront. On occasion, depending on the mood of the profession and the public, Cognitive is overtaken by Affective or Psychomotor.

The battle over which domain is the most important has endured for many years. With the exception of work by people like Rousseau, Froebel, Pestalozzi, and Neil (Summerhill School, England), most of the rest of the world—if we may generalize on such a vast scale—marches to the beat of the cognitive drummer. Although many fine opportunities for vocational education are provided by many countries, the cognitive domain remains the prestige category and is the entrée to institutions of higher learning. If our horses were pitted in an international race, Affective would come in a poor third.

Judging from the popularity of books critical of public education, the accountability movement in education, the flight to private schools, and the push for national and state assessment in the fundamental disciplines, we might conclude that the American public is partial to the cognitive domain.

---

[9]Benjamin S. Bloom, ed., *Taxonomy of Educational Objectives: The Classification of Educational Goals: Handbook I: Cognitive Domain* (White Plains, N.Y.: Longman, 1956), p. 7. Reprinted with permission.

[10]David R. Krathwohl, Benjamin S. Bloom, and Bertram B. Masia, *Taxonomy of Educational Objectives: The Classification of Educational Goals: Handbook II: Affective Domain* (White Plains, N.Y.: Longman, 1964), p. 7. Reprinted with permission.

[11]Robert J. Armstrong, Terry D. Cornell, Robert E. Kraner, and E. Wayne Roberson, *The Development and Evaluation of Behavioral Objectives* (Worthington, Ohio: Charles A. Jones, 1970), p. 22.

Although we find strong preferences both within and outside the profession for stressing cognitive learnings, I would encourage each teacher to identify and write instructional goals and objectives in all three domains, making allowances for the nature of the subject matter.

Normally, the domains overlap; each possesses elements of the other, even when one is obviously dominant. Thus, it is often difficult to categorize learnings as falling precisely into one domain. For example, we can identify learnings that are primarily psychomotor (running a football play) and secondarily cognitive and affective. We can give examples of learning that are primarily cognitive (civil rights legislation) and secondarily affective. We can offer examples of learnings that are primarily affective (honesty) and secondarily cognitive. We can also identify learnings that are primarily cognitive (constructing an equilateral triangle) and secondarily affective and psychomotor.

Many learnings will obviously fall into single categories. If we discount the bit of affective pleasure a student may feel in knowning the right answer, the formula for finding the area of a triangle (½ base × height) is pretty much a cognitive experience. Doing sit-ups, a psychomotor exercise, requires very little cognition and may even evoke an undesired affective response. Faith in one's fellow man or woman is primarily an affective goal, secondarily cognitive, and usually not psychomotor.

The classroom teacher should identify and write instructional goals and objectives in all three domains, if indeed all three are relevant. It might be asked, "From what cloth do we cut the instructional goals and objectives?" We might respond by saying, "From the same cloth from which we cut the curriculum goals and objectives—the three sources: the needs of the student, of society, and of the subject matter—with the curriculum goals and objectives themselves serving as inspiration."

TAXONOMIC LEVELS

Instructional goals and objectives should be identified at both high and low levels of learning, with greater emphasis being placed on the higher levels. It is obvious that some learnings are more substantive, complex, and important than others. Note, for example, the following learning outcomes, all in the cognitive domain, to see the differences in complexity:

- ☐ The student will name the first president of the United States.
- ☐ The student will read Washington's first inaugural address and summarize the major points.
- ☐ The student will show how some of Washington's ideas apply or do not apply today.
- ☐ The student will analyze Washington's military tactics in the Battle of Yorktown.
- ☐ The student will write a biography of Washington.
- ☐ The student will evaluate Washington's role at the Continental Congress.

The knowledge and skills required for naming the first president of the United States are at a decidedly lower level than those for each of the subsequent objectives. Each succeeding item is progressively more difficult, requiring greater cognitive powers. What we have is a hierarchy of learning outcomes from lowest to highest.

Take the following illustrations from the affective domain:

☐ The student will listen while others express their points of view.
☐ The student will answer a call for volunteers to plant trees in a public park.
☐ The student will express appreciation for the contributions of ethnic groups other than his or her own to the development of our country.
☐ The student will choose nutritious food over junk food.
☐ The student will habitually abide by a set of legal and ethical standards.

As with the examples in the cognitive domain, each objective is progressively more substantial than the preceding one.

Finally, let's look at a set of objectives from the psychomotor domain:

☐ The student will identify a woolen fabric by its feel.
☐ The student will demonstrate how to hold the reins of a horse while cantering.
☐ The student will imitate a right-about-face movement.
☐ The student will mix a batch of mortar and water.
☐ The student will operate a VCR.
☐ The student will arrange an attractive bulletin board.
☐ The student will create an original game requiring physical movements.

The first example for the psychomotor domain—simple identification of the texture of a fabric—demands a much lower level of skill than the creation of an original game involving physical activity.

Cognitive Taxonomy

Bloom and associates developed an extensive taxonomy for classifying educational objectives in the cognitive domain.[12] Of all classification systems, the Bloom taxonomy of the cognitive domain is perhaps the best known and most widely followed. It categorizes the types of cognitive learning outcomes that are featured at all levels of the educational system. Bloom and his associates classified cognitive learnings in six major categories: knowledge, comprehension, application, analysis, synthesis, and evaluation. Let's take each

---

[12]Bloom, *Taxonomy: Cognitive Domain.*

of these categories, refer back to the example previously given, and place it in the appropriate category, as follows:

☐ *Knowledge level:* The student will name the first president of the United States.
☐ *Comprehension level:* The student will read Washington's first inaugural address and summarize the major points.
☐ *Application level:* The student will show how some of Washington's ideas apply or do not apply today.
☐ *Analysis level:* The student will analyze Washington's military tactics in the Battle of Yorktown.
☐ *Synthesis level:* The student will write a biography of George Washington.
☐ *Evaluation level:* The student will evaluate Washington's role at the Continental Congress.

This taxonomy shows learning objectives as classified in a hierarchical fashion from the lowest (knowledge) to the highest (evaluation). A central premise of professional educators is that the higher levels of learning should be stressed. The ability to think, for example, is fostered not through low-level recall of knowledge but through application, analysis, synthesis, and evaluation.

Objectives in the cognitive domain are, of the three domains, the easiest to identify and the simplest to evaluate. They are drawn primarily from the subject matter and are readily measurable, usually by written tests and exercises.

Affective Taxonomy

Shortly after the appearance of the cognitive taxonomy, Krathwohl and others, including Bloom, developed a taxonomy of objectives in the affective domain, which consists of five major categories.[13] We may categorize the affective examples given earlier in the following manner:

☐ *Receiving* (attending): The student will listen while others express their points of view.
☐ *Responding:* The student will answer a call for volunteers to plant a tree in a public park.
☐ *Valuing:* The student will express appreciation for the contributions of ethnic groups other than his or her own to the development of our country.
☐ *Organization:* The student will choose nutritious food over junk food.
☐ *Characterization by value or value complex:* The student will habitually abide by a set of legal and ethical standards.

The affective domain poses a serious problem for educators. Historically, parents and educators have viewed the school's primary mission as cognitive learning. Affective learning has typically held a lesser position. As mentioned

---

[13]Krathwohl et al., *Taxonomy: Affective Domain.*

elsewhere in this text, the affective domain is still not accepted by some educators as a legitimate focus of the school. On the other hand, some educators feel that affective outcomes are more important than others.

Arthur W. Combs stated the case for affective education, tying it to the development of adequate personalities, as follows:

> For many generations education has done an excellent job of *imparting* information.... Our greatest failures are those connected with the problems of helping people to behave differently as a result of the information we have provided them.... Adequate persons are, among other factors, the product of strong values. The implication seems to be clear, then, that educators must be interested in and concerned with values. Unfortunately, this is not the case in many schools and classrooms today. The emphasis is too often on the narrowly scientific and impersonally objective.... Education must be concerned with the values, beliefs, convictions, and doubts of students. These realities as perceived by an individual are just as important, if not more so, as the so-called objective facts.[14]

Bloom, Hastings, and Madaus attested to the neglect of instruction for affective learning when they said:

> Throughout the years American education has maintained that among its most important ideals is the development of such attributes as interests, desirable attitudes, appreciation, values, commitment, and willpower. However, the types of outcomes which in fact receive the highest priorities in our schools, to the detriment of these affective goals, are verbal-conceptual in nature.[15]

Bloom, Hastings, and Madaus identified these reasons for the neglect of affective learning:

> Our system of education is geared to producing people who can deal with the words, concepts, and mathematical or scientific symbols so necessary for success in our technological society.[16]
>
> Standardized tests used by the schools ... lay stress on intellectual tasks.[17]
>
> Characteristics of this kind, unlike achievement competencies, are considered to be a private rather than a public matter.[18]

Some hold that affective outcomes are the province of the home and the church and that instruction in the affective domain smacks of indoctrination. "One of the reasons for the failure to give instructional emphasis to affective outcomes is related to the Orwellian overtones which attitudinal and value-

---

[14]Yearbook (Alexandria, Va. Association for Supervision and Curriculum Development, 1962), p. 200. Reprinted with permission of the Association for Supervision and Curriculum Development and Arthur W. Combs. Copyright ©1962 by the Association for Supervision and Curriculum Development. All rights reserved.

[15]From *Handbook on Formative and Summative Evaluation of Student Learning*, p. 200, by Benjamin S. Bloom, J. Thomas Hastings, and George F. Madaus. Copyright ©1971 by McGraw-Hill. Used with the permission of McGraw-Hill Book Company.

[16]Ibid.

[17]Ibid., p. 226.

[18]Ibid., p. 227.

oriented instruction often conjures up in the minds of teachers and the public," said Bloom and coauthors.[19]

Whose values should be taught? Are white, Anglo-Saxon, Protestant, middle-class values the ones to be promoted? Whence come the values to be selected? Although, as I noted in the preceding chapter, some people believe that values cannot or should not be taught in school, others like Theodore R. Sizer held that values can and should be taught.[20] If affective learnings should be taught and values should be among those learnings, then identifying common values is an essential task for the curriculum planner.[21] Robert S. Gilchrist and Bernice R. Roberts urged educators to include values in the educational program:

> Somehow, the notion that everyone develops and formulates his own particular value system has resulted in the educator's choice of a do-nothing position. How can we continue with this stance when the provision of experiences for the development of a value system, possibly the most important, influencing task of the educator, is hierarchically the task of the schooling process?[22]

Affective objectives are both difficult to identify and extremely difficult—often impossible—to measure, and these difficulties constitute another reason why teachers tend to shy away from the affective domain. In Chapter 12 we will discuss some approaches to the evaluation of student performance in the affective domain.

Psychomotor Taxonomies

For some reason difficult to fathom, the development and use of a taxonomy in the psychomotor domain have not been given as much emphasis as in the cognitive and affective domains. Taxonomies of the psychomotor domain do exist, but they seem not to be as widely known as the taxonomies of the other two domains.

The examples from the psychomotor domain given earlier follow the classification system developed by Elizabeth Jane Simpson.[23] Following her taxonomy, we categorize these illustrations as follows:

☐ *Perception:* The student will identify a woolen fabric by its feel.
☐ *Set:* The student will demonstrate how to hold the reins of a horse when cantering.
☐ *Guided response:* The student will imitate a right-about-face movement.
☐ *Mechanism:* The student will mix a batch of mortar and water.

---

[19]Ibid., p. 226.

[20]Theodore R. Sizer, *Horace's Compromise: The Dilemma of the American High School* (Boston: Houghton Mifflin, 1984), Chapter 6.

[21]See p. 185 of this text for one attempt to identify common values of American society.

[22]Robert S. Gilchrist and Bernice R. Roberts, *Curriculum Development: A Humanized Systems Approach* (Belmont, Calif.: Lear Siegler/Fearon, 1974), p. 13.

[23]Elizabeth Jane Simpson, "The Classification of Educational Objectives in the Psychomotor Domain," *The Psychomotor Domain*, vol. 3 (Washington, D.C.: Gryphon House, 1972), pp. 43–56. Adapted with permission.

□ *Complex overt response:* The student will operate a VCR.
□ *Adaptation:* The student will arrange an attractive bulletin board display.
□ *Origination:* The student will create an original game requiring physical movements.

Anita J. Harrow provided a clarifying description for each of the categories of the Simpson taxonomy. She identified perception as interpreting, set as preparing, guided response as learning, mechanism as habituating, complex overt response as performing, adaptation as modifying, and origination as creating.[24] Harrow proposed her own taxonomy for classifying movement behaviors of learners. Her model consists of the following six classification levels:

1.00 Reflex Movements
    1.10 Segmental Reflexes
    1.20 Intersegmental Reflexes
    1.30 Suprasegmental Reflexes
2.00 Basic-Fundamental Movements
    2.10 Locomotor Movements
    2.20 Non-Locomotor Movements
    2.30 Manipulative Movements
3.00 Perceptual Abilities
    3.10 Kinesthetic Discrimination
    3.20 Visual Discrimination
    3.30 Auditory Discrimination
    3.40 Tactile Discrimination
    3.50 Coordinated Abilities
4.00 Physical Abilities
    4.10 Endurance
    4.20 Strength
    4.30 Flexibility
    4.40 Agility
5.00 Skilled Movements
    5.10 Simple Adaptive Skill
    5.20 Computed Adaptive Skill
    5.30 Complex Adaptive Skill
6.00 Non-Discursive Communication
    6.10 Expressive Movement
    6.20 Interpretive Movement[25]

The use of the taxonomies of the three domains as guidelines can lead to more effective instruction. The taxonomies direct attention to the three major domains of learning and to the subdivisions of each. Arranged in a hierarchical fashion, the taxonomies should serve to stimulate teachers to move their learners from the lower to the higher and more enduring levels of learning in each domain.

---

[24] Anita J. Harrow, *A Taxonomy of the Psychomotor Domain: A Guide for Developing Behavioral Objectives* (White Plains, N.Y.: Longman, 1972), p. 27.
[25] Ibid., pp. 1–2. Reprinted with permission.

RULES FOR WRITING

Instructional goals and objectives should follow a few simple rules for writing. Early in this chapter we distinguished instructional goals from instructional objectives. Instructional goals defined student performance in general terms whereas instructional objectives defined it in more specific and measurable terms.

Instructional goals are often poorly stated instructional objectives. For example, "The student will know names of the first five presidents of the United States" is an instructional goal because it is not written in measurable and observable terms. We might change this instructional goal into an instructional objective by writing, "The student will name correctly and in order the first five presidents of the United States."

On the other hand, an instructional goal may serve the purpose of pointing out the direction that leads to instructional objectives. For example, the instructional goal, "The student will develop an awareness of energy needs" could lead to a multitude of instructional objectives—for example, "The student will identify the five leading oil-producing countries," "The student will identify three sources of energy that are alternatives to oil," "The student will determine how much the price of imported oil has risen in the last ten years," and "The student will propose and describe three ways Americans can conserve energy."

An instructional goal may thus be written in rather broad, imprecise terms. On the other hand, it may be stated simply as a topic—for example, "The Organized Labor Movement." Implied in the topic is the instructional goal, "The student will develop an understanding of the organized labor movement."

Though variations in style of formulating instructional goals and objectives are certainly possible, I incline toward starting instructional goals and objectives with "The student . . . " (in the singular) in order to (1) signal the meaning "each student" and (2) help distinguish from curriculum goals and objectives, which I begin with "Students . . . " (in the plural) to convey the meaning of "students in general." Although it is preferable for all plans to be committed to paper, it is possible for teachers to keep the instructional goals in mind and to move directly to the writing of instructional objectives.

Three Elements of an Instructional Objective

The literature generally recommends that three elements or components be included in an instructional (behavioral) objective:

1. the behavior expected of the student
2. the conditions under which the behavior is to be demonstrated
3. the degree of mastery required[26]

---

[26]For helpful discussion on writing instructional objectives, see Robert F. Mager, *Preparing Instructional Objectives*, 2nd ed. (Belmont, Calif.: Fearon, 1975).

Specifying Behavior. When specifying behavior, instructors should choose, as often as possible, action verbs that are subject to measurement and observation. Action words in particular distinguish instructional objectives from instructional goals. The verb "understanding," for example, is unsuitable in an instructional objective because it is neither measurable nor observable. Thus, "The student will understand his or her rights under the first ten amendments to the U.S. Constitution" is an instructional goal, not an instructional objective. If "understand" is changed to a performance-oriented verb, we can create an instructional objective, such as "The student will write summaries of the first ten amendments to the U.S. Constitution." This cognitive objective can be raised from the comprehension level to the evaluation level by modifying the statement: "The student will write a paper listing the principal rights in the first ten amendments to the U.S. Constitution and will evaluate the importance of each right to us today." The instructional objective, therefore, must include behavior expected of the learner as a result of exposure to instruction.

To help with the writing of instructional objectives, the teacher may wish to develop lists of behaviorally oriented verbs that can be used for each category of the three domains. Examples are shown in Table 10–1.

Specifying Conditions. The conditions under which the learner demonstrates the behavior should be specified, if necessary. In the objective, "Given a list of needs of this community, the student will rank them in order of priority," "Given a list of needs of this community" is the condition under which the behavior is performed. It is an essential part of the objective. As an additional illustration, in the objective "On the classroom wall map the student will point out the People's Republic of China," "On the classroom wall map" is the necessary condition. However, if students are to point out several countries on the same wall map, it becomes redundant and therefore unnecessary to repeat "On the classroom wall map" for each instructional objective. What the instructor should do in this case is write: "On the classroom wall map the student will point out. . . . " The instructor should then list all the geographical features to be pointed out.

To conserve the instructor's valuable time, obvious conditions need not be specified; they are simply understood. There is no need, for example, for the teacher to waste time placing before an objective, "Given paper and pen, the student will write an essay on the work of Mark Twain." Unless the use of paper and pen has some special significance and is not routine, it need not be specified. Adding routine and obvious conditions to instructional objectives can border on the ridiculous and can create an adverse reaction to the writing of instructional objectives at all. If we may exaggerate to stress the point, we do not wish to see the objective: "Given a tennis ball, a tennis racket, a tennis court, a net, a fair day, proper dress, and preferably an opponent also equipped with ball, racket, and proper dress, the student will demonstrate how to serve a tennis ball," "The student will demonstrate how to serve a tennis ball" is sufficient *ad diem,* as the lawyers say.

TABLE 10-1   Behaviorally oriented verbs for the domains of learning

COGNITIVE DOMAIN (BLOOM TAXONOMY)

LEVEL	VERBS
Knowledge	identify, specify, state
Comprehension	explain, restate, translate
Application	apply, solve, use
Analysis	analyze, compare, contrast
Synthesis	design, develop, plan
Evaluation	assess, evaluate, judge

AFFECTIVE DOMAIN (KRATHWOHL TAXONOMY)

LEVEL	VERBS
Receiving	accept, demonstrate awareness, listen
Responding	comply with, engage in, volunteer
Valuing	express a preference for, show appreciation by stating, show concern by stating
Organization	adhere to, defend, synthesize
Characterization by value or value complex	demonstrate empathy, express willingness to be ethical, modify behavior

PSYCHOMOTOR DOMAIN (SIMPSON TAXONOMY)

LEVEL	VERBS
Perception	distinguish, identify, select
Set	assume a position, demonstrate, show
Guided response	attempt, imitate, try
Mechanism	make habitual, practice, repeat
Complex overt response	carry out, operate, perform
Adaptation	adapt, change, revise
Origination	create, design, originate

NOTE: For a useful listing of verbs in the affective, cognitive and psychomotor domains, see Gronlund, *Stating Objectives,* pp. 26–34, 69–72. For a useful listing of verbs and direct objects applicable to the Bloom and Krathwohl taxonomies, see Newton S. Metfessel, William B. Michael, and Donald A. Kirsner, "Instrumentation of Bloom's and Krathwohl's Taxonomies for the Writing of Educational Objectives," *Psychology in the Schools* 6, no. 3 (July 1969); 227–231.

Specifying the Criterion.   The statement of the instructional objective should include the acceptable standard or criterion of mastery of the behavior if it is not obvious. For example, a French teacher might write the following statement: "The student will translate the following sentences." There is no need to write the condition, "from French to English"; the students can see that. There is no need to specify the criterion "into good English" (which should be routinely expected behavior) or "with 100 percent accuracy" or "with no errors." Unless a criterion is specified, it can be assumed that the teacher wishes students to achieve 100 percent accuracy.

Some objectives require more elaborate criteria than others. For example, let's go back to the illustration, "The student will write an essay on the work of Mark Twain." We could embellish this objective with various criteria, some of which are and are not essential. "In legible handwriting" or "free of typographical errors" should be normal expectations and, therefore, do not have to appear in every instructional objective. On the other hand, if the instructor desires an essay with no more than three spelling errors, with no more than three grammatical errors, and with all the footnotes and bibliographical entries in correct form, that information should be conveyed to the students. The criteria are particularly important if the objective is being used as a test item. It is a necessary and sound principle of evaluation that students be informed by what standards they will be evaluated.

Robert H. Davis, Lawrence T. Alexander, and Stephen L. Yelon listed six types of standards and gave examples of each, as follows:

1. When mere OCCURRENCE of the behavior is sufficient, describe the behavior. Example: The knot will be tied loosely as in the photograph.
2. When ACCURACY is important, provide a statement of acceptable range or deviation. Example: The answer must be correct to the nearest whole number.
3. If the number of ERRORS is important, state the number. Example: with a maximum of one error.
4. If TIME or SPEED is important, state the minimal level. Example: within five seconds; five units per minute.
5. If a KNOWN REFERENCE provides the standard, state the reference. Example: Perform the sequence of steps in the same order as given in the text.
6. If the CONSEQUENCES of the behavior are important, describe them or provide a model. Example: Conduct the class so that all students participate in the discussion.[27]

Novice instructors sometimes ask how the teacher decides on the criteria. How do you decide whether to permit three or four errors or whether a student should complete the task in ten rather than five minutes? These decisions are based on the teacher's past experience with students and on the teacher's professional and, if you will, arbitrary judgment. After a few years, the teacher begins to sense what is possible for students to accomplish and proceeds on that knowledge. Certain traditions may also guide the teacher. For example, 70 percent is considered by most students, teachers, and parents as so-so; 80 percent is considered not bad; 90 percent is considered good. Thus criteria in the 70 percent to 100 percent range often show up in statements of instructional objectives.

Although it is relatively simple to specify objectives in the cognitive and psychomotor domain, specifying criteria in the affective domain is enough to

---

[27]From *Learning System Design: An Approach to the Improvement of Instruction,* pp. 39–40, by Robert H. Davis, Lawrence T. Alexander, and Stephen L. Yelon. Copyright ©1974 by McGraw-Hill. Used with the permission of McGraw-Hill Book Company.

tax one's soul. We shall wrestle with the problem of establishing criteria for affective objectives in Chapter 12. At this point, however, we should mention that it is usually impossible to specify criteria for objectives in the affective domain. What criteria, for example, should we append to this objective: "The student will express a sense of pride in his or her country"? Should the Student's response be fervent? Passionate? The affective domain presents its unique instructional problems.

To the standards component, Davis, Alexander, and Yelon added a stability component—that is, the number of opportunities the student will be given and the number of times he or she must succeed in demonstrating the behavior.[28] We may illustrate the stability component with this example: "The student will type at least 50 words per minute on each of three successive tries." Analyzing this objective shows that to type is the behavior; the conditions are understood (a typewriter, paper, desk, chair, typewriter ribbon); the performance criterion is at least 50 words per minute; and the stability component is on each of three successive tries.

Generally speaking, instructional objectives should consist of at least three components: the behavior (often called the terminal behavior), the conditions, and the criterion.

VALIDATING AND DETERMINING PRIORITY OF INSTRUCTIONAL GOALS AND OBJECTIVES

Instructional goals and objectives should be validated and put in order of priority. Teachers should know whether the instructional goals and objectives are appropriate and which are the more important.

In practice, it is far simpler to validate and rank instructional than curriculum goals and objectives. Instructional goals and objectives are not normally submitted to lay groups or students for this process nor to administrators with any regularity. Nor do they need to be, since instructional goals and objectives are content-specific. To make a judgment on their validity and to decide which are essential requires a foundation both in the subject matter being taught and in the methods for teaching that subject matter. The subject matter is often technical and beyond the knowledge and skills of lay persons and students. Instructional matters are the prerogative of persons trained in their fields of specialization.

As a result, far fewer persons need to be involved in validating and establishing priorities of instructional goals and objectives than is the case with curriculum goals and objectives.

Validating and ranking of instructional goals and objectives are usually accomplished by referring to the adopted textbooks, reference books, and curriculum guides. The authors of these materials serve as the persons who validate

---

[28]Ibid., p. 41.

and set priorities. This method of validating and ordering of instructional goals and objectives is, by far, the most common.

The classroom teacher can also seek help with validating and ranking instructional goals and objectives from members of his or her team, grade level, or department, other knowledgeable faculty members, curriculum consultants, and supervisors. Consultants and supervisors trained and experienced in special fields should also be able to help the classroom teacher decide which instructional goals and objectives are appropriate to the subject and to the learners and which ones should be stressed. Finally, teachers may seek advice from acknowledged experts in the subject area outside the school system as well as from specialists in other school systems or in higher education institutions.

SUMMARY

Instructional goals and objectives are directly related to the previously specified curriculum goals and objectives. Instructional goals provide direction for specifying instructional objectives.

Learning outcomes may be identified in three major domains: the cognitive, the affective, and the psychomotor. The cognitive domain is the world of the intellect; the affective, the locale of emotions, beliefs, values, and attitudes; and the psychomotor, the territory of perceptual-motor skills.

Taxonomies of each domain classify objectives in a hierarchical fashion from the lowest to the highest level of learning. Taxonomies are useful in revealing the types of learning encompassed in each domain and in guiding instructors toward placing greater emphasis on learnings at the higher levels.

Instructional goals are statements written in nonbehavioral terms without criteria of mastery. With the possible exception of outcomes in the affective domain, instructional objectives should be written in measurable and observable terms.

Whenever practical and necessary, instructional objectives should consist of three components: the behavior that learners will demonstrate, the conditions under which the behavior is to be demonstrated, and the criterion to master the behavior.

Instructors validate instructional goals and objectives and place them in order of priority by referring to text materials written by experts and by seeking the judgments of knowledgeable colleagues, supervisors, and consultants from both within and without the school system.

QUESTIONS FOR DISCUSSION

1. In what ways do instructional goals and objectives differ from curriculum goals and objectives?
2. Is it necessary to specify both instructional goals and instructional objectives?

3. What are the purposes of writing instructional goals and objectives?
4. What are some alternatives to writing behavioral objectives?
5. Do instructional goals and objectives limit the creativity or artistry of the teacher? Explain.

SUPPLEMENTARY EXERCISES

1. Define "cognitive," "affective," and "psychomotor."
2. Define the word "taxomony."
3. Distinguish between a nonbehavioral goal and a behavioral objective.
4. Consult the Bloom taxonomy of the cognitive domain and prepare a list of verbs that might be used for writing objectives in each category.
5. Consult the Krathwohl taxonomy of the affective domain and prepare a list of verbs that might be used for writing objectives in each category.
6. Consult the Harrow or Simpson taxonomies of the psychomotor domain and prepare a list of verbs that might be used for writing objectives in each category.
7. Write one instructional objective for each of the six major categories of the Bloom taxonomy of the cognitive domain.
8. Write one instructional objective for each of the five major categories of the Krathwohl taxonomy of the affective domain.
9. Write one instructional objective for each of the major categories of either the Simpson or the Harrow taxonomy of the psychomotor domain.
10. State the three components of an instructional objective.
11. List and give examples of six types of performance standards that may be included in an instructional objective.
12. Describe what is meant by "stability component" and give an example.
13. Classify the following instructional objectives as to the principal domain and major category according to Bloom, Krathwohl, or Simpson. (Answers to this exercise follow.) This exercise is taken from a workshop prepared for the Dade-Monroe County (Florida) Teacher Education Center.
    The student will:
    a. solve ten multiplication problems in 20 minutes and achieve a score of eight correct.
    b. cut and splice a strip of film.
    c. spell 15 words correctly.
    d. respond to a call to serve on an environmental clean-up committee.
    e. using the financial pages of the daily newspaper, study the closing prices of several common stocks on one day of a particular week and tell whether the value of the stocks has gone up or down or remained the same the next day of that week.
    f. using a wall map and pointer, trace the path of the Mississippi River from source to mouth.
    g. demonstrate an awareness that school spirit must be improved.

h. write a paper of ten pages, typed double-spaced, on the topic "Traveling in Space." The paper must be scientifically accurate and in good English. It must contain at least two footnotes and a bibliography of at least five references.

i. with a compass, draw a circle that has a two-inch diameter.

j. express admiration for skills shown by a famous actor or actress.

k. identify a living American author whose works he or she believes will become classics and, by referring to the author's works, support his or her choice of author.

l. design and make a pair of earrings out of black coral.

m. demonstrate the proper way to hold the bowling ball before beginning the approach.

n. using a musical instrument, convert a classical theme to a rock or disco beat.

o. regularly donate money or goods to a charity.

p. explain reasons for his or her preference for a political party.

q. apply epoxy glue to join two pieces of wood together following directions on the label.

r. identify the smell of baking bread.

ANSWERS TO EXERCISE 13

a. cognitive–application
b. psychomotor–complex overt response
c. cognitive–knowledge
d. affective–responding
e. cognitive–analysis
f. cognitive–comprehension
g. affective–receiving
h. cognitive–synthesis
i. psychomotor–mechanism

j. affective–valuing
k. cognitive–evaluation
l. psychomotor–origination
m. psychomotor–set
n. psychomotor–adaptation
o. affective–characterization by value or value complex
p. affective–organization
q. psychomotor–guided response
r. psychomotor–perception

14. Choose one curriculum goal and write two curriculum objectives for it. Then write one instructional goal for one of the curriculum objectives and two instructional objectives for the instructional goal.

15. Using the appropriate format, explain the correct way of writing an individualized education program (IEP). In your explanation give examples of both annual goals and behavioral objectives derived from the goals.

16. In the following items, put a CG if you believe the item is a curriculum goal, CO for a curriculum objective, IG for an instructional goal, and IO for an instructional objective (answers follow):

_____ a. Students will develop an awareness of major social and economic problems of the community.

_____ b. Without using a calculator, the student will solve the following division problem, carrying out the answer to two places: $6,859 \div 27$.

_____ c. Students will increase their use of the school library as evidenced by a ten percent rise in the circulation of library books over the previous year.

_____ d. The student will develop an appreciation for *Macbeth*.

_____ e. By the end of the year, all students will have engaged in at least one community service project.

_____ f. The student will understand why the United States entered the Vietnam War.

_____ g. The student will distinguish between the sounds of ă and ā.

_____ h. Students will improve their skills in aesthetic expression.

_____ i. The student will know the functions of the executive, legislative, and judicial branches of the government.

_____ j. Students will improve their skills in composition.

ANSWERS TO EXERCISE 16

a.	CG	b.	IO	c.	CO	d.	IG	e.	CO
f.	IG	g.	IO	h.	CG	i.	IG	j.	CG

BIBLIOGRAPHY

Armstrong, Robert J., Cornell, Terry D., Kraner, Robert E., and Roberson, E. Wayne. *The Development and Evaluation of Behavioral Objectives*. Worthington, Ohio: Charles A. Jones, 1970.

Bloom, Benjamin S., ed. *Taxonomy of Educational Objectives: The Classification of Educational Goals: Handbook I: Cognitive Domain*. White Plains, N.Y.: Longman, 1956.

Bloom, Benjamin S., Hastings, J. Thomas, and Madaus, George F. *Handbook on Formative and Summative Evaluation of Student Learning*. New York: McGraw-Hill, 1971.

Brandt, Ronald S. and Tyler, Ralph W. "Goals and Objectives." In Fenwick W. English, ed., *Fundamental Curriculum Decisions*, 1983 Yearbook, 40–52. Alexandria, Va.: Association for Supervision and Curriculum Development, 1983.

Briggs, Leslie J. *Handbook of Procedures for the Design of Instruction*. Washington, D.C.: American Institutes for Research, 1970.

Burton, William H. *The Guidance of Learning Activities*, 3rd ed. New York: Appleton-Century-Crofts, 1962.

Combs, Arthur W., ed. *Perceiving, Behaving, Becoming; A New Focus for Education*, 1962 Yearbook. Alexandria, Va.: Association for Supervision and Curriculum Development, 1962.

Davies, Ivor K. *Objectives in Curriculum Design*. London: McGraw-Hill (UK), 1976.

Davis, Robert H., Alexander, Lawrence T., and Yelon, Stephen L. *Learning System Design: An Approach to the Improvement of Instruction*. New York: McGraw-Hill, 1974.

Dick, Walter and Carey, Lou. *The Systematic Design of Instruction*, 2nd ed. Glenview, Ill.: Scott, Foresman, 1985.

Dillman, Caroline Matheny and Rahmlow, Harold F. *Writing Instructional Objectives*. Belmont, Calif.: Fearon, 1972.

Gagné, Robert M. and Briggs, Leslie J. *Principles of Instructional Design*. New York: Holt Rinehart and Winston, 1974.

Gilchrist, Robert S. and Roberts, Bernice R. *Curriculum Development: A Humanized Systems Approach*. Belmont, Calif.: Lear Siegler/Fearon, 1974.

Gronlund, Norman E. *Stating Objectives for Classroom Instruction,* 2nd ed. New York: Macmillan, 1978.

Harrow, Anita J. *A Taxonomy of the Psychomotor Domain: A Guide for Developing Behavioral Objectives*. White Plains, N.Y.: Longman, 1972.

Kibler, Robert J., Barker, Larry L., and Miles, David T. *Behavioral Objectives and Instruction*. Boston: Allyn and Bacon, 1970.

Kibler, Robert J., Cegala, Donald J., Miles, David T., and Barker, Larry L. *Objectives for Instruction and Evaluation*. Boston: Allyn and Bacon, 1974.

Krathwohl, David R., Bloom, Benjamin S., and Masia, Bertram B. *Taxonomy of Educational Objectives: The Classification of Educational Goals: Handbook II: Affective Domain*. White Plains, N.Y.: Longman, 1964.

McAshan, H. H. *Competency-Based Education and Behavioral Objectives*. Englewood Cliffs, N.J.: Educational Technology Publications, 1979.

Mager, Robert F. *Preparing Instructional Objectives,* 2nd ed. Belmont, Calif.: Fearon, 1975.

Nelson, Annabelle. *Curriculum Design Techniques*. Dubuque, Iowa: William C. Brown, 1990.

Oliva, Peter F. *The Secondary School Today*. 2nd ed. New York: Harper & Row, 1972.

_____. *Supervision for Today's Schools*. 3rd ed. White Plains, N.Y.: Longman, 1989.

Orlosky, Donald E. and Smith, B. Othanel. *Curriculum Development: Issues and Insights*. Chicago: Rand McNally, 1978.

Popham, W. James. "Practical Ways of Improving Curriculum via Measurable Objectives." *Bulletin of the National Associa-tion of Secondary School Principals* 55, no 355 (May 1971): 76–90.

_____. *Systematic Instruction*. Englewood Cliffs, N.J.: Prentice-Hall, 1970.

Popham, W. James, and Baker, Eva L. *Establishing Instructional Goals*. Englewood Cliffs, N.J.: Prentice-Hall, 1970.

Popham, W. James, Eisner, Elliot W., Sullivan, Howard J., and Tyler, Louise L. *Instructional Objectives*. AERA Monograph Series on Curriculum Evaluation, no. 3. Chicago: Rand McNally, 1969.

Raths, James D. "Teaching Without Specific Objectives." *Educational Leadership* 28, no. 7 (April 1971): 714–720.

Simpson, Elizabeth Jane. "The Classification of Educational Objectives in the Psychomotor Domain." In *The Psychomotor Domain*, vol. 3, 43–56. Washington, D.C.: Gryphon House, 1972.

Tillman, Murray. *Troubleshooting Classroom Problems: A Practical Guide*. Glenview, Ill.: Scott, Foresman, 1982.

Tillman, Murray et al. *Learning to Teach*. Lexington, Mass.: D. C. Heath, 1976.

Turnbull, Ann, Strickland, Bonnie B., and Brantley, John C. *Developing and Implementing Individualized Education Programs*. Columbus, Ohio: Charles E. Merrill, 1978.

Tyler, Ralph W. *Basic Principles of Curriculum and Instruction*. Chicago: University of Chicago Press, 1949.

Vargas, Julie S. *Writing Worthwhile Behavioral Objectives*. New York: Harper & Row, 1972.

Westinghouse Learning Press. *Behavioral Objectives: A Guide to Individualizing,* 4 vols. Sunnyvale, Calif.: Westinghouse Learning Press, 1977.

_____. *Learning Objectives for Individualized Instruction,* 4 vols. Sunnyvale, Calif.: Westinghouse Learning Press, 1977.

Wulf, Kathleen M., and Schave, Barbara. *Curriculum Design: A Handbook for Education*. Glenview, Ill.: Scott, Foresman, 1984.

FILMSTRIP-AUDIOTAPE PROGRAMS

Vimcet Associates, P.O. Box 24714, Los Angeles, Calif. 90024:

Educational Objectives. 1967.

Selecting Appropriate Educational Objectives. 1967.

Defining Content for Objectives. 1969.

Identifying Affective Objectives. 1969.

Humanizing Educational Objectives. 1972.

TRAINING PACKAGE

Objectives for Instructional Programs. Insgroup, Inc., 16052 Beach Boulevard, Huntington Beach, Calif. 92647. Program on how to develop objectives, create instructional plans, and measure results. Filmstrip, audio cassette, response forms, programmed textbook, reference pamphlet, reference chart, and coordinator's guide.

VIDEOTAPES

Association for Supervision and Curriculum Development, 1250 N. Pitt Street. Alexandria, Va. 22314.

Instructional Decisions for Long-Term Learning. Four videotapes and leader's guide, authored by Pat Wolfe. Titles are:

The Student's Mind, 30 min.

Guidelines for Instructional Decisions, 1 hr.

Increasing Student Participation, 30 min.

Support for Teacher Decision Making, 1 hr.

CHAPTER ELEVEN

Selecting and Implementing Strategies of Instruction

After studying this chapter you should be able to:

1. Define style, model, method, and skills of teaching and state how each relates to the selection of instructional strategies.

2. Distinguish between generic and specific teaching skills.

3. Present a rationale for using a unit plan.

4. Relate daily lesson planning to long-range planning.

DECIDING ON INSTRUCTIONAL STRATEGIES

It's the planning period. The twelfth-grade American history teacher just left the teachers' lounge where she consumed a cup of coffee and chatted with her colleagues. She is seated now at a carrel in the teachers' work room, curriculum guide and history textbook before her. The topic to be studied by the students is World War II—the European Theater. Conscientious planner that she is, she asks herself, "What is the best way to go about teaching this topic?" "What methods shall I use?" "What strategies are possible? suitable?" "How do I put together plans for instruction?" "Which suggestions from the curriculum guide shall I adopt?" She jots down a number of approaches that she might use in creating a learning unit on the topic:

- Have the students read the appropriate chapters and come to class prepared to discuss them.
- Devise some key questions to give the class and let them find the answers as they read the chapter.
- Lecture to the class, adding points not covered in the text.
- Have each student write a paper on selected aspects of the war, such as the invasion of Normandy, the Battle of the Bulge, the crossing of the Rhine, and so on.
- Have each student select a related but different topic—for example, the opposing military leaders—and present an oral report to the class.
- Show the film *The Longest Day* on the invasion of Normandy, then follow it up with small group discussion and independent study on topics of interest to the students.
- Have the students draw charts of the tactics of both sides of selected major battles.
- Have the students read chapters in the textbook and give them quizzes in class the next day.
- Using a large classroom wall map of Europe or a small map with an opaque projector, point out the most significant geographical features of the area.
- Write a number of objective test items that will be incorporated in the end-of-unit test and drill the students on the answers as the topic is discussed.
- Invite a combat veteran of the war in Europe to recount his experiences.
- Have students choose books on the topic from the school or public library, read them, and present oral reports to the class, comparing what they have read in the library books with accounts in the textbook.
- Make comparisons between World War I and World War II as to causes, numbers of combatants, numbers of casualties, battle tactics, and aftermaths.

The teacher must decide how many days she will devote to the topic, whether she will use any or all of the approaches considered, which approaches she will use first, and how she will put the selected approaches together.

If you refer back to Figure 10–1, pp. 374–375, you will note that selecting strategies is the next step called for in the Instructional Model. In this text, "strategy" broadly encompasses the methods, procedures, and techniques the teacher uses to present the subject matter to the students and to bring about effective outcomes. A strategy ordinarily includes multiple procedures or techniques. Lecturing, for example, can include procedures such as handing out charts and calling for evaluations at the end of the lecture. It may also include techniques like set induction and closure, which are generic teaching skills.

Among the common instructional strategies are the lecture, small group discussion, independent study, library research, mediated instruction, repetitive drill, and laboratory work. To this list we can add coaching, tutoring, testing, and going on field trips. We could include the inquiry or discovery, inductive, and deductive methods. We could add programmed instruction, problem solving, and questioning. Suffice it to say that the teacher has at his or her disposal a great variety of strategies for implementing instruction.

How does the teacher decide which strategy or strategies to use? The teacher may find a curriculum guide that will detail not only strategies to be used but also objectives, suggested resources, and suggested evaluation techniques.

Unfortunately, curriculum guides do not always exist for topics that the teacher wishes to emphasize, and often when they do exist and are accessible, they do not fit the teacher's and students' purposes. Consequently, the teacher must exercise professional judgment and choose the strategies to be employed. Selecting strategies becomes a less difficult problem when the teacher recognizes that instructional strategies are derived from five major sources. Let's briefly examine each of these sources.

SOURCES OF STRATEGIES

Objectives as Source

The choice of strategies is limited at the onset by the specified instructional objectives. Although an almost infinite number of techniques for carrying out instruction may exist, only a finite number apply to any particular objective. For example, how many alternatives does the teacher have to teach the number fact that $2 \times 2 = 4$? He or she may tell the students or give a chalk-talk using the blackboard; have the students repeat again and again the $2\times$ table or use flash cards for drill purposes; have students practice using a workbook, an abacus, or a slide rule; have students practice the Korean system *chisenbop;* or let pupils use a calculator or a printed multiplication table. We are rapidly exhausting the possibilities. Of course, not all of the possible courses of action will be suitable or acceptable to the teacher or the students, which limits the range of possibilities even more.

How many techniques suggest themselves for accomplishing the following objectives? The student will

☐ purify water by boiling
☐ write an editorial
☐ sew a zipper into a garment
☐ demonstrate a high jump
☐ help keep his or her school clean

Sometimes the strategy is obvious. There is no practical alternative; in essence, as "the medium is the message" (to use Marshall McLuhan's words), the objective *is* the strategy. The student will demonstrate a high jump, for example, by performing that act. No amount of "teaching about" high jumping will permit the students to demonstrate that they can perform the high jump.

Subject Matter as Source

Subject matter provides a source of instructional strategies. With some subject matter, selecting strategies is relatively simple. If we are teaching a course in television repair, certain operations must be mastered, such as checking the circuits, replacing the picture tube, replacing the solid state components, and adjusting the color.

The teacher must zero in on the subject matter and determine what principal facts, understandings, attitudes, appreciations, and skills must be mastered by the learners. Whereas some subject areas have a reputation for being harder *to learn*—for example, calculus, chemistry, and physics—others are more difficult *to teach*. Although learners may have difficulty balancing chemical equations, the strategies for teaching this content are fairly straightforward: lecture-demonstration, followed by ample practice, followed by testing. Less apparent, however, are strategies for teaching the dictum "Thou shalt not cheat." What would be the most effective methods for inculcating an attitude of disapproval of cheating? How would the teacher test for mastery of this affective outcome?

Teaching about a subject as opposed to teaching a subject is an approach that even experienced teachers must guard against. We have alluded to this practice in the instance of teaching students to high jump. We can find other illustrations as well. For example, teachers who require students to commit grammar rules to memory often test only a knowledge of these rules rather than an ability to apply them. Rather than use the library, students are sometimes confined to studying the Library of Congress cataloging system only in the English classroom. Again, students are permitted to verbalize what a balanced meal is but are not required to select or prepare one.

It is easy to be trapped into teaching about desired outcomes in the affective domain. Students read about democracy as a way of life but are not given the opportunity—sometimes inadvertently, sometimes deliberately—to practice democracy in the school. Students are lectured on the importance of self-discipline but are not allowed an opportunity to demonstrate it.

Teaching about content can lead to verbalism—the ability to describe a behavior but not necessarily the ability to carry it out. Verbalism is more likely to result when students are placed in a passive mode. Whenever possible, the learners should be actively involved in the instructional process; they should be placed in real situations or, barring that, in simulated ones.

These comments are not at all meant to rule out vicarious learning. We would be lost without it and life would be much bleaker. Pupils cannot, of course, always be involved in real situations. History must be learned vicariously, for example. Until the day when the science fiction writer's dreams become reality, we cannot project ourselves backward in time, propel ourselves physically into the future, or project ourselves spatially into a co-existent present. For example, most of us can sail up the Amazon only through words and pictures of someone who has performed the feat and written of his or her exploits in publications like *The National Geographic Magazine*. We can only experience directly the here and now in our own little corner of the universe.

Vicarious experience is more efficient in cases too simple for direct experiencing by every student. Valuable time would be wasted, for example, by having each student in an automobile program demonstrate the changing of an automobile's air filter. A presentation by the instructor should suffice for learning this uncomplicated skill. Vicarious experience is the only option, however, when (1) resources are lacking, as in the case of learning how to use the latest model of a self-correcting typewriter when only earlier models are available; (2) facilities are lacking, as in learning to inspect an automobile's brakes when a school does not have an auto shop; and (3) the experience is too complicated or expensive, as in preparing a gourmet meal of bouillabaisse, coq au vin, and chocolate mousse.

To conclude, whether personal or vicarious in nature, instructional strategies may emerge from the subject matter.

Student as Source

Instructional strategies must be appropriate for the students. The teacher will not send the average third grader to the library to gather information from the *Encyclopedia Britannica* on the Galápagos Islands. Conversely, the teacher will not attempt to engage junior or senior high school boys and girls in a rousing game of London Bridge or Ring-Around-the-Rosie. Elementary Spanish is inappropriate for students ready for the intermediate level. Highly abstract, verbal approaches to content do not fit the needs of the mentally retarded or slow learners. Independent study is applicable only to those students with enough self-discipline and determination to profit from it.

Teachers who underestimate the ability of learners and talk down to them or who overestimate the aptitude of learners and talk over their heads follow approaches that do not recognize the pupil as a source of strategy. Unless the teacher is careful, one source of strategy may conflict with another. A particular methodology may relate perfectly to the objectives, and may be right on target as to the subject matter, but may be completely inappropriate from the standpoint of the learner. We may generalize, therefore, that any particular strategy must not run counter to any of the sources of strategies.

The teacher should enlist the aid of students in both long-range and short-range planning for instruction. The teacher cannot assume, for example, that his or her purposes are identical to the students' purposes in studying a subject; he or she must therefore make an effort to discover student purposes.

When initiating a topic, the teacher should help students identify their personal reasons, if any, for studying the material. Students should be asked to state their objectives in their own words. For example, the teacher may wish students to study the Vietnam War so (1) they can complete a section of the textbook, (2) they can fulfill a requirement of a course in American history, (3) they can become familiar with that segment of our history, and (4) they might become interested enough in history to continue studying it in college. The students, on the other hand, may wish to study the Vietnam War in order to (1) understand books, television programs, and films concerned with this topic, (2) learn what friends and relatives experienced there, and (3) find out what got us into the war, why there was so much student protest, and how we can avoid getting into such a situation again.

Students may effectively participate in planning by (1) choosing among equally acceptable topics, (2) helping to identify the instructional objectives, (3) suggesting appropriate strategies, (4) choosing individual and group assignments, (5) selecting materials, and (6) structuring learning activities.

Community as Source

The desires of parents, the type of community, tradition, and convention all play a part in determining classroom strategies. Sex education, for example, alarms persons in many communities. Some oppose the school's venturing into this area on religious grounds; others feel it is the prerogative of the home. Consequently, examining various contraceptives might be considered by many in the community as inappropriate at any level.

A survey of drug habits among youth of a community might be rejected by some citizens who feel a negative image of the community might be the result. Counseling techniques that probe into a pupil's family life, psychological and personality tests, and values clarification may disturb parents.

Learning activities that stimulate excessive competition among students in the classroom and on the athletic field may meet with community disapproval. The use of outdated methodologies like the overuse of memorization can disturb parents as can procedures that call for behaviors either beyond the pupils' capacities or below their abilities.

Community efforts to censor materials and methods occur frequently in some localities. Although teachers may experience some difficulties with the community over their choice of techniques or content, they need not abandon a course of action for this reason alone. However, as discussed early in this text, involving members of the community in the process of curriculum development is desirable. Learning about community needs, beliefs, values, and mores may be necessary before the teacher can gain support for using techniques he or she believes are most effective. Through advisory committees, parent volunteer aides, parent-school organizations, and civic groups, community opinions about the school and its curriculum can be gathered.

Teacher as Source

Instructional strategies must conform to (1) the teacher's personal style of teaching and (2) the model or models of instructing the teacher follows. Large-group instruction, for example, will not appeal to the teacher who prefers to work closely with students. A teacher who regularly follows an inductive model of teaching is not likely to be content with using a deductive model. Teachers should analyze the particular style of teaching they project and the models they find most suitable for their particular styles. They should seek to expand their repertoires by developing more than a single model of teaching.

Guidelines for Selecting Strategies

To help teachers choose instructional strategies, I have drawn up the following guidelines, which suggest that a strategy must be right for

- □ the learners. It must meet their needs and interests and be in keeping with their learning styles.
- □ the teacher. The strategy must work for the individual teacher.
- □ the subject matter. Artificial respiration, for example, is taught more effectively by demonstration and practice than by lecturing.
- □ the time available. For example, a scientific experiment requiring an extended period of several days is not possible if sufficient time is not available.
- □ the resources available. Reference materials must be available if students are required to carry out research projects that necessitate their use.
- □ the facilities. Dividing a class into small groups for discussion purposes, for example, may be impractical if the room is small, if acoustics are poor, and if the furniture is not movable.
- □ the objectives. The strategies must be chosen to fulfill the instructional objectives.[1]

---

[1] Peter F. Oliva, *Supervision for Today's Schools,* 3rd ed. (White Plains, N.Y.: Longman, 1989), pp. 127–131. Reprinted with permission.

STYLES OF TEACHING

A style of teaching is a set of personal characteristics and traits that clearly identify the individual as a unique teacher. Personal factors that make one teacher different from another include

- ☐ dress
- ☐ language
- ☐ voice
- ☐ gestures
- ☐ energy level
- ☐ facial expressions
- ☐ motivation
- ☐ interest in people
- ☐ dramatic talent
- ☐ intellect
- ☐ scholarship

Teachers consciously or unconsciously adopt certain styles. The teacher as helper, disciplinarian, actor, friend, father or mother image, autocrat, artist, big brother or sister, or expounder are examples of teaching styles. Barbara Bree Fischer and Louis Fischer defined teaching style as "a pervasive quality in the behavior of an individual, *a quality that persists though the content may change.*"[2] They observed that teachers differ in teaching style in much the same way that U.S. presidents varied in speaking style, famous painters differed in artistic style, or well-known tennis players demonstrated unique playing styles.

The teacher with a high, thin voice had best not rely heavily on lecture as a method. The teacher who is formal and proper in dress and manner will probably rule noisy games out of his or her repertoire. The teacher who lacks confidence in his or her management skills may not feel comfortable with a freewheeling, open-ended discussion. If a teacher of low-energy level or low motivation refuses to carefully read students' assigned essays or term papers, there is little point in using such strategies.

The teacher with a penchant for scholarship will likely include among his or her methods various forms of research. The teacher with an interest in people will choose procedures in which he or she and the students are interacting not only with each other but also with people both inside and outside the school.

The teacher who is confident about his or her work will invite visitors to the classroom, use resource persons, and permit audio- and video-taping of classroom activities. The teacher who is democratically oriented will design activities that permit students to participate in decision making. Unflappable individuals will be more inclined to try out innovative techniques that might

---

[2]Barbara Bree Fischer and Louis Fischer, "Styles in Teaching and Learning," *Educational Leadership* 36, no. 4 (January 1979): 245. Reprinted with permission of the Association for Supervision and Curriculum Development and Barbara Bree Fischer and Louis Fischer. Copyright ©1971 by the Association for Supervision and Curriculum Development. All rights reserved.

result in failure whereas less intrepid individuals will tend to stick to the tried-and-true.

Some teachers reject the use of audiovisual techniques because they do not feel competent enough to use the equipment or they harbor the attitude that the use of media is somehow a waste of valuable time. In the judgment of these teachers, Guttenberg provided the definitive answer to instructional media—the printed page.

Fischer and Fischer identified a number of styles of teaching, including

> *The Task-Oriented* —These teachers prescribe the materials to be learned and demand specific performance on the part of the students. Learnings to be accomplished may be specified on an individual basis, and an explicit system of accounting keeps track of how well each student meets the stated expectations.
>
> *The Cooperative Planner* —These teachers plan the means and ends of instruction with student cooperation. . . . Opinions of the learners are not only listened to, but are respected. These teachers encourage and support student participation at all levels.
>
> *The Child-Centered* —This teacher provides a structure for students to pursue whatever they want to do or whatever interests them. . . . This style is not only extremely rare, it is almost impossible to imagine in its pure form because the classroom, with its adult-child ratio and adult-responsible environment, automatically encourages some interests and discourages others.
>
> *The Subject-Centered* —These teachers focus on organized content to the near exclusion of the learner. By "covering the subject," they satisfy their consciences even if little learning takes place.
>
> *The Learning-Centered* —These teachers have equal concern for the students and for the curricular objectives, the materials to be learned. They reject the over-emphasis of both the "child-centered" and "subject-centered" styles, and instead help students, whatever their abilities or disabilities, develop toward substantive goals as well as in their autonomy in learning.
>
> *The Emotionally Exciting and Its Counterpart* —These teachers show their own intensive emotional involvement in teaching. They enter the teaching-learning process with zeal and usually produce a classroom atmosphere of excitement and high emotion.[3]

You and I no doubt find some teaching styles more appealing and more acceptable than others. We might identify some styles as negative (e.g., undemocratic behavior) and some as positive (such as concern for students). Human beings that we are, we will probably give our approval to styles of teaching that emulate our own. Fischer and Fischer made their position clear:

> We do not consider all styles of teaching and learning to be equally valid. All too often, indefensible practices are justified with the claim, "Well, that's my style. I have mine, you have yours, and each is as good as the other." . . . Since the very idea of style is based on a commitment to individualization

---

[3]Ibid., p. 251.

of instruction and the development of learner autonomy, styles that encourage undue conformity and dependence are not acceptable to us.[4]

STYLES OF LEARNING

The teacher's style obviously bears some relationship to the pupils' styles of learning. Some pupils are

- [] eager beavers
- [] mules
- [] self-starters
- [] plodders
- [] shining stars
- [] skeptics

Some express themselves better orally than in written form. Some can deal with abstractions; others can learn only with concrete materials. Some learn more effectively from aural and visual techniques than through reading. Some can work under pressure; others cannot. Some need much direction; others, little. Pupils are as different in learning styles as teachers are in teaching styles.[5] In fact, they are more different since there are more of them. Teachers must be aware that their teaching styles can have a strong impact on student achievement and that their styles can at times be at cross-purposes to their pupils'.

A teaching style cannot be selected in the same way an instructional strategy can. Style is not something that can be readily switched on and off. It is not simple to change from a task-oriented to a child-centered approach. Only with considerable difficulty, if at all, can a nonemotionally exciting teacher become an emotionally exciting one. Two questions must be asked about teaching styles: Can a teacher change his or her style? Should a teacher change his or her style?

Given a willingness to change, appropriate training, counseling, or therapy, if need be, a teacher can change his or her style. Contrary to ancient beliefs about the impossibility of changing a person's behavior, human beings can and do change. Sometimes personality change is modeled on the behavior of another person who is in some way important to an individual. Sometimes a crisis or trauma effects personality change. All religions share the basic premise that individuals can change their behavior. Thus change is possible, though it may not be easy.

Perhaps a larger question is whether a teacher *should* change his or her style. Three answers are given to this question, one of which presupposes a teacher's ability to change style. First, one school of thought holds that

---

[4]Ibid., p. 246.

[5]For analysis of students' learning styles see Rita Dunn and Kenneth Dunn, *Teaching Students Through Their Individual Learning Styles: A Practical Approach* (Reston, Va.: Reston Publishing Company, 1978). See also Pat Burke Guild and Stephen Garger, *Marching to Different Drummers* (Alexandria, Va.: Association for Supervision and Curriculum Development, 1985) and "Learning Styles and the Brain," *Educational Leadership* 48, no. 2 (October 1990): 3–80.

a teacher's learning style should match the pupils'. Consequently, we would attempt to analyze the styles of the teacher and pupils respectively, then group pupils and teachers with compatible styles. The pupils and teachers would then follow their own styles.

At first glance, ignoring the complexities of analyzing styles and grouping the pupils with compatible teachers, this position seems to be very sound and logical. Rapport between teacher and pupils would most likely be high, and the classroom climate would be conducive to learning. Herbert A. Thelen supported the concept of matching teachers and students: "We remain convinced that any grouping which does not in some way attempt to 'fit' students and teachers together can have only accidental success."[6]

According to a second school of thought, there is some merit in exposing students to a great variety of personal styles during their schooling so they will learn how to interact with different types of people. Although some students might prefer the less structured, informal, relaxed approach while they are in school, a legion of high school graduates compliment their task-oriented, subject-centered teachers for having "held their feet to the fire," thereby helping them to succeed after graduation in spite of themselves.

Richard L. Turner took this second position when he commented:

> A key feature of virtually all school organizations is that little effort is made to control the variability of teaching styles and learning styles. Schools rarely attempt to match the styles of learners to styles of teachers. Therein lies much of the strength and durability of the school as a social entity.
>
> Among any group of students, some will adapt more readily to the style of a particular teacher than others will. The strength of the school as a collective lies in the fact that over long periods of time students are exposed to many different teaching styles. By virtue of this variation, all but a few students are exposed to several teaching styles to which they readily adapt, and to some with which they must struggle.[7]

A third response to the question of whether a teacher should change his or her style holds that a teacher should be flexible, using more than one style with the same group of students or with differing groups of students. This answer combines features of both the first and second responses. Teachers vary their styles, if they can, for particular groups of learners, and by the same token, the pupils are exposed to a variety of styles. Whatever the strategy chosen, it must conform to the teacher's inimitable style. That is why it is so important for teachers to know who they are, what they are, and what they believe. Rita S. Dunn and Kenneth J. Dunn spoke about the effect of the teacher's

---

[6]Herbert A. Thelen, *Classroom Grouping for Teachability* (New York: John Wiley & Sons, 1967), p. 186.

[7]Richard L. Turner, "The Value of Variety in Teaching Styles," *Educational Leadership* 36, no. 4 (January 1979): 257–258. Reprinted with permission of the Association for Supervision and Curriculum Development and Richard L. Turner. Copyright ©1979 by the Association for Supervision and Curriculum Development. All rights reserved.

attitudes and beliefs on teaching style:

> The attitudes teachers hold toward various instructional programs, meth-
> ods, and resources as well as the kinds of youngsters they prefer working with
> constitute part of their "teaching style." It is true, however that some teachers
> believe in specific forms of instruction that they do not practice (administra-
> tive constraints, inexperience, lack of resources, or insecurity) and that others
> practice methods in which they do not believe (administrative or community
> mandates, inability to change or to withstand pressures). It is also true that
> teachers may prefer students different from those they are actually teaching.[8]

"Style" and "method" are used rather loosely—and often interchangeably—
in the professional literature. Fischer and Fischer cautioned, "Style is not to
be identified with method, for people will infuse different methods with their
own styles. For example, lecturing is not a style, in our conception, for people
with distinctive styles will infuse their respective lectures with their own unique
qualities."[9]

MODELS OF TEACHING

Whereas style of teaching is a personalized set of teacher behaviors, a model of
teaching is a generalized set of behaviors that emphasizes a particular strategy
or set of strategies. Lecturing, for example, is an instructional strategy or
method. One whose predominant strategy is lecturing is fulfilling the model of
lecturer. The contrast between model and style can readily be seen by a person
who attends presentations given by two different lecturers.

Bruce Joyce and Marshal Weil defined a model of teaching in this way: "A
model for teaching is a plan or pattern that can be used to shape curriculums
(long-term courses of studies), to design instructional materials, and to guide
instruction in the classroom and other settings."[10] The model or instructional
role that the teacher displays guides the teacher's choice of strategies. In one
sense, the model or role is the method or strategy. For example, when the
teacher plays the role of questioner, questioning is the instructional strategy
or method. If the teacher writes learning activity packages (LAPs), the use of
LAPs is the method. On the other hand, if the teacher acts as a facilitator—a
much broader role—a number of instructional strategies or methods may be
employed. Students may choose their own materials, make up their own questions, and critique their own work, all under the general facilitating supervision
of the teacher.

---

[8]Rita S. Dunn and Kenneth J. Dunn, "Learning Styles/Teaching Styles: Should They . . . Can
They . . . Be Matched?" *Educational Leadership* 36, no. 4 (January 1979): 241. Reprinted with
permission of the Association for Supervision and Curriculum Development and Rita S. Dunn
and Kenneth J. Dunn. Copyright ©1979 by the Association for Supervision and Curriculum
Development. All rights reserved.
[9]Fischer and Fischer, "Styles," p. 245. Reprinted with permission.
[10]Bruce Joyce and Marsha Weil, *Models of Teaching,* 2nd ed. (Englewood Cliffs, N.J.:
Prentice-Hall, 1980), p. 1.

Susan S. Ellis clarified the meaning of a model of teaching when she wrote:

> Models of teaching are strategies based on the theories (and often the research) of educators, psychologists, philosophers, and others who question how individuals learn. Each model consists of a rationale, a series of steps (actions, behaviors) to be taken by the teacher and the learner, a description of necessary support systems, and a method for evaluating the learner's progress. Some models are designed to help students grow in self-awareness or creativity; some foster the development of self-discipline or responsible participation in a group; some models stimulate inductive reasoning or theory-building; and others provide for mastery of subject matter.[11]

In preservice teacher education, students usually gain familiarity and some limited experience with several of the more common models of teaching, including expository teaching, group discussion, role playing, demonstration, simulation, discovery, learning laboratories, programmed instruction, tutoring, problem solving, and mediated instruction. The assumption teacher education institutions make is that students will gain proficiency in one or more of the models (methods) and identify those with which they will feel most comfortable. Given the limited time at their disposal, teacher education institutions can only introduce students to the many instructional models, encourage students to identify their favorites, and help students to develop a degree of skill in carrying out various models.

Bruce Joyce identified 25 models of teaching.[12] In their book, *Models of Teaching,* Joyce and Weil elaborated on 20 models grouped under four categories or families: (1) information-processing models—for example, Hilda Taba's inductive model and J. Richard Suchman's inquiry training model; (2) personal models, such as Carl Rogers's nondirective teaching and William Glasser's classroom meeting model; (3) social models—for example, Byron Massialas and Benjamin Cox's social inquiry model and the National Training Laboratory's T-Group model; and (4) behavioral models, like simulations and assertiveness training.[13]

Mary Alice Gunter, Thomas H. Estes, and Jan Hasbrouck Schwab explained a models approach to instruction when they described eight models: direct instruction, concept attainment, concept development, synectics, Suchman inquiry, classroom discussion, cooperative learning, and exploration of feelings/resolution of conflict model.[14]

When we speak of models rather than methods of teaching, we convey the concept that a model is a generalized pattern of behavior that can be learned

---

[11]Susan S. Ellis, "Models of Teaching: A Solution to the Teaching Style/Learning Style Dilemma," *Educational Leadership* 36, no. 4 (January 1979): 275. Reprinted with permission of the Association for Supervision and Curriculum Development and Susan E. Ellis. Copyright ©1979 by the Association for Supervision and Curriculum Development. All rights reserved.

[12]Bruce Joyce, *Selecting Learning Experiences: Linking Theory and Practice* (Alexandria, Va.: Association for Supervision and Curriculum Development, 1978).

[13]Joyce and Weil, *Models of Teaching,* 3rd ed. (Englewood Cliffs, N.J.: Prentice-Hall, 1986).

[14]Mary Alice Gunter, Thomas H. Estes, and Jan Hasbrouck Schwab, *Instruction: A Models Approach* (Boston: Allyn and Bacon, 1990), pp. 72–206.

and imitated. Although teachers may develop their own enduring personal styles (which they may not be able to change easily or desire to change), they may develop skills inherent in a variety of models. Thus we might ask the same questions about models that we asked about styles: Can teachers change their models of teaching? Should they change them?

To the first question, the answer must be yes. Were this not so, a significant portion of preservice and in-service teacher education would not be valuable. To the second question, a change of model is desirable if the teacher's stock in trade is limited to one particular model, no matter how successfully the teacher carries it out. Teachers should be masters of several models of teaching. Different models are necessary to reach different goals of instruction.

Need for Variety

Variety of modeling is essential to successful teaching. Constant exposure to a single model can lead to restlessness and boredom on the part of students. Let us fabricate a very unlikely situation. A teacher develops a successful model that his colleagues admire. In their search for the "right" and "best" method, they begin to emulate their colleague to the point where every teacher in the school adopts his model. Can you imagine what school would be like if every teacher were enthusiastic about the discovery method, for example? Life could be extremely dull for students and teachers alike.

Of course, the use of a single, consistent model by all teachers is not sound pedagogy; a model must be compatible with both the teacher's style and the students' styles of learning. Deductive thinking—in which a rule is given first, then many opportunities for applying it—is less time-consuming and more efficient with some learners than inductive thinking, in which the applications are given first and the learners determine the rule from them.

Fortunately, the use of a uniform model by all teachers is unlikely. However, we can detect sentiment among some educators that there is both a "best" style and a "best" model of teaching. Grasping for surefire solutions to instructional problems, school districts throughout the country have frequently conducted in-service education programs designed to promote a particular, supposedly universal, model of teaching.

Joyce and Weil viewed the search for the best model of teaching as a fallacy and noted that the research does not champion one model over another.[15]

TEACHING SKILLS

Up to this point we have been discussing styles and models of teaching, both of which are germane to selecting particular strategies or methods. We will now add a third dimension that bears upon selecting instructional strategies— teaching skills. A word is needed to signify the interrelationship between style,

---

[15]Joyce and Weil, *Models,* 2nd ed., p. 1; see also 3rd ed., pp. 4–5.

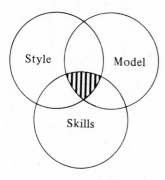

FIGURE 11–1   The teacher's approach

model, and skills of teaching. "Method" would be a tempting word to use if it did not already convey the meanings of both "strategy" and "model"— for example, the strategy of lecturing equals the method of lecturing. For want of a better term, the coining of which we will leave to others, we will use the ambiguous word "approach" to signify the interrelationship among the triumvirate of style, model, and skills. We might chart this relationship in the form of a diagram in which the shaded area represents the teacher's approach (see Figure 11–1).

Let's take a simple illustration of this relationship and see how the three aspects of the teacher's approach come together. Let's choose programmed instruction as our example. The teacher who consistently plays the role of programmer (model) is likely to be a person who is subject-centered, has a penchant for detail, believes pupils learn best in graduated bits (style), and has skill in selecting content, sequencing, writing programs, and testing (skills). At the risk of redundancy, we might say that programming is the teacher's method (or model), and the use of programs with the learners is the teacher's instructional strategy (or method).

What skills are pertinent to a particular approach? For example, what skills are required for lecturing—a method used at some time or other by most teachers? We might list the following:

- [ ] ability to enunciate
- [ ] ability to project one's voice
- [ ] ability to use proper grammar and sentence structure
- [ ] ability to "read" student facial expressions
- [ ] ability to select content to be used in lectures
- [ ] ability to sustain interest
- [ ] ability to relate content to past and future experiences of learners
- [ ] ability to speak to level of audience
- [ ] ability to deal with individuals causing distractions
- [ ] ability to stimulate thinking
- [ ] ability to organize thoughts

BOX 11–1   Florida's generic competencies

1. Applies knowledge of physical, social, and academic developmental patterns and of individual differences, to meet the instructional needs of all students in the classroom and to advise students about those needs.

2. Enhances students' feelings of dignity and self-worth and the worth of other people including those from other ethnic, cultural, linguistic and economic groups.

3. Arranges and manages the physical environment to facilitate instruction and ensure student safety.

4. Recognizes overt signs of severe emotional distress in students and demonstrates awareness of appropriate intervention and referral procedures.

5. Recognizes signs of alcohol and drug abuse in students and demonstrates awareness of appropriate intervention and referral procedures.

6. Recognizes the overt physical and behavioral indicators of child abuse and neglect, knows the rights and responsibilities regarding reporting and how to interact appropriately with a child after a report has been made.

7. Formulates a standard for student behavior in the classroom.

8. Deals with misconduct, interruptions, intrusions, and digressions in ways that promote instructional momentum.

9. Determines the entry level knowledge and/or skills of students for a given set of instructional objectives using diagnostic tests, teacher observations, and student records.

10. Identifies long-range goals for a given subject area.

11. Constructs and sequences related short-range objectives for a given subject area.

12. Selects, adapts, and/or develops instructional materials for a given set of instructional objectives and student learning needs.

13. Selects/develops and sequences learning activities that are appropriate to instructional objectives and student needs.

All of these abilities are generic teaching skills. We may define generic teaching skills as those instructional skills or competencies that are general in nature and can be employed by teachers in any field and at any level. The converse, special teaching skills, are specific abilities that must be demonstrated by teachers in a particular field or level. The foreign language teacher, for example, must be skillful in the generic competency of varying stimuli, while also being adept at projecting specific stimuli unique to the language being taught. Skill in translating one language into another is a special skill of a foreign language teacher, not a talent that must be evidenced by every teacher.

Generic Competencies

In recent years, educators have taken an interest in identifying generic teaching skills or competencies. Dwight Allen and Kevin Ryan compiled a well-known

BOX 11–1 continued

14. Uses class time efficiently.

15. Communicates effectively using verbal and non-verbal skills.

16. Creates and maintains academic focus by using verbal, non-verbal and/or visual motivational devices.

17. Presents forms of knowledge such as concepts, laws and law-like principles, academic rules, and value knowledge.

18. Presents directions appropriate for carrying out an instructional activity.

19. Stimulates and directs student thinking, and checks student comprehension through appropriate questioning techniques.

20. Provides appropriate practice to promote learning and retention.

21. Relates to students' verbal communications in ways that encourage participation and maintain academic focus.

22. Uses feedback procedures that give information to students about the appropriateness of their response(s).

23. Conducts reviews of subject matter.

24. Constructs or assembles classroom tests and tasks to measure student achievement of objectives.

25. Establishes a testing environment in which students can validly demonstrate their knowledge and/or skill, and receive adequate information about the quality of their test performance.

26. Utilizes an effective system for maintaining records of students and class progress.

27. Uses computers in education.

SOURCE: Florida Department of Education, *Study Guide for the Florida Teacher Certification Examination: Professional Education* (Tallahassee, Fla.: Florida Department of Education, 1989). Reprinted by permission.

list of 14 generic teaching skills.[16] Madeline Hunter and Douglas Russell listed seven steps—in effect, teaching skills—of planning for effective instruction.[17]

The state of Florida has identified 27 generic teaching competencies that all its teachers should possess. These competencies, which provide the basis for the Professional Education portion of the Florida Teacher Certification Examination, are reproduced in Box 11–1. All persons seeking Florida teacher certification must pass not only the Professional Education Examination but also tests in a subject area (teaching field) and in college-level academic skills. Since 1975, Florida has altered its list of generic competencies from 23 to 35 in 1984 and to 27 in 1989.

[16]Dwight Allen and Kevin Ryan, *Microteaching* (Reading, Mass.: Addison-Wesley, 1969).
[17]Madeline Hunter and Douglas Russell, "How Can I Plan More Effective Lessons?" *Instructor* 87, no. 2 (September 1977): 74–75, 88.

BOX 11–2   Texas's all-level professional development objectives

---

INSTRUCTIONAL PLANNING AND CURRICULUM DEVELOPMENT

☐ Identify stages and characteristics of development of students (birth–age 22).
☐ Apply knowledge of stages and characteristics of early childhood development from birth through kindergarten.
☐ Apply knowledge of stages and characteristics of development at the elementary level.
☐ Apply knowledge of stages and characteristics of development at the secondary level.
☐ Recognize characteristics and needs of handicapped students.
☐ Recognize the characteristics and needs of gifted and talented students.
☐ Recognize characteristics and needs of students from special populations (e.g., limited English language proficiency, migrants).
☐ Recognize characteristics and needs of educationally disadvantaged students.
☐ Understand legal requirements relating to the education of special populations.
☐ Adapt curriculum and instruction for teaching students from special populations.
☐ Analyze the influence of cultural background on the instruction of students.
☐ Apply educational goals and objectives to design curriculum.
☐ Understand principles of curriculum organization.
☐ Design instruction to enable elementary students to achieve educational goals and objectives.
☐ Design instruction to enable secondary students to achieve educational goals and objectives.
☐ Apply procedures for planning instructional lessons.
☐ Derive goals and objectives appropriate to learner needs.

ASSESSMENT AND EVALUATION

☐ Understand principles of testing and measurement.
☐ Understand methods and instruments for assessing elementary students in Texas.
☐ Understand methods and instruments for assessing secondary students in Texas.
☐ Apply principles for developing assessment instruments.
☐ Apply procedures for scoring and interpreting assessment instruments.
☐ Apply principles of evaluating an instructional program.
☐ Apply principles of evaluation to monitor student progress and evaluate student achievement.

Instead of identifying a single set of generic competencies that cut across all levels, Texas has specified 50 professional development objectives for elementary school teachers, 42 for secondary school teachers, and 50 for teachers K-12. The objectives are divided into four subareas. The first three subareas are generic teaching competencies: Instructional Planning and Curriculum Development, Assessment and Evaluation, and Instructional Methodology and Classroom Management. Principles of Education make up the fourth subarea.

BOX 11–2   continued

INSTRUCTIONAL METHODOLOGY AND CLASSROOM MANAGEMENT

☐ Apply knowledge of learning theory to instruction.
☐ Apply knowledge of principles of instruction.
☐ Analyze teaching strategies for delivering basic instruction.
☐ Analyze teaching strategies for developing higher-level thinking skills.
☐ Apply knowledge of reading skills to instruction in the content areas.
☐ Identify principles and techniques of classroom organization.
☐ Analyze uses of textbooks in instruction at the elementary level.
☐ Analyze uses of textbooks in instruction at the secondary level.
☐ Analyze uses of supplementary materials in instruction at the elementary level.
☐ Analyze uses of supplementary materials in instruction at the secondary level.
☐ Identify types and uses of audiovisual equipment.
☐ Identify types of school and community resources used for instruction.
☐ Analyze principles of instructional management at the elementary level.
☐ Analyze principles of instructional management at the secondary level.
☐ Apply principles of discipline management at the elementary level.
☐ Apply principles of discipline management at the secondary level.

PRINCIPLES OF EDUCATION

☐ Understand the purposes of education.
☐ Understand the process of educational goal setting.
☐ Identify state and federal laws related to the role of the classroom teacher.
☐ Identify rights and responsibilities in education.
☐ Apply principles of professional ethics in education.
☐ Understand the structure and functions of the state school system.
☐ Understand the local school system.
☐ Understand the role of the federal government in education.
☐ Understand procedures for hiring and evaluating personnel.
☐ Identify ways of promoting and participating in professional development.

SOURCE: National Evaluation Systems, *Study Guide, Professional Development, All-Level 01, ExCet, Examination for the Certification of Educators in Texas* (Amherst, Mass.: National Evaluation Systems, n.d.), pp. 8–13. Reprinted with permission of the Texas Education Agency.

Applicants for a teaching certificate in Texas must pass the Examination for the Certification of Educators in Texas (ExCet), which tests achievement of detailed objectives in the applicant's teaching field and mastery of the professional development objectives for the particular level(s). The stipulated professional development objectives for teachers who wish to be certified at both the elementary and secondary school levels are those shown in Box 11–2.

With appropriate training, teachers can learn to master the generic teaching skills. Although generic teaching skills may be employed by all teachers at all levels, it does not follow that any teacher at any level or in any field can use any generic skill in any given situation. Although every teacher should be able to ask probing questions, for example, each teacher will need to decide whether the nature of the content and the learning styles of the pupils will make probing questions appropriate.

Whether the skills are generic or specific, teachers must demonstrate a variety of instructional skills that can be adapted to their own styles and models. Research on teacher behaviors suggests that teaching skills can be imitated, learned, modified, and adopted.

The teachers' personal styles, the models they follow, and the teaching skills they have mastered all affect their design for instruction. For example, teachers select strategies that match their personal styles. They follow models to which they are receptive and choose strategies for which they have the requisite teaching skills.

ORGANIZING FOR INSTRUCTION

Planning for instruction involves selecting the following components:

- □ goals
- □ objectives
- □ strategies
- □ learning resources
- □ evaluation techniques

We discussed selecting instructional goals and objectives in Chapter 10 and considered selecting strategies and, indirectly, the resources needed to carry them out in this chapter. Choosing evaluation techniques is the subject of Chapter 12.

Somehow the teacher must bring all the separate components together into a cohesive plan. Both long-range and short-range planning are required. Long-range plans will be examined in Chapter 15. Let's look now at the more immediate types of plans: the short-range unit plan and the even shorter range daily plan.

Unit Plans

The unit plan—also called a "learning unit," "teaching unit," or simply "unit"— is a means of organizing the instructional components for teaching a particular topic or theme. William H. Burton defined a unit as follows: "A unit is any combination of subject-matter content and outcomes, and thought processes, into learning experiences suited to the maturity and needs (personal and social) of the learners, all combined into a whole with internal integrity determined by immediate and ultimate goals."[18]

The unit plan ordinarily covers a period from several days to several weeks. A series of units might actually constitute a particular course. The daily plan organizes the instructional components of the day's lesson(s). A unit serves as a source of a number of daily plans. Ordinarily, instructional planning progresses from course to unit to daily plans.

The writing of unit and daily lesson plans is a key skill that teacher education institutions seek to develop in preservice teachers. Some institutions insist on a degree of meticulousness and thoroughness in writing plans that is rarely seen in practice in the classroom.

You will find considerable variation in the structure of unit plans.[19] Burton offered a detailed outline for a unit plan, as follows:

- *Title*. Attractive, brief, and unambiguous.
- *The Overview*. Brief statement of the nature and scope of the unit.
- *The Teacher's Objectives*. Understandings (generalizations), attitudes, appreciations, special abilities, skills, behavior patterns, facts.
- *The Approach*. A brief account of the most probable introduction.
- *The Pupils' Aim or Objective*. The major objective which it is hoped the learners will develop or accept.
- *The Planning and Working Period*. Learning activities with desired outcomes for each activity.
- *Evaluation Techniques*. How evidence will be gathered showing that the objectives of the unit have been developed.
- *Bibliographies*. Books useful to the teacher and books useful to the learners.
- *Audio-Visual Materials and Other Instructional Aids with Sources*.[20]

Analysis of various unit outlines shows that a unit plan should contain the title, the level or course for which it is intended, and the amount of time to be devoted to the following minimum essentials:

- instructional goals
- instructional objectives (cognitive, affective, psychomotor)
- instructional procedures (learning activities)
- evaluation techniques (preassessment, formative, summative)
- resources (human and material)

Many teachers choose to include in their unit outlines of the content, a budget of time for each portion of the unit, and tentative outlines of daily lesson plans.

---

[18]William H. Burton. From *The Guidance of Learning Activities: A Summary of the Principles of Teaching Based on the Growth of the Learner,* 3rd ed., © 1962, p. 329. Reprinted by permission of Prentice-Hall, Inc., Englewood Cliffs, NJ.

[19]See, for example, Kenneth T. Henson, *Secondary Teaching Methods* (Lexington, Mass.: D. C. Heath, 1981), p. 197.

[20]William H. Burton. From *The Guidance of Learning Activities: A Summary of the Principles of Teaching Based on the Growth of the Learner,* 3rd ed., © 1962, pp. 372–374. Adapted by permission of Prentice-Hall, Inc., Englewood Cliffs, NJ.

Units are written to be used; they are living documents and should be followed where helpful, and augmented, reduced, revised, and discarded when inappropriate. Box 11–3 provides an illustration of a unit plan.

Lesson Plans

Lesson plans chart the daily instruction. Conceivably, lesson plans could (and sometimes are) written without reference to any unit plan. However, on strictly logical grounds, lesson plans that are higher in quality, better organized, and more complete are achieved more often with unit plans than without them. Creating units is essential to holistic planning.

Like unit planning, lesson planning is an individual exercise. According to Laurence J. Peter, "A lesson plan is simply an outline prepared in advance of teaching, so that time and materials will be used efficiently."[21] Peter pointed out that "various types of lessons require different kinds of lesson plans."[22] We might add, on a philosophical level, "Various types of teachers require different types of lesson plans" and "Various types of learners require different types of lesson plans." On a practical level, "Various types of administrators and supervisors require different types of lesson plans."

A six-part outline for a lesson plan that can be used generically follows:

A. Objectives
B. Activities
C. Assignment
D. Evaluation Techniques
E. Bibliography
F. Instructional Aids and Sources[23]

A sample lesson plan based on the illustrative unit plan is shown in Box 11–4.

The less experience a teacher has, the more complete his or her unit and lesson plans should be. It is desirable for both experienced and inexperienced teachers to prepare complete unit plans to fully communicate their ideas. Experienced teachers, however, will discover ways to simplify and shorten lesson plans. This practice is to be encouraged as long as the lesson plans remain serviceable to both themselves and substitute teachers. Once the unit and lesson plans have been made, the teacher can begin to demonstrate his or her style, model, and skills.

PRESENTATION OF INSTRUCTION

After planning and organizing for instruction, the teacher proceeds to direct the students' learning experiences in the classroom. Entire volumes have been written on effective means of presenting instruction. Since this text focuses on

---

[21]Laurence J. Peter, *Competencies for Teaching: Classroom Instruction* (Belmont: Calif.: Wadsworth, 1975), p. 194.

[22]Ibid., p. 194.

[23]Peter F. Oliva, *The Secondary School Today,* 2nd ed. (New York: Harper & Row, 1972), p. 313.

BOX 11–3   Illustrative unit plan

Title: Financing Our Community's Public Schools
Level: Senior High School—Problems of American Democracy
Time: Five Days

A. Instructional Goals
1. The student will understand that quality education is costly.
2. The student will understand that ignorance is more costly than education.
3. The student will become aware of sources of funding for the schools.
4. The student will become familiar with problems of financing education in our community.

B. Instructional Objectives

Cognitive

1. The student will describe the role and extent of local involvement in financing the schools.
2. The student will describe the role and extent of state involvement in financing the schools.
3. The student will describe the role and extent of federal involvement in financing the schools.
4. The student will explain the process by which public moneys are expended for the schools.
5. The student will explain what our public moneys buy for the schools.
6. The student will compare salaries of teachers in our community's schools with salaries paid outside of teaching.

Affective

1. The student will take a position on the property tax: necessary, too high, too low? Reasons must be stated for the position taken.
2. The student will take a position on the statement: Teachers are underpaid. Reasons must be stated for the position taken.
3. The student will take a position on federal aid to education: pro or con? Reasons must be stated for the position taken.
4. The student will take a position on the statements: The schools cost too much. There are too many frills in education. Reasons must be stated for the positions taken.

Psychomotor

None

C. Instructional Procedures
1. Read the district superintendent's annual report and discuss the revenues and expenditures.
2. Read last year's school budget and compare with proposed budget for next year. Account for changes in the total amounts each year.

(continued)

BOX 11–3   continued

---

3. Draw a chart of the percentages of money spent by the locality, state, and federal government for support of the community's schools.
4. Prepare a bar graph showing the total number of dollars expended this past year by the locality, state, and federal government for the community's schools.
5. Report on your family's school tax and show how it was calculated.
6. Invite a school principal to class and interview him or her about expenditures and revenues for his or her school.
7. Invite the superintendent, a member of the superintendent's staff, or a member of the school board to class and interview him or her about expenditures and revenues for the school district.
8. Report on the costs of one federally supported program in our community's schools.
9. Consult and discuss publications of the state department of education on financing schools in the state.
10. Compare amounts of money raised throughout the state by property taxes and by sales, income, and other taxes.
11. Compare salaries of teachers in our community with salaries of (1) teachers in other communities in the state, (2) teachers in other states, and (3) persons outside of teaching.
12. Account for variations in amounts of money raised for the support of education by localities of the state and in the total amounts of money available to these localities.
13. Account for variations in amounts of money raised for the support of education by the various states.
14. Compile a list of average annual costs of selected items for which schools must pay, including instructional supplies, equipment, heat, lights, water, salaries of all personnel, insurance, and maintenance.
15. Compute the costs of vandalism in our community's schools for a one-year period.
16. Write a report advocating either greater or lesser funding for our community's schools. In your report show what is to be added or cut.
17. Suggest improved ways of funding the schools.

D. Evaluation Techniques
  1. Preassessment
    Construct and administer a pretest to assess students' entry knowledge and skills. Sample questions might include:

    a. Estimate the total amount of money spent for the public schools of our community this past year.
    b. How is the property tax determined?
    c. Which spends more money on our community's schools: the locality, the state, or the federal government?

(continued)

BOX 11–3   continued

2. Formative evaluation

a. Daily oral questioning of the students by the teacher on the more difficult aspects of the lessons.

b. Daily summaries by students and teacher at the end of each lesson.

c. Teacher's evaluation of student products, as charts, graphs, etc.

3. Summative evaluation

a. Quiz on the day following conclusion of the unit. Sample test items may include questions similar to those of the pretest plus additional items. A combination of objective and essay test items may be used. Sample test items might include:

(1) Essay: Explain the process by which our community raises money locally for the schools.

(2) Objective: In reference to taxation, a mill is written as:

(a) .01

(b) 1.0

(c) .001

(d) .0001

E. Resources

Human

☐ School principal.

☐ School superintendent, member of the superintendent's staff, or member of the school board.

Material

☐ Publications of the local school board.

☐ Publications of the state department of education.

☐ Publications of the U.S. Department of Education, including:

The Condition of Education: Statistical Report. Washington, D.C.: U.S. Department of Education, Center for Education Statistics, annually.

Digest of Education Statistics. Washington, D.C.: U.S. Department of Education, Center for Education Statistics, annually.

☐ *Standard Education Almanac,* Chicago: Marquis Who's Who, annually.

☐ U.S. Bureau of the Census. *Statistical Abstract of the United States.* Washington, D.C.: Superintendent of Documents, U.S. Government Printing Office, annually.

☐ *The World Almanac and Book of Facts.* New York: Newspaper Enterprise Association, annually.

NOTE: This illustrative learning unit is based on the illustrative resource unit shown in Chapter 15.

BOX 11–4   Illustrative lesson plan

First Day
Unit: Financing Our Community's Schools
Fifty minutes

A. Objectives

Cognitive

1. The student will list three sources of funding for the schools.
2. The student will describe the source(s) of local funding for the schools.
3. The student will define "property tax," "assessed valuation," and "mill."

Affective

1. The student will take positions, giving reasons whether the property tax is equitable, too high, or too low.
2. The student will express an opinion and give reasons as to whether he or she believes expenditures for schools in the community are more than adequate, adequate, or inadequate.

B. Activities
1. Set induction: Students will listen to the teacher read a recent editorial from the local newspaper on the needs of local schools. The class will discuss its perceptions of the editorial's accuracy (eight minutes).
2. Using an overhead projector, the teacher will show transparencies of charts selected from the district superintendent's annual report to the school board. Students will respond to teacher's questions about interpretation of the charts (ten minutes).
3. Using the same data, students will prepare original charts and/or graphs showing sources and amounts of funds for the community's schools this past year. Copies of the superintendent's report will also be available for students' use (ten minutes).
4. Students will listen to teacher's description of sources of local funding. Key points: property tax, assessed evaluation, tax assessor, exemptions, and millage (ten minutes).

---

curriculum development rather than instructional methodology, I shall not attempt to discuss methods of teaching in any detail. Instead, I would like to make a few general observations about presentation of instruction and direct you to some sources for further study.

Research on effective teaching supports commonsense principles to the effect that students will learn more if teachers expect them to learn, focus on the content to be covered, keep them on task, provide adequate practice, monitor their performance, and care about whether they succeed. There is some evidence that, for certain types of learnings and for certain types of students, direct instruction of the total group by the teacher is more effective than other strategies such as small grouping, inquiry, and Socratic techniques.

BOX 11–4   continued

---

5. Students will calculate amount of school tax to be paid on the following properties (five minutes):
   a. A house assessed at $60,000; no exemptions; millage rate of 8.5 mills.
   b. A house assessed at $50,000; homestead exemption of $5,000; millage rate of 6.52 mills.
   c. A house assessed at $75,000; homestead exemption of $5,000 plus senior citizen exemption of $5,000; millage rate of 7.15 mills.
6. Closure: Teacher will ask students such questions as: Which level of government spends most on the education of young people in the community? Approximately how much money was raised locally for schools last year? What percentage of funding came from the state? What percentage of funding came from the federal government? What is the current millage rate? (five minutes).

C. Assignment (two minutes)
1. See if you can find any articles in the local newspapers about costs of education in the community, state, or nation.
2. Ask your parents how much school tax they paid last year and, if they do not object, report to the class how much it was and how it was calculated. Also ask your parents whether they believe the property tax is too high, too low, or about right.

D. Evaluation Techniques
1. Spot-check students' in-class work on charts and calculations of property tax.
2. Ask students to respond to teacher's oral questions at the end of the lesson.

E. Bibliography
1. Copies of the district superintendent's annual report to the school board.
2. Editorial from local newspaper.

F. Instructional Aids and Sources
Overhead projector and transparencies.

---

idence also shows that coaching is an appropriate technique for some types of learnings and students. Teacher training should make prospective teachers aware of the wide range of instructional strategies possible and help them develop proficiency in the use of those strategies. For research on instruction, the following references will prove helpful: David C. Berliner et al., *Phase III of the Beginning Teacher Effectiveness Study* (San Francisco: Far West Laboratory for Educational Research and Development, 1976); Wilbur B. Brookover et al., *A Study of Elementary School Social Systems and School Outcomes* (East Lansing: Michigan State University, Center for Urban Affairs, 1977); Jere E. Brophy and C. M. Evertson, *Process-Product Correlation in the Texas Teacher Effectiveness Study* (Austin: University of Texas, 1974); Jere Brophy and Thomas L. Good, "Teacher Behavior and Student Achievement," in Merlin C. Wittrock, ed., *Handbook of Research on Teaching,* 3rd ed. (New York: Macmillan, 1986), pp. 328–375; Ronald R. Edmonds, *The Characteristics of Schools that Are Instructionally Effective for All Pupils,* audiocassette (Alexandria, Va.: Association for Supervision and Curriculum Development, 1981); N. L. Gage, *The Scientific Basis of the Art of Teaching* (New York: Teachers College Press, 1978); Bruce Joyce and Beverly Showers, "The Coaching of Teaching," *Educational Leadership* 40, no. 1 (October 1982): 4–10; Lawrence W. Lezotte and Beverly A. Bancroft, "Growing Use of the Effective Schools Model for School Improvement," *Educational Leadership* 42, no. 6 (March 1985): 23–27; Donald R. Medley, "The Effectiveness of Teachers," in Penelope L. Peterson and Herbert J. Walberg, eds., *Research on Teaching: Concepts, Findings, and Implications* (Berkeley, Calif.: McCutchan, 1979), pp. 11–27; Barak V. Rosenshine, "Content, Time, and Direct Instruction," in Penelope L. Peterson and Herbert J. Walberg, eds., *Research on Teaching: Concepts, Findings, and Implications* (Berkeley, Calif.: McCutchan, 1979), pp. 28–56; David A. Squires, William G. Huitt, and John K. Segars, eds., *Effective Schools and Classrooms: A Research-Based Perspective* (Alexandria, Va.: Association for Supervision and Curriculum Development, 1983); Jane Stallings, "A Study of the Implementation of Madeline Hunter's Model and Its Effects on Students," *Journal of Educational Research* 78, no, 6 (July/August 1985): 325–337; Walberg, Herbert J. "Synthesis of Research on Teaching," in Merlin C. Wittrock, ed., *Handbook of Research on Teaching,* 3rd ed. (New York: Macmillan, 1986), pp. 214–229; Wittrock, Merlin C., ed. *Handbook of Research on Teaching,* 3rd ed. (New York: Macmillan, 1986), 35 chapters on research on teaching.

INDIVIDUALIZED VERSUS GROUP INSTRUCTION

Controversy swirls around the respective efficacy of individualized versus group approaches to instruction. Proponents of individualization maintain that instruction must be geared toward the needs of the individual learner. Thus we have seen strategies of programmed instruction, self-pacing, independent study, tutorials, guided independent study, and computer-assisted instruction practiced in many classrooms. Proponents of group instruction point out that, for some purposes, teaching entire groups is more efficient and practical in our mass educational system than attempting to individualize instruction. Consequently, teaching groups or subgroups in the classroom, be they heterogeneous or homogeneous, has been the time-honored approach to schooling. Research on teacher effectiveness has supported direct instruction of whole groups, at least for certain purposes.[24]

---

[24]See Barak V. Rosenshine, "Academic Engaged Time, Content Covered, and Direct Instruction," *Journal of Education* 160: no. 3 (August 1978): 38–66.

Interactive Video.   A newer direction in individualization is interactive video, which builds onto the technology of computer-assisted instruction and combines it with features of video presentations. Gary W. Orwig and Donna J. Baumbach provided a simple definition of interactive video when they wrote, "Interactive video is a video message controlled by a computer program."[25]

Whereas typical video presentations place the learner in a passive role, interactive video permits the student to assume an active role by responding to its presentations. Orwig and Baumbach described three levels of interactive video, albeit the first level uses no computer: (1) video disc player without a computer, the least expensive set-up, capable of the least interaction on the part of the student; (2) video disc player with internal computer; and (3) video disc player controlled by an external desktop computer, the most expensive arrangement, possessing the greatest capability for interaction.[26] Orwig and Baumbach saw interactive video as "a powerful instructional medium, and it has the potential to change the way people learn."[27] They commented:

> As interactive video becomes established in education, it will probably have a greater impact upon individualized instruction than all the self-paced workbooks, programmed instruction, drill and practice, lap-packs, computer assisted instruction, and other "individualized" techniques combined.[28]

In the years to come, we may expect to see increased use of the new technologies brought forth by computers, laser video discs, and interactive video. In many cases the electronic strategies will be incorporated into the existing curricula; in others, they will become alternatives to traditional textbook-oriented instruction.

Cooperative Learning.   New versions of group instruction as well as individualized instruction have arisen. A considerable amount of research and experimentation transpired in the 1980s on presentation of instruction through cooperative learning, which is sometimes referred to as collaborative learning. Robert E. Slavin acknowledged that the concept of cooperative learning was an old idea and went on to define it in the following manner:

> Cooperative learning is a form of classroom organization in which students work in small groups to help one another learn academic material.[29]

Slavin noted a key element of cooperative learning—group performance—when he said: "The term refers to classroom techniques in which students work

---

[25]Gary W. Orwig and Donna J. Baumbach, *What Every Educator Needs to Know About the New Technologies: Interactive Video 1* (Orlando, Fla.: UCF/DOE Instructional Computing Resource Center, University of Central Florida, 1989).

[26]Gary W. Orwig and Donna J. Baumbach, *What Every Educator Needs to Know About the New Technologies: Interactive Video 2* (Orlando, Fla.: UCF/DOE Instructional Computing Resource Center, University of Central Florida, 1989).

[27]Orwig and Baumbach, *Interactive Video 1*.

[28]*Ibid.*

[29]Robert E. Slavin, "Cooperative Learning and Student Achievement," in Robert E. Slavin, ed., *School and Classroom Organization* (Hillsdale, N.J.: Lawrence Erlbaum, 1989), p. 129.

on learning activities in small groups and receive rewards as recognition based on their group's performance."[30] Fran Lehr commented on the composition of these groups, defining cooperative learning as "an instructional system that allows students of all achievement levels and backgrounds to work in teams to achieve a common goal."[31]

Cooperative learning research brings to the forefront old arguments about the relative merits of competition, cooperation, and individualization in the classroom. Competitions among individuals for the teacher's approval, praise, smiling faces, grades, awards, and other forms of recognition have been time-honored practices in our schools. We know that competition among pupils can produce negative effects, such as stifling motivation, especially when students cannot compete on an equal basis. David W. Johnson and Roger T. Johnson called attention to more than 323 studies conducted in the past 90 years on the effects of cooperation, competition, and individualized instruction in student achievement and concluded that:

> ... generally achievement is higher in cooperation situations than in competitive or individualistic ones and that cooperative efforts result in more frequent use of higher-level reasoning strategies, more frequent process gain and collective induction, and higher performance on subsequent tests taken individually. . . .[32]

Cooperative learning, as currently defined, emphasizes the positive aspects of pupils working together to help each other. As such, it is distinguished from other cooperative methods of instruction such as small group discussion, group mastery learning and peer tutoring, and from individualized methods such as programmed instruction, individualized mastery learning, interactive video, and independent study, all of which retain individual achievement as the major goal. With cooperative learning, individuals are responsible to their group for the group's progress.

Cooperative learning techniques that are in practice place four to six pupils in groups, depending on the project under way. Groups are deliberately structured by the teacher to include a balance between high and low achievers, boys and girls, and ethnic backgrounds. You can easily infer that the goals of cooperative learning include but go beyond subject matter achievement.

Students in learning teams take responsibility for particular portions of the task, and they must share what they learn with their group in such a way that group members will comprehend. Groups may be restructured from time to time depending on the tasks to be accomplished. The teacher may assign grades both for the group as a whole and for individual members of the group. In some

---

[30]Robert E. Slavin, "Cooperative Learning," *Review of Educational Research,* 50, no. 2 (Summer 1980): 315. Copyright 1980 by the American Educational Research Association. Reprinted by permission of the publisher.

[31]Fran Lehr, "Cooperative Learning," *Journal of Reading* 27, no. 5 (February 1984): 458.

[32]David W. Johnson and Roger T. Johnson, "Cooperative Learning and Achievement," in Shlomo Sharan, ed. *Cooperative Learning: Theory and Research* (New York: Praeger, 1990), p. 33.

variations of grading under cooperative learning practices, grades represent the amount of progress made by individual members of the group. Group members' dependence upon each other serves as a motivator; in effect, it creates a positive form of peer pressure. Competition among teams provides a healthier climate than competition among individuals.

In your reading or observation, you will encounter specific adaptations of cooperative learning developed by some of those who have been carrying out research on this mode of learning. Among these are Learning Together or Circles of Learning (David E. Johnson and Roger T. Johnson), Jigsaw (Elliott Aronson et al.), Student Teams–Achievement Division or STAD (Robert E. Slavin), Team-Assisted Individualization or TAI (Robert E. Slavin et al.), and Group Investigation (Shlomo Sharan et al.).[33]

Concerning the research on cooperative learning, Slavin drew the following implications from the results of research into cooperative learning:

> Presently, the research on cooperative learning in classrooms justifies the following conclusions:
>
> 1. For academic achievement, cooperative learning techniques are no worse than traditional techniques, and in most cases they are significantly better.
> 2. For low level learning outcomes, such as knowledge, calculation, and application of principles, cooperative learning techniques, appear to be more effective than traditional techniques to the degree that they use:
>   (a) A structured, focused, schedule of instruction;
>   (b) Individual accountability for performance among team members;
>   (c) A well-defined group reward system, including rewards or recognition for successful groups.
> 3. For high level cognitive learning outcomes, such as identifying concepts, analysis of problems, judgment, and evaluation, less structured cooperative techniques that involve high student autonomy and participation in decision-making may be more effective than traditional individualistic techniques.
> 4. Cooperative learning techniques have strong and consistent positive effects on relationships between black, white, and Mexican-American students.
> 5. Cooperative learning techniques have fairly consistent effects on mutual concern among students regardless of the specific structure used.
> 6. There is some indication that cooperative learning techniques can improve students' self-esteem.
> 7. Students in classes using cooperative learning generally report greater liking of school than do traditionally taught students.[34]

---

[33] For a brief description of these techniques, see George P. Knight and Elaine Morton Bohlmeyer, "Cooperative Learning and Achievement: Methods for Assessing Causal Mechanisms," in Sharan, *Cooperative Learning*, pp. 1–7. See also Slavin, "Cooperative Learning and Student Achievement," pp. 129–156 (extensive bibliography, pp. 151–156).

[34] Slavin, "Cooperative Learning," *Review of Educational Research*, pp. 337–338.

Slavin did note, however:

What these results indicate is that cooperative learning techniques can achieve both cognitive and affective goals, but that there is still much to be discovered about when they do so—for which kinds of students, under what conditions, in which subjects, and for which techniques or components of techniques are positive effects likely to be observed?[35]

SUMMARY

Selecting instructional strategies is one of the final steps in planning for instruction. Instructional strategies are derived from a number of sources, including the objectives, the subject matter, the pupil, the community, and the teacher.

Teachers vary in their styles, models, and skills. By style we mean the unique, personal qualities that a teacher develops over the years to distinguish himself or herself from all other teachers. Mr. Chips of *Goodbye Mr. Chips* and Henry Higgins of *Pygmalion,* for example, have distinct, memorable styles.

When we speak of models of teaching, we mean a generalized role—a pattern of methods—such as discussion leader, television instructor, or foreign language informant. The so-called Socratic method of stimulating thinking is, in effect, a model. Jesus, for example, used both a model (his role as a preacher) and a method (sermonizing).

Skills of teaching are those generic and specific competencies necessary to design and carry out instruction. Lesson planning, for example, is a generic skill; that is, it is pertinent to all teachers at all levels. The ability to teach pupils to perform the division of whole numbers is an example of a specific skill. Both the models and skills must be compatible with the teacher's style. Instructional strategies must be appropriate to the teacher's style, model, and skill.

Instructional strategies, styles of teaching, and teaching skills are all selected, adopted, and implemented to successfully fulfill instructional goals and objectives. The ultimate purpose of all strategies, styles, models, and skills is to foster student achievement.

The various instructional components should be organized into, among other types of plans, short-term units and daily lesson plans. Although teachers may design their own formats for unit and lesson plans, generic outlines are suggested. As teachers gain experience, less detail in planning is possible. However, *some* planning is always necessary. The reader is referred to selections from the now large body of research on effective presentation of instruction.

---

[35] *Ibid.,* p. 338.

The chapter concluded with discussions of new strategies for presentation of instruction, called "delivery systems" by some people. The technology of interactive video furnishes a newer approach to individualized instruction; cooperative learning is a newer variation of group instruction.

QUESTIONS FOR DISCUSSION

1. How do strategies, models, and styles of teaching differ from each other?
2. How would you go about matching a teacher's style and the learners' styles?
3. How do generic teaching skills differ from specific teaching skills? Give examples.
4. How do you account for the fact that specifications of generic teaching skills differ from state to state?
5. Which do you believe is most effective in promoting student achievement: individualization, competition, or cooperation?

SUPPLEMENTARY EXERCISES

1. Select an instructional objective and design at least three strategies for accomplishing it.
2. Observe several teachers, describe their styles, and tell what makes each teacher unique.
3. Select one of the models of teaching described by Bruce Joyce and Marsha Weil (see bibliography) and describe it to the class.
4. Select one of the models of teaching described by Mary Alice Gunter, Thomas H. Estes, and Jan Hasbrouck Schwab (see bibliography) and describe it in class.
5. Describe with examples how a teacher's style affects selection of instructional strategies.
6. Observe several teachers and try to identify the models they are using.
7. Select one of the generic skills described by Dwight Allen and Kevin Ryan (see bibliography); demonstrate it in class or videotape your demonstration of the skill and critique it in class.
8. Select one of the generic skills discussed by Madeline Hunter and Douglas Russell (see bibliography); demonstrate it in class or videotape your demonstration of the skill and critique it in class.
9. Search the literature on instruction, find several outlines for unit plans, compare them, and select or create an outline you would use, stating reasons.
10. Search the literature on instruction, find several outlines of lesson plans, compare them, and select or create an outline you would use, stating reasons.
11. List several specific teaching skills for a teaching field you know well.
12. Write an essay with appropriate references in support of or opposed to training in generic teaching skills for all teachers.

13. Critique Florida's 27 generic competencies and decide whether you agree they are essential competencies for every teacher.
14. Critique the 50 professional development objectives required by Texas for all levels and decide whether you agree they are essential competencies for every teacher.
15. If your state has a required or recommended set of generic competencies, critique those competencies and decide whether you agree they are essential skills for every teacher.
16. Take a position, stating reasons, for state testing of teacher competency.
17. Design a five- to ten-day-long unit plan appropriate for teaching toward a specific instructional goal.
18. Design a lesson plan for one day based on the unit plan that you prepared for Exercise 17.
19. State your views on on-the-job assessment of beginning teachers for state certification.
20. Report on some of the recent research on effective teaching, particularly studies of time on task (academic engaged time) and direct instruction.
21. Report on the applicability and effectiveness of coaching as an instructional technique.
22. Group exercise: You are a state task force. Your task is to draw up a set of defensible generic competencies that all teachers in your state would be required to master.
23. Critique John B. Carroll's article, "A Model of School Learning." (See bibliography.) Contrast his ideas on mastery learning to those of Benjamin Bloom.
24. Prepare an oral or written report on one of the following:
    a. Mastery learning
    b. Peer tutoring
25. Conduct a demonstration of one of the following technologies adapted for classroom instruction:
    a. Computer-assisted instruction
    b. Interactive video
26. Prepare an oral or written report on one of the following adaptations of the concept of cooperative learning:
    a. Cooperative Integrated Reading and Comprehension (Nancy A. Madden et al.)
    b. Group Investigation (Shlomo Sharan et al.)
    c. Jigsaw (Elliot Aronson et al.)
    d. Jigsaw II (Robert E. Slavin)
    e. Jigsaw III (A. Gonzalez and M. Guerrero)
    f. Learning Together or Circles of Learning (David W. Johnson and Roger T. Johnson)
    g. Student Teams–Achievement Division (Robert E. Slavin)
    h. Team-Assisted Individualization (Robert E. Slavin et al.)
    i. Teams–Games–Tournament (David DeVries and Robert E. Slavin)

BIBLIOGRAPHY

Allen, Dwight and Ryan, Kevin. *Microteaching*. Reading, Mass.: Addison-Wesley, 1969.

Banks, James A. *Teaching Strategies for Ethnic Studies,* 5th ed. Boston: Allyn and Bacon, 1991.

Berenson, David H., Berenson, Sally R., and Carkhuff, Robert B. *The Skills of Teaching: Content Development Skills.* Amherst, Mass.: Human Resource Development Press, 1978.

————. *The Skills of Teaching: Lesson Planning Skills.* Amherst, Mass.: Human Resource Development Press, 1978.

Berenson, Sally R., Berenson, David H., and Carkhuff, Robert R. *The Skills of Teaching: Teaching Delivery Skills.* Amherst, Mass.: Human Resource Development Press, 1979.

Berliner, David C. et al. *Phase III of the Beginning Teacher Effectiveness Study.* San Francisco: Far West Laboratory for Educational Research and Development, 1976.

Brookover, Wilbur B. et al. *A Study of Elementary School Social Systems and School Outcomes.* East Lansing: Michigan State University, Center for Urban Affairs, 1977.

Brooks, Douglas M. "Ethnographic Analysis of Instructional Method." *Theory into Practice* 19, no. 2 (Spring 1980): 144–147.

Brophy, Jere E. and Evertson, C. M. *Process-Product Correlation in the Texas Teacher Effectiveness Study.* Austin: University of Texas, 1974.

Brophy, Jere and Good, Thomas L. "Teacher Behavior and Student Achievement." In Merlin C. Wittrock, ed., *Handbook of Research on Teaching,* 3rd ed., 328–375. New York: Macmillan, 1986.

Burton, William H. *The Guidance of Learning Activities,* 3rd ed. New York: Appleton-Century-Crofts, 1962.

Carkhuff, Robert R. *The Art of Helping III.* Amherst, Mass.: Human Resource Development Press, 1977.

Clarkhuff, Robert R., Berenson, David H., and Pierce, Richard M. *The Skills of Teaching: Interpersonal Skills.* Amherst, Mass.: Human Resource Development Press, 1977.

Carroll, John B. "A Model of School Learning." *Teachers College Record* 64, no. 8 (May 1963): 723–733.

"Collegial Learning." *Educational Leadership* 45, no. 3 (November 1987): 3–75.

Cooper, James M., ed. *Classroom Teaching Skills,* 4th ed. Lexington, Mass.: D. C. Heath, 1990.

"Cooperative Learning." *Educational Leadership* 47, no. 4 (December 1989/January 1990): 3–66.

Dishon, Dee and O'Leary, Pat Wilson. *A Guidebook for Cooperative Learning: A Technique for Creating More Effective Schools.* Holmes Beach, Fla.: Learning Publications, 1984.

Dunn, Rita S. and Dunn, Kenneth J. "Learning Styles/Teaching Styles: Should They . . . Can They . . . Be Matched?" *Educational Leadership* 36, no. 4 (January 1979): 238–244.

————. *Teaching Students Through Their Individual Learning Styles: A Practical Approach.* Reston, Va.: Reston Publishing Company, 1978.

Ellis, Susan S. "Models of Teaching: A Solution to the Teaching Style/Learning Style Dilemma." *Educational Leadership* 36, no. 4 (January 1979): 274–277.

Fischer, Barbara Bree and Fischer, Louis. "Styles in Teaching and Learning." *Educational Leadership* 36, no. 4 (January 1979): 245–254.

Floyd, Steve and Floyd, Beth with Hon, David, McEntee, Patrick, O'Bryan, Kenneth G., and Schwarz, Michael. *Handbook of Interactive Video.* White Plains, N.Y.: Knowledge Industry Publications, 1982.

Gage, N. L., ed. *The Psychology of Teaching Methods,* 75th Yearbook of the National Society for the Study of Education, Part 1. Chicago: University of Chicago Press, 1976.

———. *The Scientific Basis of the Art of Teaching*. New York: Teachers College Press, 1978.

Giroux, Henry A. *Teachers as Intellectuals: Toward a Critical Pedagogy of Learning*. Granby, Mass.: Bergin & Garvey, 1988.

Good, Thomas L. and Brophy, Jere. *Looking in Classrooms,* 3rd ed. New York: Harper & Row, 1984.

Guild, Pat Burke and Garger, Stephen. *Marching to Different Drummers*. Alexandria, Va.: Association for Supervision and Curriculum Development, 1985.

Gunter, Mary Alice, Estes, Thomas H., and Schwab, Jan Hasbrouck. *Instruction: A Models Approach*. Boston: Allyn and Bacon, 1990.

Henson, Kenneth T. *Secondary Teaching Methods*. Lexington, Mass.: D. C. Heath, 1981.

Hilke, Eileen Veronica. *Cooperative Learning*. Fastback 299. Bloomington, Ind.: Phi Delta Kappa, 1990.

Hunter, Madeline and Russell, Douglas. "How Can I Plan More Effective Lessons?" *Instructor* 87, no. 2 (September 1977): 74–75, 88.

Hyman, Ronald T. *Strategic Questioning*. Englewood Cliffs, N.J.: Prentice-Hall, 1979.

Johnson, David W. and Johnson, Roger T. *Learning Together and Alone: Cooperation, Competition, and Individualization*. Englewood Cliffs, N.J.: Prentice-Hall, 1975.

Johnson, David W., Johnson, Roger T., Roy, Patricia, and Holubec, Edythe. *Circles of Learning: Cooperation in the Classroom*. Alexandria, Va.: Association for Supervision and Curriculum Development, 1980.

Jones, Beau, Palincsar, Annemarie, Ogle, Donna, and Carr, Eileen. *Strategic Teaching and Learning: Cognitive Instruction in the Content Areas*. Alexandria, Va.: Association for Super-

vision and Curriculum Development, 1988.

Joyce, Bruce. *Selecting Learning Experiences: Linking Theory and Practice*. Alexandria, Va.: Association for Supervision and Curriculum Development, 1978.

Joyce, Bruce and Showers, Beverly. "The Coaching of Teaching." *Educational Leadership* 40, no. 1 (October 1982): 4–10.

Joyce, Bruce and Weil, Marsha. *Models of Teaching,* 3rd ed. Englewood Cliffs, N.J.: Prentice-Hall, 1986.

Kowalski, Theodore J., Weaver, Roy A., and Henson, Kenneth, T. *Case Studies in Teaching*. White Plains, N.Y.: Longman, 1990.

"Learning Styles and the Brain." *Educational Leadership* 48, no. 2 (October 1990): 3–80.

Lezotte, Lawrence W. and Bancroft, Beverly A. "Growing Use of the Effective Schools Model for School Improvement." *Educational Leadership* 42, no. 6 (March 1985): 23–27.

Medley, Donald R. "The Effectiveness of Teachers." In Penelope L. Peterson and Herbert J. Walberg, eds., *Research on Teaching: Concepts, Findings, and Implications,* 11–27. Berkeley, Calif.: McCutchan, 1979.

Oliva, Peter F. *The Secondary School Today,* 2nd ed. New York: Harper & Row, 1972.

———. *Supervision for Today's Schools,* 3rd ed. White Plains, N.Y.: Longman, 1989.

Orlich, Donald C. et al. *Teaching Strategies: A Guide to Better Instruction*. Lexington, Mass.: D. C. Heath, 1980.

Peter, Laurence J. *Competencies for Teaching: Classroom Instruction*. Belmont, Calif.: Wadsworth, 1975.

Peterson, Penelope L. and Walberg, Herbert J., eds. *Research on Teaching: Concepts, Findings, and Impli-*

cations. Berkeley, Calif.: McCutchan, 1979.

Rosenshine, Barak V. "Content, Time, and Direct Instruction." In Penelope L. Peterson and Herbert J. Walberg, eds., *Research on Teaching: Concepts, Findings, and Implications,* 28–56. Berkeley, Calif.: McCutchan, 1979.

Sharan, Shlomo. "Cooperative Learning in Small Groups: Recent Methods and Effects on Achievement, Attitudes, and Ethnic Relations." *Review of Educational Research* 50, no. 2 (Summer 1980): 241–271.

————, ed. *Cooperative Learning: Theory and Research.* New York: Praeger, 1990.

Slavin, Robert E. *Cooperative Learning.* White Plains, N.Y.: Longman, 1983.

————. "Cooperative Learning." *Review of Educational Research* 50, no. 2 (Summer 1980): 315–342.

————. *Cooperative Learning: Student Teams,* 2nd ed. Washington, D.C.: National Education Association, 1987.

————. *Cooperative Learning: Theory, Research, and Practice.* Englewood Cliffs, N.J.: Prentice-Hall, 1990.

————. *Student Team Learning: An Overview and Practical Guide.* Washington, D.C.: National Education Association, 1988.

————. "Synthesis of Research on Cooperative Learning." *Educational Leadership* 48, no. 5 (February 1991): 71–77.

————, ed. *School and Classroom Organization.* Hillsdale, N.J.: Lawrence Erlbaum Associates, 1989.

Slavin, Robert E. et al., eds. *Learning to Cooperative, Cooperating to Learn.* New York: Plenum, 1985.

"Special Feature on Cooperative Learning." *Educational Leadership* 48, no. 5 (February 1991): 71–94.

Squires, David A., Huitt, William G., and Segars, John K., eds. *Effective Schools and Classrooms: A Research-Based Perspective.* Alexandria, Va.: Association for Supervision and Curriculum Development, 1983.

Stallings, Jane. "A Study of the Implementation of Madeline Hunter's Model and Its Effects on Students." *Journal of Educational Research* 78, no. 6 (July/August 1985): 325–337.

Thelen, Herbert A. *Classroom Grouping for Teachability.* New York: John Wiley & Sons, 1967.

Turner, Richard L. "The Value of Variety in Teaching Styles." *Educational Leadership* 36, no. 4 (January 1979): 257–258.

Walberg, Herbert J. "Synthesis of Research on Teaching." In Merlin C. Wittrock, ed., *Handbook of Research on Teaching,* 3rd ed., 214–229. New York: Macmillan, 1986.

Weil, Marsha and Joyce, Bruce. *Information Processing Models of Teaching: Expanding Your Teaching Repertoire.* Englewood Cliffs, N.J.: Prentice-Hall, 1978.

————. *Social Models of Teaching: Expanding Your Teaching Repertoire.* Englewood Cliffs, N.J.: Prentice-Hall, 1978.

Weil, Marsha, Joyce, Bruce, and Kluwin, Bridget. *Personal Models of Teaching: Expanding Your Teaching Repertoire.* Englewood Cliffs, N.J.: Prentice-Hall, 1978.

Willis, Scott, "Cooperative Learning Fallout?" *ASCD Update* 32, no. 8 (October 1990): 6, 8.

Wittrock, Merlin C., ed. *Handbook of Research on Teaching,* 3rd ed. New York: Macmillan, 1986.

AUDIOTAPES

Association for Supervision and Curriculum Development, 1250 N. Pitt Street, Alexandria, Va. 22314.

The Characteristics of Schools That Are Instructionally Effective for All Pupils, narrated by Ronald R. Edmonds. 67 min. 1981.

Direct Instruction Reconsidered, Barak Rosenshine, presenter. 1990.

FILMSTRIP-AUDIOTAPE PROGRAMS

Vimcet Associates, P.O. Box 24714, Los Angeles, Calif. 90024:

Systematic Instructional Decision-Making. 1967.

Appropriate Practice. 1967.

Perceived Purpose. 1967.

Analyzing Learning Outcomes. 1969.

Knowledge of Results. 1969.

Teaching Units and Lesson Plans. 1969.

Individualizing Instruction. 1971.

Instructional Tactics for Affective Objectives. 1971.

INVENTORY

Learning Style Inventory. Price Systems, Inc., Box 3067, Lawrence, Kan. 66044. An instrument for identifying learning environments preferred by students.

NETWORK

Learning Styles Network, c/o Prof. Rita Dunn, School of Education and Human Services, St. John's University, Grand Central and Utopia Parkways, Jamaica, N.Y. 11439. Cosponsored by the National Association of Secondary School Principals and St. John's University.

VIDEOTAPES

American Association of School Administrators, 1801 N. Moore Street, Arlington, Va. 22209.

Time on Task. 26 min. 1983. Shows teachers how to make maximum use of time for learning.

Association for Supervision and Curriculum Development, 1250 N. Pitt Street, Alexandria, Va. 22314.

Cooperative Learning. Five videotapes, 20 min. to 42 min. 1990. Series features David Johnson, Roger Johnson, Robert Slavin, and Britt Tatman Vasquez showing how teachers implement cooperative learning in elementary, middle, and secondary school classrooms.

Effective Schools for Children at Risk. 25 min. 1991. Discusses the work of Ronald Edmonds on effective schools. Explains characteristics of effective schools. Richard Andrews, James Comer, Lawrence Lezotte, and Robert Slavin, presenters. Includes *Leader's Guide* and *Readings from Educational Leadership: Effective Schools and School Improvement.*

Effective Teaching for Higher Achievement. Includes two hours of videotape and leader's guide. Featured are Barak Rosenshine, Jane Stallings, Jere Brophy, Georgea Mohlman Sparks, and Dennis Sparks.

Learning—A Matter of Style. 30 min. Includes discussion guide. Rita Dunn describes examples of teachers adapting instruction to students' learning styles.

Teacher and School Effectiveness. 21 min. 1981. Barak V. Rosenshine, Ronald Edmonds, and Peter Mortimore discuss ways of improving teacher and school effectiveness.

The Teaching Strategies Library. Parts One and Two. 1987–89. Eight tapes, 40 to 50 min. Covers eight teaching strategies: mastery lecture, concept attainment, concept formation, peer practice, compare and contrast, reading for meaning, "Synectics,"™ and circle of knowledge. Richard Strong, Harvey Silver, and Robert Hanson, program consultants. Overview tape, 30 min. Two training manuals. ("Synectics" is a registered trademark for Synectics, Inc., Cambridge, Mass.)

Video Library of Teaching Episodes. Episodes 1–20. 1988–89. Twenty tapes. 15–20 min. episode with analysis.

Video Library of Teaching Episodes. Episodes 21–30. Urban Schools. 1991. Ten tapes. 15–20 min. episode with analysis.

Instructional Dynamics, Inc., 845 Via de la Paz, Suite A177, Pacific Palisades, Calif. 90272.

Mastery Teaching: Increasing Instructional Effectiveness in Secondary Schools, Colleges, and Universities. Twenty videotapes by Madeline Hunter Designed for increasing the effectiveness of instruction.

CHAPTER TWELVE ≡≡≡≡≡

Evaluating Instruction

After studying this chapter you should be able to:

1. Define preassessment, formative evaluation, and summative evaluation, and describe the purposes of each.

2. Explain the differences between norm-referenced and criterion-referenced measurement and state the purposes for which each is intended.

3. Design test/evaluation questions in the major categories of each of the three domains of learning.

ASSESSING INSTRUCTION

Assessing Student Achievement

She holds her head in her hands, eyes transfixed on the top of the desk. She looks with displeasure at the pile of examinations in front of her, each filled with red marks indicating errors. She has administrated the acid test—the examination on the unit on elections: local, state, and federal. Four weeks' work wasted! On a scale of one to 100 and a passing grade of 70, only 12 out of 36 pupils achieved the passing mark. Why? she asks herself. What went wrong? A stream of reasons floods her brain:

- □ The students are all blithering idiots who would flunk any test no matter how simple.
- □ They did not pay attention when she was going over the material.
- □ They do not study; they are more interested in drugs and sex than in the electoral process.
- □ They are too careless in answering the questions.
- □ Their parents do not force them to do their homework.

After several moments of indulging in recrimination and blaming the poor results on the students, she begins to take a look at the situation more rationally. What are some hypotheses, she asks herself, for such a high percentage of failures? After some serious reflection, she begins to wonder:

- □ Were the objectives appropriate? Were they pertinent to the subject matter? Were they within the learning abilities of the pupils? Were they relevant to the students?
- □ Did the pupils possess the prerequisite competencies before we began the unit in which they did so poorly? How do I know?
- □ Did I use the right instructional techniques? Did the strategies I chose fit the learning styles of the students?
- □ Did I make periodic checks along the way? What did they reveal?
- □ Did I alert them to the type of exam?
- □ Did the exam questions relate to the objectives? Were they clear?
- □ Did the pupils have sufficient time to respond to all the questions? Were the classroom conditions suitable for exam taking?
- □ Were the pupils at fault for their failures? Did I fail the pupils in my role as instructor? Or was there a blending of responsibilities for the low scores?
- □ Did I really find out what the students did or did not learn?
- □ And what do I do now? How shall I treat the exam results? What effect should their scores have on the next report card? How will I explain low scores to the principal, to the pupils, to the parents?

The term "evaluation of instruction" could be expanded to read "evaluation of instruction through the assessment of student achievement." In one sense, evaluation of instruction is evaluation of the effectiveness of the instructor. For example, does the teacher choose the right delivery system? Are the teacher's objectives clear? Do test items relate to objectives? Does the teacher present the material clearly? These are types of questions a supervisor asks in evaluating teacher performance. Although this book does not examine the complex and important topic of teacher performance, you will find many helpful references on this topic in the professional literature on supervision.[1] This chapter focuses on the assessment of student performance.

In another sense, evaluation of instruction is evaluation of the curriculum. It reveals the success of one dimension—how much students achieve in areas that are assessed. It may also indicate whether the content has been adequately covered. Evaluation of curriculum does not answer curricular concerns such as whether the subject matter was the right choice to begin with, whether its content is relevant, whether it meets student or societal needs, whether the profession and public are satisfied with it, whether it meets the school's philosophy and aims, or whether the content has been selected wisely. These are curricular dimensions that must be evaluated in addition to assessment of student achievement. We will look at the evaluation of curriculum in the next chapter. It is easy to see, however, that evaluation of instruction, evaluation of teacher performance, and evaluation of the curriculum are all intimately interrelated.

Cycle Within a Cycle

Instruction in the model for curriculum development followed in this text is a cycle within the curriculum cycle (see Figure 12–1). Let's once again pull out the instructional chain that makes up the instructional model. It is a submodel of the model for curriculum development presented in Chapter 5 (see Figure 12–2). To keep the model for curriculum development uncluttered, the feedback line for this submodel was depicted simply. It proceeds from the terminal component of the instructional chain—the Evaluation of instruction—directly to the beginning of the instructional model—the Specification of instructional goals.

Note that the feedback line from the Evaluation of instruction to Instructional goals demonstrates a cycle and indicates that modification in the system can be made in sequence. However, this figure would be more accurate if it showed the feedback lines to *each* component because evaluation results may reveal needed modifications in components anywhere in the system. The instructional submodel with all feedback lines is shown in Figure 12–3.

As we have seen, the instructional chain begins with specifying the goals. This cycle is not complete until we learn whether or not the instructional goals and objectives have been achieved. The problem before us now is one of evaluating the instruction that has taken place.

---

[1]For discussion of teacher evaluation see Peter F. Oliva, *Supervision for Today's Schools*, 3rd ed. (White Plains, N.Y.: Longman, 1989), Chapters 11, 12, and 13.

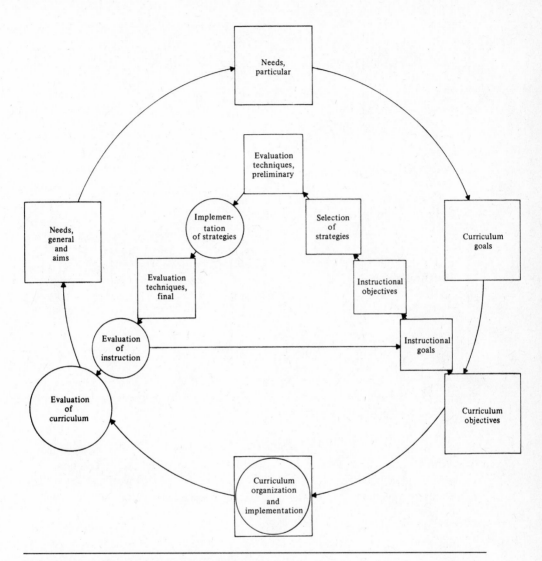

Figure 12–1 The instruction and curriculum cycles

AN ERA OF ASSESSMENT

Evaluation. Assessment. Measurement. Testing. Accountability. These words are heard with great frequency today in both public and professional circles. Specialists in measurement and evaluation are in great demand, for we are now in an era of assessment. Although this era began some time ago, its tempo began to increase considerably in the mid-1970s. In the past few years, the movement's emphasis and the sources of its impetus have changed somewhat.

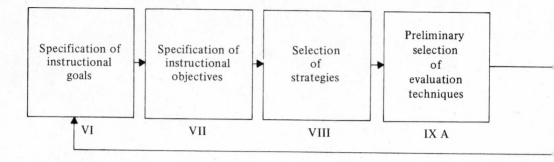

Figure 12–2   Instructional model with one feedback line

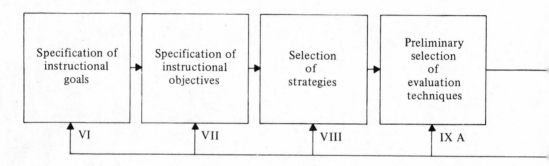

Figure 12–3   Instructional model with all feedback lines

We are all familiar with the phenomenon of mass testing that has dominated America ever since Edward L. Thorndike conceptualized the first standardized tests. The standardized SAT and GRE tests are household words in the United States in much the same way the nonstandardized baccalaureate tests are in France.

William H. Whyte, Jr., Martin Gross, and Banesh Hoffman were pointing to the dangers of mass testing in the late 1950s and early 1960s. Whyte and Gross were particularly concerned about personality testing, and Hoffman was critical of typical standardized multiple-choice tests.[2] In 1981, Andrew J. Strenio, Jr., cautioned us about "the testing trap."[3]

Definition of Terms

At this point, let's clarify the meaning of the main terms used in this chapter. These are evaluation, assessment, measurement, and testing. "Evaluation," said

---

[2]William H. Whyte, Jr., *The Organization Man* (New York: Simon and Schuster, 1956); Martin L. Gross, *The Brain Watchers* (New York: Random House, 1962); Banesh Hoffman, *The Tyranny of Testing* (New York: Crowell-Collier, 1962).

[3]Andrew J. Strenio, Jr., *The Testing Trap* (New York: Rawson, Wade, 1981).

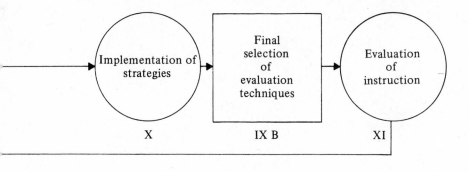

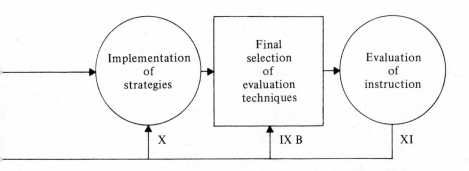

Robert H. Davis, Lawrence T. Alexander, and Stephen L. Yelon, "is a continuous process of collecting and interpreting information in order to assess decisions made in designing a learning system.[4] *Evaluation* and *assessment* are used interchangeably in this text to denote the general process of appraisal. Measurement and testing are subsumed under the general classifications of evaluation and assessment.

Measurement is the means of determining the degree of achievement of a particular competency. *Testing* is the use of instruments for measuring achievement. Thus, measurement and testing are ways of gathering evaluation and assessment data. However, we have means other than testing to evaluate student performance. When we speak of evaluating a student's performance of a competency, we may or may not measure that performance. Measurement implies a degree of precision and observable behavior.

In this chapter, we will not fully explore measurement, evaluation, testing techniques, and the by-products of evaluating instruction—marking

[4]From Learning System Design: An Approach to the Improvement of Instruction, p. 81, by Robert H. Davis, Lawrence T. Alexander, and Stephen L. Yelon. Copyright ©1974 by McGraw-Hill. Used with the permission of McGraw-Hill Book Company.

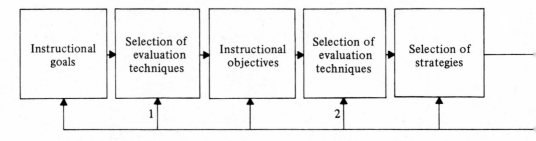

Figure 12–4   Stages of planning for evaluation

and reporting.[5] We will seek instead to develop some basic understandings about evaluating instruction, including a limited number of principles of measurement and testing.

STAGES OF PLANNING FOR EVALUATION

You will note, in referring to the proposed model for curriculum development,[6] that component IX on the selection of evaluation techniques is divided into two parts: IX A, Preliminary selection of evaluation techniques, and IX B, Final selection of evaluation techniques. This separation is made in order to convey the understanding that planning of evaluation techniques takes place both before and after instruction. However, this dual separation is an oversimplification. To be more precise, we should show planning for evaluation techniques interspersed at each stage of the Instructional Model. An expanded diagram of instruction showing the many stages of planning for evaluation is presented in Figure 12–4.

Expanded Model of Instruction

What the expanded model indicates is that the selection of evaluation techniques, including test items, is a continuous process. This concept of planning for evaluation differs from the practice of many teachers who wait until the end of the instruction, then prepare and administer a test. Evaluation techniques should be jotted down at each of the five stages shown in the expanded

---

[5]See L. R. Gay, *Educational Evaluation and Measurement: Competencies for Analysis and Application,* 2nd ed. (Columbus, Ohio: Charles E. Merrill, 1985).

[6]See Figure 5–5, p. 172.

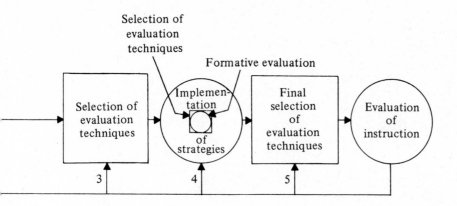

model. Three of these stages are prior to instruction; one, midinstruction; and one postinstruction. Test items should be recorded when they occur to the teacher while the content is fresh in mind. Continuous accumulation of test items and choice of other evaluation techniques can simplify end-of-instruction evaluation.

Three Phases of Evalution

The teacher needs to be able to demonstrate skill in three phases of evaluation:

☐ preassessment
☐ formative evaluation
☐ summative evaluation

These terms are technical words to connote evaluation that takes place *before* instruction (preassessment), *during* instruction (formative), and *after* instruction (summative).

Preassessment.   *Preassessment* possesses a dual nature. Walter Dick and Lou Carey described two types of tests that precede instruction.[7] These two types are an entry-behaviors test and a pretest. The *entry-behaviors test* is "a criterion-referenced test designed to measure skills which have been identified as being critical to beginning instruction.[8] This type of preassessment is conducted to determine whether students possess the prerequisite knowledge that will enable them to proceed with the new treatment. The *pretest* is "criterion-referenced to the objectives the designer intends to teach."[9] "Criterion-referenced" tests, discussed later in this chapter, measure students' achievement not by how well

---

[7]Walter Dick and Lou Carey, *The Systematic Design of Instruction*, 2nd ed. (Glenview, Ill: Scott, Foresman, 1985), p. 109.
[8]Ibid. Reprinted with permission.
[9]Ibid.

they compare with their classmates but by how well they master predetermined instructional objectives.

The entry-behaviors (or entry skills) test covers preceding (prerequisite) learnings, whereas the pretest covers subject matter to be learned. A pretest alone is not sufficient, for if students do poorly on a pretest (as they should, if future instruction is really new to them), the instructor cannot tell whether the students did poorly because they did not know the material to come (acceptable) or did not have the prerequisite knowledge or skills (not acceptable). Some means of judging possession of prerequisite skills is essential. Lack of prerequisite skills calls for remedial instruction and repetition of instruction instead of proceeding with new content.

Formative Evaluation.   *Formative evaluation* consists of the formal and informal techniques, including testing, that are used during the period of instruction. Progress tests are an illustration of formative evaluation. Benjamin S. Bloom, J. Thomas Hastings, and George F. Madaus advised instructors to "break a course or subject into smaller units of learning" and to administer "brief diagnostic progress tests."[10] Dick and Carey described an "embedded test," which consists of test items that "are included as part of the instructional strategy, and may appear every few pages, or after a major sequence of instruction."[11]

Through formative evaluation, teachers may diagnose and take remedial action to help students overcome difficulties before they are confronted with the *terminal (summative) evaluation.* Formative evaluation enables teachers to monitor their instruction so that they may keep it on course.

Summative Evaluation.   *Summative evaluation* is the assessment that takes place at the end of a course or unit. A final examination (*posttest*) is a means used for the summative evaluation of instruction. Its major purpose is to find out whether the students have mastered the preceding instruction. The astute teacher uses results of summative evaluation to revise his or her program and methods for subsequent groups.

NORM-REFERENCED AND CRITERION-REFERENCED MEASUREMENT

Norm-Referenced Measurement

Two divergent concepts of measurement compete for the attention and loyalty of instructors. *Norm-referenced measurement* is the classic approach to assessment in which a student's performance on a test is compared to the performance of other students who took the test. Following this principle, standardized tests

---

[10]From *Handbook on Formative and Summative Evaluation of Student Learning*, p. 53, by Benjamin S. Bloom, George F. Madaus, and J. Thomas Hastings. Copyright ©1971 by McGraw-Hill. Used with the permission of McGraw-Hill Book Company.
[11]Dick and Carey, *Systematic Design*, p. 109.

of achievement are administered and norms—standards of performance—are calculated for various groups who took the tests. The scores made by students who subsequently take the tests are compared to those made by the population on whom the test was standardized.

Classroom teachers follow the same principle whenever they measure the achievement of one student against or in relationship to that of other students in class. As a gross example of this approach to measurement, the teacher will administer a test, calculate the scores, rank the score from highest to lowest, find the middle score (which becomes a C grade), then grade all other tests in relationship to that middle grade. In this nonstandardized situation, students are rated in relationship to performance of that particular group on that particular test.

Criterion-Referenced Measurement

Since the norm-referenced approach to measurement is so common and so universally practiced, it might be asked, "What other approach is there?" *Criterion-referenced measurement* is the alternative to norm-referenced measurement. In this approach, the performance of students on a test is compared to criteria that were established in the instructional objectives. A student's success on a criterion-referenced test depends on demonstrated mastery of the objectives and not on his or her performance as related to others in the class.

Because of its long history of usage, the norm-referenced approach is reasonably well understood by teachers, students, and parents. Further, imbued with a sense of competition, many parents invite the kinds of comparisons that are made under a norm-referenced system.

Among the proponents of norm-referenced testing are standardized test makers, those who advocate competitive grading, those who have a need to screen or select persons (for example, college admissions officers), those who draw up honor rolls, admission committees of honorary societies, and those who award scholarships. Norm-referenced testing is necessary when a limited number of places are to be filled from a pool of applicants in excess of the number of places and when only a limited number of awards are to be distributed among a group of aspirants. Among the practitioners of criterion-referenced measurement are the instructional-design specialists and the district, state, and national assessment people. These persons desire to know whether students achieve mastery of specified objectives. If I may use the analogy of the smiling or frowning face, the norm-referenced tester frowns when all students pass an exam because it does not discriminate between high and low achievers. The criterion-referenced tester wears a broad smile when all students pass an exam, since students have mastered the objectives on which they were tested.

The emergence of criterion-referenced measurement is relatively new. Dick and Carey made reference to this phenomenon when they observed:

> In recent years, classroom testing has taken a very different turn.... As more and more emphasis has been placed on statements of explicit behaviors

TABLE 12–1   Comparison of norm-referenced and criterion-referenced measurement

NORM-REFERENCED MEASUREMENT	CRITERION-REFERENCED MEASUREMENT
1. The main function of norm-referenced measurement is to ascertain the student's relative position within a normative group.	1. The main function of criterion-referenced measurement is to assess whether the student has mastered a specific criterion or performance standard.
2. Either general conceptual outcomes (usually done) or precise objectives may be specified when constructing norm-referenced measurement.	2. Complete behavioral objectives (i.e., planning objectives) are specified when constructing criterion-referenced measurement.
3. The criterion for mastery is not usually specified when using norm-referenced measurement.	3. The criterion for mastery must be stated (i.e., planning objectives) for use in criterion-referenced measurement.
4. Test items for norm-referenced measurement are constructed to discriminate among students.	4. Test items for criterion-referenced measurement are constructed to measure a predetermined level of proficiency.
5. Variability of scores is desirable as an aid to meaningful interpretation.	5. Variability is irrelevant; it is not a necessary condition for a satisfactory criterion-referenced measurement.
6. The test results from norm-referenced measurement are amenable to transposition to the traditional grading system (A, B, C, D, F).	6. The test results from criterion-referenced measurement suggest the use of a binary system (i.e., satisfactory-unsatisfactory; pass-fail). However, criterion-referenced measurement test results can be transposed into the traditional grading system by following a set of specifically constructed rules.

SOURCE: Mary-Jeannette Smythe, Robert J. Kibler, and Patricia W. Hutchings, "A Comparison of Norm-Referenced and Criterion-Referenced Measurement with Implications for Communication Instruction," *The Speech Teacher* 22, no. 1 (January 1973): 4. Reprinted by permission.

that students must demonstrate, it has been increasingly obvious that a fair and equitable evaluation system is one that measures those specific behaviors. After students have been told what they have to do to be successful on a learning unit, they should be tested accordingly.[12]

Comparison of the Two Types of Measurement

Mary-Jeanette Smythe, Robert J. Kibler, and Patricia W. Hutchings have made a comparison of general characteristics of norm-referenced and criterion-referenced measurement systems, as shown in Table 12–1.

---

[12]Ibid., pp. 107–108.

Robert J. Kibler, Donald J. Cegala, David T. Miles, and Larry L. Barker list the following four ways that criterion-referenced tests may be used:

☐ for preassessment purposes
☐ for formative testing...that is, testing that is used concurrently with instruction for the purpose of checking the progress of students so that assistance may be provided when necessary
☐ to determine whether components of the instructional model...need modification
☐ to determine whether students have achieved the criterion levels of objectives[13]

W. James Popham described a major distinction between the purposes of norm-referenced and criterion-referenced measurement when he explained:

Since norm-referenced measures permit comparisons among people, their primary purpose is to make decisions about *individuals*. Which pupils should be counseled to pursue higher education? Which pupils should be advised to attain vocational skills?...

Criterion-referenced tests make decisions both about *individuals* and *treatments*. In decisions regarding individuals, we might use a criterion-referenced test to determine whether a learner had mastered a criterion skill considered prerequisite to a new training program. In decisions regarding treatments, we might design a criterion-referenced measure which reflected a set of instructional objectives supposedly achieved by a replicable instructional sequence. By administering the criterion-referenced measure to appropriate learners who had completed the instructional sequence, we could decide the effectiveness of the sequence.[14]

On the surface, norm-referenced tests look no different from criterion-referenced tests. However, in the first edition of their book Dick and Carey spoke of differences in construction of the two types of measures as follows:

Criterion-referenced tests include only test items that are based on specified behavioral objectives. Each item requires students to demonstrate the performance stated in an objective. Standards for acceptable performance on the test are based upon criteria stated in the objectives.

Norm-referenced tests are constructed differently. It is usually unnecessary for the exact performance desired to be described in behavioral terms prior to item or test construction. Test items are not necessarily based on instruction students receive or on skills or behaviors that are identified as relevant for student learning. Items that are developed from a given domain for norm-referenced tests are administered to a variety of students from the target population. Those items that cause the greatest spread or range in students'

---

[13]Robert J. Kibler, Donald J. Cegala, David T. Miles, and Larry L. Barker, *Objectives for Instruction and Evaluation* (Boston: Allyn and Bacon, 1974), p. 116.
[14]W. James Popham. From *Evaluating Instruction,* ©1973, pp. 25–26. Reprinted by permission of Prentice-Hall, Inc., Englewood Cliffs, New Jersey.

responses are selected for inclusion on a norm-referenced test. The range of scores is usually expected to resemble a normal or bell-shaped curve, hence the name "norm-referenced."[15]

Popham saw differences in the construction of items for the two types of tests as a matter of "set":

> The basic differences between item construction in a norm-referenced framework and item construction in a criterion-referenced framework is a matter of "set" on the part of the item writer. . . . When an individual constructs items for a norm-referenced test, he tries to produce *variant* scores so that individual performances can be contrasted. . . . He disdains items which are "too easy" or "too hard." He avoids multiple choice items with few alternative responses. He tries to increase the allure of wrong answer options. He does all of this to develop a test which will produce different scores for different people. . . .
>
> The criterion-referenced item designer is guided by a different principle. His chief purpose is to make sure the item accurately reflects the criterion behavior. Difficult or easy, discriminating or indiscriminate, the item has to represent the class of behaviors delimited by the criterion.[16]

We should take note that the tests developed by the states to assess achievements of both students and teachers are by and large criterion-referenced.

The Instructional Model suggested in this text places the specification of instructional objectives in a central position and, therefore, leans toward a criterion-referenced approach to classroom testing. This point of view, however, does not eliminate the use of standardized tests in the school or the use of norm-referenced teacher-made tests for purposes they can fulfill. It does eliminate the use of a norm-centered approach to classroom testing that permits teachers to adopt the philosophy of the normal curve and to generate scores that result in a normal distribution of grades ranging from A through F on every test. Such a practice violates the philosophy of the normal curve, which holds that traits are distributed at random throughout the general population. No single class is a random sample of the general population. Therefore, to hold A's to a mere handful, to condemn some students automatically to F's, to grant a certain percentage of B's and D's, and to assign about two-thirds of a class to the so-called average or C grade is not a defensible practice.

EVAULUATION IN THREE DOMAINS

Objectives, as we have noted, fall into three domains—the cognitive, the affective, and the psychomotor. Teachers face the task of assessing pupils' performance in the various domains. They may choose any of the numerous types

---

[15]Dick and Carey, *Systematic Design,* 1st ed. (1978), p. 88. Reprinted with permission.

[16]W. James Popham. From *Evaluating Instruction,* © 1973, p. 30. Reprinted by permission of Prentice-Hall, Inc., Englewood Cliffs, New Jersey.

of tests: actual performance, essay, or one or more objective tests—multiple choice, alternate response, completion, matching, or rearrangement.[17]

Each domain presents its unique evaluation problems. Let's look at some illustrations of test items for the major categories of each domain.

Psychomotor Domain

Objectives in the psychomotor domain are best evaluated by actual performance of the skill being taught. For example, if we wish students to be able to swim 100 yards without stopping, we require that they hop into the water and show us that they can do it. The students fail, we might say, if they sink to the bottom.

We may wish to qualify the performance by requiring students to swim 100 yards in x number of minutes. To pass the test, students would have to satisfy that criterion.

The teacher has to make some judgmental calls when students are asked to demonstrate perceptual-motor skills. Form and grace might be considered in the 100-yard swim as well as completion or speed of completion. Evaluative judgments are made when students are asked to demonstrate the ability to make a mobile in art class, to build a bookcase in woodshop, to create a blouse in home economics, to drive a golf ball in physical education class, or to administer artificial respiration in the first aid course.

Beyond the simple dichotomy—performance or nonperformance (pass-fail, satisfactory-unsatisfactory)—of a skill lie such factors as speed, originality, and quality. The teacher may choose to include these criteria as part of the assessment process. When judgmental criteria are to be used, they should be communicated to the students in advance. The teacher will find it helpful to identify as many indicators of the criteria as possible. For example, in the case of the mobile made in art class, indicators of quality might be durability, precision of construction, neatness, and detail.

There are times when teachers settle for a cognitive recounting of how the student would demonstrate a perceptual-motor skill. Ideally, psychomotor skills should be tested by actual performance. Because of lack of time or facilities, however, it is not always possible for every pupil to demonstrate every skill. For example, a group of students in home economics working together may have baked bread. A final examination question might be, "List the steps you would take in making white bread." Although not altogether satisfactory from a pedagogical point of view—most of us can talk a better game than we can play—this technique may be used. We suspect, of course, that many a forlorn loaf of bread will be turned out by the inexperienced bakers before the skill is perfected.

---

[17]For discussion of types of tests and test items see Peter F. Oliva, *The Secondary School Today,* 2nd ed. (New York: Harper & Row, 1972), Chapter 19.

Test Items of the Psychomotor Domain.   Here are examples of test items for each of the seven major categories of the Simpson taxonomy of the psychomotor domain:

1. *Perception:* Distinguish between an *s* and a *z* sound.
2. *Set:* Demonstrate how to hold a fishing pole.
3. *Guided response:* Make half-notes, following the teacher's explanation.
4. *Mechanism:* Saw a six-foot two-by-four into three pieces of equal size.
5. *Complex overt response:* Perform an auto tune-up.
6. *Adaptation:* Sketch a new arrangement for the furniture of a living room.
7. *Origination:* Paint an original landscape in watercolors.

All of these test items call for actual performance. Observe that all seven could equally be instructional objectives. We, therefore, have a perfect match between the objectives and the test items. On the other hand, let's take the following psychomotor objective. Is this objective at the same time a test item?

Objective for high school physical education: The pupil will demonstrate skill in swimming. This objective is broad, complex, and is without a stipulated degree of mastery. Although it is an objective desired by the physical education instructor, it is difficult to convert into a test item as it currently stands. Establishing a series of subobjectives from which we could derive the test items would help. For example, the student will demonstrate how to

- □ dive into the pool
- □ tread water
- □ float on his or her stomach
- □ float on his or her back
- □ do the breaststroke
- □ do the crawl
- □ swim underwater the width of the pool

The instructor might limit appraisal of the pupils' performance in these skills to "satisfactory" or "unsatisfactory."

Cognitive Domain

Achievement in the cognitive domain is ordinarily demonstrated in school by pupil performance on written tests administered to a group—usually, but not always, an entire class. To administer individual written or oral tests on a regular basis requires an excessive amount of time. The teacher should seek to evaluate, when appropriate, student achievement in all six levels of the Bloom taxonomy of the cognitive domain, using both essay and objective test items.

Test Items of the Cognitive Domain.   Whereas objective items sample knowledge of content on a broad scale, essay tests sample limited content and provide information about the student's ability to organize his or her thoughts, write coherently, and use English properly. The following test items show several ways objectives in the cognitive domain can be evaluated:

1. Knowledge
   Essay: Explain how Samuel Clemens got the name Mark Twain.
   True-False: A whale is a warm-blooded mammal.
   Completion: The United States, the Soviet Union, Great Britain, France, and _____ hold permanent seats on the UN Security Council.

2. Comprehension
   Essay: What is meant when a person says, "Now you've opened Pandora's box"?
   Multiple Choice: A catamaran is a
   a. lynx
   b. boat
   c. fish
   d. tool

3. Application
   Essay: Describe, giving at least three current illustrations, how the law of supply and demand works.
   Multiple-Choice: $4 \div \frac{1}{2} =$
   a. 2
   b. 4
   c. 6
   d. 8

4. Analysis
   Essay: Analyze the school board's annual budget as to categories of funds, needs of the schools, and sources of funds.
   Multiple-Choice: A survey of parents showed 90 percent believe schools are too lax in discipline; 5 percent too strict; and 5 percent undecided. We might conclude that these parents
   a. favor looser discipline
   b. favor smaller classes
   c. favor stricter teachers
   d. favor higher taxes
   e. favor all of the above

5. Synthesis
   Essay: Describe the origin and significance of the Thanksgiving Day holiday.
   (Since synthesis and the highest category of the cognitive domain—evaluation—require extensive narration, they are best evaluated through use of essay test items.)

6. Evaluation

Essay: Read the following planks from the platform of the Democratic or Republican Party and give your reasons for whether you believe the planks fulfill current needs in the country. Identify evidence to support your reasons.

The types of test items selected depends on the teacher's purpose and the amount of time that can be devoted to the test. As a general rule, a combination of test items provides variety and thereby stimulates interest. If essay items are used either alone or in conjunction with objective items, sufficient time needs to be provided for students to organize their answers and to respond fully to the essay questions. The passing score should always be communicated to the learners before they take a test.

Cognitive objectives, like those for psychomotor skills, are often suitable test items. For example, if we choose the objective, "The student will be able to list the steps by which a federal bill becomes a law," the teacher has a ready-made test item, "List the steps by which a federal bill becomes a law." However, if the objective is a general competency such as "The student will be able to divide whole numbers by fractions," the teacher must create specific test items that permit students to demonstrate the competency.

Affective Domain

We should refrain from using the terms "testing" and "measurement" in reference to the affective domain. As stated earlier, student achievement in the affective domain is difficult and sometimes impossible to assess. Attitudes, values, and feelings can be deliberately concealed; learners have the right to hide personal feelings and beliefs, if they so choose. Affective learnings may not be visible in the school situation at all.

The achievement of objectives in the affective domain, therefore—though important in our educational system—cannot be measured or observed like objectives in the cognitive and psychomotor domains. For that reason, students should not be graded on an A through F or percentage system for their lack or possession of affective attributes. Except for a few affective objectives like conduct (provided it can be defined and observed), these types of learning should probably not be graded at all, even with different symbols.

We attempt to evaluate affective outcomes when we encourage students to express their feelings, attitudes, and values about the topics discussed in class. We can observe students and may find obvious evidence of some affective learnings. For example, a child who cheats has not mastered the value of honesty. The bully who picks on smaller children has not learned concern for other people. The child who expresses a desire to suppress freedom of speech has not learned what democracy means. The normal child who habitually feels that he or she cannot do the work has developed a low self-concept.

Thus some affective behaviors are apparent. Teachers can spot them and through group or individual counseling can perhaps bring about a change in behavior. On the other hand, children are at school only six or seven hours a day. They are constantly demonstrating affective behaviors—positive and negative—outside of school, where the teacher will never have occasion to observe them. Are the students helpful at home? Are they law-abiding in the community? Do they protect the environment? Do they respect other people? Who can tell for sure without observing the behavior? Students may profess to behave in certain ways to please the teacher or others and then turn around and behave far differently outside the classroom.

Following the Krathwohl taxonomy of the affective domain, let's look at some affective objectives that contain ways for evaluating their achievement.

1. Receiving
   The student expresses in class an awareness of friction among ethnic groups in the school.
2. Responding
   The student volunteers to serve on a human relations committee in the school.
3. Valuing
   The student expresses a desire to achieve a positive school climate.
4. Organization
   The student controls his or her temper when driving.
5. Characterization by value or value complex
   The student expresses and exemplifies in his or her behavior a positive outlook on life.

Assessment Items of the Affective Domain.   In its evaluation of the Eight-Year Study, the Progressive Education Association assessed students' preference for newspaper reading (an objective within the affective category Receiving) by presenting them with a list of sections of the newspaper and asking them to mark each section with a U if they usually read it, an O if they read it occasionally, and an R if they read it rarely.[18] Whether students found pleasure in science activities (Responding) was evaluated by the Progressive Education Association by a list of scientific activities for each of which the students indicated satisfaction, uncertainty of their reaction, or dissatisfaction. In addition, students were asked if they had ever performed the activity.[19]

To assess the appreciation of economic factors in people's lives (Valuing), the Progressive Education Association created descriptions of economic prob-

---

[18] David R. Krathwohl, Benjamin S. Bloom, and Bertram B. Masia, *Taxonomy of Educational Objectives: The Classification of Educational Goals: Handbook II: Affective Domain* (White Plains, N.Y.: Longman, 1964), p. 116.
[19] Ibid., p. 138.

Box 12–1   Items for affective category of Organization

Gordon W. Allport, Philip E. Vernon, and Gardner Lindzey created the following items that fall in the affective category Organization

Category: Organization

Subcategory: Organization of a value system

Objective: Begins to develop dominant values

Item: *Directions*: Each of the following situations or questions is followed by four possible attitudes or answers. Arrange these answers in the order of your personal preference by writing, in the appropriate box at the right, a score of 4, 3, 2, or 1. To the statement you prefer most give 4, to the statement that is second most attractive 3, and so on.

In your opinion, can a man who works in business all week best spend Sunday in

a. trying to educate himself by reading serious books?

b. trying to win at golf, or racing?

c. going to an orchestral concert?

d. hearing a really good sermon?

Viewing Leonardo da Vinci's painting "The Last Supper," would you tend to think of it

a. as expressing the highest spiritual aspirations and emotions?

b. as one of the most priceless and irreplaceable pictures ever painted?

c. in relation to Leonardo's versatility and its place in history?

d. the quintessence of harmony and design?

SOURCE: From Gordon W. Allport, Philip E. Vernon, and Gardner Lindzey, *Study of Values*, 3rd ed. (Boston: Houghton Mifflin, 1960), pp. 8, 10. In Krathwohl, Bloom, and Masia, pp. 163–164. Copyright ©1960. Reprinted with permission of the Publisher, The Riverside Publishing Company, 8420 W. Bryn Mawr Avenue, Chicago, IL 60631. All rights reserved.

---

lems. For each problem, a number of courses of action were presented for students to indicate approval, disapproval, or uncertainty.[20]

Boxes 12–1 and 12–2 illustrate assessment items for the affective categories of *Organization* and *Characterization by value or value complex*.

Observe that some instruments are titled "tests" by their makers. The agree-disagree attitude inventory is a frequent means used to determine achievement of affective objectives. These types of questions reveal a basic problem in teaching for affective learning. If the teacher or test maker has preconceived notions of the "correct" responses, he or she is operating in a twilight zone between achievement of affective outcomes and indoctrination. Further, remember that students can and do respond to attitudinal questions as they believe the teacher or test maker wishes them to respond rather than as they actually feel.

The attainment of affective objectives is discerned by instruments such as opinionnaires or attitude inventories, by observation of the behavior of stu-

---

[20]Ibid., p. 144.

Box 12–2 Items for affective category of Characterization by value or value complex

Paul L. Dresser and Lewis B. Mayhew showed examples of items which assess objectives at the highest level of the affective domain: characterization by value or value comples.

Category: Characterization by value or value complex
Subcategory: Generalized set
Objective: Respect for the worth and dignity of human beings
Item:

1. Tom and Bob who know each other only slightly were double-dating two girls who were roommates. A sudden storm made it impossible to go to the beach as planned. Tom suggested going to a movie. After making the suggestion, he realized that Bob was without funds. As Tom, what would you do?
   a. Pay for the party.
   b. Lend Bob money.
   c. Leave it up to the girls.
   d. Get Bob to suggest something.
   e. Apologize to Bob for making the suggestion.

2. Your social organization has pledged a student who is not liked by some of the members. One of your friends threatens to leave the social organization if this person is initiated. What would you do?
   a. Talk to your friend.
   b. Do not initiate the prospective member.
   c. Get more members to support the prospective member.
   d. Vote on the prospective member.
   e. Postpone the vote until the matter works itself out.

SOURCE: From *Problems in Human Relations Test.* Cited by Paul L. Dresser and Lewis B. Mayhew, *General Education: Explorations in Evaluation* (Washington, D.C.: American Council on Education, 1954), p. 233. In Krathwohl, Bloom, and Masia, p. 170. Reprinted by permission of the Amercan Council on Education.

dents, and by essay questions that ask pupils to state their beliefs, attitudes, and feelings about a given topic. Perhaps, instead of thinking of using instruments that seek to discover students' attitudes and values through an accumulation of items administered test-fashion, we should think more of asking frequent value-laden questions and listening to students' responses. Instead of leveling a continuous barrage of factual questions, teachers can interject questions like: How do you feel about . . . ? What do you believe about . . . ? Would you be interested in . . . ? Are you in agreement with . . . ?

OTHER MEANS OF EVALUATION

Although we normally equate the word "test" with "examination" and usually think of a test in a summative context at the end of the instruction, we should remember that it is really an attempt to demonstrate mastery of objectives in whatever domain. Students can demonstrate achievement both during and at the end of instruction through means other than typical examinations. For example, synthesis in the cognitive domain can be tested by means of essay items. Competency in this skill can also be tested by written reports during the period of instruction or by term papers at the end of instruction.

A skilled instructor can tell a good deal about pupils' success just by observing their classroom performance. Individual and group oral reports may be assigned for a variety of purposes, including testing ability to speak, knowledge of the subject, and, in the case of group activities, the ability to work together. Techniques of evaluation other than examinations include student logs, notebooks, simulations, demonstrations, construction activities, and self-evaluation. Teachers should seek to develop competency in the use of a wide range of evaluative techniques.[21]

Feedback

Evaluation yields data that provide feedback about student achievement and the instructional program. It is not sufficient for evaluative data to be used solely for the purpose of measuring pupil achievement. If pupils do poorly, teachers need to find out what caused the poor showing. Teachers need to ask themselves what they must do so that subsequent groups of students—or even the same group, if repetition of the instruction appears necessary—will not encounter the same difficulties. Teachers must know what needs to be changed, and the evaluation results provide them with this evidence.

Even if pupils do extremely well, teachers should use the data to reexamine the process. The instructional goals and objectives may have been too simple; students may have been capable of achieving higher objectives. If a test was administered, the test itself may not have been valid. The questions may have been too simple, they may not have measured all the objectives. At the implementation stage, the instructor may have omitted some crucial points and thereby left some objectives unachieved. The results of evaluation provide evidence for making changes in the instructional process.

ASSESSMENT INITIATIVES FROM BEYOND THE CLASSROOM

District Assessments

Up to this point the focus of this chapter has been on assessment of student achievement through techniques (largely testing) designed by the classroom teacher for his or her own pupils. We should not leave the topic of evaluation

---

[21]For discussion of means of evaluation other than testing, see Oliva, *Secondary School,* Chapter 20.

of instruction without giving some attention to assessment on a broader scale than the individual classroom, assessments that are of special importance to curriculum workers. Since the 1960s, an almost unbelievable amount of assessing student achievement has been going on (and continues) at the district, state, national, and international levels.

Confronted with mounting criticism over both real and perceived deficiencies as evidenced by state, national, and international test scores, many school districts have restructured both their curricula and instructional methods. In so doing, they have also restructured or introduced for the first time assessments of district-wide student achievement. In the 1980s, for example, the Savannah–Chatham County (Georgia) Schools aligned their curricula. For each subject field, the district created plans that detailed objectives, activities, and resources. At the end of each nine-week marking period, students took tests developed to match the objectives in each field. District-wide assessment has been one response to public demand for accountability.

State Assessments

In recent years the assessment spotlight has focused on the state level. More than 36 six states, responding to reports such as *A Nation at Risk,*[22] have set minimum competencies for student achievement at various grade levels and for graduation from high school. Several factors motivated state legislators and departments of education to establish minimum standards of performance on tests. They were disappointed by the results of national and international assessments; they felt dissatisfied with the "products" their schools were turning out; and they heard the public clamor for concentration on subject matter and for accountability of teachers and administrators for their pupils' achievement. Assessment tests, therefore, were deemed necessary for determining whether students had achieved the competencies.

Assessment is, of course, an expected and necessary part of the curriculum-instructional process. Schools must determine the extent to which pupils have attained the objectives. The intensity of assessment, especially at the state level, is relatively new to the educational scene. Georgia, for example, mandated the administration of state-developed criterion-referenced tests for all pupils except fifth graders. In the past 15 to 20 years, states have taken more seriously than ever their role as authority over the public educational system of their state. Assessment is but one phase in the exercise of that authority. We'll return to the practice of state assessment of student achievement in Chapter 14 when the related issue of state-mandated minimal competencies is raised.

---

[22]National Commission on Excellence in Education, David P. Gardner, chairman, *A Nation at Risk: The Imperative for Educational Reform.* (Washington, D.C.: U.S. Government Printing Office, 1983).

National and International Assessments

SAT and ACT Scores.   American public education has been under repeated attack in the recent past for the poor performance of students as reflected by scores on standardized tests of achievement. For whatever reasons—some say low standards in schools, social promotions, too much time off-task, poor instruction, and irrelevant content and activities—pupils' scores on certain standardized tests declined between the 1950s and 1980s. The public and the critics of education took special note of the drop in the scores on the Scholastic Aptitude Test (SAT) and the American College Testing Program (ACT). For example, SAT scores on the verbal portion dropped 50 points between 1952 and 1982. Scores on the mathematics portion declined about 27 points during that same period. Between 1970 and 1982, the ACT scores suffered a slightly downward trend.[23] The SAT and ACT scores held constant in 1981, but the test results for 1982 and 1983 were mixed: the SAT scores began a small rise, but the ACT scores inched downward.[24] Between 1982 and 1985, SAT scores rose and have remained relatively stable since 1985. ACT scores rose between 1984 and 1986, reversing their downward trend, and except for a slight dip in 1989 have remained relatively stable since.[25]

National Assessment of Educational Progress.   Since 1969 when the National Assessment of Educational Progress (NAEP), known as "The Nation's Report Card," came into existence, it has operated with federal funding. Supported by a grant from the National Center for Education Statistics of the Office of Educational Research and Improvement within the U.S. Department of Education, Educational Testing Service currently administers this project.

In 1964, with the backing of the Carnegie Corporation, Ralph W. Tyler and the Committee on Assessing the Progress of Education began to develop criterion-referenced tests for nationwide assessment. Testing began in 1969 and encompassed ten areas:

- □ art
- □ career and occupational development
- □ citizenship
- □ literature
- □ mathematics
- □ music

---

[23]Ernest L. Boyer, *High School: A Report on Secondary Education in America* (New York: Harper & Row, 1983), pp. 22–26.

[24]Valena White Plisko and Joyce D. Stern. *The Condition of Education,* 1985 edition, Statistical Report of the National Center for Education Statistics (Washington, D.C.: U.S. Department of Education, 1985), p. 62

[25]Laurence T. Ogle and Nabeel Alsalam, eds., *The Condition of Education 1990, vol. 1 Elementary and Secondary Education,* Statistical Report of the National Center for Education Statistics (Washington, D.C.: U.S. Department of Education, 1990), pp. 36–37.

- reading
- science
- social studies
- writing

Reassessments are conducted biennially, and a "report card" showing patterns and trends is issued to the public after each assessment. Data for the areas tested have been collected from samples of children, ages 9, 13, and 17, and from young adults, ages 26 to 35. The data have been reported by geographical region, size and type of community, educational level of parents, gender, and race/ethnicity.

In recent years, NAEP has administered tests in additional fields. In 1985–86 it undertook the first national assessment of third-, seventh-, and eleventh-grade students in their knowledge and skills in using the computer.[26]

With a grant from the National Endowment for the Humanities, NAEP cooperated in 1986 with Diane Ravitch and Chester E. Finn's Educational Excellence Network in assessing about 8,000 high school juniors' knowledge of U.S. history and literature. Directed by Ravitch and Finn, this study emanated as part of their Foundations of Literacy project.[27] NAEP conducted a follow-up sampling in 1988 to determine changes that might have taken place in students' factual knowledge of U.S. history.[28] In 1988, NAEP turned its attention to geography, testing more than 3,000 high school seniors on their geography learning.[29] The sheer number of American pupils tested by NAEP is astonishing. In academic year 1987–88, approximately 130,000 elementary, middle, and secondary school students were assessed in some 1500 schools. Since its inception in 1969, NAEP has assessed approximately 9 million students in a variety of subject fields.

National test results have been somewhat inconsistent—sometimes up, sometimes down. Goodlad, for example, noted that test results reported by NAEP showed an improvement in reading skills between 1970–71 and 1979–80.[30] However, when NAEP compared the writing skills of 9-, 13-, and 17-year-olds in the United States between 1974 and 1984, it found a serious

---

[26]Michael E. Martinez and Nancy A. Mead, *Computer Competence: The First National Assessment* (Princeton, N.J.: National Assessment of Educational Progress, Educational Testing Service, 1988).

[27]Diane Ravitch and Chester E. Finn, Jr., *What Do Our 17-Year-Olds Know? A Report on the First National Assessment of History and Literature* (New York: Harper & Row, 1987). See also Arthur N. Applebee, Judith A. Langer, and Ina V. S. Mullis, *Literature and U.S. History: The Instructional Experience and Factual Knowledge of High-School Juniors* (Princeton, N.J.: National Assessment of Educational Progress, Educational Testing Service, 1987).

[28]David C. Hammack et al., *The U.S. History Report Card: The Achievement of Fourth-, Eighth-, and Twelfth-Grade Students in 1988 and Trends from 1986 to 1988 in the Factual Knowledge of High-School Juniors* (Princeton, N.J.: National Assessment of Educational Progress, Educational Testing Service, 1990).

[29]Russell Allen et al., *The Geography Learning of High School Seniors,* (Princeton, N.J.: National Assessment of Educational Progress, Educational Testing Service, 1990).

[30]John I. Goodlad, *A Place Called School: Prospects for the Future* (New York: Harper & Row, 1984), p. 13.

lack of proficiency. On the positive side, some improvement in writing was shown between 1978 and 1984.[31] However significant that improvement may have been, Arthur N. Applebee and others reported a discouraging picture of writing proficiency as a result of NAEP's 1988 assessment of writing skills of fourth-, eighth-, and twelfth-graders. Said Applebee et al.:

> Students across the grades appear to spend relatively little time each week either engaged in writing or learning to write . . . . Overall levels of writing performance remain low . . . . Further, the gap in achievement between high-socioeconomic status (SES) and low-SES groups remains large . . . . All of these findings suggest that the need for reform in writing instruction is with us still.[32]

Scores on the original ten subject areas have been inconsistent since NAEP began testing in 1969. One thing is sure, however—they have certainly been nothing to brag about.[33]

A sampling of findings from some of the NAEP reports include:

- Students generally had difficulty answering questions about computer applications and programming.[34]
- Computers are used in schools almost exclusively for teaching about computers, not for computer-assisted instruction in subject areas.[35]
- In general, student proficiency in reading, mathematics, science, and writing appears to have improved in recent assessments. Students at all three ages (9, 13, 17) were reading significantly better in 1984 than in 1971. The mathematics proficiency of 9- and 13-year-olds was higher in 1986 than in the first NAEP mathematics assessment in 1973. Seventeen-year-olds' proficiency in mathematics declined steadily from 1973 to 1982, then showed signs of initial recovery by improving significantly between 1982 and 1986. Although student proficiency in science has improved in recent assessments, the proficiency of 17-year-olds in science in 1986 was well below that of 1970. Proficiency in writing improved somewhat but remained no better in 1984 than in 1974.[36]
- Fewer than half the high school seniors assessed on knowledge of U.S. history were familiar with the U.S. Constitution and the Bill of Rights.[37]

---

[31] Arthur N. Applebee, Judith A. Langer, and Ina V. S. Mullis, *The Writing Report Card: Writing Achievement in American Schools* (Princeton, N.J.: National Assessment of Educational Progress, Educational Testing Service, 1986).

[32] Arthur N. Applebee, Judith A. Langer, Lynn B. Jenkins, Ina V. S. Mullis, and Mary A. Foertsch, *Learning to Write in Our Nation's Schools: Instruction and Achievement in 1988 at Grades 4, 8, and 12* (Princeton, N.J.: National Assessment of Educational Progress, Educational Testing Service, 1990), p. 10.

[33] Boyer, *High School*, pp. 26–29.

[34] Martinez and Mead, *Computer Competence*, p. 5.

[35] Ibid., p. 3

[36] Arthur N. Applebee, Judith A. Langer, and Ina V. S. Mullis, *Crossroads in American Education: A Summary of Findings* (Princeton, N.J.: National Assessment of Educational Progress, Educational Testing Service, 1989), pp. 7–10.

[37] Hammack et al., *The U.S. History Report Card*, p. 28.

□ On the geography assessment, most high school seniors could locate major countries of the world but had difficulty locating cities and physical land features and lacked understanding of physical and cultural geography. About a third of the students were unfamiliar with the concepts of latitude and longitude.[38]

□ Nine-year-olds gained in reading achievement from 1971 to 1980, dropped in 1984 and remained that way in 1988, but levels were still higher than in 1971. Thirteen-year-olds' achievement in reading showed some improvement between 1971 and 1980; their performance leveled off between 1980 and 1984 and remained level between 1984 and 1988. Reading proficiency of 17-year-olds was constant from 1971 to 1980 and rose between 1980 and 1988.[39]

□ On 262 cognitive items in a national test of history and literature, Ravitch and Finn found that the average of the almost 8 thousand juniors who were assessed was 54.5 percent correct on the history test and 51.8 percent correct on the literature test, which Ravitch and Finn judged to be the equivalent of failing marks.[40]

□ Of special interest to curriculum workers is NAEP's report summarizing the 20 years of assessments. In spite of all the calls for educational reform in the 1970s and 1980s the summary shows that student achievement as a whole remains relatively low and stable since 1969.[41]

From analysis of these national studies, curriculum workers can make comparisons of their local and state assessment data against national norms and can make inferences about areas in need of remediation.

When NAEP was under formation, some educators expressed great concern that the data would identify and possibly embarrass specific schools. NAEP has allayed those concerns, reporting data only for groups and not identifying schools. On the other hand, localities and states often release assessment data by school so that the public and profession can make comparisons among schools within the district and state.

In 1990 NAEP was planning to release some test results by state for those states wishing them. NAEP was also deliberating the establishment of performance standards at basic, proficient, and advanced levels of achievement, with mathematics as the first possible area.

---

[38] Allen et al., *Geography Learning,* pp. 7–8.

[39] Ina V. S. Mullis and Lynn B. Jenkins, *The Reading Report Card, 1971–88: Trends from the Nation's Report Card* (Princeton, N.J.: National Assessment of Educational Progress, Educational Testing Service, 1990), pp. 9–10. See also Judith A. Langer, Arthur N. Applebee, Ina V. Mullis, and Mary A. Foertsch, *Learning to Read in Our Nation's Schools* (Princeton, N.J.: National Assessment of Educational Progress, Educational Testing Service, 1990).

[40] Ravitch and Finn, *What Do Our 17-Year-Olds Know?*, p. 1.

[41] Ina V. Mullis, Eugene H. Owen, and Gary W. Phillips, *America's Challenge: Accelerating Academic Achievement* (Princeton, N.J.: National Assessment of Educational Progress, Educational Testing Service, 1990).

As this book goes to press, new national examinations that will reveal achievement of both students and schools are on the horizon. Dissatisfaction with our educational system runs so deep that educators, business people, parents, and others are voicing a desire for national assessment, an undertaking which would run counter to historic objections to a national curriculum and to revealing test scores of individuals and schools. As noted in Chapter 6, one of the six national goals set forth by President George Bush and the National Governors' Association in 1989 was student demonstration of competency in English, mathematics, science, history, and geography. Students would demonstrate this competency on voluntary national examinations taken at the fourth-, eighth-, and twelfth-grade levels. Plans are under way to develop these tests. The 23rd Annual Gallup Poll of the public's attitudes toward the public schools found strong public support for a standardized national curriculum (68 percent), national achievement standards and goals (81 percent), and standardized national tests (77 percent). However, 57 percent would be willing to allow the tests to be optional.[42]

Though emphasis on assessment has focused on the state level in recent years, as noted in this chapter and Chapter 14, the spotlight may well shift in the near future from the state to the national level. Advocates of national assessment, such as the President's Education Policy Advisory Committee, argue that the national testing will require schools throughout the nation to examine their instructional techniques and curricula (particularly the basic disciplines) and to take action to correct deficiencies revealed by the tests. Those who oppose national assessment, such as the National Education Association, argue that national testing will result in a national, common curriculum that cannot adequately provide for differences that exist among schools and among students in various communities.

International Assessments.   Funded by the U.S. Office of Education and the Ford Foundation, the International Association for the Evaluation of Educational Achievement (IEA) has conducted cross-national studies of student achievement in mathematics, science, literature, reading comprehension, foreign languages (English and French), and civic education.[43] Carried out on a grand scale, the study surveyed some 250,000 students and 50,000 teachers in

---

[42]Stanley M. Elam, Lowell C. Rose, and Alec M. Gallup, "The 23rd Annual Gallup Poll of the Public's Attitudes Toward the Public Schools," *Phi Delta Kappan* 73, no. 1 (September 1991): 46.

[43]See T. Neville Posthlethwaite, "International Educational Surveys," *Contemporary Education* 42, no. 2 (November 1970): 61–68. Joseph Featherstone, "Measuring What Schools Achieve: Learning and Testing," *The New Republic* 169, no. 2 (December 15, 1973): 19–21. "International Study Brings Coleman Report into Question," *Phi Delta Kappan* 55, no. 5 (January 1974): 358. See also L. C. Comber and John P. Keeves. *Science Education in Nineteen Countries* (New York: John Wiley & Sons, 1973); Alan C. Purves, *Literature Education in Ten Countries* (New York: John Wiley & Sons, 1973); Robert L. Thorndike, *Reading Comprehension Education in Fifteen Countries* (New York: John Wiley & Sons, 1973); International Association for the Evaluation of Educational Achievement, *Science Achievement in Seventeen Countries: A Preliminary Report* (Oxford, England: Pergamon, 1988).

22 countries. In 1964, the First International Mathematics Study alone surveyed more than 130,000 students taught by over 13,000 teachers in more than 5,000 schools in 12 countries.[44] The Second International Mathematics Study, funded by the National Science Foundation and the U.S. Department of Education in 1981–82, followed up the First International Mathematics Study by assessing and comparing achievement of 12,000 eighth- and twelfth-grade students enrolled in college-preparatory mathematics classes in some 20 countries.[45]

Benefiting from its experience directing the National Assessment of Educational Progress, the Educational Testing Service—with funding from the U.S. Department of Education and the National Science Foundation—cooperated with representatives of five countries in 1988 to initiate the first International Assessment of Educational Progress (IAEP). IAEP assessed mathematics and science proficiency of 13-year-olds in five countries (Ireland, Korea, Spain, the United Kingdom, and the United States) and four Canadian provinces (British Columbia, New Brunswick, Ontario, and Quebec). The U.S. average was below others in both mathematics and science.[46] Scores of U.S. students on international assessments reinforce scores made on national assessments, demonstrating that the achievement of our students remains less than desirable.

International assessments reveal how difficult it is to make comparisons of student achievement across cultures and to account for variations. Differences among nations that may affect scores include curricula, instructional strategies, social conditions, length of school year, time allocated to studies in school and at home, proportion of young people in school, number of pupils per teacher, motivation of students, dedication of parents to education, and traditions.

Whether from international or other assessments, test scores do signal strengths and weaknesses. Low test scores demand that curriculum workers determine whether the subject matter tested is essential and, if so, what measures must be taken for students to achieve mastery.

SUMMARY

Although evaluating instruction is generally perceived as an activity taking place at the end of the instructional process, teachers should begin selecting evaluation techniques as soon as they identify their instructional goals. Two types of preassessment are suggested: one to evaluate the pupils' possession of prerequisite knowledge and/or skills to begin study of the new subject matter,

---

[44] See Torsten Husén, ed., *International Study of Achievement in Mathematics,* vols. 1 and 2 (New York: John Wiley & Sons, 1967).

[45] See Curtis C. McKnight et al., *The Underachieving Curriculum: Assessing U.S. School Mathematics from an International Perspective* (Champaign, Ill.: Stipes Publishing Company, 1987). See also National Center for Education Statistics, *Second International Mathematics Study: Summary Report for the United States* (Washington, D.C.: National Center for Education Statistics, 1985).

[46] See Archie E. Lapointe, Nancy A. Mead, and Gary W. Phillips, *A World of Differences: An International Assessment of Mathematics and Science* (Princeton, N.J.: Center for the Assessment of Educational Progress, Educational Testing Service, 1989).

the other to determine whether pupils have already mastered the subject matter to be presented.

Evaluation that takes place during the process of instruction is referred to as formative evaluation and is necessary to monitor both pupil progress and the ongoing success of the instructional program. Summative evaluation is evaluation that comes at the end of instruction, as represented in a final examination.

Distinction is made between norm-referenced measurement in which a student's achievement on tests is compared to other students' achievement and criterion-referenced measurement in which a student's achievement is compared to a predetermined criterion of mastery. Norm-referenced tests are used when selection must be made from among a group of persons. Criterion-referenced tests are used to determine whether students achieved the objectives specified in advance.

The major purpose of evaluating instruction is to determine whether or not students accomplished the objectives. Instructors should design means of evaluating pupil performance in the three domains of learning—cognitive, psychomotor, and affective—whenever possible. Tests in the cognitive domain are normally written essay or objective tests administered to an entire class. Discovery of psychomotor outcomes is best carried out by means of actual performance tests of the skill being taught. Although we may speak of measurement and testing in the cognitive and psychomotor domains, we should use the more general term evaluation in reference to the affective domain. Though evaluating affective achievement is difficult and normally imprecise, teachers should engage in this activity. At times, evaluation of affective objectives will not be apparent at all. Nevertheless, affective learning is an important dimension of education, and instructors should strive to determine the best way they can the extent to which students have achieved the desired objectives.

Instructors should keep in mind that there are numerous techniques other than testing for evaluating pupil performance. Good pedagogy calls for a diversity of evaluation techniques, as appropriate.

Feedback is an important feature of the Instructional Model. On the basis of evaluative data, instructors revise the preceding components of the model for subsequent instruction. Evaluation is perceived as a continuous, cyclical process.

A great deal of assessment of student achievement is planned and administered by educators and measurement specialists from outside the individual classroom. District- and state-level assessments are designed and carried out to spot both strengths and deficiencies in the curricula of the schools. National and international assessments lend a broader perspective to student achievement. Among the many national assessments are the SATs and ACTs and the continuing assessments of the National Assessment of Educational Progress. The International Association for the Evaluation of Educational Achievement and the International Assessment of Educational Progress furnish us with cross-cultural data, comparing achievement of students in various countries and disciplines.

QUESTIONS FOR DISCUSSION

1. Are schools overemphasizing testing? Explain.
2. Are schools overemphasizing the use of objective tests? Explain.
3. Should schools use more norm-referenced tests or more criterion-referenced tests?
4. How would you recommend evaluating accomplishment of affective objectives? Give examples.
5. What value do you see in national assessments? International assessments?

SUPPLEMENTARY EXERCISES

1. Distinguish between evaluation, measurement, and testing.
2. Select a unit you will teach and prepare a pretest for it.
3. Search the literature on tests and measurement and prepare a set of guidelines for writing (a) essay, (b) multiple-choice, (c) alternate-response, (d) matching, (e) rearrangement, (f) completion items.
4. State the purposes for which essay test items are designed; state the purposes for objective test items.
5. Write a report on the use of test results.
6. Write an essay-test item and an objective-test item for each of the major categories of the cognitive domain.
7. Write a test item for each of the major categories of one of the taxonomies of the psychomotor domain.
8. Design some techniques for evaluating objectives in each of the major categories of the affective domain.
9. Deliver an oral report to the class on whether affective objectives can and should be evaluated.
10. Define formative evaluation and give some examples for a unit you are teaching or will teach.
11. Define summative evaluation and describe how you will conduct the summative evaluation for a unit that you are teaching or will teach.
12. Describe procedures you would use to evaluate
    a. oral reports
    b. group work
    c. products created by students (give examples)
    d. term papers
    e. dramatic presentations
13. Report to the class on changes in SAT and ACT scores in the last ten years.
14. Report on the district-level plan for assessing student achievement in a school district that you know well.
15. Report on results of a recent school district assessment in a particular subject area.

16. Report on your state or another state's plans for assessing student achievement.
17. Report on results of a recent state assessment in a particular subject area.
18. Choose one of the areas in which the National Assessment of Educational Progress has conducted periodic assessments and describe trends.
19. Prepare an oral or written analysis of one of the following works (see bibliography):
    a. Paul Gagnon, *Historical Literacy*.
    b. Diane Ravitch and Chester E. Finn, Jr., *What Do Our 17-Year-Olds Know? A Report on the First National Assessment of History and Literature*.
20. Prepare a position paper on national assessment, national academic standards, and national curriculum.
21. Describe findings of a recent international study of student achievement involving American students.

BIBLIOGRAPHY

Alexander, Lamar. *The Nation's Report Card: Improving the Assessment of Student Achievement*. Cambridge, Mass.: National Academy of Education, 1987.

Allen, Russell et al. *The Geography Learning of High-School Seniors*. Princeton, N.J.: National Assessment of Educational Progress, Educational Testing Service, 1990.

Applebee, Arthur N., Langer, Judith A., and Mullis, Ina V. S. *Crossroads in American Education: A Summary of Findings*. Princeton, N.J.: National Assessment of Educational Progress, Educational Testing Service, 1989.

————. *Literature and History: The Instructional Experience and Factual Knowledge of High-School Juniors*. Princeton, N.J.: National Assessment of Educational Progress, Educational Testing Service, 1987.

————. *The Writing Report Card: Writing Achievement in American Schools*. Princeton, N.J.: National Assessment of Educational Progress, Educational Testing Service, 1986.

————. *Writing Trends Across the Decade 1974–1984*. Princeton, N.J.: National Assessment of Educational Progress, Educational Testing Service, 1986.

Applebee, Arthur N., Langer, Judith A., Jenkins, Lynn B., Mullis, Ina V. S., and Foertsch, Mary A. *Learning to Write in Our Nation's Schools: Instruction and Achievement in 1988 at Grades 4, 8, and 12*. Princeton, N.J.: National Assessment of Educational Progress, Educational Testing Service, 1990.

Bloom, Benjamin S., ed. *Taxonomy of Educational Objectives: The Classification of Educational Goals: Handbook I: Cognitive Domain*. White Plains, N.Y.: Longman, 1956.

Bloom, Benjamin S., Hastings, J. Thomas, and Madaus, George F. *Evaluate to Improve Learning*. New York: McGraw-Hill, 1981.

Bloom, Benjamin S., Madaus, George F., and Hastings, J. Thomas. *Handbook of Formative and Summative Evaluation of Student Learning*. New York: McGraw-Hill, 1971.

Boyer, Ernest L. *High School: A Report on Secondary Education in America*. New York: Harper & Row, 1983.

Comber, L. C. and Keeves, John P. *Science Education in Nineteen Countries*. New York: John Wiley & Sons, 1973.

Davis, Robert H., Alexander, Lawrence T., and Yelon, Stephen L. *Learning System Design*. New York: McGraw-Hill, 1974.

Dembo, Myron H. *Teaching for Learning: Applying Educational Psychology in the Classroom*. Santa Monica, Calif.: Goodyear Publishing Company, 1977.

Dick, Walter and Carey, Lou. *The Systematic Design of Instruction,* 2nd ed. Glenview, Ill.: Scott, Foresman, 1985.

Dossey, John A. et al. *The Mathematics Report Card: Are We Measuring Up? Trends and Achievement Based on the 1986 National Assessment*. Princeton, N.J.: National Assessment of Educational Progress, Educational Testing Service, 1988.

Elam, Stanley M., Rose, Lowell C., and Gallup, Alec M. "The 23rd Annual Gallup Poll of the Public's Attitudes Toward the Public Schools." *Phi Delta Kappan* 73, no. 1 (September 1991): 41–56.

Gagnon, Paul. *Historical Literacy*. New York: Macmillan, 1989.

Gay, L. R. *Educational Evaluation and Measurement: Competencies for Analysis and Application*, 2nd ed. Columbus, Ohio: Charles E. Merrill, 1985.

Goodlad, John I. *A Place Called School: Prospects for the Future*. New York: McGraw-Hill, 1984.

Gronlund, Norman E. *How to Construct Achievement Tests,* 4th ed. Englewood Cliffs, N.J.: Prentice-Hall, 1988.

Gross, Martin L. *The Brain Watchers*. New York: Random House, 1962.

Hammack, David C. et al. *The U.S. History Report Card: The Achievement of Fourth-, Eighth-, and Twelfth-Grade Students in 1988 and Trends from 1986 to 1988 in the Factual Knowledge of High-School Juniors*. Princeton, N.J.: National Assessment of Educational Progress, Educational Testing Service, 1990.

Harrow, Anita J. *A Taxonomy of the Psychomotor Domain: A Guide for Developing Behavioral Objectives*. White Plains, N.Y.: Longman, 1972.

Hoffman, Banesh. *The Tyranny of Testing*. New York: Crowell-Collier, 1962.

Husén, Torsten, ed. *International Study of Achievement in Mathematics,* vols. 1 and 2. New York: John Wiley & Sons, 1967.

International Association for the Evaluation of Educational Achievement. *Science Achievement in Seventeen Countries: A Preliminary Report*. Oxford, England: Pergamon, 1988.

Kibler, Robert J., Cegala, Donald J., Miles, David T., and Barker, Larry L. *Objectives for Instruction and Evaluation*. Boston: Allyn and Bacon, 1974.

Krathwohl, David R., Bloom, Benjamin S., and Masia, Bertram B. *Taxonomy of Educational Objectives: The Classification of Educational Goals: Handbook II: Affective Domain*. White Plains, N.Y.: Longman, 1964.

Langer, Judith A., Applebee, Arthur N., Mullis, Ina V. S., and Foertsch, Mary A. *Learning to Read in Our Nation's Schools,* Princeton, N.J.: National Assessment of Educational Progress, Educational Testing Service, 1990.

Lapointe, Archie E., Mead, Nancy A., and Phillips, Gary W. *A World of Differences: An International Assessment of Mathematics and Science*. Princeton, N.J.: Center for the Assessment of Educational Progress, Educational Testing Service, 1989.

Linn, Robert L. and Dunbar, Stephen B., "The Nation's Report Card Goes Home: Good News and Bad About Trends in Achievement." *Phi Delta Kappan* 72, no. 2 (October 1990): 127–133.

McKnight, Curtis C. et al. *The Underachieving Curriculum: Assessing U.S.*

School Mathematics from an International Perspective. Champaign, Ill.: Stipes Publishing Company, 1987.

Mager, Robert F. *Preparing Instructional Objectives,* 2nd ed. Belmont, Calif.: Fearon, 1975.

Martinez, Michael E. and Mead, Nancy A. *Computer Competence: The First National Assessment.* Princeton, N.J.: National Assessment of Educational Progress, Educational Testing Service, 1988.

Mullis, Ina V. S. and Jenkins, Lynn B. *The Reading Report Card 1971–88: Trends from the Nation's Report Card.* Princeton, N.J.: National Assessment of Educational Progress, Educational Testing Service, 1990.

———. *The Science Report Card: Elements of Risk and Recovery—Trends and Achievement Based on the 1986 National Assessment.* Princeton, N.J.: National Assessment of Educational Progress, Educational Testing Service, 1988.

Mullis, Ina V. S., Jenkins, Lynn B., Owen, Eugene H., and Phillips, Gary W. *America's Challenge: Accelerating Academic Achievement.* Princeton, N.J.: National Assessment of Educational Progress, Educational Testing Service, 1990.

Ogle, Laurence T. and Alsalam, Nabeel. *The Condition of Education 1990, Vol. 1, Elementary and Secondary Education.* Washington, D.C.: U.S. Department of Education, 1990.

Oliva, Peter F. *The Secondary School Today,* 2nd ed. New York: Harper & Row, 1972.

———. *Supervision for Today's Schools.* 3rd ed. White Plains, N.Y.: Longman, 1989.

O'Neil, John. "Go Slow on Nat'l Curriculum, Tests, ASCD Warned." *Update* 33, no. 4 (May 1991): 1, 6–7.

Plisko, Valena White and Stern, Joyce D. *The Condition of Education.* 1985 edition. Washington, D.C.: U.S. Department of Education, 1985.

Popham, W. James. *Evaluating Instruction.* Englewood Cliffs, N.J.: Prentice-Hall, 1973.

Purves, Alan C. *Literature Education in Ten Countries.* New York: John Wiley & Sons, 1973.

Ravitch, Diane and Finn, Chester E. Jr. *What Do Our 17-Year-Olds Know? A Report on the First National Assessment of History and Literature.* New York: Harper & Row, 1987.

Simpson, Elizabeth Jane. "The Classification of Educational Objectives in the Psychomotor Domain." In *The Psychomotor Domain,* vol. 3, 43–56. Washington, D.C.: Gryphon House, 1972.

Smythe, Mary-Jeanette, Kibler, Robert J., and Hutchings, Patricia W. "A Comparison of Norm-Referenced and Criterion-Referenced Measurement with Implications for Communication Instruction." *The Speech Teacher* 22, no. 1 (January 1973): 1–17.

Strenio, Andrew, Jr. *The Testing Trap.* New York: Rawson, Wade, 1981.

Thorndike, Robert L. *Reading Comprehension Education in Fifteen Countries.* New York: John Wiley & Sons, 1973.

"What Schools Can Do About What Students Don't Know." *Educational Leadership* 47, no. 3 (November 1989): 3–91.

Whyte, William H., Jr. *The Organization Man.* New York: Simon and Schuster, 1956.

Worthen, Blaine R. and Spandel, Vicki. "Putting the Standardized Test Debate in Perspective." *Educational Leadership* 48, no. 5 (February 1991): 65–69.

FILMSTRIP-AUDIOTAPE PROGRAMS

Vimcet Associates, P. O. Box 24714, Los Angeles, Calif. 90024:

Establishing Performance Standards. 1967.

Evaluation. 1967.

Modern Measurement Methods. 1969.

Writing Tests Which Measure Objectives. 1972.

REPORTS

Reports of the International Assessment of Educational Progress may be obtained from the Center for the Assessment of Educational Progress, Educational Testing Service, Rosedale Road, Princeton, New Jersey 08541-0001.

Reports of the National Assessment of Educational Progress may be obtained from the National Assessment of Educational Progress, Educational Testing Service, Rosedale Road, Princeton, New Jersey 08541-0001.

CHAPTER THIRTEEN

Evaluating the Curriculum

After studying this chapter you should be able to:

1. Explain the major features of at least two models of curriculum evaluation.

2. Describe how one or more models of curriculum evaluation can be used by curriculum planners.

3. Select and apply a model of curriculum evaluation.

PURPOSES AND PROBLEMS OF CURRICULUM EVALUATION

Years ago in a college foreign language class, the instructor lured his students into a grammatical frame of mind by promising to reveal to them "the secrets of the subjunctive." In this chapter some of the secrets of curriculum evaluation will be disclosed. I'll make this revelation right now. The secrets of evaluation are

- ☐ to ask questions
- ☐ to ask the *right* questions
- ☐ to ask the *right* questions of the *right* people

Depending on the problems, questions might be addressed to teachers, administrators, pupils, lay people, parents, other school personnel, or experts in various fields, including curriculum.

As is often necessary in pedagogical discourse, we must first clarify terms before we can talk about them. We find numerous articles and textbooks on educational, instructional, and curriculum evaluation. The broadest of these terms—*educational evaluation*—is used in this text to encompass all kinds of evaluations that come under the aegis of the school. It includes evaluation not only of curriculum and instruction but also of the grounds, buildings, administration, supervision, personnel, transportation, and so on.

Instructional evaluation, discussed in the preceding chapter, is an assessment of (1) pupils' achievement, (2) the instructor's performance, and (3) the effectiveness of a particular approach or methodology. *Curriculum evaluation* includes instructional evaluation. Recall that the Instructional Model is a submodel of the comprehensive curriculum development model. Curriculum evaluation also goes well beyond the purposes of instructional evaluation into assessment of the program and related areas. Albert I. Oliver listed five areas of concern that call for evaluation. "The five P's," as he termed them, are program, provisions, procedures, products, and processes.[1]

The axiom that change is inevitable not only in education but also outside of education was advanced early in this text. As curriculum planners, we wish changes in education to take place for the better. Because the creations of mortals are always less than perfect, we can always seek improvement. Evaluation is the means for determining what needs improvement and for providing a basis for effecting that improvement.

You have already encountered in Chapter 7 one dimension of curriculum evaluation—the needs assessment, a process by which you can identify gaps in the curriculum. In this chapter we are concerned with the evaluation of curricula that are or have been in operation.

---

[1]Excerpts from *Curriculum Improvement*, 2nd ed., p. 306, by Albert I. Oliver. Copyright ©1965 by Harper & Row, Publishers, Inc. Reprinted by permission of HarperCollins Publishers.

Problems in Evaluation

Many concede that one place where we are vulnerable in education is in evaluating the programs we have instituted. Our evaluation is often spotty and frequently inconclusive. We should be able to demonstrate, for example, whether

- ☐ Interdisciplinary teamwork results in higher student achievement than the self-contained classroom.
- ☐ The learning of a second language helps in learning one's native language.
- ☐ Nongraded schools are more effective than graded.
- ☐ The *McGuffey Reader* is a better tool to teach reading than some of the more modern materials.
- ☐ The specification of minimal competencies improves student performance.
- ☐ One series of biology texts results in greater student achievement in biology than another series.
- ☐ An inductive or deductive approach is more effective in teaching grammar.
- ☐ Class size makes a difference in pupil achievement.
- ☐ The specification of instructional objectives leads to improved pupil performance.

Many of the conclusions reached about the success of educational innovations have been based on very limited evidence. The lack of systematic evaluation may be attributed to a number of causes. Careful evaluation can be very complicated. It requires know-how on the part of the evaluators, and, therefore, training in evaluation is essential. Further, it is time- and energy-consuming and often expensive. We could say that schools generally do not do a thorough job of evaluation and what they do is often not too helpful.

Daniel L. Stufflebeam and others observed that evaluation was ill and suffered from the following symptoms:

1. The avoidance symptom. Because evaluation seems to be a painful process, everyone avoids it unless absolutely necessary. . . .
2. The anxiety symptom. . . . Anxiety stems primarily from the ambiguities of the evaluation process. . . .
3. The immobilization symptom. . . . Schools have not responded to evaluation in any meaningful way. . . .
4. The skepticism symptom. . . . Many persons seem to argue that there is little point in planning for evaluation because "it can't be done anyway." . . .
5. The lack-of-guidelines symptom. . . . Among professional evaluators . . . is the notable lack of meaningful and operational guidelines. . . .
6. The misadvice symptom. Evaluation consultants, many of whom are methodological specialists in educational research, continue to give bad advice to practitioners. . . .
7. The no-significant-difference symptom. . . . Evaluation . . . is so often incapable of uncovering any significant information. . . .

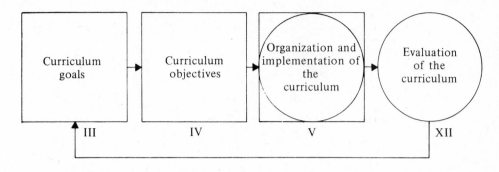

FIGURE 13–1   Curriculum model with one feedback line

8. The missing-elements symptom. [There] is a lack of certain crucial elements needed if evaluation is to make significant forward strides. The most obvious missing element is the lack of adequate theory. . . . [2]

Revising the Curriculum Model.   As in our analysis of evaluating instruction, we will develop some general understandings about curriculum evaluation and will discuss a limited number of evaluation procedures. Let's begin by taking a look at the Curriculum Model shown in Figure 13–1, which is a submodel of the proposed model for curriculum improvement.

The Curriculum Model is conceptualized as consisting of four components— Curriculum goals, Curriculum objectives, Organization and implementation of the curriculum, and Evaluation of the curriculum. A feedback line connects the Evaluation component with the Goals component, making the model cyclical in nature. We should redefine the Curriculum Model in two ways. First, as with the Instructional Model, we should show the feedback line as affecting more than just the Curriculum goals. Although the impact on Curriculum goals is felt through all subsequent components, evaluative data should feed back to each of the components of the Curriculum Model. A more precise rendering of the feedback concept would show lines from Evaluation of the curriculum not only to Curriculum goals but also to Curriculum objectives and to Organization and implementation of the curriculum, as shown in Figure 13–2.

Second, I should make clear that evaluation of the curriculum is not something done solely at the end of a program's implementation but is an operation that takes place before, during, and at the end of the implementation. Figure 13–3 shows the continuous nature of curriculum evaluation in a manner similar to the way in which the continuous nature of instructional evaluation was shown. Circles within the squares of Figure 13–3 indicate that curriculum evaluation is going on while evaluation procedures are being planned.

---

[2]Daniel L. Stufflebeam et al., *Educational Evaluation and Decision Making* (Itasca, Ill.: F. E. Peacock, 1971), pp. 4–9. Reprinted with permission.

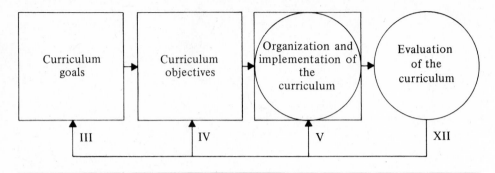

FIGURE 13–2   Curriculum model with all feedback lines

DELIMITING EVALUATION

Differences Between Instructional and Curriculum Evaluation

Some instructors and curriculum planners believe that assessing the achievement of instructional objectives constitutes curriculum evaluation. Thus, if students achieve the cognitive, affective, and psychomotor learnings, the curriculum is considered effective. To follow that line of reasoning, we would add all the evaluations of instruction together in a one-plus-one fashion presumably to determine the success of the curriculum. This position makes the mistake of equating curriculum with instruction. If this were the case, separate components for the Evaluation of instruction and Evaluation of the curriculum would not be shown in the Curriculum Development Model (Figure 5–5, p. 172).

However, instruction and curriculum are not the same. The instructional process may be very effective whereas the curriculum, like the times, may

FIGURE 13–3   Continuous nature of curriculum evaluation

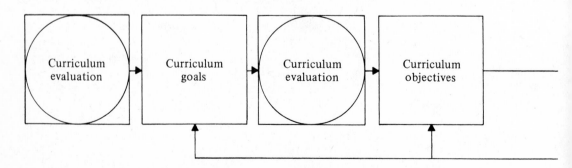

be out of joint. In Aldous Huxley's *Brave New World*, the society runs very efficiently, but few would opt to live there. Instructional evaluation may reveal that pupils are achieving the instructional objectives. On the other hand, unless we evaluate the curriculum—the programs—we may be effectively teaching all the wrong things. If I may exaggerate to make this point, we could do a beautiful job of teaching the following things to young people:

- ☐ The earth is flat.
- ☐ The earth is the center of the universe.
- ☐ One ethnic group is inherently superior to another.
- ☐ All children can be doctors and lawyers.
- ☐ White-collar workers always earn more money than blue-collar workers.
- ☐ There will always be plenty of cheap energy.
- ☐ All scientific advancements are the result of American ingenuity.
- ☐ Illnesses are caused by the evil eye.

The primary purpose of curriculum evaluation is, of course, to determine whether the curriculum goals and objectives are being carried out. However, we want to answer other questions as well. We want to know if the goals and objectives are right to begin with. We want to learn whether the curriculum is functioning while in operation. We want to find out if we are using the best materials and following the best methods. We must learn whether the products of our schools are successful in higher education and in jobs, whether they can function in daily life and contribute to society. We must also determine whether our programs are cost-effective—whether we are getting the most for our money.

Difference Between Evaluation and Research

Discussion of evaluation inevitably leads us into the area of research. Evaluation is the process of making judgments, research is the process of gathering data to make those judgments. Whenever we gather data to answer problems, we are engaged in research. However, the complexity and quality of research

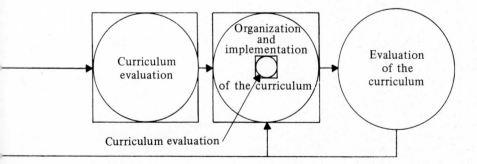

differ from problem to problem. We may engage in research ranging from simple descriptive research to complex experimental research. As an example of the former: How many library books does the school library possess per child? As an example in the latter: Do children with learning disabilities perform more effectively when they are in segregated classes or when they are mainstreamed? Most ambitious of all—and very rare—are longitudinal studies like the Eight-Year Study that compared the success in college of graduates from traditional high schools to that of graduates from experimental high schools.[3]

The field of evaluation often calls for the services of specialists in evaluation and research. Some large school systems are able to employ personnel to direct, conduct, and supervise curriculum evaluation for their school systems. These people bring to the task a degree of expertise not shared by most teachers and curriculum planners. Some school systems, which do not hire their own evaluation personnel, invite in outside consultants to help with particular curriculum problems and research. However, most evaluative studies must be and are conducted by the local curriculum planners and the teachers. The shortage of trained personnel and the costs of employing specialists are prohibitive for many school systems. Even in large systems that employ curriculum evaluators, many curriculum evaluation tasks are performed by teachers and curriculum planners.

EVALUATION MODELS

Models have been developed showing types of evaluation that schools should carry out and the processes they should follow.[4] As in the case of models of instruction and of curriculum development, evaluation models differ in detail and the points which their creators choose to include. Let's look at two comprehensive evaluation models—the Saylor, Alexander, and Lewis model, a rather easily understood model that shows the scope and nature of curriculum evaluation, and the model of the Phi Delta Kappa National Study Committee on Evaluation, a more complex model written in rather technical terms.[5]

---

[3]For an account of the Eight-Year Study see Wilford M. Aikin, *The Story of the Eight-Year Study* (New York: Harper & Row, 1942).

[4]See, for example, the following models:

Center for the Study of Evaluation, *Evaluation Workshop I: An Orientation* (Del Monte Research Park, Monterey, Calif.: CTB/McGraw-Hill, 1971).

Malcolm Provus, *Discrepancy Evaluation for Educational Program Improvement and Assessment* (Berkeley, Calif.: McCutchan, 1971).

Robert E. Stake, "Language, Rationality, and Assessment," in *Improving Educational Assessment and an Inventory of Measures of Affective Behavior*, ed. Walcott H. Beatty (Alexandria, Va.: Association for Supervision and Curriculum Development, 1969).

[5]See Stufflebeam et al., *Educational Evaluation*.

The Saylor, Alexander, and Lewis Model

Figure 13–4 shows how J. Galen Saylor, William M. Alexander, and Arthur J. Lewis charted their model.[6] The Saylor, Alexander, and Lewis model calls for evaluating five components:

1. the goals, subgoals, and objectives
2. the program of education as a totality
3. the specific segments of the education program
4. instruction
5. evaluation program

The first, third, and fourth components contribute to the second—evaluating the program of education as a totality—by, among other ways, providing data that bear on the total program. In the figure, these relationships are shown by the three arrows between the boxes, which point toward the second component. By including the fifth component—evaluation program—in their model, Saylor, Alexander, and Lewis suggested that it is necessary to evaluate the evaluation program itself. No arrow is shown from the box labeled "evaluation program," because the evaluation of the evaluation program is perceived as an independent operation that has implications for the entire evaluation process. Perhaps we could embellish the Saylor, Alexander, and Lewis model by drawing four curved arrows leading out of the right-hand side of the Evaluation Program box to the right-hand side of each of the four boxes above it.

Once again, as we look at the model, we encounter the terms "formative evaluation" (evaluation that takes place during a component) and "summative evaluation" (evaluation that takes place at the end of a component). Saylor, Alexander, and Lewis's model calls attention to both formative and summative aspects of evaluation of each component.

Evaluation of Goals, Subgoals, and Objectives.   Goals, subgoals, and objectives are evaluated (validated) in their formative stages by

1. analysis of the needs of society
2. analysis of the needs of the individual
3. referring the goals, subgoals, and objectives to various groups
4. referring the goals, subgoals, and objectives to subject matter specialists
5. use of previous summative data

Curriculum planners must make their own analyses of whether a given goal, subgoal, or objective meets the needs of society and of the learners. They should seek the judgments of students (if they are mature enough), teachers, parents, and other lay people and should further consult subject matter specialists to determine whether a given goal, subgoal, or objective is appro-

---

[6]Excerpts from *Curriculum Planning for Better Teaching and Learning,* Fourth Edition, p. 334, by J. G. Saylor and W. M. Alexander, copyright ©1981 by Holt, Rinehart and Winston, Inc., reprinted by permission of the publisher.

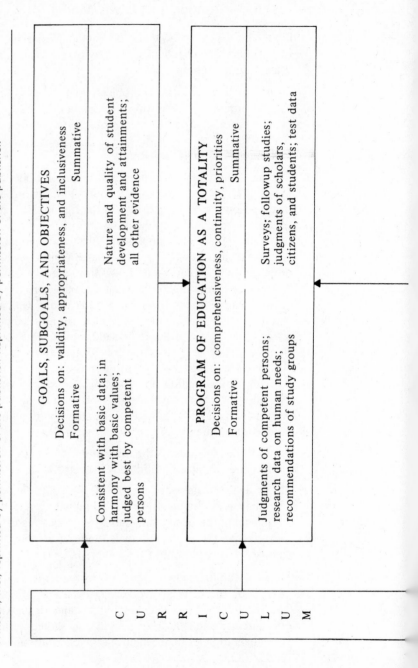

FIGURE 13–4   The Saylor, Alexander, and Lewis evaluation model. Figure from *Curriculum Planning for Better Teaching and Learning*, Fourth Edition, p. 334, by J. G. Saylor and W. M. Alexander, copyright ©1981 by Holt, Rinehart and Winston, Inc., reprinted by permission of the publisher. Reprinted by permission of the publisher.

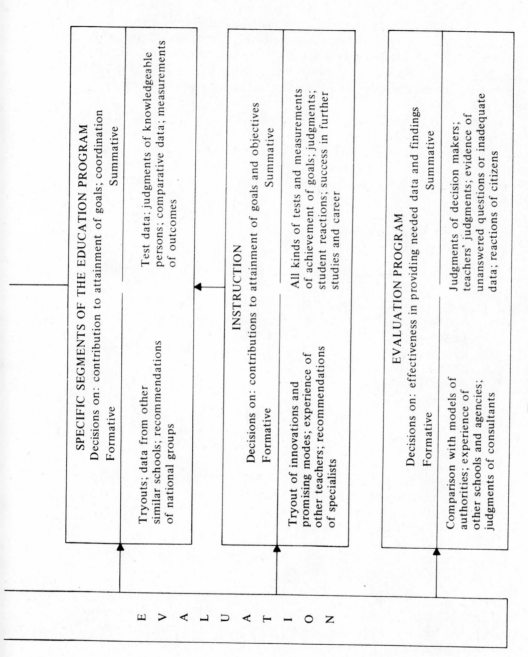

SPECIFIC SEGMENTS OF THE EDUCATION PROGRAM

Decisions on: contribution to attainment of goals; coordination

Formative

Tryouts; data from other similar schools; recommendations of national groups

Summative

Test data; judgments of knowledgeable persons; comparative data; measurements of outcomes

INSTRUCTION

Decisions on: contributions to attainment of goals and objectives

Formative

Tryout of innovations and promising modes; experience of other teachers; recommendations of specialists

Summative

All kinds of tests and measurements of achievement of goals; judgments; student reactions; success in further studies and career

EVALUATION PROGRAM

Decisions on: effectiveness in providing needed data and findings

Formative

Comparison with models of authorities; experience of other schools and agencies; judgments of consultants

Summative

Judgments of decision makers; teachers' judgments; evidence of unanswered questions or inadequate data; reactions of citizens

E V A L U A T I O N

The scope and nature of curriculum evaluation.

priate to the particular discipline. Data gained from previous tryouts of the program should be used to revise goals, subgoals, and objectives prior to the next trial. For practical purposes, instead of referring every goal, subgoal, and objective to all the groups mentioned, the curriculum planner may elect to refer the goals for validation to all groups and the subgoals and objectives for validation to just the teachers, subject matter specialists, and other curriculum specialists.

To clarify this validation process, let's take as an example the prosaic objective mentioned in Chapter 12—the baking of bread in home economics class. Although we can certainly teach young people to bake bread and can evaluate their performance in this psychomotor skill, a more fundamental question must be answered: Should the baking of bread be included in the home economics curriculum?

The question is not so simple to answer as it might first appear. A number of questions must be raised before this particular item of content can be validated. Some of these questions are as follows:

- Does society (the community, the home, the family) have any need for bread bakers?
- Is the skill of baking bread necessary or helpful to the individual?
- Does teaching the skill make sense in the light of comparison of costs of the home-baked bread versus store-bought bread?
- Does it require more energy to bake a loaf of bread at home or for commercial bakers to produce loaves for sale?
- Is there some overriding aesthetic or personal satisfaction in baking bread as opposed to purchasing it?
- Is home-baked bread more nutritious than store-bought bread?
- If baking bread is a content item, what other items were left out of the curriculum so that it could be included? Which items are the most important?
- Would experts in home economics assert that this content item is essential to the home economics curriculum?
- What percentage of families today bake their own bread?
- Is this skill something that can and should be taught in the home rather than in school?
- What has the success or failure of previous groups of students been in respect to this particular skill?

As we have seen, goals, subgoals, and objectives are established for the total program of the school. They are also established for specific program segments and for instruction. The accomplishment of curricular goals, subgoals, and objectives is revealed through an evaluation of the total program, the specific segments, and instruction.

Although Saylor, Alexander, and Lewis make the evaluation of the program of education as a totality the second component of their model of curriculum development, I would prefer to vary the sequence. Let's comment first on the two other components that impinge on the total educational program—the evaluation of instruction and of the specific segments of the program. We will return to the evaluation of the total program in a moment.

Evaluation of Instruction.   We examined procedures for evaluating instruction in Chapter 12. Saylor, Alexander, and Lewis recommended that after instructional goals and objectives are specified and validated as part of the formative evaluation process, the antecedent conditions should be examined—a process referred to by some evaluators as *context* evaluation. The learners' total educational environment, the characteristics of the learners and the teachers, classroom interaction, and the curriculum design are all evaluated and may affect the choice of instructional goals and objectives. [7] The use of criterion-referenced and norm-referenced tests and other evaluative techniques provide formative and summative data on the success of instruction.

Evaluation of Specific Segments.   The specific segments of the program require evaluation. Saylor, Alexander, and Lewis included within their concept of specific segments the following: "the plan for organizing curriculum domains, the design or designs of the curriculum for each domain, courses offered, other kinds of sets of learning opportunities provided, extrainstructional activities sponsored, services provided students, and the kinds of informal relations that characterize the institutional climate." [8]

Assessment data from district, state, and national sources should be gathered by the curriculum planners for purposes of formative evaluation of the specific program segments. At this stage data from the National Assessment of Educational Progress, for instance, can prove helpful. If, for example, the NAEP data revealed that nine-year-old children in urban areas of the southeast United States are more deficient in reading skills than children in comparable urban areas elsewhere in the country, intensive examination of the reading program of the particular school system is essential. SAT and ACT scores will provide clues. Assessments made by the International Association for the Evaluation of Educational Achievement (IEA) and the International Assessment of Educational Progress (IAEP) may also provide helpful data. [9] State and district assessments, focusing as they do on children of the state and locality, may be even more meaningful in this respect.

Evaluative Criteria.   At this stage, too, the instruments of the *Evaluative Criteria* of the National Study of School Evaluation may be used to gather empirical data about the segments for which there exist criteria.[10] These instruments assess specific areas of study and other specific segments of the pro-

---

[7]Ibid., pp. 350–352.

[8]Ibid., p. 344.

[9]See Chapter 12 for discussion of NAEP, IEA, and IAEP.

[10]National Study of School Evaluation, *Evaluative Criteria* (Falls Church, Va.: National Study of School Evaluation), various levels. See bibliography.

gram, such as student activities, learning media, and student services. Revised periodically, this particular set of standards is used by regional associations of colleges and schools of accrediting institutions. Consisting of rating scales and direct questions, these criteria permit faculties to analyze the principles related to the particular program, the evaluation techniques used, plans for improvement, and the current status.

English proposed a way of looking at specific segments of the curriculum through a technique referred to as "curriculum mapping."[11] Following this technique teachers can analyze the content that they present and the amount of time spent on each topic.

Curriculum planners must design summative measures to determine whether the curriculum goals and objectives of the specific segments have been achieved. If it was desired, for example, that 75 percent of the students in a senior high school be involved in at least one extraclass activity, a simple head count would reveal whether this objective has been realized. As is the case when evaluating instruction, sometimes the objective itself is the evaluation item. On the other hand, if it is desired that a fourth-grade class whose members average two months below grade level in mathematics at the beginning of the year raise its scores to grade level by the end of the year, pretesting and posttesting will be necessary.

Evaluation of the Total Program.   The functioning of the curriculum as a whole must be evaluated. The curriculum planners want to learn whether the goals and objectives of the total curriculum have been realized.

The aforementioned *Evaluative Criteria* provides opportunities for an overview of the school's curricula with general areas of evaluation, including sections on School and Community, Philosophy and Goals/Objectives, Curriculum/Design of Curriculum, Design for Learning, and Major Educational Priorities. The National Study for School Evaluation, the source for the *Evaluative Criteria*, also makes available inventories for teachers, students, and parents to register their perceptions about the school and its programs.

Defining an audit as "an objective, external review of a record, event, process, product, act, belief, or motivation to commit an act," English adapted the concept of a management audit to curriculum evaluation.[12] English described a curriculum audit as "a process of examining documents and practices that exist within a peculiar institution normally called a 'school' in a given time, culture, and society."[13] From documents, interviews, and on-site visits, the auditor, sometimes an external agent, seeks to determine how well programs are functioning and whether they are cost-effective. English pointed out that

---

[11]Fenwick W. English, "Curriculum Mapping," *Educational Leadership* 37, no. 7 (April 1980): 558–559. See also Donald F. Weinstein, *Administrator's Guide to Curriculum Mapping: A Step-by-Step Manual* (Englewood Cliffs, N.J.: Prentice-Hall, 1988).

[12]Fenwick W. English, *Curriculum Auditing* (Lancaster, Pa.: Technomic Publishing Company, 1988), p. 3.

[13]*Ibid.*, p. 33.

the curriculum audit is both a process and a product in that the auditor engages in collecting and analyzing data and prepares a report delineating the results. Standards applied by English to a school district's curriculum audit include district control over its people, program, and resources; clear program objectives; documentation about its programs; use of district assessments; and program improvements.[14]

Studies of the needs of society and of young people speak to the question of the school's total program. Unless one limits the school's program to purely cognitive goals, some response should be made to some of the pressing problems of the day. These studies provide formative data for the curriculum planners. Surely problems like care of the environment, conservation of natural resources, discrimination of all types, and the misuse of chemical substances should be examined by young people.

Saylor, Alexander, and Lewis recommended formative evaluation of the program of education as a totality by means of "judgments of competent persons, research data on human needs, recommendations of study groups." They recommended summative evaluation of the educational program through "surveys; follow-up studies; judgments of scholars, citizens, and students; test data."[15]

Summative evaluation of the total program is conducted in several ways. Empirical data are gathered to determine if curriculum objectives have been accomplished. School-wide test data are analyzed. Follow-up studies reveal the success or lack of success of young people after leaving the school. Finally, surveys ask teachers, parents, students, and others to evaluate the school's program.

Evaluation of the Evaluation Program. The program for evaluating the curriculum should be continuously assessed. Judgments about how evaluation will be conducted should be made before an innovation or change is put into practice. The techniques for ongoing evaluation and final evaluation must be carefully planned and followed.

Sometimes it is beneficial to enlist the services of an evaluation specialist to review the evaluation techniques proposed by the curriculum planners. Questions must be answered as to whether the instruments to be used are reliable and valid; whether the evaluation program is comprehensive, covering all the dimensions of the curriculum to be evaluated; and whether the procedures are appropriate and possible. Reactions and suggestions about the evaluation procedures should be obtained from those who are most intimately exposed to them—the students and teachers.

If research studies are to be conducted, specialists inside or outside the system should review the proposed research techniques to determine whether they meet the standards of acceptable research.

---

[14]*Ibid.*, pp. 33–34.

[15]Excerpts from *Curriculum Planning for Better Teaching and Learning,* Fourth Edition, p. 334, by J. G. Saylor and W. M. Alexander, copyright ©1981 by Holt, Rinehart and Winston, Inc., reprinted by permission of the publisher.

When data are ultimately gathered, the planners may feel the need to request the help of evaluation specialists to treat and interpret the data. It must now be determined whether all the variables have been considered and appropriately controlled and whether the evaluation measures are designed to assess the appropriate objectives. For example, a cognitive test of American history will not assess student performance of citizenship skills. The ability to recite rules of grammar does not guarantee skill in the writing.

When flaws are discovered in the evaluation program, changes should be made. Conclusions reached as a result of research and evaluation are often attacked, not on their substance, but on the evaluation processes by which they were reached.

For example, why is it that we can find skeptics for almost every curricular innovation ever tried? You name it—core curriculum; competency-based education; open education; team teaching; nongradedness; the once new, now old math; and so on—and we can find criticisms of it. Some who object do so because they are not convinced that the evaluation techniques purported to have been used actually proved the superiority of an innovation. Students of curriculum might well examine the processes for evaluating almost any program, change of program, or innovation in their school system—past or present—and at any level to find out if curricula were evaluated rigorously. Students are also likely to discover many innovations evaluated on the basis of perceived opinion of success (without adequate data), participants' feelings about the program (like/dislike), change of pace (variety as a spice), pleasure of being involved (Hawthorne effect), administrative assertion ("I say it works"), cost (if it was an expensive undertaking, it has to be good), public relations ("Look what we've done for your/our young people"), and perceived leadership ("We're in the vanguard," also known as "on the cutting edge").

To conclude, Saylor, Alexander, and Lewis have illuminated the major evaluation components that confront curriculum planners in the process of curriculum development. Less technical than some models, the Saylor, Alexander, and Lewis model offers a comprehensive view of curriculum evaluation.

The CIPP Model

The Phi Delta Kappa National Study Committee on Evaluation, chaired by Daniel L. Stufflebeam, produced and disseminated a widely cited model of evaluation known as the CIPP (context, input, process, product) model.[16] Reference has already been made in Chapter 4 to two of the major features of the CIPP model: stages of decision making and types of decisions required in education.[17]

Comprehensive in nature, the model reveals types of evaluation, of decision-making settings, of decisions, and of change. In shaping their model,

---

[16]Stufflebeam et al., *Educational Evaluation*, pp. 218–235.
[17]See p. 125 of this text.

Stufflebeam and his associates defined evaluation in the following way: "Evaluation is the process of delineating, obtaining, and providing useful information for judging decision alternatives."[18]

Stufflebeam clarified what was meant by each of the parts of the definition as follows:

1. *Process.* A particular, continuing and cyclical activity subsuming many methods and involving a number of steps or operations.
2. *Delineating.* Focusing information requirements to be served by evaluation through such steps as specifying, defining, and explicating.
3. *Obtaining.* Making available through such processes as collecting, organizing, and analyzing, and through such formal means as statistics and measurement.
4. *Providing.* Fitting together into systems or subsystems that best serve the needs or purposes of the evaluation.
5. *Useful.* Appropriate to predetermined criteria evolved through the interaction of the evaluator and the client.
6. *Information.* Descriptive or interpretive data about entities (tangible or intangible) and their relationships.
7. *Judging.* Assigning weights in accordance with a specified value framework, criteria derived therefrom, and information which relates criteria to each entity being judged.
8. *Decision Alternatives.* A set of optional responses to a specified decision question.[19]

"The evaluation process," said Stufflebeam, "includes the three main steps of delineating, obtaining, and providing. These steps provide the basis for a methodology of evaluation."[20] Before we begin to examine the various elements of the CIPP model, let's look at a figure of the entire model, shown in Figure 13–5.[21]

In flow-chart form, the model consists of rectangles (with small loops attached), hexagons, ovals, a circle, a fancy E, solid and broken lines with arrows, and three types of shading. Shaded dark, the hexagons show types of decisions; hatched, the ovals, the circle, and the big E depict activities performed; and lightly shaded, the rectangles stand for types of evaluation.

Four Types of Evaluation. The Phi Delta Kappa Committee pointed to four types of evaluation—context, input, process, and product—hence the name of the model CIPP. *Context evaluation* is "the most basic kind of evaluation,"

---

[18]Daniel L. Stufflebeam, an address given at the Eleventh Annual Phi Delta Kappa Symposium on Educational Research, Ohio State University, June 24, 1970. Quoted in Blaine R. Worthen and James R. Sanders, *Educational Evaluation: Theory and Practice* (Worthington, Ohio: Charles A. Jones, 1973), p. 129. Reprinted with permission.

[19]Ibid.

[20]Ibid.

[21]Stufflebeam et al., *Educational Evaluation*, p. 236.

said Stufflebeam. "Its purpose is to provide a rationale for determination of objectives."[22] At this point in the model, curriculum planner-evaluators define the environment of the curriculum and determine unmet needs and reasons why the needs are not being met. Goals and objectives are specified on the basis of context evaluation.

Input evaluation is that evaluation the purpose of which is "to provide information for determining how to utilize resources to achieve project objectives."[23] The resources of the school and various designs for carrying out the curriculum are considered. At this stage, the planner-evaluators decide on procedures to be used. Stufflebeam observed, "Methods for input evaluation are lacking in education. The prevalent practices include committee deliberations, appeal to the professional literature, the employment of consultants, and pilot experimental projects."[24]

Process evaluation is the provision of periodic feedback while the curriculum is being implemented. Stufflebeam noted, "Process evaluation has three main objectives—the first is to detect or predict defects in the procedural design or its implementation during the implementation stages, the second is to provide information for programmed decisions, and the third is to maintain a record of the procedure as it occurs."[25]

Product evaluation, the final type, has as its purpose

> to measure and interpret attainments not only at the end of a project cycle, but as often as necessary *during* the project term. The general method of product evaluation includes devising operational definitions of objectives, measuring criteria associated with the objectives of the activity, comparing these measurements with predetermined absolute or relative standards, and making rational interpretations of the outcomes using the recorded context, input, and process information.[26]

Stufflebeam outlined the types of evaluation in respect to objectives, methods, and in relation to decision making in the change process as shown in Table 13–1.

Four Types of Decisions.   The hexagons in Figure 13–5 represent four types of decisions, which were mentioned in Chapter 4: Planning, Structuring, Implementing, and Recycling. Note in the figure that Planning decisions follows Context evaluation: Structuring decisions follows Input evaluation; Implementation decisions follows Process evaluation; and Recycling decisions follows Product evaluation.[27]

---

[22]Stufflebeam, in Worthen and Sanders, *Educational Evaluation*, p. 136.
[23]Ibid.
[24]Ibid., p. 137.
[25]Ibid.
[26]Ibid., p. 138.
[27]Stufflebeam et al., *Educational Evaluation*, pp. 79–84.

TABLE 13–1 Four types of evaluation

	CONTEXT EVALUATION	INPUT EVALUATION	PROCESS EVALUATION	PRODUCT EVALUATION
OBJECTIVE	To define the *operating context*, to identify and assess *needs* and *opportunities* in the context, and to diagnose *problems* underlying the *needs* and *opportunities*.	To identify and assess *system capabilities*, available *input strategies*, and *designs* for implementing the strategies.	To identify or predict, in process, *defects* in the procedural design or its implementation, to provide information for the preprogrammed decisions, and to maintain a record of *procedural events* and activities.	To relate *outcome information* to objectives and to context, input, and process information.
METHOD	By describing the context; by comparing actual and intended inputs and outputs; by comparing probable and possible system performance; and by analyzing possible causes of discrepancies between actualities and intentions.	By describing and analyzing available human and material resources, solution strategies, and procedural designs for relevance, feasibility and economy in the course of action to be taken.	By monitoring the activity's potential procedural barriers and remaining alert to unanticipated ones, by obtaining specified information for programmed decisions, and describing the actual process.	By defining operationally and measuring criteria associated with the objectives, by comparing these measurements with predetermined standards or comparative bases, and by interpreting the outcomes in terms of recorded context, input and process information.
RELATION TO DECISION MAKING IN THE CHANGE PROCESS	For deciding upon the *setting* to be served, the *goal* associated with meeting needs or using opportunities, and the *objectives* associated with solving problems, i.e., for *planning* needed changes.	For electing sources of *support*, solution *strategies*, and procedural *designs*, i.e., for *structuring* change activities.	For *implementing and refining the program design and procedure*, i.e., for effecting process control.	For deciding to *continue, terminate, modify,* or *refocus* a change activity, and for linking the activity to other major phases of the change process, i.e., for recycling change activities.

SOURCE: Daniel L. Stufflebeam, an address given at the Eleventh Annual Phi Delta Kappa Symposium on Educational Research, Ohio State University, June 24, 1970. Quoted in Blaine R. Worthen and James R. Sanders, *Educational Evaluation: Theory and Practice* (Worthington, Ohio: Charles A. Jones, 1973), p. 139. Reprinted by permission.

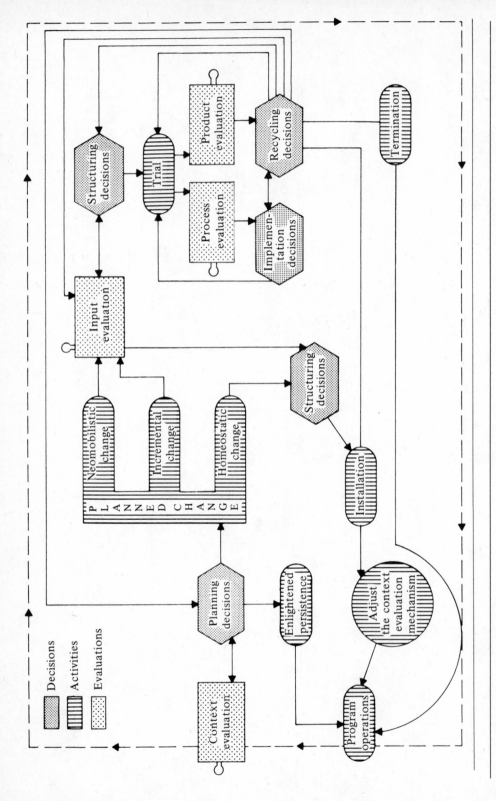

FIGURE 13–5 The CIPP evaluation model. From Daniel L. Stufflebeam et al., *Educational Evaluation and Decision Making* (Itasca, Ill.: F. E. Peacock, 1971), p. 236. Reprinted by permission.

Decision making, according to the Phi Delta Kappa Committee, occurs in four different settings:[28]

a. small change with high information
b. small change with low information
c. large change with high information
d. large change with low information

Four Types of Changes.   In these settings, four types of changes may result: neomobilistic, incremental, homeostatic, and metamorphic. *Neomobilistic change* occurs in a setting in which a large change is sought on the basis of low information. These changes are innovative solutions based on little evidence. *Incremental changes* are series of small changes based on low information. *Homeostatic change*, which is the most common in education, is a small change based on high information. Finally, *metamorphic change*, a large change based on high information, is so rare that it is not shown on the CIPP model.

The model plots the sequence of evaluation and decision making from context evaluation to recycling decisions. The committee has touched up the model with small loops that look like light bulbs on the evaluation blocks to indicate that the general process of delineating, obtaining, and providing information is cyclical and applies to each type of evaluation.

The ovals, the circle, and the E in the model represent types of activities, types of change, and adjustment as a result of the evaluations made and decisions taken. The CIPP model presents a comprehensive view of the evaluation process. Like Saylor, Alexander, and Lewis, Stufflebeam and his associates also call for evaluation of the evaluation program. Said the Phi Delta Kappa Committee: "To maximize the effectiveness and efficiency of evaluation, *evaluation itself should be evaluated.* . . . The criteria for this include internal validity, external validity, reliability, objectivity, relevance, importance, credibility, scope, pervasiveness, timeliness, and efficiency."[29]

Model with Types of Evaluation

To refine our concept of the necessary types of evaluation and to show what types are carried out at specific stages, I have rediagrammed the Curriculum Model in Figure 13–6. In this submodel of the model for curriculum development, the types of evaluation are now numbered for easy reference.

Let's review each of the numbered elements:

1. As a part of context evaluation, needs are assessed.
2. Curriculum goals are validated.

---

[28]Ibid., pp. 61–69.
[29]Ibid., p. 239.

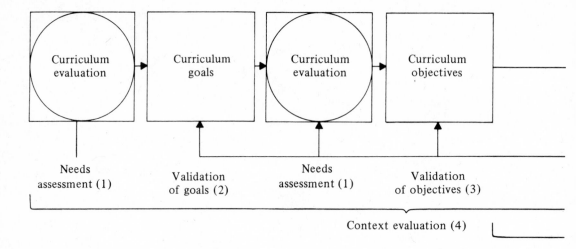

FIGURE 13–6   Sequence and types of evaluation

3. Curriculum objectives are validated.
4. Context evaluation begins with the needs assessment and continues up to the implementation stage.
5. Input evaluation takes place between specification of curriculum objectives and implementation of the curriculum.
6. Process evaluation is carried out during the implementation stage. Michael Scriven described three types of process research: noninferential studies, investigations of causal claims about the process, and formative evaluation.[30]

Noninferential studies are those observations and investigations of what is actually happening in the classroom. Investigation of causal claims is referred to by some educators as "action research." This type of research is a less than rigorous attempt to establish whether one teaching technique is better than another. Formative evaluation is assessment during the course of a study or program. To these three types of process research we might add the term "descriptive research," of which noninferential studies of teacher and student classroom behavior represent one form. The use of survey instruments and the application of such standards as the previously mentioned *Evaluative Criteria* also fall into the category of descriptive research.

---

[30]See Michael Scriven, "The Methodology of Evaluation," *Perspectives of Curriculum Evaluation*, AERA Monograph Series on Curriculum Evaluation No. 1 (Chicago: Rand McNally, 1967), pp. 49–51.

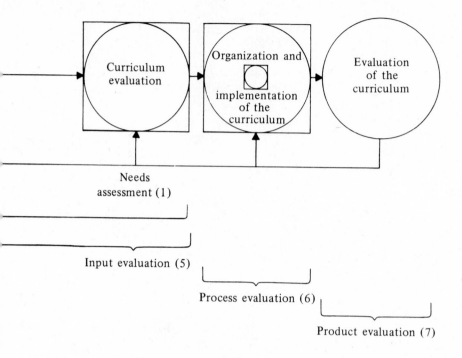

7. Product evaluation is summative evaluation of the entire process. This type of evaluation is sometimes referred to as outcome evaluation or program evaluation. Program evaluation, however, is used not only in the sense of summative evaluation but also as a synonym for the entire process of curriculum evaluation. Thus, a model for curriculum evaluation might also be called a model for program evaluation.

The Saylor, Alexander, and Lewis and CIPP models provide us with two different ways of viewing the process of curriculum evaluation. The models are similar to the extent that they urge a comprehensive approach to evaluation. They are different in the terminology they use and the level of detail they depict. The Saylor, Alexander, and Lewis model is somewhat less complex than the CIPP model and may perhaps be more readily understood by curriculum workers in general. The CIPP model may be more appealing to specialists in curriculum evaluation.

Standards for Evaluation

The use of any evaluation model will be more effective and proper if the evaluators follow some agreed-upon standards. The Joint Committee on Standards for Educational Evaluation, chaired by Daniel Stufflebeam, identified four attributes of an evaluation: utility, feasibility, propriety, and accuracy.[31] This committee proposed eight utility standards "to ensure that an evaluation will serve the practical information needs of given audiences."[32] They offered three feasibility standards "to ensure that an evaluation will be realistic, prudent, diplomatic, and frugal."[33] Eight propriety standards were advanced "to ensure that an evaluation will be conducted legally, ethically, and with due regard for the welfare of those involved in the evaluation, as well as those affected by its results."[34] Eleven accuracy standards were suggested "to ensure that an evaluation will reveal and convey technically adequate information about the features of the object being studied that determine its worth or merit."[35]

With evaluation of the curriculum, we conclude the model for curriculum development proposed in this text. However, I must stress that there is really no fixed end to the model; it is cyclical. Results of evaluation produce data for modifying earlier components. Without evaluation there can be no considered modifications and, therefore, little likelihood in improvement.

SUMMARY

Evaluation is a continuous process by which data are gathered and judgments made for the purpose of improving a system. Thorough evaluation is essential to curriculum development. Evaluation is perceived as a process of making judgments, whereas research is perceived as the process of gathering data as bases for judgments.

Curriculum planners engage in various types of evaluation and research. Among the types of evaluation are context, input, process, and product. Among the types of research are action, descriptive, historical, and experimental. In another vein, curriculum planners engage in both formative (process or progress) evaluation and in summative (outcome or product) evaluation.

Two models of curriculum evaluation were reviewed in this chapter. The Saylor, Alexander, and Lewis model seeks evaluation of five components: the goals, subgoals, and objectives; the program of education as a totality; the specific segments of the education program; instruction; and the evaluation program. The CIPP model was designed by the Phi Delta Kappa National Study Committee on Evaluation, which was chaired by Daniel L. Stufflebeam. It is more complex and technical than the Saylor, Alexander, and Lewis model. The CIPP model combines " . . . three major steps in the evaluation process (delineating, obtaining, and providing), . . . three classes of change settings

---

[31] From *Standards for Evaluations of Educational Programs, Projects, and Materials* by the Joint Committee on Standards for Educational Evaluation. Copyright ©1981 by McGraw-Hill. Used with the permission of McGraw-Hill Book Company.

[32] Ibid., p. 19.

[33] Ibid., p. 51.

[34] Ibid., p. 63.

[35] Ibid., p. 97.

(homeostasis, incrementalism, and neomobilism), . . . four types of evaluation (context, input, process, and product), and . . . four types of decisions (planning, structuring, implementing, and recycling)."[36] The creators of both these models also urge an evaluation of the evaluation program.

Curriculum evaluators from both inside and outside are employed by school systems. Much of the burden for curriculum evaluation falls on teachers as they work in the area of curriculum development. Following a set of agreed-upon standards improves the evaluation process. Attention should be given to utility, feasibility, propriety, and accuracy standards.

Evaluation of the curriculum is the culmination of the proposed model for curriculum improvement. Though placed at the end of the diagrammed model, evaluation connotes the end of one cycle and the beginning of the next. Improvements in the following cycle are made as a result of evaluation.

QUESTIONS FOR DISCUSSION

1. How do you know if a curriculum works?
2. If you evaluate instruction, is there any need to evaluate the curriculum? Explain.
3. Why is it that curriculum evaluation is often omitted or carried out ineffectively?
4. What effect should curriculum evaluation have on other components of the model for curriculum development presented by the author of this text?
5. Does the Hawthorne Effect enter into curriculum evaluation? How?

SUPPLEMENTARY EXERCISES

1. Define context, input, process, and product evaluation.
2. Report on evidence of any of the types of evaluation in Exercise 1 carried out in a school system you know well.
3. Search the literature on evaluation, and locate and report on a model of evaluation different form either of the two models described in this chapter. Contrast the model you discover to the two presented. (See footnote 4 and bibliography of this chapter for suggested models.)
4. Look up and explain to the class what is meant by internal validity, external validity, reliability, objectivity, relevance, importance, credibility, scope, pervasiveness, timeliness, and efficiency as they relate to the evaluation of evaluation programs.
5. Distinguish between instructional and curriculum evaluation.
6. Define empirical data, descriptive research, action research, historical research, experimental research, and dynamic hypotheses.

---

[36]Stufflebeam et al., *Educational Evaluation*, p. 238. Reprinted with permission.

7. Locate and present to the class a school system's job description for a curriculum evaluator.
8. Draw up a list of skills needed by a curriculum evaluator.
9. Write a position paper, using appropriate references, on the topic: When should outside consultants on evaluation be used by school systems?
10. Show with appropriate evidence that a school system you know well has used evaluative data to modify a curriculum.
11. Examine and critique the final evaluation (audit) of any state or federal program in a school system you know well.
12. Determine and provide evidence as to whether curriculum evaluation in a school system you know well suffers from any of the eight symptoms listed by the Phi Delta Kappa National Study Committee on Evaluation.
13. Explain the difference between goal-based evaluation and goal-free evaluation. Compare these two approaches and state under what conditions each is appropriate. For discussion of goal-free evaluation see David Hamilton et al. (bibliography) and articles in the literature by Michael Scriven.
14. This assignment is for four students. Refer to the publication of the Joint Committee of Standards for Educational Evaluation (see bibliography). Each student should select one of the four attributes (utility, feasibility, propriety, and accuracy) of an evaluation and describe to the class the standards suggested for it. Critique the standards as to applicability and appropriateness.
15. Describe any curriculum changes that have come about as a result of district or state assessments.
16. Read a study of one of the following and derive any implications for a school or school district which you know best:
    a. SAT or ACT scores
    b. National Assessment of Educational Progress
    c. International Association for the Evaluation of Educational Achievement
    d. International Assessment of Educational Progress
17. Report on the process and product of a curriculum audit conducted in any school system you know or reported in the literature. (See the Fenwick W. English reference on curriculum auditing for case studies.)
18. For those currently teaching: Carry out a curriculum mapping in the grade or course you teach.

BIBLIOGRAPHY

Aikin, Wilford M. *The Story of the Eight-Year Study*, New York: Harper & Row, 1942.

Apple, Michael W., Subkoviak, Michael J., and Luffler, Henry S., Jr., eds. *Educational Evaluation: Analysis and Responsibility*. Berkeley, Calif.: McCutchan, 1974.

Armstrong, David G. *Developing and Documenting the Curriculum*. Boston: Allyn and Bacon, 1989.

Beane, James A., Toepfer, Conrad F., Jr., and Alessi, Samuel J., Jr. *Curriculum Planning and Development*. Boston: Allyn and Bacon, 1986.

Bellon, Jerry J. and Handler, Janet R. *Curriculum Development and Evaluation: A Design for Improvement*. Dubuque, Iowa: Kendall/Hunt, 1982.

Brandt, Ron, ed. *Applied Strategies for Curriculum Evaluation*. Alexandria, Va.: Association for Supervision and Curriculum Development, 1981.

California Evaluation Improvement Project. *Program Evaluator's Guide*, 2nd ed. Princeton, N.J.: Evaluation Improvement Program, Educational Testing Service, 1979.

California State Department of Education. *Model Curriculum Standards: Grades Nine Through Twelve*. Sacramento, Calif.: California State Department of Education, 1985.

Center for the Study of Evaluation. *Evaluation Workshop I: An Orientation*. Del Monte Research Park, Monterey, Calif.: CTB/McGraw-Hill, 1971. Participant's Notebook and Leader's Manual.

Corey, Stephen M. *Action Research to Improve School Practices*. New York: Bureau of Publications, Teachers College, Columbia University, 1953.

"Curriculum Evaluation: Uses, Misuses, and Nonuses." *Educational Leadership* 35, no. 4 (January 1978): 243–297.

Doll, Ronald C. *Curriculum Improvement: Decision Making and Process*, 7th ed. Boston: Allyn and Bacon, 1989.

Eisner, Elliot W. *The Educational Imagination: On the Design and Evaluation of School Programs*, 2nd ed. New York: Macmillan, 1985.

———. "Educational Connoisseurship and Criticism: Their Form and Functions in Educational Evaluation." *Journal of Aesthetic Education* 10, numbers 3–4 (July-October, 1976): 135–150.

English, Fenwick W. *Curriculum Auditing*. Lancaster, Pa.: Technomic Publishing Company, 1988.

———. "Curriculum Mapping." *Educational Leadership* 37, no. 7 (April 1980): 558–559.

Guba, Egon, and Lincoln, Yvonna S. *Effective Evaluation: Improving the Usefulness of Evaluation Results Through Responsive and Naturalistic Approaches*. San Francisco: Jossey-Bass, 1981.

Hamilton, David, Jenkins, David, King, Christine, MacDonald, Barry, and Parlett, Malcolm, eds. *Beyond the Numbers Game: A Reader in Educational Evaluation*. London: Macmillan Education, 1977.

Hill, John C. *Curriculum Evaluation for School Improvement*. Springfield, Ill.: Charles C. Thomas, 1987.

Johnson, Mauritz, Jr. *Intentionality in Education: A Conceptual Model of Curricular and Instructional Planning and Evaluation*. Albany, N.Y.: Center for Curriculum Research and Services, 1977.

Joint Committee on Standards for Educational Evaluation. *Standards for Evaluations of Educational Programs, Projects, and Materials*. New York: McGraw-Hill, 1981.

Lewy, Arieh, ed. *Handbook of Curriculum Evaluation*. Paris: UNESCO, 1977; New York: Longman, 1977.

———. *Studies in Educational Evaluation*. Elmsford, N.Y.: Pergamon, 1980.

Lindvall, C. M., and Cox, Richard C., with Bolvin, John O. *Evaluation as a Tool in Curriculum Development: The IPI Evaluation Program*. American Educational Research Association Monograph, no. 5. Chicago: Rand McNally, 1970.

Miller, John P. and Seller, Wayne. *Curriculum: Perspectives and Practice*. White Plains, N.Y.: Longman, 1985.

National Study of School Evaluation. *Elementary School Evaluative Criteria*, 2nd ed. Falls Church, Va.: National Study of School Evaluation, 1981.

———. *Evaluative Criteria*, 6th ed. Falls Church, Va.: National Study of School Evaluation, 1987.

————. *Middle School/Junior High School Evaluative Criteria*. Falls Church, Va.: National Study of School Evaluation, 1979.

————. *Secondary School Evaluative Criteria: Narrative Edition*. Falls Church, Va.: National Study of School Evaluation, 1975.

Orlosky, Donald and Smith, B. Othanel, eds. *Curriculum Development: Issues and Insights*. Chicago: Rand McNally, 1978, Part 5.

Payne, David A., ed. *Curriculum Evaluation: Commentaries on Purpose, Process, Product*. Lexington, Mass.: D.C. Heath, 1974.

Plakos, Marie, Plakos, John, and Babcock, Robert. *Workbook on Program Evaluation*, 2nd ed. Princeton, N.J.: Educational Testing Service, 1978.

Popham, W. James, *Educational Evaluation*. Englewood Cliffs, N.J.: Prentice-Hall, 1975.

Provus, Malcolm. *Discrepancy Evaluation for Educational Program Improvement and Assessment*. Berkeley, Calif.: McCutchan, 1971.

Rogers, Frederick A. "Curriculum Research and Evaluation." In Fenwick W. English, ed., *Fundamental Curriculum Decisions*, 1983 Yearbook, 142–153. Alexandria, Va.: Association for Supervision and Curriculum Development, 1983.

Saylor, J. Galen, Alexander, William M., and Lewis, Arthur J. *Curriculum Planning for Better Teaching and Learning*, 4th ed. New York: Holt, Rinehart and Winston, 1981.

Schubert, William H. *Curriculum: Perspective, Paradigm, and Possibility*. New York: Macmillan, 1986.

Scriven, Michael. "The Methodology of Evaluation." *Perspectives of Curriculum Evaluation*. AERA Monograph Series on Curriculum Evaluation, no. 1, 39–83. Chicago: Rand McNally, 1967.

Stake, Robert E. "Language, Rationality, and Assessment." In *Improving Educational Assessment and an Inventory of Measures of Affective Behavior*, ed. Walcott H. Beatty. Alexandria, Va.: Commission on Assessment of Educational Outcomes, Association for Supervision and Curriculum Development, 1969.

Stufflebeam, Daniel L. "Educational Evaluation and Decision Making," an address to the 11th Annual Phi Delta Kappa Symposium on Educational Research. Ohio State University, June 24, 1970.

Stufflebeam, Daniel L. et al. *Educational Evaluation and Decision Making*. Itasca, Ill.: F. E. Peacock, 1971.

Tyler, Ralph W. *Basic Principles of Curriculum and Instruction*. Chicago: University of Chicago Press, 1949.

———— ed. *Educational Evaluation: New Roles, New Means*, 68th Yearbook of the National Society for the Study of Education. Chicago: University of Chicago Press, 1969.

Tyler, Ralph W., Gagné, Robert M., and Scriven, Michael. *Perspectives of Curriculum Evaluation*. AERA Monograph Series on Curriculum Evaluation, no. 1. Chicago: Rand McNally, 1967.

Weinstein, Donald F. *Administrator's Guide to Curriculum Mapping: A Step-by-Step Manual*. Englewood Cliffs, N.J.: Prentice-Hall, 1988.

Willis, George. "Democratization of Curriculum Evaluation." *Educational Leadership*, 38, no. 8 (May 1981): 630–632.

Worthen, Blaine R. and Sanders, James R. *Educational Evaluation: Alternative Approaches and Practical Guidelines*. White Plains, N.Y.: Longman, 1987.

————. *Educational Evaluation: Theory and Practice*. Worthington, Ohio: Charles A. Jones, 1973.

Worther, Blaine R., Sanders, James R., and White, Karl R. *Evaluating Educational and Social Programs: Guidelines for Proposal Review, Onsite Evaluation, Evaluation Contracts, and Technical Assistance*. Boston: Kluwer-Nijhoff Publishing, 1987.

Wulf, Kathleen M. and Schave, Barbara. *Curriculum Design: A Handbook for Educators*. Glenview, Ill.: Scott, Foresman, 1984.

ERIC MATERIALS

Current Index to Journals in Education. Monthly. Oryx Press, 2214 North Central at Encanto, Phoenix, Arizona 85004.

Resources in Education. Monthly. Washington, D.C.: Superintendent of Documents, U.S. Government Printing Office, Washington, D.C. 20402. Semiannual indexes available from the U.S. Government Printing Office. Annual cumulations: abstracts (2 volumes) and index (1 volume) available from Oryx Press. *Resources in Education* replaced *Research in Education* in January 1975.

Thesaurus of ERIC Descriptors. 9th ed., 1982.

FILMSTRIP-AUDIOTAPE PROGRAMS

Vimcet Associates, P.O. Box 24714, Los Angeles, Calif. 90024:

Current Conceptions of Educational Evaluation. 1972.

Alternative Measurement Tactics for Educational Evaluation. 1971.

KIT

Morris, Lyon Lyons. *Program Evaluation Kit*. Beverly Hills, Calif.: Sage Publications, 1978. The kit consists of the following volumes:

Evaluator's Handbook.

How to Deal with Goals and Objectives.

How to Design a Program Evaluation.

How to Measure Program Implementation.

How to Measure Attitudes.

How to Measure Achievement.

How to Calculate Statistics.

How to Present an Evaluation Report.

REPORTS

Reports of the International Assessment of Educational Progress may be obtained from the Center for the Assessment of Educational Progress, Educational Testing Service, Rosedale Road, Princeton, New Jersey 08541-0001.

Reports of the National Assessment of Educational Progress may be obtained from the National Assessment of Educational Progress, Educational Testing Service, Rosedale Road, Princeton, New Jersey 08541-0001.

VIDEOTAPE

Curriculum Mapping. 1981. Fenwick English explains techniques for improving the curriculum by determining what is actually being taught. Association for Supervision and Curriculum Development, 1250 North Pitt Street, Alexandria, Virginia 22314.

PART IV

Curriculum Development: Problems and Products

CHAPTER FOURTEEN

Problems in Curriculum Development

After studying this chapter you should be able to:

1. Define "scope," "relevance," "balance," "integration," "sequence," "continuity," "articulation," and "transferability" and explain their significance to curriculum workers.

2. Identify current and continuing curriculum problems that are brought about by social and political forces and explain their significance for curriculum development.

3. Identify professional problems that make an impact on the curriculum and explain their significance to curriculum planners.

CONTINUING PROBLEMS

Although a model for curriculum improvement may show us a process, it does not reveal the whole picture. It does not show us, for example, how we go about choosing from competing content, what we do about conflicting philosophies, how we assure articulation between levels, how we learn to live with change, how dependent we are upon effective leadership, what incentives motivate people to try out new ideas, how to go about finding the information we need to make intelligent decisions, and how we release human and material resources to do the job.

We already examined in Chapter 4 several major problems of curriculum development, including effecting change, group dynamics, interpersonal relationships, decision making, curriculum leadership, and communication skills. In this chapter we will consider (1) a number of perennial or continuing problems that are central to the organization and implementation of the curriculum and (2) a number of current curricular problems on contemporary issues. We will first discuss eight perennial problems of curriculum development: scope, relevance, balance, integration, sequence, continuity, articulation, and transferability. Then we will examine a number of contemporary curriculum issues and professional problems that have an impact on the curriculum.

The eight perennial problems to be discussed are not only problems of curriculum development but also are concepts that lead to principles of curriculum development. The provision of a well-functioning sequence, for example, is a continuing problem for the curriculum developer. At the same time, the curriculum developer must understand the concept of sequencing, which is essential to an effective curriculum. I will, therefore, refer to these eight problems as either concepts or principles.

All eight concepts are interrelated. We shall first examine four concepts closely related to each other: scope, relevance, balance, and integration. The last three are dimensions of scope; all four relate to the choice of goals and objectives.

We shall then consider three other closely interrelated concepts: sequence (or sequencing), continuity, and articulation. The last two are dimensions of sequencing. Finally, we shall look at the concept of transferability, which is both a curricular and instructional problem.

Scope

Scope is usually defined as "the breadth" of the curriculum. The content of any course or grade level—identified as topics, learning experiences, activities, organizing threads or elements,[1] integrative threads,[2] or organizing cen-

---

[1]Ralph W. Tyler, *Basic Principles of Curriculum and Instruction* (Chicago: University of Chicago Press, 1949), p. 86.

[2]Benjamin S. Bloom, "Ideas, Problems, and Methods of Inquiry," in *The Integration of Educational Experiences,* 57th Yearbook, National Society for the Study of Education, Part 3 (Chicago: University of Chicago Press, 1958), pp. 84–85.

ters,[3]—constitutes the scope of the curriculum for that course or grade level. The summed content of the several courses or grade levels makes up the scope of the school curriculum. J. Galen Saylor and William M. Alexander in an earlier work defined scope in the following way: "By scope is meant the breadth, variety, and types of educational experiences that are to be provided pupils as they progress through the school program. Scope represents the latitudinal axis for selecting curriculum experiences."[4]

When teachers select the content that will be dealt with during the year, they are making decisions on scope. When curriculum planners at the district or state level set the minimum requirements for graduation from high school, they are responding to the question of scope.

We encounter a problem when we equate the activities or learning experiences with scope. It is true that the sum of all activities or learning experiences reveals the scope of the curriculum. However, the activities or learning experiences are the operational phases of the topics. For example, to present the topic of the Renaissance, we can design many activities or learning experiences to teach that topic, including viewing photographs of works of art of the period, writing biographies of famous artists, reading novels about the period, reading histories of the period, writing reports on the roles of the church and state during this time, and so on.

Organizing Centers or Threads.   John I. Goodlad defined the elements of scope as "the actual focal points for learning through which the school's objectives are to be attained."[5] He wanted to convey the meaning of these elements as one term for the following reason:

> Nowhere in the educational literature is there a term that conveys satisfactorily what is intended in these focal points. The words *activities* and *learning experiences* are used most frequently but are somewhat misleading. Under the circumstances there is virtue in using the technical term *organizing centers*. Although somewhat awkward, the term does permit the inclusion of such widely divergent focal points for learning as units of work, cultural epochs, historical events, a poem, a film on soil erosion, and a trip to the zoo. The *organizing center* for teaching and learning may be as specific as a book on trees or as general as press censorship in the twentieth century. *Organizing centers determine the essential character of the curriculum.*[6]

In a similar vein, Tyler advised those who are organizing the curriculum to identify the organizing threads or elements—that is, the basic concepts and skills to be taught.[7] Thus, curriculum planners must choose the

---

[3]John I. Goodlad, *Planning and Organizing for Teaching* (Washington, D.C.: National Education Association, 1963), Chapter 2.

[4]Excerpts from *Curriculum Planning for Better Teaching and Learning,* p. 284, by J. G. Saylor and W. M. Alexander, copyright ©1954 by Holt, Rinehart and Winston, Inc. and renewed 1982 by J. G. Saylor and W. M. Alexander, reprinted with permission of the publisher.

[5]Goodlad, *Planning and Organizing,* p.28. Reprinted with permission.

[6]Ibid.

[7]Tyler, *Basic Principles,* p. 86.

focal points, the basic concepts and skills, and the knowledge that will be included in the curriculum. A central problem of this horizontal organization that we call scope is the delimitation of the concepts, skills, and knowledge to be included.

Explosion of Knowledge.   Teachers must continuously wrestle with the problem of limiting subject matter. Knowledge, spurred on by emerging technology, increases at a fantastic—and often alarming—rate. Humankind has no sooner begun to live comfortably with the computer than it has become involved in cloning, creating test-tube babies, and manufacturing new life forms. Humankind has journeyed through space but now worries about the debris floating around in our solar system. Humankind has harnessed the atom but has not learned to dispose of radioactive wastes safely. Arthur J. Lewis described the problem that has been repeatedly referred to as "the explosion of knowledge" in the following words:

> If the information explosion continues at the present pace, by the time a child born today graduates from college, the amount of information in the world will have increased fourfold. By the time the child is 50 years old, information will have increased 32 times, and 97 percent of everything known in the world will have been learned since the child was born.[8]

As long ago as 1970 Alvin Toffler spoke about the phenomenal increase in knowledge in this way:

> The rate at which man has been storing up useful knowledge about himself and the universe has been spiraling upward for 10,000 years. The rate took a sharp upward leap with the invention of writing. . . . The next great leap forward in knowledge-acquisition did not occur until the invention of movable type in the fifteenth century. . . . Prior to 1500, by the most optimistic estimates, Europe was producing books at the rate of 1000 titles per year. . . . By the mid-sixties, the output of books on a world scale, Europe included, approached the prodigious figure of 1000 titles per day. . . . Today the United States government alone generates 100,000 reports each year plus 450,000 articles, books and papers. On a worldwide basis, scientific and technical literature mounts at a rate of some 60,000,000 pages a year. The computer. . . . has raised the rate of knowledge-acquisition to dumbfounding speeds.[9]

Clearly, the problem of limiting knowledge will only intensify in the future.

Aims Procedure.   Somehow, some way, curriculum workers must select the concepts, skills, and knowledge to be incorporated into the curriculum. Many years ago Hollis L. Caswell and Doak S. Campbell suggested a procedure for

---

[8]Arthur J. Lewis, "Educational Basics to Serve Citizens in the Future," *FASCD Journal* 1, no. 1 (February 1979): 2.

[9]Alvin Toffler, *Future Shock* (New York: Random House, 1970), pp.30–31. Reprinted with permission.

determining the scope of the curriculum. Referring to the process as the "aims procedure," they outlined the steps as follows:

> First, a general all-inclusive aim of education is stated. Second, this all-inclusive statement is broken up into a small number of highly generalized statements. Third, the statement of a small number of aims is divided to suit the administrative organization of the school [for the elementary, junior high, or senior high school divisions]. . . . Fourth, the aims of each division are further broken up by stating the objectives to be achieved by each subject. Fifth, the general objectives for the subjects in each division are analyzed into specific objectives for the several grades; that is, statements in as specific terms as possible are made of the part of the subject objectives to be achieved in each grade. The specific objectives for all the subjects in each grade represent the work to be carried forward in the respective grades and indicate the scope of work for the grades.[10]

Caswell and Campbell perceived the specific objectives—not learning experiences, focal points, topics, or organizing threads—as indicating the scope of the curriculum.

Necessary Decisions.   With time so precious and the content burden so great, every organizing center included in the curriculum must be demonstrably superior to those not included. Decisions as to the superiority of the selected elements are reached by group consensus, by expertise, or by both. Curriculum planners must answer questions to which there are no easy answers, like these:

- ☐ What do young people need to succeed in our society?
- ☐ What are the needs of our locality, state, nation, and world?
- ☐ What are the essentials of each discipline?

Albert I. Oliver highlighted the levels at which decisions on scope must be made, as follows:

> Scope operates [on] at least four levels. First, there must be decisions as to what to include in the curriculum as a whole, in the major areas within which the curriculum operates. Should we concern ourselves with sex education? Shall we offer driver education? German? Geometry? . . .
>
> Within this total pattern of elements selected to achieve the school's projected goals there is a second level—the scope of an area. Whether this be called a subject field, an interdiscipline or a domain, it is a subject within the total scope. What from the discipline of mathematics is appropriate for an elementary school, for a secondary school? . . .
>
> The third level of scope determination concerns the individual teacher within the broad framework of the curriculum. What theorems shall the teacher of geometry include? . . .
>
> The fourth level relates to an individual lesson.[11]

---

[10]Hollis L. Caswell and Doak S. Campbell, *Curriculum Development* (New York: American Book Company, 1935), p. 152.

[11]Excerpts from *Curriculum Improvement: A Guide to Problems, Principles, and Process*, 2nd ed., pp. 188–189, by Albert I. Oliver. Copyright ©1965 by Harper & Row, Publishers, Inc. Reprinted by permission of HarperCollins Publishers.

As we see in Oliver's comments, decisions on the scope of the curriculum are multiple and relate to the curriculum as a whole, the various disciplines, courses or content within the disciplines, and the individual lesson. We might add an additional level before the individual lesson: the unit plan.

Curriculum workers must make decisions on scope not only within each of the three domains but also from among the domains. Within the domains they must raise questions such as the following:

☐ Shall we include a course in geology as well as biology (cognitive)?
☐ Shall we include development of charity as a value as well as the attitude of cooperation (affective)?
☐ Shall we teach typing as well as auto mechanics (psychomotor)?

Curriculum planners and teachers may find the determination of scope within a domain, albeit taxing, easier to resolve than making decisions between domains. Which domain, it must be asked, is most important? This question resurrects philosophical arguments about the nature of knowledge, the nature and needs of learners and of society. The question brings us back to Herbert Spencer's classic query, "What knowledge is of most worth?"[12] Arno Bellack addressed the same question and concluded that schools should enable teachers to develop students' knowledge in the major disciplines.[13]

Others have stressed the domain of knowledge—the cognitive domain. Jerome S. Bruner wrote: "The structure of knowledge—its connectedness and its derivations that make one idea follow another—is the proper emphasis in education";[14] Robert L. Ebel championed cognitive learning;[15] and Philip H. Phenix said: "My thesis, briefly, is that *all* curriculum content should be drawn from the disciplines, or to put it another way, that *only* knowledge contained in the disciplines is appropriate to the curriculum."[16]

Arthur W. Combs, Abraham H. Maslow, and others, on the other hand, looked beyond the realm of knowledge to the development of values and the self-concept as central to the educational process.[17] We shall not reopen the great debate between cognitive and affective learning, but we should point out that the issue looms large in determining the scope of the curriculum.

Many teachers and curriculum planners, refusing to rely on their own judgment, leave decisions on scope to others—to curriculum consultants, to writers of curriculum guides, and to the authors and publishers of textbooks. Thus

---

[12]See. p. 234 of this text.

[13]See Arno A. Bellack, "What Knowledge Is of Most Worth?" *The High School Journal* 48 (February 1965): 318–322.

[14]Jerome S. Bruner, *On Knowing* (Cambridge, Mass.: Harvard University Press, 1962), p. 120.

[15]See Robert L. Ebel, "What Are Schools For?" *Phi Delta Kappan* 54, no. 1 (September 1972): 3–7.

[16]Philip H. Phenix, "The Disciplines as Curriculum Content," in *Curriculum Crossroads,* ed. A. Harry Passow (New York: Teachers College Press, Columbia University, 1962), p. 57.

[17]See Arthur W. Combs, ed., *Perceiving, Behaving, Becoming,* 1962 Yearbook (Alexandria, Va: Association for Supervision and Curriculum Development, 1962).

the scope consists, for example, of many pages of one or more texts, and the determination is made simply by dividing the number of pages by the number of days' schooling or by dividing the number of topics and learning activities in a course of study by the number of days or weeks. Although this simplistic planning is better than none, the curriculum would be far more pertinent if, through a systematic, cooperative process, planners exercised their own combined professional judgment and selected from the entire field only those concepts, skills, and knowledge they deemed appropriate to their school, learners, society, state, region, and country.

Relevance

To assert that the curriculum must be relevant is to champion mom's blueberry pie. For who can disagree that mom's blueberry pie is one of the tastiest dishes ever concocted and is in the great American tradition? No one will stand up and argue for an irrelevant curriculum. However, the repeated demand for relevance in the curriculum—unless it is a straw man—must indicate a lack of this essential characteristic in the curriculum.

Varying Interpretations.   The difficulty of determining relevance lies in the multitude of interpretations of the word. What is considered relevant education for suburbia may not be for the inner city. What is considered relevant for the Anglo may not be for the Hispanic. What is relevant to the essentialists may not be to the progressivists. Relevance, like beauty, is in the eyes of the beholder. "Like the words 'relation' and 'relating,'" said Harry S. Broudy, " 'relevance' excludes virtually nothing, for everything mentionable is relevant in some sense to everything else that is mentionable."[18]

We should stress the word *considered* in "what is considered relevant." Whether the curriculum *is* relevant or not may be beside the point. The consumers of curriculum—the constituents and patrons of the school—will form attitudes toward relevance. Curriculum planners must deal first with perceptions of relevance before they can deal with the question of relevance itself.

Arguments about relevance swirl around immediate (as opposed to remote) needs and interests of learners. College and work, for examples, are psychologically if not chronologically far into the future for most children. They feel a need for certain knowledge *now*. Like Scarlett O'Hara, they'll worry about remote needs tomorrow.

Disagreements arise over contemporary as opposed to historic content. There is some question as to how many students would enroll in history courses—with the possible exception of American history—if the classes were not required. History teachers constantly have trouble showing young people the value of history, and the more ancient the history, the more difficulty they have.

---

[18]Harry S. Broudy, *The Real World of the Public Schools* (New York: Harcourt Brace Jovanovich, 1972), p. 179.

Conflicts come about between the academic studies and the vocational curriculum. Preparation for careers is of extreme importance to young people. They can see the value in skill courses but often do not realize that the academic areas may (1) provide a grounding needed in every curriculum and (2) open new vistas toward other careers. English teachers, for example, must feel an increasing despair that, in spite of their best efforts, the American population—arguably a more or less literate public in one of the most highly developed countries on earth—is not really a reading public. Furthermore, what is read is not of the highest quality. We can attribute the lack of reading in part to difficulties young people experience when learning to read in school. Children acquire early an aversion to reading.

We can also attribute the lack of reading to the American frontier mentality that equated reading with effete living and not with the macho men and pioneer women who tamed the West. Finally, television has delivered a significant blow to the printed word. Watching television is easier and more enjoyable to many, though perhaps less imaginative than reading.

Disagreements over relevance arise from conceptions of what *is* in society and what *should be*. The question becomes: Should curriculum planners educate young people for life as it is or as they think it should be? Should the curriculum develop the desire of citizens to read nonfiction, to subscribe to scholarly journals, to listen to classical music, and to frequent art galleries? Should the curriculum encourage young people to make money, to prefer pop fiction, to enjoy rock-and-roll music, and to artistically liven up their own homes? Should the curriculum remain neutral and abstain from all such value-laden content, or, conversely, should it expose the learners to both "highbrow" and "lowbrow" content?

Arguments arise over the relative merits of the concrete versus the abstract. Some prefer to concentrate on content that can be experienced with the senses whereas others prefer to concentrate on developing the intellect through high-level generalizations.

An Explanation of Relevance.   B. Othanel Smith clearly explained relevance when he wrote:

> The teacher is constantly asked 'Why should I learn that?' 'What is the use of studying history?' 'Why should I be required to take biology?' If the intent of these questions is to ask what use can one make of them in everyday activities, only general answers are possible. We can and do talk about the relevance of subject matter to the decisions and activities that pupils will have to make. We know, among other things, that they must:
>
> ☐ choose and follow a vocation,
> ☐ exercise the tasks of citizenship,
> ☐ engage in personal relationships,
> ☐ take part in culture-carrying activities . . .

...the question of relevance boils down to the question of what is most assuredly useful.[19]

Smith admitted that it is difficult to show the utility of abstract subject matter:

> Unfortunately, the utility of this form of subject matter is much more difficult to demonstrate. . . . Perhaps the chief reason utility of abstract knowledge cannot be demonstrated to the skeptic is that a great deal of it functions as a second-order utility. A first-order utility is illustrated in the skills that we use in everyday behavior such as handwriting and reading. The second-order utility consists of a learning that shapes behavior, but which is not itself directly observable in behavior.[20]

Uses of Knowledge. Smith classified the uses of knowledge that are not directly observable as associative, interpretive, and applicative.[21] By associative Smith meant the learner's ability to relate knowledge freely, sometimes bringing about solutions to problems. Abstract knowledge helps individuals to interpret their environment, which they cannot do without fundamental knowledge. Abstract subject matter enables learners to apply concepts to solve new problems.

Curriculum workers must, with considerable help from students and others, decide what is meant by relevance and then proceed to make the curriculum as relevant as possible.

Balance

Balance is an unusual curriculum concept that on the surface seems obvious but with some probing becomes somewhat cloudy. Nailing down a precise definition of balance is difficult. Many—perhaps most—educators feel that somehow the curriculum is in a state of imbalance. Observed Paul M. Halverson, "Curriculum balance will probably always be lacking because institutions of all kinds are slow in adapting to new needs and demands of the culture except when social change is rapid and urgent in its implications for these institutions."[22] Balance, then, is something that schools do not have but apparently should. How would we know a balanced curriculum if we saw one? This is the key question for us to examine.

The search for a definition is complicated by differing interpretations of the word "balance" as it applies to the curriculum. Halverson spoke of balancing ends and means, as follows: "A balanced curriculum implies structure and order

---

[19]B. Othanel Smith et al., *Teachers for the Real World* (Washington, D.C.: American Association of Colleges for Teacher Education, 1969), pp. 130–131. Reprinted with permission. See also Harry S. Broudy, B. Othanel Smith, and Joe R. Burnett, *Democracy and Excellence in American Secondary Education* (Chicago: Rand McNally, 1964), Chapter 3. Broudy, Smith, and Burnett discuss four uses of knowledge: replicative (repetition of a skill), associative, applicative, and interpretive.

[20]Smith et al., *Teachers,* p. 131.

[21]Ibid., pp. 131–133.

[22]Paul M. Halverson, "The Meaning of Balance," *Balance in the Curriculum,* 1961 Yearbook (Alexandria, Va: Association for Supervision and Curriculum Development, 1961), p. 7.

in its scope and sequence (means) leading to the achievement of educational objectives (ends)."[23]

Goodlad would bring the learner-centered curriculum and the subject-centered curriculum into balance, commenting:

> Much recent and current controversy over the curriculum centers on the question of what kind and how much attention to give learners and subject matter, respectively. The prospect of stressing one to the exclusion of the other appears scarcely worthy of consideration. Nonetheless, the interested observer has little difficulty finding school practices emphasizing one component to the impoverishment of the other.[24]

Ronald C. Doll looked at balance from the learner's standpoint and described it as follows:

> If a learner were to enjoy a balanced curriculum at a given time, this curriculum would completely fit the learner in terms of his or her particular educational needs at that time. It would contain just enough of each kind of subject matter to serve the individual's purposes and speed his or her development. General balance in the curriculum can be partly achieved, in the sense that certain kinds of experiences can be planned for large groups of learners according to what we know about them and about the subject matter they might learn. . . . Perhaps the best that can be done in working toward balance is to be clearer about what is valued for the growth of individual learners and then to apply these values in selecting curriculum content, grouping pupils for instruction, providing for articulation, and furthering guidance programs.[25]

In the foregoing comments Goodlad stressed the need for balance between the learner and the subject-centered curriculum whereas Doll emphasized the need for a curriculum that fits individuals through a judicious balance of group and individual experiences.

Sets of Variables.   We can apply the principle of balance in a number of ways. Given the typical elementary school, middle or junior high school, and a comprehensive senior high school, curriculum planners should seek balance between the following sets of variables. You will note below that some of the sets of variables call for proportions or splits other than a 50–50 distribution. When we speak of proportions, we distort the mathematical concept of balance as equilibrium. In reference to the curriculum, however, we cannot and probably should not always seek to achieve a 50–50 balance. There are times when a "balance" of one-third/two-thirds is defensible.

1. The child-centered and the subject-centered curriculum. This variable presupposes a balance between the conflicting philosophies of progressivism and essentialism.

---

[23]Ibid., p. 4.
[24]Goodlad, *Planning and Organizing,* p. 29. Reprinted by permission.
[25]From Ronald C. Doll, *Curriculum Improvement: Decision Making and Process,* Seventh Edition, pp. 170–171. Copyright © 1989 by Allyn & Bacon. Reprinted with permission.

2. The needs of society and of the learner. The curriculum must be not only socially but also personally oriented.

3. General and specialized education. Electives at the high school level should provide opportunities for learners in specialized areas. The Commission on the Education of Adolescents of the Association for Supervision and Curriculum Development advocated that one-third to one-half of each student's program in high school consist of general education and one-half to two-thirds consist of elective education.[26] Schools may still specialize, however, as in the case of New York City's Bronx High School of Science or Cooks' and Bakers' School. Balance can be achieved across a school system by having both general and specialized high schools. But there must be balance in schools that claim to be comprehensive in nature.

4. Breadth and depth. The curriculum can be so broad as to be superficial or conversely so profound as to limit learning. In either extreme learning is restricted.

5. The three domains, if we may create a three-way balance. We cannot ignore either the cognitive, affective, or psychomotor domain. Each has its importance in the life of the individual. Youngsters cannot find their own balance when learning is limited to one domain.

6. Individualization and mass education. We must find some way to provide for individual differences, to individualize or personalize instruction within the context of a mass educational system. Many recommendations have been made to achieve individualization—from programmed instruction to individually prescribed instruction to diagnostic-prescriptive teaching to independent study. However, of necessity, education remains largely a group process.

7. Innovation and tradition. Innovation cannot be incorporated at the drop of a hat. Tradition provides for stability and finds favor with the public. Constant innovation, often for its own sake, keeps faculties, students, and parents in a state of perpetual turmoil. We must pace innovations as to frequency and quantity in order to digest and evaluate changes taking place.

8. The logical and psychological. These variables are equated in a philosophical context with the differences between essentialism and progressivism. Some content must be organized according to the logic of the subject matter; some to the logic of the learner.

9. The needs of the exceptional and the nonexceptional child. If intelligence is distributed at random among the population, some two-thirds of the students are in the "average" range. Curriculum planners must be careful that attention to the needs of special groups does not far outstrip attention to the needs of the more numerous average student.

10. The needs of the academically talented or gifted and the slow. In recent times if we have stressed either group, we have catered to the needs of

---

[26]Kimball Wiles and Franklin Patterson, *The High School We Need* (Alexandria, Va.: Association for Supervision and Curriculum Development, 1959), pp. 9–10.

slow learners. Perhaps we assumed that the academically talented and the gifted will teach themselves in spite of school. Or perhaps we were guided by statistics; there are more slower students than academically talented (the top 15 percent) and gifted (the top 3 percent). Awareness of the needs of the gifted is coming into vogue once again.

11. Methods, experiences, and strategies. Teachers should use a mixture of techniques, including audio and visual media. Some schools rely almost exclusively on the printed word, which runs counter to the population's addiction to mediated learning—films, tapes, television, and the computer. Educators are pointing out the need for computer literacy, for example, and urging training in the use of the computer.

12. The immediate and the remote in both time and space. Some people would omit the study of ancient history (too remote) or the study of the non-Western world (too distant) and design only sparkling, new, contemporary, "with-it" curricula.

13. Work and play. At all levels youngsters need some balance, though certainly not 50/50, between academic work and leisure or physical activities. Play in the form of games, sports, and personal pursuits not only helps alleviate incipient boredom but can be an education in itself. Some of the avocations pursued by young people may become vocations or lifelong interests.

14. The school and the community as educational forces. Teachers sometimes forget that there is much to be learned outside the walls of the classroom. In fact, in many important areas of life more is learned of both a positive and negative nature outside of school than in school. Curriculum planners should build ways of using the community as an educational laboratory. If the world can be one's oyster, the community can be one's pearl.

15. Between disciplines. Disciplines, especially elective ones in the secondary school, vie with each other for student enrollment. Occasionally, a school becomes known for an exceptionally strong department in some discipline. Although excellence is to be encouraged, this situation may imply less than excellence in other disciplines. Curriculum planners should seek to foster excellence in all fields.

16. Between tracks. The college preparatory program of the secondary school often dwarfs other curricula. Curriculum planners must ensure that the general, vocational, business, home economics, and other curricula have their place in the sun as well as the college preparatory curriculum.

17. Within disciplines. The natural and social sciences, as examples, should offer a mixture of didactics and inquiry learning. The foreign language curriculum should seek achievement in comprehension, speaking, and writing as well as reading. No single phase of a particular discipline should be permitted to crowd out other important phases.

Achieving balance in the curriculum is an essential responsibility of the curriculum planner.

Integration

Curriculum workers should concern themselves with the problem of integrating subject matter. By integration we mean the blending, fusion, or unification of disciplines. Unlike determination of scope and sequence, which *must* be accomplished, the integration of disciplines is an optional and controversial undertaking. Whether or not curriculum planners choose to integrate subject matter hinges upon their philosophy of the nature of knowledge, the nature of learners, and the purposes of education. Generally speaking, educators support the conception of integrating subject matter. Tyler defined integration as "the horizontal relationship of curriculum experiences" and went on to say, "The organization of these experiences should be such that they help the student increasingly to get a unified view and to unify his behavior in relation to the elements dealt with."[27] Hilda Taba commented, "It is recognized that learning is more effective when facts and principles from one field can be related to another, especially when applying this knowledge."[28]

However, our schools have typically and traditionally behaved as if the integration of subject matter were not too important. The tenacity of the subject matter curriculum, which organizes subject matter into discrete disciplines, has been shaken only briefly by experiments like the activity curriculum and the core curriculum, discussed in Chapter 9. The activity curriculum on the elementary school level and the core curriculum on the secondary school level sought to break down the disciplinary barriers and to organize education around problems to be solved, using whatever subject matter was applicable.

Subject matter may be organized on the basis of separate disciplines with their own time blocks. Another approach is to integrate it either on a school-wide basis (as with the core curriculum) or on the classroom level (as with certain types of unit plans) without regard for disciplines.

Whether or not the curriculum is integrated and the degree to which it may be integrated are decided more on the basis of the curriculum planners' philosophies than on empirical data. It is impossible to prove without a doubt that integrating content necessarily leads to more productive, better educated citizens than organizing subject matter into separate disciplines.

Not all educators, of course, are advocates of integrating subject matter. Some believe that the various disciplines should be taught separately. Thus they reject the broad-fields approach to curriculum organization and recommend that teachers and students concentrate on the separate disciplines.

The progressives felt with considerable logic that understanding is enhanced when the artificial barriers between disciplines are removed. It is true that human beings solve their problems by judiciously selecting whatever subject mat-

---

[27] Tyler, *Basic Principles,* p. 85. Reprinted with permission.
[28] Excerpts from *Curriculum Development: Theory and Practice,* p. 298, by Hilda Taba, copyright ©1962 by Harcourt Brace Jovanovich, Inc. and renewed 1990 by Margaret J. Spalding, reprinted by permission of the publisher.

ter is needed. However, whether a program to educate the immature learner must consist of integrated disciplines is debatable. Two responses have been made over the years to reduce the separateness of disciplines. Subject matter has been both correlated and integrated. Curriculum planners have positioned themselves somewhere on a continuum that appears as follows:

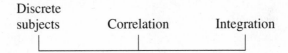

Correlation of Subject Matter.   Correlation is the relating of subjects to one another while still maintaining their separateness. Relationships between subjects taught at a particular school level are shown to pupils, as in the cases of history and literature; math and science; art, music, and literature.

Subjects may be correlated horizontally across one grade level or vertically across two or more. As an example of the latter, ancient history, taught in the sophomore or junior year of high school, may be correlated with Latin, taught in the junior or senior year. The study of Latin is therefore enriched by this progression. If the courses are taken concurrently, the study of both disciplines is enhanced.

Correlation becomes integration when the subjects lose their identities. In the cultural-epoch core approach to curriculum organization, epochs of humankind's history provide the framework; the subjects—English, social studies, science, mathematics, art, music—illuminate the cultural epochs. In the case of either correlation or integration, cooperative planning by all teachers affected is necessary.

Two Views of Integration.   Taba offered two views of integration. The first view is the one we have been discussing: the horizontal relationship of subjects. In addition, said Taba, "Integration is also defined as *something that happens to an individual.*"[29] If we follow the second view, "The problem, then, is that of developing ways of helping individuals in this process of creating a unity of knowledge. This interpretation of integration throws the emphasis from integrating subjects to locating the integrative threads."[30]

Regardless of whether the subject matter is presented to the learner in an integrated fashion by the teacher, the learner must integrate the knowledge into his or her own behavior. The distinction between an educated and an erudite person lies in the degree to which knowledge is integrated in the person. Taba remarked:

> Unification of subjects has been a theme in education ever since the Herbartians. By far the greatest number of experimental curriculum schemes have revolved around the problem of unifying learning. At the same time we are far from achieving unification, partly because of fear of loss of disciplined

[29]Ibid., p. 299.
[30]Ibid.

learning if the study of specialized subjects is discarded, and partly because as yet no effective basis has been found for unifying school subjects.[31]

Curriculum planners must decide whether they will make a conscious effort either to correlate or to integrate subject matter and, if they plan to do either, what organizational structure they will create to do so.[32] Scope, relevance, balance, and integration are interrelated principles to which curriculum workers must give attention.

Sequence

Sequence is the order in which the organizing elements or centers are arranged by the curriculum planners. Whereas scope is referred to as "the what" of curriculum organization, sequence is referred to as "the when." Sequence answers the questions of when and where the focal points will be placed. Some time ago Saylor and Alexander defined sequence as

> the order in which educational experiences are developed with pupils. Sequence refers to the "when" in curriculum planning. Determination of the sequence of educational experiences is a decision as to the most propitious time in which to develop those educational experiences suggested by the scope. If we think of scope as the latitudinal aspect of curriculum planning, sequence becomes the longitudinal axis.[33]

Once we identify the scope of the curriculum, we must put the elements into some kind of meaningful order. Let's take a simplified illustration from the reading curriculum. Suppose as reading teachers we wish students to be able to

□ read novels
□ read words
□ read paragraphs
□ read sentences
□ recognize letters of the alphabet

Is there some particular order in which pupils learn those elements? The answer is obvious here. The student should recognize letters of the alphabet first, then proceed to reading words, sentences, paragraphs, and novels. Unless one is a Mozart-like prodigy, one does not normally begin to demonstrate reading skills by reading adult tomes.

But take the following organizational threads in economics:

□ insurance
□ real estate

---

[31] Ibid., pp. 298–299.

[32] For discussion of types of integrated curricula see Gordon F. Vars, ed., *Common Learnings: Core and Interdisciplinary Team Approaches* (Scranton, Pa.: International Textbook Company, 1969).

[33] Excerpts from *Curriculum Planning for Better Teaching and Learning*, p. 249, by J. G. Saylor and W. M. Alexander, copyright ©1954 by Holt, Rinehart and Winston, Inc. and renewed 1982 by J. G. Saylor and W. M. Alexander, reprinted by permission of the publisher.

□ banking
□ stock market
□ inflation
□ recession
□ foreign exchange

What is the sequence in this case? Is there a preferred sequence? What makes it preferred? As another example, in what order should we study the American Revolution, the War of 1812, the Korean War, World War I, the Civil War, the Vietnam War, World War II, the Persian Gulf War, and the Spanish-American War? The answer in this case is simple, you say. Simply place the wars in chronological order. But could there be any other defensible way of sequencing these items?

The problem of sequencing produces questions about

□ the maturity of the learners
□ the interests of the learners
□ the readiness of the learners
□ the relative difficulty of the items to be learned
□ the relationship between items
□ the prerequisite skills needed in each case

Ways of Sequencing. How do curriculum workers decide which content comes first? Sequencing is accomplished in a variety of ways, including arranging the content in the following ways:

1. From the simplest to the most complex. We must deal with tens, for example, before we work with hundreds.
2. In chronological order. History is most often taught in this fashion.
3. In reverse chronological order. Occasionally, a history teacher will start with the most recent events and work backward to the most ancient under the assumption that pupils' attention can be grasped quicker with more recent and therefore more familiar events. Themes that exist in the present may be seen repeated as they go backward in time.
4. From the geographically near to the geographically far. Some argue that it makes more sense to study phenomena and conditions close to home and to gradually expand the learner's horizons ultimately to the world and even the universe.
5. From the far to the near. This procedure focuses on distant lands and reserves study of the home environment—the pièce de résistance—until the end.
6. From the concrete to the abstract. The pupil learns to count blocks by first manipulating them physically and only later manipulating them mentally.
7. From the general to the particular. This approach starts with the principle and proceeds to examples.
8. From the particular to the general. This approach starts with examples and proceeds to the principle.

When we are determining sequencing, we will find that there are times when the order of the units of content does not matter. When we are studying the works of twentieth-century American authors, we might want to group writers of drama, short stories, novels, and nonfiction, but it is not likely to make a great deal of difference which grouping we study first.

There are times when we will deliberately violate a sequence. The class may be studying the political structure of ancient Rome, for example, when a landmark case affecting the country's political and social system is decided by the U.S. Supreme Court. This immediate and significant case is permitted to alter the planned sequence.

Prerequisite Skills.   Frequently, pupils cannot engage in a unit of content until they master a preceding unit. The student of algebra is hard pressed unless he or she has mastered arithmetic skills. The student cannot succeed in a second-year foreign language class without mastering the skills developed in the first year. For this reason the assessment of prerequisite skills is sound pedagogy. Teachers must know whether the students have mastered the skills needed to proceed with the tasks before them.

Dubious Sequencing.   Some curriculum planners in the past, following their own notions of what constitutes prerequisite skills, have instituted sequencing that is hard to defend on any solid grounds. For years, high school students were required, for example, to take general science, biology, chemistry, and physics in that order. Actually, none is necessarily dependent upon the other. Each science depends more upon mastery of reading and mathematics than upon mastery of other sciences. We can find evidence of the same dubious sequencing in mathematics with the prescribed order of algebra I, geometry, algebra II, trigonometry, and calculus. Although it may be wise planning to start with algebra I and hold calculus for the end, there is little reason to hold algebra II until after the completion of geometry. Why is *Macbeth* invariably taught <u>after</u> *Julius Caesar?* Why does American history often come after world history? From a chauvinist point of view, we could argue that American history ought to come first in the senior high school sequence.

Conceptions of Sequencing.   Donald E. Orlosky and B. Othanel Smith discussed three conceptions of sequencing: (1) sequencing according to need, (2) macrosequencing, and (3) microsequencing. According to the first conception,

> the learner orders his own learning as he deals with a situation from moment to moment. He selects what he wants to know as the need arises. If he makes a mistake in the selection he simply goes through the process again until he finds that which satisfies his present need. This is an opportunistic notion of sequencing but those who advocate it maintain that it is psychologically sound.[34]

[34]Donald E. Orlosky and B. Othanel Smith: *Curriculum Development: Issues and Insights.* Copyright ©1978 Rand McNally College Publishing Company. Used by permission by Houghton Mifflin Company.

This perception of sequencing fits the views of some progressive educators and proponents of open education.

Macrosequencing follows principles of child development expounded by persons like Arnold Gesell, Frances L. Ilg, and Jean Piaget. Macrosequencing, said Orlosky and Smith, is

> the organization of knowledge and the formulation of instruction to co-incide with the different stages of the individual's development. For a long time teachers have arranged the knowledge of instruction roughly in accordance with the development of the child. Examining the existing program of studies of almost any school proves that it corresponds roughly to the child's development.[35]

Microsequencing is the ordering of subject matter according to the prerequisite knowledge required of each unit of content. "This assumes," said Orlosky and Smith, "that for any learning task there is a hierarchy extending from the very simple to the more abstract and complex elements which lead to the attainment of a specified objective."[36]

Curriculum planners are called upon to make decisions on placement of content at the appropriate grade levels. Using the terms "sequence" and "grade placement" together, B. Othanel Smith, William O. Stanley, and J. Harlan Shores observed:

> There are only two possible approaches to the solution of problems of grade placement and sequence. *The first* accepts the child as he is and adjusts the experience to his level of development while holding the instructional goals constant. . . . *The second approach* assumes curriculum experiences to be located at a given grade level and provides learnings to adjust the child to these experiences—that is, to get him ready for the learning.[37]

Where to Begin.   Disagreements over the process of sequencing center on whether curriculum planners should start with learners or subject matter. The first demands choosing emphases in keeping with the learners' actual growth and development; the second, placing subject matter at the grade level at which it is assumed learners will be able to master it. The latter approach to sequencing has been the historic approach.

Smith, Stanley, and Shores advocated a blending of the two approaches:

> To accept wholeheartedly the first approach, which emphasizes the nature of the child and regards the curriculum as always flexible enough at each grade level to be bent to the child's needs, is probably unrealistic. And just as unrealistic is the inflexibility of the second approach, which allows objectives and content to be so fixed at any one grade that lower grade experiences

---

[35]Ibid., p. 251.

[36]Ibid., p. 267.

[37]Excerpts from *Fundamentals of Curriculum Development,* Revised Edition, p. 171 by B. O. Smith, W. O. Stanley, and J. Harlan Shores, copyright ©1957 by Harcourt Brace Jovanovich, Inc. and renewed 1985 by B. O. Smith, W. O. Stanley, and J. Harlan Shores, reprinted by permission of the publisher.

must always prepare for this hurdle and later experiences always build upon it. Probably neither of these approaches will be used without consideration for the other.[38]

They counseled curriculum workers to take into account the maturation, experiential background, mental age, and interests of the learners and the usefulness and difficulty of the subject matter when developing a sequence.[39] The ordering of the organizing elements of the curriculum is one of the major tasks of the curriculum developer.

Continuity

Continuity is the planned repetition of content at successive levels, each time at an increased level of complexity. Tyler described continuity as follows:

> Continuity refers to the vertical reiteration of major curriculum elements. For example, if in the social studies the development of skills in reading social studies is an important objective, it is necessary to see that there is recurring and continuing opportunity for these skills to be practiced and developed. This means that over time the same kinds of skills will be brought into continuing operation. In similar fashion, if an objective in science is to develop a meaningful concept of energy, it is important that this concept be dealt with again and again in various parts of the science course. Continuity is thus seen to be a major factor in effective vertical organization.[40]

Spiral Curriculum.   The principle of continuity is represented in what has been called the spiral curriculum.[41] Concepts, skills, and knowledge are introduced and reintroduced—for example, the repetition of addition, study of democracy, writing, personal health, and conservation.

Expertise Needed.   Planning a curriculum for continuity requires a high degree of expertise, which demands both knowledge of the subject field and of the learners. For example, to plan a mathematics sequence for 12 grades with appropriate scope, sequence, and continuity requires the combined skills of subject matter specialists and teachers. Continuity is not simply repetition of content but repetition with increasing levels of complexity and sophistication. Whereas elementary school youngsters, for example, may learn that democracy means government of the people, by the people, and for the people, secondary students may wrestle with controversial and unresolved problems of democracy.

Experience will reveal to curriculum developers which units of content must be reintroduced and at what point. Preassessment, if only of the most rudimentary kind, is essential before each new organizing element is broached. Preassessment will uncover whether the learners are ready for (1) new content

---

[38]Ibid.

[39]Ibid., pp. 174–186.

[40]Tyler, *Basic Principles,* pp. 84–85. Reprinted with permission.

[41]J. Galen Saylor, William M. Alexander, and Arthur J. Lewis, in *Curriculum Planning for Better Teaching and Learning.* 4th ed. (New York: Holt, Rinehart and Winston, 1981), define sequence, continuity, and integration with slightly different interpretations from those in this text.

based on prior content and (2) prior content that will be repeated at a more complex level.

Articulation

If we view continuity as the spiraling of content upward through the grades of a particular school, we should view articulation as the meshing of organizing elements across school levels—that is, across elementary and middle or junior high schools, across junior high or middle and senior high schools, and across senior high school and college. Like continuity, articulation is a dimension of sequencing.

Horizontal and Vertical.   Oliver used the term "articulation" synonymously with "horizontal articulation" or "correlation." He equated the concept of "continuity" with "vertical articulation."[42] Regarding correlation as a halfway move toward integration, I would agree with calling correlation horizontal articulation. Sequence, continuity, and articulation are all interrelated. I would separate continuity from vertical articulation and define continuity as a reintroduction of content at progressively more complex levels and articulation as the meshing of the curriculum of the various levels of the educational ladder to provide for smooth transition on the part of the learners. This meshing may or may not involve reintroduction of units of content, progressively more difficult. When speaking of articulation, I am addressing the problem of vertical articulation.

Unfortunately, efforts at articulation between levels are in many cases feeble and ineffective. Cooperative efforts are necessary among curriculum workers if articulated sequences are to be planned from kindergarten through twelfth grade and beyond.

We find considerable unplanned repetition of content among levels. This is neither articulation nor continuity but a laissez-faire attitude that permits curriculum workers to develop their own programs without knowledge of what instructors at preceding and succeeding levels are teaching.

With our decentralized system of education, lack of articulation occurs frequently. Articulation is particularly difficult in some states where separate school districts managing different levels of schooling exist side by side under separate administrators and separate school boards. Even when all levels of schooling are centralized under a single administrator and school board, articulation remains a problem.

Gaps Between Levels.   We often find great gaps between levels. The seventh grade teacher (failing or refusing to preassess) assumes certain levels of mastery

---

[42]Oliver, *Curriculum Improvement,* p. 222. Some authors also refer to scope as a horizontal dimension of curriculum organization and sequence as a vertical dimension.

of knowledge when children enter from the elementary school; the senior high school teacher expects certain entry skills from youngsters who are promoted from the junior high school.

Personal Articulation.   There is not only a need for planned articulation of subject matter but also for pupils' personal articulation. Schools are beginning to respond to students' varied capabilities. Some junior high/middle school pupils, for example, are able to tackle senior high school subjects. Some senior high school pupils can perform ably in advanced placement courses given in the high school and in junior or senior college courses in their area of residence. Some students can skip a year of high school and enter college early or can skip the lower division of college and enroll in the upper division.

Improved articulation eases the movement of pupils from one level to the next, which can be a traumatic experience for young people. With all the problems of social adjustment as they enter a higher level, they have little need for suffering either needless repetition, exposure to subject matter that is too easy for them, or, worse yet, grasping for learnings beyond their abilities and skills. Thus curriculum planners cannot avoid the problem of articulation.

Let's recap what has been said about sequencing, continuity, and articulation. Continuity and articulation are dimensions of sequencing. Sequencing is the logical or psychological arrangement of units of content within lessons, units, courses, and grades. Continuity is the planned introduction and reintroduction of the same units of content through the grades of a school system at ever-increasing levels of complexity. Articulation is the planned sequencing of units of content across grade levels—that is, from one grade level to the next to ensure that the next grade level takes up where the previous grade level left off.

The three principles—sequence, continuity, and articulation—are interrelated and complement each other. Material must be appropriately sequenced at whatever level. Articulation must be observed to ensure that there are no gaps in a sequence from one grade level to the next, whereas continuity must be sought to permit students to achieve greater depth in a subject.

Transferability

Whatever is taught in school should in some way posses transfer value, that is, learning in school should have applicability in either a broad or narrow sense outside of school and after school years. Education for education's sake—the mark of the learned person—is simply not sufficient as a goal of education. Education should in some way enrich the life of the individual.

The transfer of learning or transfer of training, as it is sometimes called, has been discussed at some length in the literature of educational psychology.[43] Transfer gives a permanence to learning beyond the moment of its first introduction into the classroom.

Vocational education possesses a built-in one-upmanship in transferability. You can see the transfer; it's apparent. Skills learned in industrial arts and vocational education classes can be transferred to life situations. Teachers of psychomotor skills are particularly fortunate because pupils have no difficulty seeing the transfer value of these areas of study. Students can and will use the skills they learn in such areas as music, art, physical education, typing, word-processing, and home economics. Transfer is paramount with most teachers of perceptual-motor skills. Physical educators tout the carry-over value of their activities—that is, transfer.

Transfer in the affective and cognitive areas is more difficult to discern. Of course, we wish students to carry over values and positive attitudes into their daily living. We would like a student who demonstrates cooperation in the classroom to retain that behavior all his or her life. Transfer of cognitive learning is most often visible in student performance on assessment and standardized tests, in admission to and success in college, and in the evaluations employers give of the intellectual competence of their employees.

Proponents of faculty psychology (mental or formal discipline) maintained that rigorous subjects disciplined the mind; thus such education was generally transferable. Some of the essentialists have held that education is the storing of data—computer-fashion—for use at a later date when the occasion arises. Unfortunately, disuse sets in; we forget, and when we need to retrieve the supposedly stored data, we find that they have slipped away.

It has generally been believed by many—a holdover of the formal discipline days—that certain subjects lead to transfer more than other subjects. After an exhaustive study of more than 8,000 students, Thorndike concluded:

> The expectation of any large difference in general improvement of the mind from one study rather than another seems doomed to disappointment. The chief reason why good thinkers seem superficially to have been made such by having taken certain school studies is that good thinkers have taken such studies, becoming better by the inherent tendency of the good to gain more than the poor from any study.[44]

Daniel Tanner and Laurel N. Tanner pointed out that the Eight-Year Study disproved the notion that certain subjects lead to transfer:

> But probably the most stunning attack (aside from Thorndike's 1924 study) on the idea that certain subjects have superior transfer to intelligence was delivered by the Progressive Education Association's Eight-Year Study.

---

[43]See Edward L. Thorndike, "Mental Discipline in High School Studies," *Journal of Educational Psychology* 15, no. 1 (January 1924): 1–22; continued in 15, no. 2 (February 1924): 83–98. Edward L. Thorndike, *The Principles of Teaching* (New York: Seiler, 1906). Sidney L. Pressey and Francis P. Robinson, *Psychology and the New Education,* rev. ed. (New York: Harper & Row, 1944).

[44]Thorndike, "Mental Discipline" (February 1924), p. 98.

. . . the study proved that success in college is not dependent on credits earned in high school in prescribed subjects.[45]

Taba, however, explained the more current view on transfer as follows: "The recent ideas on transfer have returned to earlier assumptions of the possibility of fairly wide transfer, depending on the level of generalizing that takes place regarding either the content or the method of approach."[46] Thus, if teachers wish to encourage transfer, they must stress general principles.

Current Beliefs. Let's summarize some of the current beliefs about transfer.

- □ Transfer is at the heart of education: it is a—if not *the*—goal of education.
- □ Transfer is possible.
- □ The closer the classroom situation is to the out-of-classroom situations, the greater is the transfer.
- □ Transfer can be increased and improved if teachers consciously teach for transfer.
- □ Transfer is greater when teachers help pupils to derive underlying generalizations and to make applications of those generalizations.
- □ Generally speaking, when the learner discovers knowledge for himself or herself, transfer is enhanced. Bruner provided an example of children in a fifth-grade class learning "a way of thinking about geography" as opposed to being dished out selected, unconnected geographical facts.[47] Bruner encouraged teachers to use a discovery approach, justifying it on the grounds of "increased intellectual potency, intrinsic rewards, useful learning techniques, and better memory processes."[48]

Guided Discovery. The jury is still out on the question of the extent of use of inquiry or discovery methods. David Ausubel pointed out that some discovery techniques can be an inefficient use of time.[49] Some authorities prefer to speak of guided discovery rather than discovery per se. Whatever the process used— discovery or other—enhancement of meaning during the process of instruction should increase the degree of transfer.

Transferability is a principle of both instruction and the curriculum. When we talk about methods of teaching for transferability, we are referring to the instructional process. When we analyze what the learner has transferred, we are in the area of curriculum. Curriculum developers should specify objectives, select content, and choose instructional strategies that will lead to maximum transfer.

---

[45]Reprinted by permission of Macmillan Publishing Company from *Curriculum Development Theory into Practice*, 2nd ed., p. 323, by Daniel Tanner and Laurel N. Tanner. Copyright ©1980 by Macmillan Publishing Company.

[46]Excerpts from *Curriculum Development: Theory and Practice*, p. 124, by Hilda Taba, copyright ©1962 by Harcourt Brace Jovanovich, Inc. and renewed 1990 by Margaret J. Spalding, reprinted by permission of the publisher.

[47]Jerome S. Bruner. "Structures in Learning," *Today's Education* 52, no. 3 (March 1963): 26.

[48]Ibid., p. 27.

[49]See David P. Ausubel, *Educational Psychology: A Cognitive View* (New York: Holt, Rinehart and Winston, 1968).

Furthermore, plans for evaluating the curriculum should include means of judging the degree of the transfer of the many segments of the curriculum.

Implications of the Continuing Curriculum Problems

Given the range and the many facets of curriculum problems covered, it is useful to briefly redefine them in the light of the curriculum worker's responsibilities. Curriculum workers attend to the problem of

- *scope* when they select topics to be studied and specify the instructional objectives
- *relevance* when they "effect a congruence between the entire school system and the social order in which the young of today will spend their adult lives"[50]
- *balance* when they maintain certain sets of elements proportionately
- *integration* when they make an effort to unify subject matter
- *sequence* when they determine the order in which subject matter will be made available to the students
- *continuity* when they examine the curriculum of each course and grade level to discover where units of content may fruitfully be repeated at increased levels of complexity
- *articulation* when they examine the curriculum of each discipline at each grade level to be sure the subject matter flows sequentially across grade level boundaries
- *transferability* when they seek ways to achieve maximum transfer of learning

CURRENT CURRICULUM PROBLEMS

Several movements in recent years have had an impact on curriculum development. To gain a sense of the dimensions of these problems and their impact, let's briefly review some movements that have either changed the role of curriculum planners or caused modifications in the ways in which schools organize for curricular development.

Curriculum planners are buffeted by several strong social and political forces, some arising from pressure groups and some from the public in general. Some of the desires of both the pressure groups and the public generally have been enacted into law, primarily at the federal level.

Among the significant contemporary issues facing curriculum workers are (1) alternative choices in education, (2) emphasis on the basics and academics, (3) bilingual education, (4) cultural literacy, (5) provision for the handicapped,

---

[50]Broudy, *Real World*, p. 193.

(6) health education, (7) racial/ethnic integration and cultural diversity, (8) religion in the schools, (9) protests over schoolbooks, (10) sexism, and (11) whole language.

Alternative Choices in Education

The movement toward alternatives in education has gone well beyond free schools, storefront schools, in-district schools for children and youth with behavior problems, and magnet schools. Most of these alternative schools have been perceived as strengthening the public school system. Far more threatening to public education are the growing opportunities for parents to select (1) public or private schools other than the public schools to which their children have been assigned by the district and (2) home schools.

Selection of Public or Private School. In recent years, pressure has been building for the state to support parental choice of schools whether public or private. The Association for Supervision and Curriculum Development reported that in 1991 schools-of-choice programs existed in some 30 states.[51] Customarily, parents who have children in the public school system must send them to schools within their assigned subdistricts of the local school district. Parents may send their children to schools outside their assigned subdistricts only in special cases such as magnet schools or other programs that are not available within that assigned subdistrict. Parents have encountered even greater difficulty when they wished to send their children to public schools across school-district lines; this type of move, if permitted, may require the parents to pay tuition to the school district of choice.

Ever since the U.S. Supreme Court rendered its decision in the case of *Pierce v. Society of Sisters* in 1925, parents have had the choice of sending their children to private schools.[52] Only in recent years, however, have some states reinforced this right by issuing vouchers for payment of tuition or allowing tax credit for families whose children are being educated in the private schools. Dissatisfied with the public schools, parents have made headway in gaining the right to choose their children's schools and, in so doing, receive financial support from their state and local governments.

Since 1985 Minnesota's School District Enrollment Options Program (Open Enrollment) has allowed parents to choose a public school or program outside the district in which they live. Minnesota further allows a deduction (currently $650 per child in grades K–6 and $1,000 per child in grades 7–12) from parents' gross income for expenses incurred in sending their children to public, private, or parochial schools.

---

[51]Gordon Cawelti, "Will Competition Accelerate School Reform?" *Curriculum Update* 33, no. 2 (February 1991): 2.

[52]*Pierce v. Society of Sisters,* 268 U.S. 510 (1925).

Although two-thirds of those voting in the November 1990 elections in Oregon defeated Measure 11 (known as the Educational Choice Initiative), evidence of sizable support can be seen by the more than 100,000 signatures on a petition, sponsored by Oregonians for Educational Choice, to place the measure on the ballot. Beginning in the academic year 1991–92, Measure 11 would have allowed taxpayers a deduction from taxes owed of up to $2500 toward costs of any public or private school (secular or sectarian) or for teaching their children at home.

Though this policy has been challenged in the courts, in 1990 Wisconsin became the first state to offer to pay parents in low-income brackets up $2500 per pupil so that their children might attend Milwaukee private/nonsectarian schools. At the time this text was written legislatures of twelve states had already passed legislation granting parents the right to choose the schools their children would attend. Further, in December 1990 the Bush administration created a Center for Choice in Education within the U.S. Department of Education; the center provides information about open enrollments in public schools throughout the country and about tax credits and voucher plans for private schools.

Many people feel that, by introducing the element of competition among schools for students, provision of choice will in the long run strengthen the public schools by forcing them for economic reasons to overcome those problems with which parents are dissatisfied.

Some of the schools-of-choice may well be commercial, for-profit schools created by businesspeople who believe they can deliver a higher quality education at a lower cost than the public schools. John E. Chubb and Terry M. Moe would apply a marketplace concept that encourages creation of private schools to compete with public schools, parental choice of public or private school, and governmentally funded vouchers.[53]

Public school officials themselves may turn to private organizations for assistance in running some of their schools. For example, Dade County (Florida) Public Schools has contracted with Education Alternatives, Inc., a company in Minneapolis, to operate its new South Pointe Elementary School, which opened in the fall of 1991.[54]

Parental choice, with or without vouchers or tax credits, will likely be met with strong opposition from public school administrators and teachers who are not anxious for competition among schools and who might face the loss of revenue-generating enrollments. School personnel may argue that parental choice of schools is not the answer to the social ills that impede learning.

---

[53]John E. Chubb and Terry M. Moe, *Politics, Markets, and America's Schools* (Washington, D.C.: The Brookings Institution, 1990).

[54]Cawelti, "Will Competition?" p. 2. See also Ann Bradley, "In Dade County, Company Gears up to Help District Run a Public School," *Education Week* 9, no. 37 (June 6, 1990): 1, 16–17.

Home Schools. A growing phenomenon that also discomforts public school personnel is the increasing popularity of home schooling as an alternative to public education. J. John Harris II and Richard E. Felds observed, "Alternative education of the 1960s and 1970s is still with us, but now its impact is being felt outside the public school classroom."[55] Whereas in earlier years public schools sought to provide alternative education under their supervision and control, home schools seek to provide alternative education outside of the control of public school administrators and faculty.

The education of children in the home dates back to the "dame" or "kitchen" schools of colonial days where parents or other educated adults would tutor individuals or instruct small groups in private homes. John Holt, one of the leading exponents of home schooling, has encouraged parents to take their children out of the public schools and provide for their education at home.[56] John Naisbitt perceived the rise in home schooling as part of a nationwide self-help movement in which community groups form to solve problems not only concerning education but also crime, distribution of food for the needy, and health. Naisbitt commented:

> Self-help is the blossoming of America's entrepreneurial movement, which rejects large corporations in favor of self-employment and small business. In the schools, it is increased parental activism along with questioning of the public school system—and in some cases the rejecting of it for private schools or (more radically) home education.[57]

Home schooling has threatened the time-honored tradition of compulsory education. In the early 1980s Mississippi was reportedly the only state in the nation that gave legal sanction to home schooling. Today, however, more than twenty states either explicitly permit home schooling or maintain compulsory attendance laws that implicitly permit parents to organize home schools.[58] One of the more serious blows against state compulsory attendance laws was the U.S. Supreme Court's decision in *Wisconsin* v. *Yoder,* the First Amendment religious liberty case in which the Supreme Court ruled that Amish parents could not be required to send their children to school beyond the eighth grade.[59]

---

[55]J. John Harris III and Richard E. Fields, "Outlaw Generation: A Legal Analysis of the Home-Instruction Movement," *Educational Horizons* 61, no. 1 (Fall 1982), p. 31.

[56]John Holt, *Teach Your Own: A Hopeful Path for Education* (New York: Delacorte Press/Seymour Lawrence, 1981).

[57]John Naisbitt, *Megatrends: Ten New Directions Transforming Our Lives* (New York: Warner Books, 1982), p. 133. Reprinted with permission.

[58]Naisbitt, p. 144. See also Gregory J. Cizek, "Applying Standardized Testing to Home-Based Education Programs: Reasonable or Customary?" *Educational Measurement Issues and Practice* 7, no. 5 (Fall 1988): 12–19 and Sally Banks Zakariya, "Home Schooling Litigation Tests State Compulsory Education Laws," *The American School Board Journal* 175, no. 5 (May 1988): 45–46.

[59]*Wisconsin* v. *Yoder,* 406 U.S. 205 (1972).

J. Gary Knowles observed that advocates of home school may be found among conservatives on the right and liberals on the left.[60] The same disillusionment with the public schools that led parents to established private and parochial schools has also led to the increase in home education. Parents may choose home schooling for their children because they are dissatisfied with, among other factors, the secular, non-Christian orientation of the public schools, poor academic achievement, lack of safety in the schools, drug use among students, lack of discipline, "assembly-line" teaching, and the forced socialization of their children with others whom they deem undesirable.

The statistics of home schooling are imprecise and difficult to obtain, in part because of the nebulous definition of home school. In some cases, a home school consists of parents instructing only their own children in their own home. In other cases groups of parents band together to form a school for their children in someone's home, in their church, or at another location. Estimates of the number of children in home schools range from 50,000 to 250,000 and from 750,000 to 1 million.[61] Out of some forty million public elementary and secondary school students, one million may not seem to be a significant figure. However, because most of the children schooled at home are under the age of 12, it would be more accurate to compare the figures for home schooling to the figure of 29 million elementary school children. The spread of these schools has been rapid; in the 1970s estimates ranged from 10,000 students to 10,000 families with children in home schooling.[62] In 1990 Campbell reported about 5,000 households registered as home schools in Florida and noted that some 1,000 families per year have taken the home-school option since 1985 when Florida legalized home schooling.[63]

Restrictions on home schools vary from state to state. Iowa, Michigan, and North Dakota require home-school instructors to be certified teachers.[64] Some states require home schools to obtain approval of their curricula and to accept varying degrees of monitoring by the boards of education of their local school districts. For example, home-school instructors may have to furnish to the local school board copies of their curriculum, lists of textbooks, information on number of days and hours of instruction, attendance data, and test results.

Advocates of home schools will most likely continue to challenge both the constitutionality of compulsory attendance laws per se and the state restrictions on home schooling. Although secular public schools can never satisfy those

---

[60]J. Gary Knowles, ed., "Understanding Home Schools: Emerging Research and Reactions, *Education and Urban Society* 21, no. 1 (November 1988): 3–113.

[61]Cizek, p. 13. See also Eugene S. Frost and Robert C. Morris, "Does Home-Schooling Work?: Some Insights for Academic Success," *Contemporary Education* 59, no. 4 (Summer 1988), p. 223; Naisbitt, p. 144; "More Dissatisfied Parents Choosing Home Schools," *The Orlando Sentinel,* March 11, 1990, p. G–4; and Ramsey Campbell, "Home Schooling: The Quiet Revolution in Education," *The Orlando Sentinel,* June 3, 1990, p. A–1f.

[62]Cizek, p. 13; Naisbitt, p. 144.

[63]Campbell, p. A–1.

[64]Zakariya, p. 45.

who prefer a sectarian education, renewed academic excellence in the public schools—a result of restructuring and reform—may make the public school more attractive to some of those now involved in home schooling.

Emphasis on the Basics and Academics

In the 1970s, critics of the schools vigorously maintained that the curriculum neglected the fundamentals. Observation of student performance and test data confirmed the fact that pupils were not demonstrating mastery of the basic skills, hence the clarion call "Back to the Basics."[65] Both elementary and secondary schools resumed stress, if ever they left it, on reading, writing, and arithmetic and have since maintained the emphasis.

For several decades a growing movement has criticized schools for failing to teach pupils to read. Books such as *Why Johnny Can't Read* [66] and publications of the Council on Basic Education have laid blame on the public schools for students' inadequacies in the basic skills.

Although the Commission on the Reorganization of Secondary Education and the Education Policies Commission long ago advocated the fundamental skills, critics observed that the pronouncements of these commissions placed basic skills second on the list of cardinal principles and last on the list of ten imperative needs of youth. Champions of the basics movement see the shift toward the basics—and, by extension, toward academic disciplines in general—as righting old excesses. This movement is part of the resurgence of essentialistic doctrines in education and conservative doctrines in politics. More frequently today, we find unabashed advocacy of limiting the mission of the school to cognitive learning.

Critics of the strong emphasis on basics decry the weakening of progressive doctrines that considered the whole child and made room for affective education. Advocates of the back-to-basics movement perceive the basic skills as necessary for survival; they believe that the failure of many young people to find and hold satisfying occupations stems from their deficiencies in these fundamental skills. Placing emphasis on the basics is also popular, especially in a day and age when economies are sought by the public. Limiting the role of the school can save taxpayers considerable sums of money, an appealing move at any time.

The challenge for curriculum planners today is to meet the public's desires for graduates who are literate, educated citizens and at the same time ensure that the curriculum is broad enough to permit personal growth and development, to appeal to the individual differences, and to expose young people to areas

---

[65]See Ben Brodinsky, "Back to the Basics: The Movement and Its Meaning," *Phi Delta Kappan* 58, no. 7 (March 1977), 521–533.

[66]Rudolf Flesch, *Why Johnny Can't Read* (New York: Harper & Row, 1955). See also Flesch, *Why Johnny Still Can't Read: A New Look at the Scandal of Our Schools* (New York: Harper & Row, 1981).

of study beyond the three R's. Sometimes it seems that the curriculum planner must be not only an educator but a magician. One positive sign arising from the emphasis on basics is the identification of critical thinking as a basic skill, along with increasing efforts by teachers to help learners develop thinking skills.

Minimal Competencies and Beyond.   In the 1970s and 1980s many states, subscribing to the back-to-basics philosophy, have specified the particular standards or competencies students are expected to achieve at various grade levels and for graduation from high school.[67] The initial thrust had been to specify minimal competencies in the basic skill areas, but the process now encompasses additional subject areas.

The movement to identify minimal competencies has its origins in two related movements and has led to yet another movement. The effort to specify minimal competencies is related to the *behavioral objectives movement* and is a response to the *accountability movement*.

Examples of minimal competencies in this text are shown as statements written in terms of performance expected of the learners.[68] The behavioral objectives movement provided a formula for drafting minimal competencies; competencies are simply behavioral objectives that have been determined by their authors as the sine qua non of education.

The minimal competencies movement is a natural outgrowth of the movement for accountability—that is, for holding teachers, administrators, and schools responsible for the education of the young. With the public clamoring for proof that its educational dollar is well spent, minimal competencies are seen as an efficient way to demonstrate accountability. The competencies are usually very specific items that can be measured. Thus, if we have minimal competencies, we must teach for their achievement and we must devise ways to assess their accomplishment by the learners. Hence, the *assessment movement* has arisen. Local, state, and national assessment of competencies, with criterion-referenced measures, has proceeded at a swift pace. In some cases, successful performance on the state assessment tests is required for receiving the standard high school diploma.

The task of specifying minimal objectives is initially rather difficult for curriculum planners. Once localities, states, and the nation have developed a sufficiently large bank of competencies, the task becomes (or should become) simpler. After all, there can only be so many competencies in the basic skills. The competencies in the three R's are, hopefully, the same in Alaska as in North Carolina.

Minimal competencies tend to standardize the curriculum. Since achievement of minimal competencies is tied to accountability, teachers are prone to structure their teaching toward the competencies and therefore to the assess-

---

[67] See articles in *Educational Leadership* 35, no. 2 (January 1977).
[68] See, for example, Table 7–1, pp. 242–243 and Table 7–2, pp. 244–245.

ment tests. On these exams learners will demonstrate how successful not only they but their teachers have been.

Once the minimal competencies are identified and put into print, the role of the curriculum developer can be greatly diminished or changed. What needs to be developed when the dimensions of the curriculum have already been outlined? Curriculum planners may turn their attention to designing better ways of organizing the curriculum, devising learning activities to teach the competencies, finding ways to remedy student deficiencies in particular competencies as revealed by the tests, and designing programs that go beyond the minimal competencies.

Classroom teachers often find their curricula determined for them by either the state or the school district. State-mandated or recommended programs are common today.[69] States have spelled out minimal requirements for graduation from high school in terms not only of units but, as noted before, of minimal competencies as well. States have outlined curricular content to be covered at each grade level and in the various disciplines. To ensure accomplishment of their plans, states have coupled mandated or recommended curricula with state assessment tests that students must pass at various checkpoints ("gates") of the educational ladder.

Local school districts have mandated curricula in areas where states have not acted or, sometimes, in addition to state efforts. They, too, have specified in detail the knowledge and skills to be mastered by the learners at each grade level. They have coded the knowledge and skills to state assessment tests; they have stipulated activities and resources to be used; they have devised their own tests both to determine students' mastery of the curricula and to prepare the students for the state tests. What has happened is that more and more of the curriculum has been set for the teacher, thereby limiting the professional teacher's power of discretion over both the curriculum and the instructional process.

The previous history of curriculum movements, however, reveals that those movements that proceed to extremes will normally right themselves and move back to center. Some evidence now indicates that, with the movements to empower teachers and to encourage school-based management, the onus of curriculum development in all its phases is shifting to the local level, where many educators feel it belongs.

That the American public wants its children to learn more than the three R's can be seen in the responses on the 22nd Annual Gallup Poll of the Public's Attitudes Toward the Public Schools to the question of what subject areas they would require every public high school student to study.[70] Among the areas were drug abuse education, alcohol abuse education,

---

[69] See "State-Sponsored School Improvement: A Special Section," *Phi Delta Kappan* 67, no. 8 (April 1986): 578–596.

[70] Stanley M. Elam, "The 22nd Annual Gallup Poll of the Public's Attitudes Toward the Public Schools," *Phi Delta Kappan* 72, no. 1 (September 1990): 49–50.

AIDS education, sex education and teen pregnancy, environmental issues and problems, driver education, and character education.

Although men and women cannot live well without the basic skills, they cannot live well with the basic skills alone. There must be room for the humanities and for developing a self-concept, social skills, and lifelong interests, all of which have been part of the school's curriculum for many decades.

Bilingual Education

As ethnic groups whose first language is other than English grow in size and power, more and more curriculum workers find themselves charged with the task of developing bilingual education programs. In 1967 Amendments to the Elementary and Secondary Education Act, the U.S. Congress provided support for bilingual education programs. Although bilingual education programs are offered in more than 70 languages and dialects, the largest number of students in bilingual programs are Hispanic.

The U.S. Supreme Court's decision in the *Lau* v. *Nichols* case in 1974, which required San Francisco to provide English language instruction for the Chinese-speaking students, advanced the cause of bilingual education. The efforts of Hispanic groups (Hispanics now number about 9 percent of the U.S. population) have largely brought about the current emphasis on bilingual (and, in addition, bicultural) education.

Bilingual education is an educational, linguistic, social, cultural, political, and economic issue. As such, it has become controversial.[71] Dade County (Florida) provides an example of public discord over this issue. In April 1973, after a large number of Spanish-speaking refugees had immigrated from Cuba, Dade County was declared a bilingual community. Many "Anglos" took issue with the designation of the county as bilingual. This sentiment came to a head when county voters approved by a three-to-two vote an ordinance that forbade the county from spending county funds for the use of any language other than English, or for the promotion of any culture other than that of the United States. Thirteen years later Californians passed a controversial proposition that made English the official language of the state.

In the spring of 1990, Alabama voters overwhelmingly adopted an amendment to their state constitution recognizing English as the official language of their state government. Seventeen states now have a law or constitutional amendment that designates English as the official language of their state governments. An eighteenth state, Hawaii, has designated both English and Hawaiian as official languages of the state. In the spring of 1991 Puerto Rico passed a law that designated Spanish as the only official language of the common-

---

[71]For pros and cons of bilingual education see Rudolph C. Troike, "Bilingual—Si!," *Principal* 62, no. 3 (January 1983): 46–50 and Muriel Paskin Carrison, "Bilingual—No!" *Principal* 62, no. 3 (January 1983): 41–44.

wealth, rescinding a 1902 law that had designated both Spanish and English as official languages. At the present time, the 1991 law is under challenge from pro-statehood advocates.

The debate over bilingual education brings into sharp focus the opposing philosophies of acculturation versus pluralism that were discussed in Chapter 6.[72] The resurgence of the melting-pot concept, with its emphasis on blending has challenged the salad-bowl concept of pluralism. Proposals from both Democrats and Republicans to establish English as the official language of the federal government have surfaced in both the Senate and the House of Representatives. In 1990 the House Judiciary Committee referred to a subcommittee a recurring proposal for an amendment to the U.S. Constitution that would make English the official language of the government.

Those who support making English the official language note that throughout our nation's history immigrants have learned English. Proponents of bilingual education, however, believe that curtailment of bilingual education and designation of English as the official language would be discriminatory. They maintain that an English-only instructional approach impedes the learning of children who are not native speakers of English.

Curriculum planners as well as the public are also divided as to the exact definitions of "bilingual" and "bicultural." To some, bilingual education may simply mean setting up English classes for students who are not native speakers of English. Others often extend bilingual education to include additional dimensions. In describing a proposal for bilingual education that was introduced in the U.S. Senate in 1967 by Ralph Yarborough from Texas (a bill that became law and that was funded in 1969), Francesco Cordasco made clear the multi-faceted scope of the Bilingual Education Act:

> At long last the Congress had before it legislation which would legitimize the cultivation of individual differences in our schools.
>
> The bill recognized that Mexican-American children had been neglected by American schools. It proposed 1) bilingual education programs; 2) the teaching of Spanish as the native language; 3) the teaching of English as the second language; 4) programs designed to impart to Spanish-speaking students a knowledge of and pride in their ancestral culture and language; 5) efforts to attract and retain as teachers promising individuals of Mexican or Puerto Rican descent; and 6) efforts to establish closer cooperation between the school and the home.[73]

Since 1969 bilingual education has been provided in the schools for native speakers of many languages.

---

[72]Promoting the cause of bilingual education is the National Association for Bilingual Education, Union Center Plaza, 810 First St., N.E., 3rd Floor, Washington, D.C. 20002; promoting the cause of English as the official language of the United States is U.S. English, 818 Connecticut Ave., N.W., Suite 200, Washington, D.C. 20006.

[73]Francesco Cordasco, "The Bilingual Education Act," *Phi Delta Kappan* 52, no. 2 (October 1969): 75. Reprinted with permission.

Educators are in disagreement as to whether programs designed to promote mastery of English should allow for instruction of students in their native language until they achieve English language skills or should immerse students in English from the start. The U.S. Department of Education has usually required schools that wished to receive bilingual education funds to provide instruction in the native language. When the U.S. Department of Education sought to force Fairfax County, Virginia, to offer instruction to all students in their native language, Fairfax County brought suit on the grounds that its program of intensive English for speakers of other languages was successful as shown by their test scores. In late 1980, the U.S. Department of Education, on the strength of the success of Fairfax County students decided not to force Fairfax County to provide instruction in the native language.

Bilingual education continues to be a sensitive issue. Related issues of racial/ethnic integration and cultural diversity are discussed later in this chapter.

Cultural Literacy

Ever since schools were first created, literacy—the ability to read and write—has been the primary goal of instruction, yet, even today our educational system fails to reach that goal. An estimated third of the American population is illiterate—completely lacking the skills of reading and writing—or functionally illiterate—demonstrating severe deficiency in those skills.

Derived from the Latin word *littera* ("letter"), literacy in its purest sense pertains merely to reading and writing. Today, both professional and popular literature address computer literacy, economic literacy, geographic literacy, historical literacy, scientific literacy, and other literacies: Unfortunately, American students as a whole excel in none of these. Results of tests administered by the National Assessment of Educational Progress and the International Association for the Evaluation of Educational Achievement repeatedly reveal that American students trail European and Japanese students in most grades or disciplines.

To that roster of deficiencies critics of the schools have recently added the concept of *cultural literacy*. American children and adults, they say, do not have a sufficiently broad background of general knowledge for communicating intelligently with each other. Diane Ravitch and Chester E. Finn, Jr. reported the results of a 1986 survey of approximately 8,000 high-school juniors concerning their knowledge of history and literature.[74] This assessment, funded by the National Endowment for the Humanities and conducted by the National Assessment of Educational Progress, disclosed that the students demonstrated a disheartening lack of knowledge in the two disciplines. It is ironic that, although the public school system is presently dominated by the essentialistic

---

[74]Diane Ravitch and Chester E. Finn, Jr., *What Do Our 17-Year-Olds Know? A Report on the First National Assessment of History and Literature* (New York: Harper & Row, 1987).

philosophy, achievement of the major goal of that philosophy—transmission of the cultural heritage—has eluded far too many of our public schools' students.

In the 1980s educators and laypeople entered into serious discussion of the sometimes controversial idea that cultural literacy should be a major goal of schooling. E. D. Hirsch, Jr., professor of English at the University of Virginia, popularized the term *cultural literacy,* first in an article for *The American Scholar* in 1983 and later in a book that was widely circulated and discussed.[75]

Cultural literacy, according to Hirsch, is a broad, general knowledge that ideally should be possessed by all members of our democratic society. Although elements of this knowledge may change from time to time, most items remain the same or change slowly. A culturally literate person is one who possesses this background of knowledge. The advocates of cultural literacy state that possession of this knowledge enables a person to read with understanding, to communicate thoughts to others within our society, to contribute to the development of our society, and to open doors that lead to success in American society.

A cultural literacy curriculum would start in the elementary schools and would impart that knowledge deemed by scholars, educators, and laypeople to be important information about American culture. Hirsch pointed out that writers assume their readers possess certain cultural information. Thus, to read with understanding and to write to be understood, citizens of our society must possess a store of knowledge about the culture—people, places, facts, vocabulary, and historic and current events from our own and world cultures.

Cultural literacy rejects the concept of pluralism, in which aspects of all subcultures in the nation are studied with equal concentration. Instead, it gives precedence to a national, overriding culture and to the English language. Supporters of cultural literacy posit an American culture. They view the fragmentation of the culture and the populace's lack of commonly shared information as serious problems that schools face in their attempts to develop literate citizens.

Advocates of cultural literacy oppose the teaching of reading and writing through a culture-free skills approach. In agreement with whole language theorists and practitioners, they would use authentic materials, perhaps with more emphasis on factual materials. Cultural literacy proponents do not subscribe to efforts at teaching critical thinking as though it were a cultural-neutral skill or set of skills.

---

[75]E.D. Hirsch, Jr., "Cultural Literacy," *The American Scholar* 52, no. 2 (Spring 1983): 159–169, and E.D. Hirsch, Jr., *Cultural Literacy: What Every American Needs To Know* (Boston: Houghton Mifflin, 1987).

For a critical view of Hirsch's ideas on cultural literacy, see Thomas H. Estes, Carol J. Gutman, and Elise K. Harrison, "Cultural Literacy: What Every Educator Needs to Know," *Educational Leadership* 46, no. 1 (September 1988): 14–17. See also Hirsch's response to Estes, Gutman, and Harrison, "Hirsch Responds: The Best Answer to a Caricature is a Practical Program," *Educational Leadership* 46, no. 1 (September 1988): 18–19.

Hirsch conceptualized a two-part curriculum: the "extensive curriculum" that "constitutes the part of the curriculum that has to be known by every child and must be common to all the schools of the nation"[76] and the "intensive curriculum" that permits students to gain an in-depth knowledge of content related to student and teacher needs. Hirsch would let local schools determine how and when students will become acquainted with the specifics of the extensive curriculum; neither the extensive nor the intensive curriculum are standardized programs and methods.

Hirsch called for knowledgeable persons to develop a list of cultural items sufficiently important for incorporating in the curriculum, especially at the elementary school level. Hirsch, Joseph Kett, and James Trefil began the task by compiling a preliminary list of *What Literate Americans Know*.[77] A suitable list, Hirsch maintained, would be finite and limited in scope and would not be as formidable to assemble as some might think. He further observed that, although some items would change over time, most of the items on the list were historic and therefore would remain the same. Cultural literacy would not require in-depth knowledge of all items; in some cases an imprecise, even superficial knowledge—enough for a reader or listener to understand what a writer or speaker means—would suffice. For example, one doesn't need detailed knowledge of genes to understand the concept of Mendel's laws.

Hirsch's ideas have met with criticism. Those who espouse the teaching of reading through decoding, phonics, and word recognition object to the culture-laden approach through the use of factual material. Hirsch's acceptance of memorization (he pointed out that various cultures depend on memorization for perpetuation of their traditions) caused critics to claim that the cultural literacy movement would reduce learning to rote memorization without true understanding.

Hirsch's position that students might need only vague understanding about some cultural items has led critics to decry the cultural literacy approach as superficial and a deterrent to teaching critical thinking. On the other hand, a proponent of cultural literacy would counter that a person does not need to know all the details about nuclear fission, for example, to understand a reference to that term in a book, magazine, or newspaper article written for the general reader.

Some critics of cultural literacy feel that it is presumptuous for any individual or group to deign to draw up a list of items that all pupils in America must know. However, Hirsch and his colleagues who proposed a tentative list, urged study and review of the list by others, and made clear that their list was *descriptive*—not *prescriptive*—of information possessed by culturally literate Americans.[78]

---

[76]From *Cultural Literacy: What Every American Needs to Know,* p. 128, by E. D. Hirsch. Copyright ©1987 by Houghton Mifflin Co. Reprinted by permission of Houghton Mifflin Co.
[77]Ibid., pp. 146–215.
[78]Ibid., p. xiv.

The pluralists who reject the melting-pot concept of American culture feel that this specification of cultural items is elitist and a barrier to minorities and the disadvantaged. Hirsch attributed lower scores reported for black children on certain standardized achievement tests not to an elitist curriculum but to the schools' failure to impart the informational background needed by their students.[79] Regarding the disadvantaged, Hirsch commented:

> To be culturally literate is to possess the basic information needed to thrive in the modern world. . . . Cultural literacy constitutes the only sure avenue of opportunity for disadvantaged children, the only reliable way of combating the social determinism that now condemns them to remain in the same social and educational condition as their parents. That children from poor and illiterate homes tend to remain poor and illiterate is an unacceptable failure of our schools, one which has occurred not because our teachers are inept but chiefly because they are compelled to teach a fragmented curriculum based on faulty educational theories.[80]

Hirsch noted the general decline in verbal abilities as evidenced by SAT scores and the National Assessment of Educational Progress,[81] and he proposed tests of general knowledge to assess cultural literacy. Some critics fear that, if these proposed tests are established, teachers will structure lessons around the tests, additional testing will cause further national standardization of the curriculum, and the tests would promote rote memorization and thereby perpetuate superficiality. Some would reject the intrusion of any more tests and would claim with some justification that there is already a surfeit of assessments. However, were cultural literacy to become a goal, there would have to be some type of assessment of students' accomplishment of that goal.

Some critics have perceived lists of cultural items as trivia that can be looked up rather than stored in the brain. They feel it is impossible to draw up a list of items that should be knowledge shared by all citizens of our society for the welfare of both the individual and the nation.

There have been objections to the preponderance of items derived from British traditions on the list of cultural items developed by Hirsch and his colleagues. Hirsch explained:

> By accident of history, American cultural literacy has a bias toward English literate traditions. Short of revolutionary political upheaval, there is absolutely nothing that can be done about this. It is not a weakness of our literate culture that it has its origins in English traditions, for, like all other literate traditions connected with great national languages, the English tradition is broad and heterogeneous and grows ever more so . . . .
>
> After more than two hundred years of national life, the main elements of our vocabulary have transcended the sphere of contention and dispute.

---

[79]Ibid., p. 111.
[80]Ibid., p. xiii.
[81]Ibid., p. 4.

. . . No matter how value-laden or partisan some of these common elements were in their origins long ago, they now exist as common materials of public discourse, the instruments through which we are able to communicate our views to one another and make decisions in a democratic way.[82]

Cultural literacy may well continue to be one of the curricular issues of the 1990s.

Provision for the Handicapped

What curriculum worker has not yet encountered Public Law 94–192? This enactment of the U.S. Congress, the Education for All Handicapped Children Act of 1975, was structured to eliminate discrimination against the handicapped.[83] Schools must make special provisions to ensure that all handicapped children receive a "free and appropriate" education. To accomplish this goal, schools must develop an individualized educational plan (IEP) for every handicapped child and must ensure that each handicapped child will be placed in the "least restrictive environment." IEP's, which contain annual performance objectives for each child and must be reviewed each year, require a considerable amount of the faculty's time. Determining the appropriate educational program and the best placement for each child requires difficult judgments by teachers and administrators.

The legislation specifies that handicapped students will be "mainstreamed"—that is, taught in regular classrooms with nonhandicapped children—unless their handicaps are so severe that they cannot be taught effectively in the regular classroom. Educators disagree as to whether handicapped youngsters are best taught by placement in regular or special classes, in regular or special schools.

Susan Ohanian effectively described the dilemma teachers face with mainstreaming.[84] She noted that students are mainstreamed primarily for purposes of socialization rather than of academic achievement. Said Ohanian:

> So-called liberal doctrine holds that "special classes"—a relic of education's dark ages—produce demoralization, low self-esteem, and inferior education. And I have seen plenty of evidence that they do. In the worst cases, the special education room is just a holding tank with a curriculum of movies and M & M's; even in the best cases, the curriculum has never taken a direction very different from mainstream academics.[85]

Mainstreaming, however, may not solve the problem of providing appropriate education for all handicapped students. Citing the case of a foster father

---

[82]Ibid., pp. 106–107.

[83]See Robert W. Cole and Rita Dunn, "A New Lease on Life for the Handicapped: Ohio Copes with 94–142," *Phi Delta Kappan* 59, no. 1 (September 1977): 3–6ff.

[84]Susan Ohanian, "P.L. 94–142: Mainstream or Quicksand?," *Phi Delta Kappan* 72, no. 3 (November 1990): 217–222.

[85]Ibid., p. 222. Reprinted with permission.

who wanted his child removed from Ohanian's seventh-grade class because the boy brought home first-grade work, Ohanian commented:

> It is not easy to tell a parent that mainstreamed students *don't* fail, that his child can't read that biology book although he is passing the biology class, or that a lot of teachers—not knowing how to handle the mainstreaming dilemma—give all mainstreamed students passing marks and give higher marks to the docile ones who cause no problems. How do you explain to a parent that this is called socialization?[86]

The problem as stated by Ohanian is that "We never offer true alternatives but are lured time and again by the people who claim that everybody should learn the classics. We are very reluctant to admit that some people should be allowed—even encouraged—to be different."[87] Ohanian concluded:

> We are good at accumulating labels: minimal brain dysfunction, perceptual-motor aberration, impaired learning efficiency, sensory deficit, delayed interpretation of input, and so on. Maybe we should spend less time on labels and more time providing meaningful alternatives to all students who do not flourish in the mainstream.[88]

Some educators are concerned that parents of nonhandicapped pupils might charge that their children are being discriminated against by not having individualized educational programs designed for them.

PL 94–142 furnishes an excellent illustration of the impact that sweeping federal legislation can have on the curriculum planner.

Health Education

No better example of the convergence of needs of students and needs of society can be found than the health-related problems experienced by today's young people. In addition to offering long-standing programs of physical fitness, hygiene, and nutrition education, the schools are confronted with a number of health problems—"crises" might be a better word—that demand the close and immediate attention of curriculum planners. Specifically, the schools are seeking ways to respond to the use and abuse of alcohol, drugs, and tobacco, to the high incidence of teen pregnancies, and to the prevalence of sexually transmitted diseases, including acquired immune deficiency syndrome (AIDS).

The statistics on these health problems in the United States are startling, as the following examples will demonstrate.

Since 1975 the Institute for Social Research at the University of Michigan, with funds from the National Institute on Drug Abuse, has conducted annual surveys on the use of drugs, alcohol, and tobacco by high school seniors,

---

[86]Ibid., p. 221.
[87]Ibid., p. 222.
[88]Ibid.

college students, and young adults. In 1989 the Institute for Social Research added questions about the use of steroids to its surveys. The National High School Senior Survey, also known as *Monitoring the Future: A Continuing Study of the Lifestyles and Values of Youth,* annually samples approximately 17,000 seniors in 135 public and private high schools in the continental United States. The Institute's sample of college students (high school graduates one to four years past high school and enrolled full time in a two-year or four-year college or university) numbers about 1,200. The Institute also surveys a sample of about 6,700 high school graduates who have been out of high school from one to ten years.

Based on their 1990 study, the Institute's investigators concluded that the "use of crack and other illicit drugs has declined significantly among young Americans, but cigarette smoking and alcohol use remain high."[89] Although the use of illicit drugs has taken a downturn, a significant number of high school seniors and college students admit some use. Data from the 1990 study show that

- 32.5 percent of the high school seniors reported using at least one illicit drug during the year prior to the survey.
- 5.3 percent of high school seniors reported using cocaine sometime during the previous year.
- Percentages were similar for college students: 33.3 percent for illicit drug use during the previous year and 5.6 percent for cocaine use during the same period.

Although the consumption of alcohol has registered a small decline, its use remains high:

- 32.2 percent of the high school seniors reported heavy drinking (five or more drinks in a row) during the two weeks prior to the survey.
- 41 percent of the college students reported heavy drinking for this same period.

The Michigan studies found smoking rates little changed over the past decade. For example:

- 19.1 percent of high school seniors reported smoking cigarettes daily.
- 12.1 percent of college students reported daily use of cigarettes.

Obviously, the struggle against use of illicit drugs, abuse of alcohol, and addiction to tobacco is far from over.

The public is obviously concerned about the drug problem, for the 23rd Annual Gallup poll of public attitudes toward the public schools revealed that the

---

[89]Data from press release from News and Information Services, University of Michigan, January 23, 1991, on the 1990 annual survey of drug, alcohol, and tobacco use among high school seniors, college students, and young adults by Lloyd D. Johnston, Jerald G. Bachman, and Patrick M. O'Malley.

public continues to perceive the use of drugs as the number one problem in the schools today. Lack of discipline, which headed the Gallup poll lists for many years, has held second place, behind the use of drugs, in the most recent polls.[90]

- In 1988 James Trussell reported that, during that year, more than 830,000 women between the ages of 15 and 19 as well as 23,000 girls age 14 and under would be pregnant. Trussell observed that the rate of pregnancies in this age group has remained constant (one out of ten) for 15 years.[91] David A. Bennett and Wanda Miller pointed out that "the increase in adolescent pregnancies stems largely from an increase in the number of teenagers who are sexually active . . . Eight in 10 males and seven in 10 females now report having had intercourse while in their teens."[92]

- The National Center for Health Statistics recorded 322,406 births to unmarried women age 19 and under during 1988.[93]

- Legal abortions in the United States for the year 1985 (the most recent statistic reported in 1990 *Statistical Abstract of the United States*) numbered 1,589,000. Of these, 399,000 were recorded for women between 15 and 19 years of age and 17,000 for women under 15.[94] The total number of induced abortions has remained at approximately 1.6 million per year since 1980.[95]

- Public health data for cases of notifiable diseases reported in the United States in 1989 showed high incidence of sexually transmitted diseases: 4,692 cases of chancroid (down from 5,001 in 1988), 733,151 cases of gonorrhea (up from 719,536 in 1988), and 44,540 cases of primary and secondary syphilis (up from 40,117 in 1988). The 1988 figures revealed that 195,312 of the gonorrhea cases were young people ages 15 to 19. During this same year 3,969 15- to 19-year-olds were reportedly inflicted with syphilis.[96] Robert T. Rolfs and Allyn K. Nakashima observed, "Between 1981 and 1989, the incidence of primary and secondary

---

[90]Stanley M. Elam, Lowell C. Rose, and Alec M. Gallup, "The 23rd Annual Gallup Poll of the Public's Attitudes Toward the Public Schools," *Phi Delta Kappan* 73, no. 1 (September 1991): 55.

[91]James Trussell, "Teenage Pregnancy in the United States," *Family Planning Perspectives* 20, no. 6 (December 1988): 262.

[92]David A. Bennett and Wanda Miller, "School Clinics Help Curb Teen Pregnancy and Dropout Rate," *The School Administrator* 43, no. 8 (September 1986): 12.

[93]National Center for Health Statistics: *Vital Statistics of the United States, 1988,* vol. 1, Natality, DHHS Pub. No. (PHS) 90–1100. Public Health Service, Washington. U.S. Government Printing Office, 1990, p. 62.

[94]U.S. Bureau of the Census, *Statistical Abstract of the United States, 1990,* 110th edition. (Washington, D.C.: U.S. Government Printing Office, 1990), p. 71.

[95]See studies of research on human reproduction, family planning, sex education, abortion, and teenage pregnancy conducted by the Alan Guttmacher Institute, 111 Fifth Avenue, New York, N.Y. 10003.

[96]Centers for Disease Control. Summary of Notifiable Diseases, United States, 1989. *Morbidity and Mortality Weekly Report* 1989; 38 (54), p. 53, and Centers for Disease Control. Summary of Notifiable Diseases, United States, 1988. *Morbidity and Mortality Weekly Report* 1988; 37 (54), p. 10.

syphilis in the United States increased 34%, from 13.7 to 18.4 cases per 100,000 persons, the highest since 1949."[97]

☐ Between 1981, when AIDS was first reported in the United States, and 1985, some 11,000 cases had been diagnosed. The number of cases had climbed to an estimated 40,000 by the end of 1986.[98] By December 31, 1988, the number of cases was more than 82,000 (over 74,000 males, more than 6,900 females, and some 1300 children under the age of 13).[99] Estimates of the number of AIDS cases at the end of 1991 ranged from 195,000 to 485,000.[100]

☐ The Centers for Disease Control recorded over 100,000 deaths among persons with AIDS in the United States between 1981 and 1990. In 1988 AIDS was the third leading cause of death of men age 25 to 44 and the eighth ranking cause of death of women in this same age group. The Centers estimated that a million people in the United States are infected with the human immunodeficiency virus (HIV) and that between 165,000 and 215,000 will die during the period 1991– 1993.[101]

These health-related problems pose the classic question to curriculum planners. To what extent must the schools respond to problems of society? What can the schools do about these overwhelming problems? If educators agree that the schools can make some response, how will that response be made?

The public appears to be in rather general agreement about the school's responses to the use of alcohol, drugs, (both prescription and nonprescription), and tobacco. State legislatures, reflecting public opinion, have in some cases, mandated instruction on the use and abuse of these substances. In spite of the school's concerted attack on the use and abuse of alcohol, drugs, and tobacco, usage among young people remains high. Nevertheless, the figures show that limited gains have been made in reducing the use of these substances. Furthermore, the public supports the school's efforts to educate young people about the hazards of these products.

In the area of sex education, however, parents and other citizens of the community are in sharp disagreement. Attitudes range from support for strong sex education programs in the schools to avoidance of the topic. Attitudes of the various religious and ethnic groups differ considerably on responses

---

[97]Robert T. Rolfs and Allyn K. Nakashima, "Epidemiology of Primary and Secondary Syphilis in the United States, 1981 Through 1989," *JAMA, The Journal of the American Medical Association* 264, no. 11 (September 19, 1990): 1432.

[98]James H. Price, "AIDS, the Schools, and Policy Issues," *Journal of School Health* 56, no. 4 (April 1986): 137.

[99]"Leads from the Morbidity and Mortality Weekly Report: Update: Acquired Immunodeficiency Syndrome—United States, 1981–1988," *JAMA, The Journal of the American Medical Association* 261, no. 18 (May 12, 1989): 2609ff.

[100]Carol Ezzell, "U.S. Forecast Too Low?" *Nature* 339, no. 6227 (June 29, 1989): 651.

[101]Centers for Disease Control, "Mortality Attributable to HIV Infection/AIDS—United States, 1981–1990." *Morbidity and Mortality Weekly Report* 40, no. 3 (January 25, 1989): 41, 44.

schools should take toward sexual problems. Since sex education is value-laden, some people believe the school's program should be confined to the academics, leaving moral education to the home and church.

A survey conducted by *Time* in 1986, however, found that 86 percent of Americans favor sex education in the public schools.[102] Of over 1500 adults interviewed for the 1990 Gallup Poll, 72 percent favored making sex education courses a requirement.[103] Apparently, state legislators have listened to the advocates of sex education; according to the Sex Information and Education Council of the United States, 23 states now mandate sex education in the schools and 23 more encourage sex education programs.[104] Approximately 80 percent of the young people in the public schools systems of major urban areas receive at least some sex education.[105] Responding in 1986 to the AIDS crisis, C. Everett Koop, former Surgeon General of the United States, strongly endorsed sex education, recommending that it begin in the third grade.[106] Koop has been severely criticized for his positions on sex education, AIDS education, use of condoms, and abortion.[107]

Critics of sex education believe that exposure of young people to sex education leads to promiscuity and threatens traditional family values.[108] They are concerned about the lack of well-trained instructors and are worried that the current curricula stress the physical aspects rather than the moral issues of sex education. They claim that sex education has not been able to reduce the number of teenage pregnancies and sexually transmitted diseases. They argue instead for a sex education curriculum that promotes abstinence. In July of 1991, bowing to conservative opinions, the U.S. Department of Health and Human Services suspended a proposed five-year study of the sexual behavior and knowledge of approximately 24,000 teenagers.

Although some critics argue that education about sex should be the parents' responsibility, *Time* reported that 60 percent of Americans do not believe that parents are adequately teaching their children about sex.[109] The results of the Gallup poll confirm that a sizable majority of the public look to the schools for imparting sex information, and perhaps, values to American children and young adults.

Curriculum planners are likely to encounter controversy whatever position they take with regard to sex education. If they put sex education in the schools,

---

[102]"Sex and Schools," *Time* 128, no. 21 (November 24, 1986): 54.

[103]Elam, "The 22nd Annual Gallup Poll," p. 50.

[104]Association for Supervision and Curriculum Development, "Sexuality Education," *Curriculum Update,* November 1990, p. 3.

[105]"Sex and Schools," p. 55.

[106]Ibid., p. 54.

[107]See, for example "Disowning the Surgeon General," *Harper's Magazine* 275, no. 1647 (August 1987): 16–17.

[108]See Bennett and Miller, "School Clinics," pp. 12–14; Dryfoos, "School Systems," p. 24; and "Sex and Schools," pp. 54–63.

[109]"Sex and Schools," p. 55.

some communities will object to its presence in the curriculum. If they ignore sex education, critics say the schools are neglecting their responsibilities and not meeting the needs of learners or society. If they establish a purely biological approach to sex education or try to teach sexual content in a value-free context, criticism arises because the school has omitted the moral aspects of the subject, and many people contend that the moral dimension is more important than the biological. If they introduce moral education—that is, values—which values will be taught? For example, shall the school condemn, condone, or ignore artificial birth control measures?

An excellent example of the potential controversy exists in the presence of school-based health clinics. *U.S. News & World Report* noted that in 1986, 72 clinics had already been established in 28 cities, including Baltimore, Chicago, Dallas, Phoenix, and St. Paul. One hundred more clinics were scheduled for other cities, including Los Angeles, Miami, and Pittsburgh.[110]

Part-time and full-time physicians and other health personnel provide physical examinations and much-needed information and counseling about health problems and family planning. Clinics have been established at elementary, middle, and secondary school levels. A particular point of conflict between the school and community is the dispensing of contraceptives or prescriptions for contraceptives to middle and high school students. Some religious, political, and ethnic groups have strongly protested contraceptive services. The National Conference of Catholic Bishops, for example, in 1987 strongly protested the distribution of contraceptives and the provision of counseling about abortion in the public school system.

School systems in the United States and Canada have provided both contraceptives and counseling through their school clinics. In the fall of 1990 Baltimore became one of the first cities in the United States to distribute both birth control pills and condoms in its middle and high schools. In the spring of 1991, the New York City Board of Education, in spite of objections from religious groups, approved a plan to distribute condoms in its high schools beginning in the fall of 1991. The Philadelphia school board took a similar action in the summer of 1991.

Educators and the public, by and large, agree that the school has some responsibility for helping young people develop the knowledge and attitudes necessary to preserve and improve their own and the nation's health. Thus, exemplifying the principle of adaptation of the curriculum to the needs of the learners, society, the times, and the subject matter, schools have modified their curricula of health education, science, and the social studies to incorporate study of critical health and social problems. Curriculum planners can make a convincing argument that the preservation of the health and well-being of the

---

[110]"More Sex Clinics in Schools," *U.S. News & World Report* 101, no. 21 (November 24, 1986):34.

American people (and therefore, the nation) is the most basic survival skill of all. In urgency, it surpasses thinking skills, reading, writing, and arithmetic.

Racial/Ethnic Integration and Cultural Diversity

Ever since the decision in the case of *Brown v. Board of Education of Topeka, Kansas*[111] in which the U.S. Supreme Court ruled segregation of the races unconstitutional, efforts have been under way to eliminate vestiges of racial discrimination in the schools. Problem areas have included curriculum materials that were slanted toward white, middle-class culture to teaching methods, testing, and administrative practices such as busing, desegregation of faculties, and methods of discipline.

James S. Coleman, sociologist, surveyed some 4,000 elementary and secondary schools, 60,000 teachers, and 600,000 students to determine the extent and sources of inequality of educational opportunity among ethnic groups.[112] Authorized by the 1964 Civil Rights Act, the Coleman Report, which was issued in 1966, supported the desegregation of schools. Coleman concluded that achievement of students is influenced first by their social environment (families and peers); second, by their teachers; and third, by nonpersonal resources such as per pupil expenditures on education. A dozen years later, after observing the operation of schools that had been integrated, Coleman concluded that integration per se does not necessarily increase the achievement of black students.[113] He remained committed to integration but maintained that parents should choose whether black students attend integrated schools.

One of the storm centers of the issue of discrimination revolves around assessment practices.[114] The state of Florida is a case in point. The state legislature in 1976 mandated administration of a functional literacy test to be taken by all eleventh graders. Receipt of the standard high school diploma was to be contingent upon passing the test. After the test was initially administered in 1977, suit was brought in the federal courts, charging that the test discriminated against black children who had attended segregated schools and had not had the same educational opportunities as children of the majority. Although it ruled that the test could be administered, the U.S. District Court in 1979 ordered the state department of education not to begin denying diplomas to students who failed the test until 1983. Other states with their own tests for the high school diploma, profiting from Florida's experience, have allowed time for the tests to be phased in.

---

[111]*Brown v. Board of Education of Topeka, Kansas* 347 U. S. 483, 74 Sup. Ct. 686 (1954).

[112]See James S. Coleman et al. *Equality of Educational Opportunity* (Washington, D.C.: U. S. Office of Education, 1966).

[113]See the *Miami Herald*, September 24, 1978, p. 19–A.

[114]See Merle Steven McClung, "Are Competency Testing Programs Fair? Legal?" *Phi Delta Kappan* 59, no. 6 (February 1978): 397–400.

That not all black parents are satisfied with progress made by their children in the public schools is evidenced by the suit brought in 1986 by eight families, including Linda Brown Smith (of the 1954 *Brown v. Board of Education* decision), once again against the board of education of Topeka, Kansas. At issue was the contention by the black families that Topeka had not done enough to desegregate its schools. U.S. District Court Judge Richard D. Rogers ruled in the spring of 1987 against the plaintiffs, a decision that was reversed by a three-judge panel of the Tenth U.S. Circuit Court of Appeals in December 1989.

Other school systems are still grappling with the problem of integrating the schools. The magnet school, which was discussed in Chapter 9, has provided a partial solution to the problem of multicultural student bodies in urban settings. Busing, primarily of black children to predominantly white schools, has been a frequent court-ordered remedy since the U.S. Supreme Court's decision in the case of *Swann v. Charlotte-Mecklenburg Board of Education,* which required desegregation "with all deliberate speed."[115]

Oklahoma City may well have become a pivotal case in deciding the length of time that school systems must continue busing for the purpose of integration. Like many other school systems prior to *Brown,* Oklahoma City had maintained a de jure segregated system. Under court order Oklahoma City instituted in 1972 a busing plan designed to correct racial imbalances in the public schools. In 1984 the U.S. District Court ruled that Oklahoma City's schools were now integrated and court supervision could terminate. In 1985 Oklahoma City ceased busing of pupils in kindergarten and the first three grades and permitted parents to send their children to neighborhood elementary schools.

Because many neighborhoods in Oklahoma City were segregated de facto, the schools in those neighborhoods again became racially imbalanced once busing ceased. Black parents argued that the school system must continue busing as long as it is necessary in order to maintain racial balance. In 1989 the Tenth U.S. Circuit Court of Appeals agreed with their position and reversed the district court's decision. The case then proceeded to the U.S. Supreme Court. In January 1991 the Supreme Court took issue with the ruling of the appeals court and directed federal judges to discontinue their supervision once the court-ordered plans had successfully desegregated the schools.

Another important and closely watched case began in Kansas City, Missouri, in 1978. In this legal action, black parents in urban Kansas City sought admission of their children to suburban school districts, a desegregation measure that was permitted by the U.S. Supreme Court in an October 1990 decision. In various parts of the country members of all racial and ethnic groups are raising the question of whether allowing parents to send their children to the school of

---

[115] *Swann v. Charlotte-Mecklenburg Board of Education,* 402 U.S. 1 (1971).

their choice might not be a better solution to racial discrepancies in education than busing.

Almost 40 years after the original *Brown* v. *Board of Education* ruling, problems related to racial integration of the schools have not been completely resolved. In fact, the need to eliminate racial tensions and to design curricula that meet the needs of children and youth of all ethnic groups in America's multicultural population is a continuing problem for curriculum planners.

To reduce racial conflict and prevent racial problems from arising, many school systems have established multiracial committees whose task it is to recommend solutions to tensions and incidents of conflict among racial groups. Multiracial committees and entire faculties find that, in order to eliminate negative attitudes and conflicts, they must analyze all aspects of the school, including the "hidden curriculum"—the school climate, social relationships among individuals and groups, values and attitudes held by both student and faculty, presses on student conduct, unspoken expectations, and unwritten codes of conduct.

New Curriculum Responses.   Two recent responses to the issue of providing a suitable education for minorities are already evoking considerable controversy. The first of these developments is a proposal to desegregate the curriculum; the second is the creation of all-male, predominantly black schools.

Curriculum Desegregation. The thrust of desegregation efforts is shifting from the physical movement of pupils to secure racial balance in the schools to the reconstruction of the curriculum. Demands are increasing for the institution of "Afrocentric" curricula that would feature contributions made by early African civilizations before colonial powers expanded into the continent. Proponents of Afrocentric programs feel that the schools have placed too much emphasis on European achievements and culture. They point to Africa as the birthplace of humankind, cite African achievements in the fine arts, mathematics, and science, and take the position that the school curriculum ignores or minimizes the contributions of African civilizations.

Like bilingual education, other-centric curricula—which some people call a "curriculum of inclusion"—is an issue that goes to the heart of the debate over cultural pluralism and the melting pot of acculturation. Should the curriculum reflect and equate all cultures, maintaining their separate identities, or should schools seek to develop citizens who manifest values of a common, national American culture. For example, the Portland, Oregon, school system promotes multiculturalism through its *African-American Baseline Essays,* which present contributions attributed to African civilizations.[116] Black and white educators are found on both the supporting and the

---

[116]Portland Public Schools, *African-American Baseline Essays* (Portland, Ore.: Portland Public Schools, 1989). See also Portland Public Schools, *Multicultural/Multiethnic Education in Portland Public Schools* (Portland, Ore.: Portland Public Schools, 1988).

opposing sides of the debate over ethnocentric curricula. An ostensible purpose of Afrocentric curricula is to enhance black students' pride in their ethnic origins. Questions have been raised, however, about the historical interpretation of some of the content presented in some of the Afrocentric curricula. In addition, some educators are concerned about the extent to which ethnocentric curricula will further fragment the curriculum. Will there need to be Latino-centric, Asian-centric, Islamic-centric, and many additional other-centric curricula to reflect every culture represented in the public schools?

Most educators concede that the public schools have done a poor job of teaching about the contributions of ethnic groups. Educators generally endorse and promote inclusion of information about the contributions of males and females of all races, creeds, ethnic groups, and national origins. However, some educators state that just adding ethnocentric and multicultural content to achieve this purpose is not sufficient because it simply superimposes this content on a traditional, white, male, Anglo, middle-class curriculum structure.

Geneva Gay advocated curriculum desegregation as a means of achieving educational equality.[117] Gay classified efforts to construct curricula for culturally diverse populations as first-, second-, and third-generation curriculum desegregation. According to Gay's classification, the first generation introduced the study of the contributions of ethnic personalities, revision of textbooks to eliminate bias against and stereotypes of minorities and women, and programs such as compensatory education, Head Start, Upward Bound, and cultural enrichment. The second generation incorporated bilingual education, multicultural education, provisions for the handicapped, and efforts to eliminate sex discrimination. Gay noted that neither the first- nor the second-generation curriculum desegregation efforts changed the basic structure of the curriculum. The third and current generation of curriculum desegregation must, according to Gay, subscribe to the principle that "a pluralistic ideology must replace an assimilationist orientation" and work toward the goal of "ultimately making American society more genuinely egalitarian."[118] Gay set forth a difficult task for the schools:

> anything short of total instructional reform is likely to be ineffective . . . educational equality for diverse learners cannot be achieved within the existing curriculum structures and with present assumptions about what are valuable educational outcomes. At their very core these structures and assumptions are ethnocentric and discriminatory. . . . the foundations of curriculum . . . must become culturally pluralistic. . . . information taught about various cultures

---

[117]Geneva Gay, "Achieving Educational Equality Through Curriculum Desegregation," *Phi Delta Kappan* 72, no. 1 (September 1990): 56–62.

[118]Ibid., p. 60. Reprinted with permission.

and groups must be presented as having equal value and . . . expected outcomes must be deliberately taught. Knowledge of facts about cultural pluralism, values that promote human diversity, and skills in social activism to combat oppression and create a more egalitarian society and world should all be included in efforts to achieve curriculum desegregation.

Multiculturalism should be the driving force of subsequent efforts to desegregate school curricula. It is a reconstructive and transformative principle. Its application necessitates changing the fundamental value assumptions, substantive content, operational strategies, and evaluation procedures of all instructional programs that are planned and implemented for all students.[119]

All-male, primarily black schools. Alternative education took on a new aspect in 1990 with Milwaukee's plans to create within the public school system two African-American Immersion Schools (one elementary and one middle school). New York City drew up plans for the Ujamaa Institute, which would also focus on programs for black male students. To counter objections to the planned schools, proponents argue that the schools, located in the inner city, already have an entirely African-American student body. Opponents point out that the schools may still violate Title IX of the Educational Amendments of 1972, which outlawed discrimination based on sex. In fact, Detroit had planned to open in the fall of 1991 three schools, open to males of all races, with an African-American curricular emphasis. The American Civil Liberties Union (ACLU) and the National Organization for Women (NOW) brought suit, objecting to the exclusion of girls. In August 1991 U.S. District Court Judge George Woods ruled that the schools could not open unless females were also admitted. So that the schools might open, the Detroit school board agreed to admit girls; however, the board is expected to contest the ruling.

Dealing with Cultural Diversity. Determining what responses the schools should make to the cultural diversity of our population is one of the greatest challenges for curriculum workers. The issue of multiculturalism and plural values versus cultural mainstreaming and common values has grown in intensity on both public school and college campuses.[120] The issue is entangled in a myriad of social, political, economic, educational, philosophical, secular, and religious values.

On the positive side, all the recent efforts to empower ethnic minorities and women prove that educators are searching for ways to educate all children and raise the achievement level of those individuals and groups who are not now succeeding in the schools.

---

[119]Ibid., p. 62.

[120]See William A. Henry, III, "Upside Down in the Groves of Academe," *Time* 137, no. 13 (April 1, 1991): 66–68. See also Paul Gray, "Whose America?" *Time* 138, no. 1 (July 8, 1991): 12–17. See also Arthur Schlesinger, Jr., "The Cult of Ethnicity, Good and Bad," *Time* 138, no. 1 (July 8, 1991): 21 and Schlesinger, *The Disuniting of America* (Knoxville, Tenn.: Whittle Direct Books, 1991). See also articles on Afrocentrism in *Newsweek* 118, no. 13 (September 23, 1991): 42–50.

Religion in the Schools

In colonial America religion and education were symbiotic. The Latin grammar school prepared young men to teach and to preach. Protestants of various creeds settled in most of the colonies, and Roman Catholics settled in Maryland; clashes over Christian religious beliefs among the early colonists were inevitable. Conflicts were exacerbated over the years as immigrants of all faiths came to the New World, adding beliefs such as Judaism, Islam, Confucianism, Buddhism, Bahaism, and Shinto to those of the Native Americans and the early-arriving Christians.

There are so many varieties of Christians in the United States that it is difficult to count them. They include Baptists, Catholics, Christian Scientists, Episcopalians, Greek Orthodox, Lutherans, Methodists, Mormons, Presbyterians, and Seventh-Day Adventists. Other religions also contain divisions: Judaism has Orthodox, Reform, Hasidic, and Sephardic groups. Sunni Moslem doctrine conflicts with Shiite doctrine. The Christian denominations have divided even further. For example, Lutherans of the Missouri Synod hold differing beliefs from the Evangelical Lutherans. The Free Will, Missionary, and Southern Baptists are but three segments of that large denomination. America also is home to agnostics, deists, humanists, Unitarians, and atheists.

Forty-five simple words, written in 1791, have generated hundreds of disputes over their meaning. Disagreements over these words continue to this day and may very well continue as long as the republic of the United States lasts. The words I refer to are as follows:

> Congress shall make no law respecting an establishment of religion, or prohibiting the free exercise thereof, or abridging the freedom of speech, or of the press, or the right of the people peaceably to assemble, and to petition the Government for a redress of grievances.

These powerful words, known as the First Amendment to the U.S. Constitution, are the center of conflicts over freedom of religion, speech, press, and assembly. Almost daily there is news of a lawsuit that contends infringement of one or more of these freedoms. The question of whether religion should be included in the public schools has evoked fiery debates over the years. Time and again the U.S. Supreme Court has reaffirmed the doctrine of separation of church and state. This doctrine has been attributed to Thomas Jefferson and James Madison in particular; it was Thomas Jefferson who wrote of the "wall of separation between church and state."

The question of how high and how impregnable that wall should be has yet to be completely resolved. Decisions of the U.S. Supreme Court, the ultimate arbiter of constitutional issues, have kept that wall relatively high—much to the chagrin of those Americans who would like to see it fall and those who would fortify it even more.

Those practices with religious connotations in the school that have most often necessitated court adjudication are prayer in the classroom and at school-sponsored events, released time for religious instruction off school grounds, celebration of religious holidays, teaching of evolution, saluting the American flag, permitting religious groups to meet in the school, and extracurricular activities that require a religious test for participation.

Decisions on the constitutionality of religious practices in the schools have frequently invoked the Fourteenth Amendment (due process), which has made the First Amendment binding on the states and had figured so prominently in early racial discrimination cases. From the wealth of U.S. Supreme Court decisions, I would specify eight that have special relevance for the public school curriculum. (I have indicated the state of origin of each case in parentheses.)

- □ *West Virginia Board of Education* v. *Barnette,* 319 U.S. 624 (1943) (West Virginia). Ruled that Jehovah's Witnesses would not be required to salute the American flag.
- □ *People of the State of Illinois ex rel. McCollum* v. *Board of Education of School District No. 71, Champaign, Ill.,* 333 U.S. 203 (1948) (Illinois). Ruled that released time for religious instruction in the school was unconstitutional.
- □ *Zorach* v. *Clauson,* 343 U.S. 306 (1952) (New York). Ruled that released time for religious instruction off school grounds was permissible.
- □ *Engle* v. *Vitale,* 370 U.S. 421 (1962) (New York). Ruled that the prayer that originated with the New York State Board of Regents for use in the schools violated the principle of separation of church and state.
- □ *School District of Abington Township* v. *Schempp,* (Pennsylvania) and *Murray* v. *Curlett* (Maryland), 374 U.S. 203 (1963). Ruled that readings from the Bible and recitation of the Lord's Prayer in the school were unconstitutional.
- □ *Wallace* v. *Jaffree,* 105 S. Ct. 2479 (1985) (Alabama). The U.S. Supreme Court affirmed the decision of the U.S. Court of Appeals, which had reversed an earlier ruling by the U.S. District Court that had allowed Alabama schools to hold a period of silence for meditation or voluntary prayer.
- □ *Bender* v. *Williamsport Area School District,* 475 U.S. 534 (1986) (Pennsylvania). The U.S. Supreme Court let stand the federal district court's decision that under PL 98–377, the Equal Access Act of 1984, religious groups made up of students in the high school could meet at that school if other student groups also had access to the school's facilities.

Proponents of prayer and Bible reading in the public schools find it difficult to understand why a government founded on religious principles would declare religious practices in the schools unconstitutional. They maintain that the founding fathers had no antagonism toward religion, but rather sought to prevent the federal government from establishing a national religion.

Those who argue for religious practices in the schools, however, often assume a largely Protestant ethic. They downplay the pluralistic nature of our society and the fact that many beliefs—including non-Christian religions—are now represented in the public schools. Jewish parents and children find the New Testament unacceptable. Catholics read from Catholic versions of the Bible, such as the Douay-Rheims, rather than the Protestant King James Version. Furthermore, the wall of separation between church and state protects not only the freedom of religion but also the right of freedom *from* religion. Advocates of the separation of church and state note that *Pierce* v. *Society of Sisters* gave believers the right to send their children to private parochial schools where a religiously homogeneous student population can be instructed in the beliefs of that particular sect.

Decisions of the Supreme Court notwithstanding, supporters of the inclusion of religion in the public schools continue to press their case. Former President Ronald Reagan and President George Bush are both advocates of conducting prayer in the public schools. In 1991 George Bush's Justice Department urged the Supreme Court to permit prayers at public school graduation ceremonies. Organizations are lined up on both sides of the issue of the separation of church and state.

Numerous conflicts over the separation of church and state can be found in the annual listing of such incidents published by Americans United for Separation of Church and State. This organization recorded 192 conflicts in 46 states between September 1989 and August 1990—an increase from the 118 incidents in 38 states that were reported the previous year.[121]

Increasingly, educators and others are expressing concern over the schools' failure to include instruction about the contributions and effects of religion throughout the history of the United States and the world. Some teachers and authors of textbooks fearful that they may offend people's sensitivities, veer away from religion entirely. Many students, therefore, are to a large extent ignorant of the importance of religion in the development of this country.

A relevant curriculum would incorporate the study of comparative religions as a part of the general education of every student. Such a curriculum would focus on teaching *about* religion, not the teaching *of* religion. A person cannot fully appreciate the arts, literature, history, psychology, philosophy, or sociology—or even science, with which religion is often at odds—without studying the influence of religion on these areas of human endeavor. Certainly, students should gain familiarity with the world's great masterpieces of religious literature, such as the Bible, the Talmud, the Koran, and the Bhagavad-Gita. A knowledge about religion is one attribute of the culturally literate person.

Curriculum planners must be mindful, however, that many of those who claim the schools advocate "secular humanism" would not be satisfied with teaching *about* religion. Secular humanism implies faith in humankind and subscription to social and moral values that are not necessarily derived from

---

[121] Americans United for Separation of Church and State, *Separation of Church and State: The Ongoing Crisis: Americans United Second Annual Report on Church-State Conflict in the United States,* September 24, 1990.

belief in a divine being. Though the public schools do not, in reality, promote a doctrine of secular humanism, the absence of sectarian practices in itself provokes some people to accuse the schools of promoting secular humanism.

The debate over secular versus sectarian curricula for the public schools will be difficult to resolve because strong emotions, values, and fundamental beliefs about life and death underscore the controversy. In the following section on parental protests over schoolbooks, you will again find religion as a major source of conflict.

Protests Over Schoolbooks

Schools in many communities throughout the United States have become enmeshed in a struggle with individuals and groups in the community who seek to censor textbooks and library books and to prohibit certain types of instruction or, conversely, to promote certain types of instruction. Attempts to remove library books, textbooks, and other teaching materials from the schools have been on the rise in recent years.[122] Judith F. Krug, director of the Office of Intellectual Freedom of the American Library Association, has put the number of reported incidents at approximately 900 per year.[123] Edward B. Jenkinson observed that estimates of unreported incidents range from 25 to 50 per reported incident.[124]

Protest over schoolbooks has been a big problem in some communities. One of the more publicized and heated controversies over textbooks took place in 1974 in Kanawha County, West Virginia.[125] The conflict over a list of 325 English/language arts textbooks recommended by a committee of teachers resulted in violence, closing of schools, workers staying away from their jobs in the mines in support of the protesters, attacks on the books by ministers of some of the churches, and the resignation of the superintendent of schools. Though the books were ultimately permitted in the classroom, a set of guidelines was drawn up that required the establishment of teacher-parent committees to screen books to be adopted and retained by the school system.

Schoolbook protestors have made their appearance in communities from one end of the United States to the other.[126] Jenkinson made a conservative estimate of 200 as the number of local, state, and national organizations that

---

[122]Edward B. Jenkinson, *The Schoolbook Protest Movement: 40 Questions and Answers* (Bloomington, Ind.: Phi Delta Kappa Educational Foundation, 1986), pp.14–16.

[123]Ibid., p. 14.

[124]Ibid., p. 16.

[125]Franklin Parker, *The Battle of the Books: Kanawha County* (Bloomington, Ind.: Phi Delta Kappa Educational Foundation, 1975). See also James C. Hefley, *Textbooks on Trial* (Wheaton, Ill.: Victor Books, 1976); Edward B. Jenkinson, *Censors in the Classroom: The Mind Benders* (Carbondale, Ill.: Southern Illinois University Press, 1979), Chapter 2; and articles in *Principal* 61, no. 3 (January 1982): 4–36.

[126]Jenkinson, *Schoolbook Protest,* pp. 43–46.

protest schoolbooks.[127] People for the American Way reported 229 cases of attempted censorship of books during the school year of 1990–91.[128]

Protests against certain schoolbooks include charges that they

- ☐ portray too much sex or violence
- ☐ use profanity
- ☐ use poor English
- ☐ promote "secular humanism," are irreligious, anti-Christian
- ☐ are un-American, lacking in patriotism
- ☐ promote one-worldism
- ☐ are racist
- ☐ depict the "wrong" values
- ☐ teach the theory of evolution instead of scientific creationism

Efforts to censor topics of public discussion, reading matter, films, drama, television, and art works recur in the schools—and in society at large—with great frequency, testing First Amendment rights to free speech and press. In recent years, charges of obscenity, for example, have produced vigorous challenges to art exhibitions, novels, and films, and lyrics to musical compositions. The definition of obscenity has proved to be elusive. The U.S. Supreme Court has let local communities determine what printed and visual matter violates their community standards and possesses "no redeeming value." Many people consider the sufficient standard to be U.S. Supreme Court Justice Potter Stewart's famous statement about obscenity, "I know it when I see it."

Schools have both engaged in self-censorship and responded to pressures for censorship from outside forces. In the 1990–91 school year *Little Red Riding Hood* was under criticism, ostensibly because the main character was carrying wine to her grandmother. In various parts of the country other fairy tales and movie cartoons have been criticized for being excessively violent. This same year saw Mary O'Hara's children's classic *My Friend Flicka,* taken off the list of approved reading for some elementary school pupils apparently because some people objected to certain words that they considered unsuitable. Cases like these affirm that school administrators and boards are extremely sensitive to criticism about books and other teaching materials.

The teaching of values has come under attack by protesters who hold that some of the schoolbooks undermine traditional American values. Protesters have taken special exception to the book *Values Clarification,* ostensibly because the program that it proposes allows students to express their own views on personal problems.[129]

---

[127]Ibid., p. 70.

[128]People for the American Way, *Attacks on the Freedom to Learn* (Washington, D.C.: People for the American Way, 1991), p. 1.

[129]Sidney B. Simon, Leland W. Howe, and Howard Kirschenbaum, *Values Clarification* (New York: Hart, 1972). For a grammarian's criticism of values clarification, see Richard Mitchell, *Less than Words Can Say* (Boston: Little/Brown, 1979), pp. 79–95.

The teaching of the Darwinian theory of the evolution of humankind has long been a cause of concern to the scientific creationists, who champion the biblical account of creation in Genesis. The Scopes trial in Tennessee in the 1920s reflected the sentiments of the creationists.[130] In 1968 in the case of *Epperson* v. *Arkansas* the U.S. Supreme Court ruled that the theory of evolution may be taught;[131] however, challenges have continued up to the present and may be anticipated in the future.

Examples of the evolution versus creationism dispute are not difficult to find. In 1982 the federal district court holding that scientific creationism was a religious doctrine, struck down an Alabama statute that would have required instruction in scientific creationism in addition to the theory of evolution. In June 1987 the U.S. Supreme Court ruled unconstitutional Louisiana's Balanced Treatment for Creation Science and Evolution Science Act of 1981, which would have required that scientific creationism be given equal instructional time with the theory of evolution. In October 1990, more than 20 years after *Epperson,* the Texas Education Agency's approval of state-adopted textbooks that taught the theory of evolution made national news. Sentiment for teaching scientific creationism either in place of or in addition to evolution theory remains strong.

Often, protests over schoolbooks are not intended to force the schools to eliminate certain material but to adopt textbooks that incorporate particular topics, such as scientific creationism. Although the Supreme Court has ruled that reading the Bible and prayers for devotional purposes in the school is unconstitutional, many groups are still attempting to reintroduce or introduce these sectarian practices into the public schools' curriculum.

Of concern to teachers, administrators, and curriculum workers is the judicial decision rendered in Tennessee in the fall of 1986. In 1983 the Hawkins County schools adopted the widely used Holt, Rinehart and Winston Basic Reader Series for kindergarten through eighth grade. Christian fundamentalist families objected to the readers on the grounds that the books violated their religious beliefs and that, by requiring their children to read these books, the schools deprived them of their First Amendment rights. They demanded that their children be allowed to use alternative textbooks, which the school board permitted for a brief period of time. However, the board soon disallowed this practice and resumed requiring the adopted textbooks.

When parents forbade their children to attend classes that used the controversial textbooks, school officials suspended the children. Seven families of Church Hill, Tennessee, though they did not seek complete removal of the readers from the schools, did file suit demanding the right for their own children to use alternative textbooks. Tried in July 1986, the case attracted as much or more attention than the famous Scopes trial.

---

[130] See p. 88 of this text.
[131] *Epperson* v. *Arkansas,* 393 U.S. 97 (1968).

On October 24, 1986, U.S. District Judge Thomas G. Hull found for the plaintiffs, ruling that the school board could not force children to use textbooks that went against their religious beliefs and that the school board had violated the parents' rights to freedom of religion. By the same token the judge declared that the children had a right to a public education and that the school district must permit them to use alternative textbooks. He placed responsibility for finding the alternative texts on the parents. In addition, the judge ruled that the families could seek monetary damages from the school board for the violation of their rights. In December 1986 the judge awarded the parents more than $50,000, which included the cost of tuition for their children at private school.

Some saw in the Tennessee decision potential disaster for the public schools if other sects demanded textbooks of their own choosing and insisted that their children be permitted to opt out of instruction when textbooks that they found objectionable were used. Others felt that, in actuality, few parents would object to the use of local- and state-adopted textbooks. However, the Hawkins County school board appealed the decision to the 6th U.S. Circuit Court of Appeals. In August 1987 the Circuit Court of Appeals ruled that the First Amendment rights of the family had not been violated by the school system. In February 1988 the U.S. Supreme Court refused to hear the case, letting the appellate court's decision stand.

The Tennessee case is not an isolated episode; while the district judge was making his ruling in Tennessee, parents in Alabama were suing the Alabama board of education for the removal of state-adopted textbooks in social studies, history, and home economics because of the books' purported liberal bias toward "secular humanism." On March 4, 1987, U.S. District Court Judge W. Brevard Hand (the same judge who in *Wallace* v. *Jaffree* upheld the Alabama statute providing for silent meditation or prayer) banned more than forty textbooks from use as primary textbooks or primary sources in elementary and secondary schools of Alabama. Thirteen days later Judge Hand modified his order and allowed use of portions of the home economics books and use of the history and social studies books if they were appropriately supplemented. In August 1987 the 11th U.S. Circuit Court of Appeals reversed Judge Hands' ruling.

Underlying the protests over textbooks is the perennial conflict of differing secular and religious values in a pluralistic society. Controversy continues over interpretation of the Jeffersonian doctrine of separation of church and state and over the protections accorded by the First Amendment. Just as schoolbook protesters point to the First Amendment as the source of their rights, efforts to combat censorship have revolved around the First Amendment with its guarantees of freedom of the press, and, by extension, freedom to read.

To respond to various social and political pressures, curriculum planners need not only professional knowledge and skills but also skills in public relations and working with community groups. When dealing with controversial issues in the curriculum, they should have channels through which they may determine the seriousness of problems, the strength of community feelings, and the ways in which issues might be resolved before they become magnified and disproportionate.

Sexism

Title IX of the Educational Amendments of 1972 passed by the U.S. Congress caused school personnel to examine programs and to remove practices that discriminate between the sexes. Restricting home economics to girls and industrial arts to boys, for example, is a sexist practice. Funding of interscholastic athletics, with the lion's share traditionally going to boy's athletics, has been challenged as sexist. The integration of females into male athletic teams and males into female teams has stirred controversy within the profession and outside.

That sex stereotypes and unequal treatment of boys and girls by teachers in the classrooms still exist can be seen from recent research reported by Myra and David Sadker.[132] They studied over 100 fourth-, sixth-, and eighth-graders in four states and the District of Columbia observing language arts, English, mathematics, and science classes. The Sadkers concluded that, regardless of the subject or grade level, boys dominated classroom interaction and received more attention from the teacher than did girls.[133]

Children's attitudes about gender roles are shaped early and, like many attitudes and values, are strongly influenced by the children's significant others—parents, relatives, close friends, teachers, coaches, role models, and other persons whom they respect. A recent study by Jacquelynne S. Eccles and Rena D. Harold at the University of Michigan found that "already by the first grade, girls have a more negative assessment of their general athletic ability than do boys."[134] Athletic skills at early ages are virtually comparable regardless of gender. Not until puberty can physiological differences between boys and girls account for differences in athletic abilities. Sex roles are to a large extent culturally determined; the school often perpetuates those social determiners, either through the intentional or the hidden curriculum.

As mentioned earlier, as recently as 1972 Robert J. Havighurst perceived the achievement of a masculine or feminine social role as one of the developmental tasks of adolescence.[135] The accomplishment of these roles is no longer simple, if it ever was. Though traditional attitudes toward the roles of men and women are still held by sizable segments of the public—especially in groups of certain nationalities, certain areas of the country, and certain religious groups—the distinctions in roles have been changing rapidly. What once appeared to be

---

[132]Myra and David Sadker, "Sexism in the Schoolroom of the '80s," *Psychology Today* 19, no. 3 (March 1985): 54–57.

[133]Ibid., pp. 54, 56.

[134]Jacquelynne S. Eccles and Rena D. Harold, *Gender Differences in Sport Involvement: Applying the Eccles' Expectancy–Value Model* (Ann Arbor, Mich.: University Press, n.d.) pp. 28–29.

[135]See Havighurst, fn, p. 227 of this text.

male occupations, like truck driving, construction work, and police work, are no longer the exclusive province of the male.

Conversely, a "house-husband" is no longer unheard of, and the female can be the family "breadwinner." Men can pursue careers and avocations that were formerly considered only for women, such as nursing, elementary school teaching, and secretarial work. Schools today are counseling girls to take science, mathematics, and industrial arts, courses formerly viewed as more appropriate for boys. On the other hand, boys are advised to elect the fine arts and home economics subjects often considered particularly suitable for girls. The unisex philosophy has shaken, if not toppled, some of the stereotypes of men and women.

In response to changing attitudes about gender-based stereotypes, authors have had to "de-sex" their textbooks. They no longer use the single generic pronoun "he" to refer to both sexes. Just as authors may no longer portray all persons in their textbooks as Caucasian, so also they may no longer depict males and females as performing only socially predetermined occupations.

There is a growing awareness that women have been discriminated against in the workplace. Such discrimination includes fewer opportunities for women to gain executive positions in some occupations, and the fact that women often receive lower salaries than men do in comparable positions. For example, how many school superintendents and secondary school principals are female?

Like racism, sexist stereotypes and discriminatory practices are difficult to eradicate. Nevertheless, curriculum workers must proceed to design curricula that will help to eliminate bias based not only on race, creed, and national origin, but also on gender.

Whole Language

Literacy education—that is, the development of the linguistic skills of reading, writing, speaking, and listening—has gone through a number of transformations in curriculum and instruction. Local, state, and national assessments have consistently revealed that our pupils have deficiencies in language skills. Students' poor achievement in the fundamental processes has evoked parental and general dissatisfaction with the public school's curriculum. Pressure for reform in this area resulted in the "back-to-basics" movement.

Reading, the sine qua non of education, has been at the center of controversies over what methods are most effective and which programs most successful. The continuing controversy over methods of teaching reading can readily be found in the professional literature.[136]

Somehow the profession has managed to survive the controversy over the "look-say" methods versus phonics. Educators have argued eloquently about

[136]See, for example, Marie Carbo, "Debunking the Great Phonics Myth," *Phi Delta Kappan* 70, no. 3 (November 1988): 226–240 and Jeanne S. Chall, "*Learning to Read: The Great Debate 20 Years Later—A Response to 'Debunking the Great Phonics Myth'*" *Phi Delta Kappan* 70, no. 7 (March 1989): 521–538.

the use of worksheets, pre-primers, primers, and basal readers. Although one goal of reading instruction is to interest children in reading for pleasure, the profession notes that, in spite of commendable sales of books, magazines, and newspapers, there is still a continued disinterest in—even dislike for—reading among the majority of the American population.

The whole-language movement is a recent response to the failure of the schools to produce literate citizens. In one sense, whole language challenges the skills approach to the teaching of reading. In another sense, it is more than just a reaction against old methods. Looming large in the 1980s the whole language movement has rapidly gained champions and, as with any educational development, critics. P. David Pearson declared, "never have I witnessed anything like the rapid spread of the whole-language movement."[137]

Dorothy J. Watson observed:

> Never in the history of literacy education has there been more genuine excitement on the part of educators. Teachers, many discouraged and burned out, are ignited by a new professionalism. . . . This new professionalism, movement, philosophy, spirit is called whole language.[138]

These comments reflect the intensity of interest in the whole-language movement.

On one level, the whole-language movement is a development of a concept about language learning. On another level, whole language is a perspective on learning in general. Whole-language advocates caution teachers against viewing whole language as a specific program or set of techniques or materials. Programs, materials, and techniques for a whole-language approach will vary from school to school, teacher to teacher, pupil to pupil.

The whole-language movement borrows concepts from the progressive education movement with its premises of child-centeredness, learning by doing, and project instruction; from individualized learning with its appeal to individual needs and interests; from cooperative learning with its emphasis on collaboration; from the principle of the integration of subject matter with its fusion of various disciplines; from the principle of the integration of content within the learner with its stress on pupil choice and creativity; and from instructional methodology, which casts the teacher in the role of facilitator. Based on such concepts, whole language challenges the language arts curriculum per se, "look-say" methods, phonics, mastery learning, direct instruction, large-group instruction, and standardized tests. In some of the whole-language literature, pupils are referred to as "curriculum informants" with whom the teacher "col-

---

[137] P. David Pearson, "Commentary: Reading the Whole-Language Movement," *The Elementary School Journal* 90, no. 2 (November 1989): 231.

[138] Dorothy J. Watson, "Defining and Describing Whole Language," *The Elementary School Journal* 90, no. 2 (November 1989): 141. ©1989 by the University of Chicago Press. All rights reserved.

laborates."[139] The current buzzword "empowerment" that appears in the literature on whole language refers to the espousal of pupils' control over their own
learning and teachers' control over their own teaching.[140]

The whole-language approach allows pupils to learn to read by reading,
to write by writing, to speak by speaking, and to listen by listening. The
students create their own stories. They speak on matters that concern them.
They listen to stories that they like having read to them by their teachers and
their peers. They tell what the stories mean to them. "Authenticity" is a key
word for whole-language instructors. Whole-language proponents point to the
success of literacy education in New Zealand, where basal texts are not used
and where teachers possess considerable latitude in the selection of materials
and methods based on pupils' needs and interests.[141]

Teachers who use a whole-language approach seek to develop students'
self-concept and confidence by deemphasizing mastery and accepting errors
and partial mastery. By tolerating error, teachers encourage pupils to take the
type of risks that in a more structured situation might be met with disapproval
and censure. Whole-language advocates believe that pupils often lose interest
in reading due to picayune criticism of their spelling, grammar, and syntax.
Students learn language skills by using materials of the real (rather than the
academic) world. Whole language methods require teachers to become proficient in assessing pupils' needs and interests—a skill Yetta M. Goodman calls
"kid watching"[142]—in order to ascertain the most appropriate form of instruction.

Pupils' linguistic activities cannot take place in a vacuum because they
must use those skills in many disciplines beyond the confines of the language
class. Kenneth S. Goodman stated, "The whole-language curriculum is a dual
curriculum; every activity, experience, or unit is an opportunity for both linguistic and cognitive development."[143]

Those who promote whole language see it as a theory that is concerned
with much more than communication skills. Watson clearly expressed this sentiment: "Whole language is a perspective on education that is supported by
beliefs about learners and learning, teachers and teaching, language, and curriculum."[144] In a rebuttal to an article in which Michael C. McKenna, Richard
D. Robinson, and John W. Miller recommended a research agenda on whole

---

[139] Jerome C. Harste, "The Future of Whole Language," *The Elementary School Journal* 90,
no. 2 (November 1989): 247.

[140] Ibid.

[141] See Barbara Mabbett, "The New Zealand Story," *Educational Leadership* 47, no. 6 (March
1990): 59–61.

[142] Yetta M. Goodman, "Kid Watching: An Alternative to Testing," *The National Elementary
Principal* 57, no. 4 (June 1978): 41–45.

[143] Kenneth S. Goodman, "Whole-Language Research: Foundations and Development," *The
Elementary School Journal* 90, no. 2 (November 1989): 210.

[144] Watson, "Defining and Describing," p. 133. Reprinted with permission.

language, Carole Edelsky argued that whole language is definitely not "another way to teach reading and/or language arts." Whole language, Edelsky stressed, is "a theory in practice about education generally. It takes seriously a distinction between *using* language and doing language exercises;" it is "a set of beliefs and not methods;" it "entails congruent practice in its richest sense (not just methods and materials but research, evaluation, curriculum design, interpretive norms, preferred classroom organization, and so on)."[145] Harste commented, "All this means that although whole language developed as a theory of language, it rapidly became a theory of learning."[146]

Questions about whole language remain to be answered. Can such a high degree of individualization, no matter how commendable, be attained universally throughout our educational system, which is always strapped for funds? Can teachers successfully follow the whole language approach when they have large classes? Will schools be able to furnish the wide variety of materials needed? You will recall that one of the major deficiencies of the defunct secondary school core curriculum approach, which integrated subject areas, was the lack of a large assortment of materials. Will schools be able to secure teachers who have been trained in the whole language approach? The lack of trained teachers was one of the problems of the core curriculum approach.

Research has already shown that some pupils learn better by one method than another and for certain purposes than for others. Will a phonics approach that emphasizes word-attack skills result in higher achievement in language learning than the whole language approach? Will an approach that integrates phonics in instruction with other methods produce better results in some or most circumstances? What will longitudinal studies reveal about the achievement of youngsters exposed to the whole-language approach when they reach high school and beyond?

Because testing is a reality of education, we must ascertain how well students who have been taught by the whole-language approach will perform on the inevitable SATs and ACTs as well as on international, national, state, and local criterion- and norm-referenced assessments. Will teachers and parents who have been satisfied with the many positive aspects of whole language maintain a high level of approval if assessment results fall short? Will they be willing to accept other indices of achievement that may be more compatible to the whole-language philosophy?

---

[145]Carole Edelsky, "Whose Agenda Is This Anyway? A Response to McKenna, Robinson, and Miller," *Educational Researcher* 19, no. 8 (November 1990): 8. Copyright 1990 by the American Educational Research Association. Reprinted by permission of the publisher. See ibid. pp. 7–11; Michael C. McKenna, Richard D. Robinson, and John W. Miller, "Whole Language: A Research Agenda for the Nineties," *Educational Researcher* 19, no. 8 (November 1990): 3–6, to which Edelsky was responding; and McKenna, Robinson, and Miller, "Whole Language and the Need for Open Inquiry: A Rejoinder to Edelsky," *Educational Researcher* 19, no. 8 (November 1990): 12–13. These three articles offer insight into the disagreements among educators about some aspects of whole language.

[146]Harste, "The Future of Whole Language," p. 246.

Elfrieda H. Hiebert and Charles W. Fisher made a thoughtful observation about the future of whole language:

> Since whole language represents the vanguard of a broader set of influences on education, the experiences of students, teachers, and others as they encounter it can either support a transformation or constitute yet another short-lived pendulum swing in educational practice.[147]

To promote the movement, whole-language advocates have established a network affiliated under the aegis of The Whole Language Umbrella, which held its first conference in August 1990.[148]

Whole language is a promising curricular innovation that is gaining in popularity. Experience will demonstrate whether this approach to language and learning will supplant, supplement, or be replaced by other approaches.

THE IMPACT OF PROFESSIONAL PROBLEMS UPON CURRICULUM

Teacher Organizations

Teachers' associations and unions wield considerable influence in the schools. Many years ago Robert M. McClure spoke of the positive impact of teachers' organizations on school improvement as follows:

> Unfortunately, the anti-establishment mystique in our society has drawn greater attention to teacher militancy and the struggle between the National Education Association and the American Federation of Teachers than to the considerable impact made by the professional associations on school improvement. The less conspicuous but major efforts of the NEA and its affiliates provide an impressive list of examples: the NEA Project on the Academically Talented Student; the NEA Project on Educational Implications of Automation; the Contemporary Music Project of the Music Educators National Conference (an NEA National Affiliate); the Staff Utilization Studies of the National Association of Secondary School Principals (an NEA Associated Organization); and the NEA Project on the Instructional Program of the Public Schools (Project on Instruction).[149]

To these examples we could add the many contributions to curriculum research and study of such professional organizations as the American Association of School Administrators, the American Educational Research Association, the Association for Supervision and Curriculum Development, the Association of

---

[147]Elfrieda H. Hiebert and Charles W. Fisher, "Whole Language: Three Themes for the Future," *Educational Leadership* 47, no. 6 (March 1990): 62.

[148]At the University of Missouri-Columbia.

[149]Robert M. McClure, "The Reforms of the Fifties and Sixties: A Historical Look at the Near Past," in *The Curriculum: Retrospect and Prospect*, 70th Yearbook of the National Society for the Study of Education, Part I (Chicago: University of Chicago Press, 1971): pp. 61–62.

Teacher Educators, the national associations of elementary, middle, and secondary school principals, and associations in the specific disciplines.

The two most powerful organizations that represent the interests of teachers are the National Education Association (NEA) and the American Federation of Teachers (AFT), which is affiliated with the AFL–CIO. Although the NEA is not a union in the sense of being affiliated with organized labor, the missions of the NEA and the AFT often coincide. In fact, some years ago the two organizations talked seriously of merger.

Teachers' organizations influence the curriculum both directly and indirectly. Some curriculum decisions are made not at the customary curriculum council table but at the bargaining table, in negotiations between teachers (labor) and the school district (management). Ordinarily, these negotiations are concerned with working conditions, rights of teachers, salary, benefits, and the like. However, some items of negotiation are clearly curricular in nature. In communities in which school management and a teachers' organization have effected a contract, the process of curriculum planning will likely need to be modified from that of school systems without formal contracts. Regardless of their personal desires, school administrators are bound by the terms of a negotiated contract.

Ways need to be established to integrate efforts of the teachers' organizations into the school district model for curriculum development. As members of the teachers' organizations themselves, curriculum planners can strive to enlist the teachers' organizations in the cause of continuous curriculum improvement.

Improved Dissemination

The curriculum workers' efforts would be greatly enhanced if we had better ways of disseminating results of research and experience with innovative programs. Though we have the Educational Resources Information Center (ERIC),[150] the National Diffusion Network,[151] regional education laboratories,[152] national research and development centers,[153] and many professional journals, the results of research and experimentation do not reach the classroom teacher to the degree they should.

The rapid spread of concepts, programs, and practices such as mastery learning, critical thinking, cooperative learning, and whole language would seem to refute the premise that dissemination of curriculum innovations is slow. However, speed is a relative concept. Forty-five miles per hour may be too slow on a four-laned interstate highway but too fast on a country road. Innovations still take a considerable amount of time to permeate some 15,000 public school districts with their 59,000 elementary and middle schools, their

[150] See Appendix B.
[151] See Appendix C.
[152] See Appendix D.
[153] See Appendix E.

21,000 secondary schools, their 1.3 million elementary school teachers and their 1 million secondary school teachers.

Curriculum decisions are still made on the basis of limited information and without all currently available data. Curriculum leaders must take special responsibility to stay informed of current research so that they can channel essential information to the classroom teacher and other curriculum workers.

Improved Research

Not only do the results of research need to be disseminated, but both quantity and quality of educational research need to be expanded. The school systems need to be close partners with institutions of higher learning in the conduct of research. For instance, the National Council for Accreditation of Teacher Education (NCATE)—the voluntary accrediting agency to which schools and colleges of education may belong—promotes cooperative research between school systems and schools and colleges of education.[154]

The profession is in particular need of more experimental research and more longitudinal studies. We have many status studies and surveys of opinions and practices (favored by doctoral candidates in education) but not enough controlled research or, for that matter, less controlled action research. Curriculum planners should encourage teachers to participate in controlled research studies and to engage in their own unsophisticated action research to determine answers to simple problems that may be applicable only in their own classrooms.

Improved Preparation

Better programs are needed to prepare curriculum leaders and planners. To gain some perception of the preparation needed by curriculum developers, we might refer to Chapter 1 on the areas of learning from which the field of curriculum is derived, to Chapter 3 on the multiple levels and sectors of curriculum planning, and to Chapter 4 on the roles of various personnel in curriculum development. States might reasonably institute certificates in curriculum development. Such certificates would parallel those now offered in administration, supervision, guidance, and other specialities. Such a certificate would go a long way toward establishing curriculum as a field of specialization in its own right. Furthermore, teacher education institutions should assure that their graduates gain what might be called "curriculum literacy"—that is, knowledge about the curriculum field and basic skills in curriculum development.

Solutions to all of these problems could help to improve the efficacy of curriculum development.

---

[154]National Council for Accreditation of Teacher Education, *Standards, Procedures, and Policies for the Accreditation of Professional Education Units*, rev. (Washington, D.C.: National Council for the Accreditation of Teacher Education, 1990), p. 51.

SUMMARY

This chapter presented a number of perennial problems of curriculum development, several current curricular problems, and a few professional problems that have an impact upon the curriculum.

Eight perennial or continuing problems were considered. Each was presented as a principle to which curriculum workers must give attention.

Scope is the breadth of the curriculum—the "what." The major task in planning the scope of the curriculum is the selection of content, organizing elements, organizing centers, or integrative threads from the wealth of possible choices.

Relevance is the usefulness of content to the learner. What makes determining the relevance of a curriculum difficult is the variety of perceptions of what is relevant. A consensus of the opinions of the various constituencies and patrons of the school should be sought by curriculum workers to determine what is of sufficient relevance to be included in the curriculum.

Curriculum planners should strive for balance among a number of variables. When a curriculum gives excessive attention to one dimension or to one group of students and ignores or minimizes attention to others, the curriculum may be said to be out of balance and in need of being brought into balance.

Integration is the unification of disciplines—the weakening or abandoning of boundaries between discrete subjects. Many educators feel that integrated content helps students in the task of problem solving. Relevance, balance, and integration are perceived as dimensions of scope.

Sequence is the "when"—the ordering of the units of content. Attention must be paid to prerequisite learning requirements. Continuity is the planned introduction and reintroduction of content at subsequent grade levels and at ever-increasing levels of complexity. This concept is at the heart of the "spiral curriculum."

Articulation is the meshing of subject matter and skills between successive levels of schooling to provide a smooth transition for boys and girls from a lower to a higher level. Sequence, continuity, and articulation are all related concepts. Continuity and articulation are perceived as dimensions of sequencing.

Transferability is that characteristic of learning which when realized in one setting permits it to be carried over into another. Although there is no proof that certain subjects per se enhance the transfer of learning, there is some evidence to support the thesis that teaching basic principles of a discipline and stressing their application increases transfer. Transfer is a much-desired goal of education.

Eleven current problems of direct concern to curriculum planners were also examined. These problems, brought about by social and political forces, are alternative choices in education, emphasis on the basics and academics, bilingual education, cultural literacy, provision for the handicapped, health education, racial/ethnic integration and cultural diversity, religion in the schools, protests over schoolbooks, sexism, and whole language. Curriculum workers must be aware of the dimensions of these and other current problems as they attempt to develop curricula.

This chapter concluded with a brief discussion of four professional problems that have an impact upon the curriculum: the need to clarify the role of teacher organizations in respect to curriculum improvement, the need for better means of disseminating the results of curriculum research and experimentation, the need for more and better research, and the need for improved training programs for curriculum developers.

QUESTIONS FOR DISCUSSION

1. How do teachers and curriculum planners decide what to teach?
2. What knowledge is of most worth?
3. How do teachers and curriculum planners decide when subject matter and skills will be taught?
4. What are some current, controversial curriculum issues not included in this chapter?
5. What general guidelines would you recommend for curriculum planners to follow in dealing with controversial curriculum issues?

SUPPLEMENTARY EXERCISES

1. Outline the scope of a course you have taught or plan to teach.
2. Poll a number of teachers, students, and parents to find out what they feel is relevant in the curriculum and what relevant topics they think have been left out.
3. Determine in what ways a curriculum you know well appears to be in or out of balance. If you believe that the curriculum is out of balance, recommend ways to bring it into balance.
4. Report on any planned efforts you can find to correlate or integrate subject matter.
5. Outline and explain the rationale of the sequence of the topics or elements of a course you have taught or plan to teach.
6. Determine whether a school you know well has planned the curriculum keeping in mind the principle of continuity. Recommend improvements in continuity, if necessary.
7. Determine whether a school system you know well has planned the curriculum keeping in mind the principle of articulation. Recommend improvements in articulation, if necessary.
8. Show the transfer value of a discipline that you are certified to teach.
9. Write an analysis of J. Richard Suchman's Inquiry Training Model (see bibliography).

10. Write an analysis of David P. Ausubel's Advance Organizer Model (see bibliography).
11. Locate and summarize the content of at least one article or chapter of a book on one of the eight continuing curriculum problems discussed in this chapter.
12. Select one of the current curriculum problems facing curriculum workers described in this chapter, search the literature, review local practices, and document with references the degree to which it appears to be a problem both nationally and locally. Show your position on the problem and suggest ways for solving it.
13. Document any instances of the following current curriculum problems within the past three years in the school district you know best:
    a. racial conflicts
    b. religious disputes
    c. sex discrimination
    d. schoolbook protests
14. Consult good references on school law and report on the significance of the court decisions in the following cases. (These cases are all church-state disputes but are not necessarily curricular issues.)
    a. *Tinker* v. *Des Moines Independent Community School District*, 393 U.S. 503 (1969).
    b. *Trachman* v. *Anker*, 563 F 2d 512 (1977).
    c. *Kuhlmeir* v. *Hazelwood School District*, 607 F. Supp. 1450 (1985).
    d. *Everson* v. *Board of Education*, 330 U.S. 1 (1947).
    e. *Mergens* v. *West Side High School District*, 110 L Ed 2d 191 (1990).
    f. *Commonwealth* v. *Herr*, 229 Oa 132, 78 A. 68 (1910).
    g. *O'Connor* v. *Hendrick*, 184 N.Y. 421, 77 N.E. 612 (1906).
    h. *Tudor* v. *Board of Education of Borough of Rutherford*, N.J. 31, 100 A. 2d 857 (1953).
    i. *Board of Education* v. *Maas*, 152 A. 2d 394 (1959).
    j. *Worldwide Church of God* v. *Amarillo Independent School District*, 670 F 2d 46 (1982).
    k. *Gregoire* v. *Centennial School District*, 674 F Supp. 172 (1987).
15. Report on any activities of a teachers' association or union that have had an impact on the curriculum.
16. Select one of the professional problems that has an impact on the curriculum, search the literature, review local practices, and document with references the degree to which it appears to be a problem both nationally and locally. Show your position on the problem and suggest ways of solving it.
17. Explain the purposes of the Educational Resource Information Center (ERIC) and show how the system works. Give illustrations (see Appendix B).
18. Write the National Diffusion Network Facilitator for your state and report on exemplary programs that exist (see Appendix C).

19. Report on the work of one or more regional educational laboratories or national research and development centers. Give illustrations of their impact on the curriculum (see Appendices D and E).
20. Prepare a position paper on one of the following topics:
    a. separate schools for boys and girls
    b. separate schools for minority children

BIBLIOGRAPHY

Aiken, Wilford M. *The Story of the Eight-Year Study*. New York: Harper & Row, 1942.

Alexander, Elizabeth. "School-Based Clinics: Questions to be Answered in Planning Stages." *The High School Journal* 73, no. 2 (December–January 1990): 133–138.

Alexander, Kern and Alexander, M. David. *American Public School Law,* 2nd ed. St. Paul, Minn.: West Publishing Co., 1985.

Ambert, Alba and Menendez, Sarah E. *Bilingual Education: A Sourcebook,* New York: Garland, 1985.

"America's Crusade." *Time* 128, no. 11 (September 15, 1986): 60–68.

Annual Edition. *Education*. Guilford, Conn.: Dushkin Publishing Group, annually.

Aronowitz, Stanley and Giroux, Henry A. *Education Under Siege: The Conservative, Liberal, and Radical Debate over Schooling*. South Hadley, Mass.: Bergin & Garvey, 1985.

Association for Supervision and Curriculum Development. *Balance in the Curriculum,* 1961 Yearbook. Alexandria, Va.: Association for Supervision and Curriculum Development, 1961.

———. *Curriculum Update*. Alexandria, Va.: Association for Supervision and Curriculum Development, November 1990.

———. "Plan for 'African-American Immersion Schools' Raises Questions." *Update* 33, no. 2 (February 1991): 6, 8.

———. *Public Schools of Choice*. Alexandria, Va.: Association for Supervision and Curriculum Development, 1990.

———. *Religion in the Curriculum: A Report from the ASCD Panel on Religion in the Curriculum*. Alexandria, Va.: Association for Supervision and Curriculum Development, 1987.

Ausubel, David P. *Educational Psychology: A Cognitive View*. New York: Holt, Rinehart and Winston, 1968.

Banks, James A. *Multiethnic Education: Theory and Practice,* 2nd ed. Boston: Allyn and Bacon, 1988.

———. *Teaching Strategies for Ethnic Studies,* 5th ed. Boston: Allyn and Bacon, 1991.

Banks, James A. and Banks, Cherry A. McGee, eds. *Multicultural Education: Issues and Perspectives*. Boston: Allyn and Bacon, 1989.

Bellack, Arno A. "What Knowledge Is of Most Worth?" *High School Journal* 48, no. 5 (February 1965): 318–332.

Berman, Louise M. *New Priorities in the Curriculum*. Columbus, Ohio: Charles E. Merrill, 1968.

Beyer, Landon E. and Apple, Michael W. *The Curriculum: Problems, Politics, and Possibilities*. Albany, N.Y.: State University of New York Press, 1988.

Bloom, Allan. *The Closing of the American Mind*. New York: Simon and Schuster, 1987.

Bloom, Benjamin S. "Ideas, Problems, and Methods of Inquiry." In *The Integration of Educational Experiences*. 57th Yearbook, National Society for the Study of Education, Part 3, pp. 84–85. Chicago: University of Chicago Press, 1958.

Broudy, Harry S. *The Real World of the Public Schools*. New York: Harcourt Brace Jovanovich, 1972.

Broudy, Harry S., Smith, B. Othanel, and Burnett, Joe R. *Democracy and Excellence in American Secondary Education*. Chicago: Rand McNally, 1964.

"*Brown* v. *Board of Education* Reopens." *Contemporary Education* 60, no. 1 (February 1988): 29–31.

Bruner, Jerome S. *On Knowing: Essays for the Left Hand*. Cambridge, Mass.: Harvard University Press, 1962.

———. *The Process of Education*. Cambridge, Mass.: Harvard University Press, 1977.

———. *The Relevance of Education*. New York: Norton, 1973.

———. "Structures in Learning." *Today's Education* 52, no. 3 (March 1963): 26–27.

Butts, R. Freeman. *The American Tradition in Religion and Education*. Boston: Beacon Press, 1950.

Carbo, Marie. "Debunking the Great Phonics Myth." *Phi Delta Kappan* 70, no. 3 (November 1988): 226–240.

Caswell, Hollis L. and Campbell, Doak S. *Curriculum Development*. New York: American Book Company, 1935.

Chall, Jeanne S. *Learning to Read: The Great Debate*, rev. ed. New York: McGraw-Hill, 1983.

———. "*Learning to Read: The Great Debate* 20 Years Later—A Response to 'Debunking the Great Phonics Myth.'" *Phi Delta Kappan* 70, no. 7 (March 1989): 521–538.

Cheney, Lynne V. *Tyrannical Machines*. Washington, D.C.: National Endowment for the Humanities, 1990.

Chubb, John E. and Moe, Terry M. *Politics, Markets, and America's Schools*. Washington, D.C.: The Brookings Institution, 1990.

Coleman, James S. et al. *Equality of Educational Opportunity*. Washington, D.C.: U.S. Office of Education, 1966.

Combs, Arthur W., ed. *Perceiving, Behaving, Becoming*, 1962 Yearbook. Alexandria, Va.: Association for Supervision and Curriculum Development, 1962.

Cordasco, Francesco. *Bilingual Schooling in the United States: A Sourcebook for Educational Personnel*. New York: Webster Division, McGraw-Hill, 1976.

Cornett, Claudia E. and Blankenship, Lesley A. *Whole Language = Whole Learning*. Fastback 307. Bloomington, Ind.: Phi Delta Kappa Educational Foundation, 1990.

Cummins, Jim. *Empowering Minority Students*. Sacramento, Calif.: California Association for Bilingual Education, 1989.

"Dealing with Diversity." *Educational Leadership* 46, no. 5 (February 1989) 2–81.

Doll, Ronald C. *Curriculum Development: Decision Making and Process*, 7th ed. Boston: Allyn and Bacon, 1989.

Elam, Stanley M. "The 22nd Annual Gallup Poll of the Public's Attitudes Toward the Public Schools." *Phi Delta Kappan* 72, no. 1 (September 1990): 41–55.

Elam, Stanley M., Rose, Lowell C., and Gallup, Alec M. "The 23rd Annual Gallup Poll of the Public's Attitudes Toward the Public Schools." *Phi Delta Kappan* 73, no. 1 (September 1991): 41–56.

Feinberg, Rosa Castro, Marquez, Esther, and Valverde, Leonard, eds. *Educating English-Speaking Hispanics*. Alexandria, Va.: Association for Supervision and Curriculum Development, 1980.

Gagné, Robert M. "Curriculum Research and the Promotion of Learning." *Perspectives of Curriculum Evaluation*. AERA Monograph Series on Curriculum Evaluation no. 1, 19–38. Chicago: Rand McNally, 1967.

Gagnon, Paul. *Historical Literacy*. New York: Macmillan, 1989.

Garcia, Richard I. *Fostering a Pluralistic Society Through Multi-Ethnic Education*. Bloomington, Ind.: Phi Delta Kappa Educational Foundation, 1978.

Gay, Geneva. "Achieving Educational Equality Through Curriculum Desegregation." *Phi Delta Kappan* 72, no. 1 (September 1990): 56–62.

Gilligan, Carol. *In a Different Voice*. Cambridge, Mass.: Harvard University Press, 1982.

Giroux, Henry A., Penna, Arthur N., and Pinar, William F., eds. *Curriculum and Instruction: Alternatives in Education*. Berkeley, Calif.: McCutchan, 1981.

Gold, Milton J., Grant, Carl A., and Rivlin, Harry N. *In Praise of Diversity: A Resource Book for Multicultural Education*. Washington, D.C.: Teacher Corps and Association of Teacher Educators, 1977.

Goodlad, John I. *Planning and Organizing for Teaching*. Washington, D.C.: National Education Association, 1963.

Goodman, Kenneth S. *What's Whole in Whole Language?* Portsmouth, N.H.: Heinemann Educational Books, 1986.

Goodman, Kenneth S., Bird, Lois Bridges, and Goodman, Yetta M. *The Whole Language Catalog*. Santa Rosa, Calif.: American School Publishers, 1991.

Goodman, Kenneth S., Goodman, Yetta M., and Hood, Wendy J., eds. *The Whole Language Evaluation Book*. Portsmouth, N.H.: Heinemann Educational Books, 1989.

Goodman, Kenneth S., Smith, E. Brooks, Meredith, Robert, and Goodman, Yetta M. *Language and Thinking: A Whole Language Curriculum,* 3rd ed. New York: Richard C. Owen, Publishers, 1987.

Goodman, Yetta M. "Roots of the Whole-Language Movement." *The Elementary School Journal* 90, no. 2 (November 1989): 113–127.

Halverson, Paul M. "The Meaning of Balance." In *Balance in the Curriculum,* 1961 Yearbook, 3–16. Alexandria, Va.: Association for Supervision and Curriculum Development, 1961.

Harrington-Lueker, Donna. "Book Battles." *American School Board Journal* 178, no. 2 (February 1991): 18–21, 37.

Hass, Glen. *Curriculum Planning: A New Approach,* 5th ed. Boston: Allyn and Bacon, 1987.

Haynes, Charles. *Religion in American History: What to Teach and How*. Alexandria, Va.: Association for Supervision and Curriculum Development, 1990.

Hirsch, E.D., Jr. "Cultural Literacy." *The American Scholar* 52, no. 2 (Spring 1983): 159–169.

———. "Cultural Literacy: Let's Get Specific." *NEA Today* 6, no. 6 (January 1988): 15–21.

———. *Cultural Literacy: What Every American Needs to Know*. Boston: Houghton Mifflin, 1987.

Holt, John. *Teach Your Own: A Hopeful Path for Education*. New York: Delacorte Press/Seymour Lawrence, 1981.

House, H. Wayne, ed. *Schooling Choice: An Examination of Private, Public, and Home Education*. Portland, Ore.: Multnomah Press, 1988.

Howe, Harold, ed. "Equalizing Educational Opportunity." *Harvard Educational Review* 38, no. 1 (Winter 1968): 3–175.

Isser, Natalie and Schwartz, Lita Linzer. *The American School and the Melting Pot: Minority Self-Esteem and Public Education*. Bristol, Ind.: Wyndham Hall Press, 1985.

Jenkinson, Edward B. *Censors in the Classroom: The Mind Benders*. Carbondale: Southern Illinois University Press, 1979.

———. *The Schoolbook Protest Movement*. Bloomington, Ind.: Phi Delta Kappa Educational Foundation, 1986.

Johnston, Lloyd D., O'Malley, Patrick M., and Bachman, Jerald G. *Drug Use Among American High School Students, College Students, and Other Young Adults*. Washington, D.C.: U.S. Government Printing Office, 1986.

Joyce, Bruce and Weil, Marsha. *Models of Teaching,* 3rd ed. Englewood Cliffs, N.J.: Prentice-Hall, 1986.

Lawrence, Jerome and Lee, Robert E. *Inherit the Wind*. New York: Bantam Books, 1963.

Lewis, Arthur J. "Educational Basics to Serve Citizens in the Future." *FASCD Journal* 1, no. 1 (February 1979): 2–8.

McCarthy, Martha M. "Creation Versus Evolution: Issues and Implications." *Educational Horizons* 61, no. 1 (Fall 1982): 32–36, 51.

McClure, Robert M., ed. *The Curriculum: Retrospect and Prospect,* 70th Yearbook of the National Society for the Study of Education, Part 1. Chicago: University of Chicago Press, 1971.

Manning, Gary and Manning, Maryann, eds. *Whole Language: Beliefs and Practices, K–8.* Washington, D.C.: National Education Association, 1989.

Miller, John W. and McKenna, Michael C. *Teaching Reading in the Elementary Classroom.* Scottsdale, Ariz.: Gorsuch Scarisbrick, 1989.

Naisbitt, John. *Megatrends: Ten New Directions Transforming Our Lives.* New York: Warner, 1982.

Newman, Judith M., ed. *Whole Language: Theory in Use.* Portsmouth, N.H.: Heinemann Educational Books, 1985.

Noll, James W. *Taking Sides: Clashing Views on Controversial Educational Issues,* 6th ed. Guilford, Conn.: Dushkin Publishing Group, 1991.

Oakes, Jeannie. *Keeping Track: How Schools Structure Inequality.* New Haven, Conn.: Yale University Press, 1985.

Oliver, Albert I. *Curriculum Improvement: A Guide to Problems, Principles and Processes,* 2nd ed. New York: Harper & Row, 1977.

Orlich, Donald C. "*Brown v. Board of Education*: Time for a Reassessment." *Phi Delta Kappan* 72, no. 8 (April 1991): 631–632.

Orlosky, Donald E. and Smith, B. Othanel, eds. *Curriculum Development: Issues and Insights.* Chicago: Rand McNally, 1978.

Pai, Young. *Cultural Foundations of Education.* Columbus, Ohio: Merrill, 1990.

People for the American Way. *Attacks on the Freedom to Learn.* Washington, D.C.: People for the American Way, 1991.

Phenix, Philip H. "The Disciplines as Curriculum Content." In *Curriculum Crossroads,* ed. A. Harry Passow, 57–65. New York: Teachers College Press, Columbia University, 1962.

Phi Delta Kappa. *AIDS Education.* Bloomington, Ind.: Center for Evaluation, Development, and Research, Phi Delta Kappa, 1990.

————. *Bilingual Education.* Bloomington, Ind.: Center for Evaluation, Development, and Research, Phi Delta Kappa, 1988.

Powell, Arthur G., Farrar, Eleanor, and Cohen, David H. *The Shopping Mall High School: Winners and Losers in the Educational Marketplace.* Boston: Houghton Mifflin, 1986.

Pressey, Sidney I. and Robinson, Frances P. *Psychology and the New Education,* rev. ed. New York: Harper & Row, 1944.

Provenzo, Eugene F., Jr. *Religious Fundamentalism and American Education: The Battle for the Public Schools.* Albany, N.Y.: State University of New York Press, 1990.

Ravitch, Diane and Finn, Chester E., Jr. *What Do Our 17-Year-Olds Know? A Report on the First National Assessment of History and Literature.* New York: Harper & Row, 1987.

"Religion in the Public Schools," *Educational Leadership* 44, no. 8 (May 1987): 3–29.

Reutter, E. Edmund, Jr. *Schools and the Law,* 5th ed. Reston, Va.: National Association of Secondary School Principals, 1981.

————. *The Supreme Court's Impact on Public Education.* Bloomington, Ind.: Phi Delta Kappa and the National Organization on Legal Problems of Education, 1982.

Saylor, J. Galen, Alexander, William M., and Lewis, Arthur J. *Curriculum Planning for Better Teaching and Learning,* 4th ed. New York: Holt, Rinehart and Winston, 1981.

Schlesinger, Arthur M., Jr. *The Disuniting of America*. Knoxville, Tenn.: Whittle Direct Books, 1991.

"Schools of Choice." *Educational Leadership* 48, no. 4 (December 1990/January 1991): 3–72.

Semmel, Melvyn I. and Heinmiller, Joseph L. "The Education for All Handicapped Children Act of 1975: National Perspectives and Long Range Implications." *Viewpoints* 53, no. 2 (March 1977): 1–128.

"Sex and Schools." *Time* 128, no. 21 (November 24, 1986): 54–63.

"Sex, with Care." *U.S. News & World Report* 100, no. 21 (June 2, 1986): 53–57.

Short, Edmund C. and Marconnit, George D., eds. *Contemporary Thought on Public School Curriculum*. Dubuque, Iowa: William C. Brown, 1968.

Simon, Sidney B., Howe, Leland W., and Kirschenbaum, Howard. *Values Clarification*. New York: Hart, 1972.

Smith, B. Othanel, et al. *Teachers for the Real World*. Washington, D.C.: American Association of Colleges for Teacher Education, 1969.

Smith, B. Othanel, Stanley, William O., and Shores, J. Harlan. *Fundamentals of Curriculum Development*, rev. ed. New York: Harcourt Brace Jovanovich, 1957.

Smith, Frank. *Reading*. New York: Cambridge University Press, 1978.

———. *Understanding Reading: A Psycholinguistic Analysis of Reading*. Hillsdale, N.J.: Lawrence Erlbaum Associates, Publishers, 1986.

"A Special Section on School Desegregation." *Phi Delta Kappan* 72, no. 1 (September 1990): 8–40.

Stein, Coleman Brez, Jr. *Sink or Swim: The Politics of Bilingual Education*. New York: Praeger, 1986.

Stone, James C. and DeNevi, Donald P., eds. *Teaching Multi-Cultural Populations: Five Heritages*. New York: Van Nostrand Reinhold, 1971.

Strahan, Richard D. and Turner, L. Charles. *The Courts and the Schools: The School Administrator and Legal Risk Management Today*. White Plains, N.Y.: Longman, 1987.

Suchman, J. Richard. *The Elementary School Training Program in Scientific Inquiry*, Report of the U.S. Office of Education, Project Title VII, Project 216. Urbana: University of Illinois Press, 1962.

Swanson, Maria Medina. "Bilingual Education: What? Why? When? How? Where?" *Thresholds in Secondary Education* 2, no. 2 (Summer 1976): 19–21.

Taba, Hilda. *Curriculum Development: Theory and Practice*. New York: Harcourt Brace Jovanovich, 1962.

Tanner, Daniel and Tanner, Laurel N. *Curriculum Development: Theory into Practice*, 2nd ed. New York: Macmillan, 1980.

Thorndike, Edward L. "Mental Discipline in High School Studies." *Journal of Educational Psychology* 15, no. 1 (January 1924): 1–22; continued in 15, no. 2 (February 1924): 83–98.

———. *The Principles of Teaching: Based on Psychology*. New York: Seiler, 1906.

Toffler, Alvin. *Future Shock*. New York: Random House, 1970.

———. *The Third Wave*. New York: William Morrow, 1980.

Tyler, Ralph W. *Basic Principles of Curriculum and Instruction*. Chicago: University of Chicago Press, 1949.

Valverde, Leonard, ed. *Bilingual Education for Latinos*. Alexandria, Va.: Association for Supervision and Curriculum Development, 1978.

Vars, Gordon F., ed. *Common Learnings: Core and Interdisciplinary Team Approaches*. Scranton, Pa.: International Textbook Company, 1969.

"Whole Language: A Changed Universe." *Contemporary Education* 62, no. 2 (Winter 1991): 69–133.

Wiles, Kimball and Patterson, Franklin. *The High School We Need*. Alexandria, Va.: Association for Supervision and Curriculum Development, 1959.

Zais, Robert S. *Curriculum: Principles and Foundations*. New York: Harper & Row, 1976.

AUDIOTAPES

Association for Supervision and Curriculum Development, 1250 N. Pitt Street, Alexandria, Va. 22314.

Drug and Sex Education Programs That Work. Four titles. 1988:

Anne Arundel County Public Schools Drug Education Program. (Betsy Flemming).

Components of a Comprehensive Drug/Alcohol Program. Two tapes. (Richard Towers).

Key Issues in Family Life Planning. (Susan Wilson).

Responding to the New Jersey State Mandate for Family Life Education. (Claire Scholz).

Using Whole Language to Develop Strategies for Learning. (Marian Toth). 1990.

What 17-Year-Olds Know About History and Literature. (Chester E. Finn, Jr.). 1988.

ESSAYS

African-American Baseline Essays. 1989. Six essays (focusing on art, language arts, mathematics, science, social studies, and music) on the contributions of people of African descent from ancient times to the present. Portland Public Schools, Portland, Ore. 97227. In preparation: *American Indian Baseline Essays*.

FILMS

The Individualized Education Program. 22 min. color. Greensburg, Pa.: Instructional Media Services, 1977. Explains the procedures for developing, implementing, and reviewing the individualized educational plan (IEP) in accordance with Public Law 94-142, the Education for All Handicapped Children Act.

Inherit the Wind. 127 min. black and white. United Artists, 1960. Based on the Scopes trial in Tennessee in 1925 on the teaching of the theory of evolution. Stars Frederic March, Spencer Tracy, and Gene Kelly.

Separate but Equal. 4 hrs. ABC television mini-series, 1991. Sidney Poitier plays Thurgood Marshall, attorney in the landmark case of *Brown v. Board of Education*, in which the U.S. Supreme Court ruled segregation unconstitutional.

Supreme Court Speaks: Learning about Religion in the Public Schools. 27 min. color. Tallahassee: Florida State University, 1972. Discussion of implications of U.S. Supreme Court decisions concerning religion in the public schools. Explores teacher's role in handling religious issues.

Teaching Morals and Values. 29 min. color. Wilmette, Ill.: Films, Inc., 1977. Dr. Madeline Hunter discusses the teacher's role in developing morals and values in children.

With All Deliberate Speed. 34 min. color. New York: BFA Educational Media, 1976. Depicts events leading to racial integration in America.

JOURNALS/NEWSLETTERS

Council on Basic Education, 725 15th St., N.W., Washington, D.C. 20005.

National Association for Bilingual Education, Union Center Plaza, 810 First St., N.E., 3rd Fl., Washington, D.C. 20002.

U.S. English, 818 Connecticut Ave., N.W., Suite 200, Washington, D.C. 20006.

LESSON PLANS

K-5 African-American Lesson Plans. Sixty lesson plans in five disciplines. Portland Public Schools, Portland, Ore. 97227.

MULTI-MEDIA

Looking into AIDS. Phi Delta Kappa, P.O. Box 789, Bloomington, Ind. 47402-0789.

Curriculum for upper elementary and middle school pupils. Instructor's guide, student's book, and poster.

CHAPTER FIFTEEN

Curriculum Products

After studying this chapter you should be able to:

1. Construct a curriculum guide.

2. Construct a resource unit.

3. Identify sources of curriculum materials.

TANGIBLE PRODUCTS

The Biblical expression "By their fruits ye shall know them" can certainly be applied to curriculum workers. Walk into the curriculum laboratory of any public school or university and you may be surprised, perhaps even overwhelmed, by the evidence of the productivity of curriculum development workers. The products of their efforts are there for all to see—tangible, printed, and often packaged in eye-catching style.

Curriculum workers have been turning out products for many years. Unfortunately, some curriculum developers view the creation of products as the final rather than the intermediate phase of curriculum improvement. The products are meant to be put into practice, tried out, revised, tried again, revised again, and so on.

Creating curriculum products not only has a functional value—the production of a plan or tool for implementing or evaluating the curriculum—but also gives the planners a great psychological boost. In producing tangible materials, they are able to feel some sense of accomplishment.

Throughout this text we have already seen a number of kinds of curriculum products. Chapter 6 contained examples of statements of philosophy and aims of education. Chapter 7 included needs assessment surveys and reports, sections of courses of study and curriculum guides, and portions of a state's statement of minimal standards. In Chapter 8 we saw statements of curriculum goals and objectives. Statements of instructional goals and ojectives formed a part of Chapter 10. Unit and lesson plans were outlined in Chapter 11. Chapter 12 discussed instruments for evaluating instruction, and Chapter 13, instruments for evaluating the curriculum.

Judging from the tasks that curriculum coordinators, consultants, directors, and other workers are called on to do in the schools, there is a healthy demand for training in the production of curriculum materials. In this chapter we will discuss the creation and use of several of the more common products found in the schools.

The content, the form, and the names by which curriculum materials are known are almost as varied as the number of groups that author them. Curriculum bulletins, curriculum guides, courses of study, syllabi, resource units, and source units can be found in the curriculum libraries of school systems.

Because curriculum materials are impermanent—nonstandardized products made primarily for local use—the variations among them are considerable. To put the creation of curriculum products into perspective, we must visualize curriculum committees and individuals in thousands of school districts all over the United States constructing materials that they feel will be of most help to their teachers.

Terms for these types of curriculum materials may signal quite different products or may be used synonymously. A curriculum guide, for example, may be quite different from a course of study. On the other hand, what is called a curriculum guide in one locality may be called a course of study in another. For this reason it is difficult to predict what will be discovered in any particular curriculum product until it is examined.

The curriculum products that we will consider in this chapter are

1. curriculum guides, courses of study, and syllabi
2. resource units

We will not discuss curriculum materials that have been adequately discussed in preceding chapters, such as unit plans, lesson plans, and tests. All curriculum materials share the common purpose of serving as aids to teachers and planners in organizing, implementing, and evaluating curriculum and instruction.

CURRICULUM GUIDES, COURSES OF STUDY, AND SYLLABI

Three kinds of curriculum products are clearly related. These are (1) curriculum guides, (2) courses of study, and (3) syllabi. As already noted, some curriculum workers make no distinction among the three types. The following definitions of the terms are used in this chapter:

1. A *curriculum guide* is the most general of the three types of materials. It may cover a single course or subject area at a particular grade level (e.g., ninth-grade English); all subjects at a particular grade level (e.g., ninth-grade); a sequence in a discipline (e.g., language arts), or an area of interest applicable to two or more courses or grade levels (e.g., occupational safety). When a curriculum guide covers a single course, it may also be called a course of study. However, a curriculum guide is a teaching aid with helpful suggestions rather than a complete course of study in itself.
2. A *course of study* is a detailed plan for a single course, including text materials (content). A well-known example of a curriculum product of this nature is *Man: A Course of Study,* which has been widely used in the schools and seen on television.[1] A course of study includes both what is to be taught (content)—in summary or in complete text—and suggestions for how to teach the course. A course of study usually specifies what *must* be taught, whereas a curriculum guide may offer alternatives to the teacher.
3. A *syllabus* is an outline of topics to be covered in a single course or grade level.

---

[1]See Jerome S. Bruner, *Man: A Course of Study* (Cambridge, Mass.: Educational Services, 1965).

Curriculum Guide Formats

Let's look more closely at the creation of a curriculum guide. What is its purpose? Who should be included in the task? Curriculum guides are used in at least two ways. In less structured situations where teachers have a great deal of flexibility in planning, a curriculum guide provides many suggestions to teachers who wish to use it. In that case the curriculum guide is one source from which teachers may derive ideas for developing their own resource units, learning units, and lesson plans. In more structured situations a curriculum guide specifies minimal objectives that students must master in the discipline. It may spell out objectives for each marking period. The guide may identify teaching materials and suggest learning activities. It may be accompanied by pretests and posttests for each unit or marking period.

A curriculum guide may be written by a group of teachers or planners or by an individual. In the latter case, the guide is often reviewed by other specialists before it is disseminated within the school system. For those who write a curriculum guide, the process is almost as important as the product. The task of constructing a guide forces the writers to clarify their ideas, to gather data, to demonstrate creativity, to select content, to determine sequence, and to organize their thoughts.

Examination of curriculum guides from various school districts will reveal a variety of formats. Some school systems that develop curriculum guides follow a single format. Because the substance of guides varies from format to format, some school districts find it useful to prepare more than one type of guide. Many curriculum guides are lengthy documents, so I will not attempt to reproduce examples in this text. Instead we will look at the formats that are often employed.

From the many formats for curriculum guides we may select three that I will call, for lack of better labels, the comprehensive, sequencing, and test-coding formats.

The Comprehensive Format.   Curriculum planners following a comprehensive format would include the following components in a curriculum guide for a particular level of a discipline—for example, ninth-grade social studies.

1. *Introduction*. The introduction includes the title of the guide, the subject and grade level for which the guide is designated, and any suggestions that might help users.
2. *Instructional goals*. In this section, instructional goals (called general objectives by some planners) are stated in nonbehavioral terms. Instructional goals should relate to the schools' curriculum goals and objectives.
3. *Instructional objectives*. Instructional objectives (called specific, performance, or behavioral objectives by some planners) for the particular grade level of the subject should be stated in behavioral terms and should encompass all three domains of learning, if all are applicable.

4. *Learning activities*. Learning experiences that might be used by the teacher with pupils should be suggested and placed in preferred sequence.
5. *Evaluation techniques*. Suggestions should be given to teachers on how to evaluate student achievement. This section of the guide could include general suggestions on evaluating, sample test items, or even complete tests.
6. *Resources*. Attention should be given to human resources—persons who might be called on to assist with the content of the guide—and to material resources, including books, audiovisual aids, and facilities.

Some writers of comprehensive guides also include a topical outline of the content. No effort is made to separate the goals and objectives into time periods, nor are the components sequenced for the teacher. This format is not prescriptive. Guides of this nature are supplementary aids for the professional teacher. They offer the maximum flexibility to the teacher, who may choose or reject any of the suggested goals, objectives, activities, evaluation techniques, or resources.

Some curriculum planners prefer to cast their comprehensive guides in the following format:

TOPIC	GOALS	OBJECTIVES	ACTIVITIES	EVALUATION TECHNIQUES	RESOURCES

The Sequencing Format.   Guides of this nature

1. specify behavioral objectives for each competency area
2. indicate at what guide level(s), K–12, each competency will be taught
3. code objectives at each grade level as to whether they are introduced (I), developed (D), mastered (M), reinforced (R), or extended (E) at that level

This format provides an overall view of the sequencing of the objectives of the discipline. Teachers retain the opportunity for making decisions on when and how the objectives will be taught at each grade level.

The Test-Coding Format.   Offering teachers the least flexibility is the test-coding format, which

1. lists objectives to be mastered by the learners each marking period for each grade level of the discipline

2. codes each objective to the state and national criterion-referenced and norm-referenced tests that are administered by the school district

Though teachers may exercise choice of learning activities and supplementary resources, they are held accountable for student achievement every marking period. Locally written tests to assess student mastery of the objectives are administered at the end of each marking period.

The three formats can, of course, be combined and expanded. Test-coding can be added to the comprehensive format. Behavioral or performance indicators may be included to refine the behavioral or performance objectives. No matter what format is followed by a school system, curriculum guides should be used and revised periodically. It is an open secret that curriculum guides are often written to satisfy a local or state mandate. Having completed the task of writing the documents, teachers set them aside and allow them to accumulate dust. Teachers' failure to use the curriculum guides demonstrates once again that commitment to the process is an essential ingredient. Curriculum guides that are handed down, for example, generate little commitment. They may be followed out of necessity but without enthusiasm. Even those guides that are written by teachers rather than by curriculum consultants will be accepted only if teachers perceive the task as useful to them rather than as a response to directives from superordinates.[2]

RESOURCE UNIT

A resource unit, called a source unit by some curriculum workers, is "an arrangement of materials and activities around a particular topic or problem."[3] The resource unit is a curriculum product that falls somewhere between a teacher's learning unit and a course of study or curriculum guide. I explained elsewhere:

> The resource unit is a source of information and ideas for teachers to use. ... The major purpose of the resource unit is to provide ideas for a teacher who wishes to create his [or her] own learning unit on the same topic.... The resource unit contains a wealth of suggestions and information which will aid the teacher in supplementing material found in the basic textbook.

---

[2]For a critical view of conventional curriculum guides see Fenwick W. English, "It's Time to Abolish Conventional Curriculum Guides," *Educational Leadership* 44, no. 4 (December 1986–January 1987): 50–52.

[3]Peter F. Oliva, *The Secondary School Today,* 1st ed. (Scranton, Pa.: International Textbook Company, 1967), p. 176.

The resource unit shortens the busy teacher's planning time and simplifies his [or her] work in the construction of learning units for his [or her] classes.[4]

In essence, the resource unit serves the same general purpose as a course of study or curriculum guide. The major distinction between these types of products is that the resource unit is much narrower in scope, focusing on a particular topic rather than on an entire year, course, subject area, or sequence. Although we may encounter a course of study or curriculum guide for eleventh-grade American history, for example, we may also find resource units on topics within American history, such as the Age of Jackson, the Great Depression, or the Persian Gulf War.

The same outline that was suggested for a comprehensive curriculum guide applies to the resource unit. An example of a resource unit is given in Box 15–1.

SOURCES OF CURRICULUM MATERIALS

These illustrations of curriculum products barely suggest the types that are already available or can be constructed. In every state of the union, curriculum committees have created a wide variety of useful materials.

Curriculum developers and others who are searching for curriculum materials beyond the textbooks and accompanying teachers' manuals may locate examples in several places: curriculum libraries of colleges and universities, particularly those of schools and departments of education; curriculum centers of the public school systems; teacher education centers; the offices of curriculum consultants; state departments of education; and regional educational service agencies.

Professional organizations such as the Association for Supervision and Curriculum Development[5] and its state affiliates produce many helpful materials. Commercial firms are another source of curriculum materials that may be useful to the teacher. Many publishing firms display curriculum materials at major professional conferences. Several sources of curriculum guides are listed in the bibliography at the end of this chapter.

Great variation can be found in both the format of printed curriculum materials and in the types of available materials. Beyond typical curriculum guides, we can find curriculum materials packaged into multimedia kits consisting of films, filmstrips, charts, tapes, records, and so on.

---

[4]Ibid.
[5]Association for Supervision and Curriculum Development, 1250 North Pitt Street, Alexandria, Va. 22314.

BOX 15–1   A resource unit

Grade Level/Course:
Senior High School/Problems of American Democracy
Topic: Education in the United States

A. Introduction

   The enterprise of education in the United States consumes over 300 billion dollars per year, more than 250 billion of which are spent on public education. About 25 percent of the population is enrolled in schools from nursery through graduate level. In some way, schooling touches the lives of every person in the country, yet schooling itself is rarely studied in the schools. Although most people have their own ideas about education, their data base is often limited or lacking. The purpose of this resource unit is to provide students with facts, insights, and understandings about the American educational system.

B. Instructional Goals
   1. Cognitive
      The student will become familiar with
      a. the purposes of education in the United States
      b. the general structure of education in the United States
      c. the ways in which education in the United States is administered and financed
      d. major differences between the U.S. system of education and systems of other countries
   2. Affective
      The student will appreciate
      a. the complexity of the U.S. educational system
      b. our decentralized system of education
      c. the extent and complexity of problems facing education in the United States
      d. the achievements of American schools
C. Instructional Objectives
   1. Cognitive

      The student will be able to

      a. identify sources of funding for education
      b. explain local, state, and federal responsibilities for education
      c. state purposes of levels of education: elementary, middle, junior high, senior high, community college, senior college, and university
      d. tell the strengths and weaknesses of our decentralized system of education
      e. explain how teachers are prepared and hired
      f. describe how the educational dollar is spent
      g. account for differences in the support of education by the various states
      h. identify problems facing the schools and tell what efforts are being made to solve them
      i. account for the growth of private schools
      j. compare the American system of education with the system in another country

(continued)

BOX 15–1   continued

2. Affective
   The student will
   a. write a statement of purposes of education as he or she sees them
   b. state what he or she feels constitutes a good education
   c. state with reasons whether he or she believes compulsory education is desirable
   d. describe how he or she feels education should be funded
   e. take a position on whether public school education or private school education is better
   f. take a position on whether American education or European (or Russian or Japanese) education is better
   g. show his or her position by written reports on some controversial issues such as prayer in the schools, the teaching of the theory of evolution, censorship of textbooks and library books, busing of students for purposes of integrating the races, and bilingual education
3. Psychomotor
   None

D. Learning Activities
   1. Read provisions of the United States Constitution regarding education, especially the First, Tenth, and Fourteenth Amendments.
   2. Read provisions of the state constitution regarding education.
   3. Examine recent state and federal legislation on education.
   4. Prepare a chart showing the percentages of funding for education from local, state, and federal sources.
   5. Prepare a diagram showing overall dollars spent in any one year for education by local, state, and federal sources in the students' home state.
   6. Observe an elementary, middle/junior high, and secondary class in action, and afterward compare such aspects as objectives, materials, methods of teaching, and student conduct.
   7. Visit a community college and interview one of the administrators on the purposes and programs of the community college.
   8. Invite a private school headmaster to come to class to talk on purposes and programs of his or her school.
   9. Invite a panel of public school principals at elementary, middle/junior high, and secondary levels to come to class to talk on problems they face in administering their schools.
   10. Critique the requirements for a teacher's certificate in the students' home states.
   11. Gather and present data on the funding of higher education in both the United States and in the students' home states.
   12. Read and evaluate several statements of purposes of education.
   13. Read and evaluate a book or article critical of American public education.
   14. Report on pressure groups that influence education.
   15. Read a book or several articles on the educational system of one foreign country and describe major characteristics of that system.
   16. Find out how teachers are trained, certified, and employed in the students' home states.

(*continued*)

BOX 15–1 continued

17. Find out how school administrators are trained, certified, and employed in the students' home states.
18. Attend a school board meeting and discuss it in class.
19. Visit the superintendent's office and hear the superintendent (or his or her deputy) explain the role of the superintendent.
20. Find out what the school tax rate is in the students' home communities, how moneys are raised for the schools, and how much money is expended in the communities for schools.
21. Find out how much teachers and administrators are paid in the students' home communities and what fringe benefits they receive.
22. Examine the staffing patterns of an elementary, middle, or secondary school and determine types of employees needed to run the school.
23. Find out how serious the dropout problem is in the students' home communities and what is being done to solve it.
24. Determine whether or not student achievement in schools of the students' home district is satisfactory. If not, account for reasons for unsatisfactory achievement and report on measures that are being taken to improve the situation.
25. Debate whether teachers should have the right to strike.
26. Choose a controversial educational issue and write a paper showing positions of several prominent persons or groups and the students' own positions.

E. Evaluation Techniques
1. Give a pretest consisting of objective test items to survey students' factual knowledge about education in the United States.

   Sample test items:

   a. Responsibility for state control of education in the United States is derived from the U.S. Constitution's
      (1) First Amendment
      (2) Fifth Amendment
      (3) Tenth Amendment
      (4) Fourteenth Amendment

   b. Policies for local school districts are promulgated by
      (1) advisory councils
      (2) school boards
      (3) teachers' unions
      (4) school principals

2. Evaluate students' oral reports.
3. Evaluate students' written work—reports, charts, etc.
4. Observe students' reactions and comments in class discussion.
5. Give a posttest of objective items similar to those of the pretest.

F. Resources
1. *Books*
Armstrong, David T., Henson, Kenneth T., and Savage, Tom V. *Education: An Introduction,* 3rd ed. New York: Macmillan, 1989.

(*continued*)

BOX 15–1   continued

Cremin, Lawrence A. *The Transformation of the School: Progressivism in American Education 1876–1957.* New York: Alfred A. Knopf, 1961.

Educational Testing Service. Reports of the National Assessment of Educational Progress. Princeton, N.J.: Educational Testing Service.

Ehlers, Henry. *Crucial Issues in Education,* 7th ed. New York: Holt, Rinehart and Winston, 1981.

Goodlad, John I. *A Place Called School: Prospects for the Future.* New York: McGraw-Hill, 1984.

Halls, W. D. *Comparative Education: Contemporary Issues and Trends.* London: Jessica Kingsley Publishers and Paris: The United Nations Educational, Scientific, and Cultural Organization, 1990.

Johnson, James A. et al. *Introduction to the Foundations of American Education,* 7th ed. Boston: Allyn and Bacon, 1988.

Kurian, George Thomas. *World Education Encyclopedia.* New York: Facts on File Publications, 1988.

National Center for Education Statistics. *The Condition of Education: A Statistical Report.* Washington, D.C.: U.S. Government Printing Office, annually.

————. *Digest of Educational Statistics.* Washington, D.C.: U.S. Government Printing Office, annually.

Postlethwaite, Neville, ed. *The Encyclopedia of Comparative Education and National Systems of Education.* New York: Pergamon Press, 1988.

Standard Education Almanac. Chicago: Marquis Who's Who, annually.

United States Bureau of the Census. *Statistical Abstract of the United States.* Washington, D.C.: U.S. Government Printing Office, annually.

The World Almanac and Book of Facts. New York: Newspaper Enterprise Association, annually.

  2. *Films*

Education in America: The 17th and 18th Centuries. 16 min. black and white. Deerfield, Ill.: Coronet Instructional Films, 1958. Part of the History of Education in America series.

Education in America: The 19th Century. 16 min. black and white. Deerfield, Ill.: Coronet Instructional Films, 1958. Part of the History of Education in America series.

Education in America: The 20th Century. 16 min. black and white. Deerfield, Ill.: Coronet Instructional Films, 1958. Part of the History of Education in America series.

The Impact of Technology. 58 min. color. University of Wisconsin–Stout; Wis ETV, 1984. Discusses the relationship between technology and education. Part of the Education for a New Age series.

The Public Schools. 58 min. color. University of Wisconsin–Stout; Wis ETV, 1984. Discusses equity, excellence, and innovative reforms in the public schools. Part of the Education for a New Age series.

Technology and the Schools. 58 min. color. University of Wisconsin–Stout; Wis ETV, 1984. Discusses ways of upgrading technology and education in the schools to meet global competition. Part of the Education for a New Age series.

SUMMARY

Curriculum planners and teachers frequently engage in developing curriculum products that will be of use to teachers in their school systems. In this chapter we looked at these types of products: curriculum guides, courses of study, syllabi, and resource units.

Curriculum guides provide many suggestions to teachers for teaching a single course, a subject area at a particular grade level, an entire sequence, or an area of interest. Included in curriculum guides are suggested instructional goals, instructional objectives, activities, evaluation techniques, and resources. Sometimes an outline of the content is also included. Courses of study cover single courses and often contain a considerable amount of content material. Syllabi list topics to be covered.

Resource units are, in essence, minicurriculum guides for teaching particular topics or problems. Limited to single topics or problems, resource units offer types of suggestions similar to those found in curriculum guides.

In the creation of curriculum materials, both the process and product are important. Examples of curriculum materials can be found in school systems, colleges and universities, state departments of education, and regional educational service agencies. Professional organizations produce curriculum materials as do some business and industrial concerns.

QUESTIONS FOR DISCUSSION

1. Should writing curriculum guides be the job of the curriculum director or coordinator? Explain.
2. Should schools borrow curriculum guides from each other?
3. How do curriculum guides, resource units, and teaching units differ from each other?
4. What effect should the eight perennial problems of curriculum development discussed in Chapter 14 have on the production of curriculum guides?
5. Where would you place the production of curriculum guides, courses of study, resource units, and the like in the model for curriculum development presented by the author of this text?

SUPPLEMENTARY EXERCISES

1. Suggest your own outline for writing (1) a curriculum guide and (2) a resource unit.
2. List various curriculum products and state values you see in each.
3. List various curriculum products and state problems you see in each.
4. Locate and critique samples of curriculum guides, courses of study, syllabi, and resource units.

5. Survey opinions of teachers on the value of curriculum guides and other products listed in Exercise 4.
6. Locate and describe types of curriculum products other than those mentioned in this text.
7. Determine to what extent teachers in a school system you know well use their curriculum products. Account for their use or lack of use.
8. Locate and report on a curriculum product called a "scope and sequence chart."
9. Locate and list sources of curriculum materials available (1) in the school system, (2) in nearby colleges or universities, (3) from state departments of education, (4) from regional educational service agencies, (5) from professional associations, and (6) from business and industry.
10. Report on Fenwick W. English's alternative to the conventional curriculum guide. (See bibliography.)

BIBLIOGRAPHY

English, Fenwick W. "It's Time to Abolish Conventional Curriculum Guides." *Educational Leadership* 44, no. 4 (December 1986–January 1987): 50–52.

Glatthorn, Allan A. *Curriculum Renewal*. Alexandria, Va.: Association for Supervision and Curriculum Development, 1987.

Kemp, Jerrold E. *Instructional Design: A Plan for Unit and Course Development*. Belmont, Calif.: Fearon, 1971.

Oliva, Peter F. *The Secondary School Today,* 1st ed. Scranton, Pa.: International Textbook, 1967. Chapter 8.

Posner, George J. and Rudnitsky, Alan N. *Course Design: A Guide to Curriculum Development,* 2nd ed. White Plains, N.Y.: Longman, 1982.

Van Til, William, Vars, Gordon F., and Lounsbury, John H. *Modern Education for the Junior High School Years.* Indianapolis: Bobbs-Merrill, 1967. Chapter 11.

Winters, Marilyn. *Designing Your Curriculum Guide: A Step-by-Step Approach.* Westlake, Calif.: Las Virgines Unified School District, 1980.

Zenger, William F. and Zenger, Sharon K. *Curriculum Planning: A Ten-Step Process.* Palo Alto, Calif.: R & E Research Associates, 1982.

Appendix A

Exit Competencies

After completing this course you should be able to

1. Define curriculum development.
2. Distinguish between curriculum and instruction.
3. Describe roles of teachers, students, curriculum specialists, administrators, and parents in curriculum development.
4. Describe, giving examples, types of curriculum planning that are done at the local school, the school district, and the state levels.
5. Design and describe staff roles in a central curriculum office in a given school district.
6. Explain responsibilities and duties of a curriculum leader.
7. List skills needed by a curriculum leader.
8. Explain, identifying appropriate principles, how to go about effecting change in the curriculum.
9. Demonstrate communication skills.
10. Draw and explain a model for curriculum improvement.
11. Demonstrate skills in leading a group.
12. Write a statement of aims of education.
13. Write a school philosophy.
14. Contrast the major beliefs of essentialism and progressivism as they apply to the curriculum.
15. Conduct a curriculum needs assessment.
16. Write curriculum goals and objectives.
17. Develop a plan for organizing the curriculum of a school you know well, supporting the plan with appropriate references from the professional literature.
18. Write instructional goals and objectives in each of the three domains of learning.
19. Identify the most frequently used strategies of instruction and describe the strengths and weaknesses of each.

20. Write a unit plan.

21. Write a lesson plan.

22. Devise ways to preassess achievement of students.

23. Devise formative and summative methods of evaluating instruction.

24. Devise means of evaluating the curriculum.

25. Define and suggest ways to achieve each of the following: scope, relevance, balance, integration, sequence, continuity, articulation, and transferability.

26. Identify several current curriculum problems brought about by social and political forces and explain their significance for curriculum development.

27. Identify several professional problems and explain their significance for curriculum planners.

28. Write a curriculum guide.

29. Write a resource unit.

Appendix B ━━━━━━

Educational Resources Information Center (ERIC)

Established in 1966, the Educational Resources Information Center (ERIC) is a national system for disseminating educational information. It is, in fact, the world's largest educational database. Now under the aegis of the Office of Educational Research and Improvement (OERI), the ERIC system comprises 16 clearinghouses for information in specialized areas. The clearinghouses collect, abstract, index, and disseminate documents, which may be obtained on hard copy or microfiche. They also prepare interpretive summaries and annotated bibliographies dealing with high interest topics. Other components of the ERIC network are the ERIC Processing and Reference Facility, the ERIC Document Reproduction Service, and ACCESS ERIC.

ERIC publishes *Resources in Education,* a monthly sourcebook that contains abstracts of reports.[1] Helpful to ERIC users are *Current Index to Journals in Education,* a monthly publication that contains annotations of articles, and *Thesaurus* of ERIC Descriptors, a system of classifying ERIC documents.[2]

Following are the addresses of the current 16 clearinghouses, the other components of the ERIC network, and Oryx Press.

ERIC NETWORK COMPONENTS[3]

ERIC CLEARINGHOUSES

Adult, Career, and Vocational Education
Ohio State University
Center on Education and Training
  for Employment
1900 Kenny Road
Columbus, Ohio 43210-1090
Telephone: (614) 292-4353;
(800) 848-4815

Counseling and Personnel Services
University of Michigan
School of Education,
Room 2108
610 East University Street
Ann Arbor, Michigan 48109-1259
Telephone: (313) 764-9492

---

[1] Available from the Superintendent of Documents, U.S. Government Printing Office.
[2] Available from Oryx Press.
[3] SOURCES: *Resources in Education* (Washington, D.C.: U.S. Government Printing Office, April 1991), inside back cover; Office of Educational Research and Improvement, U.S. Department of Education, *Institutional Projects Funded* (Washington, D.C.: Office of Educational Research and Improvement, U.S. Department of Education, March 1990).

Educational Management
University of Oregon
1787 Agate Street
Eugene, Oregon 97403-5207
Telephone: (503) 346-5043

Elementary and Early Childhood Education
University of Illinois
College of Education
805 West Pennsylvania Avenue
Urbana, Illinois 61801-4897
Telephone: (217) 333-1386

Handicapped and Gifted Children
Council for Exceptional Children
1920 Association Drive
Reston, Virginia 22091-1589
Telephone: (703) 620-3660

Higher Education
George Washington University
One Dupont Circle, N.W., Suite 630
Washington, D.C. 20036-1183
Telephone: (202) 296-2597

Information Resources
Syracuse University
School of Education
Huntington Hall, Room 030
150 Marshall Street
Syracuse, New York 13244-2340
Telephone: (315) 443-3640

Junior Colleges
University of California at Los Angeles
Math-Sciences Building, Room 8118
405 Hilgard Avenue
Los Angeles, California 90024-1564
Telephone: (213) 825-3931

Languages and Linguistics
Center for Applied Linguistics
1118 22nd Street, N.W.
Washington, D.C. 20037-0037
Telephone: (202) 429-9551

Reading and Communication Skills
Indiana University
Smith Research Center, Suite 150
2805 East 10th Street
Bloomington, Indiana 47408-2698
Telephone: (812) 855-5847

Rural Education and Small Schools
Appalachia Educational Laboratory
1031 Quarrier Street
P.O. Box 1348
Charleston, West Virginia 25325
Telephone: (800) 624-9120 (Outside West Virginia) (800) 344-6646 (Inside West Virginia)

Science, Mathematics, and Environmental Education
Ohio State University
1200 Chambers Road, Room 310
Columbus, Ohio 43212-1792
Telephone: (614) 292-6717

Social Studies/Social Science Education
Indiana University
Social Studies Development Center
2805 East 10th Street
Bloomington, Indiana 47408-2373
Telephone: (812) 335-3838

Teacher Education
American Association of Colleges for Teacher Education
One Dupont Circle, N.W., Suite 610
Washington, D.C. 20036-2412
Telephone: (202) 293-2450

Tests, Measurement, and Evaluation
American Institutes for Research (AIR)
Washington Research Center
3333 K Street, N.W.
Washington, D.C. 20007-3893
Telephone: (202) 342-5060

Urban Education
Columbia University Teachers College
Institute for Urban and Minority Education
Main Hall, Room 300, Box 40
525 West 120th Street
New York, New York 10027-9998
Telephone: (212) 678-3433

OTHER COMPONENTS

Educational Resources Information Center
Office of Educational Research and Improvement
U.S. Department of Education
Washington, D.C. 20208-5720
Telephone: (202) 219-2289

ERIC Processing & Reference Facility
2440 Research Boulevard, Suite 400
Rockville, Maryland 20850-3238
Telephone: (301) 258-5500

ERIC Document Reproduction Service
7420 Fullerton Road, Suite 110
Springfield, Virginia 22153-2852
Telephone: (703) 440-1400
(800) 443-3742

ACCESS ERIC
1600 Research Boulevard
Rockville, Maryland 20850-3166
Telephone: (800) 873-3742
(Source of *The ERIC Review*)

Oryx Press
4041 North Central Avenue, Suite 700
Phoenix, Arizona 85012-3399
Telephone: (602) 265-2651
(800) 279-6799

Appendix C

National Diffusion Network

The National Diffusion Network of the U.S. Department of Education provides technical assistance and training to school systems wishing to adopt programs developed throughout the country and deemed exemplary by the Joint Dissemination Review Panel. The goal of the National Diffusion Network is to bring about school improvements by disseminating programs that have proved successful. The National Diffusion Network provides funds for facilitators whose job it is to help schools find out about, select, and adopt programs supported by the network.

NATIONAL DIFFUSION NETWORK (NDN) FACILITATORS

NDN Facilitators (located in every state, the District of Columbia, Puerto Rico, the Virgin Islands, American Samoa, Guam, and the Northern Mariana Islands) assist public and private schools that are searching for ways to improve their educational programs. Facilitators are based in local school districts, intermediate service agencies, state education agencies, and private nonprofit organizations. Facilitators supply information about exemplary programs and work with schools and institutions that wish to adopt the NDN-supported programs.

Following is a list of National Diffusion Network (NDN) facilitators.[1]

ALABAMA
Ms. Maureen Cassidy
Alabama Facilitator Project
Division of Professional Services
Room 5069–Gordon Persons
    Building
Montgomery, Alabama 36130
(205) 242-9834
FAX (205) 242-9708

ALASKA
Ms. Sandra Berry
State Facilitator
Alaska Department
of Education

Pouch F–State Office
of Education
Juneau, Alaska 99811
(907) 465-2841
FAX (907) 463-5279

ARIZONA
Dr. L. Leon Webb
Arizona State Facilitator
Educational Diffusion Systems,
    Inc.
161 East First Street
Mesa, Arizona 85201
(602) 969-4880
FAX (602) 898-8527

---

[1]SOURCES: National Diffusion Network Division, U.S. Department of Education, 555 New Jersey Avenue, NW, Washington, D.C. 20208-1525; *Educational Programs That Work* (Sopris West, Inc., 1120 Delaware Avenue, Longmont, Colorado 80501), annually.

ARKANSAS
Mr. Clearance Lovell (Acting)
State Facilitator
Arkansas Department of Education
Arch Ford Education Building
State Capitol Mall
Little Rock, Arkansas 72201
(501) 682-4268
FAX (501) 682-1146

CALIFORNIA
Ms. Barbara Duffy, Director
Ms. Joyce Lazzeri, State Facilitator
Assoc. of CA School
    Administrators
1575 Old Bayshore Highway
Burlingame, California 94010
(415) 692-2956
FAX (415) 692-1508

COLORADO
Mr. Charles D. Beck, Jr.
The Education Diffusion Group
3800 York Street–Unit B
Denver, Colorado 80205
(303) 837-1000 X2136
FAX (303) 837-1000 X2135 (ask
    for FAX, when you hear carrier
    tone, press "START" and hang
    up.)

CONNECTICUT
Dr. John Mongeau (Acting)
Connecticut Facilitator Project
    RESCUE
355 Goshen Road
Litchfield, Connecticut 06759
(203) 567-0863
FAX (203) 567-3381

DELAWARE
Ms. Carole D. White
State Facilitator Project
Department of Public Instruction
John G. Townsend Building

Dover, Delaware 19901
(302) 739-4583
FAX (302) 739-3092

DISTRICT OF COLUMBIA
Ms. Susan Williams
District Facilitator Project
Eaton School
34th and Lowell Streets, N.W.
Washington, D.C. 20008
(202) 282-0056
(No FAX)

FLORIDA
Ms. Sue Carpenter
Florida State Facilitator
Florida Department of
    Education
325 West Gaines Street
424 FEC
Tallahassee, Florida 32399
(904) 487-6245
FAX (904) 488-6319

GEORGIA
Ms. Frances Hensley
Georgia Facilitator Center
607 Aderhold Hall, UGA
Athens, Georgia 30602
(404) 542-3332 or 542-3810
FAX (404) 542-2321

HAWAII
Ms. Mona Vierra
Department of Education
Multimedia Services Branch
641 18th Avenue
Honolulu, Hawaii 96816
(808) 737-3107 or 737-9838
FAX (808) 737-5217

IDAHO
Mr. Ted L. Lindley
State Facilitator
Idaho State Department of
    Education

Len B. Jordan Office Building
Boise, Idaho 83720
(208) 334-2186
FAX (208) 334-2228

ILLINOIS
Dr. Shirley Menendez
Project Director
Statewide Facilitator Project
1105 East Fifth Street
Metropolis, Illinois 62960
(618) 524-2664
(No FAX)

INDIANA
Dr. Lynwood Erb
Project Director
Indiana Facilitator Center
Logansport Community School
  Corp.
Logansport, Indiana 46947
(219) 722-1754
FAX (219) 722-7634

IOWA
Ms. Michelle Soria-Dunn
State Facilitator
Department of Public Instruction
Grimes State Office Building
Des Moines, Iowa 50319
(515) 281-3111
FAX (515) 281-5988

KANSAS
Mr. James H. Connett
Kansas State Facilitator Project
Director KEDDS/LINK
3030 Osage Street
Wichita, Kansas 67217
(316) 833-3960
FAX (316) 833-3971

KENTUCKY
Ms. Barbie Haynes
Kentucky State Facilitator

Kentucky Department
  of Education
Capitol Plaza Tower
  Office Bldg.
Frankfort, Kentucky 40601
(502) 564-6720
FAX (502) 564-6921

LOUISIANA
Ms. Brenda Argo
Facilitator Project Director
State Department of Education
ESEA Title IV Bureau Office
P.O. Box 44064
Baton Rouge, Louisiana 70804
(504) 342-3424
FAX (504) 342-7367

MAINE
Ms. Elaine Roberts
Center for Educational Services
P.O. Box 620
Auburn, Maine 04210
(207) 783-0833
FAX (207) 783-9701

MARYLAND
Dr. Raymond H. Hartjen
Maryland Facilitator Project
Educational Alternatives, Inc.
Mail to: P.O. Box 265
Port Tobacco, MD 20677
Ship to: 115 La Grange Avenue
La Plata, Maryland 20646
(301) 934-2992 (DC line 870-3399)
(No FAX)

MASSACHUSETTS
Ms. Nancy Love
THE NETWORK
290 South Main Street
Andover, Massachusetts 01810
(508) 470-1080
FAX (508) 475-9220

MICHIGAN
Ms. Carol Wolenberg
Michigan State Facilitator
Michigan Department of Education
Box 30008
Lansing, Michigan 48909
(517) 373-1806
FAX (517) 373-2537

MINNESOTA
Ms. Diane Lassman and
Ms. Barbara Knapp
Minnesota State Facilitator Office
The EXCHANGE at CAREI
116 U Press Building
2037 University Avenue S.E.
University of Minnesota
Minneapolis, Minnesota 55414-
 3097
(612) 624-0584
FAX (612) 626-7496

MISSISSIPPI
Mr. Bobby Stacy
Mississippi Facilitator Project
State Department of Education
P.O. Box 771
Jackson, Mississippi 39205
(601) 359-3498
FAX (601) 352-7436

MISSOURI
Ms. Jolene Schulz
Project Director
Missouri Education Center
1206 East Walnut
Columbia, Missouri 65201
(314) 886-2157
FAX (314) 886-2171

MONTANA
Mr. Ron Lukenbill
State Facilitator Project
Office of Public Instruction

State Capitol
Helena, Montana 59601
(406) 444-2080
FAX (406) 444-3924

NEBRASKA
Dr. Elizabeth Alfred
Facilitator Project Director
Nebraska Department
 of Education
301 Centennial Mall
P.O. Box 94987
Lincoln, Nebraska 68509
(402) 471-3440
FAX (402) 471-2701

NEVADA
Ms. Doris Betts
State Facilitator
Nevada Department
 of Education
400 W. King Street
Capitol Complex
Carson City, Nevada 89710
(702) 687-3187
FAX (702) 687-5660

NEW HAMPSHIRE
Mr. Jared Shady
NH Facilitator Center
80 South Main Street
Concord, New Hampshire 03301
(603) 224-9461
FAX (603) 225-5428

NEW JERSEY
Ms. Katherine Wallin or
Ms. Elizabeth Ann Pagen
Education Info. & Resource Center
N.J. State Facilitator Project
700 Hollydell Court
Sewell, New Jersey 08080
(609) 582-7000
FAX (609) 582-4296

NEW MEXICO
Dr. Amy L. Atkins
New Mexico State Facilitator
Dept. of Educational Foundations
U of NM–College of Education
Onate Hall, Room 223
Albuquerque, New Mexico 87131
(505) 277-5204
FAX (505) 277-7991

NEW YORK
Ms. Laurie Rowe
State Facilitator
N.Y. Education Department
Room 860 EBA
Albany, New York 12234
(518) 474-1280
FAX (518) 473-7737

NORTH CAROLINA
Mr. William McGrady
Project Director
NC Education Department
NC Dept. of Public Instruction
116 West Edenton Street
Raleigh, North Carolina 27603-
    1712
(919) 733-7037
FAX (919) 733-3791

NORTH DAKOTA
Mr. Charles DeRemer
State Facilitator
Department of Public Instruction
State Capitol
Bismarck, North Dakota 58505
(701) 224-2514
FAX (701) 224-2461

OHIO
Mr. C. William Phillips
Ohio Facilitation Center
The Ohio Department of Education
Division of Inservice Education

65 South Front Street, Room 1013
Columbus, Ohio 43215
(614) 466-2979
FAX (614) 752-8148

OKLAHOMA
Ms. Deborah Murphy
Oklahoma Facilitator Center
101 West Broadway
Cushing, Oklahoma 74023
(918) 225-4711
FAX (918) 225-4711

OREGON
Dr. Ralph Nelsen
Columbia Education Center
11325 S.E. Lexington
Portland, Oregon 97266
(503) 760-2346
FAX (503) 760-5592

PENNSYLVANIA
Mr. Richard Brickley
Project Director
Facilitator Project, R.I.S.E.
725 Caley Road
King of Prussia, PA 19406
(215) 265-6056
FAX (215) 265-6562

RHODE ISLAND
Ms. Faith Fogle
RI State Facilitator Center
RI Department of Education
Roger Williams Building
22 Hays Street
Providence, Rhode Island 02908
(401) 277-2617
FAX (401) 277-2734

SOUTH CAROLINA
Mr. Peter Samulski
State Facilitator
Block Grant Section

Office of Federal Programs
SC Department of Education
Columbia, South Carolina 29201
(803) 734-8116
FAX (803) 734-8624

SOUTH DAKOTA
Ms. Donlynn Rice
State Facilitator
South Dakota Curriculum
  Center
205 W. Dakota
Pierre, South Dakota 57501
(605) 224-6708
FAX (605) 224-8320

TENNESSEE
Dr. Reginald High
TN Statewide Facilitator Project
College of Education/BERS–
  U of TN
Knoxville, Tennessee 37996-3504
(615) 974-1945 or 4165 or 2272
FAX (615) 974-8718

TEXAS
Dr. Judy Bramlett
Texas Facilitator Project–NDN
Education Service Center
  Region VI
3332 Montgomery Road
Huntsville, Texas 77340-6499
(409) 295-9161
FAX (409) 295-1447

UTAH
Dr. Lyle Wright
Utah State Facilitator Project
Utah State Office
  of Education
250 East 500 South
Salt Lake City, Utah 84111
(801) 538-7500
FAX (801) 538-7882

VERMONT
Mr. Howard Verman
Trinity College
Colchester Avenue
Burlington, Vermont 05401
(802) 658-7429
FAX (802) 658-7435

VIRGINIA
Ms. Judy McKnight
The Education Network of VA
3421 Surrey Lane
Falls Church, Virginia 22042
(703) 698-0487
FAX (703) 354-2013

WASHINGTON
Mr. Keith Wright
Project Director
Washington State Facilitator
15675 Ambaum Boulevard, S.W.
Seattle, Washington 98166
(206) 433-2453
FAX (206) 433-2131

WEST VIRGINIA
Ms. Cornelia Toon
WV State Facilitator
Building #6, Room B-252
State Department of Education
Charleston, West Virginia 25305
(304) 348-2193
FAX (304) 348-0048

WISCONSIN
Mr. William Ashmore
State Facilitator
Department of Public
  Instruction
125 South Webster
P.O. Box 7841
Madison, Wisconsin 53707
(608) 267-9179
FAX (608) 267-1052

WYOMING
Ms. Nancy Leinius
State Facilitator
WY Innovation Network
  System
State Department
  of Education
Hathaway Building–Room 236
Cheyenne, Wyoming 82002
(307) 777-6226
FAX (307) 777-6234

PUERTO RICO
Mrs. Iris Arbona
Puerto Rico State
  Facilitator
Evaluation Division,
  5th Floor
Department of Education
P.O. Box 759
Hato Rey, Puerto Rico 00919
(809) 753-1645
FAX (809) 250-0275

VIRGIN ISLANDS
Dr. Lois Hassell-Habteyes
State Facilitator
44–46 Kongens Gade
Charlotte Amalie
St. Thomas, Virgin Islands
(809) 774-0100 Ext. 213
(671) 472-8524
FAX (809) 774-4679

PALAU
Mr. Masa-aki Emesiochle
State Facilitator
P.O. Box 189
Koror, Republic of
  Palau 9694
(680) 488-2570 or 1003
FAX (680) 488-2830

PRIVATE SCHOOL
FACILITATOR
Dr. Charles Nunley
Private School Facilitator
Council for American Private
  Education
1726 M Street, NW
Suite 1102
Washington, DC 20036
(202) 659-0177
FAX (202) 659-0018

AMERICAN SAMOA
Mr. Rick Davis
NDN Facilitator
Department of Education
Pago Pago, American
  Samoa 96799
(684) 633-5237
(684) 633-5184
FAX 011 (684) 633-4240

NORTHERN MARIANA
ISLANDS
Ms. Paz Younis
NDN Facilitator
CNMI Public School System
P.O. Box 1370
Saipan, MP 96950
(670) 322-3194
FAX 011 (670) 322-4056

GUAM
Ms. Margaret Camacho
NDN Facilitator
Federal Program Office
Guam Department
  of Education
P.O. Box DE
Agana, Guam 96910
(617) 472-8524
FAX 011 (671) 477-4587

Appendix D ▬▬▬▬

Regional Educational Laboratories

The Office of Educational Research and Improvement of the U.S. Department of Education funds nine regional laboratories that carry out applied research, development, and technical assistance for educators, parents, and decision makers in the 50 states, Puerto Rico, the Virgin Islands, and the Pacific Basin Region. Each laboratory serves a geographic region and is governed by an independent board of directors.

Laboratories plan programs through an ongoing assessment of regional needs, a knowledge of the current trends in research and practice, and interaction with the many other agencies and institutions that assist communities and schools with educational improvement. Improving schools and classrooms is the goal of the laboratories, a goal they carry out through a common set of five tasks or functions:

☐ working with other regional organizations to apply research and improve schools. Partner organizations include state departments of education, intermediate school districts and intradistrict collaboratives, universities, colleges, and state associations of educators and parents.

☐ assisting state-level policymakers on the implications of educational research and practice for policies and programs.

☐ conducting applied research and developing materials, programs, and publications that support the mission of school and classroom improvement.

☐ collaborating with other laboratories, research centers, and national associations to extend and enhance related research and development.

☐ developing effective internal management, governance, planning, and self-evaluation, as well as reviewing regional needs and developments.[1]

Appalachian Educational Laboratory, Inc. (AEL)
1031 Quarrier Street
P.O. Box 1348
Charleston, West Virginia 25325
(304) 347-0400

Far West Laboratory for Educational Research and Development (FWL)
1855 Folsom Street
San Francisco, California 94103
(415) 565-3000

---

[1] SOURCE: Office of Educational Research and Improvement, U.S. Department of Education, *Institutional Projects Funded* (Washington, D.C.: Office of Educational Research and Improvement, U.S. Department of Education, March 1990).

Mid-Continent Regional
   Educational Laboratory
   (McREL)
Suite 201
12500 East Iliff
Aurora, Colorado 80014
(303) 337-0990

and

4709 Belleview Avenue
Kansas City, Missouri 64112
(816) 756-2401

North Central Regional
   Educational Laboratory
   (NCREL)
295 Emroy Avenue
Elmhurst, Illinois 60126
(312) 941-7677

Northwest Regional
   Educational Laboratory
   (NWREL)
101 S.W. Main Street,
   Suite 500
Portland, Oregon 97204
(503) 275-9500

Regional Laboratory for
   Educational Improvement of
   the Northeast and Islands
290 South Main Street
Andover, Massachusetts 01810
(508) 470-0098

Research for Better Schools
   (RBS)
444 North Third Street
Philadelphia, Pennsylvania 19123
(215) 574-9300

Southeastern Educational
   Improvement Laboratory
   (SEIL)
P.O. Box 12748
200 Park Offices, Suite 200
Research Triangle Park
North Carolina 27709-2748
(919) 549-8216

Southwest Educational
   Development Laboratory
   (SEDL)
211 East Seventh Street
Austin, Texas 78701
(512) 476-6861

Appendix E

National Research and Development Centers

The National Research and Development Centers focus research on topics of national significance to educational policy and practice. Each center works in a defined field on a five-year program of research and development. Each center's role is to

- exercise leadership in its mission area
- conduct programmatic research and development that advance theory and practice
- attract the sustained attention of expert researchers to concentrate on problems in education
- create a long-term interaction between researchers and educators
- participate in a network for collaborative exchange in the education community
- disseminate research findings in useful forms to education policymakers and practitioners[1]

National Arts Education Research Center
New York University
School of Education, Health, Nursing, and Arts Professions
32 Washington Place, #31
New York, New York 10003
Telephone: (212) 998-5050

University of Illinois at Urbana–Champaign
College of Applied and Fine Arts
105 Davenport House
809 South Wright Street
Champaign, Illinois 61820-6219
Telephone: (217) 333-2186

Center for Research on the Context of Secondary School Teaching
Stanford University
School of Education
CERAS Building
Stanford, California 94305
Telephone: (415) 723-4972

National Center on Education and Employment
Teachers College
Columbia University
Box 174
525 West 120th Street
New York, New York 10027
Telephone: (202) 678-3091

---

[1] SOURCE: Office of Educational Research and Improvement, U.S. Department of Education, *Institutional Projects Funded* (Washington, D.C.: Office of Educational Research and Improvement, U.S. Department of Education, March 1990).

Center for Research on Effective Schooling for Disadvantaged Students
School of Arts and Sciences
The Johns Hopkins University
3505 North Charles Street
Baltimore, Maryland 21218
Telephone: (301) 338-7570

National Center on Effective Secondary Schools
University of Wisconsin–Madison
1025 West Johnson Street
Madison, Wisconsin 53706
Telephone: (608) 263-7575

Center for Research on Elementary and Middle Schools
Johns Hopkins University
3505 North Charles Street
Baltimore, Maryland 21218
Telephone: (301) 338-7570

Center for Research on Evaluation, Standards, and Student Testing
Regents of the University of California
Center for the Study of Evaluation
University of California at Los Angeles
405 Hilgard Avenue
Los Angeles, California 90024
Telephone: (213) 825-4711

National Center for Research to Improve Postsecondary Teaching and Learning
School of Education
University of Michigan
Ann Arbor, Michigan 48918-1259
Telephone: (313) 936-2741

National Center for Improving Science Education
The Network, Inc.
290 South Main Street
Andover, Massachusetts 01810
Telephone: (508) 470-1080, or
1920 L Street, N.W.
Suite 202
Washington, D.C. 20036
Telephone: (202) 467-0652

Center for the Learning and Teaching of Elementary Subjects
Michigan State University
College of Education
East Lansing, Michigan 48824
Telephone: (517) 353-6470

Center for the Learning and Teaching of Literature
State University of New York at Albany
School of Education
1400 Washington Avenue
Albany, New York 12222
Telephone: (518) 442-5026

National Center for Research in Mathematical Sciences Education
Wisconsin Center for Education Research
University of Wisconsin–Madison
1025 West Johnson Street
Madison, Wisconsin 53706
Telephone: (608) 263-4285

Center for Policy Research in Education
The Eagleton Institute of Politics
Rutgers, The State University of New Jersey
WoodLawn–Neilson Campus

New Brunswick, New Jersey 08901
Telephone: (201) 828-3872

**National Center for
Postsecondary Governance and
Finance**
College of Education
Room 4114 CSS Building
University of Maryland
College Park, Maryland 20742-
2435
Telephone: (301) 454-1568

**Reading Research and Education
Center**
University of Illinois
174 Children's Research Center
51 Gerty Drive
Champaign, Illinois 61820
Telephone: (217) 333-2552

**National Center for Educational
Leadership**
Graduate School of Education
Harvard University
Gutman Library, 6 Appian Way
Cambridge, Massachusetts 02138-
3704

**National Center for School
Leadership**
College of Education
University of Illinois at Urbana–
Champaign
Urbana, Illinois 61801
Telephone: (217) 333-2870,
244-1122

Center for the Study of Learning
Learning, Research, and
Development Center
University of Pittsburgh
3939 O'Hara Street
Pittsburgh, Pennsylvania 15260
Telephone: (412) 624-7485

Center for the Study of Writing
School of Education
University of California, Berkeley
Berkeley, California 94720
Telephone: (405) 643-7022

**National Center for Research on
Teacher Education**
College of Education
Michigan State University
Erickson Hall
East Lansing, Michigan 48824-
1034
Telephone: (517) 355-9302

**Center for Technology in
Education**
Bank Street College
of Education
610 West 112th Street
New York, New York 10025
Telephone: (212) 222-6700

**National Center for Research
and Development in the
Education of Gifted
and Talented Children
and Youth**
To be announced

Appendix F

Curriculum Journals

Curriculum Inquiry
Ontario Institute for Studies in
  Education
John Wiley & Sons, Inc.
605 Third Avenue
New York, New York 10158
Telephone: (212) 692-6000

Curriculum Review
Curriculum Advisory
  Service
407 South Dearborn,
  Suite 1360
Chicago, Illinois 60605
Telephone: (312) 939-3010

Educational Leadership
Association for Supervision and
  Curriculum Development
1250 North Pitt Street
Alexandria, Virginia 22314-1403
Telephone: (703) 549-9110

*Journal of Curriculum and
  Supervision*
Association for Supervision and
  Curriculum Development
1250 North Pitt Street
Alexandria, Virginia 22314
Telephone: (703) 549-9110

Journal of Curriculum Studies
Taylor & Francis, Ltd.
Rankine Road
Basingstoke
Hants RG24 OPR
England
Telephone: 0256 840366

Journal of Curriculum Theorizing
Corporation for Curriculum
  Research
53 Falstaff Road
Rochester, New York 14609
Telephone: (716) 654-8010

CREDITS   *(continued from p. ii)*

Name Index

Subject Index

DATE DUE

FEB 25 1994			

Demco, Inc. 38-293